JUVENILE Delinquency
Into the 21st Century

Lewis Yablonsky

California State University—Northridge

Wadsworth
Thomson Learning™

Australia • Canada • Mexico • Singapore • Spain
United Kingdom • United States

Cover Designer: Liz Harasymczuk
Cover Image: Rick Raymond/
          Tony Stone Images
Cover Printer: Transcontinental Printing
          Division Imprimerie Gagné
Compositor: Skripps & Associates
Printer: Transcontinental Printing
          Division Imprimerie Gagné

Printed in Canada
1 2 3 4 5 6 7 03 02 01 00 99

For permission to use material from this
text, contact us:
  Web: www.thomsonrights.com
  Fax: 1-800-730-2215
  Phone: 1-800-730-2214

For more information, contact
Wadsworth/Thomson Learning
10 Davis Drive
Belmont, CA 94002-3098
USA
http://www.wadsworth.com

International Headquarters
Thomson Learning
290 Harbor Drive, 2nd Floor
Stamford, CT 06902-7477
USA

UK/Europe/Middle East/South Africa
Thomson Learning
Berkshire House
168-173 High Holborn
London WC1V 7AA
United Kingdom

Asia
Thomson Learning
60 Albert Street, #15-01
Albert Complex
Singapore 189969

Canada
Nelson/Thomson Learning
1120 Birchmount Road
Toronto, Ontario M1K 5G4
Canada

ISBN 0-8304-1425-8

This book is printed on acid-free
recycled paper.

CONTENTS

PREFACE

If you want to truly understand something, try to change it.

—*Kurt Lewin*

The past century has been marked by dramatic changes in patterns of juvenile delinquency. Notable are: (1) an increase in types of substance abuse; (2) more random and diverse youthful sexual behavior, along with an increasing number of teenage pregnancies; (3) an astounding increase in guns in the hands of juveniles, with corresponding lethal forms of violence, including gang violence; and (4) an escalation in the democratization of juvenile delinquency to include not only lower socioeconomic groups but also middle- and upper-class juveniles.

In the 1990s, substance abuse (both drugs and alcohol) is entwined with delinquent behavior. Substance abuse among juveniles has almost doubled in the past decade. Over 75 percent of the juvenile population has used some illegal substance during their teen years. Since we have not developed any viable methods for intervention, the current trend will continue.

Attitudes about adolescent sexuality and the sexual behavior of teenagers changed enormously in the second half of the twentieth century. For example, in 1950 when I began my work in a juvenile detention facility, adolescents, especially girls, were often incarcerated for "incorrigibility." This characterization was related to the now virtually discarded term "sexual promiscuity." Incarceration was often ordered by the juvenile court for a pregnant teenage girl, and her boyfriend would also become a ward of the court and be placed in a custodial institution. In recent years the sexual behavior of juveniles is virtually ignored by the juvenile courts because of a generally more liberal view toward teenage sexual behavior and the growing number of accepted teenage pregnancies. If the current trend continues without some marked intervention, we will have an increasing number of ill-equipped "child-parents." Another highly significant issue in the area of adolescent sexuality is the specter of AIDS and other sexually transmitted diseases. In this area, sexual freedom and intravenous drug abuse have become a lethal combination—and this pattern will predictably escalate in the twenty-first century.

Another general trend in the overall delinquency scene is an increase in "senseless violence," often related to the prevalence of guns and drug abuse. These two factors have had a lethal impact on youth gang violence that is unprecedented in the history of America. The indiscriminate and senseless delinquent violence and the increased use of drugs are activities found in a new type of violent gang.

Finally, a notable change in delinquency in the twentieth century is the burgeoning of middle- and upper-class delinquency, not only in numbers but also in patterns of delinquency. This increasing problem is related to the rise in substance and alcohol abuse among all adolescents. The accuracy of juvenile delinquency statistics in the 1980s and 1990s has been clouded by the fact that many middle- and upper-class juveniles who commit delinquent acts are not statistically recorded by the juvenile courts. This is because of the response of middle- and upper-class parents to their teenagers' deviance. These parents rescue their children from the juvenile court's administration of justice and place them in mental health facilities. This process has significantly affected the status definitions of delinquency and statistics on delinquency and has led to an increase in the number of mental health facilities and programs for delinquents. Juvenile delinquency is no longer restricted to lower socioeconomic and minority group children, despite the fact that they are the ones who are generally processed and incarcerated by the juvenile courts. The twenty-first century may be marked by a clearer acknowledgment that an increasing number of America's children are delinquency-prone and delinquent, despite the fact that they are not labeled delinquent by the juvenile justice system.

The twentieth century produced marked changes in the delinquent behavior of juveniles and the manner in which society responds to this behavior through the juvenile justice system. In the following pages, these issues are described and analyzed. In the final chapter, I project a plan for preventing and controlling delinquency that I am hopeful will be brought into existence in the twenty-first century.

The Author's Perspective

It is unusual for a textbook author to present a brief survey of his background and experience for writing a book on the vast and complex subject of delinquency. However, I believe it is useful for those who read this book "to know where I am coming from," to quote a 1960s phrase.

I will at times refer to my background as a researcher and group therapist for fifty years in the combat zones of crime and delinquency. My research and work have taken place in a variety of settings, including prisons, psychiatric hospitals, community crime prevention programs, and therapeutic communities. As a result of these explorations, some of my best friends are former addict/criminals and have revealed to me many "secrets" of the underworld of crime and delinquency that are valuable for students of this subject to understand. Following is a brief description of my work in the field of crime and delinquency that is the foundation of this book.

In my early years, the platitude that "some of my best friends were juvenile delinquents" certainly applied to me. My best friend during those years went to prison at the age of twenty for a federal crime. As a result of associating with these companions, I became involved in a variety of delinquent acts. I was extricated from the influence of these "friends" when I went into the navy. That part of the story, however, is being saved for a more personal autobiography. What is relevant here is that my work in the field during my graduate years at New York University and beyond prepared me for writing this treatise on delinquency.

My first major in-depth research into the structure and function of gangs and delinquency was implemented in a period from 1953 to 1958 on the Upper West Side of Manhattan in an area infested with crime and delinquency. This five-year period of firsthand research on the problem was part of a job I acquired in 1953 as director of a crime prevention program sponsored by a community organization known as Morningside Heights Inc. During this period I began my teaching career at Columbia University and the City College of New York, where I taught sociology and criminology to police officers.

I had a strategic position vis-à-vis the gang youths in the area in my role as director of the Morningside Heights Project. They had a good reason for accepting our work. To them we were not simply poking around in their lives for some vague research reason. Our agency was attempting to do something concrete to prevent and control the crime and delinquency of the area through various social, recreational, and family projects that we developed. The residents, almost a half-million people from every ethnic, racial, religious, class, and economic background, also had an awareness of our efforts, and many people in the area cooperated with our project.

The overall crime picture included robbery, burglary, homicide, drug addiction, and assault. Many of these crimes were perpetrated by young gangsters, and consequently the violent gangs in the area were considered a basic problem. My preventive work with about seventy-five gangs in the neighborhood, when I first began to implement various projects, was hindered by a lack of substantial knowledge about them necessary to develop effective methods of crime prevention. It was this limitation and the apparent lack of effective methods available to other professional and social agencies in New York City engaged in gang work that spurred my intensive gang research at that time.

In addition to some of the more formal methods of questionnaires and focus groups that were part of my research design, my daily communications with the people and conditions I was trying to change were an important element of my overall research into gangs. I learned firsthand what Kurt Lewin meant by his assertion that attempting to produce change in people was an intrinsic element in learning about the overt and underlying dynamics of their behavior.

My relationship with gang youths in the neighborhood was a two-way street. My concern with their motives and activities led to their concern with mine. Many "philosophical" afternoons and evenings were spent with gangsters in my office or on the corner, discussing "life." Much was learned on both sides about "the world." The essence and meaning of gang behavior and its violence were often more clearly revealed in these discussions than in the many formal research methods I utilized during this five-year period.

In my early research in New York City into the phenomenon of gangs and delinquency I utilized a variety of approaches. These included: (1) in-depth interviews with gangsters, individually and in groups, both in the project's office and on the street; (2) tape recordings of field notes; (3) written questionnaires; (4) the employment of two former gang leaders as paid interviewers; (5) various therapy groups; and (6) unanticipated data from a diary kept by a gang leader. My five years of gang research in New York City became the basis for my doctoral dissertation. My thesis was the foundation for my first book on gangs, *The Violent Gang* (1962).

Since these earlier experiences and publications, I have vigorously continued my research into delinquency. Notable in this regard has been my group therapy work with adolescents as a licensed therapist in several southern California psychiatric hospitals. In thousands of intensive group psychotherapy sessions in these hospitals I have learned a great deal about the social and psychological dynamics of delinquent adolescents in the context of their family backgrounds. All of these youths have contributed enormously to my understanding of delinquency. My research findings derived from this therapeutic work are incorporated into this book.

My special work since 1990 as a consultant and group therapist in the Amity Therapeutic Community projects in the R.J. Donovan Prison in California and a prison in Beaumont, Texas, has produced a considerable amount of data about criminals and delinquents and how we can transform them into law-abiding, productive citizens. In my prison work, I gathered considerable relevant data through psychodrama and group therapy sessions, individual interviews, special gang focus groups, and written questionnaires. In brief, all of my personal experiences and my fifty years as a criminologist and social psychologist are encompassed in this book.

In addition to observing and knowing many difficult and violent individuals, I have also had the experience of observing that, given a chance in an effective treatment program, many youths seemingly trapped in their self-destructive life-style can change their behavior in positive ways and facilitate positive change in their community. Individuals who started down the delinquent/criminal path have turned their lives around and become valuable citizens. As was true in the early part of my delinquency experiences, some of my best, most interesting, and most valued friends are ex-gangsters, ex-junkies, and ex-criminals who have been resocialized into a better way of life. In Part 6, "The Prevention, Treatment and Control of Juvenile Delinquency," I discuss some of these hopeful and effective methodologies. Part 7, "Therapeutic Communities," is an important part of the book since it projects a feasible plan for preventing and controlling delinquency.

My efforts in focusing on a solution are generated not only by my mind but also by my heartfelt and sympathetic emotions in response to the human waste and destructiveness that crime and delinquency produce in our society. On a personal and professional level, my work with prisoners is the most deeply affecting emotional situation in my life.

Perhaps I can explain my intensely felt emotions on this subject by describing the following recurring scenario that I observe when I enter a large California prison, the Donovan Prison in San Diego, to direct group psychotherapy and psychodrama sessions with the men in custody. After being searched and checked at the front gate of this prison, which incarcerates around five thousand men, I have to walk almost a mile through several depressing "big yards" to the therapeutic community cell block where two hundred prisoners in the Amity program reside. As I pass through these big yards, I can't help observing hundreds of prisoners along the way. They are usually engaged in typical negative prison activities, including small groups hunched together secretly discussing crimes they have committed or will commit, or simply strutting around the big yard displaying their absurd macho posturing.

Most of these young men, all formerly delinquents, are from various minority groups; many are intelligent black and Chicano individuals between the ages of eighteen and thirty who are wasting away in the cold storage of prison life. My heartfelt reaction is that the current prison system (which includes the recent politically motivated three-strikes laws) destroys the valuable human potential that exists in these unfortunate men.

All of them, even the worst sociopaths, have a spark of motivation and compassion, and if given a chance through a humanistic treatment program, these positive sparks can be ignited into flames that would lead them into law-abiding and satisfying life-styles. Their plight, which is characteristic of the approximately 1.7 million prisoners incarcerated in the United States, has motivated me to attempt to understand the causes of their onerous situation and to develop methodologies for their effective treatment. There is no question that if the current legal trend continues without some relevant policy and therapeutic interventions, in the twenty-first century we will have over 5 million of our citizens in prisons. Beyond the humanistic horror of this situation, the financial cost will dwarf the future budget for positive educational and social welfare programs.

I am hopeful that some of the insights, analyses, and possible solutions I have presented here can be developed and implemented for resocializing delinquent youths. I wholeheartedly agree with the often ridiculed comment attributed to the founder of Boys Town, Father Flanagan, that "there is no such thing as a bad boy." It is my firm belief, that all youths who are adjudicated delinquents, including the toughest sociopaths I have met, can, with the proper humanistic treatment approach, be salvaged from a life of self-destructive behavior into responsible, law-abiding citizens.

ACKNOWLEDGMENTS

In the past century, hundreds of brilliant social scientists have carried out a considerable amount of excellent research in the field of crime and delinquency. An important foundation of this book consists of distilled versions of some of their theories and empirical research. To paraphrase a comment of sociologist Robert Merton, I can see farther because I stand on the shoulders of giants. I am sincerely grateful to these many social scientists, especially Robert Merton, Edwin Sutherland, and Donald Cressey, whose theories have contributed to this presentation of the field of delinquency.

In my analysis of delinquency, I cite the theories and research of many past and present social scientists. Wherever possible, I include significant contemporary research data. However, I also include some excellent earlier studies that I believe are useful for dialectic purposes. Although these older research reports may not be *au courant*, they help students of delinquency to understand the contemporary problem.

My personal and professional understanding of crime and delinquency has been influenced by many people other than social scientists. My brilliant and beloved son Mitch, a Los Angeles County probation officer, supported me throughout the travails of researching and writing this book and pointed me in many useful directions for the acquisition of data. I am deeply grateful to my dear friends Norman Herman and Ben Krentzman, who have listened with feigned attentiveness that often bordered on sincerity to all of the good and bad concepts on delinquency that I have bounced off them over the past several years. On many occasions they contributed to my knowledge on the subject. Gregg Williford and Jeremy McMillen, two premier graduate students, read the final draft and provided editorial suggestions.

My friends and colleagues in the Amity Therapeutic Community provided a considerable amount of data on delinquency. The support of Amity Directors Betty Fleishman, Naya Arbiter, and Rod Mullen facilitated my entry into two of Amity's landmark prison programs—the California Department of Correction's Amity Right Turn Project in the R.J. Donovan San Diego Prison and the short-lived, but innovative, therapeutic community project in the Beaumont Texas Prison. Many Amity people helped me with my book. Notable in this group of people were Sheila Giddings, Fred Tent, Ernie Logan, Jessica Middleton, Rachel Curtis, and Raymond Adame. A special contributor to this project was a former Los Angeles Crip gang leader, my good friend Alex Pipkin. My dear friend and colleague, the late

Zev Putterman, one of the most intelligent ex-junkies on the planet, also contributed enormously to my viewpoint on several aspects of the delinquency problem. The late Martin Haskell, sociologist, lawyer, colleague, and good friend, deserves special recognition for influencing my viewpoint on delinquency.

I want especially to cite the contributions of Naya Arbiter, Elaine Abraham, and Al Acampora, world leaders in the therapeutic community movement, to the last chapter of the book. Their poignant success stories, which describe their transformation from criminal/addicts to significant inspirational role models and program administrators, provide a pathway for enabling young delinquents to envision the possibility of changing their lives in a positive direction.

In my work in the field of juvenile delinquency over the past fifty years I have been involved in various research, teaching, and, most notably, direct work with delinquents and criminals in community delinquency prevention projects, therapeutic communities, drug rehabilitation centers, psychiatric hospitals, and prisons. I have interacted with hundreds of people in the field and thousands of juvenile and adult offenders. All of these people have facilitated my understanding of the juvenile delinquency problem, and I acknowledge their contributions to the theories and data in this book.

PART 1

Characteristics of Juvenile Delinquency

CHAPTERS

CHAPTER 1

THE NATURE AND EXTENT OF DELINQUENCY

A lonely and alienated youth, confined in a juvenile detention facility, awaiting the juvenile court's disposition.

Juvenile delinquents are treated differently than criminals in our society, because it is assumed that they are less responsible for their deviance and that their illegal behavior has not yet solidified into a permanent criminal pattern. The courts assume that juveniles are less culpable and more responsive to positive behavioral change than adult offenders. This treatment has been in effect during most of the twentieth century, although, in recent years, especially in the 1990s, there has been a movement toward treating youths in the juvenile justice system as adult criminals.

The first statute in the United States to define a "delinquent child" and create a juvenile court to deal with dependent, neglected, and delinquent children was enacted in Illinois in 1899. The court established by this statute began operation in Cook County (Chicago) Illinois, in June of that year. The Latin phrase *parens patriae,* meaning "in place of the parent," best summarizes the legal and social philosophy upon which its policies were based. The establishment of the juvenile court thus came as a logical sequel to the creation and expansion of special and separate treatment facilities for children and the introduction of probation as a method of treatment. (The relevance and function of the juvenile court in treating delinquency is more fully discussed in chapter 2, "The Juvenile Court.")

Juvenile delinquency has a precise legal meaning in almost all jurisdictions in the United States. Juvenile delinquency involves illegal behavior by a person who, in most jurisdictions, is under the age of eighteen and who is adjudicated as delinquent in a juvenile court. Delinquency encompasses such offenses as homicide, robbery, and theft, acts that if committed by an adult would constitute a crime. Delinquency also includes deviant behavior unique to the juvenile's status in society, such as truancy, curfew violations, running away from home, and "incorrigibility." The latter is a catch-all phrase that usually means that the youth's parents can no longer control their child's behavior.

In general, in contemporary law, therefore, a juvenile delinquent is distinguished from an adult criminal by several factors:

1. In almost all legal jurisdictions, the cutoff point between delinquency and criminality is marked by age, usually eighteen.

2. Juvenile delinquents are generally considered less responsible for their behavior than adult offenders and hence are considered less culpable.

3. In the administration of justice to a juvenile delinquent, the emphasis is more on the youth's personality and the motivation for the illegal act than on the offense itself. The opposite is usually true of the adult criminal. Criminal behavior is usually determined by the evidence in the

4

case and an adversarial search for whether or not the adult committed the crime.

4. In the treatment of juvenile delinquents, after they have been adjudicated guilty in the courts, the emphasis is more on therapeutic programs than on punishment.

5. The judicial process for a juvenile originally de-emphasized the legal aspects of due process and was geared to a more informal and personalized procedure by a juvenile court judge. Although this is still largely the approach, the trend is toward greater due process in the juvenile court system. LAWYER INVOLVEMENT, LESS PERSONALIZED

Throughout recorded history we find evidence of a more benevolent treatment for young offenders and the recognition that such offenders constitute a special problem! The misbehavior of young people has been regarded as a problem apart from criminality as far back as 2270 B.C. when the Code of Hammurabi prescribed specific punishments for children who did not obey their parents or ran away from home. The Hebrews divided young people into three categories, infant, prepubescent, and adolescent, and established increased penalties as offenders became older. Old English law also indicated special treatment for juvenile offenders by providing less severe punishment for persons under sixteen. The founding of Hospes St. Michael in Rome for the rehabilitation of young people indicates a concern with this problem by the Vatican as early as the seventeenth century (Kocourek and Wigmore, 1951).

Industrialization and urbanization, with their accompanying changes in family structure and function, have resulted in an increased emphasis on juvenile delinquency. Parents working away from home have not been able to fulfill the socialization function (preparation of their children for life in the society) in the same way as was common in earlier periods of human history. The impersonal relationships that accompany urbanization in society have produced an increased tendency to resort to formal social control of children. Misbehavior traditionally handled by family and friends in smaller communities now results in complaints to the police and petitions to the juvenile courts.

In the twentieth century, the juvenile court became a significant social and legal instrument for defining who is a juvenile delinquent in American society. In recent years, however, there has also been a trend toward diverting youths who would formerly have been made wards of the juvenile court into various types of treatment clinics. In this context, they are often perceived as individuals with "mental disorders" rather than as juvenile delinquents.

FACTORS RECEIVING THE LABEL DELINQUENT

I have worked with youths like these in several private psychiatric clinics over the past two decades and have observed that if it had not been for the burgeoning of medical insurance and the growth of treatment clinics, these same youths would be placed in the juvenile court system and defined as juvenile delinquents. Parents who have medical insurance have the possibility of placing their child in a treatment facility, whereas for most other parents the cost is prohibitive. As a consequence of this development, youths manifesting the same delinquent behavior may be placed in the juvenile court system or in a mental hospital, and this diversion affects delinquency statistics.

Since 1971 data has been compiled by the Department of Justice on youths who in the eyes of the court are juvenile delinquents and are put into private facilities where they are not labeled as delinquents. Each year the Justice Department conducts a census of residential facilities that house juveniles. In this regard private facilities have played a significant role in the juvenile justice system during the past twenty years. In 1997, the Office of Juvenile Justice and Delinquency Prevention of the Department of Justice (OJJDP) published an analysis of this phenomenon. According to the OJJDP report, based on FBI and other statistics, the population of juveniles in private facilities increased 9.6 percent from 1991 to 1995. Private juvenile residential facilities held 39,671 juveniles on February 15,1995. This population stood at 36,190 in 1991. Between 1991 and 1995, private facilities experienced a substantial increase in the number of juveniles held for delinquent offenses. Over this period of time, this population grew 24.4 percent, from 14,433 in 1991 to 17,781 in 1995. About 74 percent of juveniles in private facilities in 1995 were committed by the juvenile justice system (OJJDP, 1997a).[1]

According to the OJJDP in a 1997 report, males have increased slightly as a proportion of the population in private facilities. The proportion of males increased from 71.3 percent to 73.5 percent between 1991 and 1995. The number of males held increased 13 percent in this period, from 25,801 to 29,176. The female population, on the other hand, decreased slightly from 1991 to 1993 and rose again to approximately the same number in 1995.

The delinquency status of a youth in whatever type of facility is affected by the perception of the youth's behavior by his or her parents. Some parents see a minor act of misbehavior as a criminal felony, and other parents pay little, if any, attention to the delinquent behavior of their chil-

1. The Office of Juvenile Justice and Delinquency Prevention is a component of the Office of Justice Programs, which also includes the Bureau of Justice Assistance, the Bureau of Justice Statistics, the National Institute of Justice, and the Office for Victims of Crime. When quoting from or referring to their excellent publications, I will use OJJDP.

dren. For example, one parent may see the smoking of a marijuana cigarette as an horrendous act of juvenile delinquency whereas another parent
may perceive the same act as a normal youthful experiment.* The parental
perception of certain behavioral acts is critical in determining who is
defined as a delinquent by the courts, since those parents who are more
accepting of their children's deviance do not bring them to the attention of
the authorities.

Another issue in analyzing the definition of who is delinquent
relates to the fact that norms of conduct vary from state to state, city to city,
and neighborhood to neighborhood. Moreover, whether or not these norms
are applied to a particular child may depend on the position of his or her
parents in society and the provisions of the law in that community. The
community's response is regulated by the policies and attitudes of community leaders and law enforcement officials. For example, certain delinquent
behaviors are more likely to be tolerated in a high delinquency area than
in the suburbs.

Legally, a "juvenile delinquent" is a youth who has been so
adjudged by a juvenile court. Even so, the behavior that leads to a judgment
of juvenile delinquency is vaguely defined by the statutes, and the procedures followed by the various juvenile courts are not uniform. In the final
analysis, the legal status of "delinquent" tends to depend more on the attitudes of parents, the police, the community, and the juvenile courts than on
any specific illegal behavior of a child.

Despite these vagaries and haphazard factors, my observation over
the years is that most youths who persistently violate the law end up as
delinquents in the juvenile court system and eventually are placed in an
institution for delinquents. Once arrested and in the judicial administrative
net, the youth may more easily be defined as a juvenile delinquent due to
the socialization process inherent in the judicial process. In whatever custodial situation the youth is placed, he or she is more apt to be schooled in
further delinquent behavioral patterns. Juvenile detention facilities and
other juvenile institutions often serve as training schools for more severe
future delinquent behavior.

The Differential Treatment of Juvenile and Adult Offenders

I first noted the delineation between the official handling of the juvenile
and the adult offender when I worked as a group supervisor in a juvenile
detention facility in Newark, New Jersey. In this situation, I observed many
cases of the differential treatment accorded juvenile and adult offenders.

The basic function of the juvenile detention facility where I worked was to hold children under eighteen years old in custody, pending the disposition of the juvenile court. In this situation the court was housed in the same building as the juvenile detention facility. This type of jail facility is variously referred to as a juvenile jail, a house of detention, a juvenile hall, or, in the past, a parental school. This latter designation implies, in terms of *parens patriae,* that the state has taken over the parental role in a situation in which the youth's parents are no longer in effective control of the child.

One of my functions in the custodial facility was intake. One day the police brought in two boys who had been arrested for stealing a car. In the arrest process there had been a high-speed chase, which resulted in destruction of the car, considerable property damage, but no physical damage to the boys. Both youths were intoxicated, and when taken into custody they were belligerent with the arresting officers, who had to use maximum force to make their arrest. Despite the fact that the boys had no prior serious records, because of their substance abuse and their violent behavior, the juvenile court judge in the preliminary arraignment decided that they should be held in detention and not be released to their families. At the time they were initially incarcerated, both boys gave their ages as seventeen.

It was revealed at the arraignment of the two boys that one, Matt, had given a false name and had lied about his age. He was actually eighteen years old. Matt was immediately transferred to the adult city jail. He appeared in court the next day with his lawyer, who plea bargained the case. Matt was found guilty of auto theft, given a suspended sentence, and released. There was no judicial focus on Matt's past delinquent background, his emotional diagnosis, or his family history.

In sharp contrast, seventeen-year-old Joe was treated differently because of his juvenile status. In the parental school Joe saw a social worker daily to deal with the trauma of his incarceration. After a preliminary court appearance in the informal setting of the juvenile court, the judge, who focused more on the juvenile's social and psychological background than on the offense, ordered a psychiatric and a probation-officer workup and report to guide him in the disposition of the case. The probation department was flooded with casework, as in true in most jurisdictions, and it was three months before Joe, who remained in custody, appeared again before the juvenile court judge.

The probation officer's report was quite thorough and revealed a great deal about Joe's emotional condition, his delinquent history, his poor school record, and his disorganized family background. His father was an alcoholic who had physically abused Joe's mother, sexually abused Joe's sister, and regularly inflicted beatings on Joe. This difficult family situation was considered responsible for Joe's bellicose attitude and the fact that he was involved in a number of fights while in the detention facility.

The judge also noted from the probation officer's report that Joe's poor school attendance and record was due to the fact that he had a learning disability. The judge concluded, based on the probation officer's report, that Joe's diagnosed "conduct disorder," which manifested itself in violent behavior, required further analysis before his disposition of the case. In Joe's interest, the judge ordered a more intensive social and psychiatric evaluation for him from the state's diagnostic center. This involved an additional ninety days of custody in the diagnostic center. Joe reappeared in court after six months of custody and social-psychological analysis. Joe had, by this time, turned eighteen and decided that he wanted to join the army. In lieu of sending Joe to a state training school, the judge accepted Joe's decision to join the army, and the case was dismissed on that basis.

During Joe's incarceration, I had many opportunities to talk with him and counsel him. His friend Matt often visited him and teased him about the way they were each treated for the same offense. Joe was not impressed by the judicial system's "concern and caring" for his situation. As he told me one day, "I don't understand it. Matt and I were both loaded, stole a car, and tried to kick this cop's ass. He did one day in the joint, and I did six months." This case reveals something of the inequitable system of juvenile justice and criminal justice from the viewpoint of the recipient of the state's judicial treatment. The state may perceive its approach as being caring and concerned; the ward of the court may see the same treatment as simply a "doing time" situation.

† The Status Offender

Another important aspect of defining delinquency is the concept of status offender. The status offender commits offenses that relate to the specific sociocultural status juveniles occupy in society and the behaviors that accompany their adolescent roles. A status offense is one that an adult cannot commit, for example, being a runaway or playing hooky from school (Logan and Raush, 1985).

Ruth Cavan and Theodore Ferdinard (1981) delineate various aspects of the status offender:

> Typical laws governing status offenses require obedience to parents' lawful requests, attendance at school and avoidance of immoral situations or persons. These laws are defended as related to the present or future well-being of the child. Status offenses are usually victimless—that is, harmful only to the offender. In the absence of effective control by parents, the court assumes the

role of a parent and exercises control traditionally assumed to be the responsibility of parents. It is now recognized that status offenses often indicate deep disturbance in the parental-child relationship and not simply willfulness on the part of the child. With these facts in mind, many states now require that delinquents and status offenders be kept separate within the juvenile justice system. Delinquents typically are referred to the juvenile court for a formal hearing, which may result in commitment to a state training school, whereas the status offender is usually placed on informal probation or referred to a social agency or counseling center. (P. 18)

Gwen Holden and Robert Kapler (1995) discuss the need for the special treatment of status offenders. They assert that, when juveniles of this type come before the court, it provides an opportunity for heading off more serious delinquency. They recommend that the courts should not lose this opportunity.

The attitudes and actions of parents exercise an important influence on whether or not a child is found to be incorrigible, disobedient, or a runaway. A parent may petition a juvenile court alleging that his or her son is incorrigible because he does not obey and have the child declared a juvenile delinquent; another may regard the same behavior as reflecting an independent spirit; and still another parent may not care what his or her child does.

PARENTS

Substance abuse, a rampant delinquency problem, is significantly affected by parents' reactions to their children's drug use. Some parents take swift legal action, whereas others do not. Consequently, parents' response to their child's misbehavior has a significant impact on the child's status as a delinquent. Drug-testing kits are now available that can be used by parents to ascertain their child's level of substance abuse. In a sense, with a drug-testing kit the problem of substance abuse can be handled by the parents acting as police, judge, and jury.

The diverse element of parental response significantly affects a child's legal status and, therefore, delinquency statistics. The policies of the police and the attitudes prevailing in the community also influence the chosen action. The breaking of store windows during an encounter of two groups of boys may or may not be classified as delinquency. If the boys are college sophomores "fooling around," the incident is likely to be referred to the college administration for disciplinary action. If the two groups are defined by the police as gangs and the incident is seen as gang-related, the boys are likely to be arrested, taken before a juvenile court, and adjudicated as delinquents.

COMMUNITY

Another example of the influence of community attitudes is reflected in a rape incident. In one incident, a number of young male students raped a girl in a dormitory under the absurd guise of "playing around." The youthful offenders were football players. Their punishment involved censure and "community service." In real life, outside of the school's jurisdiction, they would have (and no doubt should have) received long-term prison sentences.

Police attitudes are also significant in determining which youths are classified as delinquent. For example, in a tri-city study in Pennsylvania, Nathan Goldman (1963) determined that there were great variations in arrest practices on the part of the police. The status of juvenile delinquent depended on police attitudes and the racial background of the child, as well as the time of the day or night that the offense was committed (a lower-class youth "steals" a car, but a middle-class youth is more likely to be a "borrower" in the view of some police). It is therefore not the behavior alone that results in the label of "juvenile delinquent" but also the policies of the police, which often reflect attitudes of the community.

A significant factor in the determination of who is delinquent is the concept of "labeling." William B. Sanders (1976) commented on the process of labeling:

> When we talk about a delinquent, we refer to someone who has been labeled as such by the juvenile justice system. Once a person has been labeled, he is often forced to play the role he has been given even though he may prefer another course. Labeling theory focuses on the interactive aspects of deviance in that it takes into account not only the delinquent activity and performer but also the others who come to define the situation and the actor as delinquent. . . . For example, if some juveniles are playing in front of a house with a bird flies against a window and breaks it, then flies away, the juveniles are believed to be responsible for the act, the police may be called, and as a consequence of this definition of the situation the juveniles may be labeled delinquents. Now, we might say that they were falsely accused, but the point is that their innocence of the act does not alter the consequences. They have been defined as delinquents; on the basis of this definition, they are treated as such. (P. 51)

The procedures of the juvenile court also significantly influence the determination of delinquency. The court is more likely to deal unofficially with children whose parents show an interest in them and come to their defense. It must act officially, however, in those cases in which parents present petitions charging their children with delinquency.

Another important determinant of delinquency status is the antisocial behavior that is treated by official agencies. Welfare departments and social work agencies, and the police in certain municipalities, for example, may maintain a list of known "delinquents." These agencies include the names of all children in the community who are referred to an agency for behavior that could have brought them to the attention of a court. Indications are that less than half the children known to have committed acts classified as delinquent become part of the recorded statistics.

Many studies indicate that delinquent behavior engaged in by middle-class children does not become known to any agency, public or private. In a landmark early study that should be replicated, Austin L. Porterfield (1946) had students at three colleges in Texas record delinquent behavior they participated in while attending high school. Forty-three percent reported truancies, and 15 percent reported running away from home. Almost half of the students admitted to petty thefts in high school. Porterfield reported that, on the average, each student might have been apprehended and charged with delinquency on at least eleven occasions, yet none of them had ever been charged with an offense. Porterfield compared these student reports with offenses charged against two thousand adjudicated delinquents who had appeared in the Fort Worth juvenile court. He found that 43 percent of the delinquent boys had been charged as truants and runaways, and 27 percent had been charged with theft.

A comparison of the responses of high school boys in Seattle, Washington, with records of boys from that area committed to state training schools also revealed little difference in the type or frequency of delinquent acts (Short and Nye, 1958). On the basis of these studies, one may conclude that a large amount of delinquent behavior engaged in by middle-class children goes undetected or unrecorded by enforcement agencies. However, there is considerable evidence to support the conclusion that an even greater amount of lower-class delinquency is not reflected in official statistics.

In general, most acts of delinquency are never found out by the authorities. Researchers H. L. Wilensky and C. N. Lebeaux (1958, p. 190) noted that working-class youngsters committed many undetected and unrecorded delinquencies. Careful studies of off-the-record delinquency in Passaic, New Jersey, the District of Columbia, and Cambridge-Sommerville, Massachusetts, showed a large amount of unofficial delinquency among lower-class youths. One study of 114 boys (40 of whom were official court delinquents) conservatively estimated that they had committed a minimum of 6,416 infractions of the law in five years, only 95 of which became matters of official complaint (p. 190).

While it is difficult to develop a definition of juvenile delinquency based on behavior that would be applicable to persons in all parts of the United States or, for that matter, in any state or city, one definition is clear: A youth is defined as a juvenile delinquent when that status is conferred upon him or her by a juvenile court. A child may also become a delinquency statistic if arrested and charged by the police even when the case is not referred to a court. This type of arrest data provides the basis for Federal Bureau of Investigation (FBI) statements about the amount of delinquency in the United States. Despite the FBI statistics, about half the children arrested are never referred to a court, and of those referred even fewer are adjudicated as delinquents (UCR, 1996).

Although the twentieth century began with the Illinois law that heralded a softer approach to treating juveniles, in many states there has been a strong motivation to obliterate these special approaches to youthful offenders and to significantly lower the age of delinquency to thirteen through fifteen. This political drive is related to a viewpoint that a large number of delinquents, in terms of their violence and other offenses, behave much like adult criminals.

The original Illinois law was the blueprint for juvenile codes that were legislated in other states. This traditional family court model remained essentially intact for about seventy-five years. Most states are still committed to some version of the traditional model of juvenile justice, but a small number of states have "criminalized" the juvenile court by redefining its jurisdiction to focus primarily on juvenile criminals, changing its major purpose from the rehabilitation of the child to criminal accountability for the offense, and replacing the discretion of juvenile court judges acting in the best interests of the child with a set of rigidly structured sentencing guidelines.

When a person under eighteen is alleged to have committed a serious crime, usually murder or an extremely violent act, criminal courts can have concurrent jurisdiction with juvenile courts. Prosecuting agencies may have the option of referring to either the criminal court or the juvenile court. Some jurisdictions are required by law to prosecute the child in a criminal court. Therefore, when a serious crime is alleged, we cannot always predict whether the child will be considered a criminal or a juvenile delinquent. The action of a law enforcement agency is often the determining factor. Since juveniles have become increasingly involved with serious offenses, especially violence, the referral of juveniles to adult courts has become more common on a nationwide basis. Some official organizations have opted for a "get-tough" policy (Weiss, Crutchfield, and Bridges, 1996).

The "get tough," more punitive approach became more politically correct in the 1990s and is fueled by the public's fearful attitude toward crime based on their personal experiences. According to a 1997 *Los Angeles Times* poll of 1,143 people, a representative sample of the Los Angeles population, four out of ten people stated they personally knew someone who had been seriously wounded or killed in a violent attack (Poll of Attitudes Toward Crime, 1997). The study further revealed that one out of six adults in Los Angeles claimed to know someone who had been murdered. Blacks and young adults were most likely to have known a victim of violence. According to the poll, more than half of the blacks said they knew someone who had been shot, stabbed, or otherwise seriously wounded or slain. The same was true of half the adults aged eighteen to twenty-nine. Whites and the elderly were least likely to have known a victim of serious violence.

Violence in Los Angeles and other big cities is not just something people watch on the local news or read in the newspaper. The poll attempted to gauge not only the perception but also the reality of the danger. Seven percent of the respondents said they or someone in their household had been a victim in 1996 of a violent crime, such as homicide, rape, assault, or robbery. Another 7 percent said they or someone in their household had been a victim of a burglary or other theft in the previous year. The reality is that the Los Angeles Police Department investigated 722 homicides and approximately 35,000 aggravated assaults in 1996.

More than 40 percent of homicides in Los Angeles County are related to juveniles and are gang-related. On this fact, one mother interviewed in the *Los Angeles Times* research commented, "I am scared to go out at night, scared to do anything. The situation has deteriorated in the past ten years throughout the city. My twelve-year-old daughter rides the bus, and I am so afraid for her, especially because of other kids and gangs." Her fears have a realistic base, since in the 1990s, a number of children have been the victims of violence, including murder, on city and school buses. This type of emotional fear, combined with the reality of the violence, drives people to demand a tougher approach to juvenile delinquents, especially those who commit violent acts.

The "get tough" approach is increasingly the approved model by adults, and this general trend also impacts the judicial handling of juveniles. The "get tough" approach to adults is reflected in the "three strikes" approach to adult offenders. The thirteen states that had three-strikes laws in 1994 were California, Colorado, Connecticut, Georgia, Indiana, Louisiana, Maryland, New Mexico, North Carolina, Tennessee, Virginia, Washington, and Wisconsin. Of those, eight saw increases in violent crimes in 1994–1995. According to the Justice Police Institute study, between 1994 and 1995, both violent and overall crime rates dropped more in the thirty-seven states without the laws than in the thirteen with them. According to the survey, the violent crime rate fell 4.6 percent in non-three-strike states, compared with 1.7 percent for three-strike states.

For overall crime, the decrease was 1.2 percent for states without the mandatory sentencing provisions and 0.4 percent for those with the three-strikes provisions.[2]

The advocacy of a harsher approach reflects a pendulum approach to the juvenile justice treatment scene. The fluctuation from a policy of "getting tough" to a softer judicial attitude is a pendulum that swings back and forth in the administration of juvenile justice. Despite these fluctuations in harsh and soft treatment of juvenile offenders, the distinction between the treatment of youths and adults in the justice system remains, and this differential, in my view, should be maintained. (This issue is discussed more fully in terms of enacted state laws for juveniles and their impact in chapter 2.)

APPENDIX P.559

The Extent of Delinquency: Statistical Trends

The Federal Bureau of Investigation has annually collated arrest rates for persons under eighteen years of age.[2] These findings are derived from data reported annually by local law enforcement agencies across the country to the FBI's Uniform Crime Reporting (UCR) program. Based on these data, the FBI prepares its annual report, *Crime in the United States*, which summarizes crimes known to the police and arrests made during the reporting calendar year. This information is used to characterize the extent and nature of juvenile delinquency. The FBI's presentation of these statistics has proved to be of considerable value to students of crime and juvenile delinquency. The statistics from the FBI *Uniform Crime Reports* present a perspective on delinquency and age worthy of classroom analysis. It is clear to me, however, that citing these specific statistics here is not useful for students of juvenile delinquency, because by the time they read this data, the statistics will be less relevant and outdated. Despite this, however, a statistical analysis is valuable in depicting the size and shape of delinquency statistics at any one time.

Based essentially on FBI statistics, *Juvenile Arrests 1997* (Snyder, 1998), a publication from the Office of Juvenile Justice and Delinquency Prevention, is an excellent summary of the relevant data on delinquency. The majority of data and graphs of trends derived from this most recent *Juvenile Justice Bulletin* are presented in the Appendix; this section is most useful for those students who want to examine and analyze delinquency statistics more closely.

---

2. The FBI's *Uniform Crime Reports* and *Crime in the United States, 1997,* issued by the U.S. Department of Justice, present the most substantive data available on crime and delinquency. These publications form the basis for almost all of the statistics on delinquency cited in this text.

In the following analysis, however, general trends and data derived from these and other sources especially relevant for comprehending the nature and extent of the delinquency problem in the United States are presented. All references to "juveniles" in this section refer to youths under the age of eighteen.

Despite the fact that current statistics will change by the year 2000 the following data has relevance for analyzing some trends in delinquent behavior. In 1997, law enforcement agencies in the United States made an estimated 2.8 million arrests of juveniles—persons under age eighteen. According to the FBI, juveniles accounted for 19 percent of all arrests and 17 percent of all violent crime arrests in 1997. The substantial growth in juvenile violent crime arrests that began in the late 1980s peaked in 1994. In 1997, for the third year in a row, the total number of juvenile arrests for Violent Crime Index offenses—murder, forcible rape, robbery, and aggravated assault—declined. Even with these declines (3 percent in 1995, 6 percent in 1996, and 4 percent in 1997), the number of juvenile Violent Crime Index arrests in 1997 was 49 percent above the 1988 level. In comparison, the number of adult arrests for a Violent Crime Index offense in 1997 was 19 percent greater than in 1988. Other relevant findings from the 1997 FBI statisticts are:

Of the 2,100 juveniles murdered in 1997, 56 percent were killed with a firearm. Juveniles were involved in 14 percent of all murder and aggravated assault arrests, 37 percent of burglary arrests, 30 percent of robbery arrests, and 24 percent of weapons arrests in 1997. Juvenile murder arrests increased substantially between 1988 and 1993. In the peak year of 1993, there were about 3,800 juvenile arrests for murder. Between 1993 and 1997, juvenile arrests for murder declined 39 percent, with the number of arrests in 1997 (2,500) 11 percent above the 1988 level. Between 1993 and 1997, juvenile arrests for burglary declined 9 percent and juvenile arrests for motor vehicle theft declined 30 percent.

Juveniles were involved in 14 percent of all drug abuse violation arrests in 1997. Between 1993 and 1997, juvenile arrests for drug abuse violations increased 82 percent. Juvenile arrests for curfew and loitering violations increased 87 percent between 1993 and 1997. In 1997, 28 percent of curfew arrests involved juveniles under age fifteen and 31 percent involved females. In 1997, 58 percent of arrests for running away from home involved females and 41 percent involved juveniles under age fifteen. Arrests of juveniles accounted for 12 percent of all violent crimes cleared by arrest in 1997—specifically, 8 percent of murders, 11 percent of forcible rapes, 17 percent of robberies, and 12 percent of aggravated assaults.

In general, the foregoing arrest rates are expected to increase substantially in the early part of the twenty-first century due to the population increase projections for the ten-to-seventeen age group.

Increases or decreases in delinquency will affect the adult crime problem because there is a strong and direct connection between juvenile delinquency and adult criminal careers. Chronic juvenile offenders have a high probability of continuing to commit crimes as adults, while juveniles who were never arrested are unlikely to develop criminal careers as adults. Predictors of chronic juvenile offenses include predelinquent deviant or troublesome behavior, physiological deficits associated with abnormal brain development, poor parenting, and evidence of criminal conduct, substance abuse, and mental disorder in the parents.

It is important to note that the official FBI and other statistics reflect only a part of the delinquency problem. As previously indicated, many youths who commit acts of violence or theft or who use illegal drugs are not arrested and are thus not reflected in the statistics. A case in point would be the illegal use of marijuana. In the last decade the use of marijuana has steadily risen; however, the community and police increasingly tend to perceive its use as benign, and the official approach in terms of arrest has been to give users a pass. Consequently, statistics indicate a drop in drug arrests, despite the fact that the offense is clearly more prevalent.

Since a relatively small percentage of the children who engage in misbehavior are accorded the status of delinquent or become part of our juvenile delinquency statistics, a rise or fall in statistics does not necessarily indicate an increase in antisocial behavior. It often simply reflects changes in family, police, or community responses to children who do not conform to the expectations of their societal sphere.

The fact that families in our urban industrial society have turned more and more to community resources and public authorities for assistance in performing the family's traditional functions also affects delinquency statistics. Families who perceive various juvenile facilities as responsible for dealing with their misbehaving children tend to relinquish control over their children to these organizations, and this affects delinquency and delinquency statistics.

Another factor that affects the prevalence of delinquency is the changing cultural role of adolescents in our society. Adolescents have attained a high degree of physical maturity, and yet they are usually denied any significant economic or social role. This is especially true of the young male in depressed socioeconomic communities. He has many of the social, sexual, and material desires of a man, yet without money he tends to be deprived of a legal means for satisfying these wants.

He has two alternatives regarding school. He can either continue in school and suppress his desire to drop out or attempt to find employment or some other way of obtaining money. Unemployment, especially among sixteen- and seventeen-year-olds who enter the labor market before completing high school, helps to explain the age distribution of arrests for delinquency. Youths quit school not only because they lack interest in education but also because they need money to obtain material things. The lack of education and skills necessary to obtain worthwhile employment results in further frustration, especially for minority group children growing up in depressed socioeconomic areas.

Many young people fail to obtain employment they consider acceptable; many do not achieve steady employment of any kind. Thus, unemployed and without money, these young people find themselves on the streets with nothing to do. These are the boys and girls who are most likely to engage in delinquent activity, particularly property offenses. Many had some experience in delinquency when they were thirteen and fourteen, as indicated by the high arrest rates at these ages. While at school they were occupied part of the time. Once they dropped out of school, with their need for money not satisfied legitimately, they may, and frequently do, turn to delinquency and later to crime. The greatest incidence of school dropouts appears to coincide with the minimum age at which children can legally leave school. This confirms a relationship between dropping out of school, unemployment, and delinquency (Fleisher, 1966, pp. 83–84).

An important factor in delinquency is that substance abuse was practically nonexistent in the early part of the twentieth century and reached epidemic proportions in the latter part of the century. Also children are abusing drugs at an earlier age, and there is an escalation of substance abuse including alcohol consumption by adults. The laws on substance use and abuse are a significant part of this problem. Early in the twentieth century many drugs now regulated were not illegal. Consequently, the increasing commerce and the greater use of drugs have produced an increasing number of juvenile arrests.

Females and Delinquency

In general, female arrests for delinquency have increased in the last decade, although the ratio of male delinquents to female delinquents remains at four to one. In 1997, 26 percent of juvenile arrests were arrests of females. Law enforcement agencies made 748,000 arrests of females below the age of eighteen in 1997. Between 1993 and 1997, arrests of juvenile females increased more (or decreased less) than male arrests in most offense categories. Table 1.1 shows these trends.

Table 1.1   Percent Change in Juvenile Arrests 1993–1997

Most Serious Offense	Female	Male
Violent Crime Index	12%	9%
Murder	-36	-39
Robbery	-3	7
Aggravated assault	15	-10
Property Crime Index	10	-8
Burglary	-3	-10
Larceny-theft	14	-1
Motor vehicle theft	-19	-31
Simple assault	30	12
Weapons	-8	-24
Drug abuse violations	117	78
Liquor laws	41	30
Disorderly conduct	52	25
Curfew and loitering	102	81
Runaways	0	-4

Source: Crime in the United States—1997, table 35.

The difference between male and female arrest rates is affected by the overall cultural environment. Since men, even with the gender role changes that took place in the twentieth century, are still socialized to be more aggressive, they are more likely than females to be delinquent. Despite some changes in gender roles, females are still expected to adopt a more passive role. Nevertheless, the arrest rate of females is increasing. This may be a consequence of the narrowing of the difference between male and female cultural and occupational roles in recent years.

Increasingly, women work outside the home and are the principal breadwinners in many families. As a result of this economic gender change, they share equally with the male members of the household in the major decision-making processes that affect the family. A young girl brought up in such a home, who identifies with her mother, tends to consider herself as important as the male members of her family. She further believes herself capable of doing almost anything they can do and feels free to engage in most of the activities that they are involved in—including delinquency.

In one analysis of the gender equal opportunity–equal crime concept, Josefina Figueira-McDonough (1984) concluded that these assumptions about female delinquency have a certain complexity. She stated, "Our findings suggest that the influx of feminist orientation on illegitimate behavior is far more complex, less linear, and much more tenuous than suggested by some criminologists."

Despite the complexity of the gender issue, FBI arrest statistics reveal that between 1960 and 1995, the general crime and delinquency rate for females rose more than six times faster than that for males. The most significant increases were in burglary, armed robbery, and possession of a deadly weapon.

Freda Adler's (1975) commentary on increasing female criminality is as true for the present as it was in 1975: "The dramatic rise cannot be directly attributed to one factor. The feminist connection is that women are taking on more of the behavior of men. This also means taking on the stress, strain and frustration that males have traditionally dealt with. Many of these women, unskilled and untrained, may turn in desperation to crime. There was a time when a female confined her criminal acts to prostitution and shoplifting. Now she is committing armed robbery, auto theft, and burglary, traditionally male crimes, so that we see a definite change in both the dimension and form of female criminality" (pp. 20–22).

Women now seem to be gravitating toward the center of the action in crime and delinquency. While this is not a positive outgrowth of the women's movement, it nevertheless shows that women are behaving more like men as they increasingly think of themselves as equal to men. The general attitudes inherent in women's liberation tend to filter down to adolescent girls and are part of the causal backdrop to increased female delinquent behavior.

Rita James Simon (1975) cited statistics that showed that the percentage of women arrested for crimes of violence fluctuated between ten and thirteen percent during a twenty-year period. Her analysis of female criminality concluded that the increase was not in violence but in property offenses, such as forgery, fraud, and embezzlement. Her analysis has relevance for the twenty-first century: "It is reasonable to assume that the women's movement has had some effect on the psyche, the consciousness and the self-perceptions of many women in American society. But the extent to which it has motivated those women to act outside the law in order to gain financial rewards, vengeance, or power is still too early to assess" (p.46).

Simon's major hypothesis is that increased participation in the labor force has given women more opportunities to commit larceny, fraud, embezzlement, and other financial and white-collar crimes. "If the present trends continue . . . women will probably be involved in white collar crimes in a proportion commensurate with their representation in the society. The fact that female arrests have increased for these offenses and not for all offenses is consistent both with the opportunity theory and with the presence of a sizable women's movement" (p. 46).

Substance abuse has become one of the most significant problems for young people in American society, and the evidence reveals that it is an activity shared equally by girls and boys. It is also one of the few delinquent behaviors in which females and males are close to being equal participants. Arrest statistics do not fully confirm this assertion; however, my observations at youth gatherings and research I have carried out confirm that drug abuse is more a unisex activity than is any other type of delinquency. The reason for girls not being arrested as much as boys is related to the fact that chivalry is not entirely dead. My observation is that often in a drug arrest situation, males involved will take responsibility for the stash and "take the fall."

Another problem that has contributed to the growing statistics of female juvenile delinquency is the escalation of teenage prostitution. This problem is increasingly more a function of economic necessity for young (runaway) homeless girls than in the past, when young female prostitutes were motivated to prostitution by emotional problems.[3]

What would an alternative, egalitarian system look like in its handling of women as victims? It would undertake a massive commitment to the female victim, including:

1. Mandatory education in public schools in rape, incest, and employment rights. In addition, training of females in self-defense should be offered by the schools.

2. Employment of female staff in all parts of the criminal justice system dealing with female victims.

3. Training of all law enforcement personnel in the problems unique to female victims.

---

3. For a fuller discussion of gender issues and delinquency, see Kathleen Daly and Meda Chesney-Lind, Feminism and Criminology, *Justice Quarterly, 5* (1988), 497–538; Sally Simpson and Lori Ellis, Is Gender Subordinate to Class? *Journal of Criminal Law and Criminology, 85* (1994), 453–480; and Loraine Geisthorpe and Allison Morris, *Feminist Perspectives in Criminology* (New York: Open University Press, 1990).

4. Establishment of rape crisis centers and shelters and of other support systems to encourage bonding among female victims.

5. Encouragement of women who wish to prosecute men who have victimized them and the provision of legal assistance for these women.

In addition, necessary legal reforms would include:

1. Removal of the husband exemption in rape statutes.

2. Making restraining orders against abusive husbands a more effective legal tool for battered women.

3. Recognition of self-defense as a legitimate legal defense for women who retaliate against men who repeatedly batter them.

4. Legalization of prostitution or, at the very least, sanctions directed equally at all parties involved.

5. Adoption of more stringent laws criminalizing sexual harassment on the job. Sexual harassment should be established as adequate grounds for leaving a job without forfeiting unemployment compensation.

Rafter and Natalizia (1981) present a variety of issues related to gender roles that will significantly affect the growing number of female delinquents in the twenty-first century. For example, young girls who are sexually abused within their family are much more prone to become runaways. They usually run to the "combat zones" of large cities, where destitute and with few job skills they may become victims of male predators. Adult pimps and "tricks" tend to exploit these abused girls as prostitutes. Moreover, they are also more prone, in these onerous circumstances, to act out delinquent patterns, such as theft and substance abuse. Recent data reveal that substance-abusing mothers give birth to physically and socially defective children. These patterns, among others, contribute to the complicated and burgeoning problem of increasing female delinquency.[4]

---

4. For a fuller discussion of these issues, see Donna Bishop and Charles E. Frazier, Race Effects in Juvenile Justice Decision Making: A Statewide Analysis, *Journal of Criminal Law and Criminology, 25* (April 1996): 36–37 and Michael Lieber, A Comparison of Juvenile Court Outcomes for Native Americans, African-Americans, and Whites, *Justice Quarterly, 36* (March 1994), 58.

Minority Group Factors and Delinquency

Most of the people who migrated from Europe to the United States in the latter part of the nineteenth century and the first quarter of the twentieth century came in search of economic and social opportunities. By and large they migrated from rural areas in eastern and southern Europe and had languages and cultures differing from those of the American majority. In recent years, especially in the Southwest, large numbers of Mexicans and other Hispanic groups have entered the United States.

Generally, immigrants are poor, uneducated, honest, and willing and able to work. In the United States immigrants tend to settle in areas inhabited by members of their ethnic group, where they find others who understand their language and culture. The initial migrations were encouraged by relatives or friends in the United States, and the first residence was usually in or near the homes of these relatives or friends. This migration pattern resulted in the establishment and expansion of self-segregated neighborhoods of African Americans, Mexican Americans, Asians, Irish, Swedes, Italians, Jews, and other ethnic groups in the big cities.

Largely because of their families' socioeconomic struggles and culture-conflict issues, these groups initially experienced a disproportionately high incidence of delinquency on the part of their youths. Many violent gangs become pseudofamilies for youths who are alienated from their family struggles, conflicts, and social disorganization. Migrants to United States urban slum areas include blacks from the South, Puerto Ricans, Mexicans, and, to a lesser degree, poor whites from southern states. These groups have a higher proportionate rate of delinquency than more stable groups in American society. Children of these more recent migrants to urban areas now constitute a large proportion of delinquency cases. In California, all of the custodial institutions are populated mainly by minority groups.

Arrest rates and court statistics reveal that the highest rates of juvenile delinquency in America today are among blacks, Puerto Ricans, Mexican Americans, and more recent Latin American arrivals to urban areas. This disproportionately high incidence of delinquency in relation to their numbers in the general population is revealed in the arrest rates of minorities.

The racial composition of the juvenile population in 1997 was approximately 80 percent white, 15 percent black, and 5 percent other races, with juveniles of Hispanic ethnicity being classified as white. In 1997, in contrast to the proportions in the general population, 53 percent of juvenile arrests for violent crimes involved white youths and 44 percent involved black youths. Table 1.2 indicates the high incidence of arrests of minorities compared to the white population.

Table 1.2   White Proportion of Juvenile Arrests in 1997

Murder	40%
Forcible rape	56
Robbery	42
Aggravated assault	60
Burglary	73
Larceny-theft	70
Motor vehicle theft	59
Weapons	64
Drug abuse violations	64
Curfew and loitering	75
Runaways	77

Source: Crime in the United States—1997, table 43.

Many explanations have been given for the fact that newly arrived immigrant populations tend to have a disproportionately higher incidence of delinquency when compared to the general population. Historically, these minority groups were restricted, alienated, or excluded from full participation in the social and economic life of American society. With the exception of African Americans, minority members speak a foreign language, are expected to integrate into a society with a culture different from their own, and are often regarded as "foreigners" by members of the dominant society. Even some blacks confront a language barrier, and recently there was a discussion about using "ebonics," a black slang, in the Oakland, California, school system.

The often discriminatory societal reaction to people with different languages, cultural backgrounds, and norms makes it exceedingly difficult for the children of these minority groups to make the adjustments necessary to prepare them for roles in the dominant social system. They find it more difficult to obtain employment other than unskilled labor, partly because of lack of formal education and partly because of discrimination. These blockades to full participation in the society tend to produce a higher incidence of delinquency among minority groups.

The family structure of blacks, in particular, appears to be under even greater assault. Four out of five white children live in two-parent families; fewer than half of all black children do. Only one white child in thirty-eight lives away from both parents, whereas one in eight black children live away from their biological parents. Proportionally, there are far more black children born to unwed teenage mothers. A 1995 Census Bureau study revealed that more than half of all black babies born in the United States were born to unmarried mothers. In contrast, the study found that white unmarried women accounted for about 18 percent of all out-of-wedlock births. These statistics reflect a less favorable family situation for many black children, and this in part accounts for the higher rate of delinquency.

School behavior and its consequences also affect minority group delinquency. For example, school suspension rates for all children have increased; however, minority group children are suspended at twice the rate of other children. Minority group elementary and high school pupils are put into programs for the mentally retarded three times more often than white children. For every two black children who graduate from high school, one drops out. Due to these factors, minority group children tend to have a disproportionately higher rate of delinquency than the general youth population. The higher rate has little to do with ethnic background or skin color but a great deal to do with socioeconomic situation and lack of opportunity.

More black than white youths are committed to institutional care. This may be due to the juvenile courts' philosophy of earlier state intervention in the case of youths living under conditions of severe poverty accompanied by family disorganization. Action is taken against blacks more often and for less serious offenses than other groups. Like the immigrants of earlier periods, many black families today are restricted to depressed residential areas, which manifest more forms of social disorganization than most other areas. Vice, crime, violent gangs, and social disorder become traditional in such areas, owing to oppressive negative forces.

A veiled castelike system accounts in part for the differences between majority and minority group delinquency rates. A subordinate socioeconomic position or life-style, with its bitter implications of economic deprivation, overcrowding, substandard housing, and inadequate education, has a negative impact on the self-concepts and personalities of young children. These factors and others already noted produce a disproportionately higher rate of delinquency among minority children.

In summary, no particular ethnic or minority group has a special propensity for delinquent behavior. However, the social-psychological and economic factors that impact on a group can affect the incidence of delinquency in any given group. These causal factors and the functioning of the juvenile justice system are the significant elements that affect the nature and extent of juvenile delinquency in the United States.

CHAPTER 2
THE JUVENILE COURT

The juvenile court is the basic institution for legally defining and labelling a youth as a juvenile delinquent. The adjudication process is ususally directed by the judge, though sometimes the youth has a lawyer present.

The juvenile court is the central institution in our society for labeling and defining who is delinquent. Many elements enter into this process, including the social perceptions and norms of the community, parents, and police. The judgments of these various segments of society enter into the process and determine which children are propelled into the juvenile justice system in the first place, as well as which children are deemed delinquent by the juvenile court. These three perspectives—the community and its norms, the youth's self-concept, and the legal arm of the community (the police and the juvenile court)—all enter into the process of defining who is a delinquent. Of the three, the juvenile court process as a legal entity constructed by society has the most clarity and the best-defined consequences for a juvenile delinquent.

Three basic social-psychological perspectives are used in defining the juvenile delinquent: (1) the social perceptions of a juvenile's deviant behavior; (2) the juvenile's self-concept; and (3) the legal definition produced by the juvenile court process. The most definitive perspective is the third one, but the other two viewpoints also have real social meaning and consequences.

For example, a youth who is perceived or labeled as a delinquent by the community is very likely to experience social and personal consequences, even when he or she is not accorded delinquent status by the juvenile court process. One consequence is that the youth develops a delinquent self-concept. The labeling factor and delinquent self-concept may propel a youth into the courts, where he or she becomes a legally adjudicated delinquent. Following is a brief commentary on each of these three perspectives on delinquency and an in-depth analysis of the most definitive perspective on delinquency-adjudication through the juvenile court process.

Social Perceptions

In many communities a youth may be labeled a juvenile delinquent despite the fact that he or she has not been accorded this status by the court. For example, the youth's family, neighbors, peers, and teachers may know that he or she has committed acts of theft or violence or is a substance abuser. In the case of a female, sexual promiscuity and substance abuse are the primary criteria for delinquency status.

There are different regional and neighborhood ideas of who is a delinquent. In high-delinquency areas, theft, violence, and substance abuse tend to be viewed by the general population as the normal behavioral pattern for most youths, whereas in other communities these acts may be perceived as criminal behavior. In certain families, the discovery that a child possesses drugs may be considered a capital offense, whereas, in another family, parents and children may use drugs together. These varied perceptions have consequences, since they affect the labeling of youths as delinquents by their communities, schools, and families. In response to being unofficially labeled a delinquent by neighbors, relatives, teachers, peers, or family, a youth may or may not develop the self-concept of delinquent. The youth's awareness of being perceived as a delinquent often reinforces his or her deviant behavior.

Self-Concept

Whether a youth has a delinquent self-concept or not is a subjective matter. Many youths do not define themselves as delinquents, even when their behavior clearly points to this conclusion, and others believe that they are "bad" or delinquents based on minor norm violations. At one extreme are young people who engage in deviant acts like robbery, drug abuse, or violence, which by the judgment of most community norms are considered delinquent. At the opposite end of this continuum are youths who commit very few deviant acts, yet believe that they are delinquent. The self-concept of delinquency often does not agree with the objective situation.

Having a "delinquent" self-concept has a real personal impact. The youth who believes he or she is a delinquent is far more apt to confirm the label by acting out further deviant behavior. As one youth put it, "If they think I'm bad, I'll show them how bad I can be." A youth who acknowledges the labeling process as valid tends to feel that he or she has nothing to lose by committing more deviant acts. Some juvenile delinquents deny their status and continue their deviant behavior until they are officially defined as juvenile delinquents by the juvenile court's judicial system. Even then, many "convicted" delinquents rationalize or neutralize their deviant behavior by blaming the "system" or their parents, or claim that they are victims of discrimination. One of the consequences of this process is that the individual who denies the delinquent label also rejects treatment or change.

For example, a young substance abuser who eschews a delinquent self-concept may rationalize his or her drug addiction and the thefts necessary to support the habit. As one youth told me, "I just use drugs for recreation, and I make a little money on the side like everyone else." His denial of his delinquent condition brings to mind the Alcoholics Anonymous philosophy, which states that the first step toward resocialization of individuals is the admission that they are alcoholics and have a problem. It is likewise necessary for delinquent youths to stop rationalizing their behavior and accept a delinquent self-concept so that they will be amenable to treatment or an intervention that might change their behavior.

The Juvenile Court System

The most definitive aspect of delinquent status is the process of being adjudicated a delinquent by the juvenile justice system. The following description of the juvenile court—historical roots, how juveniles become wards of the court, the court's processes, the role of the juvenile court judge, the use of "diversion" programs by the court, and the balance of due process and social welfare in the courts—helps to explain how a youth is legally labeled a juvenile delinquent.

As recently as the latter part of the nineteenth century, children in both England and the United States were tried for their crimes in criminal courts. The age of the child was a factor in determining whether he or she should be held responsible for delinquent acts, but in most other respects, the treatment resembled that accorded an adult charged with a crime. The child was likely to be detained in the same jail as an adult criminal, tried by the same court, and sent to the same custodial facility. The common law exempted children under seven years of age from responsibility for criminal behavior, and this rule still generally applies. A child under seven could not be found guilty of committing a criminal act because of the absence of one essential element: *mens rea*, or criminal intent. But children between the ages of seven and fourteen might be tried and convicted. They were presumed to be incapable of formulating an intent to commit a crime, but this presumption could be overcome by evidence to the contrary presented by the prosecution in a criminal court.

Chancery courts, which had their origin in fifteenth-century England, also dealt with the problems of children. English common law imposed a duty on parents to provide support, supervision, and care for their children. It also provided that parents had a right to custody of their children unless they defaulted in their duties. Chancery courts were created by the king to protect children in need. If children were left without support as a result of divorce, abandonment, or death of the father, they were often destitute. The chancery court, a court of equity, assumed the duty of seeing that parents, particularly fathers, carried out their obligations to spouses and children. The welfare of the wife and child was the sole and fundamental consideration in actions by this court. The courts did not normally deal with cases in which misbehavior of children was alleged. They protected children who would now be referred to as "neglected" or "dependent" and were concerned principally with the administration of property or the ordering of financial support for dependents. The chancery court acted *in loco parentis* (in place of the parents), taking whatever steps deemed necessary to provide for the child's needs.

In 1825, with the establishment of the House of Refuge in New York City, many states began providing separate correctional facilities for children. The House of Refuge was restricted to children adjudged offenders by a criminal court. By 1860 there were sixteen such specialized institutions in the United States that were established at the insistence of reformers who objected to having children confined in jails and penitentiaries with adult criminals and subjected to potentially harmful associations and influences.

In 1841, owing largely to the efforts of John Augustus, a Boston shoemaker who helped children in trouble, a form of probation was first tried as a method of treating juvenile offenders outside a custodial institution under the supervision of a criminal court. In 1869, Massachusetts officially established probation for children and provided for the supervision of juvenile delinquents. By the end of the nineteenth century, as the states provided specialized treatment for children in training schools, the criminal courts began to send children to these schools instead of prison and to place children on probation for minor offenses. Persons interested in social reform actively sought the establishment of a specialized court for children, organized around objectives significantly different from those of the criminal courts. They wanted a court that would understand the child, diagnose his or her problems, and provide treatment that would restore the child to a constructive role in the community. The welfare of the child was considered more important than the question of guilt or innocence. It is these considerations that led reformers to seek establishment of the juvenile court and that continue to motivate its proponents today.

The first landmark statute to define a "delinquent child" and create a juvenile court to deal with dependent, neglected, and delinquent children was enacted in Illinois in 1899. The court established by this statute began operation in Cook County (Chicago) in June of that year. As previously indicated, the Latin phrase *parens patriae* (in place of the parent) best summarizes the legal and social philosophy on which its policies were based. The establishment of the juvenile court thus came as a logical sequel to the creation and expansion of special and separate treatment facilities for children and the introduction of probation as a method of treatment.

The Children's Bureau, based in the federal government, was created thirteen years after the first juvenile court and, under the leadership of social workers, exercised an important influence over the development of juvenile courts throughout the United States. By 1945, every state had passed laws providing for the special treatment of juvenile delinquents.

The juvenile court is not a criminal court, nor is it a chancery court, although, as far as children are concerned, it performs the functions of both. It is a statutory court with powers provided for and limited by statutes and procedures fixed by the judge of the court when they are not fixed by law. Juvenile court statutes do not necessarily create specialized courts completely independent of the criminal or civil court system. In many states, authority over juveniles rests wholly or in part with courts that are primarily engaged in some other function. Often the judge who presides over a juvenile court spends most of his or her time as judge of a criminal court. In most states, especially in large cities, there are completely separate juvenile courts. All states, however, have statutes providing for juvenile courts, specifying or permitting procedures that differ from those required in criminal courts. When a judge normally assigned to a criminal court sits as a juvenile court judge on a particular day of the week, that court becomes a juvenile court for that day, and the procedures followed are those legally prescribed for the juvenile court.

Overall the juvenile court justice system has grown enormously in the past century. Nationwide, the juvenile justice system consists of almost twenty thousand public and private agencies, with a total budget amounting to hundreds of millions of dollars and over fifty thousand employees. Most of the forty thousand police agencies have a juvenile component, and more than three thousand juvenile courts and about one thousand juvenile correctional facilities exist throughout the country. (National Council of Juvenile and Family Court Judges, 1995). These figures do not take into account the large number of children who are referred to community diversion programs and various psychological treatment facilities. There are thousands of these programs throughout the country, and large numbers of people are employed in them. This multitude of agencies and people dealing with juvenile delinquency and status offenses has led to the development of an enormous and complex juvenile justice system.

The Court Process

In 1995, courts with juvenile jurisdiction handled an estimated 1,555,200 cases involving delinquency charges. More than half (55 percent) of these cases were processed formally, either by filing a delinquency petition in the juvenile court or transferring the case to criminal court.[1]

---

1. The OJJDP *Fact Sheet* for March 1997, *"Trends in New Laws Targeting Violent or Other Serious Crime by Juveniles,"* presents national data on delinquency cases processed by juvenile courts from 1985 through 1994. National estimates were generated using information from the National Juvenile Court Data Archive. More than 1,800 jurisdictions containing 67 percent of the U.S. juvenile population contributed data for these national estimates.

According to United States Bureau of Justice Statistics, delinquency cases have grown 69 percent since 1985. Between 1985 and 1994, the total delinquency caseload of U.S. juvenile courts increased 41 percent. During those years, the number of formally handled cases grew 69 percent, from 505,400 to 855,200 cases annually. In contrast, the number of cases handled informally (that is, without a petition or court hearing) increased just 17 percent since 1985. The formal delinquency caseload in 1994 was 22 percent larger than the total informal caseload.

The likelihood of formal processing for delinquency cases in general increased from 46 percent to 55 percent in the years 1985 to 1994. The largest relative changes were in drug offense cases (61 percent formal in 1994 compared with 43 percent in 1985) and weapon cases (62 percent formal in 1994 versus 45 percent in 1985). The likelihood of formal handling did not change substantially in cases involving charges such as robbery, aggravated assault, and arson. One in three delinquency cases has resulted in juvenile court adjudication or waiver to criminal court. (Trends in New Laws, 1997).

A youth may be adjudicated delinquent because he or she admits to the charges in a case where the court finds sufficient evidence to judge the youth a delinquent. The most severe court actions in delinquency cases are considered to be adjudication in juvenile court or waiver to criminal court, although fewer than one in seventy such cases were transferred to criminal court in the years 1985 to 1994. The increased use of formal handling from 1985 to 1994 did not result in an equivalent increase in the proportion of delinquency cases that were either adjudicated or waived to criminal court.

In general, children are brought into the processes of a juvenile court through what is known as a petition. A petition may be initiated by a parent or another adult, but in most cases it is presented by a police officer. Children are often arrested by a regular police officer. However, in some police departments, officers with special training in handling juveniles, variously known as "youth squads" or "juvenile officers," are assigned to delinquency work. A study by McKeachern and Bauzer (1967) concluded that the number of petitions requested for juvenile court varied according to the investigating police officers. They found that police officers handled three out of four apprehended delinquents without referral to court or probation officers.

A study by Malcolm Klein, Susan Rosensweig, and Ronald Bates (1975) found juvenile arrest procedures to be vague and ambiguous. They investigated the uniformity of juvenile arrest definitions and operations, with three issues in current criminology underlying their study: (1) translating legislative intent into efficient and just administrative or operational activities; (2) developing adequate information systems for criminal justice; and (3) reporting and making decisions on the current status and progress of agencies and programs. They attempted empirical documentation of the disparate meanings that the common concept of juvenile arrest had to the various concerned people. They collected data from forty-nine separate police departments in a large metropolitan county, which included rural, suburban and urban areas. Generally, the stations were asked to report their arrest statistics to the state and federal governments, as well as to local agencies. They found ambiguous guidelines and dissimilar reporting forms in various police stations.

The use of different sets of criteria and statistics made uniformity hard to achieve. Structured interviews with forty-five chiefs of police revealed less than 50 percent agreement that "booking" was the critical point in determining arrest. Booking does not correspond to the legal definition of either arrest or recording procedures. The chiefs' lack of knowledge of and interest in this issue seemed to indicate a general tendency for juvenile officers and bureaus to be relatively independent, even in highly structured departments.

One hundred thirty juvenile officers and their supervisors filled out questionnaires, and seventy-seven juvenile officers, one in every station in the county, participated in a structured interview. Consistent with the chiefs' lack of clarity was the variation among juvenile officers in the same and different departments. To some, an "arrest" was a field contact; to others, it was bringing a suspect to the station; for still others, it constituted formal arrest.

I can confirm similar findings in my work with the police in New York City and Los Angeles. In many cases police handled juveniles outside the police station or court in a judicious way—by talking to their parents or by reprimanding or counseling the child. There is, however, considerable evidence that police contact with juveniles, especially in high-delinquency areas, is less than ideal.

Research carried out by Barbara Tomson and Edna R. Felder (1975) characterized police behavior vis-à-vis juveniles as "police pressure" and described the interaction with juveniles as follows: "In 'high-delinquency areas' police are continually harassing youth who look delinquent, and therefore police are considered enemies in lower-class neighborhoods. The gang delinquent interprets the effect of this police attitude on his or her life in a way that results in a vicious circle: The delinquent becomes more of a 'cop hater' and moves deeper into delinquency, and this causes the police officer to become more of a 'delinquent hater' " (pp. 149–50).

Based on their analysis of the situation, Tomson and Felder concluded that when the police apprehend a delinquent, they usually have several choices of action. The choice they make varies. They delineated five alternatives open to the police: outright release, release and submission of a field interrogation report, official reprimand and release to parents or guardian, petition to the juvenile court, or arrest and confinement in juvenile hall. Treatment of the minor offender depends on the youth's personal characteristics: group affiliation (is he or she a gang member?), age, race, grooming, dress, and (most important) demeanor. Tomson and Felder noted a high correlation between cooperative demeanor (exhibited by contriteness, respectfulness, and fearfulness) and police leniency. Constant police harassment of youths who presented a delinquent stereotype resulted in much negative contact between these youths and police.

Continuing interaction with police by juveniles results in their diminished concern about the police impact. As the frequency of contacts increases, the process becomes routine. Youths lose their fear of police and become indifferent and hostile, attitudes police often interpret as characteristic of a hardened criminal. The police then tend to treat them severely, reinforcing the youths' hostilities. Despite these problems, police officers have more roles, flexibility, and importance in a lower-class neighborhood than in a middle-class neighborhood, because there is often a greater need for their services in dealing with a variety of human problems, including delinquency. Despite this, some of the negative attitudes about the law and law enforcement in these communities are projected by juveniles onto all officialdom, including the juvenile court and its procedures.

Juvenile Court Procedures

The juvenile court was, from the outset, intended to be primarily rehabilitative and operated in the interest of the child. The juvenile court is a structure for helping "dependent children," "status offenders," or "neglected children" in need of care and further official attention. One ideal of the court is "individualized justice." A typical juvenile court act provides for state control as a substitute for parental control and an informal proceeding instead of a trial. An early United States Children's Bureau publication (Belden, 1920, pp. 7–10) listed some essential characteristics of the juvenile court that generally remain in current use: (1) separate hearings for children's cases; (2) informal or chancery procedure; (3) regular probation service; (4) separate detention facility for children; (5) special court and probation records; and (6) provisions for mental and physical examinations.

Official cases in the juvenile court (designated as well as specialized) are initiated by petition. If a child has been arrested by the police, the petitioner may be the police officer, the victim, or a representative of a pros-ecuting agency. The petition is similar to a complaint against a criminal in that it alleges a wrongdoing on the part of the child and requests that the court take action. It differs, however, in that it purports to be on behalf of and not against the named child.

The intake officer, usually a probation officer, schedules the case for a court hearing. If the child is in court and under arrest when the peti-tion is filed, he or she is arraigned. This means that the child is told the nature of the charge, has the right to secure witnesses, and has a right to counsel. After arraignment, the case is usually adjourned to permit the pro-bation officer to conduct a social investigation. While awaiting the hearing, the child is normally permitted to return home unless, in the opinion of the court, he or she: (1) might harm him- or herself, (2) might endanger others in the community, (3) is likely to run away, or (4) has violated probation.

Whether a child is released to his or her parents or placed in a detention facility depends on the policy of the court. The social investiga-tion, usually required by law, elicits information about the family's living conditions, neighborhood and school relationships, working conditions, health, a psychological profile of the child, and any other information that the probation officer can secure from the child or from any other source. The investigator may refer to any source or interview any person about the child without the knowledge or consent of the child or the child's family. The hearing is likely to be held in a private courtroom from which every-one is excluded except parents and witnesses.

The proceedings are generally informal, and most children are not represented by lawyers. Some judges demand proof that the child commit-ted the offense before considering the case and exclude irrelevant, imma-terial, and hearsay evidence. These judges are in the minority. In most juve-nile courts the emphasis is on social-psychological, rather than legal, evi-dence. This is the case in juvenile court, because the child is not charged with a crime and a finding of juvenile delinquency does not constitute con-viction of a crime.

In summary, the procedure followed in a juvenile court, that remains in place, may be distinguished from that of a criminal court by the following factors (Tappan and Nicolle, 1962):

1. The hearing is private. Only relevant persons are present.

2. The hearing is informal. The proceeding resembles a conference called to bring forth facts rather than an adversarial proceeding in which an attempt is made to prove that someone is guilty of some offense.

3. Juries are not used.

4. The report of a social investigation is often available to the court before the hearing.

5. It is (perhaps too often) assumed that the child committed the act that brought him or her to the attention of the authorities. The emphasis is on why he or she did it. In a criminal trial the accused is presumed innocent, and guilt must be established beyond a reasonable doubt by legal and competent evidence.

6. The disposition, in theory at least, provides for treatment rather than punishment.

At the conclusion of the hearing, the case may be disposed of in any of the following ways:

1. The case may be dismissed. This amounts to a finding of "not guilty."

2. The child may be placed under the supervision of a probation officer.

3. The child may be removed from his or her home and placed in a foster home.

4. The child may be referred to a residential treatment center or hospital for emotionally disturbed children.

5. The child may be sent to a camp or other minimum security correctional institution.

6. The child may be sent to a state training school.

7. In the case of a serious offense like an atrocious assault or homicide, the child may be referred to the criminal court system.

To these ways of disposing of a case, there is another significant vector in juvenile court justice that has become more pronounced in recent years—a concern for the victim of the child's offense. In this regard, Judge Lois Forer (1980) strongly advocated a greater concern for the victim and the provision of restitution. She cited the case of a juvenile offender who blinded his victim by shooting him point-blank in the face. Rather than imprisonment, she advocated that "every penalty must provide for the needs of the victim, society, and the offender" (p. 136). Forer asserted that since most street criminals are young, undereducated, and unemployed the sentencing judge should not ignore their need for education, employment skills, and a sense of responsibility for their own conduct. She stated that it is imperative that sentencing address these needs through the penalties available to every trial judge: suspending sentence, fine, restitution, reparation, and probation, as well as imprisonment.

I agree with Judge Forer that restitution gives the offender a greater awareness of his or her behavior and partially helps the victim of the offense through a form of reparation. There should be greater flexibility in sentencing procedures in the juvenile court.

The Judge

The juvenile court judge holds broad powers over delinquent children. These judges are the most important decision makers in determining the adjudication process, including whether or not to refer a juvenile to a higher court. The juvenile court judge's powers include the right to depart from legal procedures established for criminal courts and to deny to children and their parents privileges normally accorded defendants in civil court (National Probation and Parole Association, 1957, p. 125). Juvenile court judges may, for example, consider evidence that would be inadmissible in both criminal and civil court. There can be no doubt that these powers have at times been exercised in a high-handed manner and that rights of appeal are inadequate. The justification offered for this delegation of power over children is that it is essential if the juvenile court is to determine how best to provide care and to rehabilitate the child.

The judicial function of the court is often subordinated to the social welfare function. Individuals in tune with the original objectives of the juvenile court recognize the need for specially qualified judges and professional social workers to assist them. In many jurisdictions the juvenile court judge is expected to perform a judicial function and to administer a probation program and treatment program, including diagnostic and rehabilitative services.

In most juvenile courts the judge has the following duties and responsibilities:

1. To conduct a judicial proceeding in a fair and equitable manner. If the proceeding is perceived to be arbitrary and unfair by the children who appear in court, the judge may be contributing to disrespect for law and, in a very real sense, to the future delinquencies of children.

2. To decide, after a fair hearing, whether or not the child committed the offense alleged in the petition. The judge also has traditionally had the power to make a finding of delinquency if it is determined that the child committed some infraction other than the one alleged.

3. To protect society. The judge must determine whether allowing the child to remain in the community would be dangerous to society or to the child.

4. To determine whether the child will remain with his or her family or be taken from the family and (a) placed in a foster home, (b) sent to a psychological treatment center, or (c) sent to a custodial institution.

5. To decide what measures will be taken to rehabilitate the child.

6. If the judge decides to place the child in an institution, he or she must determine the one most appropriate to the needs of the child and the protection of society.

In addition to the foregoing, the judge is generally charged with overall supervision of probation and treatment personnel attached to the court.

Guidelines for juvenile court judges have been established by the National Probation and Parole Association. These guidelines basically require that juvenile court judges have a working knowledge of social case work, child psychology, psychiatry, and the other behavioral sciences. In recent years juvenile court judges have become increasingly aware of the need to deal with children in the context of the family system. Judges now often advocate that the child's family should be brought together whenever possible to discuss the child's behavior and their feelings about those problems with the judge, so that he or she may effectively adjudicate the case.

The Diversion Process in the Juvenile Courts

In the field of juvenile delinquency, the movement to deal with a variety of delinquents without referral to courts or other establishment agencies is referred to as "diversion." Diversion for juveniles has come to mean providing an alternative to the juvenile justice system, most particularly, the juvenile court. Prior to or immediately following an arrest, the young person is often "diverted" to an agency or activity that provides services designed to prevent delinquent behavior. School counseling, family counseling, occupational training, or some other service or therapy may be provided.

Diversion is usually instituted to minimize the negative impacts of the court process and the labeling of youngsters with a minimal record. Diversion is used for status offenders. In recent years, psychiatric hospitals have become a prevalent form of diversion.

Two noteworthy diversion programs were reported by the U.S. Department of Justice (1978), the 601 Diversion Project and the Los Angeles County Regional Diversion Program. The Sacramento County Probation Department created an experimental diversion project designed to give family crisis therapy to children on a short-term basis. The name of the project, 601 Diversion, is derived from Section 601 of the State Welfare and Institutions Code, which deals with juveniles and with delinquent problems. Cases generally involve conflict and lack of communication between youths and their families. The diversion project experimented to determine whether juveniles charged with offenses such as refusing to obey their parents or being habitually truant could be better handled through short-term family therapy, administered at the intake department by specially trained probation officers, than through traditional court procedures. The program identified a particular kind of problem—the problem of children who are beyond the control their parents—and provided a referral service for treatment. When a "601 child" is referred by the police, school, or parents, the specialized unit of the probation department arranges to see if special counseling can be of assistance. Thus, instead of the child proceeding through the juvenile court, the child and the family receive immediate family counseling services.

Since 1974, a regional diversion network has served the more than twenty-five thousand troubled and delinquent youngsters in sixty-four cities in Los Angeles County. Over thirteen diversion programs, covering 80 percent of the county, work with law-enforcement agencies, school probation departments, and other social-service agencies to identify youngsters and their families who can profit from diversion programs rather than judicial service. Funds are provided through the Law Enforcement Assistance Administration and the Los Angeles Regional Criminal Justice Planning Board. Both public and private agencies provide the services, which include crisis intervention, counseling, mental health programs, legal assistance, and vocational training. Clients range from troubled youths referred by the schools to hard-core juvenile offenders.

Many programs that are labeled diversion did not originate as formal efforts to divert people from the criminal justice process but came about through ambiguities in the law or the discretionary practices of individual agents of the justice system. Real programs of diversion specify objectives, identify a target group, outline means and activities for achieving the goals, implement programs, and produce evidence of a plan to at least attempt to evaluate whether the means employed are successful in achieving the goals desired.

Because of the variety of diversionary methods, it is essential that the community obtain reliable information concerning their effectiveness in delinquency control. More research is needed regarding diversion's impact on the justice system, the role diversion plays in crime prevention, and the relative rates of success on cases diverted from the system at different stages as compared with cases subjected to varying degrees of criminalization. Diversion programs play a significant role in crime prevention and in maintaining the juvenile justice system.

"Get-Tough" Diversion: From Juvenile to Adult Court

During the 1990s there was a definite movement to "get tough" with juveniles and increasingly refer more juveniles to the adult criminal justice system. This form of "diversion" has involved referring juveniles who commit severe delinquent acts of violence or murder to the adult courts. Increasing numbers of juveniles have been referred to the criminal courts, and some politicians have advocated the total abandonment of the juvenile court.

Jeffrey Butts (1997) cogently analyzed some of the data from the National Juvenile Court Data Archive about cases waived by juvenile court judges from 1985 through 1994. National estimates were generated using information from all jurisdictions able to provide data in sufficient detail. This involved more than eighteen hundred jurisdictions containing 67 percent of the U.S. juvenile population. The following section is based on Butts' report. The report states that "juvenile offenders are sometimes transferred to criminal court where they may stand trial as adults and various mechanisms are used to effect these transfers. Some States automatically exclude certain cases from juvenile court; others give prosecutors authority to file specific cases directly in criminal court. In all but three States (Nebraska, New Mexico, and New York), juvenile court judge may transfer certain cases by waiving the juvenile court's original jurisdiction" (p. 86).

Between 1985 and 1994, the number of delinquency cases waived to criminal court grew 71 percent, from 7,200 to 12,300 cases annually. The profile of waived cases changed considerably in that time. As recently as 1991, property offenses outnumbered person offenses among waived cases. But in 1994, the largest group of judicially waived cases involved a person offense as the most serious charge. For every 1,000 formally handled delinquency cases, 14 were waived to criminal court in 1994. In 1994 U.S. courts with juvenile jurisdiction handled more than 1.5 million cases involving delinquency offenses. Of these cases, 855,200 were processed formally in some way, either through adjudication in juvenile court or transfer to the criminal court.

Cases involving black youths were more likely to be waived than cases involving other youths, largely because of the different handling of person offenses and drug offenses. In 1994, 1.9 percent of formally processed cases involving black juveniles were waived to criminal court, compared with 1.2 percent of cases involving whites and 1.5 percent of cases involving youths of other races.

A significant factor in juvenile court procedures is the determination of the circumstances under which a juvenile offender should be referred to adjudication by a higher court. All juvenile courts in the United States provide conditions for such referral, and with the great concern about increased and more lethal violence by juveniles, this referral process is increasingly utilized. In general, a youth who commits a homicide or serious repetitive acts of violence is eligible for referral to an adult criminal court. A study by Lee Ann Osburn and Peter A. Rhode (1984) concluded that the practice of referral to a higher court in most jurisdictions was varied and somewhat capricious. They found that the subjective guidelines under which most courts operate are extremely vague and that the individualized and clinical methods used to determine the desirability of adult prosecution are unreliable. Osburn and Rhode noted that "several states recently have established objective criteria that either automatically exclude certain juveniles from juvenile court jurisdiction or create a presumption in favor of exclusion" (p. 87).

In the most drastic changes to the juvenile justice system since the founding of the first family court a century ago, almost all fifty states overhauled their laws in the 1990s to allow more youths to be tried as adults, and many states eliminated long-time protections like the confidentiality of juvenile court proceedings. The main thrust of the new laws is to get more juveniles into the adult criminal justice system, where they will presumably serve longer sentences under more punitive conditions.

Proponents of the changes say that getting tough with teenagers is the only way to stop the epidemic of juvenile crime. Over the past decade, for example, arrest rates for homicides committed by fourteen- to seventeen-year-olds have more than tripled. And with the number of teenagers projected to increase by 20 percent over the next decade because of a juvenile population increase, many criminologists expect a new surge in crime. The "get tough" approach for juveniles has already been passed into law in some states, and in other states this approach is imminent.

Minnesota enacted a detailed statutory formula to govern its waiver process. The formula combines the variables of age, alleged offense, and prior record to identify juveniles presumed to be unfit for retention in the juvenile system. Osburn and Rhode (1984) researched the Minnesota approach and concluded that "contrary to the claims of its supporters, the objective criteria adopted by the Minnesota legislature have not proven to be an adequate means for selecting juveniles for transfer to adult court. The criteria single out many juveniles whose records do not appear to be very serious and fail to identify many juveniles whose records are characterized by violent, frequent, and persistent delinquent activity" (p. 87).

In California, as violent delinquency has increased, pressure has mounted to deal with especially violent young offenders as adults. This viewpoint was reflected in a speech by former Governor Wilson of

California on April 16, 1997, in which he proposed to overhaul the Juvenile Justice System. He presented twenty bills "to get tough with violent youth crime by lowering the minimum age for the death penalty to fourteen" (Los Angeles Times, April 17, 1997). In 1997 fourteen-year-olds could be tried as adults for major felonies, but the most severe punishment they could receive was life in prison without possibility of parole.

The minimum age for execution in California is eighteen. According to Governor Wilson, "What is needed is a juvenile justice system that teaches our youngest offenders that crime is not child's play." The issue of extending the death penalty to minors for murder and other especially heinous crimes came up shortly after Wilson demanded "severe" punishment for two thirteen-year-olds accused of stomping a sixty-one-year-old man to death at a Sacramento train station as witnesses watched. In cases where a fourteen-year-old is charged with murder, Wilson's legislation would enable prosecutors to bypass juvenile court and go directly to superior court. There youths would be tried as adults. The resulting maximum punishment would be life imprisonment without the possibility of parole. Wilson, reflecting the viewpoint of many politicians in 1997 commented, "No longer will the welfare of the young felon be the primary concern of the juvenile justice system. The safety of ordinary, law-abiding citizens must be the government's top priority" (Los Angeles Times, April 17, 1997).

Michigan has enacted laws in an effort to obliterate the social welfare aspects of the juvenile justice system. A case-in-point that reflects Michigan's more stringent approach to juveniles involved Arthur, a seventeen-year-old juvenile. Arthur killed a man in a gunfight, and in 1995 he was incarcerated at a juvenile correctional facility in Michigan. Under the new law, as of January 1, 1996, teenagers who commit that same crime are given long sentences in adult prisons. Offenders as young as fourteen who commit so-called "hard" crimes like murder, carjacking, and armed robbery can be tried as adults and sentenced to do adult time in the regular prison system. Prior to the passage of the law, they would have received counseling and group sessions. Under the new law they are doing "hard time" in an adult prison.

In 1997, New York Governor George E. Pataki advocated laws to increase the minimum sentences for many juvenile offenders, to transfer all sixteen-year-olds in detention centers run by the State Division for Youth to adult prisons, and to sharply increase sentences for youths convicted of a second felony.

The most sweeping changes with regard to treating juveniles as adults in the criminal justice system were instituted in Florida in 1994. Prosecutors there now have the authority to try juveniles as young as fourteen as adults. Delinquents with three previous convictions are automatically tried as adults. Moreover, judges have the authority to confine "high-risk" juveniles in temporary detention centers indefinitely until a place becomes available in a regular secure institution. In 1997 more juveniles were sent to adult courts in Florida than in all the other states combined. In that year some seven thousand cases were referred to an adult court. This resulted in detention centers operating at 200 percent of capacity. The state was forced to let more young people out sooner and with less treatment than the law intended.

Jeffrey Fagan, director of the Center for Violence Research and Prevention at the Columbia University School of Public Health, directed a research project that compared the records of fifteen- and sixteen-year-olds charged with robbery and burglary from Newark and Paterson, New Jersey, and the New York City boroughs of Brooklyn and Queens. Under state law, the teenagers in New Jersey were treated as juveniles while those in New York were treated as adults. The survey found that offenders in both states were incarcerated for equal amounts of time, so that the juvenile court system was no more lenient than the adult courts. According to Fagan (1997), "one reason being incarcerated in adult prisons may lead to worse outcomes is that youthful offenders suffer 'contagion effects' from being housed with older, more hardened criminals. Another reason is that adult prisons tend to have fewer treatment services, like psychological counseling or job training programs" (p. 26). Fagan's research concluded that youths sentenced as juveniles in New Jersey "were significantly less likely to be rearrested than those sentenced as adults. It seemed that locking kids up as adults increases their propensity for offending, rather than lessening it" (1997, p. 48).

Fagan also noted that incarcerating juveniles in adult prisons has another serious drawback—the factor of danger for the juvenile. He cited a case where a seventeen-year-old black youth was serving a seven-to-twenty-five-year sentence in an adult prison in Ohio for acting as the lookout in a botched robbery. The youth was stabbed to death in an Ohio adult prison by members of a white supremacist group. His mother filed a $100 million wrongful death lawsuit against the prison, charging that the guards did not do enough to protect her son from the adult inmates (Fagan, 1997).

The progress toward treating juvenile offenders in a more caring and rational way initiated early in the twentieth century could be obliterated in the twenty-first century. The "get tough" punitive viewpoint generally reflects the posture of most politicians in the United States toward juvenile offenders. Most "get tough" politicians see the new laws as a way to ride the wave of public outrage at crime and get elected. But some legislators see the tougher laws as genuine deterrents to crime because a greater number of young people are committing more and more serious crimes.

The Juvenile Court, Due Process, and the Adversarial Legal System

Because of the increasing "get tough" policies and laws, the juvenile courts may, in the twenty-first century, become more like the adult criminal justice system. The juvenile court may become an adversarial system rather than a tribunal of civil jurisprudence acting on behalf of children. This issue has created controversy about the juvenile courts in recent years. The basic question raised by this issue is, How does the juvenile court protect and focus on the social welfare of the juvenile and, at the same time, provide a "due process" legal procedure? In order to answer this question, it is useful to review some of the important legal decisions in the juvenile justice system of the twentieth century that relate to this subject and are the basis for the juvenile court system of the twenty-first century.

A 1955 landmark case that went to the United States Supreme Court involved a seventeen-year-old juvenile named Holmes.[2] Holmes was arrested in a stolen car operated by another boy. He was sent to state training school by the municipal court of Philadelphia, acting pursuant to Pennsylvania's juvenile court act. His lawyer appealed the decision, contending that: (1) Holmes had not been represented by counsel; (2) he had not been informed of the specific charges against him; (3) he was not advised of his rights at his trial, particularly of his right to refuse to testify; (4) the testimony admitted into evidence at his trial was incompetent and inadmissible; and (5) the competent evidence presented at the trial did not link Holmes with any illegal acts. The reviewing Pennsylvania appeals court ruled that these objections were irrelevant and that the municipal court was not required to accord the accused the same rights that every person charged with a crime is guaranteed by the Constitution. In its decision, the appeals court held that "since juvenile courts are not criminal courts, the constitutional rights granted to persons accused of a crime are not applicable to the children brought before them" (Tappan, 1960, p. 236).

The position of the appeals court was that the state was not seeking to punish Holmes, the defendant, as an offender but "to salvage him and safeguard his adolescence." Holmes's attorney appealed the case to the U.S. Supreme Court on the grounds that the protections of the Fourteenth Amendment against deprivation of liberty without due process had been violated. The Supreme Court refused to hear the case, and the Pennsylvania verdict was upheld.

---

2. For a detailed discussion of the *Holmes* case, see Paul W. Tappan, *Crime, Justice, and Correction* (New York: McGraw-Hill, 1960), pp. 390–392.

In summarizing his opposition to juvenile court practice on the due process issue, Paul Tappan (1949), lawyer and sociologist, stated:

> It has been popular practice to rationalize the abandonment, partial or complete, of even the most basic conceptions of due process of law in the Juvenile Court. These include such matters as: the specific charge; confrontation by adverse witnesses; the right to counsel and appeal; the rejection of prejudicial, irrelevant, and hearsay testimony; adjudication only upon proof or upon a plea of guilt . . . . The presumption is commonly adopted that since the state has determined to protect and save its wards, it will do no injury to them through its diverse officials, so that these children need no due process protections against injury. Several exposures to court; a jail remand of days, weeks, or even months; and a long period in a correctional school with young thieves, muggers, and murderers—these can do no conceivable harm if the state's propose to be beneficent and the procedure be "chancery"! Children are adjudicated in this way every day without visible manifestations of due process. They are incarcerated. They become adult criminals, too, in thankless disregard of the state's good intentions as *parens patriae.* (P. 205)

Another landmark development in the battle over due process in the juvenile courts was resolved in 1967 in a landmark case that was finally adjudicated by the U. S. Supreme Court.[3] The case involved a fifteen-year-old youth named Gerold Gault, who resided in Arizona. Gault was accused of making lewd and indecent phone calls to a woman. He was arrested on June 8, 1964, and placed in custody. Gault's parents were not notified that he had been taken into custody. Gerald Gault was not advised of his right to counsel; he was not advised that he could remain silent; and no formal notice of the charges were given to Gault or his parents. In spite of considerable debate over whether Gerald Gault was guilty, he was sentenced to the State Industrial School "for the period of his minority" or until he was twenty-one. The parents engaged a lawyer who appealed the case.

On May 15, 1967, the Supreme Court considered for the first time the constitutional rights of children in juvenile courts by hearing the Gault case. In writing the majority opinion of the Court in its landmark decision, Justice Abe Fortas stated: "Neither the Fourteenth Amendment nor the Bill of Rights is for adults only. Under our Constitution, the condition of being a boy does not justify a kangaroo court." Although the decision did not give juveniles all the protections accorded adults charged with crimes, the dis-

---

3. An article by Alan Neigher, "The Gault Decision: Due Process and the Juvenile Courts," in *Federal Probation,* December 1967, p. 13, contains an excellent analysis of the *Gault* case and the constitutional rights of children after the Supreme Court decision.

enchantment with the juvenile court's lack of due process was explicit and the trend of future opinions on this issue predictable.

The appeal to the U.S. Supreme Court was based on violations of Gault's rights in terms of the following factors (Neigher, 1967):

1. The right to notice of the charges against him

2. The right to counsel

3. The right to face witnesses against him and to cross-examine them

4. The right to refuse to answer questions that might tend to incriminate him

5. The right to a transcript of the proceedings

6. The right to appellate review

The Court reversed the action of the Arizona court on the first four of these grounds. With respect to Arizona's claim that the juvenile proceeding was not a criminal proceeding, the Court said, "For this purpose, at least, commitment is a deprivation of liberty. It is incarceration against one's will, whether it is called criminal or civil. And our Constitution guarantees that no person shall be compelled to be a witness against himself when he is threatened with deprivation of his liberty." In determining its decision in the Gault case, the Supreme Court analyzed the history of the juvenile court and the specialized treatment accorded children. The *parens patriae* doctrine and the way in which it is applied by the juvenile courts was attacked in far stronger terms by the Supreme Court than those used earlier by Tappan (1949, 1960).

The Court noted that the early reformers, in establishing specialized courts and treatment for children, meant to provide "substitute parents." But these turned out to be, in effect, procedures for sending juveniles to what are, in fact, correctional institutions, in which they are confined with other juveniles sent to these institutions for offenses ranging in seriousness from minor juvenile delinquencies to serious crimes. Although the Supreme Court did not require that children be granted all the rights that adults charged with crime are guaranteed, the *Gault* decision did grant juveniles much more due process in the juvenile courts. One of the effects of the *Gault* decision was the more frequent appearance of lawyers in the juvenile court to represent the accused. Before *Gault,* few juveniles were represented by attorneys.

On the issue of attorneys representing juveniles, a survey by Marvin Finkelstein (1973) of judges in sixty-eight of our largest cities revealed that nearly two-thirds reported the presence of defense counsel in 75 percent of the cases involving a felony or serious crime. In nearly half the cities, over 75 percent of the juveniles charged with less serious crimes (not felonies) were represented by counsel. Even in PINS (person in need of supervision) and neglect cases, nearly half the cities reported that over 75 percent of the juveniles in serious cases were represented by counsel.

In the March 1997 OJJDP *Fact Sheet* new law trends were reviewed. The report documented the enormous changes in the handling of serious and violent juvenile offenders. All legislation enacted in 1992 through 1995 that targeted violent or other serious crime by juveniles was analyzed to determine common themes and trends. Telephone surveys of juvenile justice practitioners in every state provided anecdotal information about substantive and procedural changes that have occurred as a result of the new laws. The report presented a compilation of these changes, an analysis of the direction of those changes and, where appropriate, a historical perspective highlighting instances where what is considered a recent change has, in fact, been around for some time in other states. Implications for policy and practice were offered as considerations for lawmakers and policymakers.

Nearly every state has taken legislative or executive action in response to escalating juvenile arrests for violent crime and public perceptions of a juvenile crime epidemic. These actions have significantly altered the legal response to violent or other serious juvenile crime in this country. In many states, change has occurred in each legislative session since 1992, with more rapid and sweeping change occurring in 1995 and still more in 1996. This level of activity has occurred only three other times in our nation's history: at the outset of the juvenile court movement at the turn of the century; following the U.S. Supreme Court's *Gault* decision in 1967; and after the enactment of the Juvenile Justice and Delinquency Prevention Act in 1974.

The most severe modification of the juvenile justice system emanates from the 1997 federal law to try violent teens as adults. Alarmed by the "brutality and international viciousness" of juvenile crime, Congress overwhelmingly passed a get-tough bill ordering adult trials for violent Americans in their early teens. The legislation was passed because juveniles were responsible for 14 percent of all violent crime in 1995, up from 10 percent in 1980. Also in 1995, juveniles committed 9 percent of murders, 15 percent of forcible rapes, 20 percent of robberies, and 13 percent of aggravated assaults. The legislators concluded that the situation could become much worse in the twenty-first century because of an expected increase in the number of children reaching potential crime-committing ages.

The bill, if enacted, would bring about a sweeping change in federal handling of juvenile crime, ending the notion that violent offenders of fifteen, fourteen, or even thirteen should be treated as youngsters and their offenses considered childhood misdeeds. The legislation concerns federal crimes, but it also tries to persuade states to transform their own juvenile justice systems by offering $1.5 billion in incentive grants over three years. To be eligible for the money, states would have to try fifteen-year-olds as adults for serious violent crimes, require that open criminal records be established for minors after a second offense, and ensure that there are escalating penalties for every juvenile crime.

Five trends may be discerned: (1) more serious and violent juvenile offenders are being removed from the juvenile justice system in favor of criminal court prosecution; (2) in judicial disposition/sentencing authority, more state legislatures are experimenting with new disposition/sentencing options; (3) correctional administrators are under pressure to develop programs for juveniles as a result of new transfer and sentencing laws; (4) the confidentiality of juvenile court records and proceedings are being revised in favor of more open proceedings and records; and (5) victims of juvenile crime are more often being included as "active participants" in the juvenile justice process. These trends represent both a reaction to the increasingly serious nature of juvenile crime and a fundamental shift in juvenile justice philosophy. Traditional notions of individualized dispositions based on the best interests of the juvenile are being diminished by the public's interest in punishing criminal behavior. Inherent in many of the changes is the belief that serious and violent juvenile offenders must be held more accountable for their actions. Accountability is, in many instances, defined as punishment or a period of incarceration with less attention paid to the activities to be accomplished during that incarceration. Toward that end, dispositions are to be offense based rather than offender based, with the goal of punishment as opposed to rehabilitation.

The trend toward redefining the purpose of the juvenile justice system represents a fundamental philosophical departure, particularly in the handling of serious and violent juvenile offenders. This change in philosophy has resulted in dramatic shifts in the areas of jurisdiction, sentencing, correctional programming, confidentiality, and victims of crime. The more powerful role of the prosecutor and the increased use of defense attorneys makes the juvenile court more and more like an adult court, where an adversarial system reigns supreme. This trend, combined with the growing advocacy for adjudicating serious offenders in the adult courts, has increasingly diminished the original concept of social welfare in the juvenile courts that was legislated in 1899.

The Adversarial versus the Inquisitorial Court Approach

The trend to increase the number of juveniles to be tried under the rules of the adult criminal justice system raises another significant issue. There is a considerable difference between what might be termed the juvenile court "inquisitorial" system and the adult criminal court "adversarial" system. The original juvenile court system provided considerable power to the juvenile court judge and therefore to the government. The increasing use of lawyers and the adversarial system in the judicial treatment of juveniles reduces the juvenile court judge's power to that of a referee and a fact finder, usually through the probation department. Richard R. Korn and Lloyd W. McCorkle (1959) made a point about "adversarial" and inquisitorial judicial procedures that remains relevant today. They argued that in the adversary form of judicial process (the standard procedure in adult criminal cases) the role of the state is severely limited:

> The government merely supplies an impartial referee who decides judicial issues, awards the victorious "adversary," and determines the penalty or forfeit of the loser. This form of proceeding is in sharp contrast to that in which the State supplies not only a referee but a government prosecutor, who supplants the private accuser. The process in which the State initiates and presses the accusation is called "inquisitorial" (from the Latin word meaning "seek into"), and places enormously greater power in the hands of the political authorities. The political and social consequences flowing from the use of one or the other of these basic methods are far-reaching. Historically, a shift from accusatory to inquisitorial proceedings has almost invariably paralleled—has, in fact, been one of the principal instruments of—a shift toward more autocratic systems of government. (P. 382)

It may seem an exaggeration to describe the tone of the juvenile court as inquisitorial, yet the term accurately reflects many aspects of this form of judicial procedure. The juvenile court tends to hold secret hearings, there is greater emphasis on the individual's personal characteristics than on his or her offense, the accused has a limited legal defense, and hearsay evidence is not only admitted in court but vigorously sought. In this approach the juvenile court judge and the government have more power over the legal consequences meted out by the courts. Is this the judicial approach we want to continue for the next century for all defendants in court?

The shift in the juvenile justice system in the latter part of the twentieth century, reverses the 1899 juvenile court approach and tries an increasing number of juveniles in the adult criminal justice system. This perhaps provides juveniles with greater due process in the courts. It also makes the juvenile courts more adversarial in nature and brings more lawyers, especially defense lawyers, into the equation.

This raises a basic question that will greatly affect the juvenile justice system in the coming years. Is it useful to bring more defense attorneys into the juvenile justice system? Two major criminal trials of the 1990s, Menendez and Simpson, may give us pause about moving in the direction of increasingly injecting the adversarial system and more defense attorneys into the juvenile court system.

There is considerable dramatic courtroom evidence that defense lawyers have become more "creative" in devising defense ploys for their clients. In the Menendez case, the defense attorney, in her effort to free the Menendez brothers, who admittedly murdered their parents with shotgun fire, produced no credible evidence that would mitigate their behavior. In her efforts to free her clients, she claimed that the brothers were subjected to sexual molestation by their father. She also claimed that they were in imminent danger of being killed by their parents, who, in actuality, immediately prior to the murders, were watching TV and filling out a college entrance application for one of their sons.

In the other example of legal manipulation and courtroom drama, attorney Johnnie Cochran and his "dream team" convinced a jury that their client should be freed from any responsibility for two brutal murders. Cochran introduced the unfounded scenario that Colombian drug dealers, not Simpson, killed Ron Goldman and Nicole Simpson. The team of attorneys also advanced the theory that the police had framed Simpson. The jury could take their pick of these theories and set Simpson free.

The high profile Simpson and Menendez cases are only two examples of the style of defenses that now pervade American courtrooms. The adversarial system of criminal justice invites attorneys to concoct the most bizarre scenarios to free their clients. The basic and controversial question, therefore, that confronts the juvenile justice system is, Does the public want to maintain the integrity of the innovative system introduced at the beginning of this century or to modify the juvenile courts to become more like the adult judicial adversarial system?

CHAPTER 3
DELINQUENT PERSONALITY TYPES

Four of the boys in this image are engaged in a discussion while the boy in the foreground appears separated and possibly depressed. This kind of alienation sometimes produces personality problems that lead to delinquent behavior.

In the field of juvenile delinquency, there is a continuing controversy about whether delinquency is a manifestation of an emotional disorder, the result of negative social factors, such as poverty or depressed socioeconomic factors, a reflection of deviant socialization, or a combination of these factors. My observations and analyses of relevant research in these areas lead me to conclude that all of these forces create several forms of "delinquent personality."

Kenneth Adams (1985) described some of the complexity of analyzing mental health issues and delinquency:

> In the early nineteenth century, as scientific approaches to the study of crime were starting to appear, psychiatric theories vigorously stressed the notion that mental illness is the major cause of crime. These theories outlined a "medical model" of crime causation which viewed crime as a "disease of the mind" that needed to be "cured." From about the middle of the nineteenth century to about the middle of the twentieth century, psychiatric theories of criminality were widely accepted. Once the proposition that mental illness is the cause of crime was accepted, it followed logically that in order for therapeutic services to be rehabilitative in the penological sense, they must be designed to address mental health problems. From this point of view, there was little to be gained from distinguishing between correctional rehabilitation services and mental health service.

Sociocultural factors influence personality formation, so it is of value to research and analyze these factors. However, a better understanding of the general arena of delinquency is fostered by examining the emotional disorders that produce delinquent personality systems. We should comprehend not only the sociological value systems that cause delinquency but also the emotional disorders that relate to delinquent behavior. There are three aspects of the relationship between emotional disorders and delinquency.[1]

1. A basic assumption made by psychologists and psychotherapists in the field of delinquency is that delinquent behavior is a symptom of some underlying emotional disorder. There is no doubt that many delinquent acts are committed by youths who are emotionally disturbed and that some usually "normal" people commit criminal acts when under great emotional stress. Some delinquent behavior is a symptomatic acting out of underlying emotional pathology.

2. Behavior considered symptomatic of emotional disturbance is likely to receive more attention when exhibited by a person who has been

---

1. For more information on delinquency and personality, see Nathaniel Pallone and James Hennessy, *Criminal Behavior: A Process Psychology Analysis* (New Brunswick, NJ: Transaction, 1992).

charged with or convicted of an act of delinquency. A certain amount of delinquent behavior is a result of underlying emotional problems; however, because there tends to be a greater focus on the emotional background of a delinquent or criminal than on that of the average person, more emotional problems may be attributed to delinquents than to law-abiding youths. The deviant behavior may emanate from the emotional disorder, but in some cases there may not be any causal connection between the two. In other words, a delinquent may be emotionally disturbed, but the emotional disorder may not be related to his or her delinquent behavior.

3. Delinquent behavior may cause emotional disorders. Delinquent youths may develop an induced emotional disturbance as a result of detention, long-term incarceration, or the variety of abnormal social forces involved in the administration of juvenile justice. In some cases "normal" delinquent youths are hospitalized in psychiatric facilities, where the emotional stress produces personality problems unrelated to their past delinquent behavior. Being a juvenile delinquent is often an exceedingly nerve-wracking occupation or status that can cause emotional problems. The emotional disorder may be more of a status or occupational disease or a result of a delinquent life-style than a causal factor.

Delinquent youths may be grouped according to the manner in which their personality types define and affect their delinquent behavior. Following are brief descriptions of four delinquent personality types:

1. *Socialized delinquents.* These youths are no more emotionally disturbed than the average person. They become delinquent as a result of the social context within which they learn deviant values. They are more likely to become property violators than violent offenders.

2. *Neurotic delinquents.* These youths become delinquents as a result of distortions in their personality and their perception of the world around them. They may commit delinquent acts because of their insecurities about their masculinity. They may become deviant because of some anxiety or neurotic compulsion. For example, youths who become kleptomaniacs, shoplifters, and pyromaniacs have neurotic compulsions that often result in delinquent behavior.

3. *Psychotic delinquents.* Youths with severe personality disorders have a significantly distorted perception of the society and people around them. Unlike socialized offenders, they do not usually plan their crimes. Their distorted view of reality and their delusional thoughts may compel them to commit bizarre acts that violate the law. Psychotic offenders are likely to commit acts of violence, including murder. This

category includes those youths who tend to commit the most bizarre and senseless acts of violence.

4. *Sociopathic delinquents.* These youths are characterized by an ego-centric personality. They have limited or no compassion for others. Because of this character defect, they can easily victimize others with little or no anxiety or guilt. A sociopathic element is present in many delinquents, but not all delinquents are sociopaths. Many violent gangsters are sociopathic.

These four categories account for most of the delinquent population. But it should also be noted by way of preface to a more detailed analysis of these categories that there are few pure cases. Many socialized delinquents have sociopathic tendencies, and murderers often manifest a combination of socialized and sociopathic characteristics.

The Socialized Delinquent ①

In terms of Edwin Sutherland's (1965) causal explanation of "differential association," the socialized delinquent learns a preponderance of values, attitudes, and techniques that make law violation a more desirable way of life than being a law-abiding citizen. The community in which the youth grows up is apt to significantly affect his or her values, ethics, and choices in life. In high-crime neighborhoods, becoming a criminal is an attractive choice for a youth growing up with criminal role models. When the neighborhood heroes are "successful" criminals or racketeers, youths may seek to emulate them. Becoming a juvenile delinquent for many youths growing up in this social context is, therefore, more a matter of conformity than deviance.

Donald Cressey (1970) made the point that organized crime is a most attractive potential field of endeavor for poor youths growing up in urban ghettos. Cressey asserted that organized crime feeds on the urban poor. Of the thousands of people involved in organized crime, the "street men" or street-level commission agents are visible manifestations of a seductive criminal life-style, and they exert a strong influence on juvenile delinquency. The agents of organized crime have high status in their neighborhoods and are the idols of young ghetto residents; they are the men who have "made it." From the perspective of those urban youths who are socialized delinquents, the image of success is that of a hustler who promotes his interests by using others.

Cressey asserted that organized criminals influence the general delinquency rate in the inner city in three ways. First, they demonstrate to the young people that crime *does* pay. Second, the presence of organized crime exhibits the corruption evident in law enforcement and political organizations. This makes it more difficult for parents to teach their children to achieve in the world by honest labor in service to their family, country, and God. Third, organized crime, through the numbers rackets, prostitution, gambling, and drug dealing, appreciably affects and lowers the economic status of the people in the community; thus, the people have less to lose if convicted of crime. Delinquency is therefore more attractive to lower-class youths.

Cressey grouped his observations into three categories: (1) attraction; (2); corruption; and (3) contamination (1970, p. 138).

1. *Attraction.* Because of varied social forces, inner-city slum boys and girls grow up in an economic and social environment that make some participation in organized crime attractive, natural, and relatively painless. Cressey cited Irving Spergel, who, in his studies of juvenile delinquents in three different neighborhoods in Chicago, concluded that developing specific social skills is less necessary than learning the point of view or attitudes conducive to the development of organized crime. Spergel asked delinquents, "What is the job of the adult in your neighborhood whom you would want to be like?" Eight out of ten responded by naming some aspect of organized crime. Spergel's "Racketville" delinquents believed that connections were the most important quality in getting ahead. Seven out of ten chose education as the least important factor in getting ahead.

2. *Corruption.* Organized crime, in its alliances with politicians and law enforcement officials, helps, as Cressey saw it, "to break down the respect for law and order. How can a boy learn to respect authority when that authority figure is known to be on the payroll of criminals?" (p. 179).

3. *Contamination.* Cressey asserted that because the areas of low socioeconomic status in American cities have high delinquency and crime rates, it must be concluded that, in some of these areas, lawlessness has become traditional. He reasoned that in poverty-stricken neighborhoods, the values, social pressures, and norms favorable to crime are strong and constant. The individuals responsible for enforcing these moral systems and concepts are organized criminals.

Another factor in the urban ghetto, or the "hood," facilitates the socialized delinquent. Most people living in low-income or poverty areas are delinquent or criminal because they are isolated from law-abiding behavior patterns and are in close, continuing contact with criminal influences that affect forces favorable to delinquency.

Cressey summarized the urban ghetto problem by saying: "Keeping vice out of affluent areas while allowing it to flourish in the ghettos, together with corruption that supports the practice, [contributes to] the traditions of delinquency and crime characterizing our inner city areas. In these areas opposition to crime and delinquency is weak because the city is poor, mobile and heterogeneous and people can't act effectively to solve their problems" (1970, p. 137).

The contemporary version of this situation is related to drug dealing. Many urban "socialized delinquents" are making enormous amounts of money, especially in ghetto areas, by dealing drugs, especially crack, a marketable form of cocaine. Youths growing up in this type of dysfunctional social environment are more likely to become socialized delinquents—partly because their role models are criminals and partly because they have few other choices.

Socialized Delinquents: John and Jim ●

John grew up among, and was essentially socialized by, the criminal forces in the inner city of New York. I became closely acquainted with John in the course of my research on gangs in New York City and on therapeutic communities. The following is based on five lengthy in-depth taped interviews with John.

John grew up in a delinquent subculture on the West Side of Manhattan. His neighborhood "naturally" socialized him into a delinquent/drug addict life-style. The process involved the development of a delinquent mask or macho, tough-guy image that was necessary for survival on the mean streets that were his home.

John was first institutionalized by his parents at the age of ten for being incorrigible. From then on he felt extreme hatred for his parents, especially his father. In the institution, he "always felt a need to protect the underdog in a fight." He had numerous fights and found that the "home," or juvenile detention facility, he was periodically placed in was a "house of horror." He was later sent to a long-term facility for two years and learned all about crime from the older boys. When he was released from the institution at about the age of thirteen, he began running with various youth gangs on the Upper West Side. They were involved in petty theft, gangbanging, and other destructive acts.

He remembered learning to hate his father more and more. "I always stayed out late, and when he would get me at home, he would beat me up pretty badly. Then he would actually sentence me, like a judge. For example, he would give me 'sixty days in the bedroom.' I began my jail time early."

57

John, like many children in his situation, seldom went to school. During most of his adolescent years, John worshiped older gangsters and criminals and wanted to be like them. In his neighborhood there were many to imitate. One criminal he especially admired "killed a few wrong guys and died in the hot seat at Sing Sing without a whimper."

When John was fourteen, he took his first fix of heroin. In the course of his delinquent-training apprenticeship, he told me, "I used to run dope and deliver packages of heroin to older addicts. One day, out of curiosity, I asked this guy for a little. He fixed me, and that was it. I began using from then on. It's hard to describe my first feelings about heroin. The best way I can describe it is that it's like being under the covers where it's nice and warm on a cold day."

John continued to run the streets, used drugs whenever he could, and received more training for a life of crime. "In my neighborhood, when I was around fifteen, I was considered a 'cute kid.' The whores liked me, and once in awhile, for a gag, they would turn a trick with me. I admired the stand-up guy gangsters. They were my idols. My main hero at that time was the local head of the Mafia family."

John in his teenage years was a thin, baby-faced young fellow. According to one childhood friend of John, his pale, ascetic face had an almost religious quality. Because of his appearance he became known as "Whitey the Priest" in his neighborhood. He received this nickname from an addict who was kicking a habit. As John related it:

> Once, when I was in jail in the Tombs [the New York House of Detention], some Puerto Rican guy who was kicking a bad heroin habit and out of his mind came to me for help. He saw me and began to scream hysterically in Spanish that I was a priest. Later on, it was picked up by other people who knew me around the city. Some of the whores on Columbus Avenue would even "confess" to me as Whitey the Priest. First I made sure they gave me a good fix of heroin, or money for a fix, and then I would actually listen to their "confession!" They weren't kidding; they were dead serious. After the "confession" took place, usually in some hallway or in a bar, after they poured out their tragic story, I would lay a concept on them. Something like "into each life some rain must fall." I'd bless them and cut out.
>
> After winding in and out of juvenile detention, I took my first big fall at fourteen. I was sent to the reformatory at Otisville. I hated everyone there and wanted to kill the director and some of the guards. I was always fighting and spent a lot of time in the hole [solitary confinement]. This gave me a chance to think and plot different ways to kill the guards and the man who ran the joint.

At age sixteen, John was transferred from Otisville to another reformatory for older boys. Thereafter he spent time in various institutions. These included several trips to Rikers Island penitentiary, several hospitals for addicts, including Riverside Hospital, and various New York City jails. John always considered himself to be a "stand-up guy" (a criminal with ethics) and was determined to become a professional criminal.

At one point he tried to learn how to be a safecracker from an old-timer.

> Somehow I wasn't very good. I did go on a few jobs, but it wasn't right for me. Whenever I was out of jail, which wasn't too often, I would just use drugs and steal. I became a baby-faced stall for some cannons [pickpockets]. The stall sets up the mark, and the cannon picks his pocket. I made a fair living in this business. I used to like to pick pockets in museums. In fact, I don't know why, but I spent a lot of time walking around museums.

In my lengthy discussions with John, I never determined that the young man had any significant neurotic, psychotic, or sociopathic personality traits. His delinquent life-style appeared to result from the "straight-line" learning of delinquent behavior in a neighborhood milieu and institutions that stressed delinquency as a correct and logical way of life. The "socialized delinquent" growing up in a delinquent subculture acquires skills useful in crime and values and attitudes that make a delinquent career attractive. He or she learns to commit burglaries, thefts, and other property offenses and uses them to earn a livelihood.

Sutherland's and Cressey's concepts of the professional criminal parallels my sociological model of the "socialized delinquent." Sutherland's classic theory of "differential association" (simplified here, but developed more fully in chapter 11) states that delinquents learn to become delinquents by association with and learning the role from other offenders. They are trained into delinquent patterns at an early age.

Sutherland's "professional thief" is a role that the socialized delinquent will achieve if he or she becomes a specialist in a particular criminal activity. According to Sutherland and Cressey (1978), professional thieves make a regular business of theft. They use techniques that have been developed over centuries and transmit them through personal associations. They have codes of behavior, *esprit de corps*, and consensus, and have a high status among other thieves and in the political and criminal underworld in general. They also have differential association in the sense that they associate with each other and not, on the same basis, with outsiders, and also in the sense that they select their colleagues. Because of this differential association they develop a common language or argot that is relatively unknown to those not in the profession, and they have organization. A thief is a professional, according to Sutherland and Cressey (1978, pp. 80–82), when he or she has these six characteristics: regular work at theft, technical skill, consensus, status, differential association, and organization. Professional thieves have their group ways of behavior for the principal situations that confront them in their criminal activities. Consequently, professional theft is a behavior system and a sociological entity.

This model of professional criminals characterizes them as resourceful, well trained, and effective, members of a profession (albeit illegal) with certain ethics and values that dictate their conduct. In criminal jargon, professional thieves have "class." They would not "rat on their buddies," and even certain victims are proscribed. Unlike the emotionally disordered offender, assault and violence are used as means to an end, not as ends in themselves.

Jim, like John, fulfilled the prototypical criteria for a socialized delinquent. Following is Jim's story as he told it to me:

> When I was sixteen or seventeen, I used to hang around a pool hall in our neighborhood a lot. I could shoot pool pretty good, and once in a while I would make a couple of bucks. But there were older guys there who were really doing good. They had good reputations in the neighborhood, and they always had money, cars, and broads. Me and some kids my age were doing a lot of petty stealing at this time, cars and things from cars, but we didn't know how to make any real money. What we wanted to do was get in with the older guys we admired so we could learn something and make some real money.
>
> One day, I remember, I had just got out of juvenile hall for some petty beef, and one of the older thieves, a guy that was supposed to be one of the slickest safe men around, came over to me and talked to me for awhile. This made me feel pretty good. Later, one of his friends asked me if I wanted to help him carry a safe out of some office. We worked half a night on that safe and never did get it out of the place. But from then on I was in with this older bunch. Every once in a while one of them would get me to do some little job for him, like "standing point" [lookout] or driving a getaway car or something like that; and once in awhile when they had snatched a safe, I would get to help open it.
>
> I was learning pretty fast. By the time I was eighteen, me and a couple of my buddies had real solid names [reputations] with the older thieves. We were beating a lot of places on our own, and we handled ourselves pretty well. But we were still willing to learn more. We used to sit around some coffee shop half the night or ride around in a car listening to a couple of the old guys cut up different scores [crimes]. We would talk about different scores other guys had pulled or scores we had pulled,

and we would also talk about how you were supposed to act in certain situations—how to spend your money, how to act when you got arrested.

We discussed different trials we knew about. We even talked about San Quentin and Folsom, and prisons in other states, because usually the older thieves had done time before in these other places. We talked about the laws, how much time each beef carried, how much time the parole board would give you for each crime. I guess we talked about everything that had anything to do with stealing and crime. Of course we didn't talk about it all the time. Lots of the time we just shot the bull like anyone else. But by the time I was eighteen I had a pretty good education in crime.

John and Jim learned their criminal behavior in a relatively normal fashion, and it is my clinical opinion that neither of them had any special personality problems. They became criminals as a result of the deviant value system they were exposed to as youths growing up in a neighborhood where becoming a criminal was a "legitimate" and "desirable" way of life. They were thus socialized into a criminal life-style and can be clearly categorized as "socialized delinquents."

The Neurotic Delinquent (2)

Emotional disorders include neurotic and psychotic categories. Neurosis is a less severe form of emotional disorder than psychosis. Neurotic compulsions can cause certain types of delinquent behavior. Youths suffering from neuroses are usually capable of functioning in everyday life. Unlike the psychotic, the neurotic generally does not have sharp distortions of reality. Moreover, neurotics usually are aware that there is something wrong with their thinking and behavior.

A principal symptom of neurosis is anxiety, which involves a visceral sense of fear and personal distress not brought about by any clear stimulus in the environment. In mild cases of neurosis, anxiety may be expressed directly. In some severe cases, a neurotic person may appear to be in a state of panic. According to psychiatrists, anxiety may also be expressed indirectly, showing up as a variety of other problems such as blindness, deafness, exhaustion, inexplicable fear of objects or particular situations, and compulsive activity, including offenses like kleptomania, pyromania, and shoplifting.

Some burglars manifest neurotic tendencies in their *modus operandi*. Eric, a sixteen-year-old offender whom I worked with in a juvenile jail, presented a clear pattern of neurotic compulsion. He was a compulsive

61

house burglar. When he was finally arrested, the police cleared more than sixty burglaries committed over a three-month period. Eric's burglary pattern took the following compulsive form. He would locate and break into a house whose residents were on vacation. Once inside the house, he would make himself at home. He would cook himself a meal, read a paper, and then take a nap. Upon awakening, he would loot the house of all valuables. Prior to leaving, almost as an afterthought, he would return to the bedroom and defecate on the bed.

I had many lengthy counseling sessions with this neurotic delinquent. We concluded that this last act of defiance and hostility was related to his hostility toward his parents. He felt that they had never provided him with an adequate home situation, and his delinquency revolved around his unconscious hostility toward people who had "nice homes." Eric's neurotic burglaries and defiant acts of defecation were a form of revenge directed at "good homes." He talked about how he would sometimes walk around for days with an inner feeling of fear and hostility—manifestations of his anxiety. He explained that when he acted out his compulsion in a burglary, his anxiety was relieved, and he would feel better for a period of time.

Freud and others have hypothesized that neurotic anxiety is reduced by various ego defense mechanisms. Following are several of these basic mechanisms and their relation to the neurotic delinquent.

1. *Denial of reality:* Protecting the self from unpleasant reality by refusal to perceive or face it, often by escapist activities like using drugs or acting out delinquent behavior.

2. *Fantasy:* Gratifying frustrated desires and imaginary achievements. The violent gang in many ways has a pseudoreality component, where youths picture themselves as heroic, embattled individuals fighting a courageous war for their turf.

3. *Projection:* Placing blame for difficulties upon others or attributing one's own unethical desires to others. Gang members and other violent youths project onto others their own violent motivations, often in a paranoid way.

4. *Reaction formation:* Preventing insecure feelings from being expressed by exaggerating opposed attitudes and types of behavior and using them as a "barriers." The delinquent boy who is insecure about his power and masculinity acts out in violent and deviant delinquent acts to prove that he is a "powerful man." This is a basic mechanism for violent gang youths.

5. _Displacement:_ Discharging pent-up feelings, usually by hostility, on objects less dangerous than those that initially aroused the emotions. Displacement is a common defense mechanism for neurotic delinquents, and it accounts for the violent behavior of many delinquent youths.

The Psychotic Delinquent ③

Psychosis is a more severe type of mental disorder than neurosis. Individuals diagnosed as psychotic have their own unique version of reality and are usually unable to perform the roles expected of them in everyday life. Consequently, treatment of psychoses commonly involves involuntary confinement. Psychotics generally suffer from delusions, hallucinations, deep changes in mood, or an inability to think, speak, or remember. While psychiatrists have found that some psychoses are organic—a result of actual physical damage to the brain or of chemical imbalances in a person's system—they claim that most types of psychosis are caused by defective socialization.

One of the more common psychoses is schizophrenia. This term is applied to people who are extremely withdrawn from their surroundings or who act as if they are living in another world. Schizophrenics' thoughts may appear disorganized and bizarre, their emotions inappropriate to the situation, and their behavior unusual. Various types of schizophrenia have been identified and categorized. Individuals who exhibit delusions of being persecuted by others are called paranoid schizophrenics. Catatonic schizophrenics act in an excessively excited manner or, alternatively, exist in a mute, vegetative state.

When psychotics are in their excited state, they can explode into murderous acts of epic proportions. Cases of this sort include the University of Texas rampage of Charles Whitman, the Hillside strangler murders in Los Angeles, the murderous spree of Herbert Mullin, and the "Son of Sam" murders by David Berkowitz that terrorized New York City. These horrendous murders were committed by offenders with psychotic personalities. The cases of Charles Whitman, Leo, and Kenneth Bianchi ("The Hillside Strangler") graphically and dramatically reveal some of the patterns of psychotic murderers.

Charles Whitman

On the afternoon of August 1, 1966, a blond, husky young man strolled into a hardware store in Austin, Texas, and asked for several boxes of rifle

63

ammunition. As he calmly wrote a check in payment, the clerk inquired with friendly curiosity what all the ammunition was for. "To shoot some pigs," the young man replied. At the time, the answer seemed innocent enough, for wild pigs still roamed not far from the capital. The horror of his true intent became obvious a few hours later, when the customer, Charles Joseph Whitman, twenty-five, a student of architectural engineering at the University of Texas, became the perpetrator of one of the worst mass murders in U.S. history.

That morning, Charles Whitman entered two more stores to buy guns before ascending, with his arsenal, to the observation deck of the tower 307 feet above the University of Texas campus. There, from Austin's tallest edifice, he took command of the 232-acre campus. Whitman had visited the tower ten days earlier in the company of a brother and had taken it all in. Today, though, he had no time for the view. Methodically, he began shooting everyone in sight. Moving along the tower's walk, he shot his bullets at people on the campus below, then at those who walked or stood or rode as far as three blocks away. His victims fell as they went about their usual routines. By lingering perhaps a moment too long in a classroom or leaving a moment too soon for lunch, they had unwittingly placed themselves within Whitman's reach.

Before he was killed by police bullets, Charles Whitman murdered thirteen people and wounded thirty-one more, for a staggering total of forty-four casualties. It was later discovered that he had also slain his wife and mother, bringing the total dead to fifteen. It was later determined that Whitman had emotional problems stemming from early childhood and his relationship to his mother and had sought psychiatric help. He had had several counseling sessions, but apparently the depths of his emotional disorder had not been fully revealed.

Leo

The case of Leo (not his real name), a twelve-year-old killer I worked with, reveals the dynamics of a psychotic delinquent. When Leo was eleven, he would often get into fights in the school playground. His grandmother told him that it was wrong to fight. But she also told him that it was all right to defend himself "with whatever he could get hold of." Leo's parents had been murdered and he lived with his grandmother and her son, who had records for gang-related crimes, including assault with a deadly weapon. Authorities believed that Leo's home environment played a large role in shaping his violent behavior. By the time he was twelve, Leo had been suspended from school several times for fighting, had killed a boy with a knife, and had stabbed another boy with a pencil while in juvenile hall. One of his teachers said about Leo, "He was the kind of kid who would walk up to some kid and just coldcock him—punch him in the stomach with no rhyme or reason. He didn't know the kid. It was just his way of being macho."

Leo's history of spontaneous and indiscriminatory violence peaked two weeks before his twelfth birthday, when he stuck a four-inch knife into the heart of another student. Many of those who dealt with Leo at school, where he had a reputation for bullying smaller children, agreed with a teacher who said that she was not surprised that he had committed murder. "I think Leo was striking out for help," she said. A school psychologist had noted a year before the murder that Leo had "a very short temper and [was] verbally and physically aggressive toward peers and adults." In an attempt to divert him from what seemed to be an inevitable course of violence, Leo was counseled, tested, twice evaluated by a psychologist, punished, placed in special classes, and referred to other experts for more of the same.

Leo came from a dysfunctional and criminogenic family. When Leo was born, his unmarried parents were fifteen and sixteen. When he was five, his father, who had been in jail and prison for offenses including rape, was shot to death. When he was eight, his mother was stabbed to death. Both parents had street-gang affiliations.

Leo told authorities that when he was eleven he was "jumped into" a street gang by the uncles he lived with at his grandparents' home. When Leo's grandmother testified in Leo's murder trial, she was asked if she ever told Leo that "what happened to his mother and father was wrong." "No," she answered. "Did you ever tell him not to kill people?" Again she answered no.

The boy Leo stabbed lived forty-six days in a coma before he died. A probation officer interviewed Leo for an hour and a half and said, "He appeared to be fighting back a smile, and did not seem shaken by the offense, nor did he seem to show any sign of remorse." While in juvenile hall awaiting trial, Leo boasted of murdering his victim and showed no remorse for what he had done. Prior to sentencing to the California Youth Authority, while awaiting his murder trial, Leo fought with a boy who also had a reputation for picking fights. The other boy, thirteen, suffered superficial puncture wounds when Leo stabbed him in the neck and stomach with a pencil. His probation officer said, "Leo obviously learned nothing from the murder he committed and in fact threatened to shoot juvenile hall counselors as soon as he got out of custody." Leo was finally sentenced to the California Youth Authority (CYA) for murder and assault with a deadly weapon. At CYA he was closely supervised until age twenty-one, when the juvenile court lost jurisdiction.

Kenneth Bianchi—The Hillside Strangler

Psychotic murderers do not confine their homicidal tendencies to one outburst. There appears to be an increasing number of serial psychotic murders in the United States. One such case involved the so-called Hillside Strangler, Kenneth Bianchi. Bianchi was responsible for the murders of over twenty young women during a one-year period. Almost all the victims were found nude and strangled. They had been tortured and sexually assaulted prior to their deaths. Almost all the cases involved sexual intercourse, and all of the bodies were found on hillsides.

After Bianchi's arrest, John G. Watkins, professor of psychology at the University of Montana, interviewed him and put him under hypnosis. During the time Bianchi was under hypnosis, Watkins found him to have multiple personalities. Under hypnosis the personality of "Steve" came to life. Unlike Bianchi, who was polite and courteous most of the time in his sessions with Watkins, "Steve" was rude and hostile. Watkins identified the killer personality as "Steve."

"Steve" told Watkins that he hated Ken because Ken was always nice to people. "Steve" also said that he made Ken lie and that he liked to hurt anyone who was nice to Ken. "Steve" related how one night he went to his cousin Angelo Buono's house. He walked in while Angelo was killing a girl, and he joined in the murder. "Steve" said that he and Angelo talked a lot about killing women. "Steve" asked Angelo what it was like to kill someone and how many others he had killed. About a week later, "Steve" and Angelo went out together and picked up a girl. They both had sex with her and then killed her.

According to Bianchi, this was the first of a series of killings that they would commit together. "Steve" explained that, whenever the murders took place, he was in control of Ken's body, and Ken would have no recollection of what had happened. "Steve," Bianchi's hidden personality, told Watkins that he could become sexually aroused only when he knew he was going to kill a woman. Ken, on the other hand, had a normal sex life with his girlfriend.

Ralph Allison, a theorist in the field of abnormal psychology, also put Ken into a state of hypnosis. Allison asked Ken to tell him when he had started to have problems at home. Ken responded by going back to when he was nine years old. He said that the Bianchis were having financial problems at that time, and Mrs. Bianchi was constantly upset. Ken said she was always yelling at him or hitting him. Ken felt he needed his mother's approval, and when she became upset with him, he would hide from her. It was at this time that "Steve" appeared. "Steve" was at first Ken's imaginary friend. This is a normal occurrence for some children, but most of these imaginary people disappear in time. In this case, however, "Steve" became the "bad" Ken Bianchi. This enabled Bianchi to defend his "self," so he did not have to accept personal responsibility for his homicidal behavior. He could displace this negative side of his self onto "Steve."

Bianchi was examined for several months by a number of psychiatrists and psychologists. He was diagnosed by several as psychotic with multiple personalities. But several psychiatrists disputed the validity of the "Steve" personality that appeared under hypnosis. They alleged that Bianchi was faking the "Steve" personality in order to mount an insanity plea and escape the death penalty.

If the personality "Steve" was not faked by Bianchi, we can speculate that Bianchi's multiple personality was a complex, defensive psychotic syndrome emanating from an early life that involved severe problems with his mother. One psychiatrist's analysis related Ken's psychosis to his mother's prostitution. In one interview, Bianchi revealed his hostility toward his mother stemming from hearing her having sex with various men in the room next to his bedroom.

One aspect of Ken Bianchi's repressed hostility toward his mother was revealed in psychiatric observations made when Ken was a child. Early clinical reports stated that she beat him physically, often without any justifiable reason. Later, when he was interviewed and hypnotized, the videotaped sessions supplemented the earlier data. Under hypnosis, Ken described the violent assaults by his mother. Ken said she "hit me almost every day. Most of the time she hit me for no reason. I was mad at her all the time, but I would never hit her back. I was fully controlled by her and under her thumb." The psychiatric videotapes revealed that Bianchi repressed all of his enormous hostility toward his mother and avoided any encounters with her. It was during these childhood years that he developed "Steve" to help him deal with his anger and his feelings toward his mother.

Bianchi's torment and anger were expressed later in life in his ritualistic brutal murders of young women. His homicides can be partially explained as the expression of the rage he felt as a child toward his mother, which was later displaced through the torture and murder of his female victims. In a sense he practiced a kind of role reversal. When he was a child, his mother had all of the power. She was the offender, and he was the victim. As an adult, he had all of the power, and the women he killed became the helpless victims of his rage. In this way he achieved a revenge against his mother.

Many homicidal psychotics like Bianchi develop another personality that is held responsible for their heinous acts. I have encountered several violent delinquents who attributed their darker side to a manufactured "other person" in their body. This other personality, they alleged, took over and committed the horrendous act. This enabled the psychotic delinquents to rationalize their violence, to deny responsibility for their deviance, and maintain a self-concept of being a good person. In Kenneth Bianchi's case, "Steve" was the villain, and Ken remained a good guy.

Whitman, Leo, and Bianchi all became psychotic criminal personalities as a result of defective socialization processes. Their murderous acting out was a reflection of their early childhood problems that festered in their delusional psychotic personalities.

The Sociopathic Delinquent

For many years the label "psychopath" was applied by psychiatrists to all individuals whose behavior deviated markedly from normal yet who could not be clearly categorized as severely neurotic or psychotic. In the past decade, the term *sociopath* has been used interchangeably with *psychopath* to describe individuals who, because of a severe character defect involving a lack of compassion, act out self- and other-destructive behavior. My viewpoint is that the terms sociopath and psychopath are interchangeable and describe the same personality type. In the following analysis I use the term *sociopath* to describe this personality disorder that delineates a significant number of delinquents.

Defining the Sociopath

The sociopathic offender is characterized by what has varyingly been called a "moral imbecility" or "character disorder." This type of offender may know right from wrong but lacks any coherent, appropriate discretionary ability in the realm of compassionate, moral behavior. A number of sociologists and psychologists have attempted to define this delinquent personality syndrome. Paul Tappan (1960) described the sociopath as follows: "He has a condition of psychological abnormality in which there is neither the overt appearance of psychosis or neurosis, but there is a chronic abnormal response to the environment" (p. 137). According to psychologist Harrison Gough (1948), the sociopath is "the kind of person who seems insensitive to social demands, who refuses to or cannot cooperate, who is untrustworthy, impulsive, and improvident, who shows poor judgment and shallow emotionality, and who seems unable to appreciate the reactions of others to his behavior."

Albert Rabin (1961) succinctly described the basic trait of a defective social conscience apparent in a sociopath's personality:

> There are two major related aspects to this notion of defective conscience . . . . The first aspect is represented in the inability . . . to apply the moral standards of society to his behavior; he cheats, lies, steals, does not keep promises, and so on. He has not absorbed the "thou shalts" and the "thou shalt nots" of his society and cultural milieu. The second aspect is that of absence of guilt. Guilt is an important part of any well-developed conscience. When a normal person violates the moral code he feels guilty; he feels unhappy and blames himself for the transgression. . . . Guilt is an unknown experience for the personality with no superego. There is none of this automatic self-punishment that goes along with the commission of immoral and unethical acts. The psychopath [sociopath] continues to behave irresponsibly, untruthfully, insincerely, and antisocially without a shred of shame, remorse, or guilt. He may sometime express regret and remorse for the actions and crimes which he may have perpetrated; however, these are usually merely words, spoken for the effect, but not really and sincerely felt.

In the section entitled "Adolescent Disorders" in the American Psychiatric Association's *Diagnostic and Statistical Manual of Mental Disorders (DSM-IV, 1987)*, juvenile psychopath or sociopath is characterized as a conduct disorder syndrome: "The essential feature is a repetitive and persistent pattern of conduct in which either the basic rights of others or major age-appropriate societal norms or rules are violated" (p. 49). *DSM-IV* delineates four specific subtypes of sociopathic conduct disorders: (1) undersocialized aggressive; (2) undersocialized nonaggressive; (3) socialized aggressive; and (4) socialized nonaggressive. These subtypes are based on the presence or absence of adequate social bonds and of a pattern of aggressive antisocial behavior in the delinquent behavior of this type of juvenile. The category "undersocialized aggressive" fits the delinquent sociopath category.

In *DSM-IV*, the juvenile psychopath is described as a person characterized by a failure to establish a normal degree of affection, empathy, or bond with others. Peer relationships are generally lacking, although the youth may have superficial relationships with other youths. Characteristically, the child does not extend him- or herself to others unless there is an obvious immediate advantage. Egocentrism is shown by readiness to manipulate others for favors without any effort to reciprocate. There is a general lack of concern for the feelings, wishes, and well-being of others, as shown by callous behavior. Appropriate feelings of guilt or remorse are generally absent (*DSM-IV*, 1987, p. 52). Psychiatrist Hervey Cleckley contributed significantly to our understanding of the sociopath in his aptly titled book *The Mask of Sanity* (1976). He defined the sociopath (in his terms, the psychopath) as follows:

> This term refers to chronically antisocial individuals who are always in trouble, profiting neither from experience nor punishment, and maintaining no real loyalties to any person, group, or code. They are frequently callous and hedonistic, showing marked emotional immaturity, with lack of responsibility, lack of judgment, and an ability to rationalize their behavior so that it appears warranted, reasonable, and justified. (P. 238)

Cleckley developed comprehensive criteria for viewing this delinquent personality, asserting that most psychopaths (sociopaths) manifest a number of deviant personality traits.

1. Superficial charm and good "intelligence." Typical psychopaths, when first encountered, seem friendly and well adjusted and appear to have many interests. They are also likely to possess superior intelligence.

2. Absence of delusions and other signs of irrational thinking. Psychopaths can recognize the physical realities around them, do not "hear voices," and reason logically.

3. Absence of "nervousness" or psychoneurotic manifestations. Psychopaths are usually free from minor reactions popularly called "neurotic," and they are typically immune to anxiety and worry such as might be considered normal in disturbing situations.

4. Unreliability. Psychopaths, after making substantial gains personally and often financially, will for no predictable reason abruptly throw their gains away in an irresponsible manner.

5. Untruthfulness and insincerity. Psychopaths seem confident and comfortable when making a solemn promise they will never keep. They will lie recklessly, but with great conviction, to extricate themselves from an accusation.

6. Lack of remorse or shame. Psychopaths cannot accept blame for misfortunes that they bring on themselves or others. Although they may claim (insincerely) some responsibility for troubles they have created, this is probably done to elicit confidence and trust from others. Also, they display virtually no sense of shame, even though their lives are filled with immoral exploits.

7. Inadequately motivated antisocial behavior. Psychopaths generally follow a course of behavior that is antisocial—cheating, lying, and fighting—even when such actions do not serve any purpose.

8. Poor judgment and failure to learn by experience. Although more than capable of rationality, psychopaths display terrible judgment about

how to get what they want. There is no evidence that they ever learn from their continuing negative experiences. Psychopaths compulsively repeat their failures, even to the point of repeating antisocial behaviors that lead to second or third incarcerations.

9. Pathologic egocentricity and incapacity for love. Though psychopaths often manifest the overt signs of affection and love, there is no indication that they experience these emotions in any real sense. They do not form enduring relationships. Despite surface indications of love and compassion, psychopaths are usually callous and destructive toward others.

10. General poverty in major affective reactions. Psychopaths display peevishness, spite, and false affection but are incapable of experiencing deeply such emotions as pride, anger, grief, and joy.

11. Specific loss of insight. Psychopaths have limited insight and are apparently not introspective. They cannot see themselves as others do. If they have committed a crime, they assume that the legal penalties do not or should not apply to them.

12. Unresponsiveness in general interpersonal relations. Although they may be superficially courteous in minor matters, psychopaths are incapable of sacrifice or true generosity. They do not demonstrate appreciation when others perform acts of trust or kindness toward them.

13. Bizarre behavior. Psychopaths typically use alcohol (and drugs) to excess. Unlike most alcoholics, psychopaths under the influence of even a modest amount of alcohol may become extremely irrational and destructive. This bizarre behavior can continue even when they are not drinking or using drugs.

14. Suicide threats rarely carried out. Sociopaths often threaten suicide but rarely carry it out. The lack of real guilt or shame about their behavior does not produce a true motivation for suicide. The threat is used for egocentric immediate personal advantage.

15. Impersonal, trivial, and poorly integrated sexual activity. The sexual life of both male and female psychopaths is generally promiscuous and, for the most part, emotionally unfulfilling. The sexual partner is viewed as an object rather than as a person with feelings. Psychopaths often seem to choose sexual exploits solely to put themselves, as well as others, in positions of sharp indignity and distastefulness.

The sociopath can be distinguished from the psychotic, a person whose reasoning is disturbed by delusions and hallucinations (by applying

Cleckley's criteria), and from the neurotic, a person who suffers from an excess of anxiety and guilt. The sociopathic personality can also be distinguished from the "normal" personalities of the previously described syndrome of Jim and John, who are socialized delinquents. The diagnostic criteria employed by Cleckley clearly illuminates the sociopath as a special delinquent personality type.

Two social scientists, William and Joan McCord (1964), described the delinquent sociopathic syndrome. The McCords' profile of the psychopath (or sociopath) parallels Cleckley's categories and further defines the sociopathic delinquent:

1. Psychopaths are asocial. No rule, however important, stops them. The professional criminal, the gang delinquent, and others may be asocial or antisocial, but they do not share the character structure of the true psychopathic personality. Any adequate study of the psychopath must look beyond asociality.

2. Psychopaths are driven by uncontrolled desires. Much of their asociality can be traced to this quest for immediate pleasure. Psychopaths often seem to know no greater pleasure than constant change. They do not seem to receive satisfaction from productive work.

3. Psychopaths are highly impulsive. Unlike the normal person, or even the average criminal, their adventurres often seem purposeless. Even their crimes are rarely planned. They have no stable goals.

4. Psychopaths are aggressive. They characteristically react to frustration with fury. Their uninhibited search for pleasure often clashes with the restrictions of their society. The conflict frequently results in aggressive action.

5. Psychopaths feel little guilt. They have no conscience in the usual sense. They can commit any act with barely a twinge of remorse. They show very little anxiety, worry, or inner conflict.

6. Psychopaths have little capacity for love. They have been characterized by the phrase "lone wolf." They seem cold and compassionless. They treat people as they do objects—as means for their own pleasure. Either because they are incapable of forming them or because their experience has not shown them how to form them, psychopaths avoid close attachments.

The Charm of the Sociopathic Personality

The Mask of Sanity, the title of Cleckley's book mentioned earlier, is descriptive of a dominant characteristic of the sociopath. In Cleckley's

(1976) analysis, the sociopath appears to have "superficial charm and good intelligence. Typical psychopaths, when first encountered, seem friendly and well adjusted and appear to have many interests. They are also likely to possess superior intelligence" (p. 187).

In my efforts to understand violent sociopaths, I interviewed and attempted to treat several hundred criminals with sociopathic personalities. A number of these individuals had committed violent acts, including murder. I found that most of the time, sociopathic killers behave like the average person. A sociopath can present the appearance of being an intelligent, charming, considerate person except when he or she is acting out pathological violent behavior. The sociopath's usually charming overt appearance belies his or her underlying character disorder.

An example of a charming sociopath was serial killer Ted Bundy, who murdered over twenty women. It is a testimony to his sociopathic charm that he was able to kill this many women over a number of years without being caught or convicted. He was finally caught after killing several women in Florida. The judge, when sentencing Bundy to death, was impressed by his behavior in court, acting as his own attorney, and commented, "It's too bad you went down the wrong path . . . you would have made a good lawyer" (A & E *Biography*, 1997).

Jeffrey Dahmer, the flesh-devouring madman, kept the severed heads of victims in his refrigerator so, as he said "they wouldn't leave." In court, he appeared to be a gentle person who was accepted by the people in the apartment where he lived as a "nice guy" and a quiet neighbor.

Kenneth Bianchi, the Hillside Strangler, who with his cousin Anthony Buono tortured and killed twenty women, was characterized by his live-in girlfriend as "a wonderful husband and father to my daughter who could never have killed anyone." Most violent sociopaths have these two divergent personalities, and most people untrained in the psychology of the sociopath have a difficult time separating the killer from the nice guy.

In an encounter I had with Charles Manson at the Haight-Ashbury Free Medical Clinic in the late 1960s, before his "family" went on their murder spree, I found him to be a nice fellow. At the time he was concerned with getting "his girls" the medical treatment they needed at the clinic for their various sexual diseases. Although he was spouting platitudes about the crazy state of American society, on the surface he appeared to be the benign loving hippie of that era.

Another example of this personality disorder is Susan Smith who drowned her two children by driving them into a river. For several weeks before her lies unraveled, she fooled the world by acting out the role of a normal, kind, and sympathetic mother who had lost two children to a carjacker. Her story about the kidnapping of her children masked the underlying sociopathic personality that enabled her to commit this violent act.

Most of the killers I have described can be defined as sociopaths. And most individuals who fit this characterization appear to be normal human beings most of the time. Their pathology is unmasked only when they commit some deviant act that draws close scrutiny of their behavior.

A significant aspect of the sociopath is the absence of feeling guilt for their antisocial behavior, and this facilitates their ability to act as if they have done nothing wrong. Guilt is an important part of any healthy personality. When a normal person violates a moral code, he or she feels guilty; he or she feels unhappy and blames him- or herself for the transgression. Guilt is an unknown experience for the sociopath, who has no controlling superego. Sociopaths have no automatic self-punishment that goes along with the commission of immoral and unethical acts. They behave irresponsibly, untruthfully, insincerely, and antisocially, without a shred of shame, remorse, or guilt. Sociopaths may sometimes express regret and remorse for the actions they have perpetrated; however, these are usually meaningless words, spoken for their effect or to extricate them from a punishing situation. In most cases, the murderer can convince him- or herself and others that he or she did not commit the act.

In summary, sociopaths' overt personality and behavior traits would include most, if not all, of the following factors: (1) limited social conscience; (2) egocentrism dominating most interactions, including the "instrumental manipulation" of others for self-advantage; (3) inability to forgo immediate pleasure for future goals; (4) a habit of reckless pathological lying to achieve personal advantage; (5) the rationalization of their violent behavior in the face of overwhelming objective evidence; and (6) the total absence of the ability to express any regret for their crimes.

●Sociopathic Gangsters

The violence of sociopathic offenders in violent gangs who "gangbang" reveals a form of group sociopathic behavior. The gangsters' unpremeditated violence is characterized by the following factors:

1. No evidence of prior contact or interaction between the assailants and their victims.

2. The violent act often occurs in an unpremeditated, generally spontaneous, and impulsive manner.

3. In some cases there is a degree of prior build-up to the act; however, the final consequence (often homicide) is not anticipated.

4. The offenders' expressed reaction to the violent behavior is usually lacking in regret and is inappropriate to the act committed.

The following comments made by a sociopathic youth involved in a brutal gang homicide reveals the compulsive, abnormal behavior of the sociopath as defined by Cleckley and the McCords:

> Momentarily, I started thinking about it inside; I have my mind made up I'm not going to be in no gang. Then I go on inside. Something comes up, then here all my friends coming to me. Like I said before, I'm intelligent and so forth. They be coming to me—then they talk to me about what they gonna do, like kill this guy! Like "Man, I just gotta go with you." Myself, I don't want to go, but when they start talkin' about what they gonna do, I say, "So, he isn't gonna take over my rep, I ain't gonna let him be known more than me." And I go ahead, just for selfishness. (Yablonsky, 1997, p. 46)

The senseless, other-directed violence of such sociopathic gangsters is perpetrated for ego status—for kicks or thrills. The kicks involve a type of emotional euphoria that the sociopathic delinquent maintains "makes me feel good." He or she does it out of selfishness. The goals of this type of delinquent are self-oriented, with material gain as a secondary consideration. The socialized delinquent would not place him- or herself in jeopardy for this type of senseless gang-violence offense. Instead, violence is used as an instrument for material gain, which serves to validate his or her existence. It is used in a rational way as an instrument in the delinquent activities of the socialized delinquent. (Issues related to the sociopathic gangster are more fully developed in chapters 8 and 9.)

Factors Related to the Causation and Development of a Sociopathic Delinquent

An adequate social self develops from a consistent pattern of interaction with rational adult parents in a normative socialization process. The parent or adequate adult role model helps a youth learn social feelings of love, compassion, and sympathy. The proper adult role models necessary for adequate socialization are often absent from the social environment of youths who develop sociopathic personalities. The basic ingredient missing in the socialization process is often a loving parent or adult.

The concept of adequate self-emergence and socialization through constructive social interaction with others, especially parents, is grounded in the theoretical work of Charles Horton Cooley, later developed by

75

J.L. Moreno, George H. Mead, and others. According to Mead (1934, p. 236): "The self arises in conduct when the individual becomes a social object in experience to himself. This takes place when the individual assumes the attitude or uses the gestures which another individual would use and responds to it himself. Through socialization, the child gradually becomes a social being. The self thus has its origin in communication and in taking the role of the other."

On the issue of parental impacts on the development of the sociopathic delinquent, the McCords state (1959, p. 107): "Because the rejected child does not love his parents and they do not love him, no identification takes place. Nor does the rejected child feel the loss of love—a love which he never had—when he violates moral restriction. Without love from an adult socializing agent, the psychopath remains asocial."

Psychiatrist Marshall Cherkas interviewed several hundred delinquent sociopaths. In his view:

> Children are extremely dependent upon nurturing parents for life's sustenance as well as satisfaction and avoidance of pain. In the earliest phase of life, in their first year, infants maintain a highly narcissistic position in the world. Their sense of security, comfort, reality, and orientation is focused on their own primitive needs with little awareness and reality testing of the external world.
>
> As the normal infant develops, its security and comfort is reasonably assured. There occurs a natural attachment, awareness, and interest in "the other." As the child matures, the dependency upon "the other," its parents, diminishes, but the strength of the self is enhanced, and the child develops an awareness that its narcissistic needs are met through a cooperative, adaptive, and mutually supportive relationship to its parents and others. In other words, the child recognizes that even though its selfish (narcissistic) needs are extremely important, they can best be served by appropriately relating to other people, especially its parents.
>
> This cooperative process is repeated many times in the development of the individual, and there are stages of recapitulation where dependence and narcissistic interest are heightened. There are other stages where the child's sense of social recognition and cooperativeness are greatly increased, with less emphasis upon its own narcissistic needs. Infants whose needs are not adequately met because of the parents' own exaggerated narcissistic needs develop feelings of mistrust, insecurity, and wariness about the capacities of their provider. In order to protect itself, the child may perform many tasks to gain attention, support, and interest from the parent.
>
> A child socialized in this manner begins to feel that it cannot trust others, and that its needs can only be met through self-

interest. The child who cannot count on its own parents begins
to become egocentric and therefore sociopathic in its behavior.[2]

Edwin Megaree and Roy Golden (1973) carried out research into
the issue of causation related to the sociopath. They based their research on
the reasoning that the psychopathic offender has a significantly poorer relation with his parents than does either the nondelinquent or the normal
(social) delinquent. The purpose of the study was to partially test these formulations by comparing the parental attitudes of psychopathic and subcultural offenders and a nondelinquent group of comparable socioeconomic
status.

Megaree and Golden (1973, pp. 427–439) hypothesized in their
research that:

1. Psychopathic delinquents' attitudes toward (a) their mothers and
   (b) their fathers would be significantly more negative than those of nondelinquents.

2. Psychopathic delinquents' attitudes toward (a) their mothers and
   (b) their fathers would be significantly more negative than those of subcultural delinquents.

3. There would be no noteworthy difference in the subcultural delinquents' and nondelinquents' attitudes toward (a) their mothers and
   (b) their fathers.

Using various psychological inventories, they cross-compared a sample of
identified sociopaths from a federal correctional institution and a matched
control group of students attending a technical trade school. Both institutions were located in Tallahassee, Florida. The correctional institution's
final sample of thirty-one was divided into two groups of "subcultural delinquents" and "psychopathic delinquents." (The subcultural delinquents
would parallel socialized delinquents.) The delinquent groups (both psychopathic and socialized) were contrasted with the nondelinquents with
regard to parental relationships.

On the basis of their research, Megaree and Golden (1973,
pp. 433–437) came to the following conclusions. The nondelinquents
expressed the most favorable attitudes toward both their parents, and the
psychopathic delinquents, the most negative. For these two groups there
was little difference between ratings for their mothers and the fathers. The

---

2. Adapted from an unpublished paper, "The Sociopathic Delinquent Personality," by permission of the
   author, Marshall Cherkas.

subcultural (socialized) delinquents displayed a different pattern, however; their attitude toward their mothers was as favorable as that of the nondelinquent group, but their attitude toward their fathers was as negative as that of the psychopathic sample. The data highlighted the important role played by the mothers. While the attitude toward fathers was the crucial variable separating the delinquents from the nondelinquents, it was the attitude toward mothers that differentiated the subcultural from the psychopathic delinquents. One might speculate that the positive relationship with the mother permits subcultural delinquents to appear well adjusted and capable of loyalty to a group and adherence to a code of values, albeit a socially deviant code.

A sociopathic personality is basically produced by a socialization process that does not include loving parental or other positive role models. Because of this absence of loving role models, the sociopathic delinquent tends to be self-involved, exploitative, and disposed toward violent outbursts. This individual lacks social ability, or the ability to assess adequately the role expectations of others. He or she is characteristically unable to experience the pain or the violence he or she inflicts on others since this individual does not have the ability to identify or empathize with them.

The sociopath is thus capable of committing spontaneous acts of senseless violence without feeling concern or guilt. Sociopathic delinquents are highly impulsive and explosive youths for whom the moment is a segment of time detached from all others. Their actions are unplanned, guided by whims. Sociopathic delinquents are aggressive. They have learned few socialized ways of coping with frustration. They feel little if any guilt. They can commit the most appalling acts yet view them without remorse. Sociopathic delinquents have a warped and limited capacity to love and be compassionate. Their emotional relationships, when they exist at all, are shallow, fleeting, and designed to satisfy their own egocentric desires. Some measure of the negative personality factors found in the prototypical sociopathic delinquent are found in all types of delinquents.

● A Classic Sociopath: The Case of Jose

The emergence of the sociopathic delinquent personality is a process that has not been fully explained. Yet there are patterns that recur consistently enough to enable us to identify them as probable causes of the development of the sociopathic personality. As noted earlier, one is the lack of a loving and compassionate parental role model. By love, we mean the ability to involve oneself with another human being without egocentric designs.

Most sociopaths have grown up in a predatory, exploitative, and manipulative social situation. Love and compassion are generally foreign to their life-style. The evolution of the sociopath may be seen in the case of a boy we shall call Jose whom I met while researching sociopathic gang youths in New York City.

Jose had participated in the stabbing and killing of another youth and was convicted of homicide. I had the opportunity to observe his behavior on the streets prior to the murder and to interview him several times in the state reformatory where he was incarcerated after the murder.

Jose migrated from Puerto Rico to New York City with his family when he was eight years old. At first he disliked the cold and dirt. "It's always summer in Puerto Rico," he explained. Although he had lived in a run down area called La Perla in San Juan, it was heaven to him compared to the slum he now lived in on Manhattan's Upper West Side. Jose could step out of his shack on the island into sunlight and ocean breezes and the friendly greetings of his neighbors. In New York City he would leave his tenement to enter a cold world of hostile and indifferent strangers. On the island Jose was somebody. He had an identity. Although the Perez family was poor, the Perez name meant something, and Jose sought to live up to it. His family and friends identified him as an individual; he had a position in the community, even though he was still a child.

Everyone in the huddle of poor shacks where he had lived in San Juan knew everyone else; they all had some concern for one another. In New York, Jose was shocked to discover that he was considered "different." The first time he was called a "dirty spick" at school he became severely upset and angry. His response became aggressive: he retaliated. He began to attack other children without provocation in anticipation of their insults. Whites and blacks were not his only antagonists. He was often picked on by other Puerto Ricans who had lived longer in New York City. To them he was a foreigner. He embarrassed them because he was a Puerto Rican greenhorn and had not yet become assimilated. Other Puerto Ricans, suffering from self-hatred as a result of their low status, took out their resentment on someone they regarded as even more inferior.

Jose had a good school record in Puerto Rico, but in New York City he hated school and became a habitual truant. His despised identity as a "spick" was accentuated by his inability to speak English. His teacher tried to help but, overwhelmed by a large number of students with various problems, she had limited success. Her students' personal problems, combined with their language difficulties, made teaching any specific subject matter almost impossible. The school guidance counselor tried to talk to Jose, but by this time Jose was thought of as having a serious behavior problem. His hatred for school became more intense each time he played hooky. Going back to school seemed increasingly difficult, if not impossible. He spent his days at the movies when he could raise the price of a ticket by petty thievery, or he simply sat and daydreamed.

Jose alternated between fantasy and direct acts of violence, increasingly delivered to undeserving and often unsuspecting victims. Lectures and threats to send him to a reformatory meant little to Jose. He already knew from a friend that the state reformatory was "all filled up, and they ain't going to send you there for just playing hooky." Roaming the streets led to other delinquent activities, including vandalism and muggings. To Jose, people became things you manipulated to get what you wanted. He discovered that "being nice" was often useful but only if it helped get what you wanted. When caught stealing, he learned that "sometimes if you hang your head down right and look pitiful, you could avoid punishment."

Few people in Jose's world ever considered another person's feelings or welfare unless they expected to get something in return. The two most successful types of behavior were manipulation and violence. When one did not work, the other would. Jose found violence and the threat of violence very effective.

As Jose's reputation for sudden, unexpected violence grew, others responded by complying with his egocentric needs. Jose learned to manipulate others and to use violence "properly." He never learned to feel affection for anyone, not even the other members of his family. No one taught him to express positive emotions or to set an example by displaying human feelings. In the hostile and asocial world that surrounded him, he learned the most effective adaptation, and his sociopathic personality became more developed with each day's experience.

Jose's family was of little help to him in New York City. His family's rules, language, and appearance were considered old-fashioned and inappropriate. Also, his parents and older brothers were busy battling their own enemies in the city. His family was not available to fill his needs for humanism and compassion. He sometimes thought with fondness about pleasant evenings in Puerto Rico with his family. They used to go to a park near their home. Mostly the children would play, and the adults would sit and discuss the day's events. Children and adults talked easily with each other. In those days, now gone, Jose had the opportunity to discuss his personal troubles with his parents and older brothers. It was even pleasant to be criticized, since it gave Jose a secure feeling to know that someone was concerned. Not only his own parents but relatives and other adults had taken an interest in the children.

In Puerto Rico, there were men who took the boys swimming. A group of older men from a social club formed a baseball league for the younger boys. Jose had belonged to a community. All of this changed in New York City. Jose's father earned a modest amount when he worked, but he was often unemployed. During these periods, quarrels and conflict developed between his parents, and his father became less and less the man of the house—the role he had clearly occupied in Puerto Rico. Beset with their own overwhelming problems, Jose's parents sometimes violently attacked their children, who increasingly became a burden to them.

There was no one for Jose to talk to about his feelings. His father began to drink excessively to escape from reality and a sense of inadequacy he could not face. The more he drank, the more violent he became. In his senseless rages, he beat Jose's mother and often attacked Jose for no apparent reason. Senseless violence surrounded Jose, and he became indifferent to his family.

About his father Jose said, "I'll ask him to take me boat riding, fishing, or someplace like that, a ball game. He'll say no. He don't go no place. The only place where he goes, he goes to the bar. And from the bar, he goes home. Sleep, that's about all he do. I don't talk to my parents a lot of times. I don't hardly talk to them. There's nothing to talk about. There's nothing to discuss about. They can't help me."

Jose increasingly resolved his problems outside the home. In his barrio, Jose met a violent gang leader called Loco. As his name implies, Loco was thought to be a little crazy, and this did not displease him. His reputation for sudden violence made him greatly feared.

The gang provided a vehicle for expressing much of the hatred, disillusionment, and rage that existed in Jose. His gang involvement also enabled him to express the manipulative sociopathic personality he had developed. Violence was expressed at the right opportunity or opportunities were created. The gang helped minimize feelings of guilt and anxiety about violence at the increasingly rare times such feelings existed in Jose. Any limited concern about his feelings of worthlessness were diminished by the recognition that there were others like himself.

The violent gang gave Jose a feeling of power. He was a core member and accepted the mutually supported gang fantasy that he was now "a leader." He found it gratifying and exciting to strike out at others for whom he had no feeling. Violence was a useful instrument for him, and he was well trained for this activity. Inevitably, in a gang-war situation, he killed an enemy gang member, and by that time he was old enough to be sent to a state prison. The negative factors that developed his sociopathic personality on the streets were enhanced by the macho violent behavior Jose had to develop to survive in prison.

Attempts to Treat Sociopaths

Despite the large number of delinquent sociopaths in our institutions, little progress has been made in providing treatment for them. This is partly due to the fact that most experts consider the sociopath to be untreatable. Hervey Cleckley (1959) noted that, in spite of the fact that psychoanalysts reported some success in the treatment of patients regarded as psychopaths, analytic treatment of the psychopathic personality had proven a failure. He noted further that "all other methods available today have been similarly disappointing in well-defined adult cases of this disorder with which I am directly acquainted" (p. 321). He suggested setting up facilities specifically designed to deal with problems of the psychopath and pointed out that state and federal psychiatric institutions were organized for psychotic patients and were not well-adapted for handling psychopaths.

Despite the pessimistic viewpoint of Cleckley and others about the possibilities of effectively treating sociopathic delinquents, a number of promising therapeutic modalities have been developed recently for treating the variety of offenders, including sociopaths. Notable among these therapeutic modalities is group therapy, especially in the setting of a "therapeutic community." These approaches to the treatment of delinquents effectively enlist the aid of ex-criminal/addicts in the therapeutic process. (These new and innovative methodologies are discussed in Part 6, "The Prevention, Treatment, and Control of Delinquency.")

CHAPTER 4
SOCIAL CLASS AND DELINQUENCY

Minority group youths are too often unfairly labelled as delinquents. A continuing and increasing problem is found among youths from the middle and upper strata of society. The parents of these youths generally have more power, and when their child is arrested, they can help their child to avert being identified and ajudicated as a juvenile delinquent.

A complex element in defining delinquency is social class. It is apparent that individuals in the lower socioeconomic strata of society are often frustrated and blocked by unemployment, prejudice, and discrimination in their quest for the American dream. These blockades to equal opportunity and success tend to produce a high incidence of delinquency. This is reflected in the disproportionate number of juveniles from these strata of society who are adjudicated "delinquent" by the juvenile courts.

More privileged young offenders are often diverted into other social facilities, or their behavior is absorbed by their family. They are not as likely to be accorded delinquent status by the juvenile court. Despite the fact that most youths who appear in juvenile court are from the lower strata of society, it does not necessarily follow that they comprise the majority of the delinquent population. Research data lead to the conclusion that police biases, legal vulnerability, and parental decisions affect which children wind up in court and are adjudicated delinquent. These factors are related to social-class attitude and power in society and tend to determine who will be officially labeled a delinquent.

Many researchers have explored this issue. Most social-psychological studies that have investigated delinquents and nondelinquents have compared institutionalized delinquents with children who have not been adjudicated delinquent. The assumption is made that those children who have not been judged delinquent by a court have not engaged in delinquent behavior. This assumption may not be totally true. Even though the majority of the children found to be delinquent by the courts were from the most socioeconomically deprived segments of our population, and a general appraisal of welfare data reveals that there is a higher incidence of adjudicated delinquents from welfare families, it doesn't necessarily follow that only those youths adjudicated by the courts have committed delinquent acts. Many "nondelinquent" youths have violated legal norms without being arrested or at least without being adjudicated delinquent. Various studies in which anonymous questionnaires were used indicate that middle-class children are involved in delinquent behavior similar to that of lower-class adjudicated delinquents.

Theory and Research

The United States as a democracy views itself as a classless society; however, class position in American society is a significant, albeit complex issue. The following section examines a wide spectrum of theories, research, and analyses that deal with the issues involved in determining social class factors that relate to delinquency.

Despite the fact that Karl Marx was not the first social philosopher or economist to analyze the concept of social class, his writings on the subject are widely known and have exerted an influence on many economists, psychologists, and sociologists in the United States. Marx (1909) defined class in terms of its relationship to power, and the ownership of land and capital. According to Marx, there are two basic classes: the bourgeois capitalists, who own capital and property, and the masses (the proletariat), who do not possess capital or property. The latter constitute the working class, whose members depend on their labor to live. In simplistic terms, he asserted that members of each class, by virtue of their position in the economic order and relationship to property, have common experiences, economic and political interests, and ways of life.

Class conflict, according to Marx, arises when proletarian class consciousness emerges because of the difficulties experienced by the members of the working class. Implicit in Marx's theories is the assumption that the dominated group (the masses) has less of a stake in the system and that the lower class is likely to be rebellious. This rebellion, according to Marx, often takes the form of delinquent and criminal behavior.

In 1916, William A. Bonger, a Dutch criminologist, related Marxist theory in more depth to the crime and delinquency problem. Bonger (1916), building on Marxist theory, asserted that the members of the working class and the unemployed become disproportionately involved in crime because of the economic demands of the capitalist system. This view of society was referred to by Bonger as "economic determinism." Describing people as both altruistic and selfish, Bonger concluded that capitalism stimulates the selfish side of people. People produce for profit rather than for personal consumption, and this fact results in, among other things, intense competition between capital and labor for the fruits of labor. Employers try to purchase labor at the lowest possible price; workers try to sell their labor for the highest possible price. The "selfish egoistic competition fostered by the capitalist system," according to Bonger, transforms the business person into a "parasite" who lives without working, feels no moral obligation to his fellow humans, and regards workers as things to serve and entertain him. Thus, crime and delinquency are, by Bonger's definition, expressions of human selfishness. This selfishness and social irresponsibility causes unemployment, lack of education, and other disabilities of the poor that lead to their commissions of crime (1916, pp. 401–402).

Richard Quinney (1980), a contemporary criminologist, building on the theories of Marx and Bonger, presented a Marxist view of the crime problem in American society. He maintained that, since 1 percent of the population owned 40 percent of the nation's wealth and nearly all power in American society is concentrated in the hands of a few large corporations,

85

government and business are inseparable. According to Quinney, as a capitalist society the United States has two major classes: one that owns businesses and controls government, and a working class. Professionals, small-business people, office workers, and cultural workers may cut across class lines. However, the ruling class owns and controls the means of production and through its economic power uses the state to dominate society. The dominant class is the ruling class.

Although Quinney's criminological theories appear to be extinct in light of the fall of many socialist countries, his viewpoint is still popular among a number of criminologists. The essence of this theory as it relates to class and delinquency is that the "deprived" and alienated people in society act out their delinquent behavior to strike back at the society that created and maintains their inferior position in the social system. Many minority group leaders explicitly and implicitly subscribe to this perspective on American society.

Lower-Class Culture as a Generator of Delinquency

Applying Bonger's or Quinney's thinking to contemporary conditions, one would conclude that the poor, people on welfare, the unemployed, and workers who consider themselves exploited might favor the commission of crimes against the more privileged and against the economic and political establishment controlled by the wealthy. The underprivileged classes, having little or no voice in their destiny, would be expected to be alienated, hostile, and in favor of retaliatory activities, which would be defined as crimes.

In encouraging unrestrained egoism, self-interest, or rugged individualism, a capitalist society inspires attacks on the social organization by those who consider themselves disadvantaged. Because of this situation underprivileged working-class people might be expected to have, and in fact do have, higher delinquency rates. Urban slum areas, inhabited by the lower socioeconomic classes, do have the highest rates of violent gangs and juvenile delinquency, the highest arrest rates of young people, the largest number of court referrals, and the largest number of recidivists (repeaters). Also, according to recent statistics, these areas produce the largest number of young people who belong to violent gangs or are in correctional institutions.

A Juvenile Delinquency Project of the National Education Association, directed by William C. Kvaraceus and Walter B. Miller (1959), published a report delineating how various factors in lower-class culture affected the delinquency problem in the United States. Kvaraceus and

Miller's research contrasted lower-class culture with middle-class culture and described the ways in which lower-class culture contributed to the delinquency of lower-class children. Their report concluded that the preponderant proportion of the delinquent population consisted essentially of normal lower-class youngsters. According to Kvaraceus and Miller, the concerns, values, and characteristic patterns of behavior of the lower socioeconomic class are the products of a well-formed cultural system. They estimated that between 40 and 60 percent of the total population of the United States share or are significantly influenced by the major outlines of the lower-class cultural system. Many youngsters growing up in these areas are "normally delinquent" if they conform to their culture. Behavior of those in a given cultural system is said to be motivated by a set of "focal concerns"—concerns that receive special emphasis within that culture.

In lower-class society, according to Kvaraceus and Miller (1959), the following concerns are dominant: trouble, toughness, smartness, excitement, fate, and autonomy.

1. *Trouble.* A boy or girl may be accorded recognition or prestige by being successfully involved (in trouble) with the authorities (police or school) or for avoiding such involvement (staying out of trouble).

2. *Toughness.* Physical prowess, "masculinity," endurance, athletic ability, and strength rank high in the concerns of lower-class adolescents, as is evident by the kinds of heroes they select—tough guy, gangster, tough cop, combat infantryman, and "hard" teacher. Boys in the hoods or barrios boast of acts that indicate toughness and belittle those who appear soft.

3. *Smartness.* Skill in duping and outsmarting the other guy is admired, as is the ability to avoid being duped by others. The con man is the hero and model. The victim of a con man is seen as a sucker or fool.

4. *Excitement.* The search for thrills and stimulation is a major concern when life is monotonous and drab.

5. *Fate.* Drinking, gambling, and fighting are popular as sources of excitement. Lady Luck is a reigning goddess of lower-class society. Success is attributed to good luck, failure to bad luck. Gambling is viewed as a way of testing one's luck.

6. *Autonomy.* Lower-class adolescents say in no uncertain terms that no one is going to boss them. Yet they frequently seek out, through norm-violating behavior, situations in which they will be told what to do, when to do it, how to do it, and whether it is right when done.

Several class factors enter into a lower-class child's commission of acts of delinquency: (1) certain cultural practices that comprise essential elements of the total life pattern of lower-class culture automatically violate certain legal norms; (2) in certain instances, when alternative avenues to valued objectives are available, the law-violating route frequently entails a relatively smaller investment of energy and effort than the law-abiding one; and (3) the demanded response to certain situations recurrently engendered within lower-class culture calls for the commission of illegal acts. The lower-class youngster who engages in a long and recurrent series of delinquent acts that are sanctioned by his or her peer group is acting to achieve prestige within his or her reference system or gang.

In a theory similar to those of Kvaraceus and Miller, Bonger, Quinney, and others, Albert K. Cohen (1983) perceived the delinquency of what he termed "the working-class boy" as a form of rebellion against the middle class and its values. He describes the delinquent subculture as "nonutilitarian, malicious, and negativistic." Cohen contends that in addition to such obviously nonutilitarian delinquent acts as vandalism, even stealing by those involved in the delinquent lower-class subculture is nonutilitarian. He says, "In homelier language, stealing 'for the hell of it' and apart from considerations of gain and profit is a valued activity to which attaches glory, prowess, and profound satisfaction. There is no accounting in rational and utilitarian terms for the effort expended and the danger run in stealing things which are often discarded, destroyed or casually given away. . . . Unquestionably, most delinquents are from the more 'needy' and 'underprivileged' classes, and unquestionably many things are stolen because they are intrinsically valued" (p. 87). Cohen also asserts that most elementary, middle, and high schools in the United States are essentially structured for middle-class children. Lower socioeconomic class children who are alienated from or reject the larger society do so specifically by dropping out of school. Those who are not dropouts tend to produce the most behavior problems in the schools.

Cohen concludes that many activities of lower-class delinquents are even less motivated by rational, utilitarian considerations. He notes that there is a kind of malice apparent, an enjoyment in the discomfiture of others, a delight in defiance against taboos. Cohen sees the acts of adherents to the delinquent subculture as essentially negativistic. He sees an element of spite in their flouting of rules, defiance of teachers, and misbehavior in school, a revolt against the middle class and its values by the working-class boys. He says, "All this suggests also the intention of our term *negativistic.* The delinquent subculture is not only a set of rules, a design for living which is different from or indifferent to or even in conflict with the norms of the 'respectable' adult society. It would appear at least plausible that it is defined by its 'negative polarity' to those norms. That is, the delinquent sub-culture takes its norms from the larger culture but turns them upside down. The delinquent's conduct is right, by the standards of his subculture, precisely because it is wrong by the norms of the larger culture" (1983, p. 28).

Cohen (1983, pp. 28–32) asserts that juvenile delinquency in general, and the delinquent subcultural in particular, are overwhelmingly concentrated in the male, lower-class sector of the juvenile population. Acknowledging that police and court biases may account in part for the correlation between juvenile delinquency and social class, he nevertheless concludes that almost all statistical analyses of juvenile delinquency indicate that delinquency in general is predominantly a working-class phenomenon.

Cohen and other sociologists who have studied the phenomenon of class and delinquency have come to a consensus that lower-class children are evaluated in accordance with middle-class standards set by middle-class teachers, social workers, ministers, and adults who work with them. Delinquency then becomes a rebellion against the middle class, a form of class conflict. Frustrated by the fact that their socialization in lower-class culture handicaps them for success in the middle-class status system, they rebel against it and find a solution in delinquency. In the context of middle-class norms and values, lower-class youths see themselves as not likely to succeed in school, at work, or anywhere else that middle-class norms are applied. They see themselves at the bottom of the heap and develop a sense of hopelessness. Therefore they join with others like themselves in rejecting middle-class culture and develop a subculture (the violent gang) that acts out in defiance of the larger society (Cohen, 1983, pp. 36–44).

Self-Reporting Studies, Social Class, and Delinquency

The explanations offered by Kvaraceus, Miller, Quinney, Cohen, and others assume that delinquency is largely a lower-class urban phenomenon. Although this assumption is supported by most available statistics, there is a body of research that indicates a growing difference in magnitude between lower-class delinquent behavior and middle-class delinquent behavior. The delinquencies of middle-class children are often not adequately reported because of police bias in making arrests, parental intervention in the judicial process, and the referring of middle-class children into various nonlegal therapeutic modalities.

Researchers have developed a method for obtaining middle-class delinquency data from the source other than the official police and court statistics. This research approach essentially involves a questionnaire in which young people are asked to report instances of delinquent behavior on a self-reporting basis. Another method is the in-depth interview, granting anonymity to the respondent, in which similar information is elicited.

Using this research methodology in their study of social class and delinquency, Ivan Nye, James Short, Jr., and Virgil Olsen (1958, pp. 381–389) obtained their data using anonymous questionnaires. Their research attempted to answer a basic question: Does delinquent behavior occur differentially by socioeconomic status? These researchers rejected studies of delinquent behavior based on court records, police files, records maintained by correctional institutions, and other official sources. Such studies, they maintained, might be adequate for an examination of official delinquency but are unreliable as an index of delinquent behavior in the general population.

The distinction between the concepts "official delinquency" and "delinquency behavior" was considered important by these researchers. From their viewpoint, delinquent behavior is behavior violating legal norms; it becomes official delinquency only when it results in action by official authority, such as police and the courts. Official delinquency in their view represents a reaction of society to delinquent behavior.

In general, when sociologists refer to youths as members of the lower, middle, or upper class, they base their differentiations on the economic status of the child's family. The occupation of the head of the family, family income, educational attainments, or some combination of the three are generally used as criteria for placing a child in a particular class. In other words, the class position of the family is ascribed to the child. In the research of Nye, Short, and Olsen (1958), the father's occupation was used to place the child in one of four status groupings: (1) unskilled or semiskilled labor; (2) skilled labor and craftsmen; (3) white-collar workers and small businessmen; and (4) professionals and large businessmen. The sample for this study was drawn from high schools in several Western and Midwestern communities.

In all, 756 differences were tested for and 33 were found to be significant. That is, 33 significant differences were found in the proportion of acts committed by a particular socioeconomic category. The two middle status groups had the highest proportion of delinquency in four instances; the upper status group in thirteen instances; and the lower status group in sixteen instances. From this, the researchers concluded that either middle-class delinquent behavior is underreported or middle-class parents are more effective in socializing their children and controlling their behavior.

In another study comparing delinquent behavior of boys and girls in different socioeconomic strata, Harwin L. Voss (1966) also used self-reported data. The subjects of his study were 620 students in a public inter-mediate school. Attention was focused primarily on the information pro-vided by 284 male respondents. The data were gathered in Honolulu, a metropolitan center in which the majority of the population is Oriental. Anonymous questionnaires were administered to a 15.5 percent random sample of seventh-grade students. The researcher recorded on a chart the number of times a youth had committed a particular act and the minimum frequency required for the youth to be classified as delinquent. Children were placed in four classes based on the socioeconomic position of the father. The four strata were (1) unskilled and semiskilled labor, (2) skilled labor and craftsmen, (3) white-collar workers and small businessmen, and (4) professionals and large businessmen (1966, pp. 314–324).

The data were subjected to three tests in an attempt to locate sig-nificant differences in the incidence of delinquent behavior. In the first test the distributions of most and least delinquent groups of boys and girls by socioeconomic status were tested. The girls in the various status levels were found not to differ significantly. However, for boys, socioeconomic status was found to be significantly related to incidence of delinquent behavior. In this study, boys in the two upper social strata reported more extensive involvement in delinquent activity than did boys in the other two groups. The number of those who "purposely damaged or destroyed property" was reported to be higher in the two upper strata. The researchers concluded that the incidence of admitted illegal behavior of lower-status children did not differ significantly from those of middle- and upper-status children.

In another significant study on the issue of social class and delin-quency, Erickson and Empey (1965, pp. 268–282) used self-reported data in an attempt to understand how peer pressure in different strata affects delinquency. They were concerned primarily with studying the relation-ships of children to their peers. They noted that explanations of delin-quency are often based on the assumption that class position and exposure or lack of exposure to educational and other socializing activities are directly related to delinquent behavior. Because lower-class children lack the "successes and satisfactions" of upper- and middle-class children, it is generally believed they are more frequently inclined to become delinquent.

One theory suggested by Erickson and Empey (1965, p. 281) is that "a lower-class child joins with delinquent peers and participates in delin-quent activities because these things represent an alternative means for acquiring many of the social and emotional satisfactions that other children obtain from conventional sources." If their theory is accurate, it would indi-cate that (1) delinquency is more indicative of the lower class than of the middle or upper classes, (2) peer relations are more predictive of delinquent or nondelinquent behavior than is lower-class position, and (3) children

91

from the lower class are more apt to associate with and have a commitment to delinquents than are children from middle and upper classes.

Twenty-two delinquent acts were defined by the researchers. Each subject (only boys were investigated) was interviewed personally and asked: (1) Have you ever committed any of these offenses? (2) If so, how many times? and (3) How often have you been caught, arrested, or brought into court? More serious crimes, such as narcotics and arson, were eliminated, because they did not play a significant or frequent role in the lives of the youths in the sample. Erickson and Empey found no significant correlation between class position and delinquency. In regard to association with delinquents, the results showed that those boys who were already delinquent were more apt to associate with other delinquents. All classes responded negatively to "informing on a peer" or "ratting." The researchers concluded from their results that social-class position is less predictive of delinquency than is association and identification with delinquent peers (Erickson and Empey, 1965, p. 292).

Based on his analysis of the problem Clemens Bartollas (1993, p. 46) states about self-reporting that: (1) there is considerable undetected delinquency; (2) both lower- and middle-class juveniles are involved in considerable illegal behavior; (3) many undetected serious crimes are committed by juvenile delinquents each year; (4) lower-class youths appear to commit more delinquent acts and are more likely to be chronic offenders than middle-class youths; (5) African-American youths are more likely than white youths to be arrested, convicted, and institutionalized when both have committed the same offenses; and (6) female delinquents commit more offenses than the statistics indicate.

A study of police officers by Marcia Garrett and James F. Short (1975) supported a hypothesis that there are different perceptions of lower-class delinquents by members of the community. The Garrett and Short study dealt with police attitudes toward delinquents. Data were analyzed to determine police images of delinquency; police estimates of the delinquent involvement of boys from different social-class backgrounds; and police predictions on the basis of first official contacts. Data were collected in three cities. Ninety-three unstructured interviews of police were conducted, and questionnaires were also administered to 453 officers. Officers' predictions about future delinquency were tested over a six-year follow-up period. Police in widely different settings based their judgments on "street" experience and similar theories of delinquency causation linking social-class background, parental neglect, and delinquent behavior. In general, police perceived lower-class minority group boys as more likely to be involved in serious delinquent conduct than boys with "higher" social-class backgrounds.

Limitations of Self-Reporting

If we accept the various studies based on self-reporting as valid, we must conclude that there is a minimal difference between the amount of delinquent behavior committed by lower-class boys and by middle-class boys. In this regard, several reasons for a closer analysis of the findings of self-report studies with respect to the relationship between social class and delinquency were suggested by Travis Hirschi (1969, p. 70): (1) the self-report measure of delinquency is invalid for this purpose; (2) the samples used in these studies deal only with a restricted class range; (3) the measures of socioeconomic status are invalid; (4) the effects of socioeconomic status are suppressed by the effects of some third variable; and (5) contrary to their assertions, some of the "no-difference" self-report studies do show a relation between socioeconomic status and delinquency.

The acts reported by middle-class youths, although technically illegal, may not be truly comparable with offenses charged against lower-class youths. For example, a fourteen-year-old middle-class boy, a subject in one self-report study, took a can of beer from his mother's refrigerator without permission and drank it. He reported himself guilty of two delinquent acts, stealing and illegal use of a drug or intoxicant. This offense can hardly be considered comparable to a violent carjacking, dealing drugs, or an armed robbery—acts for which a lower-class youth might more likely be found delinquent in court (Brown, 1984).

Some Explanations of Middle-Class Delinquency

Although there is ample evidence that the vast majority of young people adjudicated delinquent by the juvenile courts are from lower-socioeconomic-class families, there are many whose families are middle class. If we take into consideration research indicating more favorable treatment of middle-class children by the police and the courts, we must conclude that there are probably far more middle-class delinquents than the statistics indicate. Furthermore, the self-report studies suggest that the incidence of delinquent behavior among middle-class children may be as great as that among lower- or working-class children.

In general, there are more dysfunctional families and absentee fathers in lower-class families due to the negative social factors they confront. Some research also reveals that middle-class parents provide socialization strongly favoring conformity to the law, and middle-class children have few, if any, economic needs not satisfied by their parents. Given these factors, how can we account for what is claimed to be a large and growing amount of delinquent behavior among middle-class youths? Some efforts to account for this phenomenon are presented in this section.

William Kvaraceus and Walter Miller (1959), who related lower-class delinquency to such focal concerns of the lower class as trouble, toughness, smartness, and autonomy, considered middle-class delinquency in relation to the focal concerns of the middle class. They noted that middle-class concerns were centered around such factors as achievement through directed work effort; deferment of immediate pleasures and gains for future goals; personal responsibility; and maintenance of the solidarity of the nuclear family. Kvaraceus and Miller believed that orientation toward these concerns deterred middle-class children from delinquency and that the legal codes supported these middle-class focal concerns. These middle-class traditions exerted pressure on children to postpone gratification. Self-denial and impulse control were encouraged. The increase in middle-class delinquency may be attributed, in part, to a weakening of these traditional values.

Kvaraceus and Miller also asserted that when serious delinquency occurs in middle-class groups, it may be a portent of pathological behavior since it is conduct counter to the definitions of a significant reference group. They pointed out that "the middle-class youngster who engages in norm-violating behavior may often be viewed more usefully as a "behavior problem" than as a "delinquent." My observations as a group therapist in a number of psychiatric hospitals for delinquents support this viewpoint. The mostly middle- and upper-class parents I worked with tended to see their child's misbehavior not as delinquent behavior but as deviance emanating from psychological problems.

Talcott Parsons' (1947) view was that in our society the mother has the dominant role in socialization. The father is preoccupied with his occupational role and is away from home most of the time. Because of this, the child, particularly the middle-class suburban child, is likely to perceive his or her mother as a principal exemplar of morality, source of discipline, and object of identification. According to this viewpoint, the middle-class male delinquent knows it is shameful for a boy to be like a woman and feels constrained to rebel against impulses that suggest femininity and to exaggerate behavior that connotes masculinity. In Parsons' context, "goodness" represents femininity and "badness" masculinity. Hence, middle-class male delinquency may be a form of masculine protest.

Some sociologists explain the rise in middle-class delinquency in relation to changing social and economic conditions. They observe that the patriarchally controlled family has given way to a more "democratic" family unit in which children share in the decision-making process. The family atmosphere has become more permissive and achievement goals more difficult to inculcate. The school, too, has become more permissive. As a result, the adolescent role has become vague, and the distinction between right and wrong is soft-pedaled. The adolescent is left to define what is "right" conduct (Frease, Polk, and Richmond, 1974).

Many of the theories and research findings reported here are of interest in accounting for the middle-class delinquency in the past and, to some extent, for a great deal of the hidden middle-class juvenile delinquency of the present. However, contemporary middle-class delinquency is best explained in relationship to the enormous increase in substance abuse by middle-class juveniles. Drug addiction, including alcoholism, among middle-class youths is rampant and is a delinquency problem in its own right. It also accounts for a considerable amount of middle-class delinquent behavior, including parent-child conflicts, driving under the influence, sexual acting out, family conflict resulting in running away from home, learning problems and truancy, and theft and prostitution to obtain money to support a drug habit (McGee, 1992).

The juvenile social problem of substance abuse, which was mainly a lower-class phenomenon in the first half of the twentieth century, has become more democratic and now exists among juveniles from all social classes. Entwined with substance abuse, including smoking marijuana—which is considered a benign delinquent act by most youths—is theft and violence to acquire money for drugs. In general, the increase of drug use among most adolescents has contributed enormously to a significant rise in middle-class juvenile delinquency. (This issue is addressed in Part 4, "Substance Abuse.")

Class Differences and Delinquency: Two Portraits

Statistics, various theories, and the social-psychological analysis of class and delinquency provide many insights into the relevant issues that surround delinquent behavior. However, case analysis adds a more in-depth understanding of the issue of class and delinquency. The following cases of a lower-class delinquent substance abuser, Baby Love, and an upper-middle-class female delinquent, Jill, provide insights into some of the differences in the sociocultural background of lower-class and upper-middle-class delinquency.

Baby Love

In lower socioeconomic groups, drug and alcohol use has become an arch tranquilizer for youths locked into a ghetto or barrio, who see little opportunity or hope for their future. Drugs have become an adjunct to a life of poverty and hopelessness that leads to delinquency and criminal behavior. The following portrait of Baby Love, from an article by James Wilde (1981) reveals the blood and guts social context of the lower-class delinquent:

> Baby Love sits on the stoop, rolling the largest, fattest joint in the world. He wastes little: in go twigs, seeds, everything, until it seems as big as a torpedo. Other joints are tucked over each ear, and more are secreted in plastic bags under his hat. It is Friday night, the night to get high, get drunk and strut. Baby Love's entire wrecking crew is here, sprawled over cars, squatting on the sidewalk, jiving. There is Shistang ("He be cool with dice"), Little Spank, Gugu, Snake Eyes, Shilo, Spider Man, Daddy Rich, Little June, Snatch Pocket Earl and Snootchy Fingers. "We be in the streets hangin' out an' gettin' high," says Baby Love. He is a very skinny, very small, very lethal fourteen-year-old. His eyes are slate gray, flashing to blue when he laughs. Mischief is etched across his face as a bittersweet smile. Like his crew, he is dressed in mugger's uniform; designer jeans, T-shirt and $45 Pumas, the starched laces neatly untied. A wolf in expensive sneakers.
>
> Baby Love is a school dropout, one of more than 800,000 between the ages of fourteen and seventeen in the United States. Baby Love inhabits a world few white folks ever see, a Dickensian hell of cheap thrills, senseless deaths and almost unrelieved hopelessness. He lives in Brooklyn's Bedford Stuyvesant section, one of the oldest black settlements in the United States. Unlike the burned and ravaged South Bronx, ten miles to the north, Bedford Stuyvesant does not resemble a war zone; most of its owner-occupied row houses, brownstones and churches are more or less intact. But high unemployment and a 60 percent dropout rate among black high school students make it a very dangerous place. One Bed-Stuy precinct, the 77th, has the highest murder rate in the city: eighty-six killings last year. Baby Love is trapped. He can barely read or write, even though he would have been in the seventh grade this year. Because he is nearly illiterate he could never hold even the meanest job for long. He has been running wild so long now that he may be beyond redemption.
>
> Ghetto children today are seduced much earlier by drugs and the street, some of them as young as eight or nine. That is the time they need help. Sinbad Lockwood, a Bed-Stuy street artist who tries to wean boys like Baby Love away from the streets to painting, says (in Ebonics), "It be the parents' fault, they gets rid of the kids by sending them to the candy store where they be buying reefer and beer. These kids ain't no monsters—they be raising themselves, that's all."
>
> Baby Love is almost always stoned. He rises late, plays basketball in the park or galactic-warfare games at the pinball arcade all day. If there is any money left over, he and Daddy Rich go to karate movies. He juggles four chicks with Casanova skill, and he makes enough from gambling and stealing to be a real

sportin' man. For Baby Love, stealing means survival. He is the best gold chain snatcher on the block. "I pretends to be making a phone call when the bus be comin' along," he explains, "so the driver won't warn the passengers. Then when it be by, I's leapin' in the air with my hand through the window and gone befo' anyone sees." He breaks into laughter, slapping skin all around. He has been caught five times this summer for pickpocketing. At Macy's he was caught boosting eight blue Izod Lacoste shirts in his Adidas bag. He has just finished sixty days' probation.

Baby Love lives on the fourth floor of a crumbling, turn-of-the-century tenement with his aunt and legal guardian, Cora Lee. He sleeps on a stained mattress in a small room he often shares with his cousins, Butter and Buckeye, and with an army of roaches that waddle fatly across the floor. His two younger sisters, Shantia, eleven, and Sarah, eight, are also in Cora Lee's charge. Baby Love's mother, Rose, stays there too. They are all receiving welfare payments. There have been three bad fires in Baby Love's building in the past couple of years. The fifth floor is gutted. He and his crew now use it as their clubhouse. Baby Love uses the roof as an escape route from police. He jumps across a yawning chasm to the next building, then he is down the stairs and away. "We be doin' this when we drunk," says Baby Love with an impish smile.

A born hustler, he is slick at pool and dice. He gambles Friday nights in front of BeeGee's candy store with men who feed him chiba chiba, a Puerto Rican expression for an especially potent kind of marijuana, the reefer that zoots you out. He thinks Bruce Lee is a cool dude, but "Richard Pryor is the Man," says Baby Love. "He's got power." The violence Baby Love sees on the screen is not much different from what he faces on the street. He was thirteen when he first saw a man blown away with a shotgun. He has faced down a few gunslingers himself. He sometimes carries a .25 automatic. "All my friends got guns." . . .

Tough, mean young men shoot it out like Western heroes of old. The dead are dumped in trashed buildings. Some of Baby Love's friends did not live through the summer. A cheeky dude like him risks death or injury every time he steps outside. Being small does not help. He was always getting beaten up until he learned to steal. Now he can bribe would-be assailants with reefer. He sometimes spends $20 a day on the stuff.

On Friday nights the crowds along Fulton and Nostrand Avenues ebb and flow like a tide. Dudes are gambling up and down the streets. The sweet smell of reefer is everywhere, and wine bottles are passed around. Up the block, twelve-year-old hookers teeter on high heels, flouncing their boyish hips. There are drunken brawls, skin-and-bone addicts overdosing, police sirens screaming and the rattle of the el in the distance.

A procession of dudes pause to talk to Baby Love. Most have done hard time. Some push dope, many are boozers. All have bitter wisdom. Crocodile comes by waving a bottle of vodka, his eyes gleaming yellow. He tells Baby Love, "Wait till you do hard time, boy. They'll pat your butt, they'll feel you. You'll come home swishing like a girl." A huge dude, his muscles rippling, speaks in a cool bass: "I got a pair of $600 lizard shoes and I got silk shirts. I'm the Man, boy. I changes my clothes fifteen times a day. Learn to hustle girls, and you can wear dark shades and sharkskin suits and ride a big white Caddy."

Riff the horn player sniffs in disgust. "You've got to have dignity, boy, you be nothing without dignity. The only way to beat the Man is by going to school. Go back to school, boy." Baby Love sneers. He stands up. "I'm goin' get all I wants," he says, "and I don't care if I gotta steal to get it. I'm not afraid of doin' time so long as I kin do it fast." Then he goes up to the clubhouse with Daddy Rich. He lies on a mattress puffing on an El Producto cigar hollowed out and filled with chiba chiba. There is a bottle of 150-proof Bacardi rum by his side. The cassette player throbs and, for a moment, Baby Love is warm and secure, at peace and flying high. . . .

Where did Baby Love go wrong? His mother, Rose, thirty-one, does not deny that she was a drug addict. "I'm an alcoholic too," she adds. She gave up legal custody of her children to Aunt Cora last year. According to Rose, Baby Love's father is an alcoholic, a drug addict and a bisexual. He was doing time at Attica during the prison's 1971 riots, shrugs Rose, and "he flipped his brains. That's why I divorced him." His father beat Baby Love up often with his fists, says Rose, and once he did so with an extension cord. When Baby Love retaliated with a piece of heavy steel pipe, she recalls, his father took him to the police and demanded, futilely, that he be locked up. Baby Love rebelled against his mother when she started sleeping with other men. Once, when she nearly overdosed, he dragged her from the kitchen, poured hot and cold water on her feet and burned her arms with a lighted cigarette to revive her.

Baby Love walks with a slight limp. His mother explains that he had a serious accident while playing ball in the streets when he was four. He was run over by a car and his left leg, right arm and most of his ribs were broken. Rose then did one of the few constructive things she has done in her sad life: she sued the driver and got a settlement of $3,000, which is now in trust. Baby Love will get the money when he turns 21. If he lives that long. (Pp. 36–41)(Reprinted by permission of Time Life Syndication.)

Jill: A Middle-Class Delinquent

In sharp contrast to Baby Love was Jill (not her real name). Jill had never been arrested, despite the fact that she was a heavy drug user and addict. She was a well-mannered, well-dressed sixteen-year-old when she took part in my therapy groups over a ten-month period in a psychiatric hospital. Jill's substance abuse and delinquency flowed from a different social-psychological context than Baby Love's.

Jill came from an affluent family background where any material need was immediately met. While Baby Love had limited or no access to upward mobility in the social system, Jill was already there in terms of material success and status. Yet, for Jill, her status, her private, elegantly furnished room in a large house, and material acquisitions did not prevent her heavy drug use and delinquent behavior.

I first met Jill after she had been in juvenile court and was remanded for treatment to the psychiatric hospital where I worked. At the time of her entry into the hospital she was suffering from depression, had been addicted to cocaine, alcohol, and a variety of pills for several years, and had attempted suicide. Her parents considered her "incorrigible," a common middle-class synonym for "delinquent."

During the ten-month period that I worked with Jill in the hospital, her treatment included individual psychiatric counseling and group therapy with professional therapists. In particular, I worked directly with her in a drug addict encounter group and a psychodrama group. In addition to these sessions, I interviewed her several times on an individual basis for this case analysis toward the end of her therapy at the hospital.

Jill, an only child, began smoking marijuana at thirteen—around the time her parents divorced. She lived with her mother. She found her mother cold and unfeeling. The following "self-described" assessment of Jill's delinquent behavior is derived from many individual discussions and group sessions I had with Jill over a ten-month period.

> My mother just bored me to death. She never talked to me. When I learned some psychiatric jargon I would say she was catatonic. It was like living with a stone. I missed my father terribly—and saw him rarely—because he was always traveling on business and out making money. Around the time I was fourteen, I met Jim. You could say for me he was an older man. He was twenty-five. I realize now it was all bullshit, but he had this revolutionary line that got to me. He was always talking against society and how people rip each other off and how fucked society was. That's how he justified why he committed a lot of burglaries and robberies. In the meantime, he was really exploiting me. I really thought I was in love with him, and he was my one and only. But I found out later I was only one of his girlfriends. He was just a terrible liar, and he ripped me off in a lot of ways. I now know he was the worst kind of sociopath.
>
> About a year after my parents split, my father got married again, and I got to go live with him. His new wife, my stepmother, seemed OK at first but turned into a total bitch. I had fooled around with some coke with Jim, but my new stepmother

really turned me on to coke. My father didn't know how heavy she was using. All he cared about was that she screwed him whenever he wanted to. She would get stoned and tell me that's how she held on to him. After my dad went off to work, I would have a nice breakfast with my stepmom. She would put out a good spread. It consisted of scrambled eggs, coffee, and several lines of coke. If it wouldn't make me late to school, instead of snorting the coke I would smoke some crack.

For my lunch break at school, I would smoke a joint, and on other days when it was available I would do some more coke or have a few ludes. This routine went on until I was fifteen. My boyfriend Jim and I did lots of drugs, sex, and once in a while I drove the car when he went to rob a house. In my drug haze, I fell madly in love with Jim, and almost worshiped him. I knew my stepmom was partying and making it with lots of other guys when my dad was away on his business trips. The bitch was into younger guys, and she often flirted openly with Jim. He denied any interest in her. You guessed it. One day I came home early from school and there they were fucking in my father's bed. They hardly stopped when they saw me. I got into a big screaming hassle with the two of them. They tried to calm me down. We all did some coke, and they just giggled about what had happened.

I was smashed by the incident and felt horrible. But it didn't seem to bother them at all. Later, when I was alone, I screamed at Jim how I loved him and how could he do this to me. He was totally cold to my feelings. Finally he said, "If you don't like it bitch, get lost." To show you how stupid I was at that time, that night I went over to his house and found out he wasn't home. I told his parents I would just wait on the lawn for him. They must have gone to sleep. So I'm sitting out there in terrible emotional pain full of pills, smoking a joint, feeling all alone, sorry for myself, and getting more depressed by the minute. The only one I felt I had in the world was Jim, and he had abandoned me. He never showed up that night, and I found out later that he had fucked some bitch that night.

Out on the lawn, around 4:00 A.M. when I came down from my coke high, I was very depressed. I had thought a lot about suicide around that time. I carried some razor blades in my purse. (They were also good for cutting up hash and lining up coke.) So there I was all alone and depressed, and I decided to do it. I cut my wrists, and they were bleeding lightly. I was still partially stoned and actually felt mellow watching blood ooze out of my wrists. That'll show them all, I thought.

Then I got this crazy idea. I thought it was logical for me to write Jim a letter in my own blood. I had a pen in my purse and would dip it in my blood. The writing was red and blue from the pen. I talked about my grief, depression, loneliness, what a dick he was, and on and on and on. His parents must have seen what I was doing through the window. They called the police and my father. They scooped me up and rushed me to the emergency ward. I really hadn't lost that much blood, but I was obviously nuts.

In a way my suicide attempt worked. My father, for the first time in ages, began to talk to me. I told him about his bitch wife and how she had served me cocaine at breakfast time and how she made it with Jim. Well that blew it for her. My father knew we both had to get some therapy. For me, it was the start of around six drug programs. They were all sixty- to ninety-day detoxification programs with a little bullshit group therapy. None of them worked, and as soon as I was out the door I would use again.

Along the way, over this year or so when I was in these programs, my dad divorced the bitch. Then he got himself another one, who was just as bad. My father became distant again as I went in and out of these psychiatric hospitals. In a few of them I was able to have friends smuggle in drugs. Jim and I were on again, off again. I still felt I loved him in spite of the fact that he continued to use me. He was always off with other girls, and I never forgave him for fucking my stepmom.

During this period in the hospital, Jill participated in the psychodrama group I directed, plus a special drug encounter group for adolescents that I codirected with several recovering ex-addicts who lived in a therapeutic community. In psychodrama she confronted some of the basic underlying issues that she was working on with her psychiatrist. These included her problems with her father, her mother, and Jim, whom she once characterized as "a father substitute because my dad was never around."

The several psychodrama sessions I had with her that related to her father involved the basic theme of feeling emotionally alienated from him and her sense of his lack of real caring for her. "He gave me all the money and things I wanted, but no caring or real love." In several psychodramas, a male nurse played the role of her father. In these dramatic, tearful sessions she would implore this stand-in for her father to love her, spend some time with her, and make her feel cared for. She felt especially abandoned by her father when she reached puberty.

I recorded her concluding commentary in one session: "Dad, I was always your special little girl and you adored me. You used to hug me and hold me on your lap and tell me how pretty I was. Then when I was thirteen, you pushed me off your lap like I was some 'thing.' Our family broke up and you left me with mom. I love mom, but she's like a dead person. She never talks or feels anything. You were the important one in my life. When I began to use drugs, it killed the pain of my feeling alone, and it always made me feel better."

Drugs became Jill's self-administered therapy; the emotional effects were more reliable than her parents. In various sessions several fourteen-

and fifteen-year-old girls shared similar feelings of being abandoned by their fathers at puberty. In the group discussions that followed the role playing, several psychological points were made that seemed to fit Jill and many teenage girls. When they make the transition from childhood to adolescence, many teenage girls feel abandoned by their fathers. This is often because their fathers, especially if they are insecure men like Jill's father, repress some of the sexual feelings they might have for them by coldly rejecting them. Of course, this is superior to the problems that ensue from fathers who act out their sexual feelings, either flirtatiously or directly. What is more appropriate is an honest awareness of these sexual feelings and dealing with them without rejecting their daughters. These issues were discussed by the group after Jill's psychodrama.

Jill also learned from several psychodrama sessions and discussions with her psychiatrist on this theme that she had limited control over "getting her father back"; however, she had total control over her response to her feeling that her father had rejected her. Her therapy also helped her to conclude that the onset of her drug problems was related to her feelings of low soft-esteem, which stemmed from being rejected by her father. Her self-destructive drug abuse was connected to her conflict and alienation from her father. She said, "I learned from my therapy that I'm not the only girl with these feelings of being abandoned by my dad. And I also see how I attempted to substitute an older man, Jim, for the father I felt had abandoned me." Her overall insight was that this was a family problem, and she was the "identified patient." This insight relieved some of her sense of being a "bad, sick girl," which had propelled her into drug addiction.

This is only a brief sketch of some of the psychodynamics that were related to Jill's drug abuse symptom syndrome, which were considerably relieved and resolved during her overall therapeutic program. She went back to school, developed a more optimistic viewpoint, and at last report was leading a drug-free, relatively happy life.

Baby Love and Jill: An Analysis

Jill's middle-class perspective on her personal problems and her substance abuse were acquired first from her friends and relatives. She had read some self-help books, had discussed psychological issues with her friends and family, and was receptive to and had access to one of the best treatment systems available to help her resolve her problems.

In contrast, Baby Love, a lower-class delinquent, was in an entirely different social milieu. First of all, he didn't have the financial means or any motivation to have his problems treated in a psychiatric hospital. His "counselors" were streetwise criminal pimps and hustlers, who would advise him mainly on how to become a more effective juvenile delinquent. He saw these people as role models and helpers in his battles for "success" on the street.

It is apparent that the social-class, cultural, law-enforcement, and economic context that surrounds adolescents like Baby Love and Jill were considerably different. Baby Love was attracted to the drugs and hustling behavior that surrounded him and was relatively normal in his environment. Children like Baby Love see little opportunity or hope in their future in the larger society. This partly accounts for their disinterest in school and their gravitation toward the criminal role models in their neighborhood who have, in their eyes, "made it."

Drugs were a pain killer for hopelessness and a commodity for profit in Baby Love's life situation. Drugs and theft are an intrinsic part of this delinquent system. It is highly unlikely that families like Baby Love's would have the health insurance or the financial means for treatment.

Inevitably, lower-class youths like Baby Love will be incarcerated in a state institution where the delinquent value system and behavior will be reinforced. In the state facility they will be exposed to other young men who will collectively rationalize their plight and be eager to learn more in their juvenile apprenticeship for a later life of crime.

Despite these differences, in some ways Jill's and Baby Love's delinquency emerged from similar causes. They both felt alienated and helpless and turned to drugs for relief from their pain. Their class position in the social system, however, clearly propelled them in different directions. Jill's family had wealth and attitudes about emotional problems that motivated them to place her in a psychiatric facility that might help change her behavior. The chances of Baby Love being resocialized in an appropriate treatment center were slim to none.

The foregoing analysis encompasses some of the central reasons why teenagers from different class backgrounds become and remain delinquent. It is apparent that middle- and upper-class youths like Jill have a greater chance of being resocialized than youths from a lower socioeconomic background. In the United States, correctional institutions are predominantly filled with males like Baby Love and females of similar background. In contrast, children with Jill's background are rarely incarcerated in state institutions and have greater access to a variety of contemporary treatment facilities. Baby Love's prototypical lower-class delinquency and Jill's prototypical middle-class delinquency exemplify the two types of delinquency that exist in American society.

PART 2

The Juvenile in a Violent Society

CHAPTERS

CHAPTER 5

VIOLENCE AGAINST CHILDREN AND ITS IMPACT ON THEIR DELINQUENT BEHAVIOR

Children who are abused emotionally and physically are more likely to become delinquent.

In the past century there has been an escalation of juvenile violence and sexual abuse and exploitation of children. These two factors are in many respects intertwined. Based on my years of working with delinquents in the community and in custody, I am persuaded that more than 80 percent of youths who are adjudicated delinquent have been emotionally, sexually, or physically abused or exploited. Children who are abused or exploited have in effect been subjected to violent treatment. This fact of their socialization process is a significant contributory element in their later violent behavior.

Children who are violently abused by their parents or other significant people learn that they are objects that do not deserve caring and love. The consequence of this negative socialization is to produce low self-esteem and rage in these children. A side effect of low self-esteem is not caring about what happens to oneself, and this inner rage often produces violent behavior that is often displaced on innocent victims. These two factors affect a youth's propensity for committing acts of violence. (Violent behavior is more fully addressed in chapter 13, "Sociological Causation Theories.")

This chapter is divided into two parts. The first part deals with the climate of violence that exists in American society, including the impact of the mass media, and the second part examines various patterns of child abuse and exploitation of children that affect their violent behavior and delinquency.

The Sociocultural Climate of Violence in American Society

People in contemporary society are constantly bombarded by reports of violence in the news. A shoot-out in Los Angeles that ended in the death of two bank robbers was a typical event in the life of that city. The impact of this dramatic violence on the populace, including children, was analyzed in a *Los Angeles Times* article:

> The bloodstains have faded from the pavement along Archwood Avenue. The bullet holes on the Bank of America wall have been patched. The flowers have stopped arriving at the North Hollywood police station. The televised gun battle that mesmerized a city—and left two bank robbers dead and seventeen bystanders and police officers wounded—is but a memory, last week's news, now giving way to gun-control debates and speculation about paramilitary groups. Or is it? What about among residents of that quiet North Hollywood neighborhood, trapped in their homes as their streets were strafed with gunfire? And

customers of that Bank of America branch, huddled in fear inside a vault, wondering when the rat-a-tat of the machine guns outside would reach them. And passersby, felled by bullets and forced to cower behind parked cars until the shooting stopped?

The story may have stopped leading the nightly news, but it will probably haunt the lives of those who lived through it for weeks, months, even years to come. There will be fear and loathing, anger and anxiety, nightmares, tears, and temper tantrums. "These two guys didn't just rob a bank," said Barbara Cienfuegos, who coordinates disaster response for the county Mental Health Department. "They robbed all of us. . . . They stole our sense of security, of feeling safe and good in our homes, on our jobs, in our community. Those are very real losses, and now we have to deal with that."

I have a friend—call her Linda—who manages a San Fernando Valley outlet of a national restaurant chain. Eight months ago, just after she opened for business one morning, two men barged in with guns drawn, directed a stream of obscenities at her and her customers, and demanded money. She remembers going into a "politeness mode—'yes sir,' 'no sir,' 'I'm getting it as fast as I can, sir' "—as she knelt and opened the safe, with the cold steel muzzle of a gun pressed hard against her temple. She handed over the cash and when she stood up, was staring directly into the barrel of his gun. "And he was looking at us, and I thought, 'He's going to shoot me, he's going to shoot all of us, just for the hell of it.' I could feel the color drain out of my face from the fear of it all. And that's the thing I keep playing over in my mind . . . the incredible sense of fear. It felt like an eternity, and I didn't know if I was going to live or die." She lived. The robbers fled, the police were called, the customers were comforted, and the overturned tables and chairs set right. Life went on; the restaurant reopened within hours, and Linda and her staff finished their shifts and went home.

Over the next few days, she recounted the robbery to her husband, her children, her friends; everyone told her how lucky she was to have survived unhurt. But she didn't feel lucky or unhurt. She felt scared. And angry. And bewildered at feeling scared and angry. "I was really unprepared for that," she recalls now. For weeks, she was afraid to go into stores, restaurants, anyplace where more than a few people might congregate. "I started worrying for the first time about things like whether the kids were safe at school," she said. "I never thought about that kind of stuff before. It was like suddenly I realized I wasn't in control . . . that at any moment, anything can happen to you. That's a hard feeling to handle." There were no TV skycams recording her robbery, no dramatic shootouts or police news conferences. But Linda shares with the victims of the North Hollywood siege feelings familiar to anyone who has ever been held up, shot at, raped, beaten . . . those anonymous folks victimized in crimes that never make the news, but whose lives are changed nonetheless. (Banks, 1997) (Reprinted by permission of the Los Angeles Times Syndicate.)

This crime is typical of the violence that has become an everyday occurrence in contemporary society. Almost all children are exposed to episodes of violence in real life, not just depicted on TV. The emotional impact of these events on juvenile violence is difficult to ascertain.

Violence in contemporary society, for most people is a reality they have learned to live with. There are still some types of senseless and bizarre violence and homicide that produce emotional reactions like the cannibalistic homicides of Jeffrey Dahmer or the serial murders of women by Ted Bundy. For the most part, however, people benignly accept the reporting of violence on television or in the newspapers and accept movie violence.

As they observe violence in the mass media, many people, especially children, are not fully capable of separating "real" violence from fictional violence.[1] For many, real violence shown on television news is not so different from the fictionalized violence of a so-called docudrama shown on television. A case in point is the sexual, violent drama of Amy Fisher and Joey Buttafuco. In a period of one week, the real-life violence of fifteen-year-old Amy Fisher shooting Mrs. Buttafuco in the head was portrayed three different ways by three major television networks in three docudramas. The evolution of violence in films reflects the acceptance of increasingly bizarre depictions of death and mayhem.

In the music industry, rap records sold to young people graphically advocate suicide and murder, with a special emphasis on killing the police. The rappers themselves have been killed by unknown assailants. Notable among these murders are the drive-by killings of two hip-hop recording stars Tupak Shakur and Notorious BIG. In an interview shortly before he died, BIG was philosophical: "There's nothing that protects you from the inevitable," BIG said, two weeks before his death. "If it's gonna happen, it's gonna happen, no matter what you do. It doesn't matter if you clean your life up and live it differently. What goes around comes around."[2] In the end, his death underscores and perhaps tragically validates the alarming message that is at the heart of gangsta rap. Many other murders have taken place in the lower echelons of the music business that are not as widely publicized as the death of the industry's stars. Although the deaths of these rap stars are deplored and eulogized by fans and the press, they seem to stir the cauldron of violence in many young people, both white and black, who are devoted fans of these pied pipers of violence.

In many films, violence is presented as an effective way of handling problems not only for ordinary people but also for "heroes" and

---

1. For a further analysis of this issue, see C. Hale, "Fear of Crime," *International Review of Victimology,* April 1996.

2. Interview on MTV, July 15, 1995.

representatives of the state, police officers, and people in authority. If we accept the available data on the relationship between viewing violence on television and increased aggressive behavior in children, we might conclude that watching violent films is likely to increase violent crime. People who watch film and TV stars perform violent "hero" roles are likely to consider violence as an approved way of asserting masculinity and of solving life's problems. This is particularly true for children who have emotional problems. There has been research on this subject; however, for the most part, we can only speculate about how violence in films has affected juvenile violence. A steady diet of this violence negatively affects many people in our society and may cause young people to be indifferent to the effects of violence.

A case in point is the response of one sixteen-year-old youth who witnessed an actual homicide. His father, a fifty-year-old psychologist, relates the following story of his son's reaction to a real-life murder and his own reaction to his son's behavior after witnessing the murder:[3]

> The movies I saw during my childhood years contained simple human stories and had very little violence. Today the movies are full of mutilations, grisly murders and outrageous horror scenarios. My son is an afficionado of these modern horror films, and I detest them. He thinks they are fun and exciting, and I think they are crass examples of the product of the typical banal, mercenary Hollywood mind. He sees them all, and I see only a few for purely psychological interest in understanding modern tastes. In this context of our different perspectives, my son recently had what would have been a horrendous emotional experience for me. The experience and his reaction to it reveal something about the conflict of perceptions in this generation gap.
>
> During the past summer he became friends with a young man—I will call him Jim—a twenty-five-year-old who seemed more like sixteen, my son's age at the time. The "man" was quite immature and had the basic personality of the standard Hollywood hustler who had no special talent yet was trying to break into the film and music business. He would do anything but work for his glorified and exorbitant goals. He did not have to work because he had a wealthy father who sent him a sizable allowance. My son would tell me about his friend's escapades with dope and prostitutes.
>
> Jim's story is rather complex, but the bottom line is that one day he got into an altercation (in my son's presence) with a man who lived near his apartment. Apparently Jim owed him money for drugs and refused to pay up. The man assaulted Jim. Jim went into his apartment, got a gun he had bought that day, and shot his adversary in the head, killing him. My son was an eyewitness

---

3. The sixteen-year-old youth was my son, and I was the "fifty-year-old psychologist."

to this horrible event. He was interrogated by the police for several hours. Knowing something about the psychological impact of such bizarre emotional events, when I saw my son after the police interrogation, I pressed him to open up and freely discuss his deeper emotional feelings about what I perceived as a dreadful experience. He ran through it one time, and in response to my continuing concern about how it affected him personally, he finally said in an exasperated voice: "Dad, I know what you're getting at. But it really doesn't bother me that much. I've seen plenty of killings on the tube and in the movies. You don't have to worry about me. I'm really okay." And apparently he was. I never saw any later evidence in my son's behavior that would indicate that he was fazed by the violence he had witnessed, despite the fact that it had a profound effect on me. My socialization on the horrendous nature of violence was apparently entirely different than the impact of violence on my son.

Acts of violence seen on a movie screen may be replicated in real life. For example, one of the notable assassination attempts of the twentieth century was John Hinkley's effort to assassinate President Ronald Reagan. The violent act was ignited by Hinkley's obsession with the movie *Taxi Driver*. The film depicts an alienated "hero" who plans the assassination of a political figure. The film apparently dramatized for Hinckley his sense of alienation and loneliness.

In the film, the protagonist portrayed by Robert DeNiro is a taxi driver who moves through an anonymous crowd. He is jostled, ignored, hassled, and abused, but he is untouched by his alienation because of his own secret fantasy world and his inability to communicate with people. The taxi driver is a lonely "everyman" who is aching to be noticed, recognized, and loved, but unable to attain any human contact. At the end of the film, the "heroic" taxi driver goes on a brutal, senseless mass murder spree, claiming at least five lives.

The fictional image of the alienated taxi driver had its impact on Hinckley, and he became obsessed with the film, DeNiro, and the film's other star, Jodie Foster. Hinckley later claimed he attempted to shoot the president to gain Jodie Foster's attention and love. Many young sociopaths commit acts of violence based on the media, literary, and historical materials in the larger society. These cultural models tend to synthesize the violent fantasies they already harbor in their minds.

The Nazi model of violent behavior is often adopted by sociopathic youths, for example, youths who become skinheads and modern-day members of the American facsimiles of the Nazi party. They use the organization as a cloak of immunity to mask their dehumanized sociopathic personalities. In the context of these violent organizations, their own violence is viewed by the general public as having some level of rationality. In fact, their delinquent behavior is an acting out of a sociopathic emotional disorder.

An example of this sociopathic syndrome is revealed in the following case history of a young man, who, like Hinckley, read many books about the Nazis. Greg was fifteen when he killed his parents with an ax and then threw himself to his death from a water tower. An analysis of his background revealed that his underlying violent persona was kept a secret. His teachers liked him, and his neighbors saw him as thoughtful and courteous. In dozens of interviews with his friends, teachers, physicians, and law-enforcement officials conducted after the murders and suicide, another picture of Greg emerged—that of an adolescent tormented by unattained and secret aspirations, who sought solace in a secret room and in secret dreams.

On the day Greg killed his parents and himself, his German teacher recalled he had asked Greg what he had been doing the night before. "I read Shirer's *The Rise and Fall of the Third Reich*," the boy answered. In a room in his attic were a mattress, a lamp, books, empty liquor bottles, canteens of water, and a number of Nazi emblems and insignias. It was the fifth time he had read the book.

War, parental violence (overt and covert), institutionalized violence by political leaders, mass media presentations of violence—all are factors that produce this violent ethos for today's youths. The violent nature of a society affects the degree of violence committed by young people who live in the society. In a nonviolent social system, most people would not ordinarily commit acts of aggression. The opposite would also hold true. Within the violent climate of Nazi Germany, for example, it would be expected that youths would be amenable to violent behavior. In this context, it is apparent that a person (young or old) in Nazi Germany would be more likely to follow orders and commit brutal acts than people in more humanistic societies.

Milgram's Research into the American Sociocultural Predisposition for Violence

One set of experiments that reveals the average person's predisposition to commit acts of violence was carried out by psychologist Stanley Milgram (1965) at Yale University. His research remains relevant to present-day institutionalized violent behavior. Milgram was concerned with the conditions under which people would be obedient or disobedient to authority in the commission of violent acts. He investigated a variety of experimental settings and varied modifications of this basic theme. In his overall project, which extended over a period of several years, almost a thousand individuals were subjects in his research.

The results were frighteningly uniform. On the basis of his research, Milgram concluded that a majority of "good people," who in their everyday lives were responsible and decent, could be made to perform "callous and severe" violent acts when they were placed in situations that had the "trappings of authority."

The following description of one of Milgram's research experiments in which this behavior took place more clearly illustrates the general research approach that was used. The subjects in this example of Milgram's experiments on obedience were a random sample of New Haven adult males who came to Milgram's Yale Research Center in response to a newspaper advertisement. They were paid by the hour and individually brought to a laboratory and introduced to their "partners," who were in reality members of the research team.

Each research subject was told that he was going to participate in a learning experiment with his partner. One was to be the "teacher "and the other, the "learner." The experiment was contrived so that the research subject always wound up as the teacher, and the Yale research assistant always became the learner. The subject was then told that the research was being conducted to determine the effects of punishment on learning.

The subject, now the teacher, witnessed a standard procedure by which the learner (in reality a member of the research staff) was strapped into a chair that apparently had electrical connections. The teacher was then taken into another room and told to ask the learner certain questions from a questionnaire he was given. The teacher was told to administer electric shocks every time the learner gave a wrong answer. (In some cases, before the learner was strapped into his electric chair, he would comment, "Take it easy on me, I have a heart condition.")

In the room with the "teacher" (the research subject) was another member of the Yale research team who served as an authority figure and as a provocateur. The teacher was told that the authority figure was present to make sure that the teacher administered the proper shocks for incorrect answers. The teacher was told by the authority figure to give progressively stronger shocks to the learner when the learner's answers were incorrect.

In front of the teacher was an elaborate electric board that, as far as the teacher knew, controlled shock levels from 15 volts to 450 volts in 15-volt gradations. The last two switches were ominously labeled XXX. The researcher in the room told the teacher to increase the shock for each incorrect answer. In a short time the teacher was repeatedly, as far as he knew, giving shocks of up to 450 volts to the learner in the next room. The learner would often dramatically pound the wall and shout, "Stop it, you're killing me!" Some teachers balked at continuing but proceeded on the orders of the authority figure, who would simply say, "You must continue the experiment."

At a certain point the learner, after pounding on the wall, would "play dead"—act as if he had passed out. The researcher in the room would instruct the teacher to count "no response" as an incorrect answer. He would then order him to continue to shock what the teacher could only conclude was an apparently inert or dead body with continuing XXX heavy electric shocks.

In several cases, when the teacher refused to act out the violent behavior of continuing to shock the learner because he was afraid he had killed him, the researcher would say, "Go on with the experiment." The authoritative voice of the Yale researcher caused more than half of the teachers to continue to shock what might very well have been a dead body!

Some teachers refused to continue, saying "That guy in the other room is in bad shape—I can't do this anymore." The researcher would tell the teacher to continue, "Go ahead, I'll be responsible for what happens to the learner." When this was said, some teachers would say, "OK, I'll continue, but remember, you're responsible, not me!"

This experiment, conducted with forty subjects, was typical of the experiments carried out. All forty subjects complied by shocking their "victims" with up to three hundred volts. Fourteen stopped at that point or at slightly higher levels. But the majority, twenty-six subjects, were obedient to the commands of the research authority figure and continued to administer increasingly severe shocks beyond what they thought was 450 volts. This was beyond a switch in front of them marked "Danger: Severe Shock." Thus 65 percent of this representative sample of "good people" conformed to the dictates of an experimental authority situation to the point that they believed that they had inflicted severe pain or possibly death on another human being. The research validated the assumption that people would conform to dictates of those in authority even when they knew they were inflicting severe harm on another person up to and beyond homicide. Authority in a legitimate social context produced obedience and conformity to inhuman goals—even in America.

It would be difficult to measure the degree of violent components in an individual and perhaps even more difficult to estimate the number of such individuals in a society. A speculation that could be extrapolated from the overall Milgram experiments would be that more than half of the population, within the context of obeying the orders of a person in authority, would commit acts of violence.

The Role of Alienation

One reason for the contemporary climate of violence that affects juveniles is the alienation of people in our social system. One observer of the societal scene, Lynne B. Iglitzin (1972), commented: "By far the most potent source of violence is the ubiquity of feelings of alienation and anomie which plague so many human beings in modern society. Feelings of normlessness and meaninglessness, of estrangement from one's self and from others are generally accepted characteristics of alienation. The alienated person is out of touch with himself and with other persons; he is at the mercy of his technological creations, a 'thing' dependent on unknown powerful forces" (p. 97).

R.D. Laing (1967), the British psychoanalyst, described the alienation that underlies violence as: "The pervasive condition of estrangement from ourselves and from the human community provides a setting in which people have perpetrated incredible acts of violence upon each other and have been able to rationalize such behavior as 'normality' " (p.xiii). Laing conceptualized that "the condition of alienation, of being asleep, of the unconscious, of being out of one's mind, is the condition of the normal man." As support for this premise, he noted that "normal men have killed perhaps 100 million of their fellow normal men in the last fifty years" (p. 12).

Local and International Warfare

In the 1990s, in Africa, the Balkans, the Middle East, and other areas of the world, well over a million people were killed for bizarre and difficult to understand political reasons. This international situation is a backdrop for the slaughter on the streets of America by violent juvenile gangs. Kody Scott (1993), a gang leader known as Monster, has an interesting viewpoint on gang warfare: "Who fired the first shot? Who knows? But, too, who cares, when one of theirs is lying in a pool of blood with his brains blown out. This question becomes weightless in the aftermath of a shooting where someone has died. Thus the goal becomes the elimination of the shooter or as many of his comrades as possible. This inevitably leads to war—a full-scale mobilization of as many troops as needed to achieve the desired effect: funerals" (p. 136).

Researcher Henry De Young (1976) accounted for adolescent violence as follows.

> First of all, and perhaps most relevant, there is television, which contributes immensely to the "unreality" of death and the gener-

ally low value ascribed to human life. Every night of the week, children may see as many as two dozen shootings, hangings, knifings, poisonings, assaults with clubs and automobiles, and countless other forms of mayhem. Furthermore, such assaults on life are rarely depicted as wrong, or even objectionable; they're perpetrated, often as not, by the good guys—police officers, cowboys and cowgirls, private eyes, cartoon characters—against the bad guys, or those who are perceived to be bad. To further confuse the young and undiscriminating mind, the victims of this senseless violence never seem to be really dead. An actor who "dies" on TV at 7:30 P.M. is often magically resurrected to appear, unharmed and little the worse off for his ordeal, an hour later on *S.W.A.T.* Dying in TV-land is also a nice, clean way of departing this life. There's rarely any blood, and never an honest depiction of what violent death is really like. "If every kid under ten could see what a gunshot does to people in real life," observes a Chicago police officer, "I have little doubt that our homicide rate would be cut in half. It's an ugly sight." (P. 89)

James Sorrells, Jr. (1980) delineated the sociopathic personality of children who kill in the following way: "These juveniles see other people solely in terms of their own needs—to be used if useful, to be eliminated if presenting an obstacle or threat. The question, 'How will that person feel if you harm him?' has little meaning and almost no relevance to this group of juveniles. It never occurs to them that other people have a right to life and feelings, too. They lack the capacity to experience empathy or identification with, or compassion for, other human beings" (pp. 156–157).

Many youths who commit acts of violence, including murder, are sociopaths who have no concern or compassion for their victims. This type of violent delinquent behavior is more likely to occur in a social system where there is a backdrop of alienation and where violence is perceived by children as normal behavior in the larger society.

The Mass Media Impact on Juvenile Violence: Research Findings

Over the past thirty years there has been considerable research into the effects of television on children. The findings have been varied. Some researchers concluded that watching television negatively influences adolescent behavior; other researchers concluded that television has a minimal impact on the average psychologically healthy child.

Television and Growing Up (1972), an early study on the impact of TV violence on children conducted by the surgeon general reported that three out of ten dramatic segments on TV portrayed violence. About 70 percent of all leading characters studied were involved in some violence, and the odds were two to one in favor of the leading character being a killer and seven to one that the killer would not be killed in return. An aspect of violence on television is that killing someone is an approved method of solving problems. What does the hero do when he or she encounters the villain? Draw a weapon and shoot. No action is taken against the hero. This may influence the young viewer to seek similar solutions to his or her problems. He or she can be a hero and resolve problems by killing somebody.

The study examined the TV habits of a group of 475 children over a ten-year period and determined that children were heavy viewers and that they preferred cartoon programs that included an enormous amount of violence. One finding of the research concluded that of ninety-five cartoon films analyzed, only two did not contain violence. An analysis of the findings in this study led to the conclusion that watching violent television programs in early years influenced aggressive behavior later on in life. A number of other studies concluded that viewing televised violence caused the viewer to become more aggressive. The advisory committee indicated that in general "there is a convergence of the fairly substantial experimental evidence for short-run causation of aggression by viewing violence on the screen and the much less certain evidence from field studies that extensive violence viewing precedes some long-run manifestations of aggressive behavior."

In another research project on the relationship of TV viewing and violence, two psychologists, Ronald S. Drabman and Margaret Hanratty Thomas (1975), studied the relationship between television violence and violence in real life. They specifically analyzed to what extent exposure to televised aggression makes children more tolerant to the real thing. One of their experiments involved forty fifth-graders from a lower-middle-class parochial school. Each child watched either a fifteen-minute segment from a television detective series that contained several shootings and other acts of violence or a fifteen-minute segment of a baseball game. Then the experimenter said he had to leave for awhile and asked each child to keep an eye on two kindergartners playing in a nearby room. The children were told that the toddlers were being filmed by a camera and could be watched on the television screen. If anything went wrong, the fifth-graders were to get help.

What the children actually saw was a staged videotaped sequence in which the kindergartners became more and more unruly until they apparently knocked over the camera and the monitor went blank. The researchers were interested in how long it would take the fifth-graders to seek help after seeing this real-life violence. The children who had watched the detective show took much longer to respond than did the baseball watchers. Five children in the aggressive film group (two boys and three girls) never went for help at all, as opposed to only one girl in the control group. Fifty-eight percent of the control children ran to get help before the kindergartners began slugging it out. It took a lot more aggression to stir the children who had seen the violent film; 83 percent of them waited until the kindergartners physically battled before they sought help.

Drabman and Thomas suggested two possible reasons for the apathy of the test group. Perhaps violence on television teaches children that aggression is a way of life, not to be taken seriously. Or perhaps real-life aggression simply seems bland when compared to the vicious violence on television.

There is insufficient research to conclude firmly that media violence does or does not cause violent behavior in children. Despite the inconclusiveness of the evidence, however, occasionally events occur that produce simplistic cause-and-effect observations and demonstrate that fictionalized violence in the mass media is sometimes replicated in real life. One example was the response of a gang of delinquents to the film *Fuzz* (1986) after it was aired over network television. In the film, teenage boys are shown setting fire to skid-row bums along Boston's waterfront.

Two nights later after the TV showing of the film, a woman was burned to death by a group of youths in Boston. The woman, a Swiss divorcé, had moved to Boston only five days earlier and was living in a small commune in Roxbury. While she was on her way home from a job-hunting trip, her car ran out of gasoline in the center of Roxbury's business district. Returning to her car with a two-gallon refill can from a service station, the young woman was forced into a trash-filled backyard along Blue Hill Avenue by six teenagers, beaten, and ordered to douse herself with the fuel. After the terrified victim complied, one of them set her afire with a match. Before dying five hours later, she told the police that three of her assailants had been part of a black group that had called her a "honky" the previous day and warned her that whites were unwelcome in Roxbury. Thus a combination of racism and a murder shown in a TV film may have caused this real-life homicide.

Heat, a 1995 movie starring Al Pacino and Robert DeNiro that involved a "cat and mouse" interaction between a cop and a robber, ended in one of the most violent scenes ever depicted on film. In the final scene, a shoot-out with automatic weapons after a botched bank robbery, about fifteen people, including innocent civilians, are brutally murdered. The real-life bank robbery in 1997 that took place in Hollywood was almost a replica of the scene in *Heat*. Two bank robbers in full-body armor and wearing ski masks indiscriminately shot their AK-47s, injuring over seventeen police officers and civilians. The event was like the scene in *Heat*—the only difference was that the bandits were shooting real bullets.

Another notable study that attempted to discover the impact of media violence on youths was carried out by psychologist Leonard Berkowitz (1964) at the University of Wisconsin. Berkowitz told student volunteers that he was simply interested in their physiological responses to a variety of stimuli. He even took blood pressure readings to strengthen his camouflage. In reality, he was after something quite different. Each experiment involved two subjects; one of them, as in the Milgram experiments, was actually Berkowitz's assistant.

The first test presented was an intelligence test. Berkowitz's conspirator always finished first, whereupon he would lean over to the subject and with a sly smile make a remark such as, "You're certainly taking a long time with that." This was usually enough for the subject to develop a dislike for his co-worker. Then both were shown a seven-minute film sequence taken from the 1949 movie *Champion*, in which Kirk Douglas is brutally beaten. The last test involved the floor plan for a house, which the conspirator had supposedly drawn up. The subject was to indicate his degree of disapproval of the plan by pressing a button that he was told would administer electric shocks to his co-worker. In this way, Berkowitz attempted to create a situation, mirroring real life, when someone who is nursing new anger happens to attend a movie depicting physical violence and soon afterward is given the opportunity to vent his feelings.

The test results were illuminating. In the cases where Berkowitz's conspirator refrained from making any insulting remarks during the intelligence test, or when peaceful travel scenes were used instead of the fight sequence, the conspirator received fewer shocks during the floor-plan experiment. But the conspirator felt a barrage of shocks when the volunteer subjects were treated to the full course of insults and the violent boxing sequence.

This research study, according to Berkowitz, showed that so-called "justified aggression" triggers the greatest violence. In briefing his subjects on the overall plot of the movie, Berkowitz told some that Douglas was an "unprincipled scoundrel." Others were told he was about to go straight. Those who watched what they believed was a bad guy getting beaten almost always delivered more shocks. According to Berkowitz, "If it was all right for the movie villain to be injured aggressively . . . then perhaps it was all right for them to attack the villain in their own lives" (1964, p. 87).

Despite his findings, Berkowitz did not believe movies can make a delinquent out of a teenager. "The effect of filmed violence is temporary. But by the same token, a normal average citizen who is angry about something and then sees a case of justified aggression is more likely to attack,

120

apparently because what he has seen has weakened his normal inhibitions against committing aggression" (1964, p. 72).

Another study that focused on the effects of TV violence on children was carried out by psychologist Albert Bandura (1963). For Bandura, the basic issue was what happens to a child who watches violence on television. He designed a series of experiments to determine the extent to which children copy the aggressive patterns of behavior of adult models in real life, as real people on film, and as cartoon characters on film.

One group of children observed real adults. The children were brought into a room, one by one. In one corner, the child found a set of play materials; in another corner was an adult sitting quietly with a set of toys, including an inflated plastic Bobo doll and a mallet. Soon after the child started to play in his corner, the adult began attacking the Bobo doll ferociously—sitting on it, punching it on the nose, pounding it with the mallet, tossing it up in the air, and kicking it, while saying: "Sock him in the nose!" "Hit him down!" "Throw him in the air!" "Kick him!"

Another group of children saw a movie of the adult attacking the Bobo doll. A third group watched a movie, through a television set, in which an adult dressed as a cartoon cat attacked the doll. A fourth group served as a control group, did not see any aggressive behavior, and allowed comparison with the actions of the first three groups. At the end of ten minutes, each child was taken to an "observation room," where he or she was watched through a one-way mirror. The child had access to "aggressive toys" and "nonaggressive toys" for a twenty-minute period.

According to a team of psychologists-observers, those youngsters who had previously been exposed to the aggressive model showed almost twice as much aggression in the observation room as did the children in the control group. From this Bandura reached two important conclusions about the effects of the aggressive models on a child: (1) the experience tended to reduce the child's inhibitions against acting in a violent, aggressive manner, and (2) the experience helped to shape the form of the child's aggressive behavior. Most of the children from the first three groups sat on the Bobo doll, punched its nose, beat it on the head with a mallet, tossed it into the air, and kicked it around the room. And they used the familiar hostile remarks, "Hit him down!" "Kick him!" and so forth. This kind of conduct was rare among the children in the control group who had not observed any violent activity.

Bandura's findings led him to a third, highly significant conclusion. He noticed that a person who behaved violently on film is as influential as one who behaved violently in real life. The children were not too interested in imitating the cartoon character, but many children copied precisely the actions of both real-life and film models. From these observations, Bandura concluded that televised models are influential sources of social behavior whose impact on personality development cannot be ignored. He pointed out that, as audiovisual technology improved, television would become even more influential on violence.

In contrast to research findings that TV affects aggression and violent behavior, a comprehensive study by two psychologists, Robert M. Kaplan and Robert D. Singer (1972), concluded that there was no justification for censorship of television programming because of the violence it portrays. Kaplan and Singer reviewed more than one hundred twenty studies of television violence and concluded that "the accumulated research does not show aggressive behavior because too much of the research that draws a correlation between television violence and aggressive behavior is conducted in an unrealistic laboratory setting" (p. 23). According to Kaplan and Singer, "The lab setting doesn't seem to generalize to the real world. We're trying to argue that research should meet certain criteria before it is used to justify changes in public policy. When you look closely at the [past] research, television doesn't show potent effects on aggressive behavior. It is fascinating that so many hours of research and so much money has been spent and directed at the possible effect of TV violence on aggressive behavior, when it is most likely that television is not a significant cause of human aggression. Instead of castigating the networks it may be more useful to ask why the public is so fascinated by programs portraying violence" (p. 23).

Kaplan and Singer concluded that (1) violent television programming has not been shown to have the effect of reducing aggressive behavior by allowing a person to "drain off" his or her aggressive tendencies while watching violence on television; (2) there still remains the possibility that violence on television may contribute to violent behavior by "disturbed" viewers; and (3) there is a difference in the influences of fantasy violence and real violence—as portrayed on news shows—on aggressive behavior. In summary, they stated: "As in so many other areas of juvenile delinquency, we have to conclude, based on many studies, that a clear causal connection between mass media violence and actual violent behavior is still inconclusive. Yet it is our observation that several studies indicate a degree of brutalization occurs from certain types of programs" (p. 24).

A study financed and reported by the National Cable Television Association (NCTA), based on research from four universities, found that violence on TV escalated in the 1990s. The study was conducted by independent researchers from the University of California—Santa Barbara, the University of North Carolina, the University of Texas, and the University of Wisconsin. The researchers determined that 61 percent of all shows in the 1995–96 television season contained violent scenes, compared to 58 percent during the preceding season. Moreover, the researchers concluded, the new television ratings system was likely to have a "forbidden fruit" effect, enticing children to watch the violent programs that their parents want to keep from them (*National Cable Television Report,* 1997).

In analyzing the content of television shows, researchers at the University of California identified more than eighteen thousand violent incidents in a sample of more than two thousand hours of programming drawn from twenty-three cable and broadcast channels. Using random sampling techniques, they created a composite week of programming to analyze the 1995–96 television season. They found that television continued to portray violence as glamorous. Of the programs that depicted violence, very few—just 4 percent—portrayed it in a way that conveyed an antiviolence theme. And television violence frequently was sanitized. In more than half of the violent incidents on television, victims of the violence showed no physical injuries and had no pain, unlike real life violence.

The NCTA research also uncovered a troubling paradox. They determined, as earlier studies had found, that the most egregious examples of violence were concentrated in cartoon programs targeted specifically to children under the age of seven. The study analyzed all programming for high-risk portrayals of aggression, in which several violent plot elements come together in one scene. It was found that the vast majority of these high-risk portrayals were contained in cartoons. The researchers concluded that of all channel types, child-oriented basic cable—the Cartoon Network, the Disney Channel, and Nickelodeon—posed the highest violence risk for children.

We need to keep in mind one factor implicit in the varied research conclusions about the impact of violence on TV. The psychological state of the observer of mass media violence is a significant factor. For example, many people saw the film *Taxi Driver*, but no one else reacted to the film in the same way as John Hinckley. The emotional state of the viewer of violence is of enormous significance. A juvenile with a low boiling point is apt to be more directly influenced and set off by television or movie violence than a person who has a relatively normal, nonaggressive personality.

One way to combat the negative influences of violence in the mass media on children is with psychodrama. In working with adolescents who had a propensity for violence, I utilized an approach involving psychodramatization of actual instances of violence. But instead of glamorizing violent behavior, my psychodrama sessions focused on a discussion of the causes or reasons for the violent behavior. The causal reasons usually indicated some weakness in the personality or social relationships of the violent individual.

I directed various psychodramas of this type in university class-rooms featuring role-playing conversations with students playing the role of the Hillside Strangler, Kenneth Bianchi, or Charles Manson. In this exercise a student played the role of a violent offender and would, in response to other students' questions, defend his or her violent behavior on the basis of his or her family context of abuse and abandonment as a child. This led to heated discussions of the causes of violent behavior and its meaning in the larger, sociocultural context of violence.

Child Abuse, the Exploitation of Children, and Juvenile Delinquency

Child Abuse

Most delinquents who become violent offenders have been either physi-cally, emotionally, or sexually abused and/or abandoned by their parents. In too many cases they have been abused in all of these ways, by their par-ents or others. This abuse produces low self-esteem and a level of rage that is not present in children in a healthy social environment. The significant issue of child abuse and its effect on delinquent behavior, especially vio-lence, promises to be an area of extensive research in the twenty-first cen-tury. Coupled with research on the causes and effects of child abuse will be a focus on developing effective methodologies for treating this social virus that has an enormous effect on the degree of violence in American society.[4]

The issue of child abuse was in the past not as widely recognized or discussed as it is today. The problem has become familiar not only to individuals working in the medical and helping professions, social services, and law enforcement agencies but to the general public as well. From a legal standpoint, child abuse is viewed as any harm that is done to a per-son under the age of eighteen, whether it is done by the child's parents, a relative, a guardian, or caretaker, or by a total stranger. Nonlegal definitions typically regard abuse as a physical injury requiring medical attention or, more generally, as an intentional infliction of harm to a child, usually by a parent or other caretaker.

The California Penal Code defines child abuse as "a physical injury which is inflicted by other than accidental means on a child by another per-son. Child abuse also means the sexual assault of a child or omission . . .

---

4. For a fuller discussion of this issue, see Katherine Beckett, "Culture and Child Abuse," *Social Problems*, February 1996; and Keith Kaufman, "Comparing Male and Female Sexual Abuse Victims Reports," *Journal of Impersonal Violence*, September 1995.

(willful cruelty or unjustifiable punishment of a child . . . or . . . corporal punishment or injury). 'Child abuse' also means the neglect of a child or abuse in out-of-home care."

A definition of child abuse by Everstine and Everstine (1983) incorporates both acts of commission, which are more frequently considered to represent child abuse, and acts of omission, which are often alternatively referred to as "negligence." They define child abuse as "the intentional non-accidental use of force or intentional non-accidental acts of omission on the part of the parent or caretaker interacting with the child in his care, aimed at hurting or destroying the child" (p. 46).

Frederic Wertham (1973, p. 17) called child abuse "the maltreatment syndrome." Another researcher in the field, Vincent Fontana (1973), concluded that child abuse is a more widespread practice than we are willing to admit. According to Fontana, "It is a myth that in this nation we love our children." He estimated that each year at least seven hundred American children are killed by their parents or parent surrogates. Fontana maintained that "some 10,000 are severely battered every year; 50,000 to 75,000 are sexually abused; 100,000 are emotionally neglected; and another 100,000 are physically, morally, and educationally neglected" (p. 37). The tragic stories behind these appalling statistics were related by Fontana in his book, *Somewhere a Child Is Crying*, and his profiles of James Earl Ray, Arthur Bremer, and other convicted violent criminals. They illustrate the fate of some of yesterday's violently battered children who retaliated in kind against society. In 1997 there were approximately 1.6 million convicted people in long-term custodial institutions. Almost all of these men, women, and children were victims of some form of child abuse.

In the twentieth century, child abuse by parents, the exploitation of children, and the lack of any concerted effort by agencies to control this phenomenon led to the murder of many innocent children. An extensive study by social worker David Kaplun and psychiatrist Robert Reich (1975) reveals many interesting and significant dynamics of the relationship of child abuse to murder. Kaplun and Reich studied the records of the chief medical examiner in New York City and found, in a one-year period, 140 cases of apparent homicides of children under the age of fifteen. They reviewed the postmortem reports and police inquiries for the 112 victims who could be identified. They also examined the case reports of the city's public assistance and child welfare agencies for sixty-six of the victims' families. Poverty seemed to be a strong factor in the child murderer's background. Seventy percent of the victims' families lived in areas of extreme poverty. Many of the murderers in these families were involved in alcoholism, narcotics use, criminal activity, or assault other than child abuse. Many of the victims were infants; over half were under a year old.

According to Kaplun and Reich's (1975) study, the murderers usually killed out of rage—beating and kicking the child to death. One mother of three, estranged from her husband, was described by her social worker as "a sweet-tempered, affectionate young woman overburdened with home responsibilities." A short time later her three-year-old son was hospitalized with bruises, burns, and a leg fracture caused, said the mother, by a fall from a crib against a hot radiator. Because the mother was so attentive and affectionate toward her child, the hospital and social worker decided she was not to blame. A year later the boy was killed. The mother again attributed his injuries to an accident, an accident that police investigation disclosed could not have happened. She was not charged, but her two other children were taken from her.

In the search for the causes of various patterns of violent behavior in delinquents, many studies reveal a correlation between brutal parents and violent children. The use of harsh discipline or abuse to discipline children in the family is a significant factor in producing violent people.

Violent Families and Youth Violence

Parents are role models to their children. It logically follows that husbands and wives who are violent with each other are prone to be violent with their children. This is how children learn to settle their frustrations or disputes by acting out violently. In 1995, Murray Straus and Richard Gelles reported on their National Family Violence Survey of 8,145 families. Their overall research data validate the fact that violent families produce violent children.

In another extensive report on the impact of violent families on youth violence, Terence P. Thornberry (1994) summarizes some significant research on children growing up in violent families. The research addressed two questions: First, are children who are victims of maltreatment and abuse during childhood more apt to be violent when they are adolescents? And second, are children who are exposed to multiple forms of family violence, not just maltreatment, more likely to be violent?

The data for this analysis was derived from the Rochester Youth Development Study, which Thornberry directed. His ongoing study of delinquency and drug use began with one thousand seventh and eighth grade students attending the public schools of Rochester, New York, in 1988. Youngsters at high risk for serious delinquency were sampled. The youths and their primary caretakers were interviewed every six months until the adolescents were in the eleventh and twelfth grades. Students who left the Rochester schools were also contacted. The overall retention rate was 88 percent. In addition to personal interviews, the project collected data from schools, police, social services, and related agencies. Delinquency was measured by self-reports of violent behavior. Every six months the interviewed youths indicated their involvement in six forms of violent behavior, ranging from simple assault to armed robbery and aggravated assault. The measure used in this analysis was the cumulative prevalence of such behavior over the course of the interviews.

Thornberry found that 69 percent of the youths who had been mal-treated as children reported involvement in violence as compared to 56 percent of those who had not been maltreated. A history of maltreatment, therefore, increased the chances of youth violence. Other analyses of these data indicated that maltreatment was also a significant risk factor for official delinquency and other forms of self-reported delinquency.

The research also attempted to answer the questions, Does direct childhood victimization increase the likelihood of later youth violence, and does more general exposure to family violence also increase the risk? To address these questions, researchers used three different indicators of fam-ily violence: partner violence, family climate of hostility, and child mal-treatment. It was found that, for each type of family violence, adolescents who lived in violent families had higher rates of self-reported violence than did youngsters from nonviolent families. The results for partner violence illustrated this finding. Seventy percent of the adolescents who grew up in families where the parents fought with one another self-reported violent delinquency as compared to 49 percent of adolescents who grew up in families without this type of conflict. Similar patterns can be seen for the other two indicators of family violence.

The final issue examined by the research project was the conse-quences of growing up in families experiencing multiple forms of violence. While 38 percent of the youngsters from nonviolent families reported involvement in violent delinquency, this rate increased to 60 percent for youngsters whose family engaged in one of these forms of violence, to 73 percent for those exposed to two forms of family violence, and further increased to 78 percent for adolescents exposed to all three forms of fam-ily violence. Exposure to multiple forms of family violence, therefore, increased the risk of self-reported youth violence.

The researchers concluded that adolescents who had been direct victims of child maltreatment were more likely to report involvement in youth violence than nonmaltreated adolescents. Similarly, adolescents who grew up in homes exhibiting partner violence, generalized hostility, or child maltreatment also had higher rates of self-reported violence. The highest rates were reported by youths exposed to multiple forms of family violence. In these families, over three-quarters of the adolescents self-reported violent behavior. In other words, children exposed to multiple forms of family violence reported more than twice the rate of youth violence as those from nonviolent families.

Parental violence and its consequences for children is not a phenomenon restricted to the United States. A cross-cultural study by psychiatrist Leopold Bellak and psychologist Maxine Antell (1975) suggests that child abuse varies from society to society and is linked to the socialization of violent offenders. Bellak and Antell noted that "the Nazis who goose-stepped their way across Europe in the 1940s may have begun their training as toddlers on the playgrounds of Germany, and the child-rearing practices that produced Hitler's war criminals may still be creating violence" (p. 38). Bellak and Antell analyzed the biographies of the Nazi leaders and concluded that nearly all of them were cruelly abused as children.

The Violent Exploitation of Children

Child abuse is generally perceived to be parental abuse in the home in the socialization of the child, especially discipline practices. Another form of child abuse, one that occurs outside the home, is the exploitation of children in the larger society. The problem is bound to become more severe in the twenty-first century. In response to the growing problem of the abuse and exploitation of children, the United States Department of Justice, Office for Victims of Crime, produced a monograph in 1995 appropriately entitled *Child Sexual Exploitation: Improving Investigations and Protecting Victims.* The monograph cogently delineates the need for victim services by describing the effects of sexual exploitation of children.

> The effects of sexual exploitation can be devastating. The emotional consequences of child sexual abuse can range from low self-esteem to serious mental health problems. Children and youths who become involved in other forms of sexual exploitation often have additional emotional burdens to bear. Many exploited youths suffer from having been manipulated rather than explicitly coerced into these activities. As a result, they may feel responsible for, or at least complicit in, the sexual behaviors that are foisted upon them as victims. (U.S. Department of Justice, 1995, pp. 53–58)

The monograph presents several brief case summaries of four types of child exploitation and then describes what may be considered an "optimal" response to combat the problem. These four types incorporate a range of scenarios that may be present in any given child sexual exploitation case.

128

Case 1: Child Prostitution

Children and youths who are involved in prostitution are often run-aways who have left abusive homes for the perceived benefits of inde-pendence on the streets. Some have consciously chosen the excitement of the street over the boredom or restrictions of their homes. Lacking formal education or job skills, they survive by whatever means they can. They may steal, sell drugs, or trade their bodies for a meal or a place to stay. As a result, they may enter the criminal justice system as offenders rather than as victims. However, these young people are addi-tionally burdened by their early problems and/or victimization in their homes, by the exigencies of life on the street, and by the compounded trauma of having been exploited by a number of adults over a long period of time. They are also at high risk for contracting HIV and other serious health problems.

In one case, a police officer, while processing a young woman arrested during a routine police sweep for prostitution, noticed that her identification—a driver's license—had been altered. Upon questioning, the girl admitted that she was fifteen years of age and had been given a forged driver's license by her boyfriend. The "boyfriend," who was thirty-two years old, was arrested when he came to the precinct house to post bail for the girl. A check of his arrest record revealed that he had a criminal record for drug charges and breaking-and-entering in a neigh-boring state. Additional questioning of the girl revealed that she had met the man she called her boyfriend in the neighboring state after she had run away from home. He had convinced her that easy money could be made through prostitution and had paid for her bus ticket to the city in which the arrest was made. Because state lines had been crossed, the U.S. Attorney's Office and the FBI were notified.

Given the girl's age and history, a decision was made (and approved by the local prosecutor) not to prosecute her on the prostitu-tion charge if she would testify against her pimp on the federal charges. However, a records check revealed that the girl was a ward of the court in her city of origin, had a history of running away from home, public drunkenness, and minor drug offenses, and was subject to an outstand-ing warrant for grand theft auto, since she had taken her stepfather's car when she left home. Because of this, the girl was placed in secure deten-tion until arrangements could be made to return her to the Division of Youth Services in her home state.

Several different types of offenders exploit runaway and home-less youths. Some are pimps who seduce or intimidate young girls into prostitution. (It is far less common for males who engage in prostitution to have a pimp.) However, the girl often thinks of this individual as a protector, lover, or surrogate family member rather than an exploiter and therefore is reluctant or even afraid to testify against him. Others who exploit runaway youths include customers who trade shelter, drugs, food, or money for sex. Again, the young runaway may not think of such a relationship as prostitution but rather will think of the older individual as a "boyfriend" or "sugar daddy" and see no reason to assist police or prosecutors in their efforts to bring charges against her perceived benefactor.

Case 2: Computer Exploitation

A police precinct received a call from a woman who found that her twelve-year-old son had been receiving sexually explicit messages via a sports-oriented computer bulletin board. The woman and her husband had demanding jobs and could not spend much time with their son, nor did they share his interest in sports. The boy was not very outgoing and had few friends. He spent much of his time in his room with his computer. The messages, purportedly received from another twelve-year-old boy, included graphic descriptions of sexual experiences, offers to send pornographic pictures via electronic mail, and suggestions that the two boys meet for some "fun." The messages also urged the boy not to reveal this correspondence to his parents or anyone else, as they would not "understand" the friendship.

The investigating officer contacted a state police expert in computer crime, who in turn contacted the field office of the FBI. A check with the telephone company revealed that the number of the computer bulletin board was registered to a twenty-eight-year-old man whose rap sheet included several convictions for sex offenses. Investigators acquired a search warrant for the man's home. The search of the suspect's home was conducted by a team from the local police, state police, FBI, and the prosecutor's office. This approach allowed both federal and state crimes to be pursued. A small collection of child pornography was seized, along with a number of nonpornographic photographs of boys, including some picturing the boys with the suspect. The archived messages in the suspect's computer revealed that he was corresponding with a number of young boys he had met through the bulletin board. Material contained in a database in the suspect's computer led to the identification of some of the boys in the photographs. Questioning by the child abuse unit, with help from the victim assistance staff, revealed that at least two of these boys had engaged in sexual activities with the suspect.

The suspect ultimately pled guilty to several counts of statutory rape and agreed to cooperate with the police in identifying all of his victims as well as the sources of his child pornography. The victims were referred to community mental health agencies for counseling.

Youths who become the victims of computer-initiated crimes often have similar characteristics to those who become the victims of other forms of sexual exploitation. They tend to be emotionally vulnerable, withdrawn from their peers, and have parents who do not have the desire or capacity to spend much time with them. Victim assistance personnel can be particularly effective in assessing and meeting the emotional needs of these youngsters and their parents, who often blame themselves for their children's victimization.

Case 3: Child Pornography

An informant in a child prostitution case revealed to the police that he knew of a man in another state who claimed he could procure child pornography. This information was passed on by the local police to a U.S. postal inspector. The postal inspector asked the U.S. Customs Service to see if they had any information on this suspect. The police in the suspect's home town reported that the suspect was currently on probation for child molestation.

The postal inspector began corresponding with the suspect under the guise of being a collector of erotic art. This correspondence continued, with the suspect subsequently advising that he might be able to provide both photographs and videotapes of children and teens performing sexual acts once he had ascertained that his correspondent was not an "undercover agent." The postal inspector asked the suspect to detail what type of material he was specifically interested in (ages and type of sexual activity) and what exactly the suspect had available to exchange. Based on the suspect's response, the postal inspector sent the title pages of several archived, commercially produced child pornography magazines, photocopied in such a manner as to display only the titles. Also provided were the titles of archived, commercially produced 8 millimeter child pornography film transferred to videotape. The suspect then wrote the postal inspector and specifically requested several of these items. He further offered not only to provide the inspector with original child pornography but also to introduce the inspector to young children whom the inspector could photograph.

Based on this evidence, a controlled delivery was arranged and executed by the postal inspector and the local police department. A search warrant was obtained promptly following receipt by the suspect of the controlled delivery material. This search revealed a large collection of foreign-produced child pornography, plus an extensive collection of correspondence with other men sharing a sexual interest in young children. Some of this material originated in Southeast Asia. The suspect's collection also included Polaroid photographs of very young children in sexually explicit poses with adults. The suspect's probation on the state child molestation charge was revoked, and he was sent to prison to serve the remainder of his sentence. The postal inspectors began to investigate other men with whom the suspect had corresponded by initiating correspondence with them.

Many child molesters produce, collect, trade, or sell child pornography. While some collectors of child pornography do not molest children, others do. Thus, an investigation involving child pornography (especially that of very young children) should be thought of as a potential investigation of child sexual abuse. If the suspect states, by telephone or mail correspondence, that he has molested a child or is currently molesting a child, every attempt should be made to identify the victim. Many child molesters have a strong need to validate their behavior by communicating with others who share their sexual interests.

Case 4: Sexual Abuse and Pornography

A fifteen-year-old girl confided to her teacher that she had been molested by her uncle. The girl also claimed that her uncle had photographed her in the nude. When these allegations were reported to the child protection agency, a multidisciplinary abuse team was convened. This team consisted of representatives from child protective services, the child abuse unit of the police department, the prosecutor's office, and the victim assistance program. A search warrant was obtained and executed. During the search of the uncle's house, a small collection of pictures of young people, some naked and in sexually explicit poses, was discovered. Some of these photographs were of the girl who had made the allegations. Others were of her thirteen-year-old male cousin (the suspect's son).

All of these cases have common characteristics. A young person does not usually have the knowledge and ability to resist the kinds of exploitation visited on them by pathological adults. In a sense, all of these adult pathological behaviors visited upon the children are a form of rape. The social science literature on rape concludes that rape is an extreme form of violence. Consequently, not only are children like those depicted in these various cases sexually abused, but the abuse is also violent.

Missing Children and Their Exploitation

In the 1990s, there appeared to be an escalation of random violent acts by adult sex offenders resulting in missing children. Many of these children were kidnapped by pedophiles, sexually assaulted, and then murdered. Although these cases were not numerous, they were dramatic and understandably produced enormous fear among parents in any community where an event of this type took place. The violent impacts of this criminal behavior could often affect an entire community or city (Laney, 1995).

Notable among these cases was the kidnapping and brutal murder of seven-year-old Megan Kanka in 1996. This homicide led the state of New Jersey to pass a law that mandated the publicizing of a released pedophile's name and location in a community. Although this law is considered by some legal analysts to be unconstitutional, many states have passed similar legislation. The law, popularly known as "Megan's Law," reveals the degree to which the general population is concerned about these violent acts perpetrated on children.

A federal law, the Missing Children's Assistance Act (1984),[5] was passed to deal with this type of violence against children. It established a Missing and Exploited Children Program in the Office of Juvenile Justice and Delinquency Prevention (OJJDP). In addition to authorizing assistance for research, demonstration, and service programs, the act authorized the use of federal resources to establish and support a national resource center and clearinghouse dedicated to missing and exploited children issues.

Between 1984 and 1995, a government agency known as the National Center for Missing and Exploited Children (NCMEC) received over 905,000 calls ranging from requests for publications and technical assistance to sighting reports of missing children. Substantive information is immediately forwarded to the appropriate law enforcement agency. NCMEC hotline staff coordinate lodging and transportation assistance for families traveling for the purpose of joining their children. The NCMEC works with corporations to provide free lodging and transportation to families unable to pay.

---

5. Law Act of 1974, Public Law 93-415, as amended by the Missing Children's Assistance Act of 1984.

NCMEC is electronically linked with forty-six state-level missing children clearinghouses. Information and images can be transmitted instantly through this on-line network. NCMEC promotes active information exchange with state clearinghouses and provides pictures of missing children, lead information for local law enforcement, and responses to technical information requests.

The Impacts of Child Abuse: Runaways, Suicidal Tendencies, and Youth Violence

Youths who are relatively happy and well adjusted at home and school do not become runaways. Children who are physically, emotionally, or sexually abused by their parents often become runaways. A research report from the U.S. Department of Justice by Kathleen Maguire and Ann L. Pastore (1996) reveals that a disproportionate number of runaways become victims of predatory and criminal adults. As a result of being alienated and on the streets, these victims often become violent delinquents. The report states that runaways were more than twice as likely as adults to be victims of rape, robbery, and violence. More than sixty of every thousand teenagers were victims of violent crimes each year, compared to just twenty-seven of every thousand adults. The study also found that teenagers were nearly twice as likely as adults to be victimized by theft. The teenage victim rate for theft was one hundred and twenty-three per thousand teenagers compared to sixty-five per thousand for adults. Victims of violent teen crime usually knew their assailants, and more than 60 percent of such violent teen crimes were committed by offenders under age eighteen.

The report further revealed that offenses against teenagers are not reported as often as crimes against adults. Two-thirds of the violent crimes against teenagers from ages twelve to fifteen were not reported to the police. Also unreported were nearly 60 percent of the violent crimes against persons sixteen to nineteen years old. In contrast, more than half of the violent crimes against adults were reported to police. Teenage violence is more prevalent than it appears in official records, and other teenagers are most likely to become victims of this violence.

Many runaways become teenage prostitutes (male and female). These youths have low self-esteem and often have suicidal tendencies, which makes them more vulnerable when they place themselves in dangerous situations that average emotionally healthy adolescents would clearly avoid.

Suicidal Tendencies

It seems logical to assume that youths who place themselves in vulnerable situations tend to have suicidal tendencies. There has been a dramatic increase in suicide by young people since the 1960s. Researchers at the U.S. Centers for Disease Control have estimated that about 50,000 youths (under eighteen) commit suicide each year. Nearly 62 percent of these suicides were carried out with firearms. In 1950 the rate was 4.5 suicides per 100,000 population, and in 1995 the rate was 12 suicides per 100,000 population. The Centers for Disease Control reported that the 1995 nationwide suicide rate of children ten to fourteen years old had increased 120 percent since 1980, the biggest jump of any age group. Each year, the federal government estimates, at least 276,000 teenagers across the nation attempt suicide and fail (Maguire and Pastore, 1996).

The suicidal attitudes of many youths are reflected in their reckless behavior behind the wheels of automobiles or playing Russian roulette or getting stoned on intense mind-altering drugs. The accessibility of guns has also introduced an increasingly lethal factor in the suicide equation. In homes with firearms, according to FBI statistics, the risk of suicide among family members is nearly five times higher than in homes with no firearms (UCR, 1996). In 1995 an estimated 41 percent of the nation's households had guns. Many are loaded and not locked away—a dangerous combination for a troubled and impulsive youngster to kill someone else or himself. There is no reason to believe that the suicidal tendencies pattern of violence will not escalate in the coming years.

In my group psychotherapy and psychodrama sessions with delinquents in several psychiatric hospitals, I determined that more than half of these incarcerated youths had attempted suicide at least once. This leads me to the speculation that a considerable amount of contemporary youth violence reflects the victim-precipitated interactional thesis: Many youths start out as the perpetrators of violence, not caring what happens to them, and often end up as the victims.

Suicidal Gangsters

My extensive research (Yablonsky, 1997) into violent gangs also confirms the low self-esteem–suicide hypothesis, which explains a considerable amount of violent behavior among juveniles. Many gang youths I have interviewed would agree with one who told me: "I don't give a fuck about myself, so when our gang gets into a fight I don't care who goes down, even me. What do I have to live for? Who gives a fuck. I don't care if I get killed or I kill someone else" (Yablonsky, 1996).

Because of their dysfunctional backgrounds, sociopathic gangsters have a limited concern about whether they live or die. In a real sense they manifest suicidal tendencies in their everyday behavior by their involvement in dangerous and deadly situations. On a number of occasions, in the process of directing therapy groups with gangsters, I have raised the issue of gang behavior as tantamount to suicidal behavior. The usual response I received was an angry denial: "Hey man, you're crazy. I ain't suicidal." I would then have the group review as many incidents as they could when they had exposed themselves in fights, drive-by shootings, and other gang activities in "enemy" territory where they made themselves vulnerable to being shot and killed. Often after extensive discussions, they would acknowledge that their gang behavior might be potentially suicidal.

I recall a fifteen-year-old gangster with whom I worked in a custodial setting, who accounted for his being wild in the streets in this way: "My father always beat me up since I was a little kid. When I hit fourteen we would still wrestle and fight. Sometimes I would beat him up—but mostly he won. Our fights would totally piss me off, and when I hit the streets I was full of rage and looking for trouble. I had fights every day, and when our gang went gangbanging I was always up in the front line. I never cared what happened to me or anyone else. Everybody dies!"

Another case in point related to the suicidal tendencies of gangsters was brought to my attention by Tonya (not her real name), a female who was part of the "female-auxiliary" of a gang. She came from a dysfunctional family and had been sexually abused by various "fathers," "uncles," and brothers for most of her childhood. She became a crack cocaine addict who hung out with gangs for kicks and drugs. She was usually sexually available to any member of the gang who had the right amount of cocaine. In brief, she was, in the lexicon of the gang culture, a "coke-whore."

Tonya's relationship to the gang was prototypical. Most gangs have female counterparts like Tonya. The females participate in the gang in many ways including fighting and drug commerce, and often, like Tonya, they will indiscriminately sexually service their male homies. They have a fierce loyalty to "their" gang.

Tonya was an unusual case in that her mother at one point had a job that provided health insurance. The parents of most gangsters do not have this benefit, so the gangsters do not appear in psychiatric hospitals for treatment. After an arrest for drugs, the judge gave Tonya a choice of jail or psychological treatment. Tonya was hospitalized, and I worked with her in several sessions in an adolescent therapy group in a psychiatric hospital. Because of her past of sexual and physical abuse, Tonya manifested low self-esteem. One result of her apparent low self-esteem was self-mutilation. She slashed herself with razor blades and almost died on several occasions.

At the end of one encounter group therapy session she attended, I delivered a diatribe about the deadly, destructive effects of drug abuse and gang behavior, emphasizing that "drug addiction is a form of slow suicide." As I spoke I noticed Tonya's eyes light up and a smile come over her face. I later asked her about her curious response to my sermon, and she commented, "Your lecture on drugs and gangs really came through to me. Now I know why I do drugs. I feel like a worthless piece of shit, and if I had enough courage I would kill myself. I often feel, especially when I smoke crack, maybe I'll die painlessly and suddenly from an overdose. I want to die, and your talk gave me the insight that my choice is to kill myself slowly with drugs." The insight Tonya gained from my lecture was that she was suicidal, and her choice was to carry out her own death by the continuing use of drugs.

Summary

The many violent social and psychological forces that have emerged in the twentieth century aid in the creation of violent delinquents. As a result of these sociocultural forces, America has become one of the most violent industrialized countries in the world. The rage and violent activity of young offenders emanates from this cauldron of the violent behavior of adults and the rampant child abuse and exploitation that pervade American society.

Delinquent adolescents who are violence prone are more contentious than adults and will commit violent acts that endanger their lives. This is especially true of both male and female delinquent runaways, who, because they have no resources, live on the streets in dangerous, high-violence areas of the city. Drug abuse contributes to their vulnerability and suicidal tendencies. Because of their suicidal tendencies these youths are much more prone to become both victims and perpetrators of violence.

Child abuse is criminal violence in its own right, and its impact on producing violent delinquents is significant. From my research and therapeutic work with a variety of delinquents in the combat zones of the streets, juvenile institutions, and psychiatric hospitals, I conclude that about 80 percent of those who act out violent behavior were abused or neglected by one or both parents.

In summary, my perspective on the social-psychological dynamic process involved in child abuse and delinquent violence is as follows:

1. Being a victim of child abuse produces humiliation, low self-esteem, and rage in youths.

2. Because of low self-esteem and rage, abused delinquent youths develop a low threshold for violence, low impulse control, and are apt to react violently when even slightly provoked. In many cases abused children attempt to create situations where they can act out or displace their inner, often unconscious violent rage.

3. Most violent youths do not attack those who abuse them because they are intimidated and fear the wrath of their parents or other adult abusers, many of whom would retaliate with greater violence.

4. As a consequence of their fear of being "hit back" by the persons who have abused them, they displace their rage and act their violent emotions out against victims who are weaker than they are.

5. Youths who have low self-esteem because they have been violently abused, usually by their parents, feel despondent, don't see much to live for, and have suicidal tendencies. If no one else values or cares about them, they don't value their life. Consequently, they are more apt to place themselves in death-defying violent situations than are youths who value their life.

CHAPTER 6
PATTERNS OF DELINQUENCY VIOLENCE

The prevalence of guns in American society, combined with parental approval of their use, is a serious problem that affects violent delinquent behavior.

A variety of patterns of violence are acted out by young people. Most violent acts committed by juveniles are difficult to understand and can be categorized as "senseless violence." Evidence indicates that unless there is some radical intervention in the social system, the twenty-first century will produce an increasing amount of juvenile violence. With the proliferation of lethal firearms available to juveniles in the United States, it is predictable that homicidal violence will increase. This chapter analyzes various forms of juvenile violence, with an emphasis on lethal, "senseless" violence.

"Normal" Juvenile Violence

In general, most violent acts perpetrated by juveniles are never officially recorded because some violence is considered relatively "normal behavior" for youths in certain social conditions. Children, up to the age of twelve, at some point in their interactions with other children, are likely to become involved in some act of violence—as either a perpetrator or a victim. This pattern of violence, however, is apt to be unpremeditated, spontaneous, and not necessarily harmful. This relatively benign pattern of limited violence is found among most elementary and middle-school children in the United States. It involves a moderate pattern of arguments followed by pushing, slaps, and, in the extreme, punching. This violent behavior does not usually result in any great harm, and it is seldom defined as illegal or brought to the attention of the police or school authorities.

However, even at this early age, in many inner-city schools in large cities of the United States, this pattern of "normal" and for the most part accepted violence is apt to be a serious problem. A well-trained, sensitive schoolteacher who taught in an elementary school in Los Angeles perceived violence in her school as follows (personal interview):

> My experiences teaching in an elementary school in Watts have been varied, but the number one problem I confront is discipline and dealing with problem students in violent situations. During my first year of teaching, I went through a period of shock. My students were disrespectful, did not want to learn, and did not understand my style of language, nor did I theirs. Most of my time was devoted to disciplining and controlling violence, not teaching subject matter.
>
> My ideals about teaching and education that I learned at the university were shattered, and I felt like a failure. During the time I was in the classroom, I was continuously breaking up fights. Once I used karate in order to keep one of my students from killing another one by bashing his head against the stairs. Another time, I used my arm to prevent a child from being hit in the head by a dictionary thrown by another student. The slight-

est *conflict between students, boys or girls, would bring on a fight. The other students would then gather around and cheer for one or the other side. Ironically, after all of the hostility and anger subsided, the battling participants would later be the best of friends. Remedies for dealing with these problem children are hard to come by. (Very little of this violence is ever brought to the attention of the school authorities or the police.)

*Calling or involving a violent child's parents in this situation to rectify their child's behavior can often backfire and lead to a more severe problem. Sometimes, dealing with the parents pours gasoline on the fire. The parents are either disinterested or become defensive and belligerent. In some cases calling a parent can lead to child battering. After my call, one of my students was beaten with an extension cord by his father. When I found this out, I stopped calling that parent. Another time, after calling home about one of my student's violent behavior in class, I found out that the child was burned with a hot iron. He appeared in class the next day with welts all over his arms.

As a last resort, I will send a severe discipline problem to the principal. *That is often ineffective, due to the school bureaucracy. Most principals are reluctant to suspend a child because every suspension goes on record downtown and reflects negatively on the principal and his school record. For these varied reasons, violent behavior is often tolerated and pushed on from grade to grade.*There is limited room for the special problem child to be placed in a special class. Because of their continued presence, the rest of the children suffer and do not acquire the education they are entitled to.*Most of a teacher's energies are devoted to the problem kids and the disruptive and violent situations they create in the classroom.

This teacher's worries about teaching in the current climate of violence in the schools is representative of the plight of many well-educated and dedicated teachers. Because of problems that exist in the children's home and community, the maintenance of discipline becomes a teacher's major objective. The teacher's avowed main task of conveying knowledge is subverted by the climate of violence that surrounds the educational situation.

One aspect of the juvenile violence problem is middle-class teachers who attempt to teach children from a different sociocultural background. Many adolescents quickly resort to violence when under pressure. They respond in this violent way because they have been socialized to believe that this is the way to resolve a conflict or a disagreement. For example, to many adolescents, especially gangsters, any sign of being "dissed," or disrespected, is immediately met with an act of violence.

In my work with gangs, both those in custody and those on the street, I observed flare-ups of assault for something that from my perspective was a minor conflict or disagreement. The "macho syndrome" for gangsters is a significant catalyst for violent behavior; adolescents who have a low self-concept of their masculinity attempt to prove their manliness through violent behavior. Any "diss" that implies that a gang member is less than masculine by referring to him as "pussy" or "faggot" will result in a violent reaction. In my research into the so-called Mexican Mafia gang, I learned that this pattern was a part of their code of honor and violent behavior. In fact, a death contract was put out by the Mexican Mafia on Edward James Olmos for depicting Mexican Mafia gangsters in his film *American Me* homosexually sodomizing a convict in a prison scene. (This concept is discussed more fully in chapter 7.)

Violent behavior in certain adolescent situations is considered a "normal" behavioral response; and this behavior is perceived differently by people who are socialized in different sociocultural contexts. Middle-class teachers tend to view the "normal" expected violent behavior of lower-class children from a different perspective than the youths who engage in the violence view it. Consequently, teachers are more likely to label this "normal" violent behavior as delinquent.

This issue of "normal" aggressive behavior being labeled "delinquent" is a complex social-psychological phenomenon. Some youths who are perceived as violent by middle-class standards are, from the youths' viewpoint, "just fooling around." In my gang research, I have witnessed "friendly combat," where I thought a youth was getting killed, analyzed by the combatants as "fooling around." I remember one gang kid dragging another down concrete steps, his head bouncing on the concrete. Although some blood came from the victim's bruised forehead, both youths wound up laughing about what I perceived as an extremely violent activity.

Howard Becker, in his book *The Outsiders* (1963), asserted that labeling a child as a delinquent is often more related to the "social perception" of society's labeler than the definition of the child who is acting out. He makes the point that labeling students as delinquents for their aggressive behavior should be done cautiously. "This often takes place in the middle-class school setting where the conduct of the lower-class child is apt to deviate significantly from middle-class attitudes and values" (p. 28).

Becker said that deviant behavior, including violence, does not refer to some intrinsic quality of a specific act, but rather is external to the act; it is a property conferred upon some form of behavior by observers. He stated his case as follows: "Social groups create deviance by making the rules whose infraction constitutes deviance, and by applying these rules to particular people and labeling them outsiders. From this point of view, deviance is not a quality of the act the person commits, but rather a consequence of the application by others of rules." A violent act committed by a youth from a gang subculture may be considered normal behavior according to the norms of the gang, even though it may clearly be considered illegal delinquent violence within the context of the juvenile court of the larger society (1963, pp. 53–54).

School Murders

Beyond the "normal violence" of juveniles, inner-city schools have been plagued with severe violent behavior, especially gang murders. This form of violence has been prevalent and persistent in the end of the twentieth century. In the United States in 1999 there were around 50 million students in 100,000 public schools. In general the great majority of these schools, until recently, have experienced moderate and rare incidents of violence.

A pattern of homicide has emerged in a number of public schools that demand special attention. From February 1997 to April 1999 there were 28 students killed and over 50 students wounded by gunfire. This new pattern involves unforeseen violent eruptions by students shooting classmates in a brutal fashion. A distinctive characteristic of these murders is that, unlike the large number of murders that have taken place in the inner-city areas of America, these homicides were committed by youths with no prior violent background in formerly violence-free small-town schools.[1]

1. On February 19, 1997, Evan Ramsey, sixteen, killed his school principal and a fellow student and wounded two other students in Bethel, Alaska.

2. On October 1, 1997, in Pearl, Mississippi, Luke Woodard, sixteen, killed his mother at home, his ex-girlfriend, and another student, and wounded seven other students at his high school.

3. On December 1, 1997, Michael Carneal, fourteen, shot at a group of students who were in a prayer group, killing three and wounding five others in a West Paducah, Kentucky, high school.

4. On March 24, 1998, in Jonesboro, Arkansas, Mitchell Johnson, thirteen, and Andrew Golden, eleven, opened fire on their classmates, killing five students and wounding ten more persons.

---

1. The following list is compiled from various sources including: "Tragedy in a Kentucky Town, *Newsweek*, December 15, 1997; "The Schoolyard Killers," by Trent Gegas, Jerry Adler, and Daniel Petersen, *Newsweek*, April 6, 1998; "Burials Begin in a Grieving Arkansas Town," by Julie Cart, *Los Angeles Times*, March 28, 1998; "A Son Who Spun Out of Control," by Patricia King and Andrew Murr, *Newsweek*, June 1, 1998; "Guns in Schools: A Survey," CNN Internet report, June 19, 1998; and CNN Internet report, April 22, 1999.

5. On April 24, 1998, Andrew Wurst, fourteen, opened fire at a school dance in Edinboro, Pennsylvania, killing a teacher.

6. On May 19, 1998, in Fayetteville, Tennessee, Jacob Davis, eighteen, killed a classmate three days before graduation.

7. On May 21, 1998, Kip Kinkel, fifteen, killed his mother and father, then went to his high school in Springfield, Oregon, and opened fire in the cafeteria. He killed two students and wounded twenty-two others.

8. The most violent school event of the century took place on April 20, 1999, when two students, Eric Harris, 18, and Dylan Klebold, 17, shot and killed 12 students and a teacher and seriously wounded 22 others at Columbine High School in Littleton, Colorado. In addition to the shootings, their murderous rampage involved planting 50 homemade bombs in different locations in the school in a planned effort to blow up the entire school in a blaze of fire. When they were finished killing and wounding their fellow students they committed suicide.

These violent offenses were committed by individuals, and in the case of Columbine High by a small group. Because Harris and Klebold committed suicide, only a sketchy record remains of their motivation. According to their parents and many of their friends, their planning and violent activity was kept a secret until the massacre erupted.

Most of the youths who committed school murders came from homes that were relatively stable. There is limited evidence of a dysfunctional family background, and the families were not criminogenic. For example, the parents of Kip Kinkel were both respected high school teachers, and none of the other parents manifested severe family problems. With the exception of some minor issues regarding school disciplinary action, none of the killers had a prior record of severe delinquency. Most of them, however, seemed to experience some form of alienation or separation from their high school classmates. One was reputed to be involved in a form of devil worship, and the Columbine High killers were apparently involved in this and a white supremacist group. In one incident, several students in a school hallway were gunned down as they were praying, possibly supporting the devil worship hypothesis.

As outsiders, most of these killers claimed to have some grievance about being taunted or ridiculed by their peers. In particular, Luke Woodard complained in the aftermath of the murders he committed that no one liked him, including his mother, and he always felt very lonely. Many of the school killers manifested suicidal tendencies. A significant common denominator for all these youths was their fascination with guns.

The "Trench Coat Mafia"

The Columbine High School murders were the most shocking case of all of the school murders at the end of the century, and received the greatest horrific response in the United States and around the world. This mass murder of 13 people was appropriately perceived as a national disaster. The President, the press, and many others held numerous townhall and community meetings in an effort to analyze the event and assuage the emotional pain and sorrow experienced by many people. The killings became the subject of a mass media barrage for several weeks, while social science and law enforcement experts attempted to make some sense out of the tragedy. Following is my analysis of the Trench Coat Mafia's role in the Columbine killings, other sections of the book present data on gangs, guns, emotional disorder, and violence that are relevant to and dovetail with this analysis.

The known perpetrators of the massacre, Eric Harris and Dylan Klebold, were leaders of a group self-identified and known as the "Trench Coat Mafia." This apparently white supremacist gang wore black trench coats, talked in German, displayed Nazi symbols, and carried out their murders on Hitler's birthday, April 20 (1999). Harris and Klebold were also avid violent video game players, and had a Web site that advocated and threatened violence. According to a police report, as Eric Harris planned the assault on Columbine High School, he wrote in a diary that he envisioned killing as many as 500 students, going on to attack neighboring homes, and then hijacking a jet airplane and crashing it in New York City. Harris' Web site writings, prior to the murders, provide a clue to his state of mind: "Well, all you people out there can just die. You all better hide in your houses, because I'm coming for everyone soon, and I will be armed to the teeth, and I will shoot to kill, and I will kill!"

Although law enforcement officials did not uncover, arrest, or prosecute other "members" of the Trench Coat Mafia, it is my speculation, based on my knowledge of violent gang organization, that there were a number of individuals who helped to carry out the massacre. The planting of 50 bombs, including 5 large propane tank bombs, could not have been accomplished without the aid of other individuals. Despite an effort by the authorities to piece together the event, the scenario and sequence of the murders is sketchy because of Harris and Klebold's suicides. However, the main events of the rampage can be pieced together from comments by several of the survivors of the incident. Their commentary provides some insights into the dynamics of the Columbine killings (CNN, April 21,1999):

> An unidentified male student: "I looked out the window and there was a kid with a trench coat and a shotgun and pipe bombs in the parking lot. And then he shot a girl outside and then he

came into the cafeteria and you could hear, like, bombs and shotguns going off. And then he came into the library and shot everybody around me. Then he put a gun to my head and asked if we all wanted to die and that he was going to kill us if we were of color, and if we had a hat, and if we played sports. I just started screaming and crying and telling him not to shoot me and so he just shot the girl in the head in front of me, and then he shot the black kid, because he was black, in the face."

Student Casey Brackley: "It was around 11 a.m. or so. It was soon after that they started shooting and when they went into the lunch room and started firing rounds. There was a girl about 50 yards away from us laying against the curb who had been shot in her leg. Another kid was lying face down at the bottom of the steps and he had been shot in the back point-blank. Then the one kid who shot the kid in the back went up a hill and threw a bomb into the parking lot and that exploded. Then they went inside and continued to shoot at people."

Student Jamie Roark: "One of them opened his cape and had a shotgun. Finally, I started figuring out these guys shot to kill, for no reason.... They didn't care what race you were. It didn't matter. They wanted to shoot to have fun. They're sick people."

Based on various media reports and my own research into gangs, following are my summary observations on the Trench Coat Mafia:

1. The Trench Coat Mafia were an alienated white supremacist clique that attempted in some ways to emulate the more prevalent and established hate groups in America. From my viewpoint, they were a minor version of the "skinhead" collectivities, the Klan, and the so-called "White Aryan Race" gangs. There is some evidence that they read the perverted and illogical racist literature of these violent groups on the Internet.

2. The group dynamics of this and other white violent gangs, in a number of ways, resemble the more prevalent minority violent gangs like the Crips, Bloods, and Mexican Mafia. Like minority gangs, the participants in the Trench Coat Mafia manifested the American gun culture-psychosis. This unfortunate cultural pattern of romanticizing guns exists primarily in the United States. No other Western society has the same obsessive attitudes about firearms (an apparent correlate to this fact is that no other country in the world has this level of homicidal problems in their schools). Further, a significant element in the massacre was the availability of guns. In this context, a national survey by the Parents Resource Institute for Drug Education (PRIDE) revealed that around one million students brought guns to school in 1997, and that 154,350 stu-

dents between the ages of 10 and 18 had witnessed deadly shootings during the same year (CNN news report, 1997).

3. The Trench Coat Mafia's comment about themselves in the school year-book ("It's healthy to be insane") characterizes the gang's leaders. One of them was under psychiatric care, and was receiving a psychoactive drug for his emotional problem. In this type of gang, emotionally distorted behavior is central to and coalesces around one or two leaders who are totally committed to their attitudes. From them, it spreads out to more peripheral followers, who accept their leaders' viewpoints.

4. Delinquent groups like the Trench Coat Mafia are constituted of alienated youths, full of rage. They generally have a low self-concept and mask their underlying feelings of inferiority and powerlessness by a reaction formation of posturing macho images of power. At Columbine High School the group was seen as outsiders, characterized by the other students as "freaks" and "crazies." Their hurt feelings simmered under these verbal attacks, and then exploded into their acts of senseless violence.

5. Based on my extensive work with youths in psychiatric hospitals I have observed a pattern of suicidal tendencies among youths who have the kind of emotional problems manifested by the killers. Youths with suicidal tendencies by definition have a limited concern for their own lives and consequently care less about the lives of others. This seemed apparent in the behavior of Harris and Klebold in the year before the killings, and was validated by their homicidal behavior on the day of the rampage that climaxed with their suicide.

The Impact of Guns on Delinquent Violence

The increasing availability of guns clearly escalated the violent delinquency problem in the latter part of the twentieth century. When I began working with violent gangs in the 1950s, youths rarely had guns. Gangsters were mainly involved in direct hand-to-hand combat and occasional stabbings. Some enterprising youths made and used so-called zip guns or what was referred to as "home-mades." A pipe was used for a barrel, and a makeshift trigger was hooked up to it with some rubber bands. When a youth shot at someone, the "gun" might blow up in his hand or shoot 45 degrees to the left of the intended victim. The currently used rapid fire automatic guns can spray bullets at a target. As a consequence, in a drive-by or walk-by shooting, accuracy is not a requirement for hitting a target. The spray of bullets acts like a shotgun, and a number of people can be killed or injured with a few squeezes of the trigger.

In the 1990s, about 20,000 people were murdered each year, and about 70 percent of these crimes were committed with firearms of various kinds. It is estimated that there are more than 250 million firearms in the possession of American citizens. This translates into the fact that there are enough guns available for almost every man, woman, and child in the United States. This lethal societal condition has an enormous impact on the violent behavior of juvenile delinquents. The availability of handguns is clearly related to the increase in juvenile violent crime, especially murder and robbery. The homicide rate per capita in the United States is estimated to be thirty-five times higher than the rate in Germany or in England, and even higher than that in countries like Japan, where few citizens own guns. In 1997, England passed a law totally banning all handguns.

In recent years, juveniles in the inner cities, especially those who are gangsters, have come to see guns as acceptable instruments for controlling or killing "enemies." In the larger society, well-meaning, law-abiding citizens perceive owning and carrying guns as their constitutional right; for the most part they use their guns for hunting. This societal attitude and perception of guns contributes to the approximate 22,000 homicides and countless woundings of people by firearms that have taken place each year in the United States. The "right to bear arms" has contributed to the climate of violence and the increasing acts of violence committed by juveniles in the past century (Blumstein, 1994).

The increase and availability of guns can be attributed, in large part, to the work of the National Rifle Association. The NRA rationalizes their promotion of violence with their slogan, "Guns don't kill people, people do." This flies in the face of the fact that arguments that end in physical battering and even stabbings are seldom lethal if there are no available guns. Guns in the hands of sociopathic juveniles contribute to mayhem on the streets of America.

As a case in point, the following prototypical example of the juvenile gun problem involves a series of armed robberies committed with handguns by two adolescents. Their violent activity is derived from a June 1996 police report. These teenagers, in a three-hour period one night, went on a bloody rampage with handguns that resulted in the deaths of four people. The two teenagers started their homicidal spree at dusk on the streets of West Los Angeles. Their first stop involved a man who had no cash, only his infant in a stroller. They let him pass and kept walking. They next encountered a man and his wife at a nearby intersection. The couple quickly handed over $8 and two wristwatches, then fled. Next, the boys intercepted two elderly Oriental women and pulled out a pistol. When one woman tried to push the gun out of her face, ten bullets were fired, killing both women.

The boys kept walking. They came upon a trio of friends out for an evening stroll. They took a watch and a few dollars and, without so much as a word, killed one of the three, a French citizen visiting Los Angeles for the first time. They next found a seventy-six-year-old man in front of a restaurant. They asked him for his money, and he refused to comply with their request. They argued with him for less than a minute and then shot him to death. Their evening over, they climbed into an old sedan and drove off into the night. The four killings were committed in plain view and without cause in a neighborhood where murder was usually not a fact of life. All the dead were strangers to the killers.

A notable case of a random murder was the death of Ennis Cosby, son of Bill Cosby. Cosby was in the act of changing a flat tire when several bullets slammed into him from an unknown assailant. The Cosby case touched deeply the emotions of millions of people in America because Ennis was the son of a much-loved national figure; however, this type of homicide is experienced daily by hundreds of average citizens. The Cosby murder was confirmed a month later to be an act of random violence, committed by an eighteen-year-old youth with a long record of delinquent violence.

In an article in the *New York Times*, Jane Brody (1997) cogently delineated the impact of guns on juvenile violence:

> A few years ago, a young Las Vegas family was shattered by a three-year-old girl who found her father's loaded revolver in a desk drawer. Thinking the gun was a toy, she aimed it at her pregnant mother, who was asleep on the sofa, and pulled the trigger. The mother died on her way to the hospital. Earlier this month, a thirteen-year-old Brooklyn boy, whom a neighbor described as a good person who "always did the right thing," was shot and killed while he and his friends were playing with a gun. In Montgomery, Alabama, a nine-year-old boy accidentally shot his seven-year-old brother with a gun he had found in the glove compartment of the family car. The boy died, even though the incident occurred in a hospital parking lot, where the father had left the car and the boys while he ran an errand.

These incidents are the tip of the iceberg of deaths related to guns in and around people's homes. Nearly half the households in the United States contain firearms and one-fourth have handguns. More than half a million guns are stolen from homes each year. Deaths caused by firearms, most of them handguns, number about 40,000 each year in the United States. More than 1,600 of these are accidents. The number of nonfatal injuries caused by gun accidents is four to six times as high. According to

Josh Sugarmann (1997), "In the United States, guns are the second most deadly consumer product, after cars, on the market."

National polls have consistently shown that about two-thirds of citizens support stricter gun-control laws, and a 1993 poll found that 52 percent of adults favored a federal ban on ownership of handguns. The Johns Hopkins School of Public Health has a Center for Gun Policy and Research that is pressing for personalization of handguns to prevent all but the authorized users from firing them. The center, established in 1995, has pointed out that "while personalized handguns will likely reduce the risks of some gun deaths, reliable studies still teach us that possessing a gun in the home is more perilous than protective" (CNN News, June 15, 1995).

Studies published in medical journals since 1990 have documented the fact that guns are more likely to cause than prevent harm to innocent people. A recent report published in the *Archives of Internal Medicine* (1997), found that gunshot wounds were the single most common cause of death for women in the home, accounting for 42 percent of suicides and 46 percent of homicides. In the wake of these alarming statistics, a number of medical organizations have responded with efforts to control guns.

The American Academy of Pediatrics, noting the failure of lesser measures to control gun-related tragedies, has suggested amending the constitutional right of citizens to bear arms. According to a report in the *Journal of Pediatrics* (1996), a publication of the academy, data from "several rigorously conducted studies indicate that home ownership of guns" increased the risk of homicide among teenagers and young adults more than threefold and the risk of suicide more than tenfold (p. 43). In these studies, guns were used in nearly three-fifths of the suicides and a third of the homicides that occurred in the victims' homes.

Researchers who examined suicides and murders in the homes of female victims in three metropolitan counties concluded that the presence of a gun in the home increased the risk of being murdered and committing suicide. Although many people say they own a gun for self-protection, the gun is more likely to be used against them, most often in the heat of a domestic argument or jealous rage (Straus and Gelles, 1995).

The availability of a gun greatly increases the likelihood that a suicide attempt will succeed. Nationwide, firearms—mostly handguns—are used in about 19,000 suicides each year. Among young people from ten to nineteen, more than 1,400 suicides are committed with guns each year (UCR, 1996).

The belief of many gun advocates that teaching children how to use a gun properly will prevent accidents is belied by one West Coast surgeon's account. He told me in a personal interview (June 1997) about a gun incident that involved a father and a son. The surgeon left the operating room to tell a young couple that their little boy was dead, having accidentally shot himself while playing with his father's handgun. According to the doctor, the boy's father, who said he was a member of the National Rifle Association, became visibly angry, and said, "I taught the dumb kid how to use it right." This was also the primary defense of the father whose son murdered five people in the Jonesboro, Arkansas, killing spree.

In 1997, in addition to gun control laws, law-enforcement authorities began installing a new generation of sophisticated security devices that are expected to lead to technology that will let police officers spot people on the street who are carrying concealed guns. Justice Department officials have developed highly sensitive weapon detectors that are being installed for final testing at a federal courthouse in Los Angeles and a prison in North Carolina. The device for which officials hold the most hope is one that uses a camera employing electromagnetism to enable the police to detect a weapon hidden under someone's clothing from thirty to sixty feet away. A version of this gun control approach is expected to be accessible by the year 2000.

In schools in high delinquency areas, this new technology could more easily detect juveniles carrying guns than metal detectors in current use. Although these devices could prevent some lethal gun violence, their use raises the controversial issue of whether or not we want to expose youths to high-tech surveillance in the schools in a democracy.

Delinquency, Guns, and Violence in the Schools

The availability and lethal nature of guns have become significant because of the escalating violence of delinquents in the formerly sacrosanct halls and environs of schools. There is evidence that an increasing number of adolescents carry guns and bring them to school. The day before fifteen-year-old Kip Kinkel killed two of his fellow students in Springfield, Oregon, he was suspended from school for having a loaded gun in his locker.

The issue of school safety has been high on the national agenda since U.S. Senate hearings in the 1970s. In 1994, the National Council of the Great City Schools reported that 83 percent of urban superintendents and school board members listed violence and gang activity as their top concerns. Such findings have caused many to believe that schools, particularly those in areas such as Los Angeles, are dangerous.

A recent two-year study of schools in Los Angeles, a study that represented the geographic diversity of the schools, revealed that one in seven Los Angeles high school students say they carried a weapon to school for protection at least one time. The survey, which covered 1,802 Los Angeles

Unified School District high school students, was conducted in 1995 and 1996 by the American Civil Liberties Union of Southern California, with the help of researchers from California State University—Los Angeles and the University of Southern California ("Guns in Los Angeles Schools," 1996). The study revealed that about 49 percent of the students said they could easily get a gun, and 25 percent said they would have to pay less than $50 for one. As indicated earlier, 14 percent carried a gun on campus at least once, and 2.5 percent of the students questioned at eleven high schools said they brought a gun on campus every day, making it as much a part of their school materials as a textbook or a calculator. These gun-toting students were not deterred by the Los Angeles Unified School District's policy of making random checks with metal detectors. Nearly half were unaware their schools had such a policy.

The survey found that students worried more about violence off campus than on campus. An eleventh-grader said that fights might stem from disputes that start in school but usually don't occur there. "They plan it in school and take it elsewhere, so they won't get caught. Students sometimes bring weapons to school to prepare for off-campus battle. You can't run to your house and pick up a gun after school" (1996, p. 18). While 14 percent of students surveyed said weapons are a means of repelling on-campus attacks, 39 percent said it was fear of gang-related violence that led students to arm themselves. Another 30 percent said a weapon offered protection getting to school and back home.

Other facts revealed by the survey involved the race factor: 9 percent of the white students, 13 percent of the Asian-Pacific Islanders and Latinos, and 22 percent of African-American students said they had carried a weapon to school. Most students were fearful and aware of potential danger. Seventy percent of the students at one high school said they had witnessed a drive-by shooting near campus. More than a third of the respondents in the survey had seen a fellow teenager shot in their neighborhood, and 41 percent had witnessed a drive-by shooting.

One of the most disturbing findings of the study was that the Los Angeles school district "has clearly been unsuccessful" in implementing a consistent policy for using metal detectors to deter pupils from carrying weapons. In 1993, after fatal shootings at Reseda and Fairfax High Schools, the district began requiring administrators to conduct daily, random searches of some students using a handheld metal detector. The idea was not to find all weapons but to make students worry that, if they brought one to school, they might be caught and face expulsion. Nearly half the surveyed students said they were unaware of the policy, and two-thirds said the devices had no impact on the number of weapons on campus.

Most violent youths who are involved in gangs and drug dealing and who carry guns rarely if ever attend school. Consequently, children inside the school are safer there than they are in the islands of violence that surround the schools, where guns are a pervasive part of the adolescent community. This is supported by a landmark study carried out by George Knox with David Laske and Edward Tromanhauser (1995). The authors note, however, that research over the past decade reveals a direct correlation between the presence of guns and gangs in and around schools and increases in school violence.

Controlling the Availability of Guns ✶

The Second Amendment to the U.S. Constitution legalized "the right to bear arms." However, when this amendment was written over two hundred years ago, it was appropriate and relevant for an entirely different United States than contemporary America. The Founding Fathers could not have envisioned the United States of the twenty-first century and its 20,000 murders each year. The amendment was written when a musket fired one shot and took some time to load. They were not thinking in terms of sociopathic juveniles and violent gangbangers enacting senseless and lethal drive-by killings with automatic weaponry that could kill a large number of people with one spray of bullets.

Pete Hamill (1981) summarized the easy availability of guns in the twentieth century:

> Go ahead: Sell the kid a gun. What the hell . . . He's got the money, he gets a gun. A Luger. A .357 Magnum. A .38 Smith and Wesson police special. Sure are beautiful, aren't they? Nice weight, beautiful finish. Why buy just one, kid? Here, buy two. They're on sale. And have some extra ammo. Where you going, kid? Washington, huh? Hey, I hear it's pretty there this time of year, with the cherry blossoms and all that. Well, have a good time, kid. All right, who's next?
>
> John Warnock Hinckley, Jr., came to Washington with at least one gun. But he was carrying a lot of extra baggage with him. There was his unrequited love for Jodie Foster, the star of a blood-and-guns movie called *Taxi Driver*. He had photographs of her. He wrote letters to her in the corrupted language of the fan magazine. He didn't know her, of course, any more than he knew Ronald Reagan. He never met the real Jodie Foster, a person of flesh and blood, no doubt burdened with the usual ration of human frailties and folly. She was part of his baggage anyway, a shimmering illusion glimpsed in a darkened theater, shaped by the deceptions of art. But when the art was over, when the men who made this movie were finished splattering phony blood

around their celluloid world, someone yelled "cut" and the actors got up and went to a bar.

Last Monday, in the drizzle of T Street in Washington, nobody yelled "cut" over James Brady; a real bullet had carved a real tunnel through his real brain. Timothy Delahanty did not go to a bar, and neither did the President of the United States. They all had real bullets slammed into their real bodies. They had bullets in their bodies . . . because someone sold guns to a young man named John Warnock Hinckley, Jr.

The general American attitude and policy on guns is out of sync with the reality and history of the past century. England has developed a more rational viewpoint and policy on guns. The British do not subscribe to the view held by many in the United States that every citizen is entitled to own a gun. Under Britain's firearms control laws, no one may own a firearm without a police certificate, except for antique weapons and certain types of airguns. To get a certificate, the applicant must have a "good reason," which in the vast majority of cases is the desire to have a weapon for hunting or sport shooting. Membership in a gun or hunting club is usually the way to get the certificate. Gun clubs are aware of the danger of a person joining for the purpose of getting a certificate that might otherwise be withheld. Virtually all clubs have a six-month probationary period for new members that enables the club's officers to find out if the new member is really interested in sport shooting. The police in England are not required to state a reason for rejecting an application unless the applicant challenges the rejection in court.

Aside from the "good reason" requirement, the applicant must show, usually through completion of a safety course, that he or she knows how to handle a firearm properly. The minimum legal age for possession of a firearm is seventeen. There are especially heavy penalties in England for possession of an unauthorized firearm, whether or not it is used in the commission of a crime; the use of a fake gun in the commission of a crime carries a maximum penalty of fourteen years in prison. This is only one of eighty different offenses linked to the illegal possession of firearms. As a result, firearms play a relatively small role in British crime (Trimborn, 1975). British police generally are not armed and there are no shootouts like the one described earlier that took place in Los Angeles in 1997. British police may use firearms, as the government rules state, "only when necessary to protect the life of the police officer or some other person. The responsibility for using a weapon rests with the police officer; and the unnecessary use of firearms might constitute a criminal offense" (1975, p. 59).

Why is there so much opposition to greater and, in my view, vitally needed gun control in the United States? For one thing, the manufacture and sale of firearms is a big business. Gun owners spend an estimated $1 billion each year on guns. Gun and ammunition manufacturers, retail gun dealers, gun-magazine publishers, *Soldier of Fortune* magazine, and hunting resort owners make a great deal of money from the sale and distribution of weapons. They also spend a good deal of money in the form of contributions to the political campaigns of congressional and state legislative candidates. The National Rifle Association is probably the most effective lobby in Washington, and the organization carries on a continuous campaign against any gun-control legislation. Its officials have boasted that they can get their members to send at least half a million letters to Congress on seventy-two-hours' notice.

The NRA's 1998 stand as explicated on TV by their new president Charleton Heston, in favor of automatic weapons is difficult to understand. These guns, which can spray bullets over a wide area, can kill a number of people with one blast. This type of gun is not useful for hunting. The automatic AK-47 or Uzi would eviscerate or blow apart any animal shot by a hunter. Their only use is in a war zone or for young gangsters and others to randomly and senselessly kill people. Yet the NRA will not budge in its efforts to keep these guns legal.

A factor that may help us understand the resolute NRA attitude is that of the "weapon's effect" as presented by psychologist Leonard Berkowitz (1981). He asserts that past and present research reveals that weapons have an aggressive effect on our behavior. Based on his studies and those of others, he believes that the sight of a weapon increases any aggressiveness that one is already experiencing and that the "weapon's effect" can occur even without any previous frustration or rage felt by an individual.

Berkowitz refers to several studies that have shown that, when children are given toy guns to play with, they act more aggressively than when they play with other toys. Berkowitz offers two theories as to why the weapons effect occurs: (1) weapons function as a conditioned stimulus eliciting associated responses, and (2) guns remind people of earlier occasions when they have seen aggression rewarded (as on television and in movies).

The attitude toward guns in American society is a product of the "weapons effect," which has a profound impact on juveniles. On countless occasions, in my research interviews with violent offenders, especially gangsters, I have heard some variation of the comment: "A gun is the great equalizer. A gun puts you in charge of any situation, and makes you feel nine feet tall."

In my work with delinquents and violent behavior over the past fifty years, I have witnessed the enormous increase in lethal violence that has emanated from the availability of the variety of firearms. As a witness to the mayhem and destructiveness of guns, I have developed a zero tolerance for weaponry in the hands of civilians. In my view, the only truly legitimate use of weaponry should be in the hands of law enforcement and the military. If we really want to substantially control violence in America, we should ban all guns for civilians, and severely restrict the role of the hunter. Target shooters' guns can be stored in the buildings where they practice their target shooting. In my opinion, these restrictions on the use of guns would be a valid trade-off that would save tens of thousands of lives and would have a profound impact on minimizing juvenile violence in American society.

Vandalism as Violence

Most of the juvenile violence discussed to this point has involved people against people. But historically, violent youths have committed acts of delinquency by destroying or defacing property. Vandalism of this type is an expression of inner rage. A 1990s version of this displaced aggression has been referred to as "tagging." The tagger defaces property by writing his name on walls and other places of prominence.

I have interviewed over one hundred youths who have been characterized as taggers. Vandalism is often construed as senseless violence, yet a closer analysis of this delinquent act reveals that there are some definitive motivations in these acts, often motivated by a desire to commit violence on a person displaced onto an inanimate object. For example, one youth who had destroyed a door in his house said, "My mother trashed my room looking for marijuana. I was really pissed at her, and I was so mad I wanted to hit her. I put my fist through the door instead of hitting her." Another example of vandalism as displaced aggression is the destruction of school property by children who hate school.

One researcher who studied vandalism, British criminologist Stanley Cohen (1973), maintained that despite the fact that most people view vandalism as "mindless, random action, there are meanings and motives that surround various forms of vandalism." Cohen asserted, after careful study, that vandalism has more structure to it than most people believe.

> Vandalism—the illegal and deliberate destruction or defacement of property—might be labeled differently according to circumstances and might not always be considered a crime. Some groups are given a sort of collective license to commit vandalism. Much routine property damage (such as graffiti) becomes accepted or condoned, and there are forms of official vandalism such as the destruction of buildings of architectural merit in the name of urban "renewal." From the outset the words "wanton," "senseless," "malicious," and so on used by social scientists, the mass media and the public to describe vandalism have obscured

any real attempt to understand what such behavior is all about. In property-oriented societies such as ours, it is incomprehensible that someone could destroy property without any apparent gain. Theft is easy to understand in straightforward economic terms; even personal violence usually seems intelligible. But for most people the only way to make sense of vandalism is to assume that it does not make sense—that it is mindless, random action. Research in England and America suggests that there are clear clusters of meanings and motives around the various forms of vandalism. (Pp. 238–241)

Cohen described several forms of vandalism.

1. *Acquisitive vandalism:* Damage to acquire money or property: breaking open telephone coin boxes, stealing material from construction sites.

2. *Tactical vandalism:* Damage as a conscious tactic used to advance some other end: breaking a window to be arrested and get a bed in prison; jamming a machine in a factory to gain a rest period.

3. *Ideological vandalism:* Similar to some tactical vandalism, but carried out to further an explicit ideological cause or to deliver a message; breaking embassy windows during a demonstration; chalking slogans on walls.

4. *Vindictive vandalism:* Damage done to gain revenge; breaking windows of a school to settle a grudge against a teacher.

5. *Play vandalism:* Damage done as part of a game: who can break the most windows of a house, who can shoot out the most street lamps.

6. *Malicious vandalism:* Damage as an expression of rage or frustration, often directed at symbolic middle-class property. It is this last type that has the vicious and apparently senseless facade that many find so difficult to understand.

A central proposition of Cohen's analysis is that vandalism, or violence against property, is more apt to flourish against an anonymous enemy—"them." This study is supported by my own observations and research during the five-year-period when I directed a delinquency-prevention program on the Upper West Side of Manhattan, near Columbia University. The program was largely sponsored by Columbia University, which was adjacent to a neighborhood that contained violence of all types, especially muggings and gang violence. Many young people who were bored, deprived, and full of hostility would choose Columbia University as a target for their frustrations. They would often ventilate their aggression by breaking windows and generally vandalizing the property. One youth told me how he always felt better after he destroyed something at Columbia. To him, the anonymous gray buildings were inhabited by enemies who he felt took care of rich kids.

Over a period of several years, I set up a delinquency-prevention program that helped provide access for several hundred poor, minority, gang youths to facilities at Columbia. The gymnasium, swimming pool, and baseball fields were opened up for use by neighborhood youths under controlled conditions. The results were that vandalism related to the buildings was sharply reduced. The cold, anonymous "them" became part of the juveniles' real community, and they saw no point in destroying property that, in part, now belonged to themselves. The program broke down their formerly aggressive we-they stance.

A research project by Richard A. Berk and Howard E. Aldrich (1972) supports my observations that vandalism against property by youths is often a displaced act of aggression against a particular person or class of people. Berk and Aldrich concluded, based on their research, that "patterns of attack during civil disorders strongly imply choices by some rioters. Civil disorders cannot accurately be described as 'irrational' or 'mindless' destruction. We are not arguing that the overall events were planned, but rather that individual participants appear to have been selecting many of their targets. . . . Apparently some believe consumer goods are distributed unfairly, label the villains and take collective action against them."

The Berk and Aldrich hypothesis was confirmed during the 1992 Los Angeles riots. Most black-owned businesses in the riot area remained untouched, whereas many other business establishments were burned to the ground. African-American rioters particularly targeted Korean-owned grocery stores where they felt they had been mistreated and charged unnecessarily exorbitant prices for products.

A novel view of juvenile vandalism was recounted by Pamela Richards, Richard Berk, and Brenda Foster (1979). Their book *Crime as Play* presents the results of an extensive questionnaire study in which almost three thousand teenagers, ranging from fifth graders to high school students, told the investigators about their activities concerning vandalism, drugs, and theft and other forms of deviant behavior. The authors assumed that shoplifting and other vandalism can be explained as a choice that, to the "delinquent," produces a maximum return on his or her investment of time and energy. They state, "As is the case with other economic choices, the returns consist of capital formation (in this case, the learning of skills), commodity production (the stolen or destroyed goods), and consumption (enjoyment, fun)" (p. 187).

Another facet of vandalism as violence is its relationship to a youth's participation in a gang. Andrew L. Wade (1967) made the point long ago that vandalism is one means of producing group solidarity among alienated youngsters. Wade viewed aggressive juvenile vandalism as a "social act" of fraternity, despite the fact that the results may be destructive. The act of vandalism, according to Wade, functions as a means of ensuring group solidarity. Conformity to the peer group occurs because involvement tends to satisfy the adolescents' need dispositions for status, recognition, and response. Identification with societal property norms becomes subordinate to the demands of the peer group. Adolescents will participate in acts of property destruction in order not to appear "chicken." In other words, youths can, through this involvement, maintain a satisfying self-definition and avoid becoming marginal members of the group. Even though they may recognize the act to be "wrong" or "delinquent," they find some comfort in the guilt-assuaging rationalizations present in adolescent subcultures.

Wade comes close to my own "senseless violence" hypothesis of vandalism when he states:

> Some property destruction appears to function for the adolescent as a protest against his ill-defined social role and ambiguous status in the social structure. Other meanings are more specific. If a boy has suffered frustration, he may express his resentment by a revengeful act of destruction: "Well, he accused us of stealing some stuff out of his joint. He didn't come right out and say it was us, but the way he talked he made it sound like it, particularly us. We were kidding him about an old rifle he had. It was about ninety years old, and he wanted $15 for it. . . . We left and came back later. I told my buddy ,"Let's go down and break those windows." He said, "Okay," and we went down there and picked up some rocks along the way. We got down there and stood in front of the place till there weren't any cars very close to us, and we threw the rocks and ran. (1967, p. 168)

In another case example Wade (1967) describes, the theme of vandalism as displaced aggression toward a person is apparent. A youth stated, "I know of some friends of mine who went over to school and we decided to break some of Mr. X's windows for the simple reason that we absolutely despised this teacher. There were about four or five of us. . . . Many windows are broken in our school. In one room in particular in which one unpopular teacher holds classes, about twenty-five panes a year have to be replaced" (p. 174). The vandals believed that this was a way to "get back at" a teacher.

Tagging—writing one's name on walls and elsewhere—became a widespread fad in the 1990s. Earlier, before this activity was labeled tagging, Claire Berman (1976) described how a prototypical truant spent his time on the streets of New York City. She noted how school truancy dovetails with wanton vandalism.

> The fifteen-year-old boy pointed to his signature "Dune 1"—an artfully spray-painted nom de graffiti in bold, four-foot letters on the concrete wall of a school playground. "Everybody knows my name, I painted it all over the city." His proclamations notwithstanding, Dune 1 is a nobody to a city school system that lost track of him more than two years ago. He is one of possibly 90,000 youngsters listed by the Board of Education as long-term absentees—and frequently referred to as "ghosts." Instead of going to school, they crowd department stores, the Port Authority bus terminal, the Bronx Zoo, Central Park, Coney Island. They wander the hallways of other schools. They join gangs. They spend hours on the subways, their transistor radios blaring. Many like Dune 1 have learned to decorate the trains, using cans of spray paint "lifted" from the shelves of local stores. (P. 182)

The Rise and Impact of "Senseless Violence"

Acts of wanton vandalism are part of an enormous increase in what has been termed "senseless violence." This pattern of violence has become increasingly spontaneous and "wild," prompting a number of serious crimes, including murder, to be referred to as "wilding." This term was used by a group of juveniles who brutally assaulted and raped a woman in Central Park, New York City, in June 1995. The woman was beaten so badly by the "wilding" gang that she almost died. When they were interviewed, the perpetrators could not explain their vicious behavior.

Given that it is almost impossible to anticipate random and spontaneous violent events and that it is difficult to defend against their occurrence, this type of violence is most feared by the general population and, of course, by many children. In the pantheon of American history, the following cases were highly publicized and for that reason are most notable: the assassinations of John F. Kennedy, Martin Luther King, Jr., and Robert Kennedy by apparently psychotic killers; the serial killing of eight student nurses by Richard Speck in Chicago; the mass killing of nine people in a home in Victorville, California; the brutal ritualistic and senseless murders committed by Charles Manson's "family"; the murder of over twenty-five migrant farm workers by Juan Corona; the Hillside Strangler Murders; the some thirty random, serial killings committed by Ted Bundy; the random killing of Ennis Cosby on a lonely road; and the murders perpetrated by Jeffrey Dahmer in Milwaukee, Wisconsin.

Another relatively unpublicized case example occurred in 1973—the murders of more than twenty-eight teenagers over a three-year period in Houston, Texas, by Wayne Henley, David Brooks, and Dean Corll. These senseless, grisly murders were described by Brooks in his statement to the police: "In all, I guess there were between twenty-five and thirty boys killed, and they were buried in three different places. I was present and helped bury many of them but not all of them. . . . On the first one at Sam Rayburn [Reservoir] I helped bury him, and then the next one we took to Sam Rayburn. When we got there, Dean and Wayne found that the first one had come to the surface and either a foot or a hand was above the ground. When they buried this one the second time, they put some type of rock sheet on top of him to keep him down" (*Time*, 1973).

Many killings are committed by two or more killers in concert, in "buddy-killer" form. The so-called Los Angeles Freeway Murders are a case in point. Although several other individuals were involved in the Freeway Murders in Los Angeles, there were two principals—Vernon Butts and William Bonin. Their twenty-one teenage victims, most alleged to to be homosexuals, were sodomized, tortured, and then killed. The following description of Butts provides some of the characteristics of this brand of pathological "buddy-killers."

> When Vernon Butts kept telling his co-workers that he slept in a coffin, they thought he was putting them on. But now that he is accused of being an accomplice to "Freeway Killer" suspect William Bonin, they aren't so sure. What is for sure, investigators say, is that Butts had two coffins in the Norwalk apartment he occupied until last January. One was used as a coffee table and the other was rigged up as a telephone booth. Bonin, a thirty-three-year-old convicted sex offender, has been accused of killing twenty-one victims with assistance from Butts in at least six of the slayings, which authorities said involved torture and homosexual acts. The victims, mostly teen-age boys, were picked up while hitchhiking and their bodies dumped near freeways throughout southern California, giving rise to the "Freeway Killer" label. (Farr and Lindgren, 1980, p. 48)

There has been limited intensive research to date on buddy-murderers. Some of the questions that could be investigated are: Do the two killers set each other off psychologically? What do they talk about during and after their buddy-murders? How does one dominate the other(s)? Is there any kind of superego or moral quotient that surfaces between the two to stop their horrendous spree? Are buddy-murderers individuals whose pathological backgrounds have similarities?

Another development in twentieth-century America was the increase in the number of serial killers. Based on several studies and my own observations, I would conclude that serial killers have the following characteristics. Most are white males twenty-five to thirty-four years of age. They are likely to be intelligent or at least "street smart." They are charming and charismatic, and most of them are sociopathic. Many known serial murderers were born out of wedlock or came from apparently dysfunctional families. As children many were physically, sexually, or emotionally abused. These killers tend to abuse alcohol or drugs, and often this abuse exacerbates their sadistic fantasies. Many were intimately involved with women who had no knowledge of their partner's homicidal activities.

Richard Ramirez, known as "The Nightstalker," is a prime example of a serial murderer who perpetrated senseless violence on a large number of victims. In one year he was alleged to have killed more than fifteen people in a murder spree in California. He was sentenced to life in prison. (In 1996, a seemingly sane woman "fell in love" watching Ramirez on TV and was allowed by the authorities to marry him in prison.)

All of these cases, many of them highly publicized, have their impact on the juvenile delinquency problem. Because of their visibility on TV, some youngsters watch these "negative role models" and emulate them in deviant acts of their own. One example of this impact is the fact that one of the best selling T-shirts in the United States was one with a picture of Charles Manson emblazoned on the front.

✦ Victim-Precipitated Violence

A considerable amount of senseless violence by juveniles has an interactional quality, where the aggressor who initiates the violence often winds up as the victim. A child who comes home crying about being hit may have a perceptive parent who raises the question, "What did you do to provoke being hit?" Victims of violence are often participants in their victimization.

This pattern of violence, termed "victim-precipitated violence," was first analyzed by Hans von Hentig in his classic work, *The Criminal and His Victim* (1948). Von Hentig's concept was further developed and researched by Marvin Wolfgang (1957). Von Hentig and Wolfgang posited that violence has a dual frame of reference that involves both the victim and the perpetrator. Although Wolfgang and Von Hentig refer mainly to the ultimate violence of murder, the concept is also useful in explaining lesser forms of assault and violence. The concept of victim-precipitated violence is relevant to the analysis of violent juveniles and why many juveniles are disproportionately likely to be victims of violence. Wolfgang explains: "In many crimes, especially in criminal homicide, the victim is often a major contributor to the criminal act. Except in cases in which the victim is an innocent bystander and is killed in lieu of an intended victim, or in cases in which a pure accident is involved, the victim may be one of the major pre-cipitating causes of his own demise" (1957, p. 46). Wolfgang initially researched the pattern of victim-precipitated homicide in a study of over 588 consecutive homicides committed in Philadelphia during a four-year period. Wolfgang concluded that 150 cases, or 26 percent, fit the model of victim-precipitated homicide.

Various theories of social interaction, particularly in social psy-chology, have established the framework for the present discussion. In criminological literature, however, von Hentig (1948) provided the most useful theoretical bases for analysis of the victim-offender relationship. In chapter 12 of his book, "The Contribution of the The Victim to the Genesis of Crime," he discussed this "duet frame of crime" and suggested that homi-cide is particularly amenable to analysis in this context. The victim is char-acterized as being the first person in a homicide drama to use physical force directed against his or her subsequent slayer. The victim-precipitated cases are those in which the victim was the first to show and use a deadly weapon and to strike a blow in an altercation—in short, the first to com-mence the interplay or resort to physical violence.

In the context of Von Hentig's and Wolfgang's interactional hypoth-esis, David Abrahamsen (1973), asserted that:

> The relationship between criminal and victim is much more com-plicated than the law would care to acknowledge. The criminal and his victim work on each other unconsciously. We can say that as the criminal shapes the victim, the victim also shapes the crim-inal. While the law looks upon this relationship from an objective, nonemotional viewpoint, the psychological attitude of the partici-pants is quite different. The law differentiates distinctly between the attacker and the victim. But their relationship may be, and often is, quite close, so that their roles are reversed and the victim becomes the determining person, while the victimizer in the end becomes his own victim. . . . Trapped and helpless, and beset by inner conflicts, the murderer encounters his victim, who also is full of conflicts. Through the foreplay—comparable to foreplay pre-ceding sexual intercourse—and interplay between attacker and victim, intentions and motivations may be spelled out, because the protagonists do not understand themselves. Instead they act out what they harbor in their mind. There is a victimizer and a victim; and the border between them during the victimization is as blurred as their self-image. Intertwined with each other, they represent on every level of the conscious and unconscious mind a stream of fluid and transitory emotions that can hardly be deciphered.

In my own research on the crime scenes of violent juvenile delin-quent behavior, I have found that the theory of victim-precipitated violence is a useful model for analyzing violent situations. I would conjecture that about 70 percent of juvenile violence fits this interactional hypothesis. In only about 30 percent of the violent attacks that occur among juveniles is there a clear victim and a clear offender. In most cases there is an interactional process that precedes the violence; the strongest youth is apt to become the "perpetrator," and the weaker youth will become the "victim."

This interactional concept has been integrated into the law. I served as a consultant/expert witness in two cases that are notable in that they reveal how the legal system deals with the senseless violence of juvenile delinquents.

Case 1

I was engaged by the defense in a case that involved a gang murder. The alleged killer was sixteen years old. However, because this was a murder case, it was tried in an adult superior court in Los Angeles before a jury. The defendant, a gangster, admitted that he had stabbed the victim, an individual he perceived as a gangster from an enemy gang, with a large knife on the streets of Hollywood. The defendant claimed that the youth he killed had invaded his turf, that he feared for his life and consequently stabbed the intruder to death.

The defendant claimed what is referred to in the law as "imperfect self-defense." This legal concept alleges that the perpetrator of an act of violence believed that he or she was in imminent danger from another individual and consequently struck the first blow. In this case the defendant claimed the youth he killed was a gangster who appeared on his turf with the trappings and colors of an enemy gang. The defense attorney in the case (who hired me) was not attempting to get an acquittal—he was trying to get the charge of first-degree murder changed to second-degree murder. As in the Menendez Brothers case, the imperfect-self-defense effort was unsuccessful, and the defendant was convicted of first-degree murder and received a life sentence.

Case 2

This case involved a sixteen-year-old youth who was shot six times and as a consequence of his wounds was paralyzed and confined to a wheelchair. The youth's attorneys charged that the pinball and game arcade establishment in a mall where the shooting took place was responsible for their client being shot, because they did not take proper security measures to control this kind of violence. The establishment was a known hangout for Vietnamese gangs, and a number of violent acts had occurred in the past. The victim sued the owners of the establishment and the mall where the shooting took place for $15 million.

I was hired by the defense as a consultant/expert witness. After ana-lyzing a number of depositions of eyewitnesses, the deposition of the "vic-tim" who was suing, the police investigation report, interviews with the local police, and an analysis of the crime scene, I wrote the following report of my findings for the defense attorney who was preparing to go to trial.

Summary Findings of My Research into Case [name of case] as Discussed in My Deposition on February 13, 1997

Based on my forty-five years of research into the structure and behavior of gangs delineated in my two books (*The Violent Gang*, Macmillan, 1962, and *Gangsters*, New York University Press, 1997), the investigation of the Little Saigon area and envi-rons as this general community relates to gang violence, inter-views with Mark Nye, detective, Westminster Police Department Target Gang Unit and various police reports, the analysis of var-ious depositions, and an analysis of the plaintiffs' background and deposition, I have come to the following conclusions about the violent event that took place on November 24, 1994.

1. The Little Saigon area and environs is a high-risk area for gang violence. Given the varied Asian gangs operating in the area, violent gang incidents have occurred throughout the area and could occur at any time throughout this geo-graphic area. This viewpoint is supported by my police drive-along with Detective Nye, who pointed out various gangsters in cars cruising the area.

2. In this context, the TRG gang is a significant gang in this area, and in recent years, according to the police, is respon-sible for many violent incidents, including murder. Notable among the violent incidents perpetrated by TRG gangsters is the case of a TRG home invasion robbery which resulted in murders of a family of five people. In brief, the TRG group is a dangerous and lethal gang, which, according to Detective Nye, has been responsible for approximately twenty gang murders since 1987.

3. It is my opinion that the plaintiff is a member of the TRG gang, and was active in his gangster role the night of the incident. The fact of his TRG tattoo on his chest is clear proof of his affiliation. In my research with several thousand gangsters, I have never known nongangsters who had a gang tattoo on their body. This representation by an outsider would not be tolerated by a gang.

4. His observed belligerent behavior on the evening of the inci-dent reinforces my conclusion that he was acting in the role of a gangster. His behavior as a small individual attacking a large enemy gangster is consistent with an effort to enhance his reputation, or in gang terms his "rep." As one witness stated in her deposition, and as noted in a police report, Pee

Wee (his gang name) struck the first blow by walking up to Lam Nguyen (the accused shooter) and punching him in the face. This witness also stated that seven TRGs jumped in on the plaintiff's side in the gang fight that ensued after the plaintiff struck the first blow. In my opinion the fact that the shooter singled out the plaintiff to receive all of the shots fired would lend credence to the fact that the plaintiff was the main person who began the violence that resulted in the gang fight. The shooter did not shoot anyone else. The plaintiff's behavior in the incident is consistent with the role of a gang member involved in a gang fight.

Summary. I conclude from my analysis of all the data in this case that the plaintiff was the initial perpetrator of the event that backfired into his becoming a victim. He simply was responsible for his own injuries. This is consistent with the suicidal gangster behavior I have observed in thousands of individuals who participate in gang activity. In their continuing efforts to achieve a "rep" and macho power, they place themselves in the vulnerable position of becoming victims of violence. Gangsters are almost always responsible for the physical harm, and sometimes death, they bring upon themselves in the context of "gangbanging" violence. It is my considered opinion that the plaintiff, in his role as a gangster, was responsible for the unfortunate physical condition that resulted from his gangster behavior in the gang fight.

In regard to another aspect of this case, I have observed that it is almost impossible to control the spontaneous gang violence that occurred in this case. Gang violence in a gang area can and does erupt at the slightest provocation of being "dissed" (disrespected), real or imagined conflict, and the motivation of an angry gangster to enhance his macho reputation. Violent gang incidents often explode in the proximity of the most effective law enforcement efforts to control this behavior.

Following are two notable situations that make this point: (1) the Los Angeles Police Department's Crash Unit is especially trained and equipped to control gang violence in South Central Los Angeles—an epicenter of the national gang violence problem. Despite Crash's expertise, numerous gang murders have been perpetrated in the proximity of the Crash Unit when they are on active patrol. Also, in this regard, Detective Nye informed me of an incident involving a gang shooting which took place within 20 feet of a police patrol car in the Westminster area. (2) Gangs tend to dominate the California Department of Corrections prison system, and The California Youth Authorities institutions for delinquents, and despite the high security systems in place, including armed guards on surveillance in the prisons, volatile and often deadly gang violence is a persistent problem in all of California's prisons, including the California Youth Authority institutions. In brief, it is almost impossible to control the spontaneous outburst of violence that is characteristic of violent gang behavior.

Despite my deposition, analysis, and conclusion that the establishment was not liable or responsible for the "victim's" disability, the company that insured the establishment decided not to go to court. They settled the case for $4.5 million.

The pattern of victim-precipitated violence is often acted out by youths who have a chip on their shoulder. Such youths, by their demeanor, provoke violence. And it is often difficult to ascertain who is the offender and who is the victim.

A Paradigm of Patterns of Violence

There are many forms of delinquent violence and many factors that delineate what I would term "logical" from "senseless" violence. Three factors enter into the consideration of all violent behavior: (1) the *legality* of the act; (2) the *sanctioning* of the act within the societal context; and (3) the *rationality* of the act as perceived by most people in the society.

Using these factors, I posit four categories that encompass almost all patterns of violence—including "senseless violence."

1. *Legal, sanctioned, rational violence.* Many violent acts are supported in law, sanctioned, and considered rational. The soldier is rewarded as a hero for the intensity of his violent action. In fact, a nonviolent soldier may, under certain conditions, be court-martialed and executed. Police officers enact another role that is supported by legal violence. Other legally justified violence is found in certain aggressive sports, such as football and boxing, and in certain acts of self-defense.

2. *Illegal, rational, sanctioned violence.* A significant factor in any analysis of violence is social sanction or support. No one would argue that an assault committed by a deceived spouse on an adulterer was not illegal, but many would sanction this violence. Even when homicide is the result, the "unwritten law" has wide support. Other examples of violence that are illegal yet sanctioned and considered rational include violent responses to insults or an attack upon one's honor. This pattern accounts for most youth gang violence. Violence, even when it is illegal, has varying degrees of acceptance within different segments of American society. S. J. Ball-Rokeach (1980) commented on what he termed "social violence," a pattern that fits into this category: "If a violent act is primarily goal-oriented and therefore rational human behavior, then it permits exploration of 'normal' social processes and 'functioning' personal and social systems as possible causes of violence. The issue becomes not whether violence is prescribed, but how violence is incorporated into everyday systems of social action.

Violence caused by 'normal' social and personal processes may be called 'social' violence to distinguish it from 'asocial' violence."

3. *Illegal, nonsanctioned, rational violence.* Some violent acts that are neither legal nor sanctioned are considered rational in a delinquent context. A prevailing form of delinquent act, violence for financial gain, fits into this category. Robbery and assault upon a person or the commission of violence within the framework of a drug deal would be considered rational behavior to a delinquent. Gang violence may or may not be rational. For example, killing an enemy gangster who has infringed on one's drug-selling territory would fall into the category of illegal and nonsanctioned; however, the murder would have a degree of rationality. On the other hand, it could be argued that the drive-by murder involving spraying bullets into another gang's hood is irrational or "senseless" violence.

4. *Illegal, nonsanctioned, irrational violence.* This is the category I define as senseless violence. It includes such varied crimes as William Bonin's "freeway murders"; Whitman's shooting and killing of fifteen people and the wounding of thirty-one from a university tower; the Hillside Strangler murders; the stabbing and bludgeoning to death of a fifteen-year-old polio victim by a teenage gang; the Manson murders; Jeffrey Dahmer's cannibalistic murders; the random killing of Ennis Cosby; and the Menendez brothers' slaughter of their parents. A basic characteristic of this type of violence is that there is no social sheath of rationality to the act. In order to understand this seemingly senseless behavior, the inner psycho-dynamics of the perpetrator must be analyzed. This category of senseless violence includes psychotic delinquent youths who are paranoid and have delusions that people are out to get them. Their response is to retaliate with violence and assault or kill imagined enemies before they can do any harm. From my perspective most "gangbanging" is senseless violence.

A considerable proportion of acts of senseless violence by juveniles can be accounted for by the sociopathic delinquent personality described earlier. An aspect of the sociopathic youth's senseless violence may be termed "existential validation." When a youth with this personality syndrome feels constantly alienated from other human beings, he begins to lose the sense of his own humanity and requires increasingly heavier doses of bizarre and extreme behavior to validate the fact that he really exists. The extreme, violent behavior gives the sociopathic youth a glimmer of emotions when nothing else does. As one gang killer of this type told me in an interview, "When I stabbed him once, I did it again and again, because it really made me feel alive for the first time in my life" (Yablonsky, 1997). At least three of the 1997-1998 school murderers were alienated sociopaths.

Eminent playwright Arthur Miller (1962), drawing upon a study he made of gangs in a New York City neighborhood, described this pattern of sociopathic senseless violence as stemming, in part, from the malaise of boredom:

> The boredom of the delinquent is remarkable mainly because it is so little compensated for, as it may be among the middle classes and the rich who can fly down to the Caribbean or to Europe, or refurnish the house, or have an affair, or at least go shopping. The delinquent is stuck with his boredom, stuck inside it, stuck to it, until for two or three minutes he "lives"; he goes on a violent raid around the corner and feels the thrill of risking his skin or his life as he smashes a bottle filled with gasoline on some other kid's head. In a sense, it is his trip to Miami. It makes his day. It is his shopping tour. It gives him something to talk about for a week. It is life. Standing around with nothing coming up is as close to dying as you can get. Unless one grasps the power of boredom, the threat of it to one's existence, it is impossible to "place" the delinquent as a member of the human race.

The commission of a violent murder is not the equivalent of a vacation from boredom; however, many violent acts are committed to give the perpetrator a sense of "being," or "existential validation." An act of murder committed by the central character in Albert Camus' novel *The Stranger* is justified in part because it made the murderer feel some emotion where none had existed. Many acts of senseless violence are committed by delinquents in order to experience a "high." Young people play "chicken" in two cars headed for a collision. They dare each other to commit senseless, suicidal acts, fight with each other, and go out on "gang bangs" out of the feeling of boredom described by Miller and explained by the concept of "existential validation."

A Prototypical Act of Illegal, Irrational, and Nonsanctioned Senseless Violence: The Milpitas Murder

Juvenile violence is not restricted to gang violence, adolescent drug deaths, and suicide patterns of children from a lower socioeconomic family background. The case history of a murder committed by a middle-class juvenile from a "good home" in Milpitas, California, exemplifies a type of senseless violence that may portend a pattern for the twenty-first century. The killer and his friends who were brought in on this event showed little emotional response to the murder, which in some respects foreshadowed the spate of school killings in the late 1990s.

This case became a spectator event when the young murderer, who had killed his girlfriend for no apparent reason, brought his friends to witness the dead victim's body over a period of several weeks. During this time no one revealed the secret of the murder. Elizabeth Kaye (1982) described some of the forces at work in this senseless murder and its bizarre aftermath.

> At moments in history, events occur that mirror society in so fundamental a way that they become metaphorical and reveal us to ourselves with the indisputable clarity of a traffic signal. An event such as this gave rise to the notoriety of Milpitas, a Northern California town. On a Tuesday, a sixteen-year-old named Jacques Broussard cut school with a fourteen-year-old named Marcy Conrad. This, in itself, was unexceptional. Jacques and Marcy were stoners.
>
> Stoners smoke a lot of pot and cut school often. They are also given, as are many children nowadays, to the utterly unchildish apprehension that life is not necessarily getting better, for they are part of the first generation of Americans raised by parents who no longer have reason to believe the sustaining tenet of the American dream: that the reward for hard work and sacrifice is the privilege of making one's children's lives far better than one's own. As members of that generation, they view the world through the tarnished prism of their parents' disappointment and conclude that they may as well live for today since being young may very well be the best thing that will ever happen to them.
>
> So it may have been in the name of living for today that Jacques and Marcy cut school and eventually went to his house, a one-story, dark green house six blocks from hers, with a Beware of the Dog sign on the door, in the sort of neighborhood where houses are neatly centered between tiny front and back yards and where the color television is, as a rule, the focal point of the living room. Homes such as these were once a mere rung on the American ladder of acquisition and success, but in this era of diminished prospects they simultaneously constitute the end of the line and the apogee of a certain level of middle-class attainment. Jacques's family had lived in this house for many years, and it was here that his mother had died. His mother's death was one of two things that set Jacques apart from everyone. The other was that he was black, while all his friends were white. Of these two things, his mother's death was the more significant by far.
>
> Gloria Broussard died when her son was eight years old. Jacques was the one who found her body, so the impact of her death transcended grief and became one of abject horror. On what was an otherwise ordinary day Jacques came home from school, and the harbinger that something was dreadfully wrong was the living room rug, which was sodden with water. When he heard the shower running he treaded his way to the bathroom door, opened it, made his way through the water-soaked room, and drew back the shower curtain. He saw his mother's naked body. She had died of natural causes a few hours earlier.
>
> Jacques never quite recovered from that day, and all his friends knew it, which is why it was understood among them that

they never breathed a word to Jacques about his mother. But Marcy Conrad dispensed with this crucial amenity, it seems, and said something about her, something truly mean. Or so Jacques told his friends. He also told them that is why he killed her. Marcy became a corpse on Jacques's living-room couch.

The corpse was half naked, and this was because before Marcy died Jacques either made love to her or raped her. Were stoners at all interested in irony or observation, Jacques might have been taken by the fact that the corpse was clad in nothing but a tank top with the words *Spoiled Rotten* on it and a necklace decorated with a gold marijuana leaf-shape charm.

Once Marcy was dead Jacques was confronted with a succession of practical considerations, to which he apparently responded quite methodically. First he went outside, backed his pickup truck into the garage, and set about gathering up Marcy's purse, jeans, and schoolbooks. He then lifted her body from the couch and began the formidable task of getting it out of the house. Jacques weighed 280 pounds and stood six foot four, and Marcy was just a little girl, but she was dead weight now. Jacques would later tell his friends that he had one hell of a time moving her. But finally he got the body into the back of his truck.

The white truck was an unlikely hearse, with its KOME and KSJO stickers that appear on the cars of most stoners, letters that also appear as patches on their jeans and as decals on their schoolbooks. They are the call letters of two rock stations. The only thing the average stoner likes as well as weed is fine rock music . . . . Jacques drove on to Old Marsh Road, and then the scenery abruptly changed, and the trees and grass beside the road became as sensuously moist as those in the center of a rain-soaked forest.

The spot is a gathering place for many young people in Milpitas, and the pungent blanket of fallen leaves and bright green clover that covers the earth shares its space with empty, crushed beer cans and shards of broken wine bottles. It is here that Jacques scattered Marcy's purse, jeans, shoes, and schoolbooks. Then he drove on, a half mile or so, to where Old Marsh Road merges again with the sun, and where the land to the south of the road slants down sharply to a barbwire fence. . . . This place was selected by Jacques Broussard as his final destination. He stopped the truck and took the half-naked corpse from it. He carried it down the incline and pushed it beneath the barbwire fence. The body rolled and was stopped by the thick trunk of the oak tree. There it remained for the next two days, in the sun and the wind and the cold and the dark, face down.

In the days that followed, the murder of Marcy Conrad assumed its allegorical significance and ultimately became that rare event of equal interest to newspaper reporters and to poets. It is at this stage in the narrative that the focus shifts and both the murderer and victim become oddly peripheral to its telling. Events center instead on nine young people, all of whom are self-described stoners.

In retrospect, it seemed inevitable that others be drawn into it. It was not all that likely that a sixteen-year-old could indefinitely keep to himself the amazing fact that he has just become a killer. So it was, on the day following the murder, that three teenage boys were told of it by Jacques Broussard himself. They did not believe him, so he took them up the hill and showed them what all the horror movies and all the televised violence they had ever seen could not have conceivably prepared them for, just as they had hardened them to it.

There was no requiem at the oak tree. There was only gazing. And there was this thought in the mind of one of the boys: "Jacques is in real trouble now." The hours that followed were extraordinary only for their ordinariness, only for the ways the three boys managed to proceed as if nothing had occurred that was in the least unusual. One fell asleep in his room listening to the radio and did not wake up for dinner. Another would later say he thought the body was a mannequin and didn't think any more about it. The third was met at his door by his mother, who told him not to come in. She had discovered he had stolen her marijuana. This was something that had happened before; he had been warned that he would not be welcome in the house if it happened again.

The boy's name is John Hanson. He went out into the night and later met up with a friend named Robby Engle. He told Engle about the corpse, and when Engle wanted to see it, Hanson said he would show it to him the next day since it was now too dark to see anything. Instead, they walked to Engle's house, went to his room to smoke some dope, and fell asleep.

The night air was cool. In the hills where Marcy Conrad's body lay it was even cooler. Both boys slept dreamlessly. All the next morning at Milpitas High, the huge bulk of Jacques Broussard traversed the grassy campus, telling students that he had killed Marcy and conveying that information with the reckless resolve of a man committing suicide because he is afraid of dying.

Among the students, many of whom knew Marcy, though she had been enrolled at another school, the consensus was that Jacques couldn't have killed her, that he was simply "bragging" about it. Students at Milpitas High do not place too high a premium on the subtleties of words, which may be why the thought that bragging about a murder is kind of a contradiction in terms did not seem to occur to any of them.

Later in the day, Jacques, perhaps resenting that the most significant thing he had ever done had proven too significant to seem feasible, took a young girl and two boys up the hill so they might make witness to his claim, and having done so they, too, joined the circle of silence, increasing its number to six. And now the passive silence was augmented by an action, when one of the boys aided Broussard in covering the corpse with a plastic bag and a scattering of leaves. Eventually he would be charged as an accessory after the fact, sentenced to three years at a county ranch for delinquent boys, and his existence would become a study in the curious way an entire life can be irrevocably altered in a single moment.

After lunch hour at the high school, John Hanson made a second sojourn to Old Marsh Road. He took Engle and two other friends, Mike Irvin and Dave Leffler, with him. Hanson was low on dope that day, so he bet Irvin a joint that the human form at the foot of the giant tree was an actual corpse. All right, he was told, but if it isn't, you give me your shoes and socks and walk home barefoot.

It was on this note that they began to drive up the hill. They parked the car just as the oak tree became discernible. They scrambled down the incline. They stopped when they saw what they had come to see. The four young men stared down at Marcy Conrad's earthly remains. Moments passed; nothing was said. The only sound was the insistent yammering of a few distant birds. Then Hanson wanted to collect on his bet. Leffler said, "This is no time to smoke," but they climbed up the incline and smoked anyway.

On the way down the hill Mike Irvin said he was going to the police. Hanson and Engle wanted to go back to class. "As far as we're concerned," Engle said, "the body doesn't exist." All Hanson could think of was that he had seen the corpse the day before and not reported it and that if he got involved at this point he might be arrested as an accessory. And he thought of how he had hated the time he once spent in juvenile hall after committing a burglary. And he thought of one of the terms of his parole, which was that he not associate with Mike Irvin, his alleged partner in that crime, the same young man who wanted to go to the police at this moment.

So Hanson and Engle went back to class, and Irvin and Leffler drove to the Milpitas police station. Leffler waited in the car. It was left to Irvin to walk alone up the sidewalk and open the thick glass door and, once inside, tell of the incredible thing ha had seen in the hills, so that 48 hours after the murder of Marcy Conrad, the silence of the young people who knew she had died would be forever broken.

While Mike Irvin was in the office of the Milpitas police, Sergeant Garry Meeker was driving on Interstate 680. Meeker is the homicide and assaults investigator for Santa Clara County. . . . He takes a cop's pride in being tough and when he is summoned to view a corpse tries to regard it not as a body but as a piece of evidence. He often apologizes for the coldness of that attitude but has never doubted that if he's going to do his job, that's the way to do it.

It was two-thirty in the afternoon when he got the radio dispatch about the body up on Old Marsh Road. Meeker knew the area well. For one thing, it was something of a dump ground for corpses. . . . When Meeker got to the oak tree, five of his colleagues were already there, men who were also paid to think of

Marcy Conrad as a juvenile female, deceased. Before they left, two or three cars came up the hill and turned around when they drew near the police.

Meeker did not give it much thought at the time; an hour or so would pass before he would learn of Broussard's boasts and the young people who had not reported the murder, and then he figured that the cars must have been those of young kids coming to see for themselves whether or not Broussard was lying. The Milpitas police picked up Jacques Broussard later that evening. Shortly afterward Meeker questioned the young people who had gone up the hill to see Marcy's body.

It had been an unsettling experience, though it was not the murder that was troubling. Meeker had seen a lot of murder victims, and murder itself was as old as dirt. There was really nothing else you could say about it. But this case was different, and what made it so was the silence of the youngsters.

"They were supposedly normal people," Meeker said. "But people who see dead bodies get shook. It bothers them. It still bothers me if you want to know the truth. But these kids . . . it didn't seem to bother them." The silence of the children was the issue. The silence was the metaphor. And the only question of pertinence was, metaphor for what? "That's a moral breakthrough somewhere," Meeker concluded. "That's what this thing represents. And it's not the kids' fault. The kids are a product of what we made them."

The murder was shocking, in and of itself but not nearly as unsettling as the circle of young people who knew what had happened and maintained their silence for forty-eight hours. It wasn't "reefer madness" that produced their response. Smoking marijuana does not usually produce the extreme indifference noted in this case. It may be, however, that a steady day-to-day diet in our violent society of smoking dope, dropping pills, watching horrendous acts of violence on the television and in the movies, and the continuing nonuse of intellectual capacities lead to a cool boredom that produces this indifference to human life and breeds senseless violence. Unless there is some profound intervention in the treatment of delinquents, this senseless violence will increase in the next millennium.

PART 3

The Gang Problem

CHAPTERS

CHAPTER 7

THE CONTEMPORARY GANG PROBLEM

Graffiti is a method used by gangs for staking out their territory. It is an "art form" found in most large American cities.

On any given evening, along with the weather report and sports scores, the TV news in large and small cities throughout America present the toll of assaults and deaths that result from gang violence. The incidence of gang violence over the years has escalated, and the patterns of gang violence have become increasingly lethal.

Juvenile gangster violence and gang warfare in the United States during the twentieth century may be divided into four periods. The first fifty years were characterized by youthful camaraderie, a concern with territorial control, various acts of delinquency, and violence—largely involving fistfights and knife assaults. The second identifiable period is the post–World War Two era—the 1950s to the mid-1960s. This period showed a shift toward violence related to territorial disputes acted out in more severe ways, including stabbings and an occasional murder using a gun. The third period, the 1960s through the early 1980s, saw a hiatus in gangs, gang violence, and warfare, partly as a consequence of various quasipolitical groups like the Black Panthers and the Brown Berets. These groups and others involved many black and Chicano youths who might have participated in gangbanging violence in relatively positive efforts for social change through political activities. The current period is one of contemporary violent gang problems, which is entwined with the business of drugs and characterized by drive-by murders, high-powered lethal automatic weapons, and extreme violence.

Types of Gangs

Based on my research and work with gangs, especially in New York, Texas, and California, I have identified three basic types of gangs: (1) social gangs, (2) delinquent gangs, and (3) violent gangs.

The Social Gang

A social gang has a relatively permanent organization that typically centers its activities in a specific stable location such as a restaurant, candy store, or clubhouse. All the members know one another, and there is a sense of comradeship and a "we" feeling. Some wear club jackets or sweaters with an insignia that identifies the members to the external community. Most of their activities are "socially oriented" and require a degree of responsible social interaction in the group. Their activities include organized athletic participation, personal discussions, organizing dances, and other socially acceptable activities characteristic of adolescence. Membership is not based upon "self-protection" (as in the violent gang) or on social athletic prowess (as in an athletic team) but upon feelings of mutual attraction and a level of camaraderie.

This type of gang seldom participates in delinquent behavior, gang warfare, or property theft except under unusual conditions. Members become involved in minor gang clashes but only under great pressure. The social gang has considerable permanence. Its members grow up together and often develop permanent lifelong friendships that continue when they become adults. The social gangs of the 1950s were a natural part of the community, and many youths of that era belonged to the community centers that were part of the neighborhood.[1]

The Delinquent Gang

Delinquent gangs persist today. These collectivities are primarily organized to carry out various illegal acts. The "social" interaction part of the gang is a secondary factor. Prominent among the delinquent gang's behavior pattern is the commerce of drugs, especially heroin, burglary, petty thievery, mugging, assault for profit (not simply kicks), and other illegal acts directed at monetary gain. Delinquent gangs are generally tightly organized cliques that steal or commit acts of robbery with maximum effectiveness. In recent years some gang researchers have termed the delinquent gang "corporate" or "entrepreneurial." In the past decade, the most prevalent form of this type of gang is involved in the drug trade and to some extent in carjacking for profit.

The delinquent gang is comprised of a cohesive group of emotionally stable youths socialized into illegal patterns of behavior. Violence is employed as a means of acquiring material and financial profit. In contemporary violent gangs, delinquent gang cliques are often referred to as "crews" that operate within the framework of the larger multipurpose violent gang. Wannabees and middle range gangsters doing work in the gang often become part of a delinquent gang crew to earn a reputation and status in the overall violent gang.

The Violent Gang

Violent gangs have changed significantly over the past fifty years. A primary function of the violent gang in the 1950s was to provide a vehicle for

---

1. See Frederic Thrasher, *The Gang* (Chicago: University of Chicago Press, 1926) and William Whyte, *Street Corner Society* (Chicago: University of Chicago Press, 1943). Their research is presented in more detail in chapter 8.

acting out hostility and aggression to satisfy the continuing and momentary emotional needs of its members. The gangs were convenient and malleable structures quickly adaptable to the needs of emotionally disturbed youths who were unable to fulfill the demands required for participation in more normal groups.

In the 1950s, members of violent gangs killed and maimed for no logical purpose. They were groups whose members, when later describing their killing of a youth in a gang fight, commented: "I just went like that, and I stabbed him with the bread knife. You know, I was drunk, so I just stabbed him. [Laughs] He was screamin' like a dog" (Yablonsky, 1997). One of his brother gang members who did not want to be left out of the action, said: "After he was stabbed he was layin' on the ground bleeding. I was watching him. I didn't wanna hit him. Then I kicked him twice. He was laying on the ground looking up at us. I kicked him on the jaw or someplace; then I kicked him in the stomach. That was the least I could do, was kick him" (Yablonsky, 1997).

Violence for acceptance and acquiring a reputation was common in the gangs of the 1950s and probably set the model for contemporary violent gangs. As one gang member who participated in a gang murder told me: "I didn't want to be like . . . you know, different from the other guys. Like they hit him, I hit him. In other words, I didn't want to show myself as a punk. You know, ya always talkin', 'Oh, man, when I catch a guy, I'll beat him up,' and all of that, you know. And after you go out and catch a guy, and you don't do nothin' they say, 'Oh, man, he can't belong to no gang, because he ain't gonna do anything' "(Yablonsky, 1997).

The contemporary violent gang differs from violent gangs of the past in several significant ways:

1. *Gun firepower.* Today's gangs have access to and pack more lethal weapons than at any time in the history of America.

2. *Interracial violence.* In the first half of the twentieth century, minority gangs tended to band together and fight gangs from different racial and ethnic backgrounds. Today's gangs, especially black and Chicano gangs, participate in internecine warfare, with black on black and Chicano on Chicano violence.

3. *The use and commerce of drugs.* In the past fifty years there has been a marked increase in the involvement of gangsters in the use and dealing of drugs.

4. *The multipurpose gang.* In the past, gangs tended to have simple functions for their participants. Youths joined gangs for a sense of belonging and to "protect" their territory. Today, gangs provide more deviant

opportunities for their participants, including violent activities, drug use, the commerce of drugs, and the possibility for participating in the illegal activities of organized burglary and robbery.

Since there are diverse definitions of the word *gang*, it is useful to clearly define today's violent gang:

1. All gangs have a name and a territorial neighborhood base, and they maintain a fierce proprietary interest in their neighborhood. They fight for the territory they claim as their own and attack any interlopers—members of other gangs—who come into their "hood."

2. Joining a gang often involves a form of "jumping in" ritual that ranges from informal verbal acceptance to a violent initiation rite; leaving the gang takes many forms.

3. Delinquent and criminal acts involving burglary and theft are important gang activities for achieving a "rep" (reputation) and status in the gang.

4. Senseless violence, including drive-by shootings and "gangbanging" (fighting other gangs), is a basic gang activity.

5. The commerce of drugs, their use, and violent acts for the maintenance of drug territory are part of the gang configuration.

6. Gangs provide social life and camaraderie that usually involves gambling, getting high, hanging out, and partying.

Violent Black and Chicano Gangs—In and Out of Prison

Various types and forms of gangs exist in the United States, such as white gangs in urban and suburban areas, motorcycle gangs, white skinhead racist gangs, Asian gangs, Jamaican gangs, South American gangs, independent female gangs that are unconnected to male gangs, and other groups that could be characterized as gangs. Many of these gang-type collectivities are responsible for acts of racism, violence and crime. These gangs, however, are not nearly as prevalent as black and Chicano male gangs. Most of the gang problems in urban areas throughout the United States are caused by violent black and Chicano male gangs.

Black gangs occur in some form in the "hoods" of almost all American cities across the United States. For the obvious reasons of migration and immigration, and the proximity of many Southwest cities to the

Mexican border, a large number of Chicano or Hispanic gangs are found in the Southwest. Puerto Rican gangs are located on the East Coast, especially in New York.

Some Characteristics of Chicano and Black Gangs

Chicano gangs and black gangs have many similarities. Chicano gangs tend to involve several generations in the stable barrios, such as those in Los Angeles, El Paso or San Antonio in the Southwest. Growing up in a barrio, therefore, tends to present a youngster with gang role models and a history of gangs. In contrast, black gangs tend to be more transient.

Another difference between these two types of gangs is related to family background. Most Chicano gangsters tend to be socialized in cohesive, albeit dysfunctional families. Black gangsters are likely to be raised in dysfunctional families with divorced or absentee fathers. Many black gangsters, because their parents are separated or divorced, live with their grandparents or are out on their own at an early age.

In terms of the commerce and use of drugs, Chicano gangs, over the years, have become heavily involved with marijuana and heroin, although more recently crack-cocaine has come onto their scene. Black gangsters in the past were involved with heroin and more recently deal and use crack-cocaine. Black and Chicano gangs are similar in their participation in the basic violent gang activities of drive-by shootings, gangbanging, delinquency, drugs, and crime.

Chicano Gangs

Diego Vigil (1988) describes Chicano gangs in California and in cities throughout the Southwest. He notes that Chicano gangs are made up largely of young males from thirteen to twenty-five years of age. According to Vigil, the Chicano gang is a response to the pressure of street life and serves to give some barrio youths a feeling of familial support, goals and directives, and sanctions and guides.

Vigil states that most Chicano gang activities are similar to those found in any neighborhood where adolescents congregate.

> They talk, joke, plan social events, and exchange stories of adventure and love. Their alcohol consumption and drug use shows some parallels with that of other American adolescents. Yet it is their other, violent, socially disruptive activities that distinguish gang members from most adolescents. Reflecting the tendency among adolescents to develop new modes of dress and

speech, Chicano gang members have adopted a distinctive street
style of dress, speech, gestures, tattoos, and graffiti. (1988, p. 45)

The gang's style is called *cholo*, a centuries-old term referring to
Latin American Indians who are partially acculturated to Hispanic-based
cultures. The term when applied to Chicano gangsters reflects the cultural
transition of Mexican Americans in the Southwest, a process strongly
affected by underclass forces and street requisites. Many of the *cholo* customs are related to identification with the gang, although many nongang
members in a barrio copy the style. Vigil observes that there is a wide difference among members in degree of commitment to the gang, and that
youths with the most problematic lives tend to become the most core participants in the Chicano gang.

Joan Moore (1978), like Vigil, produced some significant contributions to the understanding of Chicano gangs. She perceived of Chicano
gangs as fiercely territorial. The gang's major concerns, according to
Moore, were "protecting" their territory by fighting for it when they deemed
it necessary and using drugs, especially heroin. According to Moore, all
Chicano gangs are fighting gangs, and most, if not all, use drugs. In fact, the
gang is the principal context for both the use and marketing of heroin. She
noted that the Chicano youth gang is a specialized structure of the barrio
and has its own set of values, norms, traditions, and concepts of status and
honor. The gang *klika* (clique or "set") usually involves a lifelong membership and a basic reference group for some but not all members of the gang.
A meaningful source of cohesiveness is related to fighting for their barrio.
During adulthood, the Chicano gangsters' primary loyalty may be reinforced by confrontations with racism and experiences in various custodial
institutions (Moore, 1978, p. 132).

Culture Conflict and Chicano Gangs

In general, as a partial consequence of being in a minority position in a new
community, immigrant parents often have difficulty providing effective
socialization for their children. Many sociologists have pointed out how
this problem of culture conflict, the conflict of norms from one society to
another, can lead to delinquent behavior and the formation of gangs by the
children of immigrants. The factor of culture conflict is significant in the formation of Chicano gangs. For example, many children of Mexican immigrant families are affected by language differences at home and at school.
The lower socioeconomic status of their parents and poor living conditions
also affect youths, who turn to the gang for status and recognition that is not
accorded them in the larger society.

The immigrant parents are consumed with succeeding economically and socially in the United States, and the family structure is often severely affected in the process. This was true of the Jewish, Irish, and Italian families on the lower East Side of New York and black families in New York, Detroit, and Chicago. In recent years, many Asian youths have also created gangs in an effort to cope with the cultural conflict they and their families confront in the new society.

The context of such social factors as culture and language conflict, a lower socioeconomic status, poor living conditions as compared to families in the larger society, and to some degree discrimination and prejudice has spurred the formation of Chicano gangs on both coasts. In the Southwest, there are many barrio Mexican-American gangs; and on the East Coast, especially in New York, culture conflict has resulted in the creation of Puerto Rican gangs.

Black Gangs

Black gangs represent a large proportion of the violent gangs in large and small cities throughout the United States. They generally emanate from and are populated by alienated and hostile youths who in many ways experience varied forms of prejudice and discrimination. These youths feel a sense of despair and hopelessness about their opportunities for success through the normal pathways to success in the larger society. The gang provides them with a pseudocommunity and a sense of power that they do not experience in the institutions of the larger society.

The majority of young men who are raised in the black ghettos of America rise above the deleterious social forces that exist in their hood and become hardworking and successful citizens. However, given the poverty of many black ghettos, those young men who experience the most negative social pressures of their depressed socioeconomic situation create the violent gang as a viable option for success and achievement. In the gang they can achieve a sense of personal power, and the gang serves as a vehicle through which they can act out their rage about the hopeless situation they experience. For these alienated and rebellious youths, the violent gang becomes a vehicle for expressing their personal feelings of hopelessness and rage, and at the same time, provides them with a kind of family and community.

A component that fosters the formation of the violent gangs is the breakdown of the family. A disproportionate number of black youths grow up without fathers. And too many black gang youths "father" children without any responsibility for their proper socialization or welfare. One of the key factors highlighted in the much heralded 1995 Million Man March on

Washington was the necessity for black fathers to effectively assume responsibility for their families.

Another significant cause of black gangsters' rage is the discrimination blacks experience in American society. Young black men find when they are in white communities that people tend to fear them. In general, they find that they are likely to be the last hired and the first fired. The police, who represent the larger society's law enforcement, too often target young black men unfairly in their policing activities. An astounding statistic cited by the National Institute of Justice[2] is that around 30 percent of all young black men are enmeshed in the criminal justice system—courts, jails, prisons, and probation or parole.

The following case history of a Los Angeles "original gangster" (OG) Crip follows a prototypical black gangster through his gang life cycle. Los Angeles has been a center of gang violence, and the Crip gang structure and function have been exported throughout the United States.

Ed's Story: Case History of an OG Crip

The fiery, violent crucible of the 1965 Watts riots in Los Angeles and the despair in the hood that followed in part influenced the formation of two now notorious black gangs, the Crips and the Bloods. These gangs and their gang forms have spread to hoods all over America. Ed (not his real name) was a prototypical Crip who rose in the ranks from a wannabee to an OG. He grew up in Watts and South Central areas of Los Angeles, and from the age of nine ran with a number of gangs in his hood. He was on the scene when the first Crips gang began in 1968. Among the many notorious Crips that he knew over the years was Monster Kody, with whom he spent four years in cell block C in California's Soledad prison. Ed did it all. At one time or another he had participated in gangbanging, drive-bys, and the Crips' drug business, and he had organized and directed an armed robbery crew that specialized in holding up jewelry stores. Along the way he participated in several gang murders.

Ed rose through the ranks of the Crips to become a respected OG. His thirty-year run with the Crips from their inception, in and out of prison, reveals this black gang's structure, function, and activities in dramatic detail from a gang expert's point of view.

The first time I met Ed was in 1995. I had traveled to the Texas Department of Correction's Beaumont Prison to carry out a series of group and individual research interviews with young gangsters incarcerated in

2. OJJDP, Internet, 1998.

this medium security prison. Ed, at that time, had become a responsible citizen. He had been drug and crime free for over five years as a consequence of his treatment and participation in Arizona's Amity Therapeutic Community program and was working as a paraprofessional staff employee for Amity in the Beaumont prison. Given the fact that he was now a law-abiding citizen who trusted me because we were colleagues in our work with incarcerated gang youths at Amity, he felt free to fully reveal his criminal past with considerable insight and candor.

On one of my visits to the Beaumont prison to direct a gang focus group, Ed was standing at the front gate of the prison ready to usher me into the special cell block within the walls that was known as Amistad de Tejas. This was an Amity Therapeutic Community project in the cell block for about four hundred prisoners, most of whom were black and Chicano gangsters. The project was administered by a staff of forty ex-criminal/addicts, including Ed, who had been rehabilitated in the Amity Therapeutic Community facility located at that time in Tucson, Arizona.

Accompanying Ed at the front gate was thirty-seven-year-old Sheila, the director of the therapeutic community prison project, herself a former addict/criminal who had been clean for over ten years and who was a valued employee of the Amity Therapeutic Community. As Ed and Sheila ushered me into the Amity Project cell block, they received a flow of friendly greetings from inmates who were in various prison big-yards behind barbed wire fences, taking their recreation hour. I basked in the reflected glow of the inmates' acceptance and apparent affection for Ed, Sheila, and the Amity program. (The therapeutic community approach is discussed more fully in chapter 7.) Over a two-day period, because of the trust that was accorded Ed, Sheila, and the Amity staff, I was able to garner some significant research data through interviews with individual gangsters and several special and extraordinary gang focus groups. Because my respondents truly liked and accepted Ed and the Amity program, they were exceptionally open and forthcoming about their life as gangsters in and out of prison.

In the process of several focused gang research groups, with Ed at my side, I was able to learn about his life as a Crip. He had "been down" with the South Central Los Angeles Crips gang from the age of twelve for a span of almost twenty-five years in and out of California prisons. He had been an active OG participant in the gang through various phases of the gang's development and growth. At the time we met, he had been out of the gang and drug free for five years. This gave him a unique perspective on his former life as a Crip. My bonding with Ed as a friend and colleague involved a significant element of trust, and my several intensive interviews with him provided an unusually revealing and valuable case history of a Crip gangster.

I was born in Los Angeles in 1956 and grew up in Watts. I had six brothers and two sisters. My father left us when I was four. My mother had to raise all of us, and of course she had a helluva time trying to keep the family going. I've since learned that we had what you all would call a dysfunctional family. Also, Watts was what you might call a dysfunctional neighborhood. The message in Watts was that everything that was right was wrong, and everything that was wrong was right. I was fucked up from the beginning.

We moved from Watts to another South Central Los Angeles neighborhood, but I brought my stealing and going to juvenile hall along with me to the new hood. All of my six brothers, with the exception of my oldest brother, who was raised in the South, went to prison for various offences. Three of them, including me, did some long, hard time in the state prisons. I eventually went to Soledad a few times, and one of my brothers was in Folsom.

When I was around ten or eleven, I began to hang out with a small gang of kids called the Pigmies. They came from a family of around twenty kids, and we all used to go into stores and steal shit. At thirteen, after several trips to juvenile court and detention in the county's juvenile jail, I was sent to a juvenile camp for various thefts, burglaries, and stealing cars right off of people. The new word for that is carjacking. Back then it was just car theft.

One of my older brothers was in a gang called the "Ex-Cons." In South Central Los Angeles you were automatically in a gang if you lived in the hood. When I was around twelve, I joined by just going along with the homies. There was no big initiation like they talk about these days. I think most of those jumping-in stories are bullshit. Alls you have to do to be down is start running with the homies and do what they do. Back then you just had to show you had heart and you began to do what the older dudes did. This involved stealing, burglaries, violence, and of course helping out in gangbanging when your turf was invaded or disrespected.

Around that time in 1967, when I was gangbanging and all that, we didn't pay any attention to black politics. I now know a lot more about political leaders like Ron Karenga and of course Martin Luther King, Jr. The only group we paid any attention to and respected were the Black Panthers' chapter in South Central Los Angeles. But we were still doing our gang thing, and they didn't affect our crime and gangbanging.

Around that time our gang was called the Avenues. Most of us did weight lifting, and we had like twenty-inch arms. In those days, if you had the muscles, you had the power. We weren't into any heavy violence with guns. It was mainly stealing, especially from people in other areas. Like we would fight a guy and take his nice leather coat. We would go to parties, drink, smoke weed, and shit like that. That we would get into fistfights, sometimes knives, and just bust some heads.

At that time, the Avenues was a close-knit neighborhood gang around Hoover Avenue in around a one square mile area. We had about forty guys, and we all knew each other. I had around ten to twelve arrests and did a few tours at the Probation Camps for burglaries and robberies.

Along the way I became a Crip. The Crips began around 1968. The name came about in a funny way. At that time we were doing a lot of robberies. We were mugging a lot of people on the streets when the situation was right. A rich target for a mugging were some of these Japanese ladies who lived in the hood. We found out that the cops in the area from the 77th Division of the LAPD had these block meetings with the citizens, including the Japanese ladies. At these meetings, citizens were told [that] if someone was robbing you the thing to do was to scream, make a lot of noise, and wave your arms so the police will come.

After one of these police block meetings a group of old Japanese ladies were walking on Central Avenue. A group of dudes, including Raymond Washington, a well-known OG who was the leader of his gang, started to rob them and take their purses. The old ladies started yelling and making noise, the gang ran, and the police came. The women were all excited when they were talking to the police. And one Japanese lady, who could hardly speak English, kept repeatedly yelling "a crip, he was a crip." The police finally figured out that one of the attackers had a cast on his leg, and the woman was trying to say she had been attacked by a "cripple." So that's how the name Crip came about.

After that, our dudes accepted the name Crips for our gang. Another group from Pirue Street who were our enemies began to stand up to us. They called themselves the Pirus and later on they changed their name to the Bloods. Other gang sprung up around the area using the name Crips, like the West Side Crips.

We were the original gangsters from the streets, and that was where the label OG Crips came about. Our original group of guys became known as OGs. The dudes who joined in the camps or CYA [California Youth Authority] were known as "jailhouse crips," and there were some wannabees. Yes, we did use that expression back then for kids who were claiming things they weren't and had not yet put in their work. We would use expressions back then like OG, jailhouse, or a wannabee Crip.

I'll give you an example of a wannabee. If some dude wanted to be down with the gang and they weren't in, we OGs would say, "You wannabee in the gang, well you're going to have to put in some work by taking this gun and shoot someone." For example, there was this young kid around fourteen, and he wanted to be with us all the time and go to parties and things. We liked him and we let him be with us. One time we had this problem, and we went on a drive-by. I said, "You wannabee with us, take this gun, and when we spot these motherfuckers we'll see what you do." So when it was going down, he took the gun and shot this guy standing in front of his house. I don't know whether he killed him because we didn't stop to check it out, but I saw the guy go down.

Some OGs would use wannabees to do their dirty work. For example, in a burglary it can be dangerous to enter a house. You don't always know if there is some motherfucker sitting there with a gun who might blow you away. So you might say to a wannabee who's with you on his first job, "You go in the window first, cause you're smaller." Or you might hand the kid a gun in a store robbery.

When we would do a drive-by, you never knew for sure if you killed anybody. None of us really had any training with guns. Everything would be spur of the moment, and you were never sure exactly who you hit. You try to do as much damage as you can. And you might look in the paper the next day to see if you killed anyone, but you can't be sure. I'm sure that over the years I killed three people, one in a drive-by and two times in robberies. Other times, I never stopped to find out if a guy I shot was just wounded or dead. The advice I was always given by my homies was, "Fuck man, don't worry about it, what's done is done."

In those days we would do some crazy shit like going to a funeral home and fucking up our dead enemy's casket and even his body. We were pretty crazy. After we killed a guy we would sometimes do some more shooting at the funeral parlor because we knew our enemy's homeboys were going to be there. Once me and a couple of my homeboys got arrested for shooting up a funeral. This was around the third time we had done this crazy shit, and the police were waiting for us. To this day, if you see a dead homie's funeral, you can bet his homies will be there with guns, and the police will be watching for an attack by his enemies.

You know, Lew, when I'm telling you these things, I can't believe I did this shit like fucking up some dude's body at a funeral home, but it's good for me to get all of this shit out of me. You have to know that back then my mom was working two jobs. When I went to school, which I rarely did, when I got home there was no one there. My homies were the only people around for me. I had no one else. In a way they became my family. We did a lot of wrong, but my homies were the only people who accepted me. There were few places for me to go. In those days there were some clubs where you could lift weights. And if you weren't in the gang you couldn't get into the club. Being part of the game made me somebody.

At that time I did a lot of things that in my mind I really didn't want to do. But belonging to the gang was my life. For example, me and two dudes from my set, Kenney and Eddie, would stand on the corner by our school and just rob kids coming or going to school. We would take their lunch money and go buy some beer or weed. I liked some of these kids we stole from, but if they didn't do what they were supposed to and give us their money fast, we would beat the shit out of them. I didn't like it, but I knew what side I wanted to be on. I would rather be on the side of giving the beating than on the side of the guy that was getting the beating. If you weren't part of the power in my hood, than you were the prey. I didn't always like what I did, but I felt I had to do it to be down with my gang. Looking back, it wasn't much of a family, but it was the only family I had that I trusted. The only love and trust I got from anyone back then came from my homies.

If you were part of the gang, you could trust your homies. For example, no one would snitch on you. In those days your homies stood up for you. Nobody snitched, so no one could find anything out about what we did. There may have been a few snitches, but most of the time a gangster would rather go to the joint than give up a homie. Going to prison wasn't that big a price to pay for keeping quiet, because many of your friends were in the institution. And the snitch always ran the risk of getting killed.

I was arrested around twenty-five times from around the age of twelve to seventeen. Most of the time I was cut loose from the Juvenile Court with a warning. A few times I would be in Juvenile Hall or sent to Probation Camp for six months. Finally, when I was seventeen, I was sent away for four years to CYA (California Youth Authority) for robbery, rape, kidnapping, and grand theft.

We had kidnapped this white lady. I remember her name was Jane. We took her down by Redondo Beach. We robbed her, and then me and my partner raped her. She refused to get out of the car, so we knocked her out and stole the car. After we left, like a fool, I ran a red light. A police car stopped us and checked us out. I had no license, and it was a stolen car.

They wanted to try me as an adult at seventeen, but I was fortunate enough to get sent away to CYA in 1972 as a juvenile. If I was eighteen I would probably still be in prison for kidnapping and rape. Back then, you would be arrested maybe twenty to thirty times before you would get sent to CYA. Many of the dudes in CYA were in for robbery, murder, and really heavy crimes.

The Crips had been going on in the hood for around five to six years by the time I went away to CYA. By then, even though I was pretty young, I had done a lot of work and was a highly respected OG. There were around twenty Crips from my neighborhood during my four years in CYA. In CYA they reviewed me at the end of two years, but my conduct was so bad, they kept me another two years until I was twenty-one.

When I got out of CYA, I was only on the streets for around two months. Then I got busted for grand theft. This was for pickpocketing around the Forum in Los Angeles. I was trying to steal with more finesse, but I got caught. This time I was sent to a real prison at Soledad in 1975.

In Soledad, some of the older prisoners hated the Crips, because on the streets in Los Angeles some of their relatives had been killed. In the prison, there weren't too many of us Crips, but we had to stay strong and together for our own protection. The prison gangs at that time included the Mexicans' La Familia and the beginning of the Mexican Mafia, the Black Guerrilla Family, and the Aryan Brotherhood, and there were white biker-type gangs. The main problem in prison was always racial, although there was some black on black and Mexican against Mexican violence.

Back then these groups ran the prison. As Crips, we had to watch our back all of the time, because we didn't have too many homies there at that time. But then later on, when Crips and Bloods started going to prison in bigger numbers, we began to get a lot of power. Even in prison the Crips and Bloods hated each other, but because we were getting a lot of violence from the Mexicans and whites, we would join forces at times.

When I got my release date and was thirty days away from getting out of Soledad, some real shit went down. This black dude, one of our Crips, had snitched, and there was a big shakedown in some cells, and they found different weapons. He was one of ours, and we had to take care of him. We had this meeting, and I got the contract. Now, I didn't want to do it, because I was set to go home in thirty days. A good friend of mine took it over from me, and he killed this snitch with a shank (a knife).

When I got out, I noticed people began to look at me differently in my hood. I was now a big homie because I had been to prison. I got more respect, and people were afraid of me. I enjoyed the way people were treating me. I had no intention of getting a job or anything like that. I was an OG in the 89th Street East Coast Crips.

Around that time I got involved in a drive-by. One of my younger homeboys had been killed, and we knew the gang that did it. Someone stole a car, and we loaded all of our weapons in the car. We rolled into their neighborhood, and we knew where they would be kickin' it. We pulled up as close to them as we could get, and then we unloaded on them. I knew I had hit and killed this one motherfucker, and when I got back to the hood I was braggin' on it. We talked about it for a week. At that time we would think it was funny if a dude who got shot screamed or cried like a bitch when he got hit.

It seems crazy to me now but back then with all the violence there was love for your homies. Like three of my homies that got killed, younger guys, I remember them with love. I had a strong rep and I tried to help them, but they got killed gangbanging. These kids kind of idolized me, and when I was in the penitentiary they would go to my house and drop $200 to $300 on my mom to send to me to buy things in prison. They were my friends, and in a kind of memorial, I have their three names tattooed on my back.

During my being locked up in prison, for a few years, I decided that money was more important than gangbanging, so in the early 1980s, when I was in my late twenties, I became involved in armed robberies. Making money from my crimes began to make more sense to me than crazy gangbanging. My specialty was jewelry stores, because these jobs were very profitable.

I asked, "Why did you switch over to robberies from gangbanging?"

Gangbanging was OK for the kids in my set who were coming up. They were putting in work to make their reputation. And when they came to me for advice about some problem with another set, I would tell them what to do. But at that time I wanted to make some real money. The crew that did robberies would still do gangbanging, but these were the guys with plenty of weapons out to make some money. These were the guys who had nice cars, apartments, and all that.

Right now, let's say there are around thirty Crip sets in Los Angeles. Every set has an OG who has organized a crew that does robberies. He will, as I did, use a younger homie in a robbery who showed heart, was cool, and had no fear in his crew. An important thing I always made sure of, if I brought a kid along in my crew for a robbery was that the kid, if caught, would not snitch.

The most important things about a younger homie that I would take in my crew would be, Will he shoot to save my life? I wouldn't want anyone with me who wouldn't pull that trigger if my life was in danger. I wasn't into killing anyone in a robbery for senseless shit, but if he was going to kill me, I'll get him first, and every one in my crew has to be there to watch my back.

I asked, "Why rob stores? Why didn't you get more into the drug thing?"

My thing was robbery. Some crews and gangs were mainly involved with drugs. I tried to get into selling drugs. But I'm no dope dealer. I tried, but I can't sell no dope. I would use it or give it away. When I tried to sell dope, if someone came to me with a bullshit story, and had no money, I would just give him the shit. In order to sell dope you got to be a coldhearted chickenshit person.

I did have a personal bout with drugs. One time when I got out of prison and I was trying to sell rock cocaine, I experimented with the shit and got hooked on crack. That was the worst time in my life. I did a lot of stupid shit for crack. I would sometimes be beggin' my homies for crack or money to buy it. I carried a pistol, and I would sometimes rob a homie for the shit. If anyone trusted me I would burn 'em and that wasn't like me. I even was put out of the gang at that time. If anyone tells you that gangsters are using drugs, that's bullshit. They smoke weed and drink, but they don't fuck with that hard-core shit. I lost a lot of respect from my homies behind that shit.

Some dudes made a fortune selling drugs. One guy I knew was Freeway Rick. He was with the dudes from the Hoover Crips. Rick was a wild man! He would put ninety keys of dope in a car and drive somewhere like a madman. He was one of the first guys I saw who used guns with silencers. With all his money and drugs he had to have firepower.

I don't know about Freeway in particular, but a lot of guys would kidnap a rich dealer and hold him for ransom. The last I heard was that Freeway was getting drugs from the police and then he turned informant on them. I don't know what really went down, but I believe he's doing time now.

"So, in a way, what you're telling me is that today's gangs have many purposes," I said.

That's right. The gangs now are like a big melting pot. In my earlier days, the groups were smaller, tighter, and more like a family.

I was sent back to Soledad a few times. I was there between 1981 and 1983. I was also in Chino [prison] for what they call diagnosis for a time. When I was there I got into some trouble. Me and my homies attacked a guard, and I was sent to the hole for about four months. But I liked it there. You got away from the prison bullshit, and you could kick back, read, and think. From Chino, they sent me back to Soledad in 1984.

My last long stretch was from 1984 to 1989 in Soledad. You asked me about Monster Cody. I met him around 1986 in C-Wing in Soledad. He immediately, when he got in, started organizing the Crips in the prison. You had to respect Monster. He was intelligent and sharp. We respected each other and got along, even though we were from different Crip sets. I knew he was going to move out of the black-on-black violence because he was being educated by some older dudes in the joint who were political and against that shit. Like he taught me some Swahili. He was into his African roots, and this had calmed his violence down.

But he wasn't totally out of the Crips and he organized us. One time, he did beat up some guy who was supposed to stand "post." Standing post is like standing guard. Like when we black guys were showering, someone had to stand post to guard us from the Mexicans and whites. When you're showering you are naked, vulnerable, and have no protection. This guy fucked up and went off his post to watch some TV program. Monster later on punished him by beating the shit out of him. Normally he would have been killed.

I got out of Soledad in 1989, and some of my homies had made a lot of money selling dope. They staked me for awhile, then like a fool I got hooked again on crack. After a while they just cut me loose, and I had to earn some money on my own. I began to rob jewelry stores on the West Coast.

Ed became involved in a series of jewelry store robberies around the Southwest that landed him in jail in Tucson, Arizona, in 1990. He was also accused of conspiracy to commit first-degree murder. For various reasons the murder charge was dropped, and a set of circumstances arose that motivated Ed to enter the Amity Therapeutic Community. As a result of his entrance into Amity in 1990 he remained free from drugs and crime for over seven years. In 1997, Ed died of a heart attack. Over one thousand people attended his funeral.

Gangsters and Gangs in Prison

In general, the structure of gangs is more cohesive in prison than on the outside. This is largely due to the close physical proximity of gangsters in prison and also to a more intense need for security and protection from other prison gangs. This was validated by about 80 percent of the respondents to my questionnaire on the subject. One gangster interviewed shortly after he was released from California's Folsom prison responded succinctly to my query about the difference between gangs in and out of prison: "In prison there's no place to go or hide."

My friend and colleague sociologist John Irwin was incarcerated for armed robbery for five years in Soledad prison. He later returned to Soledad as a graduate student to research his doctoral dissertation. His research was the basis for his book *Prisons in Turmoil* (1980). Irwin described some of the fundamental problems of prison gangs that exist in Soledad and most other prisons around the country. Irwin asserted that violent racial and ethnic prison gangs in the pursuit of loot, sex, respect, or revenge will attack anyone who is not in their group. This, Irwin told me, "has completely unraveled any remnants of the old codes of honor and tip networks that formerly helped to maintain order in prison. In a limited, closed space, such as a prison, threats of attacks like those posed by racial and ethnic groups cannot be ignored. Prisoners must be ready to protect themselves or get out of the way. Prisoners who have chosen to continue to circulate in public in prison, with few exceptions, have formed or joined a clique or gang for their own protection. Consequently, violence-oriented gangs dominate most, if not all, large men's prisons in the United States."[3]

Irwin emphasized that gang-type structures are developed along racial lines in prisons, and the level of violence and potential violence has escalated in recent years.

> Racial conflicts among blacks, whites, and Hispanics in American prisons have produced a situation in which groups of prisoners regularly rob and attack other prisoners and retaliate when members of their clique or gang have been threatened or attacked. This has intensified the fear and widened the gap between prisoners, partic-

3. John Irwin, personal interview, June 1996.

ularly between prisoners of different races. The problem of racial conflict has substantially increased the level of prison violence and made many prisons almost impossible to manage. (1980, p. 36)

In my work with prison gangs, I encountered the secrecy and violence noted by Irwin. In a group session at the R. J. Donovan Corrections Prison in San Diego, I videotaped a group interaction. There were about fifteen men in the group who had volunteered to talk to me about gang structure and behavior in and out of prison. Two were caucasians, and the rest were Chicano and black convicts who had extensive experience with gangs. I assured them that I wanted only to discuss the general aspects of gangs and that I was not interested in specific names or criminal behaviors that might get someone into trouble.

Before the discussion began, two Chicanos raised their hands to tell me that they would not discuss anything until the video camera was turned off. I decided I wanted to keep it on, and five Chicanos excused themselves from the session on the basis of their fear of Mexican Mafia retaliation. I later determined that their fear had a basis in reality.

Their resistance was related to the violent aftermath of a movie about Mexican prison gangs. The award-winning film by Edward James Olmos, *American Me*, is a documentary on Chicano gangs in and out of prison. Two individuals who were familiar with Mexican gangs, and especially the Mexican Mafia, served as technical consultants on the production of the film. The Mexican Mafia felt that the film was disrespectful, so in retaliation, they arranged the assassination of the two technical advisers. The Chicano prisoners in my gang research focus group were well aware of these brutal homicides and chose not to participate in my research. But a sizable number of Chicano gangsters in the prison did cooperate with my research and provided valuable and insightful data.

Chicano gangs in recent years are more coherent and cohesive in prison than black gangs. Two major and powerful prison gangs in the Southwest are the Mexican Mafia in California and the Texas Syndicate in Texas. These gangs deal in drugs and maintain their strong position through assassinations. Both gangs, but especially the Mexican Mafia, known as "Eme," Spanish for "M," have gang sets in each prison with connections throughout the California and Texas prison systems.

The East Los Angeles barrio is the spawning ground for Eme. Many youngsters growing up in this area have limited choices, since their fathers, uncles, grandfathers, and other role models are gangsters. In recent years the problem of racial violence has been accentuated by the evolution of more clearly defined prison gangs. Almost all of these groups have some connection to the neighborhood gangs the inmates belonged to in their communities.

Mexican prison gang battles began when Chicanos were sent to prison in large numbers in the late 1960s for drug trafficking. These new Chicano prisoners were often greeted by groups of *veterano* Los Angeles Mexican Mafia with disdain and ridicule. The older inmates sneered at the new young convicts and regularly preyed on them for money and sex. The victims responded in kind and formed a new Chicano prison gang known as La Familia. Pitched battles for power between these two gangs became common in prisons. This conflict resulted in a number of assassinations committed by La Familia. Later, La Familia merged with the Emes and accepted their name.

In earlier years the Eme gang operated openly under an informal system of peaceful coexistence with state prison officials. Eme leaders were sometimes permitted to roam the halls at will, to enter the normally secure solitary areas for private meetings, and even to use the prison's staff conference room. One veteran California Department of Corrections worker commented, "We were trying to use them as a way to control the violence inside. It didn't work."

A large number of rivals and gangsters who didn't follow the rules of secrecy and conformity to the rigid contract of the gang leaders were assassinated. A rough estimate is that around two hundred murders were carried out in the California system from 1970 to 1990, and many more gang murders emanating from the prison conflicts were committed in the barrios of California. Mexican-American youths participated in Eme in their barrios and inside prisons. A gangster's street reputation followed him from his neighborhood into prison and vice versa.

Chicano gang youths tend to assume a high visibility in the prison world. They wheel and deal. They dress in what is known in prison as a "bonnarue" style with sharp, well-laundered prison garb. They are meticulous about their appearance and use their prison connections to get better clothes. Mexican *veteranos* have a number of young gangsters who do their bidding and carry out their orders without question. Many Chicano gangsters in prison entertain little or no hope for life on the outside. Their youth has been spent learning to optimize the quality of the environment inside the camps, youth facilities, and prisons that are too often their homes for most of their lives.

For *veterano* gangster prisoners with prestige in the world of organized crime related to drugs, prison is a time for laying low, for avoiding attention from the authorities, and for maintaining the street business of drugs outside the walls. This commerce in drugs came to a head in 1995 as a result of an FBI investigation and a large number of indictments. I had an opportunity to meet with several agents involved in the FBI Gang Task Force and learned a great deal about the FBI's findings and gang dynamics.

The arrests and indictments revealed that the Eme's power extended to getting a cut of the commerce of drugs in and out of prison. The Chicano gang ensured the success of their powerful enterprise by arranging assassination for anyone who got in their way. The assassinations produced enormous fear in the barrios and compliance with Eme's dictates. The coldness of their violence is revealed in a case involving a seventeen-year-old who was on probation. He was a "mule" who transported drugs for the gang. At one point in his gangster career, he wanted to quit the gang and was told that it was not allowed. He was informed that if he quit, his family would die. In response to this admonition, in order to save his family, the young man attempted suicide, with the belief that if he was dead, they would not go after his family. After the failed suicide, he continued to do his "job" of running drugs for Eme.

The federal indictment revealed a great deal about the Eme. The FBI indicted twenty-two members and associates of the Mexican Mafia prison gang, who for several years relied on murder and intimidation in an attempt to organize drug trafficking among hundreds of Latino street gangs in Southern California. The twenty-two people, ranging from the organization's reputed leader to street-level enforcers, were charged under RICO—the federal Racketeer Influenced Corrupt Organizations Act—with crimes including murder, extortion, and kidnapping. One of those arrested was accused of helping plot the death of the two consultants who had worked on Edward James Olmos' film *American Me.*

The indictment marked the first time that RICO was used against a gang in Southern California. The eighty-one-page indictment painted a chilling picture of this Los Angeles underworld and its organization and ruthlessness in the long and bloody history of Chicano gangs in and out of prison.

The indictment and trial indicated that one of the principal goals of the Mexican Mafia was to control narcotics distribution by street gangs. Two of the kingpins indicted were at the time incarcerated at the California Pelican Bay Prison. The authorities attempted to get a conviction under the RICO act in part because it would allow them to have key Eme gangsters transferred to a federal prison. The goal was to remove them from the gang's power base in the California penal system. The indictment and trial revealed that Eme was "the gang of gangs," with a membership of four hundred in prison and control over hundreds of youths in street gangs on the outside. The gang was reputed to control narcotics distribution, gambling, and prostitution at many state prisons, and their power reached from the prison into the community.

In one instance, the indictment charged that Eme kidnapped a local drug dealer who failed to pay $85,000 in "taxes" as part of the extortion arrangement. Eme eventually let him go after he agreed to pay four kilos of cocaine to settle the score. To deal drugs in a two-block area near downtown Los Angeles, the indictment charged, drug dealers were required to pay the Mexican Mafia $15,000.

The FBI alleged that the money-making potential and violent power of organizing the estimated sixty thousand Latino gang members from four hundred and fifty gangs in Los Angeles County alone was enormous. Eme's power emerged in the summer and fall of 1993, when Eme members held a series of meetings with gang members from Riverside to Los Angeles. Relying on fear, intimidation, and rhetoric steeped in cultural unity, Eme ordered the street gangs to halt drive-by shootings and settle their differences face-to-face or face the deadly wrath of the gang's hit ability from behind bars. Their move was not altruistic. It was for the purpose of controlling the senseless gangbanging in order to improve the lucrative drug business. The move, which initially resulted in a drop in Latino gang killings, was welcomed by many residents of the barrios. The violence continued, however, as evidenced by the one hundred and twenty gang-related murders committed by Mexican gangs in Los Angeles in 1993.

The trial was held in the federal court building in Los Angeles. Thirteen defendants were seated in three rows, chained to their chairs, their attorneys at their side. The FBI showed videotapes of the gangsters discussing various aspects of their drug enterprise. The tapes were facilitated by an Eme informant who was a gang member. Some of the gangsters in the court learned for the first time that their beloved homies plotted their demise. The trial ended on May 30, 1997, with the conviction of twelve members of Eme.

A Common Bond: The Macho Syndrome and the Machismo Characteristic of Gangsters

The most violence-provoking epithet one can hurl at a black or Chicano gangster is one that accuses him of having feminine characteristics or homosexual tendencies. A gangster cannot allow a serious intentional attack on his masculinity to go unpunished, especially if it takes place in front of his homies.

Most gangsters spend a good part of their life in custodial institutions. In this context prison homosexuality has always created identity problems for gangsters. Long before today's era of racial-ethnic prison gangs, many prisoners, particularly those with youth prison experiences, regularly or occasionally engaged in homosexual acts as the dominant sexual partner with prison "queens," "kids," or "punks," though not without some cost to their own masculine self-definition and reputation. There is a cynical accusation repeated frequently in the informal banter among prisoners that those inmates who engage in homosexual life too long finally learn to prefer it and, in fact, become practicing homosexuals. On the issue of homosexuality and violence in prison, John Irwin (1980, p. 87) stated:

> Violence has always been a popular solution for inmates in prison conflicts. Short of a prison riot, violence is a constant element in contemporary prison life. This super-macho form of violence involves an exaggerated form of masculinity. This pattern of super-macho toughness is the most important value and attitude in the violent men's prisons. It means, first, being able to take care of oneself in the prison world, where people will attack others with little or no provocation. In addition to threats of robbery, assaults, and murder, the threat of being raped and physically forced into the role of the insertee (punk or kid) has increased in the violent prison world. It was a jocular credo that after one year behind walls, it was permissible to kiss a kid or a queen. After five years, it was OK to jerk them off to "get 'em hot." After ten years, "making tortillas" or "flip-flopping" was acceptable and after twenty years anything was fine. [These expressions refer to the homosexual "turning out " of some prisoners.]

In my encounters with tough criminals of all ages, in and out of prison, I have always felt that their extreme macho posturing had a ridiculous tinge to it. However, I have always been careful not to challenge it for fear of a violent reaction. Many men are "macho," and this kind of posturing is not necessarily pathological. It is pathological when it becomes an extreme perspective on life that pervades an individual's thoughts, physical posture, and verbal expressions. Being a macho man is characterized by the way a gangster walks and talks. One can often tell that someone is a macho gangster by his unique swaggering walk down the street or in prison.

I define the term *macho syndrome* as a pathology that involves an attitude and posturing of being a superman for the purposes of survival in a real or imagined hostile world. Almost all gangsters have this affliction, which affects most of their social interactions and relationships. It is a tough-guy mask that states for self-protective reasons a posture and an attitude that is reflected in the one liner I have heard many times from gangsters: "Don't fuck with me or you will regret it."

The macho syndrome stems, in part, from the traditional and somewhat perverted perspective on gender roles that has changed only slightly in the past decades. American men are supposed to be supertough and invulnerable; women are supposed to be supersensitive and vulnerable. An aspect of the macho equation for males growing up in a gang environment is the notion that "the world is a hostile place, and in order to survive I have to always be on guard and present a tough masculine posture to others." In this sense the macho syndrome is a rational response to a hostile environment. It reflects a rational motivation to not be violated or victimized.

On many occasions I have heard the following gangster rationale expressed in one form or another: "I can never let anyone see me as a punk. They always know what I'll do, if anyone messes with me." This rationale accounts for the continuing and often bizarre acting out of senseless violence by gangsters for the maintenance of their status in the gang and their hood. In this context, being a superman, feared by others, is a shield against being in the opposite role of a feminine punk who is violated and victimized. "A good offense is the best defense."

The macho syndrome is in part caused by gangsters' early life experiences. Studies of youths who become gangsters reveal that they suffer a disproportionately high number of the indignities of physical, emotional, and sexual abuse when compared to youths who are socialized in a more normal or positive family environment. They are more often than not physically abused by one or both parents and older siblings. In a defensive reaction formation to this early life treatment, they believe, with some justification, that their continued existence requires a tough guy, macho attitude.

One prototypical example of this abuse phenomenon was a young man I will call Roy, who was in prison and took part in my group therapy session. Roy blamed his two older brothers for his criminal behavior and incarceration. In a role-playing session, he confronted his two older brothers, roles played by two other inmates in the group. At one dramatic point in his session, Roy said, "You motherfuckers put me in this place. All my life you fucked with me. Kickin' my ass when I was a little kid five years old. You fuckers, joking around, forced me to smoke dope when I was eight, and that kicked off my drug habit. And the main way you fucked me up is that I don't trust anyone. I am always suspicious of people, and I really don't know how to have any friends. Even in my gang I was always a loner."

A factor that contributes to the macho syndrome for some gangsters is sexual molestation at an early age. In various therapy groups, personal interviews, and therapeutic community group sessions focused on this issue, I have heard a large number of gangsters reluctantly disclose their sexual victimization experiences. Many of these youths revealed how their fathers, mothers, and sometimes older brothers and sisters sexually abused them. In one case, a young Chicano told how his father, who was a minister, sexually abused him. He went on to state, "Now that I am in therapy, I have talked more openly to my sisters and brothers and found that he had also sexually abused them."

Most youths who become gangsters spend time in juvenile jails of various kinds. For several years I worked in a juvenile detention facility.

200

Here, despite the efforts of staff to prevent the phenomenon, a variety of acts of sexual abuse, including rape, by older inmates on younger ones was a common occurrence. A common warning in a lock-up is, "When you are showering, never bend down to pick up the soap." I recall one incident where two youths in a juvenile institution were standing in a cafeteria line. Suddenly, one of them turned around and with his metal tray began to severely beat the boy standing in back of him. He later explained his violent behavior: "I could tell that the motherfuckin' faggot was eyeing me, and I wanted to let him and everyone else know I am not a punk faggot." His macho violence was his defensive way of asserting his masculinity.

I once held an individual therapy session with a sixteen-year-old gangster who was notorious for manipulating and forcing younger kids to "give him a blow-job." He would also rape them. In discussing his proclivities for these violent homosexual acts, he vehemently denied the possibility that he was a homosexual. At a certain point in our discussions, he revealed that he had been raped by his older brother and later on by older inmates in an institution where he had been incarcerated. I asked him, "You know how horrible you felt when you were victimized, how could you do the same thing to another kid?" Through this youth's response and the responses of other youths with whom I have discussed this situation, I have concluded that being in the role of the controlling perpetrator of the homosexual act removes the rapist as far as he possibly can get from being the punk victim. In a convoluted and pathological way, being a super-macho gangster rapist validates the perpetrator's masculinity and places him in a less vulnerable, nonvictim position.

In the gangster macho syndrome, especially in prison, a sexual gang rape involves multiple rapists attacking one victim. In some cases this form of gang rape is often enacted with the curious rationale of punishing a person who has snitched or violated some important gang rule or code of honor. This punitive sodomizing sexual act is vividly enacted in the film *American Me*. In one dramatic scene, a Mexican prison gang punishes a gangster who has violated the gang's code of honor by having five gang leaders, each in turn, sodomize the helpless victim.

Machismo and Chicano Gangs

The macho syndrome, or machismo, is a significant factor in Chicano gangs. Machismo may have its roots in the early history of Mexico. The Mexican revolution for land and liberty, led by Pancho Villa and Emilio Zapata in the early years of the twentieth century, created a bond involving a fight for honor. Most peasants in the Villa army were poor, illiterate, and untrained as soldiers. They made up for their deficiencies by what they considered to be fearless acts of super masculinity. In this context, a basic element of machismo became a willingness to kill or be killed for their brothers-in-arms, their land, and their freedom. Honor and pride as a man, or machismo, in this context was worth the sacrifice of one's life.

There was, of course, a logical reason for the revolution led by Villa and Zapata. Poor peasants were fighting for land and rights of freedom that were their due, and victory was a sought-after and valued achievement. This honorable code of machismo of that era has been transferred in a perverted way to become an important value in the Chicano gangs of the barrios in many cities of the Southwest.

A Chicano nicknamed Munchie, an ex-*veterano* gangster who had been a drug dealer for over thirty years, presented some interesting observations on the concept of machismo. I worked alongside Munchie as a colleague in an Amity Therapeutic Community prison project in a special cell block for two hundred prisoners in the California R. J. Donovan Prison. Munchie has become a legendary figure in the resocialization of Chicanos in prison. He described for me the absurdity of machismo in contemporary violent gangs:

> In today's Chicano gangs our kids are killing themselves in astronomical figures for the simple reason of demonstrating their machismo. This characteristic is so embedded in Chicano gangsters that they don't blink an eye in killing somebody or getting killed. In the process, they stupidly cause the destruction of two lives—one dead, the other doing twenty years to life in prison. This simultaneously affects two families with irreparable damage, not to mention the killing of a blood brother.

While directing Chicano prisoner groups, Munchie often presented his view on the absurdity of machismo in the gang. In one session he gave the following message to a group of Chicano gangsters, who viewed him as a positive role model and appeared to absorb his commentary:

> The guy who puts so little value of appreciation on his life and is not concerned about those who are victimized (children, spouses, relatives on both sides) is not in my estimation a man of high values or worthy of respect. It takes much more machismo to maintain a job, be responsible to our dependents, meet our debts, and be respected for living up to our commitments. This kind of machismo would also involve a man becoming a good role model as a father to his children.

Using Munchie's logical viewpoint, I directed a psychodrama session with Raoul, a Chicano *veterano* gangster in the Amity program, who was concerned about his son who was following a machismo gang life-style. Raoul was almost forty years old and had spent half of his life in prison for a variety of offenses. He was in the process of turning his life around in the Amity program. He was convinced that his son was follow-ing a pathway into a life of crime and prison, and he wanted to learn how he might be able to handle this unfortunate situation. In the psychodrama, a younger inmate plays the role of his son. The pivotal "moment of truth" in the two-hour session was Raoul's diatribe to his son about machismo, drugs, and gangs. In part, he told him:

> Listen, man, there's no glory or honor in killing a blood brother just because we had a fight over some drugs that he was sell-ing in my territory. I know, I've done that. And now that I've come to my senses, it's hard to live with that memory. I can still see his face when I blew him away. And over what? Some stupid white powder bullshit that we were fighting over. Because I was in the gang, I had to kill him or look like a pussy and lose the respect of my homies. Look at me now. Look at the price I'm paying with my life in this joint just to show those guys that no one can fuck with Raoul and get away with it. I see everything differently now. Don't be a machismo asshole like I was. It's not worth killing someone and losing your free-dom for life.

In another situation, an ex-gangster I will call Ricardo revealed to me a murder he had committed to maintain his machismo honor. At the time he was twenty-eight years old, had been through a therapeutic com-munity rehabilitation program, was functioning as a paraprofessional drug counselor, and had been clean for almost five years. When he was driving me to the airport after I had directed a group session in the prison where we both worked, I asked him to give me his viewpoint on machismo. He responded by telling me the following story:

> When I was about thirteen, I was in a gang and I was trying to get my reputation. One day, this older twenty-year-old guy, a *loco-vato* in the gang, got me alone in back of this building. We smoked some good weed that he had, and then when we were both loaded he forced me at knifepoint to suck his dick. At that time I was a weak kid without any power. I never told anybody this story because it was too humiliating to me. I just took my time and waited for my opportunity to get my revenge. He was still around, and around five years later we were in this group just hangin' out on the corner and talking about this and that. I told him that I had some good shit, a kind of inhalant, and why don't we go and get loaded. The two of us went to a private place and got high on this shit. When I could see that he was kind of mum-bling and out of it, I took this rope I had hidden in my jacket, put

it around his neck, and strangled the motherfucker until he was dead. For me, with my thinking at that time, there was no way I was going to let him get away with what he had done to me. I was honor bound to kill him for the way he had disrespected me when I was a kid. I never told anyone until now how and why I killed him.

In summary, the basic concept of machismo as originally rooted in Mexican culture, involving honor, respect, and reputation as a man, is a laudable concept. The attitude is perverted in contemporary Chicano gangs into a rationale for many violent acts that have no relationship to logical and respectful behavior. This form of a macho syndrome is rampant in both black and Chicano gangs. In some ways it is derived from the larger society. Many contemporary films depict pathological killing as heroic and honorable behavior. Not only gangsters, but average citizens, young and old, pay millions of dollars to see blockbuster movies that glorify sociopathic macho-syndrome behavior and homicide. A partial fallout of macho violence that is too often affirmed, honored, and patronized by the larger society in the mass media is that it validates a parallel form of sociopathic violence by gangsters in the context of their gangs.

CHAPTER 8

THEORETICAL VIEWPOINTS ON GANGS

Prison gangs are a major problem in the prison community. This photo depicts former gangsters participating in a seminar in the Amity Therapeutic Community in a California prison. A major topic of discussion is how their gang affiliations affected the criminal behavior that landed them in prison. The author's theories on gang structure and behavior were greatly influenced by the information derived from interviews with the participants in these seminars.

This chapter reviews some of the theories on gang structure and function that have been developed in the past century. A number of significant sociological and social-psychological theories and research efforts have contributed to the understanding of the structure and function of gangs. The theories of Richard Cloward and Lloyd Ohlin, Albert Cohen, Herbert Bloch, and Arthur Niederhoffer, and Walter Miller are briefly summarized since their theories are presented more fully as explanations of delinquency in general in chapter 13.

Major Theorists

The earlier theories of Frederick Thrasher, Clifford Shaw, and others of the Chicago School are the foundation of gang research in the past century; however, in many respects these earlier theories were descriptive of a different genre of gangs. Post–World War II gangs are more lethal and involved with drugs than earlier gangs. For this reason, the theoretical perspectives presented here are more relevant to understanding gangs that emerged in the second half of the twentieth century.

Albert Cohen

In his book *Delinquent Boys,* Cohen (1955, p. 45) viewed the gang as a subculture with a value system different from the dominant ones found in the inclusive American culture. Working-class children, according to Cohen, used the delinquent subculture (the gang) as a mode of reaction and adjustment to a dominant middle-class society that indirectly discriminated against them because of their lower-class position (p. 31).

The thesis developed by Cohen is that working-class youths, trained in a different value system, are not adequately socialized to fulfill the status requirements of middle-class society. Despite this different socialization and subculture value condition, they are unfairly exposed to the middle-class aspirations and judgments they cannot fulfill. This conflict produces in the working-class youth what Cohen termed "status frustration." In a reaction to this problem, these youths use the gang as a means of adjustment. In the gang youths act out their status frustrations in "non-utilitarian, malicious, negativistic" forms of delinquency that, according to Cohen, are their way of reacting against the described status dislocation of the social system (1955, p. 59).

The delinquent subculture described by Cohen represents a collective effort on the part of the youths to resolve adjustment problems produced by dislocations in the larger society. In the gang the norms of the larger sociely are reversed so that "nonutilitarian" deviant behavior (especially violence) becomes legitimized activity. The gang thus provides a legitimate "opportunity structure" for working-class youths to strike back at the larger society that produces their "status frustration" problems (1955, p. 132).

Herbert Bloch and Arthur Niederhoffer

In their book *The Gang*, Bloch and Niederhoffer (1958) view gang behavior as a universal and normal adolescent striving for adult status. They assert that the gang pattern may be found in all cultures as a vehicle for achieving manhood. The gang pattern, they maintain, is more pronounced in cultures where youths are normally cut off from the possibility of manhood for a prolonged period (p. 99).

Bloch and Niederhoffer studied the differences and similarities of the adolescent condition in a variety of societies.

> The adolescent period in all cultures, visualized as a phase of striving for the attainment of adult status, produces experiences which are much the same for all youths, and certain common dynamisms for expressing reaction to such subjectively held experiences. The intensity of the adolescent experience and the vehemence of external expression depend on a variety of factors, including the general societal attitudes towards adolescence, the duration of the adolescent period itself, and the degree to which the society tends to facilitate entrance into adulthood by virtue of institutionalized patterns, ceremonials, rites and rituals, and socially supported emotional and intellectual preparation. (1958, p. 143)

However, today's gangs have distorted Bloch and Niederhoffer's concept of "manhood." The gangster's idea of manhood is earning money by any means necessary, using violence to settle disputes, perceiving women as objects and ornaments, and strutting this status in a violent manner. Manhood in contemporary gangs involves the macho syndrome, which goes beyond the "striving for manhood" delineated by Bloch and Niederhoffer (1958, p. 136).

Walter B. Miller

Miller (1959) described his lower-class adolescent theory of gangs in a fashion somewhat similar to Cohen's position. He maintained that the values of lower-class culture produce deviance because they are "naturally" in discord with middle-class values. The youth who heavily conforms to lower-class values is thus automatically delinquent.

207

Miller, like Bloch and Niederhoffer, suggested that gang activity is, in part, a striving to prove masculinity, and females are exploited by gangsters in the "normal" process of relating. They are "conquest objects" utilized to prove and boost the masculinity of the streetcorner male (1959, p. 37). Miller emphasized that lower-class youths who are confronted with the largest gap between aspirations and possibilities for achievements are most delinquency prone. Such youths are apt to utilize heavily the normal range of lower-class delinquent patterns of "toughness, shrewdness, cunning, and other devices in an effort to achieve prestige and status . . . [as well as] physical prowess, skill, fearlessness, bravery, ability to con people, gaining money by wits, shrewdness, adroitness, smart repartee, seeking and finding thrills, risk, danger, freedom from external constraint, and freedom from superordinate authority" (1959, p. 48).

Richard Cloward and Lloyd Ohlin

In their book *Delinquency and Opportunity*, Cloward and Ohlin (1960) presented an in-depth analysis of the lack of fit between American success goals and means of achieving these goals available to lower socioeconomic groups in American society. The explanation presented by Cloward and Ohlin for the emergence of gangs is derived from the goals, norms, and anomie theories of Durkheim and Merton: "Pressures toward the formation of delinquent subcultures originate in marked discrepancies between culturally induced aspirations among lower-class youth and the possibilities of achieving them by legitimate means" (1960, p. 56).

Cloward and Ohlin's thesis is based on Emile Durkheim's original theory of anomie. Durkheim, in describing two categories of need—physical and social—makes the point that physical needs are satiable, whereas social gratification is "an insatiable and bottomless abyss" (1950, p. 52). Cloward and Ohlin state that, when men's goals become unlimited, the "norms no longer control men's actions" and a state of "normlessness" or anomie exists (1960, p. 126).

Building on the theoretical base of anomie (originally presented by Durkheim and later developed by Robert Merton), Cloward and Ohlin stated the core of their theory:

> The ideology of common success-goals and equal opportunity may become an empty myth for those who find themselves cut off from legitimate pathways upward. We may predict, then, that the pressure to engage in deviant behavior will be the greatest in the lowest levels of the society. Our hypothesis can be summarized as follows: The disparity between what lower-class youth are led to want and what is actually available to them is the

source of a major problem of adjustment. Adolescents who form delinquent subcultures, we suggest, have internalized an emphasis upon conventional goals. Faced with limitations on legitimate avenues of access to these goals, and unable to revise their aspirations downward, they experience intense frustrations; the exploration of nonconformist alternatives may be the result. (P. 132)

Cloward and Ohlin viewed gangs as an alternative road to social "success goals." Alienated youths band together in the collectivity of the gang in an effort to resolve mutually shared problems. Cloward and Ohlin posited that there are three types of delinquent gang norms and activities: violence, theft, and drug use. Each of these provides the focal concern of three basic gang types: (1) conflict gangs, (2) criminal gangs, and (3) retreatist gang drug users (p. 52).

↳ CRITICISM ↴

Although there is considerable merit in Cloward and Ohlin's conceptualizations of gangs, especially in their analysis of anomie and opportunity structures, their delineation of three types of gangs—conflict, criminal, and retreatist—is not useful for the analysis of contemporary gangs. One major flaw in the Cloward and Ohlin model with regard to today's gangs is related to their "retreatist subculture." Most contemporary gangsters use alcohol and smoke marijuana. However, the gangster who gets too involved with drugs, especially crack-cocaine or heroin, becomes a gang dropout. The gangster who becomes addicted gets on the drug-seeking treadmill and becomes unreliable as a gangster. His primary aim in life is to get high and get the money necessary to get high by any means necessary. His concern with anyone else is simply as a "mark," a victim to be conned or cheated, or possibly as a criminal accomplice in a "quick score" for acquiring drugs. The flux of the addict's life condition provides no stability for group formation, even one with very limited cohesion. Drug addicts, as social isolates, may be in some physical proximity to each other, but their lack of ability to relate even minimally makes a social group unlikely. The "retreatist subculture" thus cannot be regarded as a category of contemporary gangs.

5
✱ **James F. Short, Jr., and Fred Strodbeck** (1974)

Short and Strodbeck, together and individually, carried out a number of gang studies in Chicago over a number of years. They wrote a series of articles that contributed enormously to our understanding of gang behavior. Among the conclusions of their varied studies was the assertion that aleatory (chance) elements play a considerable part in gang behavior. According to Short and Strodbeck (1974), gang activities, whether for fun or profit, usually involve a degree of risk. Most of the time these activities are engaged in without serious consequences, but sometimes something goes wrong, and the outcome is calamitous. They discuss the implications of these aleatory risks:

CHANCE

> Our use of the term aleatory does not restrict it to events which are independent of the actions of the persons involved. It was incidentally true that the events in question were not, for this stratum, punished by society. However, we now wish to go beyond this feature and direct the argument to instances of serious aggression in which the outcome is not desired either by the boys or the community, and for which serious consequences, like imprisonment, may result from the response by the larger society. We do not say that all cases of serious aggression result from action with such an aleatory element, but that, etiologically, those which do should be distinguished from cases in which serious injury is the clear intent of the actor. (1974, p. 19)

Short and Strodbeck adopted an approach consistent with the earlier poverty area research of Clifford Shaw and Henry McKay and the group delinquency perspective found in the theories of Cohen, Cloward and Ohlin, and Thrasher. They found that it was difficult to locate gangs that corresponded to those described in most theories. This led them to examine in greater depth the processes and values that lead to gang delinquency.

★ Short and Strodbeck specified five specific indices of gang activity: (1) conflict; (2) institutional social activities; (3) sexual behavior, hanging out, and selling alcohol; (4) homosexuality, fathering illegitimate children, and common law marriages; and (5) involvement in minor correlated crimes, conflict, and alcohol use. They observed that these behaviors were not greatly different from the more routine activities of adolescent males (1974, p. 34). They determined that gangs had a shifting membership and structure, with allegiances vacillating over time. Leadership was seldom strong and generally incapable of exacting discipline from members. Concomitantly, few strong group norms laid claims on the behavior of individual gang members. They found in Chicago gangs, as I had in Los Angeles gangs, that threats to the status of the gang were particularly important, and conflict often emerged from disputes about the reputation of the gang.

Barbara Tomson and Edna R. Felder (1975)

Tomson and Felder, in their book *Gangs: A Response to the Urban World*, analyzed the impact of the neighborhood on gangs. Their general assumption was that gang membership is a response to the difficulties of the depressed urban slum situation. Their research dealt with gang members' response to the urban structure, the political structure, and the mass media.

According to Tomson and Felder, "These are institutions in which they are unlikely to have formalized individual contacts. . . . For youngsters who are not in touch with the larger society, the gangs provide a positive identity for their individual members" (1975, p. 122). They summarized their viewpoint as follows:

1. The urban setting in which gangs thrive reduces varied pressures: the need to deal successfully with strangers, the need to deal with a money-based economy, loneliness, and lack of privacy. The delinquent responds to these pressures by identifying with the gang, which offers him symbols of identity, activities, and helps him obtain money, companionship, and friends.

2. The purpose of the political machinery is to provide services and resolve conflicts for members of the society. Delinquents assess the political situation correctly by concluding that they do not belong to society and are not wanted. They can, however, identify with and be understood by their gang. (1975, p. 87)

Irving A. Spergel (1964) (1995) CHANGE

GANGS

In his first book on gangs, *Racketville, Slumtown, Haulberg*, Spergel (1964) explored three different styles of delinquency in three different lower-class areas of a large eastern city. Spergel's study, based on firsthand field study interviews, contains the verbatim responses of gang youths. Spergel's assumptions parallel Cloward and Ohlin's theories of gangs. He asserted that delinquent subcultures use socially unacceptable means for achieving acceptable goals. He described three major types of delinquent youth subcultures: one characterized by racket activities, another by violent conflict, and a third by theft. These subcultures, according to Spergel, depend on the interaction of conventional and criminal opportunities. Spergel stated that "drug addiction . . . develops mainly as a variant and transitional pattern for older adolescents and young adults, many of whom have been participants in the major delinquent-youth subcultures" (1964, p. 39).

In his most recent book, *The Youth Gang Problem*, Spergel asserts that there are four basic strategies for dealing with youth gangs: (1) local community organizing and mobilization of citizens, community groups, and agencies; (2) social intervention, often outreach counseling, and detached work; (3) provision of social and economic opportunities, especially jobs, training, and remedial education targeted to gang youths; and (4) suppression, including both formal and informal mechanisms, of control (1995, p. 37). Spergel states that the ideal plan of intervention and suppression, as well as prevention, depends on appropriate analysis of the community's gang

211

problem and the resources available to deal with it. Spergel emphasizes the importance of suppression by police and interrelating these strategies with strategies of community mobilization. He specifies that violent gangs should be selected for special attention, based on shared organizational and community group information. Gang youths should be targeted for special controls, social services, and provision of social opportunities in the following order of priority: first, leadership and core-gang youths; second, high-risk gang-prone youths who give clear evidence of beginning participation in delinquent or criminal gang activities; and third, regular or peripheral members with special needs for social control and intervention through a variety of educational and socializing services (1995, p. 53).

Malcolm W. Klein (1971)

Klein, in his role as director of the University of Southern California Delinquency Control Institute, carried out a large number of research projects dealing with gang structure and behavior. Klein's decades of research on gangs, and the work of other notable gang researchers and theorists, are incorporated in a book edited by Klein, Cheryl L. Maxson, and Jody Miller, entitled *The Modern Gang Reader* (1995).

Based on his studies of Mexican-American and black gangs in Los Angeles, Klein (1971) defined gangs as "any denotable adolescent group of youngsters who (a) are generally perceived as a distinct aggregation by others in their neighborhood, (b) recognize themselves as a denotable group (almost invariably with a group name), and (c) have been involved in a sufficient number of delinquent incidents to call forth a consistent negative response from neighborhood resident and/or enforcement activities" (p. 58). Klein concluded that gang leadership is not a position, as many have theorized, but rather is a collection of functions. Leadership varies with the activity, such as fighting, athletics, and interacting with girls. He asserted that gang leaders are often difficult to identify except by the reactions of other members and that age is an influence in leadership. According to Klein's findings, gang boys portray a caricature of adolescence.

> They behave and react in excess, and they definitely overplay roles. Gang boys have little confidence in themselves and are insecure with respect to their own abilities and social relationships. These feelings of inadequacy often result in a dependence on the peer group and, consequently, on arrest-provoking behavior. Adolescents float together as they reject and are rejected by their community. Thus the gang is a cluster of youths held together by their individual incapacities rather than common goals or interests. It serves a need satisfaction and leads to delinquency only secondarily. (1971, p. 89)

212

Martin Sanchez Jankowski

In his book *Islands in the Streets* (1991), Jankowski reports on ethnographic studies of gangs in New York, Boston, and Los Angeles conducted over a ten-year period. In the process of his research, he was a participant-observer of thirty-seven randomly selected gangs representing several different ethnic groups (including Chicano, Dominican, Puerto Rican, Central American, African American, and Irish). His work, based on "living the gang life," provides a distinctive viewpoint on gangs. He describes gang members as "defiant individualists," who possess distinctive character traits, including competitiveness, wariness, self-reliance, social isolation, and strong survival instincts.

Jankowski perceived the gangs he studied as "formal-rational" organizations having strong organizational structures, well-defined roles, rules that guide member activities, penalties for rule violations, an ideology, and well-defined means for generating both legal and illegal income. He observed that gangs function much like most groups and maintained that many gang members have positive relationships with people in their neighborhoods, often performing essential functions such as looking out for the well-being of the community in which they live. In this regard the functions he observed included such things as protection against unscrupulous businesses as well as organized crime. He labeled the links between gangs and their neighborhoods as a form of "local patriotism" (1991, p. 56). Jankowski, in his research of over thirty inner-city gangs, utilized a number of gangsters to assist him in his research. He noted that they were involved with a territorial imperative that included violence for the protection of their territory. He perceived gangs as having a significant level of intense camaraderie that involved the recreational act of "kicking back" (hanging out). He concluded that the use of drugs, with the exception of heroin, was condoned by the gang.

Jankowski is one of the few gang researchers who focused on personality factors in his research. He observed that the juveniles who joined gangs were those with "defiant individualism." He perceived these youths as the most competitive individuals in a community, who organized and joined gangs for the purpose of acquiring the scarce resources that exist in lower socioeconomic communities. He noted that their competitive edge to win these resources accounts for gangbanging behavior. Jankowski concluded that gang behavior was often an appropriate response to the pathological conditions that exist in the inner cities of the United States.

10
William B. Sanders (1994)

Sanders's book *Gangbangs and Drive-Bys* (1994) is based on research with gangs over a ten-year period in the San Diego area. Sanders utilized what he terms "by any means necessary research." His approach employed participant observation, ethnography, and statistical analysis. His book effectively delineates an excellent research approach for studying and analyzing gangs. He examined a panorama of gang issues, including the gang's motivation for violence, organizational characteristics, leadership factors, and territorial imperatives (p. 42).

Sanders defines the gang as "any transpersonal group of youths that shows a willingness to use deadly violence to claim and defend territory, and attack rival gangs, extort or rob money, or engage in other criminal behavior as an activity associated with its group, and is recognized by itself and its immediate community as a distinct dangerous entity. The basic structure of gangs is one of age and gender differentiation and leadership is informal and multiple" (p. 5).

11
Jerome H. Skolnick (1995)

Skolnick has contributed to the understanding of gang behavior in a number of articles. Notable among these is his analysis of "drug gangs" (1995, p. 36). Based on his extensive interviews with prison inmates and police, Skolnick concluded that there are two types of gangs, entrepreneurial and cultural. His basic premise is that as gangs become more enmeshed in the drug trade, they become less a strictly cultural phenomenon and more a business enterprise. This evolution, he concludes, poses a significant problem for law enforcement officials (p. 138). Skolnick believes that the cultural gang is more likely to take part in gangbanging and some social activities. Those gangsters involved in the drug trade are a part of what he refers to as the entrepreneurial gang.

12
John M. Hagedorn (1994)

Hagedorn, in his varied writings, has focused on the injection of the drug business in gangs and how this factor has affected the gangs' structure and function in recent years. Based on his research on gangs in Milwaukee, he posits that most adult gang members cannot be described as committed long-term gang participants in the drug economy. Most of the gangsters he interviewed revealed that they were sporadically involved in the drug trade, and that they moved in and out of gangs and conventional labor activities (1994, p. 24).

214

Hagedorn developed a typology of adult gang members and specified four categories. He placed the four ideal types on a continuum of behavior and values: (1) "Legits" are those few gangsters who have gone legitimate and matured out of the gang; (2) "Homeboys" are those gangsters comprising a majority of both African-American and Latino adult gang members who alternately work conventional jobs and take various roles in drug sales; (3) "Dope fiends" are those gangsters who are addicted to cocaine and participate in the drug business as a way to maintain access to drugs; and (4) "New Jacks" are gangsters who regard the drug business as a career (1994, p. 27).

George Knox 13

Knox, as editor and founder of *The Journal of Gang Research*, has made a major contribution to the understanding of gangs. The many important and diverse articles published in the journal by Knox and his colleagues in the New Chicago School have presented a considerable amount of valuable data about gangs. Apart from his contributions to the journal, Knox has written a number of significant articles and books on various aspects of the gang phenomenon. His book *An Introduction to Gangs* (1995) is an important contribution to the field.

Notable among Knox's publications is *Schools Under Siege*, an extensive study of gangs in schools, written with David Laske and Edward Tromanhauser (1992). The authors note that research over the past decade reveals a direct correlation between the presence of gangs in and around schools and an increase in school violence. They assert that the relationship between gangs and schools hinges on several factors:

A. Street gang members have easier access to weapons than do non-gang affiliated students and are more likely to use these weapons.

B. Gangs can more easily afford to purchase weapons using the money earned from drugs.

C. Historically territorial conflicts fuel gang violence because entrepreneurial street gangs, involved in drug trafficking use terror to protect their sales market area.

D. The presence of street gangs in schools increases the percentage of students who carry guns. Both gang affiliated and non-affiliated students begin to carry weapons for protection.

E. The school environment brings rival gang members in close proximity to one another and blurs haphazard turf lines, which leads to confrontations and challenges within schools, on school property, and on the streets surrounding the schools. (1992, p. 134)

Schools under Siege is a useful book for school administrators since it presents viable methods for dealing with gang violence in and around the school.

In 1995, Knox and his associates completed a comprehensive study entitled *The Economics of Gang Life*, which involved gathering information from over one thousand gang members. The premise of their research was "to understand the costs and benefits associated with gang life in America today." The research involved collecting data in different types of social contexts, including adult and juvenile correctional facilities and community programs. Data was obtained from five states—California, Illinois, Iowa, Michigan, and Ohio. Knox and his associates determined that there were differences in organizational sophistication between gangs: "The higher level gangs were more organizationally sophisticated and appeared to have a number of formalized economic functions and capabilities." The researchers determined that most of the gangs they analyzed were fairly sophisticated; they had some formalized rules and their own argot or gang language. Their sample of gang members included both youths and adults, "but the top leaders were for the most part adults with long tenure in the gang" (1995, p. 96).

Summary and Conclusions

Several themes emerge from the various theories and research reports reviewed here. Most gang researchers share the following viewpoints: (1) gangs have a fierce involvement with their territory in their hood or barrio, and gangs will fight and gangbang to protect their turf; (2) gangs have different levels of participation, partially based on age, and gang members can be characterized as core or marginal participants; (3) different gangs have diverse patterns of leadership; (4) many gangs and gangsters participate intensely in the commerce and use of various drugs; and (5) gangs are, in part, generated by their cultural milieu in a response to a society that blockades their opportunity to achieve the success goals of the larger society.

My review of the literature reveals that many gang researchers have amassed a wealth of significant data on gangs; however, as sociologists are wont to say, "more research is needed." At the 1995 Academy of Criminal Justice Sciences meetings in Boston, sociologists Scott Decker and Ronald Huff presented a valuable seminar based on their extensive research into the field that attempted to summarize early and recent field studies of gangs. Notable in their presentation was data from Ronald Huff's book *Gangs in America* (1991). They concluded their presentation with a number of suggestions for future research on gangs that were contained in a paper written by Scott Decker (1995). These include:

(1) Does gang membership precede the onset of serious criminality? (2) What effect, if any, does gang membership have on
other members in the family, and conversely, what effect does the
family have on gang members? (3) What is the process by which
gang members leave their gang? (4) How do gangs grow in size?
(5) How do gangs spread from one city to another? (6) Are there
links between gangs and organized crime groups? (7) What is the
genesis of intergang and intragang violence? (8) How are roles
within the gang established, and how are individual selected for
those roles? (9) What role do economic factors and motivation
play in the actions of gangs and gang members? (10) What is the
relationship between gang members and social institutions?
(11) What are the protective factors that insulate some individuals from gang membership? and (12) How does the gang change
over time?

Two areas of conflicting viewpoints are revealed in gang theory and
research that require additional research and analysis. One involves the personality characteristics of youths who participate in gangs. Do gangsters
manifest emotional pathologies that differ significantly from nongangster
youths? The second is related to the structure of gangs. Are gangs the cohesive groups perceived by some theorists or the inchoate structures that I have
found in my research? The following section presents some additional clar-
ification on these two significant issues in the context of my theory of the
gang as a near-group.

The Violent Gang as a Near-Group It YABLONSKY

The development of an adequate theory on the violent gang requires an
extensive foundation of relevant research data. The importance of such
research for theory building and the pitfalls of not carrying out such empirical investigation were cogently expressed by sociologist Robert Merton
(1957): "Empirical research initiates, reformulates, refocuses, and clarifies
the theories and conceptions of sociology. It is evident that any theorist who
is remote from all research, of which he learns only by hearsay, runs the risk
of being insulated from the very experiences most likely to turn his attention in fruitful directions" (p. 131).

Research Issues in the Development of
Gang Theory

The diverse sociological and psychological viewpoints on the organization
and the behavior of gangs is partly explained by the chameleon nature of

gangs, the changes in their structure and behavior in different time periods, and perhaps more importantly the perspectives of the researchers. Different researchers have studied gangs from different perspectives. Camera positions in the production of a film serve as a relevant metaphor. Some gang researchers operate from an academic distance and have no direct communication with the gangster subjects of their research. They base their theories on reports from the gang battlefront and have a long-distance viewpoint. In film parlance, they are viewing the gang from a camera "long shot." Other researchers perceive the gang in a "close-up." Their perception of the gang is based on a close study of one or two gang entities up close and personal. Somewhere in between is a "two shot." My research camera has attempted to encompass all of these perspectives, including what might be termed a "long tracking shot" over a time span of close to fifty years.

Differing perspectives on gangs may also be explained by the old story of the six blind men and the elephant. After each man had inspected a part of an elephant by feeling it in a particular place, each was asked to describe the appearance of an elephant. The man who felt the trunk described the snakelike characteristic, the man who touched the leg described it accordingly, and so on.

Research Problems and Pitfalls

The generally suspicious violent gangster is not easily approached in his habitat on the streets of his barrio or hood. Also, most gangs tend to change over a period of time, with such factors as family movement, arrests, incarcerations, police pressure, and drug involvement. These factors tend to change the personnel and structure of a gang and also impact researchers' findings. Consequently, certain techniques of formal sociological research are not useful for researching gangs.

The development of an effective methodological design for systematically studying gangs remains a challenging and formidable research problem. "Long distance" views about gangs emanating from questionnaires that are not administered directly to gangsters, outdated research findings, or research related to delinquency in general rather than to the gang in particular are prone to lead to theoretical misconceptions.

Another issue that relates to some of the contemporary viewpoints on gangs is that too many current theoretical conceptions of gangs rely heavily on the theories and empirical data contributed by the early Chicago School. It is apparent that there have been significant social changes in American society over the past fifty years, and these changes have altered the sociocultural causal context and the structure of gangs.

The earlier methodologies of using personal documents, case materials, and direct interviews, characteristic of the Chicago School research approach, remain vibrantly valid; however, drawing conclusions about contemporary gang structures with outdated gang data can lead to erroneous theories. The development of accurate gang theories requires an innovative type of research that gathers a variety of documentary data about gangs through diverse methods in different settings. William Sanders, in his book *Gangbangs and Drive-Bys* (1994) refers to this type of data gathering as "research by any means necessary" (p. 24). His utilization of various research methods for data collection serves as a viable model for studying gangs.

An appropriate model for current gang research might well be the anthropological field study approach usually reserved for more "exotic" foreign cultures. In this type of field-study research, the researcher moves into a barrio or hood and experiences the various social forces operating in the community. From this vantage point he or she is in the most ideal position for gathering the wide range of data that would prove most useful toward the development of gang theory. Such data would include information about various types of gangs, leadership patterns, the meaning of membership, activity analysis, violence patterns, gang language, and gang-youth personality types. William Whyte lived in "Cornerville" near Boston, and to some extent Martin Sanchez Jankowski utilized this approach for his book *Islands in the Streets* (1991, p. 56). I utilized this approach in my early gang research in New York and to some extent for studying gangs now, since I live close to the gang area of Venice, California.

In the development of my theory of gangs, I have carried out gang research utilizing all of the approaches described so far with two additional methods that have seldom been employed. My fundamental data on gangs is derived from traditional field research in the community, interviews with individual gangsters, and use of an extensive questionnaire that elicited over sixty responses. My work with gangsters in prison gang focus groups, group therapy, and psychodrama proved to be valuable for enhancing my understanding of the phenomenon of violent gangs. I found that because my gangster respondents were bored with prison life, they contributed enormously to my research data. In prison, my captive audience, having nothing better to do and having plenty of time on their hands, sat for hours in individual interviews, gang focus groups, and therapy groups. They were much more amenable to discussing their gang organization and behavior, past and present, when they were in prison than when they were on the streets.

An important facet of their willingness to cooperate with my research interests when they were in prison was related to the fact that they were already convicted and sentenced. They had little resistance to discussing their past violent gang behavior, because their revelations would not result in additional punishment. Of course, the murders some of my gang subjects had committed and admitted to had no statute of limitation and were discussed with a certain level of obfuscation and discretion, and an assurance on my part that I would not reveal this information.

Most of the gangsters I studied were in a therapeutic community treatment program that stressed the open and public discussion of their past and present personal life. My role as a group therapist and psychodramatist in the program enabled me to collect data on the participants in my groups from a more logical vantage point than simply interviewing them about their motivations and personal life. A considerable amount of personal data emerged in the context of the group therapy sessions. At times, after an emotional therapy session, I would follow up with a one-on-one discussion about a particularly relevant subject with an individual who had become emotionally wide open and was highly motivated to explore a significant personal issue in his life.

In the context of therapeutic community groups, former rivals from different gangs were more amicable toward each other. In the nonviolent and nonthreatening environment of a prison therapeutic community they could share their past experiences in an effort to better understand their violent emotions. The positive social environment enabled former deadly enemies to see each other as human beings.

In the general prison population, gangsters were housed according to their racial and ethnic backgrounds by choice. This was facilitated by the prison administration. In a therapeutic community, about two hundred Chicano, black, and a few white convicts were integrated in one cell block. This integration factor enabled me to bring a Crip and a Blood or a Chicano and a black face-to-face in a focus group and have them discuss the nature of their hatred of each other as enemy gangsters. After placing them in chairs directly facing each other, and after a heated discussion, I would say, "Here is a guy who has many of the same problems of family and feelings about society that you have. In a way, despite the racial and enemy gang bullshit that divides you, you have essentially the same kinds of problems as human beings. Why do you hate and kill each other?" In the discussions that usually ensued from this kind of confrontation, some gangsters would see the foolishness of their hatred for each other and the senseless nature of gangbanging, and reveal a great deal of personal information that was most useful in understanding their motivation for participating in gangs. These insightful dialogues produced invaluable data on the general structure and function of gangs. From this conglomeration of research data I have developed and constructed my definition of gangs and a basic theory on the structure of violent gangs.

What Is a Gang?

Sociologist Emile Durkheim (1950, p. 65) exhorted the sociologist to be explicit: "Every scientific investigation is directed toward a limited class of phenomena, included in the same definition. The first step of the sociologist, then, ought to be to define the things he treats, in order that his subject matter may be known. . . . A theory, indeed, can be checked only if we know how to recognize the facts of which it is intended to give an account."

The term *gang* has been used to describe Thrasher's gangs, the Capone-like adult gangs of the roaring twenties, and the Mafia, Whyte's Norton Street group, Bloch and Niederhoffer's Comanche adolescent groups, Cohen's "delinquent boys," Cloward and Ohlin's "conflict gangs," and the contemporary Crips and Bloods. The contemporary violent drug gang, in my view, incorporates the following basic characteristics and activities:

1. All gangs have a name and a territorial neighborhood base, and they maintain a fierce proprietary interest in their neighborhood. They will fight for the territory they claim as their own and will attack any interlopers who come into their "hood" who belong to an enemy gang.

2. Joining a gang often involves a form of "jumping in" ritual that ranges from informal verbal acceptance to a violent initiation rite, and leaving the gang takes many forms.

3. Delinquent and criminal acts involving burglary and theft are important gang activities for achieving a "rep" (reputation) and status in the gang.

4. Senseless violence, including drive-by shootings and gangbanging (fighting other gangs), is a basic gang activity.

5. The commerce of drugs, drug use, and violent acts for the maintenance of drug territory are part of the gang configuration.

6. Gangs provide a form of social life and camaraderie, involving gambling, getting high, hanging out, and partying.

Gang Structure: The Gang as a Near-Group

Based on their research perspective, many theorists have determined that gangs are cohesive entities. Others have depicted gangs as loose structures. My research has led me to perceive the violent gang as somewhere in between a highly defined group and a loosely organized mob—what I term a *near-group*. My view of the gang as a near-group is illuminated by defining a "group" in sociological terms. A standard group is an identifiable, coherent, and finite entity of people who relate to each other on the basis of defined norms and rules for interaction. Membership in a group is clearly defined and involves some form of self-identification and recognition by other group members that an individual belongs to the group. In most groups the role of each member entails certain rights, duties, and obligations that are clearly defined. When all of these factors are clear, the members of a bona fide social group can reciprocally interact with each other in terms of the accepted norms of the group.

Social groups have defined values, and the behavioral expression of the values of most groups are openly accepted in the larger society. Deviant and illegal groups, whose values and behavioral enactments are considered antithetical to the values and goals of the larger society, tend to be less clearly defined, partly because they operate outside of the norms and laws of society. Because the behavior of individuals who participate in deviant groups is often illegal, the rights, duties, and obligations of participants are apt to be less clearly defined. In most criminal and deviant groups, including the violent gang, the definition of who is a member, the norms of the group, and the expected behavior of participants in the group are less clear than they are in groups that are socially acceptable and conform for the most part to the acknowledged norms of the larger society.

In terms of structure, in the overall social system there are three basic types of groups or collectivities, which can be arranged on a continuum: (1) social groups, (2) mobs or crowds, and (3) near-groups. Social groups are coherent entities that have norms that are clear to both the members and society. At the other end of this continuum of group organization are mobs or crowds. These are spontaneous collectivities that meet sporadically for some event, have limited or no continuity, and are not basically interactive. The people who participate in mobs or crowds have no membership status or clear roles. On the continuum, in terms of structure and behavioral function, near-groups are somewhere in between mobs or crowds and defined social groups. In a near-group the definition of membership, the leadership, and the norms and values of the collectivity are not as chaotic as those of a mob and not as coherent as those of a socially acceptable group. Based on these criteria, the violent gang is a near-group.

In summary, the violent gang has a near-group structure and has the following characteristics that enable a socially disabled gangster to have a sense of belonging and of community:

1. Participants in the near-group violent gang are generally sociopathic personalities. The most sociopathic are core participants or leaders, and the less sociopathic are more marginal members. These individuals belong to the near-group gang because they do not have the social ability to belong to more coherent and demanding social groups.

2. For the socially disabled gangster, the near-group gangs serves as a desirable adjustment pattern that not only accepts but aggrandizes his macho-syndrome behavior.

3. Because they are imprecise, the nondemanding roles that characterize the near-group violent gang structure satisfy the emotional needs of gang participants, who lack the ability to become members of more socially demanding groups.

4. The behavioral expectations for participating in the gang are diffuse and vary for each participant. Behavior is essentially emotion motivated within loosely defined boundaries. There is a limited consensus of normative expectations for behavior in the near-group gang.

5. In the near-group, cohesiveness decreases as a participant gangster moves from the center of the collectivity to the periphery. Core participants are at the center of the gang, and there are many marginal gangsters who sporadically participate less often and less intensely in the gang's varied activities.

6. Limited responsibility is required for belonging. Leadership is often self-appointed and varies with the activities of the gang at a particular time. There is a shifting and personally defined stratification system. Participation is often in flux, and it is difficult at any point in time to define the exact number of participants that comprise the gang.

7. There is a limited coherent and defined consensus among participants in the collectivity as to the near-group gang's functions and goals.

8. Norms and behavior patterns are generally deviant and consequently in conflict with the inclusive social system's prescriptions for behavior.

9. Interaction within the collectivity and toward the outer community is often hostile and aggressive, with spontaneous outburst of violence to achieve impulsively felt goals. Violent behavior, especially extreme and bizarre violence, is a highly regarded value and contributes enormously to the felt power and status of gangsters in the near-group violent gang.

A number of researchers have corroborated my viewpoint on the gang as a near-group. Notable among these researchers are Howard and Barbara Myerhoff (1964), who have carried out extensive empirical and theoretical research into gang structures in general and near-group theory in particular. They state:

The sociological literature about gangs contains at least two sharply conflicting descriptions of the extent of gang structure and the nature of their values. In the most prevalent view, the gang is seen as a kind of primary group, highly structured, relatively permanent and autonomous, possessing a well-developed delinquent subculture which is transmitted to new members. . . . Cohen has identified the primary needs met by the gang as those of resolving status frustration for lower-class boys, and providing an expression of masculine identification for middle-class boys. Parsons has also emphasized the achievement of sexual identity as a problem dealt with by delinquent behavior in a gang.

Cloward and Ohlin, following Merton's conception, have specified the discrepancy between aspirations toward success goals and opportunities for achieving them as the problem giving rise to gang behavior. Kvaraceus and Miller have stressed the inherent conflict between lower- and middle-class values and the delinquent's predisposition to the former in explaining gang behavior. Eisenstadt and Bloch and Niederhoffer have pointed to the gang as a collective response to the adolescent's striving toward the attainment of adulthood and the frustrations attendant on the transition from one age status to another. These authors identify different components of the gang subculture according to their interpretation of its function, but implicit or explicit in all these positions is the view of the gang as an integrated and relatively cohesive group.

A strikingly different interpretation of the structure of gangs describes them as more informal, short-lived, secondary groups without a clear-cut, stable delinquent structure. Lewis Yablonsky has suggested a conceptualization of the gang as a "near-group," specifying the following definitive characteristics: diffuse role definitions, limited cohesion, impermanence, minimal consensus on norms, shifting membership, emotionally disturbed leaders, and limited definition of membership expectations. On a continuum of the extent of social organization, Yablonsky locates the gang midway between the mob at one end and the group at the other. . . . The supervisor of a large, long-lived detached worker program in Los Angeles, with many years of gang experience there and in Harlem, has given a description much like that of Yablonsky. He observed that delinquent gangs . . . and their antisocial activities are committed in small groups. . . . He found communication between members to be meager and sporadic, reflecting the same limitations in social abilities that Yablonsky identified. (P. 348)

✶ Factors That Define the Violent Gang as a Near-Group

The following summarizes the most significant characteristics that define contemporary violent gangs as near-groups.

Emotional Characteristics of Gangsters

A gangster's personality is formed in the depressed, deprived, and violent cultural milieu of their hood or barrio. For youths growing up under onerous conditions, often including a dysfunctional family, the gang becomes their only source of identity, status, and emotional satisfaction. Ill-trained to participate with any degree of success in the dominant, middle-class world of language and norms foreign to their own, they construct their own community—the gang. In their gang they set goals that are achievable; they build an empire, partly real and partly fantasy, that helps them live through the confusion of life as an adolescent into early adulthood. All of these factors impact on their emotional characteristics.

A disproportionate number of gangsters are sociopathic, if not clearly in their basic personality, then certainly in their behavior. Their sociopathic personality is manifest in their senseless violent behavior. Pathologic gang youths have difficulty functioning in normal groups. The demands for performance and responsibility in the cultural context of the gang are readily adapted to the personal needs of these youths. The larger society, with its foreign values and expectations, is not compatible with their perception of the world.

A primary motivation of a gangster is his continuing quest for respect, reputation, and a sense of personal power that he feels are lacking. The acquisition of "respect" and some kind of reputation, even one as a killer, is sought to nourish underlying feelings of low self-esteem. He "puts in work" in the gang by committing acts of senseless violence in an effort to achieve the respect and personal power he feels is missing in his inner life. Many gangsters are willing to die for respect. This drive helps to explain their suicidal tendencies.

A social-psychological perspective that I have found helpful in analyzing the personality issue in a gangs youth's motivation is the concept of "existential validation"—a gangster's sense of alienation from human feeling or meaning. Most relatively normal people have a sense of identity and existence in their everyday activities. They do not require intense emotional excitement to know they are alive, that they exist. In contrast, some pathological people, including sociopathic gangsters, need extreme forms of emotional arousal in order to feel that they are alive. Their sense of ennui and alienation requires increasingly heavier doses of bizarre and extreme emotional behavior to validate the fact that they really exist. Extreme, violent behavior is one pattern that gives the sociopath a glimmer of being someone. In some respects, in this context, violence is an addiction. Many gangsters have told me that they are addicted to the emotional rush they experience in an act of bizarre and senseless violence.

Belonging

Because of their personality problems, most participants in the violent gang cannot be clearly or fully defined as members, since the gang's values, norms, and expectations for participation in the gang or the out-group society are not clearly defined. If a youth lives in a particular hood or barrio, joining and belonging to most violent gangs is a relatively easy process. Membership has a quality of vagueness.

The ritual of being formally "jumped-in" to join a gang is often a myth presented by gangsters to demonstrate that their gangs are more defined than they really are. There are no high standards for entrance placed in the way of a "wannabe" who wants to do the deviant "work" associated with becoming a member and rising in the hierarchy. The main criterion for belonging to the gang is a proclivity toward violent and delinquent behavior. There is a mythology built up around joining and initiation rites, such as the requirement that a potential member steal something or assault someone, but these entrance demands are not always fulfilled or really expected to take place. In some cases, however, a new member, at the whim of his homies, may run a violent gauntlet, be forced to commit an act of violence, or simply be accepted because he lives in the hood and begins to hang out with the gang.

There is little precise definition of role behavior in the gang. If qualifications and standards for belonging were more precise and definite, most gangsters would be unable to participate, since they usually lack the social ability to relate to others in a definitive way, an ability that is necessary for assuming responsibilities and belonging to a socially acceptable group.

The usual overt rationale given by gang boys for joining a gang is related to their felt needs for a "family" and involves their defense, protection, and a feeling of security. Although this is the usual surface reason given, on a deeper level of analysis it is revealed that the gang is a malleable vehicle for adjusting the members' personal problems and feelings of inadequacy. A youth's desire for community and belonging to something has more value for him than the spurious nature of the security and affection that is provided in reality by his associates. He seldom finds the love and caring of a family or the community he seeks in the violent gang; however, this reality is less important than his desire for some form of belonging that gives the illusion of being in a family or community.

Participation in and "belonging" to the violent gang does provide a sense of power. It also provides a channel for expressing a retaliatory aggression related to other emotions and difficulties, such as a response to discrimination or an acting out of racial prejudice. Thus, many youths, in an effort to cope with a variety of emotional problems, act out their personal frustrations and aggression through the gang. The gang provides a sense of "self-protection" in the hostile world that the gangster himself has helped to create.

The expectations for participation in the near-group violent gang's activities are unclear. Leadership and leaders are characterized by megalomania, strong needs to control territory, and an emotionally distorted picture of the gang's organization. The image and size of the gang's membership is often exaggerated and glorified by gang members to enhance their own feelings of power. The sociopathic disorder that exists in many gangsters fuels violent behavior even in their own set. A considerable amount of the gangster's time is spent in a pattern of needling, ridiculing, or fighting with his homies; consequently, a great deal of the "social" participation and camaraderie is of a negative nature. The underlying theme of these playful but often violent street-corner activities is an attempt to prove oneself by disparaging others. There is continual verbal and sometimes physical attack and defense going on. In most of these "playful" but aggressive encounters the underlying theme is one of expressing a felt hostility and rage that emanates from the gangster's depressed life situation.

There is a myth in many violent gangs that one can never rescind "belonging." In the Chicano gangs, the expression *por vida* (for life) is the standard. Yet, many youths do separate from gangs in a variety of ways. They don't usually resign from a gang and give up their participation in a formal way. After a sojourn in prison or jail, gangsters can voluntarily decide to give up the gang life. Most of the time, if they are making an effort to go straight, they will not be hassled in their efforts. In fact, in many instances, their desire to get a job and change their deviant life-style is encouraged by their homies.

In some cases leaving the gang can result in violent retribution; however, this is often done sporadically at the whim of other gangsters. There are no hard-and-fast rules about quitting the gang, as when a member resigns or retires from a corporate entity. Gangsters do not receive pink slips per se; however, on some occasions a pink slip may take the form of an assassination by a homie or a drive-by shot from an enemy.

A gangster can gracefully retire from gang activity without any retribution from his associates. This is most true for *veteranos* or old gangsters (OGs). They can retire with dignity. As one active OG told me about another OG who had retired, "He's thirty and he put in his work. He was shot eight or nine times fighting for his homies, and he did about ten years in the joint. He's married and has kids. He's got a little job. He just hangs out with us sometimes, gets loaded, and talks about the old days when he was gangbanging. People respect him for what he did, and if a kid wants some advice, or a war starts, we might get his opinion on what to do."

Belonging to and leaving a gang is not as clearly or formally defined as it is in more coherent social groups.

Levels of Participation: Marginal and Core Gangsters

Gangsters participate in their gangs at different times with different levels of involvement. Some individuals are marginal and have a limited participation in a gang, even though they appear to be gangsters by their demeanor and the way they dress. These marginal gang youths may present a gang appearance for the purposes of protection.

The core category includes those who are at the center of the gang's structure and are the most dedicated and involved gangsters. Core participants in a gang tend to know each other on a face-to-face primary group level. They live in close proximity to each other in the hood, hang around the same location, play together, fight among themselves, worry together, and plan gang strategy for warfare. The solidarity of the core gangsters is much greater than that of the outer ring of more marginal gang participants. Gang involvement is close to the core gangster's lifeline of activity, and the gang constitutes their primary world. Their ego strength, position in the world, and any status or pleasure they enjoy are tied to gang activity. Their turf and activities, particularly the gang's violence, give meaning to their existence.

Leaders and Leadership

In response to a question on leadership one gangster commented, "We don't have anyone as a special leader. We certainly don't elect anyone as a leader. If a homie puts in a lot of work like hurting or killing some enemies, or backing up his homies with action rather than bullshit he is looked at as a leader. Also, OGs are leaders, because they've been with the gang for a long time, they've earned their stripes, they know our history, and people respect them for lots of things they've done to help the gang be known."

Most gang leaders are essentially self-appointed and tend to assume a leadership role in a particular activity of the multipurpose gang. OGs have a level of leadership status based on their longevity in the gang and the violent quality of the work they have put in as gangsters. Many gangster leaders manifest paranoid delusions of persecution and grandeur. In some cases they attempt to compensate and adjust serious personality disorders by acting in the role of powerful pseudoleaders. Their wild dreams of glory often serve their personal pathological needs.

The Drug Factor

Crack-cocaine and heroin are the main drugs of use and commerce for gangsters. Crack is a commodity for both black and Chicano gangs; however, heroin in the 1990s became an important part of Chicano gang culture. Crack is a heavily addicting drug that has dominated hoods and barrios throughout the United States since the mid-1980s. Gangsters are involved in the distribution and sale of these drugs at all levels. Some gangsters have direct contact at the very top of the drug business with manufacturers and distributors on an international level. Those at the lower rungs of the drug business ladder deliver and sell drugs on the street.

The commerce of drugs (especially crack-cocaine) and the use of drugs by gangsters has an impact on the overall structure of the gang. The gangsters who are centrally involved in the commerce of drugs tend to form a more coherent and cohesive structured subgroup in the context of the multipurpose gang. They are in a business that involves the performance of specific roles in the buying and selling of drugs, and this requires some coherence to their behavior. They have to handle specific amounts of money, launder the money, and protect their territory from incursions by dealers who are not part of their organization. They have to call the shots on hurting or killing anyone who intrudes on their profit-making business. In some cases they have the responsibility of exporting their drug business into new markets.

The entrepreneurial corporate drug-dealing subgroup of the multipurpose gang has most of the qualities of cohesiveness that exist in most normal coherent groups. However, within this framework, there are a number of factors that affect this structure. These include the fact that the drug subgroup of the gang is involved in an illegal enterprise involving secrecy and the constant threat of being arrested, incarcerated, or killed.

Another problem that exists in the commerce of drugs is that some of the purveyors of the commodity get hooked on their product. This usually leads to the abuser being ostracized from the gang. However, even in the harsh world of the violent gang, there is sometimes room for compassionate help. I was told by a number of hard-core gangsters that they would often make an effort to counsel their homies when they were hooked. These "drug-counselors" discussed their "clients" and the difficulties of "treating" a crackhead. Although negative attitudes about crack and heroin prevail in the gang, marijuana and alcohol are perceived as harmless drugs that are used on a day-by-day basis. The evidence is overwhelming that the persistent use of any mind-altering drug by participants in a group has a negative impact on the structure and function of the group, and in this regard many gangs are near-groups because of the drug factor.

Violence: Gangbanging and Gang Warfare

Illegal violence is a basic characteristic of the violent gang. The use of illegal violence, either rationally or irrationally, necessarily affects the structure of any collectivity. There are two types of violence enacted in the near-group violent gang. One has a level of rationality—defense of drug territory, administration of a drug business in an area, or punishment of a "snitch" who violates the gang's code of secrecy. The other form of gang violence, the gangbanging pattern, is irrational. This violent behavior is motivated by emotional issues. It has no clear purpose for or consensus of definition by the participants.

In most cases, gang wars originate over trivia: territorial violation, a "bad look," an argument over a girl, paranoid revenge, or a remark that is perceived as disrespectful. These reasons are exaggerated and spread through gang networks in distorted ways to inflame gangsters into battle. Such provocations give disturbed youths a *cause célèbre* and a legitimate banner under which they can vent hostilities related to other issues in their life situations. The gangsters' emotions are fanned through interaction and produce a kind of group contagion. What starts out as a "bad look" from one youth toward another can thus develop into a major battle with a real or imagined enemy. Each youth who becomes involved can project into the battle whatever angers or hostilities he has toward school, his family, the neighborhood, prejudice, or any other anger-provoking problems he may be living through at the time.

In gangbanging that is not related to the drug business, at an "actual" gang-war event, or in a drive-by, participants may have little or no idea of why they are there or what they are expected to do except assault someone who appears to be an enemy. Gangsters and their leaders, citizens, the police, and the press are often caught up in the fallout of gang-war hysteria. The gang war can result in injury and often homicide. The confused nature of the near-group gang with its fantasy qualities helps make it more highly destructive than it would be if the violence was orchestrated in the more deliberate and coherent fashion of La Cosa Nostra.

Since the 1950s, gang warfare has escalated from one-on-one fist-fights and knifings to rat-pack group attacks to the grand form of the drive-by murder—the dramatic approach to murder that was invented by organized crime gangs in the 1920s. These early adult gang drive-bys had a precise target. Contemporary drive-bys sometimes target a real enemy who has invaded a gang's drug territory; however, more often than not they are spontaneously organized random hits on an imagined enemy fueled by the unspecified rage of gangsters who are high on alcohol or drugs. Gangbanging for some youths is a social narcotic.

The following description of a prototypical drive-by reveals the near-group nature of the violent gang:

> We were hangin' out, talkin' shit, and getting loaded. This cat, "Little Snowman," we called him that because he had a cold heart, kept talkin' about how these bloods had dissed him the day before. My homies had some guns that we had stole out of this house, and we had a car. Pretty soon we're talkin' about how we had to teach those motherfuckers a lesson they wouldn't forget. Myself, I didn't want to go—but there was no way to back down.
>
> The next thing I remember we're in the car and rolling on our enemy's hood. The closer we got to their hood, the higher I got. I remember my homie, OG Willie, who was leading our attack, screaming, "We're going to show those motherfuckers no love!"
>
> I only had a pistol, but my homie, with an automatic, sprayed these guys on the corner. Like in the movies—they all ducked and I saw two guys get hit and go down. We split, and for the next week that was all we talked about—who did what and how those motherfuckers deserved it. And how funny it was to watch this one dude get hit, and fall into some garbage cans. That week we all watched our backs—'cause we knew they would be coming back at us.

This drive-by was a spontaneous action, with no special planning or motive. The targets of such a drive-by include anyone who is in the line of fire; the shooters are typically high on some substance. Their participation in the violence provides an even greater emotional high, and the more bizarre the violent act, the greater the status the actor is accorded in the gang's postviolence dialogues.

Paranoid Pseudo-Communities: Why Gangsters Join Near-Group Violent Gangs

Norman Cameron's (1943) insightful social-psychological concept of the "paranoid pseudo-community" provides a theoretical perspective on why gangsters join and become enmeshed in violent gangs and further illuminates my viewpoint of the gang as a near-group. Cameron's concept, briefly stated, is that the emotionally disordered individual who is paranoid creates a pseudo-community in his mind, and sometimes these delusions find credence in reality. This concept is useful in analyzing those gangsters who perceive enemy gangs as out to harm them. In response to this impending violent doom, they organize their lives around the gang in a continuing defensive stance. Of course, there is some reality to this perspective on the hostile world that surrounds them; however, more often than not, their perception of enemy gangs as being out to "get them" is delusionary (p. 35).

The creation of this mental pseudo-community, according to Cameron, results from a series of events that impact on an individual. He posits that, in general, a group makes certain demands upon its participants, and in the normative pattern of life, the individual gives in to group demands. Most normal individuals find their participation in a group a satisfying experience and are willing to adhere to the normative demands of the group. In their daily level of group interaction, their participation is validated by other individuals in the group (p. 37). However, under certain circumstances individuals with socially inadequate personality development (like gangsters) fail progressively to adhere to the group's (society's) minimal requirements for behavior. This results in their becoming "socially disarticulated," and very often these individuals have to be set aside from the rest of their community to live under artificially simplified conditions. In my view, the violent gang is a creation that provides these "artificially simplified conditions."

Cameron further posits that some people with socially inadequate personalities become paranoid. He states, "The paranoid person, because of poorly developed role-taking ability, which may have been derived from defective social learning in earlier life, faces his real or fancied slights and discriminations without adequate give-and-take in his communication with others and without competence in the social interpretation of motives and intentions" (p. 40).

The gangster, whose role-taking skills are impaired in this way, lacks the ability to appropriately assess the behavior of others in their interaction with him. He begins to take everything the wrong way, and because of his social inabilities to think as others do, he becomes increasingly alienated and disassociated from the consensual world of reality that is perceived by most people. In this context, the gangster's delusional fantasies become hardened, and he begins to see and experience things not consensually validated or similarly felt by others. He lives in the context of what Cameron termed a "paranoid pseudo-community." The actions and attitudes ascribed by him to enemy gangs do not fully exist in reality. They exist mainly in his mind.

Cameron's description of a "paranoid person" fits the description of the sociopathic gangster. A "bad" look or any "diss" (disrespect) becomes a major issue for the gangster. He too often responds with a level of violence that is out of proportion to the act that he believes has been perpetrated by another gangster or people in the larger society. He often feels people are "out to get him."

The fact of the real community's response to and retaliation for his deviant behavior serves to strengthen the gangster's suspicions and distorted interpretations about the social system and its institutions. He utilizes this as further evidence of the unfair discrimination to which he is being subjected. He comes out into the open with overt action against his real and supposed enemies and manages to bring down further social retaliation. Society's retaliation includes arrest and incarceration. This makes the gangster's internal pseudo-community more objective and real to him. As Cameron stated, "The reactions of the real community in now uniting against him are precisely those which he has been anticipating on the basis of his delusional beliefs" (1943, p. 42). Even though most gangsters are aware that they are locked up because they have violated the law, they tend to perceive society's response to their deviance as unfair. Most incarcerated criminals, gangsters included, see themselves as innocent victims of a discriminatory society.

In summary, adapting Cameron's theory of the paranoid pseudo-community, there are four main phases in the process of a gangster becoming enmeshed in the paranoid pseudo-community of the near-group violent gang:

Phase 1: Most gangsters have been physically, emotionally, or sexually abused. This negative socialization by dysfunctional families produces a disproportionate number of sociopathic youths with limited social conscience and little ability to relate effectively to other people and groups in society. They are, as Cameron indicated, in a state of "social disarticulation."

Phase 2: Because of their paranoid sociopathic tendencies, these youths are alienated from the more consensually real and constructive community of the larger society. Their negative self-feelings of "difference," social ineffectiveness, and rejection become reinforced and hardened by society's response to their illegal and violent behavior.

Phase 3: A youth's sociopathic personality is articulated in a pathological paranoid reaction to the world around him. Participating in a gang gives the sociopathic youth some illusionary ego strength and contributes to a reaction formation that takes the form of a "tough-killer" macho syndrome.

Phase 4: The violent gang becomes, for this type of youth, a convenient paranoid pseudocommunity, one that is functional in at least temporarily alleviating his personal inadequacies and problems. The structure of the near-group violent gang, with its flexibility of size, power roles, and delusionary possibilities, make it a most convenient and acceptable collectivity for the sociopathic gangster.

Policy and Treatment Implications Derived from Perceiving the Gang as a Near-Group

It is axiomatic in a medical model that a correct diagnosis is vital for the solution of a physiological problem. The same reasoning applies to the effective solution of social problems. The current general perspective on the gang as a cohesive group that is presented by many theorists is not in accord with the drug-dealing, gangbanging, drive-by murderous character-istics of contemporary multipurpose gangs. A consequence of this view of the gang is that it leads to ineffectual treatment policies.

The therapeutic community (TC) provides the most promising approach for teaching gangsters how to relate to constructive groups in a positive community. The TC approach involves removing the gangster from a destructive gang and integrating him into the "positive gang" in a TC. A gangster's participation in a TC can modify his sociopathic personality and resocialize him to effectively participate in a law-abiding manner in soci-ety. (Chapter 17 delineates a projected plan for accomplishing the complex and difficult feat of resocializing delinquents and gangsters in a therapeutic community.)

PART 4

Substance Abuse

CHAPTERS

CHAPTER 9

GROWING UP IN A SUBSTANCE-ABUSING SOCIETY

An inner-city youth smoking crack cocaine. Various drugs are used by youths who feel a sense of hopelessness growing up in their "hood."

Since the 1950s, substance abuse has been a burgeoning national problem. The measures brought into play to counter the problem include a federal "war on drugs."

Juvenile Substance Abuse

The substance-abuse problem has reached awesome proportions in the United States and internationally. Most consumers begin using drugs at a young age, resulting in a large population of adult substance abusers. The problem affects not only the self-destructive abuser but also his or her family and has intruded into the political relationships of nations. In the countries of the world who supply the drugs (and have their own share of addicts) and those that illegally import the various drugs, the problem is increasingly part of everyone's life. As nations agonize and attempt to develop blockades for preventing the flow of drugs across their borders, too often we lose sight of the simple fact that, if there were no eager consumers, there would be no drug problem.

The statistics on juvenile substance abuse are almost irrelevant, since the patterns and fads of use shift like the changing ocean currents. Yet some general statistics serve as indicators of the problem. When I attended South Side High School in Newark, New Jersey, in the 1940s, practically no one used drugs. I recall that a few people were known to smoke marijuana, then called "reefers," and one individual later became a heroin addict. There were few adolescent alcoholics. My high school had about two thousand students. In 1997 the juvenile courts in the United States dealt with over 250,000 cases involving drug law violations. The figure is considerably higher when the estimated several million young drug users who never get arrested is added to this figure.

Almost every American teenager has tried some kind of drug, and around 20 percent of this population has bordered on addiction. Marijuana is the most widely used illegal drug by both youths and adults. Early in the century, marijuana use was restricted to a handful of people, mainly musicians. Since then, many new addicting drugs have become part of American culture. Heroin and cocaine, second in use to marijuana, have become the drugs of choice. They are used in a variety of ways by a sizable portion of the population. Marijuana use has become as American as apple pie, and in 1997 several states passed legislation legalizing the substance for "medical use."

In 1997, the Partnership for a Drug-Free America collected statistics on juvenile substance abuse worth noting. One relevant statistic cited in the Partnership's report, entitled *Juvenile Drug Abuse* (1997), is that 2.4 million youths have used some form of illegal substance. Teenage marijuana and other drug use in the United States has doubled since 1987, and there has been a parallel increase in marijuana use among preteens in the nine to twelve age group. Citing their ninth annual study of United States drug use, the Partnership states that marijuana use among preteens increased from 230,000 in 1995 to 460,000 in 1996. The study also found that in 1995, nearly one in four children aged nine through twelve, or 24 percent, said they had been offered drugs.

The children studied in the Partnership report indicated a decrease in the amount of antidrug information they were getting from outside sources, such as school, television, movies, televised public service announcements, and friends. The Partnership, a nonprofit coalition of advertising agencies and media professionals known for their antidrug advertisements, aimed to reverse this trend by an intense media effort to educate children about the negative effects of substance abuse.

Statistics collated by the National Institute of Drug Abuse (1996) reveal that there are 5 million regular cocaine users; 20 million to 24 million people have tried cocaine; there were 563 cocaine-related deaths: 30 percent of all college students had tried cocaine by their senior year; 42 percent of all college students had tried marijuana; and there are about 500,000 hard-core heroin users. Over 80 percent of high school students reported having used some illegal substance.

Smoking cigarettes is a widespread practice among adolescents, and the revelations from the Federal Drug Administration about the addictive and negative health consequences of smoking has focused attention on this issue. Although this section on juvenile substance abuse concerns *illegal* drugs, it is important to note that smoking nicotine is a devastating *legal* drug problem. It should also be noted that smoking by juveniles remains an illegal behavior, despite the fact that the law is seldom, if ever, acted upon. If the so-called stepping-stone concept of escalating drug use has a degree of validity, smoking nicotine may be the first step on the ladder for some youths to a life of more severe substance abuse.

Almost all illegal substances negatively affect people emotionally and physically; however, nicotine's primary negative effect has been on people's health and longevity. The consequences of smoking tobacco, with the active ingredient of nicotine, have been so devastating than in 1997 a number of private citizens who had members of their family die from smoking and a number of state attorneys general have sued the tobacco companies. States have also sued companies on the basis of the billions of dollars they have had to spend on the health problems of people negatively affected by smoking, and the war on nicotine is escalating.

A research report issued by the California Department of Health (*Report on Smoking Habits,* 1997) reveals a national trend of smoking patterns.

Researchers surveyed a representative sample of eight thousand adults and two thousand children, ages twelve to seventeen. The report states that smoking among California adults, which had been dropping for more than a decade, rose sharply in 1996 to 18.6 percent of the adult population. Nationwide, about 25 percent of the adult population smokes tobacco. The California Department of Health's research includes findings that point toward a future increase in smoking among children. The percentage of children considered "susceptible" to smoking tobacco has increased to 45 percent from 25 percent a few years ago. Smoking among adults continued its overall decline among whites and Latinos, but the new surveys show that smoking increases were particularly evident among African Americans and Asian Americans. In addition, smoking increased among people who had less than a high school education and were between the ages of eighteen and twenty-four and among men ages thirty-five to forty-four. Clearly, smoking has not declined, and various research predicts that the rise will continue for several years.

Smoking among youths fell to 8.7 percent in 1992, but starting in 1994, smoking among teenagers increased. In 1996 the percentage of teenagers admitting to survey takers that they smoked was 11.6 percent. The survey also showed that increasing numbers of teenagers viewed smoking as acceptable. In 1993, researchers identified 25 percent to 30 percent of the teenagers interviewed as being "susceptible" to smoking. In 1996, that number had risen to 45 percent. The number of seventeen-year-olds addicted to cigarettes increased from 9.9 percent in 1993 to 12 percent in 1996. The study defined "addicted smokers" as a person who had smoked at least one hundred cigarettes and stated that research shows that the vast majority will need sixteen to twenty years to quit.

The escalation in substance abuse has become more "democratic." Earlier in the past century, severe addiction was primarily restricted to the lower socioeconomic segments of society. Today, the problem is found among people in all walks of life. People of all ages and occupations have become addicted to drugs and alcohol. The current problem has affected people with high and low statuses in different social organizations. Consequently, the crippling effects of substance abuse have had a profound negative impact on all major social institutions in American society.

Various research indicates that adolescents who continue their education beyond high school tend to continue their substance-abusing behavior. Substance abuse among college students appears to be escalating. Colleges and universities that receive federal money are required by law to make yearly reports on crimes committed on their campuses and to make these reports available to students and employees. A survey by the *Chronicle of Higher Education* (Drug abuse in colleges . . .,1997) revealed that drug arrests on major college campuses climbed by almost 18 percent in 1995. The survey covered all four-year colleges and universities enrolling five thousand students or more. While the survey highlighted the rise in drug arrests, college health specialists said alcohol abuse posed a far greater problem. There were 6,797 arrests for drug violations in 1995, up from 5,764 the previous year, and 15,208 arrests for liquor-law violations, up from 15,027. An official at one university appropriately commented that almost all of the sexual assaults in the previous year were alcohol-related.

The abuse of drugs in high school is often referred to by adolescent users as "recreational drug use." This casual attitude about substance abuse is often carried by adolescents into their adult life, and this tends to exacerbate the overall problem.

Another factor related to the general substance-abuse problem in the United States is the proliferation of a variety of drugs in the illicit marketplace. The former staples of substance abuse such as alcohol, marijuana, and heroin have been joined by PCP, LSD, "ecstasy," "designer" drugs, cocaine (in various forms, including "crack"), and an increasingly larger selection of addictive medications. Certain drugs that were thought to be harmless have turned out to have long-term and even lethal consequences in their effects on the users. Notable in this context is marijuana and especially cocaine. Juveniles who began smoking marijuana several years ago for "fun" discover too late that they have become strongly psychologically dependent on the drug.

Cocaine, formerly a rich person's party drug, has in a more marketable form known as "crack," penetrated into usage in all segments of society and has had a destructive effect on many users. A number of well-known athletes, men in perfect physical condition, have died from heart failure shortly after using cocaine. On the contemporary substance-abuse scene, adolescents are heavily into the use of crack, and too many have succumbed to the lethal consequences of this deadly drug.

Another problem related to substance abuse, especially for delinquents, is the complex relationship that exists between intravenous use of drugs and AIDS. Recent research in the United States reveals that nearly 50 percent of intravenous drug users carry the AIDS virus. Delinquents, especially teenage runaways of both genders involved in prostitution, are especially vulnerable.

Defining the Substance Abuser

How do we know when a person is truly addicted and when some form of help is needed? In most cases, when family and friends believe that a person is addicted to a drug or alcohol, the person denies his or her addiction.

Because of self-deception and denial, the person refuses to take the first step in treatment—admitting he or she is a substance abuser.

Based on my research and observation of young substance abusers, the following five elements are present when a person has crossed the line from being a "recreational" or "casual" user to becoming a substance abuser or addict.

1. *Overwhelming need.* People become substance abusers when they have an intense conscious desire for their drug of choice or a variety of drugs. They have a mind-set where acquiring and using drugs becomes the paramount fixation or concern in their lives. The need or motivation to use drugs emanates from a number of complex situations in the substance abusers' social-psychological sphere. These needs or motivations come from one or several of the following forces: (a) *Self-medication.* This involves the use of a drug to relieve some specific emotional or physiological pain. (b) *Addictive continuance.* After an individual has become addicted, he or she needs to continue to use an addictive substance to relieve the potential pain of withdrawal. (c) *"Recreational."* This form involves an effort to temporarily alter one's mood and "have fun" under the influence of a drug. (d) *Peer pressure and conformity.* Adolescents are often motivated to use drugs or alcohol in order to conform with the substance-abuse behavior of their friends and peer groups. (e) *Hallucinogenic use.* The user wishes to alter his or her state of consciousness in an attempt to reach a higher level of awareness. (f) *Releasing inhibitions.* The user has a need to remove mental blockades in order to enact behavior he or she wouldn't ordinarily act out. A drug is sometimes used to "party," to remove sexual inhibitions, or attempt to perform more effectively on an intellectual level. These are only some of the modalities that motivate substance abuse. For some adolescents peer pressure is a primary motivation. Others take drugs as a way of self-medicating their emotional problems. For most, however, their need for drugs is motivated by a number of these forces.

2. *Controlled by substance.* Having one's life controlled by a substance is a significant criterion in determining who is a substance abuser. This issue is the Alcoholics Anonymous first step: the substance has taken power over the person, and his or her life has "become unmanageable."

3. *Self-deception and denial.* Almost all substance abusers in the early phase of the addictive process practice self-deception and denial. Their denial often takes the form of stating in one form or another, "I can quit any time I want to." However, they almost never quit on their own

unless some strong outside pressure is brought to bear on them. The denial syndrome also takes the form of lying to others and themselves about the amount of drugs they use; the degree they are dominated by their drug habit; the fact that the drug has become an integral part of daily life; and that their use of drugs has negatively affected their personal relationships. I developed in my work with adolescents what several youths in one of my therapy groups named the "Yablonsky Principle." This principle asserts that the amount of drugs or alcohol the substance abuser admits to when first asked the question, How much drugs or alcohol do you use and how often? can be immediately multiplied by three. In support of the "Yablonsky Principle" in therapy groups I have directed, I have routinely asked adolescent substance abusers this question. The interviewee will at first answer the question with a false response. In almost all cases upon further probing, the addict will admit to at least three times the amount and frequency of use beyond his or her initial response.

4. *Periodic abstinence.* Most addicts occasionally become drug free for a period of time when their habit becomes too onerous or they are in a custodial institution. They may quit for a brief period to prove to themselves that "I can quit anytime I want to." The period of abstinence is usually very short compared to the length of time of their overall abuse syndrome. I have known substance abusers who have used drugs for over twenty years and during that period of time have "quit" over fifty times.

5. *The addict self-image and primary group relationships.* After a period of time, the addict's substance abuse becomes a central focus of his or her behavior and in many cases represents his or her identity. The addict no longer denies being an addict after he or she has tried to quit a number of times and failed. The true addicts now begin to feel most at ease with peers, "friends," and cohorts who have the same drug problem they have, and these "friends" more and more comprise their primary group. Adolescents refer to themselves with a self-identifiable term like "druggies" or "stoners." These substance-abusing collectivities increasingly become alienated from people, friends, and family who are not drug abusers. They become identified by others with labels such as alcoholics, "junkies," "cokeheads," or "potheads." The perceptions and responses of others tend to affect the addicts' self-concept. The perceptions of other people reinforce the addicts' self-image and identity as drug abusers. The delinquents now have a firm self-concept of being part of a substance-abusing subculture, and this helps to perpetuate their addiction.

Patterns and Trends in Substance Abuse by Delinquents

Drug abuse has been a part of all social systems since the beginning of recorded history. The Bible cites cases of the use of substances that were no doubt antecedents of contemporary substance abuse. In the past century, most societies have had problems with the abuse of alcohol, morphine, opium, heroin (a derivative of morphine), cocaine, and marijuana.

In the 1940s very few youths used illegal substances. Some used alcohol, however, the alcoholic problem among teenagers was moderate. Marijuana in general, and heroin in particular, were part of the juvenile drug scene in the ghettos of large cities. Cocaine was restricted to the wealthy and some jazz musicians. In this period, the opiate drugs, especially heroin, were used by minority youths to block out their onerous social environment, to attempt to resolve personal problems, and to escape into a state of pleasant reverie. Heroin, especially among lower socioeconomic groups, has posed a persistent drug abuse problem. Although heroin has been used to some extent by young people in the middle and upper segments of society, it has been and remains a predominantly lower-class phenomenon in American society.

In the 1950s, with the advent of rock-and-roll concerts, marijuana and alcohol became more widely used by adolescents. Heroin and marijuana remained a problem in this period, especially among minority youths growing up in depressed socioeconomic conditions.

In the 1960s and early 1970s, the "greening of America" was the philosophical pretext for raising consciousness and for mind expansion. The 1960s in particular was a peak period in the use of drugs by adolescents, sparked by the hippie era. Beginning in the early 1960s, Timothy Leary, then professor of Psychology at Harvard and his associates experimented with hallucinogenic drugs, a catalyst for adolescent substance abuse. Leary's early pop-culture admonition to youth to "turn on" (use drugs, especially psychedelic substances), "tune in" (explore your inner emotional world through "consciousness-raising" drugs), and "drop out" (quit bureaucratic societal game playing) was followed by a major explosion of psychedelic substance use and abuse by young people throughout the country.

A variety of psychedelic substances were advocated and used by a large number of adolescents. Most teenage and young adult dropouts used psychedelic hallucinogenic substances (LSD, mescaline, "mushrooms") in the context of a new sociocultural awakening free from the "heavy trips" of the larger society. In the hippie orbit, marijuana was the "black-bread staple" drug used on a daily basis by millions of young people to maintain their plateau of being and staying high. They referred to this process as "maintaining." LSD and other psychedelics were an important part of this social-exploration scene. This period saw an enormous increase in adolescent substance abuse. The so-called hippies of that era set an ethos of embracing drugs as a way of exploring one's inner world and raising a person's level of consciousness. Mind-altering drugs for the first time in American history were perceived as not deleterious to a person's emotional or physical health. To some extent, this attitude was carried over into the latter part of the century and affects our contemporary drug problem (Yablonsky, 1968).

In the 1970s many youths began to "crash" and run into serious emotional problems from substance abuse. More potent drugs, including heroin, methamphetamine, "crystal," or speed began to appear. In the depressed socioeconomic areas of the city, marijuana and heroin continued as the drugs of choice. Although hallucinogenic drug use was waning, the 1970s was a period of increased acceptance of drug use by many people who had been part of the "psychedelic revolution" and had now moved back into the mainstream of society. This more accepting attitude toward drug use made marijuana in particular an easily accessible drug tacitly condoned by parents, many of whom had been substance abusers in the 1960s. Some of these parents used drugs with their children, partly to rationalize their own substance abuse as acceptable behavior.

The 1980s and 1990s were strongly impacted by the commercialization of cocaine in the form of crack. A consumer could easily purchase $10 to $50 worth of rock in a "rock house," on the streets, or in the business sections of large cities during his or her lunch break. Drug use and abuse reached grotesque proportions and caused the federal government to escalate what they call a "war" on this severe national problem that has pervaded all segments of society. Youths growing up under these conditions have become heavily involved in substance abuse. Although crack has become a particularly popular drug, all other substances continue to be used (Fagan and Ko-Lin, 1991).

The impact of the general substance-abuse pattern has had a profound impact on the delinquency problem. I estimate that over 90 percent of all delinquents have used illegal substances, and a large percentage of this group has, or has had, a serious substance-abuse problem. Therefore, substance abuse has now become an integral and significant part of the overall juvenile delinquency problem in the United States.

The Sociocultural Context of Substance Abuse by Delinquents

A major influence in the creation of the growing adolescent drug problem is adult substance abuse, with special emphasis on parents as negative role models. Research data supports the theory that the children of substance-abusing parents, especially alcoholic parents, are likely to become substance abusers. This parent-child drug syndrome was especially prevalent in the late 1960s and early 1970s. The attitudes and behavior regarding drugs during that time set the stage for the explosion of drug abuse by adolescents in recent years.

There are several theories about parental substance abuse and its impact on children: (1) parents may influence the child to become an abuser because of their substance-abuse role modeling; (2) nonusing but severely disciplinarian parents may cause their children to rebel against their harsh norms, and the rebellion may include substance abuse; (3) substance-abusing parents may genetically or physiologically transmit the problem to their children, since there is clear evidence that the children of addicted mothers are often born addicted to the same drug their mother was abusing; (4) in some cases, a parent clearly and directly influences children's drug use by using drugs with them. This connection was cogently described by Mike Granberry (1986).

> Bob is forty-one. His daughter, Melissa, is sixteen. They first "did drugs together" when she was eleven. Their basic high? Marijuana. "I never considered marijuana a drug," he said. "I thought it a sacramental religious experience. I actually quit drinking before I quit using marijuana." Melissa says that her mother, Doris, thirty-nine, also used drugs. By the time she was fifteen, Melissa was smoking marijuana, drinking, "doing crystal and coke, LSD, mushrooms. . . . The way I got into drugs was totally through the family," she said. "They were so [screwed] up, I had to start using, just to fit in." Once, in front of friends at a birthday party, Melissa was given a "giant joint" tied with a bow and ribbon— Mom's gift to her. "I thought it was so cool," Melissa said. "I think back on it now and realize how bizarre it really was."
>
> Today, Bob and family appear to be normal middle-class Americans, living in the San Diego suburb of Chula Vista. They agreed to be interviewed as long as their real names were not used. They are "recovering drug addicts and alcoholics," under the care of a program for the children of alcoholics in San Diego. They shared their story, hoping it might give some insights to parents giving drugs to children.
>
> At the end of the interview Bob remarked, "I can't smoke

one joint, and I can't drink one beer. If I do, I lose my entire sobriety. My chief symptom was denial—even to giving drugs to my kid. Denial is what keeps you going. It can keep you going for a very long time." He glanced at the floor, then at his daughter's face. "Wow," he said. "I could have killed her."

In my own work I have encountered many situations of the type described by Granberry. In one case, a fourteen-year-old girl in a drug treatment group I directed revealed that she had been turned on to the drugs by her grandfather, who was a substance abuser.

The Effects of Quasi-Legal Substance Abuse

Children are inundated by television and other advertisements for nonprescription headache and sleeping pills. This social climate sets the tone for the belief that emotional problems, or for that matter any problem, are easily cured by ingesting pills. Each year millions of legal prescriptions are written by physicians for psychoactive drugs, such as tranquilizers, amphetamines, and barbiturates, and most of the time these prescriptions are for rational medical purposes. However, a substantial portion of this pill-popping is related to feeding a drug habit in a quasi-legal context. These drugs are essentially used by "right-thinking," generally conservative, middle- and upper-class people who have no reason to believe they are doing anything deviant. This pattern of drug use, however, gives children the message that drugs are an acceptable way to cope with the stresses and strains of living. It is ironic that adults can use these drugs with impunity. However, when an adolescent uses the same drugs by buying them from a drug dealer to solve problems or simply to get high, he or she may be labeled "juvenile delinquent."

In an article on prescription mind-altering drugs in America, Lennard, Epstein, Bernstein, and Ransom (1970) came to some interesting conclusions. Their central theme was that America's pharmaceutical companies were engaged in promoting drug use, and a proportion of these drug sales fed the habits of quasi-legal substance abusers. They asserted, "In order to extend the potential market for its product, the pharmaceutical industry, in its communications to physicians, all too often practices mystification in relabeling an increasing number of human and personal problems as medical problems, and drugs are the solution. It is apparent that the pharmaceutical industry is redefining and relabeling as medical problems, calling for drug intervention, a wide range of human behaviors which, in the past, have been viewed as falling within the bounds of the normal trials and tribulations of human existence. Much evidence for this position is to be found in the advertisements of drug companies, both in medical journals and in direct mailings to physicians."

The researchers presented a number of examples to illustrate their point. The first involved the potential personal conflict a young woman might experience when first going off to college. On the inside front cover of a journal an advertisement stated: "A Whole New World . . . of Anxiety . . . to help free her of excessive anxiety . . . adjunctive Librium." Accompanying the bold print is a full-page picture of an attractive, worried-looking young woman, standing with an armful of books. In captions surrounding her, the potential problems of a new college student are foretold: "Exposure to new friends and other influences may force her to reevaluate herself and her goals. . . . Her newly stimulated intellectual curiosity may make her more sensitive to and apprehensive about unstable national and world conditions." The text suggested that the product together with counseling and reassurance "can help the anxious student to handle the primary problem and to 'get back on her feet.' " Thus, the normal problems and conflicts associated with the status change and personal growth that accompany the college experience are relabeled medical-psychiatric problems and as such are subject to amelioration through a legal drug.

Another journal they used as an example had an advertisement that advised a physician on how he or she could help parents deal with their children with such everyday anxieties of childhood as school and dental visits. This advertisement portrayed a tearful little girl and in large type appeared the words: "School, the dark, separation, dental visits, 'monsters.' " On the facing page the physician is told in bold print, "The everyday anxieties of childhood sometimes get out of hand" and in small print below, "A child can usually deal with his anxieties. But sometimes the anxieties overpower the child. Then, he needs your help. Your help may include [product name]." The advertisements, in effect, presented a skewed conception of normal behavior and behavioral change. Potential anxiety engendered by new and different situations is defined as undesirable, as constituting a medical and psychiatric problem that requires the intervention of a physician and, most particularly, the prescription of a psychoactive drug.

Physicians and parents with a low tolerance for their own anxiety, or who are unable to meet the demands of even a temporarily troubled child, are more prone to believe that the child is disturbed and in need of drug treatment. There is, however, no substantial evidence that prescribed drugs facilitate children's participation in school situations. What is especially disturbing about advertisements is that they tend to enlist the help of physicians to introduce children to a pattern of psychoactive drug use. Paradoxically, such drug use at a later time in their lives, without a physician's prescription, is deplored both by the medical profession and the community at large.

Lennard and his colleagues deplored the fact that psychoactive drugs played a much too important role in many parent-child relationships. In another relevant example, the authors describe an ad on the box of a physician's sample of a psychic energizer used to to combat depression. On the box is a picture of an adolescent girl. About the picture in bold print is the legend, "Missing. Kathy Miller." Below the picture we read, "$500 reward for information concerning her whereabouts." Alongside in white print we read the plea, "Kathy, please come home!" Inside the box is a letter entitled, "Kathy, We love you. . . . Please come home." The ad states: "Dear Doctor: For parents, inability to communicate with their children is a significant loss. The 'What did I do wrong?' lament of the parent may be accompanied by feelings of incapacity, inferiority, guilt, and unworthiness. Many may, in fact, be suffering from symptoms of pathological depression. What can [product name] do for your depressed patient?" The advertisement then described how the product relieved these symptoms.

From my viewpoint, drugs are a peculiar method for handling a delinquent runaway, that is, remove the delinquency problem from the realm of family dynamics, then convert it into a medical problem that can be "cured" by drugs. The parents, rather than dealing with the behavioral situation, are encouraged to allay their fears and anxieties with a drug. In this way, drug use is set up as a model for the false resolution of an intrafamily problem. When a physician prescribes a drug for the control or solution (or both) of personal problems of living, he or she does more than merely relieve the discomfort caused by the problem. He or she simultaneously communicates a model for an acceptable way of dealing with personal and interpersonal problems.

In the foregoing case of a juvenile runaway, the parents may have been mishandling the situation, and faced with feelings of "incapacity, guilt, depression, and unworthiness" might change their behavior and become better parents—so their child would not want to become a runaway. The palliative of what is in essence a tranquilizer might have a negative impact on the family system, because it would mask the reality of the situation and would lead to only a temporary "feel good" resolution. In the long run the parents and their child who wants to run away into delinquency require human counseling to effectively resolve their problem. Drugs provide a temporary and false feeling that a solution has been effected.

Another gross error in rationality is depicted in the advertisements of the pharmaceutical establishment. Their promotion pieces describe specific psychotropic drugs as altering specific emotional states and affecting specific psychological processes. This sells a single result from the drug, even though it has been clearly established that any mind-altering drug has side effects that are often deleterious.

Pharmaceutical companies describe the desired effects of a drug's impact and label these "main effects." All other effects are labeled "side effects," regardless of whether they are positive or negative, merely uncomfortable or highly dangerous.

Using the pharmaceutical companies' rationale for their psychoactive drugs, an advertisement for heroin or cocaine could read: "Here is the solution to all your problems. Relief is just a fix away. Warning: may be addictive." Essentially the statement about the immediate relief by ingesting the drug is true. But it is totally misleading, because it fails to mention that the addictive "side effects" are so horrendous that they clearly negate the positive benefits of the drug that are touted by the advertiser.

Lennard and his colleagues concluded their analysis of the drug problem created by pill-popping in the following way:

> Drug giving and drug taking represent all too brittle and undiscriminating responses, and ultimately, in our view, they will breed only more frustration and more alienation. Changing the human environment is a monumental undertaking. While seeking to change cognitive shapes through chemical means is more convenient and economical, the drug solution has already become another technological Trojan horse. The ultimate task is to alter the shapes of human relatedness and social arrangements that determine the context and the substance of our existence. To maintain, as do significant groups within the pharmaceutical industry, the medical profession, and the youth culture, that this can be accomplished merely through chemical means is indeed to have fallen victim to mystification. (1970, pp. 438-441)

There is little doubt that this widely accepted concept of "mystification" and the power of psychoactive drugs affected the patterns of drug use by young people in the 1970s. The concept of drug use to alter and resolve human problems has been a central theme of many youth movements. The tremendous growth of drug use among young people stems in part from the affirmation of its use by adults in "legal form." Allen Geller and Maxwell Boas (1971) described succinctly the adult influence on juvenile drug use of the seventies: "Today's teenagers entered a world in which mood-changing substances were a fact of existence; sleeping pills, stimulants, tranquilizers, depressants and many other varieties of mind-altering chemical compounds have long been absorbed into the nation's pharmacopoeia, and popping pills, swallowing capsules, and downing tablets were a national habit. Our youngsters' indulgence in drugs can hardly be blamed on some sinister outside influence; they witnessed firsthand the tranquilizer-amphetamine-barbiturate boom as their own parents took eagerly to psychic delights. They grew up regarding chemicals as tools to be used to manipulate the inner mind" (p. xvi).

Physicians, who are often referred to as "Dr. Feelgoods," have become vigorous drug-dealers in the escalation of pill-popping in the past century. This pattern of quasi-legal substance abuse was described by George Reasons and Mike Goodman (1978) in an article in the *Los Angeles Times*. They wrote:

> The president of the state's Division of Medical Quality estimates there are "between 500 and 1,000 drug-pusher doctors" in California. They are illegally giving out close to a million pills a day, and they do it by writing prescriptions for anyone who can pay their fees. They operate in almost every community. Many doctors know who they are but will not expose them, said Dr. Eugene Feldman, president of the Division of Medical Quality. Although it is estimated that less than 2 percent of the state's doctors are involved, narcotics agents say, the doctors now illegally supply about 90 percent of all pharmaceutical drugs on the street. Some of these doctors earn $1,000 a day writing illegal prescriptions for anyone who can pay the $10 to $20 fee, preferably in cash. A doctor with a pencil and prescription pad has a ticket to a fortune, one narcotics agent said. "He works great hours and makes no house calls, doesn't need medical equipment or medical employees. The drugs they deal are powerful narcotics that can transform young men and women into helpless addicts whose drug tolerance grows along with their drug dependence."

The Physician's Desk Reference is the drug manual for members of the medical profession. It clearly warns of the danger to patients who use drugs without careful supervision. The most sought-after pills on high school and college campuses across the nation all carry warnings as to their danger in this reference source. Many psychoactive drugs are swallowed by the handful, but often they are dissolved and injected into the bloodstream with hypodermic needle and syringes, known as "outfits." The outfits sometimes are supplied by pharmacists who work with doctors, cashing thousands of their prescriptions a week for up to 100 percent profits. There are hundreds of these pharmacies in the United States.

Some of these quasi-legal drug-dealing doctors run assembly-line operations. Their waiting rooms are often jammed with addicts, pushers, and teenagers. The doctor's office sometimes becomes a meeting place for the drug culture. Those awaiting their turn often make their wait a social event by swapping information on new doctors and "easy" pharmacies, trading prescriptions and pills, and selling marijuana and sometimes heroin.

Drugs distributed in this way have become a national problem that fosters substance abuse by delinquents. A narcotics officer told me that "often these pharmaceutical pills wind up in the hands of large-scale dealers in Las Vegas, Seattle, Chicago, New York, and Miami. A clearly criminal Los Angeles doctor working with the syndicate wrote prescriptions for more than a million pills, delivered to his confederates by the boxload. In another case, 200,000 pills were seized in the office of an Oakland doctor who confessed to 'indiscriminately and recklessly dispensing huge quantities of dangerous drugs' over several years. A San Francisco doctor was caught driving a panel truck loaded with 1.7 million amphetamines destined for the street. One West Los Angeles doctor sold thousands of prescription blanks to a dealer who filled them out, got the drugs, and sold them to criminal syndicates in Las Vegas and New York."[1]

One substance-abusing young man who utilized this type of quasi-legal drug situation to support his habit described his participation in the following way:

> I was living off these doctors. A lot of my friends were, too. The doctors helped me become a junkie. They kept me well supplied with a powerful narcotic pain-killer. I was shooting it up and selling it. I always carried my "outfit" (syringe, needle, and drugs). I needed a fix about every two hours. I would do this in toilet stall doors closed tightly so no one could see me "tie off" and fix. I would crush the tablet, drop the powder into the spoon, put some water on top, fire underneath, cook it, draw it, and fix. It took four or five minutes. Once a week I performed the important ritual of visiting my main doctor. I was getting eighteen to twenty tabs a day from the doctor. The tabs I didn't shoot I sold on the street. My drug habit grew until it was all I thought about. It consumed my life.

The distribution and usage of these Dr. Feelgood drugs are indirectly facilitated by large pharmaceutical companies, who have no real concern about the potential users of their products or the fact that their customers might become addicted. They are prime examples of profits taking precedence over human life. A student told me the following story about the large pharmaceutical firm he worked for: "My company doesn't care who uses their drugs or who gets addicted. They are only involved with sales and profits. In one case they received an order and shipped a staggering amount of amphetamines to a drugstore in a small town in Mexico. I would estimate that the shipment would keep every man, woman, and child in that town loaded for fifty years! Our executives knew it was a crooked deal, and that those drugs would be sold back across the border, probably in San Diego and Los Angeles in the illegal drug market, and that California high school kids would be using those

---

1. Personal interview, June 15, 1993.

drugs. But they didn't see that part of it as their problem. They were and are in business to sell drugs."

The widespread and insidious problems created by the enormous sociocultural impact of quasi-legal pill production and use, with a special emphasis on its impact on adolescent substance abuse, may be summarized as follows:

1. There are valid reasons for a person, including parents and their children, to use some form of physician-prescribed tranquilizer to get through a life crisis or in a therapeutic situation.

2. Despite this legitimate use, the wide acceptance of psychoactive substances tends to relabel "human problems" as "medical problems." It sets up an ethos where drugs are used in an attempt to solve problems that might be better solved by discussing the problem with a friend, introspection, or therapeutic counseling. This drug ethos that exists in the larger society is not lost on youths. They adopted this described adult "philosophy" on drugs, and this facilitates their substance abuse.

3. An ironic situation exists in our society where it is legitimate for a doctor to give an adolescent drugs; however, if a juvenile administers the same drug to himself or herself, he or she is violating the law and may be adjudicated as a delinquent.

4. Supplying psychoactive drugs to adolescents may be more beneficial for the parents and doctors who give them the drugs than it is for the juveniles. Giving children psychoactive drugs may calm them down; however, it doesn't solve the problems. An adolescent under the influence of a psychoactive drug is sedated, more compliant, and not usually belligerent or argumentative. As in Aldous Huxley's *Brave New World*, where the soma pill tranquilized the people, adolescents will become more malleable in their sedated state; however, their underlying emotional problems persist.

5. When proponents advocate the extensive use of behavior altering drugs, they tend to emphasize only the immediate positive effects and not the longer term negative side effects. For example, a good case can be made for the powerful energy and short-term "happiness" and "self-confidence" that can be quickly achieved on cocaine or amphetamines; however, the longer term consequences can be depression when the user stops using the drug. The user may become addicted and have to confront the painful consequences of being hooked on drugs— and the difficult process of "kicking a habit" and learning how to live without drugs.

6. Finally, the use of psychoactive substances may sidetrack individuals from getting effective psychotherapy or counseling, which, over the long run, would be more beneficial to their health and future life situation.

Female Substance Abuse and Delinquency

In the overall sociocultural context of American society, both adolescent females and males have achieved equality as substance abusers. There are, however, some special issues and hazards related to female substance abuse that deserve emphasis: (1) substance abuse when pregnant affects the fetus, and (2) mothers are the primary socializing agent for children. An addicted mother is often more harmful to her child than a father, because an addicted father is more likely than the mother to be an absentee parent. Research suggests that many young women are turned on to drugs by male companions. Lee Bowker (1978) found that girls' use of alcohol and marijuana is influenced more by their boyfriends than by their girlfriends. For boys, he noted, peer influences appear to be "homosocial" (that is, boy influencing boy), whereas, for girls, peer influences appear to be "heterosocial" (boy influencing girl). It appears that drug use spreads more from males to females than from females to other females. There is a good deal of evidence that males provide illicit drugs and receive sexual favors in return. Bowker summarized this situation as follows:

> The combination of biological and social pressure may lead to ambivalence about sex among females. For males the pressures are all toward engaging in sexual behavior. As a result, males try to get their girlfriends to agree to participate in sexual intercourse. Females are socialized to please males (on dates and everywhere else), yet expected to avoid pleasing them so much that they ruin their reputations. A reasonable solution to this double-bind dilemma is for females to join their boyfriends in recreational drug use and use it as an excuse for participation in initial and subsequent drug seduction (I'm not that kind of girl, but I was just so drunk). (1978, p. 90)

Prostitution and Delinquency

While working with substance-abusing adolescents, I became acquainted with a phenomenon referred to by adolescents as the "coke-whore syndrome," sexual favors accorded males who supply females with drugs. Many girls and women support their drug habits through the "coke-whore syndrome," which is a less dangerous form of the female addict-prostitution syndrome. The female in this context does not have to get involved with the more dangerous form of street prostitution where she "turns tricks" to get money for her drugs from a stranger. The behavior of most female delinquents is explained by the addict-prostitution syndrome. Following are some typical examples of this syndrome.

Paula

My interview with Paula, who had been a New York prostitute and heroin drug addict for many years, revealed the problems that an addict-prostitute confronts on the streets. Her story provides a case history of the path traveled by many girls who begin as "incorrigible" delinquents who are abandoned by their families and later in life become substance-abusing prostitutes.

> Before I was nine or ten, I was a problem child. I was put into a problem child's institution at a very early age. I think I was a year or a year-and-a-half old when I was abandoned by my parents and placed in an institution. I progressed from there to different institutions until I was sixteen. The last reformatory I was in was a so-called treatment center. Here I got my final street education. Most of the kids there, including myself, were considered incorrigible. Most of the guys had long criminal records for drug use and violence. Some of the girls had been runaways and whores from the age of twelve.
>
> The guys were violent, and some were accomplished thieves and con men. I absorbed all of their teachings readily. I enjoyed it. I think I always knew I was going to use drugs. I used my first form of drugs when I was twelve. There were two guys who lived in the same apartment house where my family lived. I admired and looked up to them. They were about seventeen or eighteen at the time. I was allowed home visits once or twice a year for a weekend when my behavior in the institution I was in at the time was good enough.
>
> Whenever I did manage to get a home visit, I looked forward to hanging out at night in front of the house with these guys. They seemed to know I was hurting inside and tolerated me. One summer night I saw them going to the roof of the house, and I followed them. They were smoking marijuana. It smelled good to me, and I asked for a hit. I turned on. I remember that I felt it was the most beautiful thing that ever happened to me. I was very happy and started to imitate all the singers I liked at that time. The guys gave me lots of approval for my singing. From then on, I was one of them and got all the pot I could use.
>
> After that year, I was introduced to cocaine by the same two guys and horned it whenever the opportunity arose. For fourteen years I enjoyed all the drugs I could get my hands on. Heroin crept up on me. I normally weighed 125 pounds. There was a period when I was badly strung out on heroin and weighed 90 pounds. I thought my clothes had stretched! I had a six-year

period of using every form of narcotic and everything that went with it.

Maybe if I describe the average life of a female addict in New York City, you will get an idea of what my life was like. My hours were from six to six. That is, six in the evening to six in the morning. I'd get up as late as possible, because the sun hurt my eyes. I didn't want people to look at me. You know something's terribly wrong. You're different. Squares are scurrying around, bumping up against each other. They look insane to you. Addicts talk a lot about how crazy squares are. You get dressed, and if you happen to have some drugs you take your morning fix. From there on in, you begin to scramble for bread and drugs, and anything goes.

I would buy and sell drugs. Most dealers are addicts. They're not the big-time people you read about with beautiful apartments. The heavier dealers (those with large quantities of drugs) are usually addicts too. That's the reason they're dealing. It's a simple matter of economics. You buy a quantity. You cut the drugs yourself. You sell a little bit. You make a little money to buy more dope. Most of the time you're broke, so you use your wiles. You'll use anything you've learned. You con, and being female you have a few tools that guys don't have.

I got pretty mean with my life when I turned out as a whore. I participated in many degrading acts. If you check Krafft-Ebbing, you will find a pretty good catalog of what I had to do to make my money. If you get drugs that are pretty strong, you can go along on them for a few hours. But usually drugs are so weak and cut down, you have to fix six or eight times a day to feel normal. When you have a real heroin habit going, you don't really get loaded like you see acted out in the movies or read about. You need the drug to feel normal.

After the first few months of addiction, the stuff takes over. The demand builds higher and higher and the supply is never enough. You need more and more drugs and money. I spent as much for myself as I did for my old man. (You would call him a pimp. I didn't think he was.) If I made $500 a day, it would be spent on drugs.

[handwritten margin note: TAKES OVER LIFE]

Maria

Paula could have become the mother of Maria, a thirteen-year-old crack-cocaine addict-prostitute. Maria lived with her prostitute-addict mother, turned tricks, and used drugs with her in San Francisco. Maria was torn between two worlds when she cleaned up her habit in a drug rehabilitation therapeutic community. Her mother often called, begging her to return to their life on the streets.

I interviewed Maria after she was drug free, and she commented as follows: "The most important lesson I've learned in the program is that I'm worth something." Maria at thirteen looks twice her age. A small "12" tattooed on her hand reveals her past. It was tattooed one night after she did a lot of cocaine. Now it reminds her of the twelve stages of her drug-abuse recovery program.

Maria's family background is prototypical for an incipient drug addict. When she was five, her drug addict parents left her to be raised near Oakland by her grandmother. She was seven when she began experimenting with marijuana and PCP. At eleven she went to live with her mother and joined her world of sex and drugs. She turned to prostitution when her habit reached $200 a day. She returned to her grandmother the following year, but soon she ran away. She was raped twice and arrested for heroin use, and even when she moved back to her grandmother's house, she continued using crack.

One night she returned home intoxicated and high on PCP. "I walked into the house, then I fell on the floor kicking and screaming, telling my grandmother to kill me." Instead, her grandmother enrolled her in the drug-treatment program. Maria commented, "It was the first time I was strong enough to say, 'That's it.' "

The beginning of her treatment program was difficult. She was hard to reach, cold and distant. "I don't always trust others with my feelings," she said. Soon, however, she was talking openly in groups that discussed family problems along with detoxification. The program taught Maria that she would probably never be free of the urge to use drugs or the pressures of the world outside. Despite her problems, Maria was learning to live one positive drug-free day at a time in the therapeutic community.

Maria is typical of many teenage addict-prostitutes who have been resocialized in recent years in a "therapeutic community."

Andrea

The social-cultural forces that produced Paula and Maria's substance-abuse problems emanated from a lower socioeconomic class situation. The contemporary substance-abuse scene for adolescent females appears at all levels of society. The following case example of Andrea depicts the substance abuse etiology of a middle-class girl.

Andrea had it all. She was a cheerleader in an affluent suburban city, a member of the homecoming queens court, and an honor student who thought that taking drugs was dumb. But Andrea did an abrupt about-face when she was suspended from the cheerleader squad for, of all things, putting on lipstick during class.

She bleached her hair white and cut it in a Mohawk. As her mother remembers, "She went from preppy to punk in seven months." No longer in the teenage social elite, Andrea sought acceptance in the school's drug culture. "I just wanted to be 'it' again, and I was, with another group." Soon her grades dropped to F's, she couldn't wake up in the morning, and she had screaming fights with her divorced mother. Andrea commented, "I was strung out on coke, acid, everything I could put into my body." Her mother suspected she was using drugs, but when she broached the subject, Andrea ran away. Friends found her a sanctuary in a rundown crack-house where she had been smoking crack-cocaine with some criminal and violent male cohorts, who sexually abused her.

Andrea called an old school friend, giving her a phone number "in case anything happens to me." The call probably saved her life. The friend finally betrayed Andrea's secret to her frantic parents. Two juvenile officers plucked her from the seedy apartment about 4:00 A.M., and later that day she was committed to a drug-rehabilitation center for youths. She screamed and carried on, but shortly after admission Andrea became determined to come clean. She was half dead at that time and wanted help. Andrea's most vivid memory of treatment was being able to see colors again. In the depths of her addiction, she saw everything in shades of black and gray. She stayed in the locked inpatient program for seven months, then attended public school part time for five months. After that, she was released to the third phase of the program in the community, where she attended group therapy and twelve-step meetings. She was on her way to recovery.

Janet

I interviewed Janet in the Amity Therapeutic Community. Her father had been a criminal and an addict who had been successfully rehabilitated in Synanon. She loved and respected her father, who when she knew him was a functioning person and a good father. Her problems arose when her father died in an accident when she was fifteen. A year later, she ran away from her mother, who had remarried. Janet apparently suffered an emotional trauma from the loss of her father, and in some respects her drug use was related to a search for her father.

> I am a twenty-six-year-old woman who feels as if she has lived many lives. I started shooting heroin at fifteen after running away from home. I found my true love in the spoon and with the needle. Upon coming to Amity, I had been strung out for ten years on a variety of drugs ranging from heroin to methadone.
>
> I lost my father at the age of fifteen. That's when my troubles began. He was my hero, my protector, my friend, and I idolized him. But, I never grieved his death, because I didn't know how to deal with the loss of a person I truly loved. I let that sense of loss,

258

anger, and grief rule my life. I tried in my own way to destroy myself through many years of heroin addiction and prostitution.

I was raped at seventeen, and that became another problem for me. I felt an incredible sense of shame. I felt like no decent man would ever want me again. I felt dirty, ugly, and used up! Hate became my way of showing the world that I could handle my pain. I shot dope to sleep, and when I was semi-awake, I hung around with people who were angry and violent. I hated the world, and I blamed everyone around me for the pain I felt.

At eighteen I found myself standing in front of a Los Angeles judge in handcuffs. I was being charged with petty theft with a prior. As I stood before him, I begged for a drug diversion program. He told me that I was a hopeless addict! I was sent to the Sybil Brand Los Angeles County Jail to kick a bad heroin and methadone habit cold turkey. I felt hopeless and pathetic.

I am five feet, seven inches tall, and at that the time I was about ninety pounds. My arms looked terrible, with black tracks running down both of them. I had collapsed veins throughout my entire body. I sat in jail just begging God or somebody to take the pain away. I will never forget that prison experience.

When I got out of jail, I of course returned to prostitution and heroin, since my jail experience was of absolutely no use. I married a man who lived a life of violence and crime. All of my hate and anger was OK with him, because he was like me. I thought I had found my protector again, and in some strange way, a piece of my father. My husband became my emotional baggage. He became a person who needed me, and he validated all of my insecurities. He was also the person who turned me out into the sex industry. He showed me the ropes. He walked me to work at the peep shows every day. He walked me to work at the strip clubs every night. I became his mother, his room and board, and paid for his daily fix with my body.

As a prostitute and a stripper, I worked in the sex industry for quite a few years. I lived for my fix, and I would do anything to get it. I danced set after set so loaded that I would trip over myself. I remember many nights working the Tenderloin [San Francisco] streets. Sometimes I'd get a sick, weird, and violent trick, and I would just be grateful to make it out of a hotel room alive.

Finally, through some real friends, I found my way into the Amity Therapeutic Community. I have been at this treatment center for over a year, and I am doing great. I am healthier than ever, and I have friends who help me in my groups to understand my past life as a junkie.

I'm happy, but the groups have stirred up many of my past experiences that I have to deal with and understand—all of my dancing with life and death—despite the healthy pain of looking at myself, which is productive. I no longer wake up "dope sick" with that horrible ache and fogged view of the world. I can see many things clearly now, and it's a really neat feeling. I feel lucky to have lived through these experiences. The main thing that has helped me in my changing and growing process are the friends I have made in Amity. I have developed friendships with many people, and sometimes they know me better than I know myself. These people, with small gestures of humanity and caring, have made me feel much more like a good human being.

I write this with the hope that it will be useful to other women who are killing themselves with drugs. I have lived the life of a "street junkie," and today I am living the life of a "square." In my opinion that gives me a wealth of knowledge about both worlds. I am sharing my life here with the hope that my experience will help someone else who is going through the hell I experienced. I represent thousands of other women in the United States who are on the streets or sitting in juvenile or adult prisons. Since I have been able to save my life through Amity, I believe these other women should know that there is hope for them to change and live a decent and happier life.

Female Substance Abusers as Mothers

Paula, Maria, Andrea, and Janet are examples of adolescent females substance abusers and how they managed to recover their lives. Millions of adult females have somewhat different patterns of substance abuse, and the processes of their recovery are more complex. It is of significance to explore this aspect of the female substance abuse problem, because these women are mothers who too often foster the substance abuse and delinquency of their children.

A true story that was reported to me by a student reveals one aspect of the enormous problem of pill-popping mothers. A nine-year-old became increasingly angry about what was, from his point of view, a situation where his mother never seemed to stop picking on him. She was on his case from morning to bedtime about such things as cleaning his room, eating the right food, and doing his homework. According to his sister, my student, the child burst into an angry diatribe at his mother and said, "Why don't you leave me alone? Why don't you behave like my friend Jimmie's mother? She lays on the couch all day, and she never picks on him." According to my student, Jimmie's mother was addicted to a tranquilizer. Like thousands of American mothers, she was on tranquilizers most of the time and never disciplined her son or assumed her parental role.

Psychoactive-drug pill-popping has increasingly become a social problem in America. One consequence of this pattern of substance abuse is that many parents do not enact their proper parental role. The severity of this problem for women is often revealed when they attempt to kick their often secret drug habit (Gordon, 1981).

Treatment Issues

Ann Japenga (1982) analyzed how one woman kicked her habit in a rehabilitation center especially created for women. "Barbara, a thirty-eight-year-old medical technician, got off drugs the hard way. She just stopped. The first days without . . . , a sedative her doctor had first prescribed for sleeplessness, were bad—anxiety, the shakes. But on the seventh day she lost control of her muscles. To survive the following weeks, she clung to a scrap of paper on which she'd written, 'This is withdrawal. You're not crazy.' "

Some people think of tranquilizers as the choice of housewives and substance abusers who do not have a severe habit. What they don't know, and what the women who take them (67 percent of prescriptions for psychoactive drugs go to women, according to the National Institute on Drug Abuse, 1993) don't know is that the withdrawals can be as terrifying as anything experienced by a street-hardened junkie.

A medical doctor, Josette Mondanaro, who was director of a California substance abuse program, opened a special facility for women. Dr. Mondanaro believed that established detox programs weren't being used by middle- and upper-class women because the services were geared to the male street-drug addict and consequently were unequipped to handle withdrawal from prescription drugs—a long-term project. Dr. Mondonaro's rationale was: "There are reasons women aren't using the programs: image. A woman who talks, thinks, and looks like the mainstream of society has a hard time going to place a reserved for junkies. She doesn't think of herself as an addict and she's not easily identified as one. The only clue that something is wrong may be recurring backaches, migraines, or insomnia" (quoted in Japenga, 1982).

Dr. Mondonaro described a woman who came to her drug facility, called Wingspread.

> Mary is one who didn't believe drugs were her problem until she came to Wingspread. "I thought I was crazy . . . my mother had a medicine cabinet full of drugs. If anything was out of whack, you took a pill." Mary dresses expensively, furs complementing her silver-gray hair. At forty-one, she's twenty years older than the average client in a street-drug program. Like most of the women at Wingspread, she's been addicted more than fifteen years. Her doctor prescribed diet pills when she was fifteen. Later, she was in a traffic accident and another doctor gave her an open prescription for Codeine and Dalmane for neck pain. This month she celebrating a year of sobriety. Over the slow course of recovery at Wingspread, she said she's been able to admit to part of her problem: she's an alcoholic, but her self-image won't allow

her to identify with pill-heads. "The drug addict part I still really have a problem with. And none of my family (she has two teenage children) believes I've ever been an alcoholic or drug addict." (Quoted in Japenga, 1982)

I interviewed a number of adolescent girls and women who were addicted to tranquilizers. The interviews took place in a psychiatric hospital where I directed group therapy sessions. When a female is dependent on a tranquilizer, her nervous system is depressed, and during withdrawal, it rebounds with a fury. Some women have a feeling of imminent death. In addition to psychological symptoms, muscles twitch. Some female patients can't sleep or their bodies jerk violently in their sleep. Some sweat profusely, have a bad taste in their mouth, and suffer from severe and constant headache. Some have seizures. These are the kinds of symptoms that make addicts think they're crazy. They don't realize that the discomfort is due to withdrawal. The effects of withdrawing from some prescription drug often don't appear until seven days after stopping the drug, so many people don't associate the symptoms with withdrawal. After taking a drug for five to ten years, it is difficult to quit "cold-turkey." Therefore, the drug to which the patient is addicted is generally doled out in decreasing dosages a day at a time. The actual detox process can take from six to eight weeks. Many of the women I worked with were parents. When they were addicted, their ability to parent was severely impaired. This usually had a devastating impact on their children.

Psychologists Richard Brotman and Frederic Suffet (1976) drew a number of conclusions about female addicts from their analysis of several studies. When they reviewed the findings on female drug use, Suffet and Brotman found that whether the drug is marijuana, heroin, or cocaine, women are usually initiated into the scene by men. In a study of needle sharing, it appeared that most men (68 percent) but few women (29 percent) injected themselves. Most studies of drugs for recreational and pleasure use indicate that males tend to be the regular users, although among the very young the gender gap narrows. While females are still more likely than males to spurn many illicit drugs, they are the major consumers of psychoactive drugs like barbiturates, sedatives, tranquilizers, antidepressants, and amphetamines.

When research subjects in the Brotman and Suffet analysis were asked what they used to cope with life, more men reported that they drank alcohol, while women said they took pills. When addicts were asked why they first dabbled in drugs, women were more likely than men to cite "the relief of emotional disturbance." Brotman and Suffet also found in their analysis of relevant research that female addicts held conventional values, despite the fact that most of them turned to prostitution to support their habits. Based on their research, Brotman and Suffet ventured a prediction about the future of female drug use. According to these researchers, "As women take their rightful place in the work world, they will be subject to the same pressures men experience. They may continue to pop pills or they may turn to booze to forget the strains of the office." It is apparent from recent statistics that females, especially minor teenage girls, are increasingly becoming serious substance abusers.

Female Addicts, Pregnancy, and AIDS

Female addicts who become pregnant have a special problem that relates to future generations. This problem is transmitting their substance-abuse problems and possibly HIV and AIDS to their child at birth. A substance-abusing pregnant woman has a drug-induced physical impact on her child at birth. Mary presents a case example of the addicted teenage mother. She was thirteen years old when her teenage boyfriend shot her up with heroin for the first time. "I like the way it felt, and I wasn't thinking then about babies." Addicted to heroin, Mary became pregnant two years later. After she knew she was pregnant, she tried to end her addiction to heroin and cocaine. The consequences were devastating. Her severe physiological withdrawal killed the fetus. After that, Mary gave birth to two children during a period when she used "speed" and cocaine. She was using a considerable amount of cocaine while she carried the first of these two, a son. The boy was born premature. He was brain-damaged, and exhibited the irritability, jitteriness, and slow development that is characteristic of children who are born addicted to cocaine. When the second child was born, Mary went into premature labor after injecting herself with crystal methamphetamine ("speed"). Her daughter nearly died at birth. The infant spent three weeks in intensive care and was then placed by social workers in a foster home.

Mary's case, which is unfortunately typical of thousands of teenage girls each year, raises a number of difficult questions. When and how should society intervene to protect a substance-exposed baby from its addicted parent? Should a pregnant mother be held legally accountable for not following sound medical advice during pregnancy? These questions are compounded by the fact that many of these addicted AIDS-prone women are already in prison.

Alcohol abuse remains a major danger for teens. Research reveals that about ten thousand children are born annually with fetal alcohol syndrome, and another thirty-six thousand are born with more subtle forms of alcohol-related damage. This malady is characterized by distinctive facial and body malformations, mental retardation, and inhibited growth. Karen Ann Farr (1995) carried out extensive research on these issues.[2] She states:

> During the 1980s, concern about fetal harm resulting from a pregnant woman's use of illegal drags escalated, and prosecutions of pregnant drug users for harm against the fetus, or fetal abuse, were undertaken in several states. Because of constitutional and statutory problems, as well as concerns about fairness and effectiveness, efforts to criminalize fetal abuse have typically failed to withstand judicial scrutiny. Evidence suggests that criminal prosecution for fetal abuse relies on questionable procedures, is unevenly applied, and may keep women from seeking drug treatment or prenatal care. Besides legal questions, there are also concerns about issues of fairness and effectiveness. Most notably, there is clear class and race unevenness in the reporting and likelihood of fetal abuse. Poor women and women of color are more likely than others to give birth in hospitals where drug testing is done, to be tested (and have their newborns tested) for drug use, to be reported to child welfare authorities for drug use, and to be prosecuted for fetal abuse.

A lack of money and understanding prevent needed prevention, intervention, and rehabilitation programs—from detoxification, counseling, and social work for pregnant drug users to special nursery care and developmental follow-up for drug-affected newborns. The growing numbers of teenage addicted mothers exacerbates the problem.

In summary, several factors influence the substance abuse patterns of juveniles: (1) the direct influence of parents who use drugs with their children; (2) negative substance-abusing adult-parental role models who say "do as I say, not as I do"; (3) a pill-popping philosophy that erroneously states that human problems can be resolved with psychoactive drugs; and (4) substance-abusing mothers who directly transmit addictive and health problems to their children.

All these factors converge to significantly affect the widespread substance-abuse attitudes and behavior of children and adolescents in contemporary society. It is painfully clear that unless realistic an effective treatment interventions are introduced, it is a certainty that the twenty-first century will be polluted by an even more deleterious substance-abuse problem for juveniles. Drug addict behavior will substantially enlarge the juvenile delinquency problem.[3]

2. See also Rita A. Isbell and William H. Barber, "Fetal Alcohol Syndrome and Related Birth Implications," *Journal of Special Education*, June 1993, and Don C. Des Jarlais and Samuel R. Friedman, "A.I.D.S. and Intravenous Drug Use," paper presented at the 15th Institute on Drug Abuse, Amsterdam, The Netherlands, April 1986.

3. For a fuller discussion of these issues, see Ronald Akers, *Drugs, Alcohol, and Society* (Belmont, CA: Wadsworth, 1992); Howard Abadinsky, *Drug Abuse* (Chicago: Nelson-Hall, 1993); and James Inciardi and Karen McElrath, *The American Drug Scene* (Los Angeles, CA: Roxbury, 1995).

CHAPTER 10

DRUGS USED, THEIR IMPACT, AND TREATMENT ISSUES

Psychodrama is a basic method used in many therapeutic communities and psychiatric hospitals for treating adolescent substance abusers. In this photo, Dr. Yablonsky, assisted by his staff, is directing a psychodrama with a 16-year-old recovering addict. The girl, hitting the chair with a soft bat, is acting out her hostility towards a stand-in for her father, who physically and sexually abused her. She attributes her addiction to his abuse, and is role-playing to enact her repressed rage and attempt to resolve her problem.

In the first half of the twentieth century, there was a limited effort at controlling the substance use of American citizens. Laws prohibiting alcohol were passed in the 1920s; however, the prohibition laws were seen as a failure—alcohol usage actually increased while alcoholic beverages were legally prohibited. Drugs like cocaine and heroin were primarily used in the music culture and by minority groups. Marijuana was used freely, it was perceived as a problem after it became characterized as the "devil's weed" in films such as *Reefer Madness.*

There may have been some cause-and-effect relationship to the type of drugs used in any given period in American history; however, this connection would be difficult to ascertain. Perhaps the clearest period of drug use where some connection could logically be made between the cultural ethos of the time and the type of drug used would be the 1960s. Marijuana and the psychedelic drugs of that era were used by juveniles primarily for self-exploration and breaking free from what many young people perceived as an onerous, controlling, bureaucratic social system (Yablonsky, 1968).

In the history of substance use and abuse in the twentieth century, there has been a social and legal bifurcation that enabled adults, but not juveniles to use certain drugs. The legal controls include the proscription of all drugs, including alcohol and tobacco, for juveniles. Now that nicotine is perceived as an addictive drug there is a strong movement to eliminate smoking by young people.

One constant in the overall drug controversy in the past century has been the prohibition of drug use by juveniles. In fact, any boy or girl under the age of eighteen who uses these substances has violated the law and could be adjudicated a juvenile delinquent. Despite the laws, many young people use a variety of drugs; juvenile drug use has escalated, and this trend will most likely continue in the twenty-first century.

In the following sections, I examine some of the basic substances used and abused by juveniles. Emphasis is on the emotional effects of the drugs, the social context in which the drugs are used, and how each type of substance abuse impacts the overall delinquency problem.

Alcohol

The use of alcohol by an adolescent is a "status" delinquent defense, since it is illegal for a juvenile to drink alcohol. Alcohol, next to marijuana, is probably the substance most used by youths in the United States, and when used in excess leads to alcoholism. Alcoholism is a chronic behavioral disorder manifested by repeated drinking of alcoholic beverages in excess of the dietary and social uses of the community to an extent that interferes with the drinker's health or his or her social or economic functioning. According to the National Institute on Alcoholic Abuse, in 1996 there were 2.5 million alcoholics in the United States. Alcoholism is considered one of the nation's greatest health problems, and since it results in serious consequences to the alcoholic and his or her family, its easy availability contributes substantially to delinquency.

The National Council on Alcoholism reports that the proportion of high school students who drink has doubled in almost every decade since 1970. There is also persuasive evidence that the age of alcoholism in children has dropped from twelve to nine. According to Wright and Kitchens (1976), "The drinking patterns of children tend to model those of their parents and the immediate sociocultural milieu. . . . Like father, like son is true in many areas, and as a result boys are more likely to drink than girls" (p. 97).

A study by the Research Triangle Institute for the National Institute of Drug Abuse (*Research Triangle Institute Report,* 1995) concluded that most American teenagers drink alcoholic beverages and that one-third of the nation's high school students are "problem drinkers." The study showed that, despite laws against minors purchasing alcohol, seven of ten high school students said they could "usually" or "always" obtain it.

Probably because drinking alcoholic beverages is a source of recreation and pleasure for about half the population, the person addicted to alcohol is not rejected by society to the same extent as are other types of addicts. Alcoholism is usually regarded as a disease that requires hospitalization and treatment. Evidence to support this position is based on physiological and psychological data. Excessive use of alcohol results in such physical complications as malnutrition, cirrhosis of the liver, polyneuritis, and gastrointestinal bleeding. Psychologists and psychiatrists note the compulsive nature and self-destructive characteristics of the alcoholic's drinking patterns. The actions of the alcoholic so closely approximate those of an emotionally sick individual that alcoholism is viewed as a disease.

Every state has a law against drunk driving. Driving while inebriated is a common way for juveniles to acquire delinquent status in the juvenile court. Drunk drivers account for a disproportionate share of automobile accidents and death on the highways. The use of alcohol affects delinquency directly and indirectly:

1. Directly: The use of alcohol by a minor is a "status offense." Also, drunkenness that interferes with others is forbidden in most states. Where state laws do not provide penalties for such behavior, county, municipal, or other local laws usually do.

2. Indirectly: The excessive use of alcohol contributes to the commission of serious delinquent acts such as robbery and violent behavior.

Many delinquents admit that they have committed serious delinquent acts under the influence of alcohol. Grace Barnes (1984) concluded, based upon her research:

> Adolescent alcohol abuse is a complex issue which has been shown in this work to be related to other problem behaviors as well as to other general socialization factors such as parental nurturance. It is clear from this study that heavier drinkers have more specific alcohol-related problems and a greater prevalence of problem drinking in general than do infrequent to moderate users of alcohol. A profile of adolescent problem drinkers emerges from this study. Problem drinkers have a variety of other problem behavior or problems in living. They are characterized as having negative attitudes toward school, receiving poor grades in school, having poor interactions with parents, and placing little value on parental advice in decision making. In addition, there is a strong relationship between heavy drinking and various other deviant behaviors, including staying out later than parents allow, running away from home, skipping school, and using marijuana. (P. 36)

Despite the fact that alcohol remains illegal in most jurisdictions for young people under eighteen, drinking alcoholic beverages appears to be a growing pattern of accepted behavior in juvenile peer groups. Most youths drink because of the positive immediate effects it has on their personality. Drinking tends to mask feelings of inadequacy, gives some youths a sense of power, provides euphoric feelings, and in some instances is used to overcome inhibitions.

Some sociologists see adolescent drinking as a form of rebellion. Robert Bales (1959) reasoned that abstinence norms may actually encourage the use of alcohol as a symbol of aggression against authority. He wrote. "The breaking of the taboo becomes an ideal way of expressing dissent and aggression, especially where the original solidarity of the group is weak and aggression is strong. This total prohibition sometimes overshoots the mark and encourages the very thing it is designed to prevent. This situation is frequently found among individual alcoholics whose parents were firm teetotalers and absolutely forbade their sons to drink" (pp. 263–267).

Based on a study of the drinking patterns of 1,410 high school students, Norman Alexander (1967) affirmed Bates's observations:

> It has been shown that the likelihood of drinking and of legitimating the use of alcohol (in opposition to parental expectations) is inversely related to the closeness of the adolescent to an abstinent father. Furthermore, among drinkers who lack peer support for alcohol use, the rejection of their father is associated with frequent disobedience of parental authority in order to "get even" with them. . . . The rejection of parental authority is associated with fre-

quent and excessive drinking leading to extreme intoxication, and drinking for psychological rather than social reasons is an expression of rebellion against the parental authority figure. (P. 548)

Psychiatrists Henri Begleiter, Bernice Porjesz, Bernard Bihari, and Benjamin Kissin (1984) saw genetic factors as part of the alcoholic syndrome, especially as it pertained to fathers and sons. Based on their research they asserted:

> Genetic factors may be involved in the development of alcoholism. Sons of alcoholic fathers represent a special group at high risk for developing alcoholism even when they are separated from their biological parents soon after birth. Studies of male adoptees indicate that the biological rather than the adoptive parent is predictive of later drinking problems. Further evidence for a genetic predisposition comes from twin studies indicating that the concordance rate for alcohol abuse among identical twins is almost double the rate for fraternal twins; patterns of alcohol consumption are also highly concordant among identical twins. This evidence suggests that a genetic factor may be involved in the presence of natal pathophysiology associated with alcohol abuse. (P. 280)

G. Lawson, J. Peterson, and A. Lawson (1983) identified four parent types associated with the development of alcoholism in children. According to these researchers, alcoholics typically have one or both parents in one or more of the following categories:

1. The alcoholic parent: While alcoholic parents encourage development of alcoholism in their offspring in many ways, the most important way is through role modeling. Thus, if the child's parent deals with problems by drinking, so too will the child.

2. The teetotaler parent: In general, teetotaler parents provide their children with rigid rules and expectations which are unrealistic and inconsistent with basic human needs. In response, the child of a teetotaler parent may display his or her contempt for such unreasonable expectations by abusing alcohol, typically during adolescence or early adulthood.

3. The overdemanding parent: The high expectations of overdemanding parents make it impossible for the child to develop a positive self-image. In response, such children may turn to alcohol, drug abuse, or become mentally ill.

4. The overly protective parent: As a result of being overly protected, children of these parents have been deprived of opportunities to develop self-confidence or feelings of self-worth or to learn how to deal with life's problems. Thus, such children may respond to problems by drinking. (P. 134)

Another significant aspect of alcohol abuse and delinquency is that it is perceived as a "stepping stone" to the use and abuse of stronger illegal substances. In a study by John W. Welte and Grace Barnes (1985) the "stepping-stone" theory of progression into drug use was examined based on the alcohol and other drug use of over 27,000 seventh- through eighth-grade students in New York State. Welte and Barnes found that students do not use illicit drugs unless they also use alcohol.

> White, black, and Hispanic students all tend to initiate the use of drugs in the following order—alcohol, marijuana, pills, and "hard" drugs. Among blacks and Hispanics, pills are not as important a transition between marijuana and hard drugs as they are among whites. Cigarettes form an important step between alcohol and marijuana use for younger students, particularly for females. Since alcohol serves as the gateway to all other drug use, prevention approaches that control and limit alcohol use among adolescents may be warranted. . . . While a great deal of emphasis on the stepping-stone theory has centered around marijuana use, it is critically important to note that alcohol precedes marijuana in the developmental sequence and that alcohol serves as the gateway to other drug use. Stated simply, alcohol use precedes all other drug use. These results tend to justify a negative and prohibitive view of the use of alcohol by adolescents. (P. 228)

Marijuana

Marijuana is used daily by many adolescents and most delinquents in the United States. "Grass" or "weed" is plentiful; usually the only questions raised about it concern its strength. It is generally used by juveniles without question, without guilt, and with little self-examination. Although marijuana remains an illegal drug, because of the increasing acceptance of its usage, the laws against its use which were vigorously enforced at the beginning of the twentieth century now are seldom enforced. The situation is reflected in various statistical reports on marijuana use. Most reports show that juvenile arrests for marijuana use in California are down. This decrease in arrests does not reflect the fact that marijuana use among adolescents has significantly escalated in the 1990s. The police in recent years seldom arrest users. They usually give them a citation that carries a small fine. Consequently, arrest rates for marijuana use do not reflect the escalating usage.

There are mixed opinions on the deleterious effects of marijuana on users; however, it is increasingly perceived as a harmful drug, particularly for juveniles. In an early study on marijuana's deleterious effects, researcher Constandinos J. Miras (1966) studied chronic users in

Greece, where marijuana is quite strong. Miras defined a chronic user as one who smoked at least two marijuana cigarettes a day for two years. Dr. Miras found that chronic users had "slowed speech, lethargy, and lowered inhibitions, and some users became suddenly violent without any apparent provocation." Miras's most serious charge was that prolonged marijuana use produces brain damage. Miras studied the effects of THC, tetrahydrocannabinol, the active chemical in marijuana, which is found in all parts of the plant. Chronic users, according to Miras, are prone to anemia, eye inflammations, and respiratory infections, and there is also good evidence of abnormal brain-wave activity.

It is important to note that Miras's research was conducted using Greek subjects, and there is evidence that the marijuana used in Greece when Miras did his research was somewhat different in nature and strength from the type used in the United States and northern Europe. Recent research reveals that the marijuana used in the United States has steadily increased in toxicity and is now probably as strong as the marijuana used in Greece when Miras performed his research.

In a discussion of the pharmacologic effects of marijuana, pharmacologist Frederick H. Meyer (1972) concluded that "the effects of marijuana, both operationally and in its mechanism of action, correspond exactly to those of other sedatives and anesthetics, especially alcohol. The apparent distinctiveness of marijuana is due mostly to the use of a route of administration that permits the rapid development of an effect and to properties of the active components that lead to rapid decrease in the effects. One is driven to the conclusion that the differences between the dominant attitudes and consequent laws toward marijuana and alcohol are unrelated to the pharmocologic effects of the drugs but are due to a conflict between the mores of the dominant society and one or more of the subcultures in this country."

Norman Zinberg (1976) carried out extensive research into several major areas of concern about marijuana including: emotional impact, possible psychosis, brain damage, chromosome damage, marijuana as a stepping stone to heroin, sex impairment, and general health hazards. On the basis of all evidence on the subject, Zinberg summarized his conclusions:

> Obviously there are areas of concern. Drawing any hot substance into the lungs cannot be good for anyone, but we should remember that no marijuana smoker in this country uses as many cigarettes a day as tobacco smokers do. Also, marijuana is an intoxicant; and despite the research showing that someone high on marijuana does better on a driving simulator than someone high on alcohol, driving under the influence of any intoxicant

must be considered a real danger. Finally, it is my absolute conviction that adolescents below the age of eighteen should not use intoxicants of any kind, whether nicotine, alcohol, or marijuana. The fourteen-, fifteen-, or sixteen-year-olds struggling to develop themselves for their future life in this complex society need as clear a head as possible. One argument made some years ago for the legalization of illicit substances was based on the possibility that parents and other authorities could more readily control above-ground use of licit substances than they could control the underground use of illicit substances. In the end, after all this work and all these words, I still find myself echoing the remark made by Dr. Daniel S. Freedman of the University of Chicago after a Drug Abuse Council conference on marijuana. "Nobody can tell you it's harmless. Each person must decide for himself what he wants to do." (P. 58)

A study by Robert Heath of the Tulane University School of Medicine (1981) showed that regular marijuana smoking may, in the long run, widen the gaps (synapses) between nerve endings in vital parts of the brain. Heath administered marijuana smoke and its active ingredient, tetrahydrocannabinol (THC), to rhesus monkeys over a period of six to eight months. At doses that are comparable to those inhaled by a moderate-to-heavy smoker, THC caused structural changes, widening synapses by 35 percent. The most marked effects occurred in the septal region (associated with emotions), the hippocampus (concerned with memory formation), and the amygdala (responsible for certain behavioral functions).

In a study carried out by the Institute of Medicine of the National Academy of Science (Internet, 1996) data indicated that persistent marijuana usage can produce severe health problems. Their research revealed that over 25 million Americans spent some $24 billion for the illegal privilege of regularly smoking marijuana. Another 25 million have tried the drug at least once, making it the most widely used illegal substance in the country. This study determined that the principal active element in marijuana, tetrahydrocannabinol (THC), like alcohol, impairs motor coordination, the ability to follow a moving object, and the ability to detect a flash of light. Since these functions are necessary for safe driving, among other activities, impairments suggests a substantial risk on the highway.

Marijuana Research and Its Impact on Usage in the Twenty-First Century

In the 1930s and 1940s marijuana was perceived as the "killer weed." From the 1950s to the 1980s marijuana use became "hip"—it was the drug of choice. By the 1990s its use became increasingly accepted with a minimum of legal restraint or control. It is now used by people of all ages, social statuses, and all occupations with a general sense that smoking marijuana is a safe recreational activity, useful as a relaxant or aphrodisiac with minimal deleterious effect. However, many researchers conclude that the increased strength of the marijuana used results in negative effects on users. The pendulum is swinging back to a perception of marijuana by researchers and nonusers as a serious and destructive drug, although it is not perceived in this way by regular users.

The war on drug smuggling from foreign countries has caused an increase in home-grown marijuana production, especially in California. Domestic marijuana growers and foreign suppliers have developed stronger marijuana. In the 1990s many American marijuana producers traveled to Amsterdam, where marijuana is legal and used widely, to attend conferences that focused on the most effective and modern ways for growing marijuana.

In 1985 I interviewed long-time researcher in the field of drug research Sidney Cohen of UCLA. He estimated that THC, the active ingredient in marijuana, comprised about seven to fourteen percent of the content. In contrast, in the mid-1970s, the content was from .5 to 2 percent. Researchers who have tested the potency of the marijuana smoked in the United States in recent years estimate that it is now about ten times stronger than it was a few short years ago. Cohen asserted that the marijuana in use was almost a different drug. He and other researchers found that the new stronger marijuana had some of the following deleterious effects: THC caused changes in the reproductive systems of test animals. Marijuana smoking among pregnant women could adversely affect fetal development. Extensive lung damage had been documented in chronic marijuana smokers. THC impaired the immune system in test animals and decreased resistance to infections. These findings have serious implications for adolescents who are still maturing. Cohen commented that animal studies indicated that THC interferes with the immune system. In tests with guinea pigs, the drug was shown to decrease resistance to herpes simplex virus. And other studies had shown that THC appears to inhibit the production of lymphocytes, which are important in the synthesis of antibodies.

Darryl Inaba and David Smith, researchers at the Haight-Ashbury Drug Clinic in San Francisco, in an interview I had with them in 1991, noted that as more potent California marijuana has become available, they have treated patients suffering from "acute anxiety reactions." At first those at the clinic assumed the marijuana was laced with PCP, but it was just high-grade pot. Inaba stated, "The patients who now come to the clinic smoke too much strong marijuana too fast. They require talk-down treatment like the treatment used on a bad LSD trip. Ten years ago people would have laughed at the idea that marijuana could cause such an adverse reaction or that users would have a difficult time giving up smoking pot. Now many patients check into the detoxification clinic because they cannot quit smoking this potent "pot."

In a study at Brigham and Women's Hospital in Boston, the children of mothers who smoked marijuana had five types of malformations, including congenital heart disease and spinal problems, at a rate twice as high as a control group. The researchers concluded that although the overall rate of all malformations was only slightly higher in the study—which surveyed about 12,000 women, 1,200 of whom smoked marijuana—the association between marijuana usage and major malformations is "suggestive" and "merits further investigation." (Science News Report, 1986).

A parole officer colleague of mine who does marijuana drug testing informed me in 1996 that THC stays in a person's system from three to five weeks. Many researchers and medical experts maintain that it is significant that marijuana smokers retain the drug in the system for so long. Cocaine and heroin are water-soluble, quickly metabolized, and usually cannot be detected by urine tests after forty-eight hours. But marijuana, which is fat-soluble, lodges in the body's fat deposits and can be detected in chronic smokers up to forty days after use.

Many doctors are concerned about the effects of the stronger strains of marijuana on people's reproductive systems. Primate research has revealed that THC induces decreases in the female sex hormones estrogen and progesterone, thus interfering with ovulation and other hormone-related functions. Marijuana use is also associated with a reduction of the male sex hormone testosterone. The administration of THC to male mice in one study for as little as five days resulted in a reduction of sperm production and in abnormal sperm forms. Although some of these changes are reversible when marijuana use is halted, many questions remain about long-term use.

On the issue of marijuana's effect on the lungs, Donald Tashkin, a professor at UCLA Medical School, who has been studying the effects of marijuana smoking since 1972, concluded that chronic marijuana smokers face a greater risk of developing lung cancer than cigarette smokers. In a study of seventy-four subjects, Tashkin found that "even smoking one joint a day for at least two years causes abnormality of air passages and increases the effort necessary to breathe by 25 percent. One marijuana cigarette is as deleterious as twenty tobacco cigarettes" (Science News Report, 1986).

Tashkin completed a study of 275 marijuana smokers who had smoked at least two marijuana cigarettes a day for several years. About half of the group also smoked tobacco. He conducted bronchoscope studies, which allowed him to view and biopsy samples of lung tissue. According to Tashkin, "The marijuana smokers who didn't smoke cigarettes had extensive lung changes—things you wouldn't expect to see in young individuals. They were the kinds of changes you see only in older, long-term cigarette smokers. Some of the changes could be considered precursors of lung cancer. Every marijuana's smoker had some kind of abnormality." Because marijuana is smoked in a different fashion than cigarettes—marijuana is inhaled deeply and held in the lungs longer—those in the test group had damaged different parts of the throat and lungs. As a result, according to Tashkin, they could run a greater risk of lung cancer and cancer of the larynx than tobacco smokers, even though they smoked much less. Tobacco smoking further exacerbates the problem. Tashkin concluded, based on his research, that "marijuana smoking is where cigarette smoking was in the 1940s. With something like smoking, you've got a precancerous smoldering and it takes decades for the cancer to develop (Science News Report, 1986).

The Socialization Process, Marijuana Use, and Delinquency

All of these recent studies by researchers point to the harmful social, physiological, and psychological consequences of smoking marijuana. There is, however, another negative consequence which I found in my own research into marijuana usage as it affects young users. This is the impact on the socialization of children, adolescents, and young adults. The harm I perceive is related to two aspects of the learning and social development process: (1) the loss of learning basic social and educational data and skills during a significant developmental period of life; and (2) the amotivational syndrome. These factors are interrelated. The following observations on these two issues are based on my study of five hundred adolescent marijuana users that I interviewed and directed in a number of group therapy sessions over a ten-year period. All of these young males and females smoked marijuana almost daily for a period of eighteen months to five years. Although many of the youths in this sample also used other drugs like alcohol, cocaine, and LSD, their primary constant drug of choice was marijuana.

It should be noted by way of preface, that there are some heavy marijuana users who acquire good grades in school, relate well to their family, have healthy personalities, are sociable, and enter their adult life phase with no special social deficits. These "invulnerables" are exceptions to the general negative results I have observed in my research.

Social and Educational Deficits

About 90 percent of the marijuana users in my study had educational problems. These took the form of excessive truancy and a poor learning ability. This resulted in their missing out in learning educational processing techniques and the subject matter that is acquired by most relatively normal adolescents. This deficit learning is cumulative and results in an increasingly alienated posture toward school and working.

About 90 percent of the sample I studied presented a flat, listless personality in their social relationships. They were often alone or in the presence of peers who shared their posture of low-level social interaction. Basic human interaction in their lives was blockaded by their almost constantly "stoned" condition and made almost impossible by a continuing intrusive diet of loud music or television. Their speech patterns were curt and minimal. There were limited or no signs of intellectual curiosity or concern. Almost all of these youths had family problems. It was difficult to ascertain whether family problems caused the marijuana-abuse syndrome or their drugged behavior created a problem between the abusers and their parents.

In some cases it appeared that abusing or neglectful parents caused the use of marijuana in the adolescents. That is, the adolescents used the drug to cope with or block out the emotional pain that resulted from their pathological and emotionally painful family situation. In some cases the drug abuse was the "identified patient" and smoked marijuana as a self-administered therapeutic sedative. In others it appeared that the family was reasonably healthy, and the use of marijuana by the youth created a rational concern and disruption in the family situation. In about 90 percent of the cases, the long-term, almost daily, use of marijuana (from one to five years) produced a deficit in learning basic social skills required for effective participation in society. Marijuana abuse interfered with or blockaded the youths from going through the normal developmental phases required for proper socialization in American society. As a consequence, these youths had severe deficits in their educational and social abilities.

The Amotivational Syndrome

The complex of social-psychological problems caused by marijuana use results in what may be termed an "amotivational syndrome." This is not the immediate "listless, withdrawal" effects of marijuana intoxication. Amotivational syndrome refers to the long-term personality consequences of the prolonged abuse of marijuana. Amotivational syndrome characterizes a person who: (1) has limited ability to concentrate on any subject for any length of time; (2) does not learn any new data brought to his or her attention commensurate with his or her basic intelligence; (3) has difficulty relating to others and carrying on a normal social conversation; (4) has difficulty acquiring employment because of deficits in his or her attention span and occupational ability; (5) has a high level of apathy and boredom in relationship to subjects that go beyond his or her immediate life situation (a form of sociopathic egocentrism); and (6) in general has difficulty relating on a meaningful and intimate level to other people. In sum, the adolescent with amotivational syndrome that results from marijuana use is an alienated, bored, "vegged-out," and self-centered person. Apart from the fact that the adolescent marijuana abuser is already delinquent due to buying and using an illegal substance, long-term abuse renders the user susceptible to other kinds of self-destructive deviance. Abusers are prone to lie, cheat, or commit acts of theft to support their habit. In order to acquire their drug, they are necessarily in relationships with an illegal underworld.

Both males and females are more prone to participate in sexual acts with partners they would not select if they were not under the influence of the drug. They are also less likely to take precautions to avoid unwanted pregnancies. Because of the contemporary proliferation of sexually transmitted diseases, especially AIDS, unsafe, irresponsible sex can be enormously self-destructive and may lead to death.

In summary, based on my research and the research of others, I conclude that marijuana abusers are more prone to commit self-destructive acts of delinquency than nonabusers. Most marijuana users—about 90 percent—have family, school, and personal problems, and are victims of self-destructive behavior and the emotionally crippling amotivational syndrome.

Hallucinogenic Drugs

The use of hallucinogenic drugs, such as LSD, peyote, and various "magic mushrooms," did not begin with the psychedelic revolution. However, their usage was accelerated by the "hippie," "counterculture," consciousness-raising movement of the 1960s. Among the various hallucinogenics, LSD sporadically remains a drug of choice among adolescents in the 1990s. I will concentrate on the use and abuse of LSD, or "acid," in the following discussion because its social context of use and its effects are similar to those of other hallucinogenic drugs. Although LSD (lysergic acid diethylamide) is much abused, the mental distortions produced by the chemical have an emotional impact that often meshes with the user's search for emotional liberation or consciousness raising. The following discussion of LSD is based on a number of meetings I had with David Smith, founder of the Haight-Ashbury Free Clinic, and on an article he published in the *Journal of Psychedelic Drugs* in 1967.

The ergot alkaloids are a group of drugs obtained from an ergot fungus that grows on rye and gives rise to a great number of medically useful compounds, such as ergonovine and ergotamine. These compounds are used medically to contract the uterus after childbirth and to treat migraine headaches. LSD was first synthesized in 1938 as an intermediate stage leading to the synthesis of ergonovine. Its profound psychological effects were completely unknown at that time. In 1943, Albert Hoffman, a Swiss medical doctor, was one of the people involved in the original synthesis of LSD. At the time he was seeking a stimulant using lysergic acid (the base of all the ergot alkaloids) in combination with a chemical similar in structure to nikethamide, a central nervous system stimulant.

While working with these drugs, Hoffman began to experience some peculiar psychological effects, which he later described:

> On the afternoon of April 16, 1943, when I was working with these drugs and had ingested some, I was seized by a peculiar sensation of vertigo and restlessness. Objects, as well as the shape of my associates in the laboratory, appeared to undergo optical changes. I was unable to concentrate on my work. In a dreamlike state I left for home, where an irresistible urge to lie down overcame me. I drew the curtains and immediately fell into a peculiar state similar to drunkenness, characterized by an exaggerated imagination. With my eyes closed, fantastic pictures of extraordinary plasticity and intensive color seemed to surge toward me. After two hours this state gradually wore off. (Smith, 1967, p. 2)

When a person ingests an average dose of LSD (150 to 250 micrograms), nothing happens for the first 30 to 45 minutes. The first thing the individual usually notices is a change in the way he or she perceives things. The walls and other objects may become a bit wavy or seem to move. Colors are much brighter than usual. As time goes on, colors can seem exquisitely more intense and beautiful than ever before. It is also common to see a halo or rainbow around white lights. Hallucinations, or false sensory perceptions without any basis in external reality, are rather rare with LSD. More common are what may be called pseudohallucinations. The individual may see something out of the ordinary, but at the same time he or she usually knows it has no basis in reality. For example, if an LSD user sees dancing geometric forms or brilliantly colored pulsating shapes, he or she realizes that they don't really exist.

For the user of LSD, there is another kind of rather remarkable perceptual change referred to as synesthesia—a translation of one type of sensory experience into another. If the LSD user is listening to music, for example, vibrations of the music may surge through his or her body, or the actual notes may appear to move or colors beat in rhythm with the music. Another change of perception is in cognitive functioning, or ordinary thinking. There is no loss of awareness, and the user is fully conscious and usually remembers most of the experience. Thoughts move much more rapidly than usual. He or she doesn't necessarily think in a logical way or on a basis of causal relationships. Things that are normally thought of as opposites can exist in harmony and in fact become indistinguishable; black and white or good and bad are equal. A person may feel heavy and light at the same time. There is a kind of breakdown of logical thinking; but if the user is asked to perform some ordinary task—write his or her name or take a psychological test—he or she can usually do it, although resenting the interruption of the drug-induced experience.

The user's time sense is frequently affected. Past, present, and future get mixed up. Strange bodily sensations may occur. The users body may seem to lose its solidity and distinctness and blend into the universe. Sometimes a person's hands seem to flicker and become disconnected from the body. The LSD user may feel his or her neck elongate and experience other *Alice in Wonderland* phenomena.

The effects of LSD are largely psychological and can be divided into acute, immediate effects and chronic aftereffects. When a person takes LSD, he or she may lose control of him- or herself. Under this circumstance, some people panic. In their desperation to escape from this powerless state, they sometimes run in blind terror. If they do not run away, they may become excessively fearful and suspicious of the people who are with them. Convinced that their companions are trying to harm them, they lash out at them. People under the influence of LSD often show very poor judgment in other ways as well. More than one person has jumped out of a window under the impression that he or she could fly. There have been reports that LSD users have committed suicide by strolling into the ocean, feeling they were "simply part of the universe." I vividly recall that when I was researching material for *The Hippie Trip* (1968), I encountered a young man on the edge of a cliff in Big Sur, California. He informed me that he was going to merge with the universe. For my viewpoint, he was about to jump off the cliff and die. From his viewpoint, on acid, he was going to have a profound spiritual experience by jumping into the waves that were crashing on the shoreline. At least, on that afternoon, I was able to walk him back to a safer environment for experiencing his high. Many other people on LSD who experienced feelings of invincibility and omnipotence have stepped confidently into the paths of cars and trains and never stepped anywhere again.

Further adverse effects sometimes occur after the acute effects of the drug have apparently worn off. Some people have had prolonged psychotic reactions to their drug experience. These psychotic consequences do not appear to be totally irreversible, but in some cases the emotional disorders have lasted for many months, and a few cases involved long-term hospitalization.

The adverse side effect known as the "flashback" is a recurrence of the acute effects of the drug many days and sometimes weeks or months after the individual took the drug. This recurrence of symptoms can have a frightening impact. The flashback phenomenon is relatively rare and seems to occur more frequently in individuals who take the drug regularly. The "crash" or self-destructive condition that has emerged for many young psychedelic drug users is a personality pattern that defies description. It is hard to know in many cases whether the hallucinogenic drug-induced personality is a traditional psychosis or a flashback phenomenon that is a consequence of an extended period of drug abuse.

The LSD-induced hallucinogenic experience seems to produce personality reactions that shatter older modes of definition. Some individuals who take LSD as part of a religious experience or consciousness raising may end up in a psychotic state in a psychiatric hospital. One case of this type that I studied was a sixteen-year-old boy who claimed to have been on a "religious trip." He had taken LSD about forty times and "smoked pot as a daily religious sacrament." He was taken to a psychiatric hospital by his parents because he claimed he had talked to God. Shortly after he was admitted, we had the following conversation:

> L.Y.: How old are you?
>
> BOY: You obviously want to know my chronological age. In your terms I am sixteen. However, in my reality I have lived for four thousand years. [Long monologue about reincarnation and the cosmic view of life.]
>
> L.Y.: Tell me about your family.
>
> BOY: You are obviously referring to a mother, father, and two sisters. However, my real family is in a commune in northern California. That's where my spiritual heart is. [Long monologue about the Family of Man and Nature.]
>
> L.Y.: Do you believe in God?
>
> BOY: I am God. God is in me. When I have had some good acid [LSD] I am tuned into the Universe. I can now tune into God and communicate with him without drugs. I can meditate and reproduce the acid experience. Acid helped me get to this point, but I can achieve this state without drugs now.

Was this young man deeply religious or spiritual? Or was he a psychotic having a flashback experience? These are questions for which there are no simple answers. All of these roles, emotions, and states of being tend to overlap. One of the primary characteristics of most psychoses is a belief in a fantasy world rather than the reality felt by the majority of people. Many hallucinogenic drug-induced "psychotics" can balance several worlds adequately. They are not usually blocked from communicating with anyone in terms of the "real" world, and yet many appear to be on their own cosmic trip.

The fact that people in this drug-induced state can communicate on an "everyday" reality level tends to minimize the likelihood that they are clinically psychotic. The confusion of the usual psychological categories by the impact of psychedelic drugs has produced many problems for standard psychotherapeutic practitioners. Clients often view the "headshrinker" forced upon them by their parents with mingled feelings of spiritual superiority, condescension, and even pity, because they have no self-concept of having a problem or any pathology.

Another type of drugs in the hallucinogenic category is the so-called of designer drugs. Many were developed in laboratories to avoid restrictions imposed by the U.S. Drug Enforcement Administration. In this group of hallucinogenic substances, MDMA, or "Ecstasy," was placed on the administration's dangerous-drug list in 1986. At that time, these hallucinogenics were not widely used by adolescents.

The use of LSD and other hallucinogenics in the 1960s was a part of the "hippie" consciousness-raising movement. Hallucinogenic drugs are still used in the 1990s; however, they are used more for recreation or simply to get high.

PCP: "Angel Dust"

A drug that is sporadically used in urban areas around the nation is PCP (phencyclidine), or "angel dust." In the 1990s its usage diminished considerably. PCP is a potent hallucinogenic anesthetic agent. Exhibiting high potency with almost no respiratory depressant effect, it seemed to fulfill the promise of a "perfect" anesthetic. It is sold on the streets with names like "angel dust," "crystal," "hog" "key-jay," and "rocket fuel." Often, because of its extreme potency, it may be misrepresented as a "consciousness-altering" drug like cocaine, LSD, mescaline, or psilocybin (Gay, Rappolt, and Farris, 1979).

Chronic abusers of PCP usually roll it into a joint of marijuana or tobacco leaves. This and snorting ("horning") permit the user to control to some degree his or her level of intoxication. The effect is rapid, and profoundly incapacitating symptoms occur at relatively light levels of anesthesia. Oral ingestion of PCP is now rare for the sophisticated drug user, although this method may be employed in a clear suicide attempt.

Even the mildly intoxicated PCP user presents a bizarre clinical personality. The following is a typical description of a PCP user by a nurse in an emergency ward in 1990. "The PCP patient is sometimes 'zombielike' but quite often 'combative and hostile.' Many patients come in after they punched out a window or something and they make animal sounds . . . barking, growing, and gorilla-like snorting. . . . They have enormous strength, crazy strength. It takes a lot of people to hold them down. You can hit them in the face, break their noses, and that doesn't stop their violent behavior. On PCP it just agitates them." This description of the out-of-control and superstrong person on PCP is supported by police officers, who have the difficult job of restraining someone on PCP. People high on PCP have been known to break out of standard police handcuffs. Disorientation, hallucinations, extreme agitation, loss of motor control, drooling, and vomiting are symptoms of a person high on PCP. The mildly intoxicated person who is still upright will exhibit a slow, stiff-legged, lurching gait. Rappolt, Gay, and Farris (1979) described the symptoms of PCP in the following case history:

> Dr. Gay called to see a young person who had smoked a "duster" at a Led Zeppelin rock concert (one of thirteen people so seen that day). The patient was a thirteen-year-old Chicano from the South San Francisco Bay area. She was of slight habitus, and reportedly had just inhaled "only a few tokes." History available indicated that she was not new to this form of recreational drug use. The patient arrived by stretcher to a medical field tent. She was comatose, and her posture was a board-stiff extensor rigidity. Her extremities showed a tonic-clonic spasticity, accentuated by stimulus (movement of the stretcher, loud noises). Her eyes were open and staring, nonblinking. She was moved to a quiet area, and counselors proceeded to talk gently to her and to massage the muscles of her legs, upper back, and arms. At fifteen minutes her muscle spasms appeared much improved, but she was still unresponsive to voice. . . . At thirty minutes she appeared visibly more relaxed, and responded to voice. Within an additional fifteen minutes she was sitting up, appeared weak but with voluntary muscular control, and was sipping water and conversing. One hour after admission she was released to the care of her friends, and walked out unassisted. (P. 78)

Heroin

Heroin is a drug primarily used in the urban ghettos of American cities. In the 1990s it became popular among middle and upper socioeconomic class drug users. The drug has been used by delinquents to escape from the oppressive conditions of poverty in the hoods and barrios. For many youngsters, heroin, a strong anesthetic, provides a way to blank out a dim future of limited opportunity and little hope.

A dramatic portrait of the meaning of heroin to a ghetto youth is provided by Piri Thomas (1967), a former addict, in his perceptive book on New York's Spanish Harlem:

> Heroin does a lot for one—and it's all bad. It becomes your whole life once you allow it to sink its white teeth in your bloodstream. . . . Yet there is something about dogie-heroin—it's a super-duper tranquilizer. All your troubles become a bunch of bleary blurred memories when you're in a nod of your own special dimension. And it was only when my messed-up system became a screaming want for the next fix did I really know just how short an escape from reality it really brought. The shivering, nose-running, crawling damp, ice-cold skin it produced were just the next worst step of-like my guts were gonna blow up and muscles in my body becoming so tight I could almost hear them snapping.

Heroin use is again on the rise, judging from the increase in heroin-positive urine samples collected from arrestees and the growing number of people entering addiction programs.

Beginning in the 1970s, many middle-class youths became heroin addicts. At the beginning of this escalating trend, George Gay and Ann Gay (1972) stated:

> It is no longer buried in black and Puerto Rican ghettos, no longer confined to the "ignorant" poor. Heroin is in the suburbs, and white parents are beginning to know the impotent range of fear and despair that black parents have lived with for decades; the call from school, from the police, from some hospital somewhere, the call that rips you from complacency and tells you the cold, mean, street-corner truth: your kid has been arrested; your kid is a junkie. Your daughter, the lovely, clear-eyed child who was going to marry a nice, attractive, sensible, hard-working young man, who was going to give you grandchildren and comfort in your old age—well . . . she ran off with a greasy slob on a motorcycle. When he got tired of fucking her, he split, so now she is turning tricks on the street, hustling for enough bread to cop a balloon of heroin. (P. 201)

One of the early signs that the heroin trade was no longer off-limits to middle-class shoppers came in 1979, when David Kennedy, a son of the late Senator Robert Kennedy, reported that he had been beaten and robbed in a Harlem hotel that police said was a notorious heroin "shooting gallery." Recreational drug users on pills or cocaine are vulnerable to becoming heroin addicts. An ex-addict told me, "The same people who would have run out of the room at the mention of heroin a few years ago are buying it. It's become another white powder to them, and they don't have to inject it or cop it on the street. Where you used to go to someone's house and he'd say, 'Do you want some cocaine?' You now hear, 'Would you like some Uptown [cocaine] or Downtown [heroin]?' " But there may be a more compelling connection between the two drugs. Because cocaine produces a swift, surging high, users often need something to "come down" with, once the initial euphoria wears off. As a result, drug connoisseurs often take cocaine and heroin together—a potent mixture called a "speedball."

With the use of heroin by middle-class junkies, heroin arrest figures do not always reveal the prevalence of heroin addiction. Wealthier heroin users don't have to steal toasters and TV sets to support their habits. Indeed, one difference in middle-class addicts may be that they do their stealing at home. One patient in a therapeutic committee commented that to pay for his heroin he was looting his father's business. "Once I got $100 from my grandmother to buy some clothes, and I went out and spent it on heroin. I wrote bad checks for a while. I never had to steal, because somebody always gave me money, and I could steal stuff out of my house" ("Middle-Class Junkies," 1981).

One reason for the rise in all addictive drugs, including heroin, is that people get a message that they don't have to deal with pain from headaches to anything that's bothering them. The use of all drugs continues to rise among all classes of people—from alcohol and over-the-counter potions through prescription drugs like Prozac to hard drugs like heroin.

Despite the fact that heroin is now used at every level of society, it remains most widely used in the ghettos by the poor. It has become so integrated into city life that it is packaged, advertised, and sold with identifying brand names. In one study that remains relevant, Paul Goldstein (1983) and his co-workers researched the marketing process developed by New York City heroin vendors. They found that "heroin dealers are doing everything but advertising on television."

Heroin in many cities around the country is being distinctively packaged prior to sale. The labeling of street heroin entails stamping, writing or pasting a name, symbol, or number, usually in a specific color, on the bag containing the drugs. The bag may then be sealed with colored tape. Heroin users always try to purchase the most powerful heroin that is available. They express little fear of overdose. If word gets out on the street that somebody has overdosed from a specific dealer's wares, that heroin is eagerly sought.

One female addict described her copping procedure as follows:

> I don't know how the word gets around which is the best, but the word gets out. If you're going up to the bar on 116th and Eighth, it's "get the red and black tape." Or "today it's the yellow" or whatever, and that's how you get off. When I used to go uptown, I'd usually talk to the people outside the bar, who's got what and what is it. I don't know how the word gets out that morning, but

it does. If you try different kinds of dope, and some are better, you can go back and buy the good stuff. There are so many different people selling a dealer's stuff you have to be able to identify it. People mark bags to sell their product. Say you've got fifty people out there selling narcotics and you don't know who's who. And you hear the name "The Joint," well, this is the best. And you hear somebody on the street saying "Red Tape" so you say, "Nah, I heard Red Tape ain't nothing. Let's try The Joint. It's supposed to be better. Marked bags identify who the dealer is. It gives people an idea of which is the best stuff." (Goldstein, 1983)

The social realities confronting heroin purchasers may be summarized as follows: Most addicts have limited capital to expend on heroin. There are a multitude of street dealers to choose from. Getting beat or "burned" on a heroin purchase or buying inferior quality heroin is an omnipresent risk. Also, buying relatively high quality heroin can lead to death. In a two-week period, a form of potent heroin from Mexico known as "black tar" resulted in more than two hundred overdose deaths in Los Angeles County. Heroin is a lethal drug.

The ruthlessness of the commerce of heroin use is revealed in a CNN news article on the Internet: "Luz Marina Ocampo might have survived after a balloon containing heroin ruptured in her stomach upon her arrival from Colombia. But no one rushed her to the hospital. Instead, members of the forty-four-year-old Colombian's drug ring simply let her die, cut her open to remove the rest of the heroin, then set her corpse ablaze beside a suburban highway. At $85,000 a kilo wholesale in New York City, compared to $16,000 a kilo for cocaine, Colombian heroin is a lucrative trade. Four people have been arrested for Ocampo's death, but thousands of similar arrests have done little to stem the influx of Colombian heroin" (CNN, 1997).

The growing tide of high-purity heroin that began arriving from Colombia in the 1990s poses new challenges to law enforcement. Because pure heroin can be smoked or sniffed rather than injected, it is more palatable to thousands of potential users. The attraction of new users has brought an increase in overdoses. Heroin-related emergency room cases have skyrocketed nationwide since Colombian-produced heroin appeared on the scene—from 5,400 in 1989 to 11,000 in 1995 (CNN, 1997).

Cocaine

The heroin problem, despite the fact that it remains a drug widely used by people of all ages and socioeconomic strata, has been dwarfed by the enormous increase in cocaine abuse and the social problems caused by the use of this lethal drug, especially in the form of "crack." Cocaine, in its earlier use pattern, notably by the wealthy and by musicians in the 1920s and 1930s, was considered the Rolls-Royce of drugs. In the 1980s and 1990s it became a drug abused by people of all ages, in all strata of society. The drug has been snorted in powder form, smoked and inhaled in a "freebase" form, "slammed" (injected intravenously), and smoked in a pipe in the form of "crack" or "rock."

To the Incan people the coca leaf was believed to be a gift from Manco Capac, son of the Sun god, bestowed as a token of esteem and sympathy for their labor. Coca served as a stimulating tonic to these working in the thin mountain air of the Andes. Anthropologic research indicates that the highly sophisticated surgical procedure of trephination was repeatedly successful in this era, as the operating surgeon allowed coca-drenched saliva to drip from his mouth onto the surgical wound, thus providing an adequate (and a very real) anesthesia. This permitted the operation to proceed effectively in relative quiet.

In 1884, a cocaine "kit" was delivered to Sigmund Freud in Vienna. Ever the visionary experimenter, Freud began to use coca in the treatment of various medical and psychologic disorders. Between 1884 and 1887, he wrote five papers extolling coca as a wonder drug. His "coca euphoria" subsided however, when he began to experience the devastating negative side effects of addiction. He subsequently deleted these laudatory writings from the collected papers of his autobiography.

When cocaine was first used in the United States, the historical pattern of injection was largely supplanted (in a needle-fearing society) by inhalation, in which a "line" of coke was "horned" or snorted. This was often done by elite users through a rolled-up Federal Reserve note of high denomination (to denote affluence) or through a red, white, and blue sipping straw. In some cases, users bought various expensive instruments sold in boutiques to inhale their cocaine. A side effect of this nasal method of ingesting of cocaine was septal perforation due to intense and repeated vasoconstriction. Snorters were also prone to infection of the nasal mucosa and upper respiratory tract due to chronic local irritation.

Smoking crack cocaine, or "freebasing," introduced a much more expensive habit and a method whereby a much greater quantity of substance was introduced (almost equivalent to the rate of intravenous use) with a concomitant increase in euphoria, leading to extreme toxicity, and, in some cases, death. Prolonged or chronic use of cocaine may lead to an irrational effect not unlike paranoid schizophrenia. Plagued with the dark shadows of increasing nervousness, inability to concentrate, and disturbed sleep patterns, the chronic user is increasingly prone to violence. Because of these paranoia-producing qualities, coupled with the legal sanctions against possession of cocaine, the user will seldom be seen in offices or emergency rooms of traditional medical facilities.

Freebasing cocaine, a method adopted by many users, is exceedingly dangerous. In 1988, comedian Richard Pryor almost died of burns from an explosion while freebasing the drug. In this method the purified cocaine base is smoked in a water pipe or sprinkled on a tobacco or marijuana cigarette for a sudden and intense high. The substance reaches the brain within a few seconds. However, the euphoria quickly subsides into a feeling of restlessness, irritability, and depression. The freebase posthigh is so uncomfortable that, to maintain the original high and to avoid crashing (coming down), smokers often continue smoking until they are either exhausted, pass out, or have run out of cocaine. Smoking cocaine is much more serious than snorting the drug. An enormous craving results from the rapid high-low shifts, and the smoker tends to become compulsive and less able to control the amounts of the drug used. Consequently, dosage and frequency of use tend to increase rapidly, so that cocaine smokers are likely to develop extreme dependency.

Crack cocaine is used differently than powdered cocaine. Two researchers, Dorothy Hatsukami and Marian Fishman (1996), reported on these two approaches to the use of cocaine.

> Cocaine hydrochloride is readily converted to base prior to use. The physiological and psychoactive effects of cocaine are similar regardless of whether it is in the form of cocaine hydrochloride or crack cocaine (cocaine base). However, evidence exists showing a greater abuse liability, greater propensity for dependence, and more severe consequences when cocaine is smoked (cocainebase) or injected intravenously (cocaine hydrochloride) compared with intranasal use (cocaine hydrochloride). (P. 49)

Hatsukami and Fishman further comment that

> the immediacy, duration, and magnitude of cocaine's effect, as well as the frequency and amount of cocaine used is more important than the form of the cocaine used. Furthermore, cocaine hydrochloride used intranasally may be a gateway drug or behavior to using crack cocaine. Based on these findings, the federal sentencing guidelines allowing possession of one hundred times more cocaine hydrochloride than crack cocaine to trigger mandatory minimum penalties is deemed excessive. Although crack cocaine has been linked with crime to a greater extent than cocaine hydrochloride, many of these crimes are associated with the addiction to cocaine. Therefore, those addicted individuals who are incarcerated for the sale or possession of cocaine are better served by treatment than prison. (P. 56)

From a historical perspective the cocaine problem in the United States has increased enormously with the advent of crack cocaine. A significant aspect of the problem may be related to the degree to which crack cocaine has pervaded the lives of adolescents in all strata of society. The federal government's failed attempts to interdict smuggling from Central and South America has allowed a flood tide of cocaine to reach consumers of all ages in this country. Prices are down, purity is up, and dealers do not care if the buyer is a juvenile or an adult. Crack is widely available at low prices within the financial reach of the young. The new coke goes by many names on the street, but it is usually called crack or rock. It is smoked, not snorted, and the resulting intoxication is far more intense than that of snorted cocaine—much quicker, much more addictive.

There is no such thing as the "recreational" use of crack. Crack is simply a variant on freebasing, which is the conversion of sniffable cocaine crystals into a smokable "base" form of the drug. Dealers make crack by mixing cocaine with common baking soda and water, creating a paste that is usually at least 75 percent cocaine. The paste hardens and is cut into chips that resemble soap or whitish gravel. A small piece, sometimes called a "quarter rock," produces a twenty to thirty minute high. Its low cost and accessibility is probably a major reason that cocaine abuse among the young is on the rise. Dealers of crack are usually adult; however, crack is widely peddled by juveniles primarily because teenagers, by law in most states, do not normally face heavy penalties when arrested.

Crack, with its enormous profits and the violent crime associated with it, has transformed the ghetto. To a striking degree, the coke boom is a youth phenomenon; in both Los Angeles and New York, crack houses are protected by armed teenagers. Other teens hawk crack on street corners, and in some cities dealers ply their trade from cars and make quick curb-side sales. The contagion has already spread to suburbia, where dealers flourish in abandoned buildings. A teenager working in a crack house can make big money. He or she can sit in the house for six or seven hours and earn $300 a day. Consequently, the dealing and use of crack cocaine has reached epidemic proportions ("Kids and Crack," 1986).

Research reveals that the percentage of high school seniors who have tried cocaine nearly doubled from 9 percent to 17.3 percent since 1985. Overall, marijuana remains the most widely used illicit drug among high school seniors: 49.6 percent say they have used it within the past year. It is followed by stimulants (15.8 percent) and cocaine (13.1 percent). Predictably, because of the pattern of cocaine distribution from South America, school-age cocaine abuse is higher on the East and West Coasts, but it has also increased significantly in all areas of the country. There is no other industrialized country in the world that has a comparable proportion of young people involved with illicit drugs (Maguire and Pastore, 1996).

Treatment Approaches for Juvenile Substance Abusers

In the past fifty years, substance abuse has escalated steadily and at a staggering rate. There is no era in American history that compares to the way drugs have taken hold of the youth population. Teen-age substance abusers are difficult to treat. In my work with teen-age addicts over the past several decades, I have learned about some of the basic characteristics of their substance abuse and the approaches that are needed to stop drug use. These approaches include: (1) the juvenile courts; (2) a national policy and strategy for treating the problem; and (3) comprehension of the basic adolescent attitudes about drugs and how their resistance can be effectively dealt with in treatment programs.

The Juvenile Drug Court Movement

Marilyn Roberts, Jennifer Brophy, and Caroline Cooper (1997) advocate a special juvenile court to deal with adolescent substance abuse.

> Many nonviolent, substance-abusing adult and juvenile offenders are repeatedly cycled through the judicial system because of a lack of intervention measures that would provide the sanctions and services necessary to change their deviant behavior. To address this problem, some communities have established adult and juvenile drug courts. Beginning as a grassroots initiative, drug courts have spread across the nation. Currently more than 244 drug court programs are under way or are being planned, with 25 dedicated to juveniles. Local teams of judges, prosecutors, attorneys, treatment providers, law enforcement officials, and others are using the coercive power of the court to force abstinence and alter behavior with a combination of intensive judicial supervision, escalating sanctions, mandatory drug testing, treatment, and strong aftercare programs. (P. 78)

According to Roberts, Brophy, and Cooper, the populations and caseloads of most juvenile courts changed dramatically during the 1990s. Delinquency and dependency became far more complex, involving more serious and violent criminal activity and escalating degrees of substance abuse. Recently, several jurisdictions have tried to determine how juvenile courts can adapt the experiences of adult drug courts to deal more effectively with the increasing number of substance-abusing juvenile offenders. Juvenile drug courts, however, face unique challenges not encountered in the adult drug court environment. These include: counteracting the negative influence of peers, gangs, and family members; addressing the needs of the family, especially families with substance abuse problems; complying with the confidentiality requirements for juvenile proceedings while obtaining information necessary to address the juvenile's problems and progress; and motivating juvenile offenders to change, especially given their attitudes of invulnerability and lack of maturity (1997, p. 134).

The innovative use of drug courts for juveniles may have an impact: however, it is difficult in treatment to convince adolescents that using drugs is ultimately self-destructive. At the time they are using drugs, the pleasure far outweighs the pain and the fear of problems they will have to face in the future. In my group treatment work with adolescent abusers, I utilized the services of recovering substance-abuse veterans who were once in the teenagers' position. They can often convey the fact to adolescents that drug abuse involves deficit emotional spending, and that eventually they will pay a high price of future pain for their current euphoric lifestyle. Juvenile drug courts should utilize the services of ex-addicts who have been through the mill of drug use to counsel youths just beginning substance abuse.

The National Drug Policy Council's Plan for Controlling Teenage Substance Abuse

A national policy for preventing and controlling adolescent substance abuse is necessary if we are to succeed in overcoming this significant social problem. In 1996 President Clinton appointed a National Drug Policy Council that developed a manifesto for dealing with the drug abuse of juveniles. The following section reviews selected parts of the council's strategy plan derived from their larger statement together with my viewpoint based on my work in the field of juvenile substance abuse.

The National Drug Policy Council's strategy focused on some of the practical reasons for preventing and controlling juvenile drug use. The council asserted that bringing teens to adulthood free of substance abuse will provide them and the nation with greater potential; and that if youths grow up without using illegal drugs, alcohol, or tobacco, they are more likely to remain drug free for the rest of their lives. Rarely does a person begin drug abuse after the age of twenty. The intention of the council, therefore, was to enable children to recognize toxic, addictive substances as alien, self-destructive, and antisocial. To this end, their strategy fosters initiatives to educate children, parents, and mentors. They seek to mobilize civic and antidrug organizations, businesses, and the communities that focus on the best interests of children.

The policy statement properly notes that "substance abuse among children is a complex, multidimensional problem. Nonetheless, it is a problem that can be affected by concerted and sustained action. This strategy proposes a comprehensive, long-term approach designed to mobilize and leverage federal and state resources and to raise awareness through well-coordinated initiatives allowing the vast majority of our youth to mature drug-free" (National Drug Policy Council, 1997, p. 132). The council's initiatives include the following ten strategies and approaches:

1. *Broadening "drug-free zones."* Youths are more likely to use illegal drugs, alcohol, and tobacco if these substances are readily available or if their use is encouraged directly or subtly in youth-oriented materials. It is therefore critical to keep drugs out of areas where children and adolescents study, play, or spend leisure time. All who seek to communicate with youths, no matter what the medium, must depict these substances and effects in accurate ways. (President Clinton appropriately in 1997 criticized adolescent clothing ads that used young models with the gaunt and wasted "heroin addict look.")

2. *Expanding school-based prevention programs.* Because schools offer both formal and informal opportunities for developing attitudes toward drugs, the council asserts that the classroom is a place where students can receive accurate, comprehensive information that will help them understand the importance of avoiding illicit drugs, alcohol, and tobacco. School programs can teach students why they should discontinue drug use before the onset of dependency. These programs must be comprehensive and focus on reducing risk factors, teaching avoidance skills, and building collaborative antidrug relations between students, teachers, and parents. The council cites the Drug Awareness Resistance Education (D.A.R.E.) program and the Bureau of Alcohol, Tobacco, and Firearms' Gang Resistance Education and Training programs as examples of useful school-based programs.

3. *Expanding youth-oriented antidrug messages.* The power of the media in molding public opinion is enormous. Young people are particularly susceptible to such influences. The council notes that in recent years the number of drug-related public service announcements carried by television, radio, and print media has decreased markedly. The council seeks to reverse this trend by developing a public education campaign that supplements antidrug announcements already offered by organizations like the Partnership for a Drug-Free America and the National Center for Advancement and Prevention. Youths should be warned through the media about the hazards of illegal drugs and shown the advantages of a drug-free life-style. Information-based material should be repeated with sufficient frequency to reinforce learning and motivate youths to reject illegal drugs.

4. *Preventing alcohol use by youths.* Underage drinking continues to be a significant problem. The council notes the following researched statistics on alcohol use by youths. Approximately one in four tenth grade students and one-third of twelfth graders report having had five or more drinks on at least one occasion in a normal week. The average age of first drinking is declining and is now 15.9 years, down from a 1987 average age of 17.4 years. To counter these behavior patterns, the council recommends: educating youths, their mentors, and the public about the dangers of underage drinking; limiting youth's access to alcoholic beverages; encouraging communities to support alcohol-free behavior on the part of youths; and creating both incentives and disincentives that lead to less alcohol abuse by young people (Merrill, Fox, Lewis, and Pulver, 1996).

5. *Preventing tobacco use by youths.* Despite a decline in adult smoking, the use of tobacco products is on the rise among American youths. In 1995, more than a third of high school seniors were cigarette smokers— a greater number than at any time since the 1970s. The vast majority of smokers (over 80 percent) start smoking before age eighteen. Each day three thousand more children become regular smokers; one-third of these youngsters will have their lives shortened as a result. The statistical correlation between tobacco and drug abuse is high. Youths aged to twelve to seventeen who smoke are about eight times more likely to use illicit drugs and five times more likely to drink heavily than nonsmoking youths. Of adults who use cocaine, 83 percent identified cigarettes as a gateway to other drugs. The council seeks to reduce children's access to tobacco products, diminish the appeal of cigarettes for young people, and educate youths about the lethal effects of tobacco (Merrill, Fox, Lewis, and Pulver, 1997).

6. *Reducing drugged driving.* Twenty percent of high school seniors polled stated that they had smoked marijuana in a car. The initiative on drugs, driving, and youth is intended to reduce drug use by young people as well as driving under the influence of drugs. The major feature of this initiative, which affects both young and adult drivers, is drug testing for driver's license applicants. This will send the message that drugs and driving don't mix. The council also recommends identifying youths who should be referred to drug assessment and treatment.

7. *Drug abuse and violence.* The council issued the following statement regarding the relationship between drug abuse and violence:

> The social ruin fostered by drug-related crime and violence mirrors the tragedy that substance abuse wreaks on individuals caught in its tentacles. The psychological, civic, and economic consequences of illegal drugs and their trade lead to disruptive,

volatile, antisocial behavior. Significant percentages of domestic violence cases are tied to the use of illegal drugs—especially methamphetamine, which induces violent, erratic, and abusive behavior. A large number of the 12 million property crimes committed each year are drug-related as are almost 2 million violent crimes. (UCR, 1996)

8. *Drug abusers and the juvenile justice system.* The council noted that drug use is pervasive among individuals entering the justice system and that the system has been strained by high rates of recidivism among drug offenders. Approximately half of the felony drug offenders on probation in 1986 were rearrested for another felony within three years. For parolees with histories of heroin and/or cocaine addiction, studies suggest that up to 75 percent return to drug use within ninety days of release. In a 1992 comparative study conducted in Delaware, inmates who received treatment in prison and during work release programs were 75 percent drug free and 70 percent arrest free after eighteen months. But 80 percent of the prisoners who did not receive treatment went back on drugs, and two out of three were arrested again (Bureau of Justice Statistics, 1992).

The council correctly asserted that drug treatment in the justice setting can decrease drug use and criminal activity, reduce recidivism, and improve chances for subsequent employment while improving overall health and social conditions. In this regard, the 104th Congress passed legislation requiring states to test prisoners and parolees for drug use as a condition for receiving prison grants. States that do not meet this requirement were ineligible for prison funds in 1998. This strategy encourages an integrated effort to rid criminals of their drug habits. The coercive power of the criminal justice system can be used to test and treat drug addicts arrested for committing crimes. (Chapter 17 presents an effective therapeutic community approach for treating substance abusers in prison.)

9. *Expanding alternatives to incarceration.* The council noted that alternative judicial processes can motivate nonviolent offenders to abandon drug-related activities and thereby lower recidivism rates. More than two hundred drug courts and community programs are already helping nonviolent offenders break the cycle of drugs and crime. These programs feature close supervision and mandatory drug testing and treatment, reinforced by escalating sanctions for offenders who fail to become drug free. These programs promise to reduce incarceration costs while providing strong incentives to abide by the law.

10. *Chronic substance abusers.* The council noted that chronic drug users are at the heart of America's drug problem. Two-thirds of the nation's supply of cocaine is consumed by about 20 percent of the drug-using

population. Chronic users maintain drug markets and keep drug traffickers in business. Not only are these drug users responsible for a disproportionate amount of drug-related crime, they are frequently vectors for the spread of infectious diseases like hepatitis, tuberculosis, and AIDS. There are methods for identifying chronic drug users before they get caught up in the adult criminal justice system.

Most youths who use marijuana on a regular basis are not aware of the facts related to the drug, and how this can propel them into the adult criminal justice system. A study published in the *Journal of Science* found that "people who regularly smoke large amounts of marijuana may experience changes in their brain chemistry that are identical to changes in the brains of people who abuse heroin, cocaine, amphetamines, nicotine and alcohol. The findings provide strong support for the emerging idea that all addictive drugs corrupt the same brain circuits, although to varying degrees, and suggest that chronic marijuana use may literally prime the brain for other drugs of abuse, a notion known as 'the gateway effect' " ("Brain Studies," 1997). Therefore, some young chronic marijuana users, through the marijuana route, may find themselves more heavily involved in other, more dangerous drugs. According to this new hypothesis, addictive drugs like nicotine, heroin, and cocaine all work through common pathways in the brain. There is now scientific support for the idea that experience with marijuana primes the brain to be more receptive to other more dangerous drugs.

Through focusing on 3.6 million chronic drug users in America, the council stated that it is possible to lessen the national demand for drugs at the retail level while helping this suffering group recover. Treatment options include therapeutic communities, pharmacotherapies, outpatient drug-free programs, inpatient hospitalization, therapy-based (or psychiatric inpatient) programs, twelve-step programs, and multimodality programs. The effectiveness of each method is a function of the type of substance abused, individual history of abuse and treatment, personality, and social environment of the user. Providing treatment for 3.6 million chronic users of illegal drugs is a compassionate and economically sound proposition ("The Need for Delivery of Drug Abuse Services," 1995).

A 1992 California Department of Alcohol and Drug Programs survey (Gerstein et al., 1994) on the effectiveness, benefits, and cost of substance abuse treatment concluded that a treatment approach for addicts is more effective than punishment through incarceration without treatment. The principal finding was that treatment can generate a seven to one return on investment. The study estimated that the $209 million cost of providing treatment to 150,000 individuals generated an estimated $1.5 billion in savings.

Illegal drug use by participants dropped by 40 percent as a result of treatment. Treatment reduced drug-related illness. Hospitalization rates dropped by a third after treatment. Post-treatment criminal activity correlated with the length of treatment programs. While overall criminal activity of surveyed individuals dropped by two-thirds after completion of treatment, the greater the time spent in a treatment program, the greater the reduction in individual criminal activity. All populations—men and women, young and old, African American, Hispanic, and white—experienced generally equal treatment effectiveness for each type of program studied ("The Persistent Effects of Substance Abuse Treatment," 1996).

Basic Issues to Be Confronted in the Treatment of Juvenile Substance Abusers

If the juvenile drug court approach or the federal plan is to be successful, the therapeutic agents or counselors who assist the court must be aware of a number of relevant issues generally related to the effective treatment of juvenile substance abusers. The following issues are based on my research and treatment experience with young addicts in custodial institutions and in community drug programs. They reveal some of the basic characteristics of juvenile substance abusers and the problems in treating and resocializing delinquent substance abusers.

1. *Addict-alcoholic self-concept.* Even after an addict has entered treatment and has evidence that he or she is an addict or an alcoholic, the person continues to deceive him- or herself about this fact. An encounter-group process is vital in order to constantly remind the potentially self-destructive addicts about their problem. Delinquents' self-delusion and denial in this area can block their receiving treatment and lead them back into their former life-style.

2. *The "co-addict" or "enabler" issue.* A considerable amount of research has established the fact that a family's attitude can reinforce addiction in a youth. A mother's admonition to her addicted teenager, "It's OK for you to drink at home, but don't smoke marijuana or use cocaine," is one example of the way some addicts' family members facilitate the addict-alcoholic's return to self-destructive addiction. In treatment extreme language and harshness is often required to communicate to young addicts and their families the ways in which families reinforce the addicts' habit. Juvenile substance abusers need to understand how their families may subtly push them toward drugs. They need to be internally vigilant so they can assess when a loved one or friend is unconsciously facilitating their

slide back to drug abuse. In many cases, as described earlier, substance abuse is reinforced or facilitated by the fact that the addict's mother or father is a substance abuser.

3. *"Friends" and "peers."* A teenager in an encounter group I directed remarked: "My best friend offered me some 'crack' yesterday when I was at school, and he knows I'm trying to quit drugs." It takes an extreme amount of energy and discussion in the group to prove to a substance abuser the iron clad rule, "No one who uses drugs or offers you drugs is a 'friend.'" Peer pressure is a most significant factor in delinquent substance abuse. It is enormously difficult to extricate youths from their substance-abusing peer group and involve them in the dynamics of an antidrug support group.

4. *Projected despair: A life without drugs or alcohol.* One of the most difficult issues young substance abusers must confront is a research-established fact that they can never "use" again. For most addicts or alcoholics, this issue produces feelings of gloom and despair. I have heard the following comment many times from adolescents recovering from substance abuse when confronted with the "never again" hypothesis: "You mean, later on I can't have one drink or smoke one joint without falling back into my habit? That's really depressing." Most young addict-alcoholics who want to stop using continue to harbor the idea that, some day, after they have been drug-free for a period of time, they can successfully use drugs again on a "recreational basis." The treatment group has to hammer away at this self-deceptive, self-destructive notion. The Alcoholics Anonymous concept of staying drug-free "one day at a time" is often a helpful slogan for the recovering person to keep in mind.

5. *Are drugs "fun" or destructive?* The fact that drugs are pleasurable in the short run is another issue that requires repeated group discussion and analysis in order to point to the long-term destructive effects of substance abuse. Many recovering addicts believe on an emotional level that giving up drugs will take away their main or only source of recreation. The recovering substance abuser fights this issue in a variety of ways. He or she tends to remember the pleasurable aspects of drug abuse more readily than the long-term negative effects. The recovering substance abuser needs to be constantly reminded of the real long-term impacts and consequences of his or her drug use.

6. *Slippage-regression.* Many young substance abusers slip at some point in their recovery process and return to their habit. This is one situation in the psychodynamics of drug abuse where verbal punishment deters substance abuse when properly administered in a treatment group. Individuals who have regressed or "slipped" should know that if they use a

drug, they can expect to be verbally brutalized by the indignant group of addicts who comprise their support group. A group "attack" can prove most humiliating and yet enormously helpful when the group pours out its indignation at the "offender." The fear of this flood of wrath from the group often serves as a valid deterrent when temptation appears. I recall a youth commenting to his fellow group members, "I was in a situation when I was about to slip. When I weighed it up against what you guys would do to me when I copped-out in this group—something I would have to do—it wasn't worth it."

7. *Painkiller and/or social lubricant.* "Why do I use drugs?" is a topic that is repeatedly discussed by recovering addicts. Two of the most common responses by addict-alcoholics to this question (beyond deeper psychodynamic reasons) include variations on "It helps kill the pain of my personal problems" and "It's the only way I feel a sense of belonging in a group." The response is: "It's difficult, but the only way you'll resolve your problems is to encounter them head on, without submerging or complicating them with drugs." Drugs do provide a short-term "sense of belonging" and assuage feelings of alienation, but it is necessary for the abuser to learn how to relate and communicate with people without the help of drugs. It is difficult for the recovering addict-alcoholic to learn how to confront day-to-day life situations without drugs as a "painkiller" (for depression) or "social lubricant." The addict and the alcoholic, in their "using" life situations, had friends and activities that validated their addiction identity. They often resist giving up this past identity because of a fear of having to relate drug free to another set of friends in a drug-free social setting.

8. *The life-and-death factor in drug abuse.* An allegation often hurled at an addict in a drug-treatment group is: "You are committing suicide with drugs." This is a critical and often dismal subject for a substance abuser to discuss in a group, because many group members are forced to confront the fact that on some level their drug use is suicidal behavior.

In an adolescent group I directed, a fifteen-year-old girl revealed how she immediately went back to drugs when she left the group. She talked about her despair of ever stopping: "I have no self-control." Because of her openness and vulnerability, the group was very supportive. One group member, trying to pull her out of her abject state of depression, asked her to "tell us about some of your positive fantasies." She responded, "I do have one positive fantasy." The group members eagerly awaited her response, hoping that her comment about something positive would cheer her up. They asked, "What's that?" She replied, "My positive fantasy is being dead and free from my depression and pain."

It is obviously difficult for a young addict to confront the fact that his or her drug use may constitute an unconscious suicidal tendency. Yet it is a significant issue that must be encountered by all addict-alcoholics. The life-death issue in substance abuse leads to a basic premise about the delinquent abuser: On some level his or her behavior is a self-destructive pattern, which in its extreme form is short- or long-term suicidal behavior.

In general, the willingness of young drug users to undergo treatment is influenced by the availability of treatment programs, affordability of services, access to publicly funded programs or medical coverage, personal motivation, family and employer support, and potential consequences of admitting a dependency problem. In many communities, the demand for help far exceeds treatment capacity. Being unable to enter treatment may discourage users from maintaining a commitment to end drug dependency. Parents may hesitate to enter a child in a program for fear of his or her exposure to greater drug risks from associating with addicts who use other substances. The challenge is to reduce these barriers so that increasing numbers of juvenile substance abusers can avail themselves of effective treatment.

PART 5

The Causes of Crime and Delinquency

CHAPTERS

CHAPTER 11

THE FAMILY AND THE SOCIALIZATION PROCESS

The breakdown of communication between parents and their children is a significant causal factor affecting delinquent behavior.

In Western societies, religious leaders, philosophers, economists, and most recently, psychologists and sociologists have considered that the family is the basic socializing agent that affects positive behavior or deviant behavior. In the search for the causes of delinquency, we look at the family system and its socialization process for explanations for delinquent behavior. When we analyze theories of crime and delinquency in this and subsequent chapters, it is useful to bear in mind several causation issues as guides to the rationality and scientific validity of these theories:

1. A relationship of factors does not necessarily constitute a causal nexus. The fact that a preponderance of criminals and delinquents come from broken homes does not necessarily mean a broken home must cause delinquency and crime.

2. No single theory explains all crime and delinquency. Different patterns of crime and delinquency require different causal explanations. The sexual psychopath, the burglar, and the violent gang youth do not necessarily emerge from the same causal context.

3. Primary and secondary causes should not be confused. A lack of social workers and poor school facilities are not primary causes of delinquency; however, a dysfunctional or criminogenic family may be a primary causal factor.

4. Causation is a multifactored condition. It is difficult to isolate one single cause of crime or delinquency. The relative weight of each factor is difficult to determine. In some cases the family is a major factor in causing delinquent behavior; however, in some cases other factors are more significant.

5. In examining causal explanations based on research with offenders, we have the problem of separating family factors from the impacts of the administration of justice (arrest, jail, courts, prison).

Family Impacts on Delinquency

The social configuration that exerts the most profound causal influence on every youth's personality is his or her family. Dislocation in a youth's family, the absence of the family's potentially positive effects, or a severe emotional disorder in one or both parents that results in the abuse or neglect of a child can produce devastating negative impacts, including juvenile delinquency. The fundamental significance of the family's responsibility in socializing children was expressed by Robert Bierstedt (1957):

Of all of the groups that affect the lives of individuals in society, none touches them so intimately or so continuously as does the family. From the moment of birth, when young parents gaze with adoration upon their very own creation, to the moment of death, when sons and daughters are summoned to the bedside of a passing patriarch, the family exerts a constant influence. The family is the first social group we encounter in our inchoate experience, and it is the group with which, in one form or another, we shall have the most enduring relationship. Every one of us, with statistically small exceptions, grows up in a family and every one of us, too, with perhaps a few more exceptions, will be a member of a family for the larger part of his life. The family, almost without question, is the most important of any of the groups that human experience offers. Other groups we join for longer or shorter periods of time, for the satisfaction of this interest or that. The family, on the contrary, is with us always. Or rather more precisely, we are with it, an identifiable member of some family and an essential unit in its organization. It is the family, in addition, that gives us our principal identity and even our very name, which is the label of this identity, in the larger society of which we are a part.

Given the enormous significance of the family in everyone's life, a person's family or the absence of positive family life is an important determinant of whether or not a child will become delinquent. The family, as the basic agent of socialization, determines a child's socioeconomic class, and its structure and process is vital in the personality formation of the individual. All of these factors—socialization, class, and dynamics—impinge on the development of either a law-abiding or a delinquent child.

The family into which an individual is born is obviously a condition over which he or she has no control. In this sense, the person's destiny has already been determined. This event has determined the social class he or she will initially move in, along with the values, advantages, and disadvantages of the class. Class membership usually controls a person's economic position, which in turn determines the neighborhood, friends, and school the person attends. It also affects the kind and quality of other community agencies and resources that will be available. A person's economic resources effect his or her physical development and the efficiency of biological functioning in terms of dietary standards and access to medical care. An individual's parents set some limits on his or her intelligence and emotional makeup, and give that person a physical appearance that may work to his or her advantage or disadvantage in a culture where a certain appearance is considered superior.

A child has no control over the actual structure of the family: whether one, two, or no parents are available and whether or not grandparents are present. The family composition of siblings is also not within a child's control. A child also has limited, if any, control over the family's emotional problems, which may stem from the family's system of relationships. For example, some children become family scapegoats and are blamed for the family system's problems. A child may become the symptomatic carrier of a family pathology that stems not from the child's personal problems but from the family's structural problems. Therapists who are sensitive to a family's dynamics are well aware of the concept of the "identified patient" in a troubled family. This concept posits that, in a pathological family situation, one member is identified as the "sick" one, despite the fact that the overall family system is dysfunctional. Many children who become delinquent are the "identified patients "in this family situation. Emotionally disturbed, substance-abusing parents may blame their child for their own problems. In family groups that I have worked with as a marriage and family therapist, I have heard parents say, "if it wasn't for you, we would all get along, and I would quit drinking. You're the problem in our family." This type of scapegoating and identifying a child as the "sick one" is often used by emotionally disturbed parents to project their problems onto their children. This parental behavior is too often a significant cause of a child's delinquent behavior.

The Socialization Process

It is important to understand a child's total family system and socialization process to understand the child's delinquent behavior. Socialization refers to the process by which one acquires social skills and learns to participate effectively in society. This lifelong process may be divided into two stages. The first stage occurs between conception and approximately five years of age, when the primary socializing agent is the family. During this time the child must learn and master a number of activities if his or her later development is to proceed without difficulty. Children must master basic motor control and then advance to more complicated skills. They must learn breath control if language and communication are to develop. They must develop and understand basic concepts about themselves, other people, and the world around them. They must learn that things have names and that events occur together. They must absorb a cognitive, aesthetic, and moral value system.

Later in the socialization process, children must learn to relate to other people and to society on a personal basis. The second stage of the socialization process occurs from the time the child engages in group interaction until his or her death. Throughout an individual's lifetime, he or she is constantly forming, evaluating, and refining social skills for effective group interaction. Gerald Patterson and Thomas Dishion (1985) comment on this issue:

> From a social interactional perspective, delinquent behavior is thought of as the outcome of an extended process characterized by two general stages. The first stage usually begins during pread-olescence; it is initiated as a result of a breakdown in family management procedures. This disruption produces both an increase in antisocial child behavior and an impairment in the child's development of social and academic skills. Given that the pread-olescent child is exposed to this process, he is placed at risk for rejection by normal peers and eventual academic failure. In the second stage, during adolescence, continued disruptions in the parents' monitoring practices and poor social skills place him further at risk for contact with a deviant peer group like a gang. The association with deviant peers, poor parental monitoring of the child, and academic failure during adolescence all contribute directly to the likelihood he will engage in high rates of delin-quent activities. (Pp. 63–64)

Erik Erikson on Socialization and Developmental Stages

Erik Erikson's theories on developmental phases reveal how family structure and the socialization process can break down and facilitate delinquency. Erikson (1963) focused on the behavioral problems that a child has to solve, with or without the help of his or her family, in order to achieve a healthy adult personality.

Erikson posits a number of developmental stages in the early life of every individual, which, if properly handled, will produce: (1) trust instead of mistrust; (2) autonomy instead of shame and doubt; (3) initiative instead of guilt; (4) industry instead of inferiority; (5) identity instead of role diffusion; and (6) intimacy instead of alienation. (Erikson delineates two other phases; however, these are related to adult behavior and are not relevant to adolescence and delinquency.) Youths who do not effectively and properly complete these stages of personal development are more apt to become involved in delinquent behavior.

Trust

According to Erikson, a sense of trust develops in the first year of life and is built upon rewarding experiences and satisfaction of basic needs in the family. The baby's feelings of hunger are anticipated and food is supplied; its feelings of uneasiness or anxiety are assuaged by the comfort and warmth of being held closely and securely. Babies learn to trust others and themselves when they reach for an object and are able to grasp it. They learn to trust when objects that disappear, like mother's face, consistently and invariably reappear. This sense of trust in others, in oneself, and in the world may well be the most important elements in a healthy person who does not become delinquent. Most delinquents are distrustful of adults and authority figures.

Autonomy

According to Erikson, a "sense of autonomy" usually starts developing when children are twelve to fifteen months old. For the next two years, they try to assert that they have a mind and a will of their own. If all goes well, each child comes to feel that he or she is an independent and separate human being who nevertheless can still depend on the help of parents and others in certain situations. This stage is decisive for the proper balance between love and hate, giving and receiving, and expressing and control-ling feelings. If children are successfully socialized, they will be able to maintain proper self-control without any loss of self-esteem. If unsuccess-ful, they will have doubts about themselves and others and feelings of shy-ness and shame.

Donald Peterson and Wesley Becker (1965), speaking from a more classical psychoanalytic framework, supported Erikson's viewpoint in their assertion that there are four basic childhood needs: (1) the security and the backing of two present parents; (2) parental love and understanding; (3) an optimum period of gratification for infantile sexual desires; and (4) oppor-tunities to express hostilities, antagonisms, and aggressiveness, so that the child can learn what these feelings are like and how to deal with them in their relationships.

Initiative

A "sense of initiative," said Erikson, occurs in the fourth and fifth years of childhood. This is a period of experimentation and imagination, play and fantasy, when children want to find out what they can do. With the arrival of "conscience," a child wants to know the limits of how far he or she can go without being inhibited by "pangs of guilt." The superego, or censor, must allow the young boy or girl the freedom to "move." Denial of this free-dom by manipulative and controlling parents often results in a rigid and constricted personality accompanied by resentment, bitterness, and a vin-dictive attitude toward the world. If this occurs, a child would be more prone to be delinquent.

306

Industry

A "sense of industry" begins at around the sixth year and extends over the next five or six years. The slow acquisition of skills and knowledge go on during this period. A child learns fair play and cooperation and the "rules" for becoming a social being in the larger society. The positive outcome is a sense of duty and personal accomplishment, as opposed to feelings of inadequacy and inferiority. This leads to involvement in a meaningful occupation. Most delinquents resist hard work in a conventional work situation.

Identity

A person's "sense of identity" begins roughly with the onset of adolescence, a period of physiological changes and rapid physical growth. The central question to be answered during this period is, "Who am I?" Adolescents try to find out who they are: whether they are capable of becoming husbands and fathers or wives and mothers, how they will make a living, and whether they will be a success in life or a failure. An effectively socialized child will develop an ego identity and an occupational identity that will provide hope and confidence in him- or herself and the future. Some adolescents, according to Erikson, can't seem to "get hold of themselves" or "find themselves." They don't seem to know who they are or what their place in life really is, and are thus more disposed toward delinquent behavior.

Intimacy

Erikson postulates that a "sense of intimacy" can come only after a sense of personal identity has been established. The individual must have sufficient mastery over mind and body and sufficient ego strength to take the risks involved in order to develop personal relationships, close friendships, sexual intimacy, and love. The inability to achieve such relationships may result in excessive egocentrism and a deep sense of isolation and alienation. This sense of alienation can make a youth more vulnerable to delinquency. The inability of delinquents and criminals to develop a true sense of intimacy with other persons is reflected in the difficulty they have in relating to their family members. And in more cases than not, their families are corrupted by substance abuse and other forms of criminal behavior.

Criminogenic Families and Delinquency

It can be inferred from Erikson's stages of development that inadequate socialization within the framework of the family leads to delinquent behavior. The effective socialization of the child by the family through these developmental stages is the best safeguard against delinquency. Children who become delinquent are often brought up in dysfunctional families where their socialization is more likely to be influenced by deviant values than by law-abiding values. These families have been labeled "criminogenic families" by Hiram and Ruth Grogan (1971), who stressed that in families disorganized by unresolved and recurring internal conflicts, the process of socialization, of teaching the child by precept and example, is difficult. The family that is beset with chronic conflict and tension labors under a handicap in meeting its socialization responsibilities effectively. The consequence is a pathological family or, as the Grogans called it, a criminogenic family. This type of family produces an inadequately socialized child, one who is ill-prepared to face and accept values, standards, and codes of conduct that are socially acceptable. As this child grows older, the Grogans asserted, he or she may turn away from the family and seek comfort in a clique or gang, where he or she eagerly accepts all the antisocial or delinquent values of the group.

The criminogenic family is a phenomenon common to many urban areas. In an article in the *Los Angeles Times*, Joy Horowitz (1981) traced the pattern as described by a perceptive police officer who worked with delinquents. The officer, Tom Corey, on the basis of an extensive analysis of a criminogenic family and delinquency, proposed a radical and controversial treatment involving removing children from the criminogenic family. Following is a description of this family and Corey's recommendation for dealing with this social problem.

> A Family Tree of Delinquency. When the case file landed on his desk last fall Officer Tom Corey figured it was a routine matter. He began to read the arresting officer's report: Two children had been caught shoplifting two plastic toy motorcycles and an orange toy car worth a total of $3.97 from the J. C. Penney store in Pasadena. It would be up to Corey, a teacher-turned-cop assigned to the Pasadena Police Department's Youth Services Division, to dispose of the case.
>
> He carefully reread the report. It indicated that the children—cousins, eight and nine—had no prior police record and needed "no further counseling." Corey decided otherwise. On the last page of the report, the name of the children's family—Wilson—popped out at him like a bad omen. "Oh my God!" he remembers thinking when he realized the fathers of both

children were serving time in prison. "Where will it stop? There's got to be something better for these kids." Like other local police and probation officers, Corey, an eight-year police veteran, was more than familiar with the activities of the Wilson (a fictitious name) clan—a large, poor family spanning three generations and living adjacent to an area known for its low-income housing and high incidence of drug dealing and other crimes. . . . Because of the extensive criminal involvement of the Wilson children's grandparents, uncles, aunts, and parents, who had been in and out of jail or prison for offenses including robbery, burglary, assault, larceny and prostitution, the thirty-five-year-old police officer was determined to "break the cycle of crime" in the family. He and his superiors agreed it was time to goad the legal system, to test the court's commitment to preventing crime in the name of protecting children.

In this case, Corey reasoned, it could best be done by taking the children from the parents and placing them in foster homes. If not, he believed, "there's a 99 percent chance these children are going to become criminals." So Corey initiated court proceedings to remove the third generation of Wilsons from their home, an action that may wind up setting a startling legal precedent, court observers say. His decision was not based on the home's physical condition ("I've seen a lot worse") or on battering or on lack of adult supervision—all standard criteria for court intervention. "My judgment," Corey explains, "was based on the parents being criminal role models." In his report, Corey offered a three-generation family tree of the Wilsons—based strictly on their criminal records. "It's the kind of thing we see a lot in police work," he says, rocking back in his desk chair. "The parents are criminals. Their kids are criminals. And the kids' kids are just starting to become criminals. It's a criminal family."

In a precedent-setting decision, the Juvenile Court ruled on the "Wilson" case described here. Bill Hazlett (1981) reported the decision as follows:

Juvenile Court authorities Tuesday removed four children from their Pasadena home because their parents and relatives have a history of four hundred arrests in the last ten years. "The parents—and even the grandparents—have been in and out of jail like a revolving door," Deputy County Counsel Sterling Honea said. A temporary order making the children, ages ten, nine, eight, and one and one-half years, wards of the Juvenile Court was issued by Superior Court Judge Elwood Lui on recommendation of Honea and Pasadena Juvenile Officer Tom Corey. The four children have three mothers, who are sisters, and share the home with various members of their family group.

Two of the fathers of the children are in prison; the whereabouts of the third father is not known. The children and their mothers are members of a family group that police and juvenile officers call the "Wilsons," though that is not the real name because an effort is being made to protect the youngsters' identities. The family group lives in a small section of Pasadena called "The Pit." There is an unusually high rate of drug-related crime in The Pit. But the Wilsons' criminal history is not limited to such offenses. It also includes petty theft, prostitution, and other problems.

"These minors," Corey said in one court document, "spent their formative years in a family environment in which it was the norm for family members to be arrested and incarcerated. Nearly all the adult members of their immediate family have double-digit arrest figures and even their great-aunt was arrested twice this year." Honea said one box of criminal records brought to his office during the investigation of the Wilson clan "weighs about 40 pounds." Corey, who began investigating the family after two of the children's cousins were caught shoplifting last September, said his goal was to "give these kids a chance to be around some other adults who don't lead a life of crime."

Most family laws and courts do not support removing children from their biological families. In fact, wife and child batterers often receive custody of their children. In extreme cases family law even allows a parent who murders his or her spouse to acquire custody of children. Even though he was held responsible in a civil court trial for the brutal death of his wife, O.J. Simpson received custody of his children. In another case the same judge gave custody of two children to a mother who had attempted suicide. She later murdered herself and her children.

In a research study on the issue of criminogenic families, Raymond R. Crowe of the Department of Psychiatry at the University of Iowa College of Medicine carried out a study to determine whether or not any genetic basis for antisocial behavior emerged from the family. Crowe (1975) studied two groups of adoptees—one that included forty-six children of convicted female felons (90 percent) and misdemeanants (10 percent) and the control group made up of forty-six adoptees specially chosen to parallel the other group demographically. The offspring of mothers with criminal records had more marks against them socially than did the controls. Seven of them were arrested as adults. All seven had been convicted at least once, some had multiple arrests and convictions. Three were considered felons, and six had spent time incarcerated either as an adult or as a juvenile—one as both.

Of the control group only one person had been arrested and convicted. In the experimental sample, eight subjects had been referred by the courts, and seven of the eight were treated for antisocial behavior. Although the controls had been treated for antisocial behavior, none had been remanded by the courts, and none had arrest records. Crowe concluded that "the unique finding in the present study is that the unfavorable [family] environment influences were associated with the development of antisocial personality in the subjects but not in the controls" (1975, p. 67). Of the many factors that contribute to delinquency, most important are absentee or criminal fathers, mothers who are inadequate for a variety of reasons, and substance abuse by parents.

Absentee or Criminal Fathers

A significant factor in the development of delinquency is the role of the father. Most boys who become delinquents have no positive adult role models. Their fathers, older brothers, and uncles are involved with drugs and gangs, and in too many cases, are frequently in and out of prison. The issue of absentee criminal fathers as negative role models was dramatically revealed in a psychodrama session I directed in a cell block that housed two hundred men who were taking part in a California prison therapeutic community project. The project, administered by ex-criminal addicts who were graduates of the Amity Therapeutic Community, was one of the most effective approaches I have ever participated in with regard to changing criminogenic families. Notable was a banner sign that hung on the prison cell-block wall: "Don't forget, we are the fathers of 617 children."

The subject in the session was Fernando (not his real name), a fifty-year-old, longtime Chicano gangster who had been in and out of prison most of his life. In the process of changing his way of life in the Amity program, Fernando developed a sincere concern for his three teenage sons. It was clear to Fernando and the group that if there was no intervention, Fernando's sons would join their father in prison. Despite the fact that Fernando had been away from his sons and in prison most of his life, the boys wanted to emulate their criminal father—he was their role model and hero. Fernando, as a result of his change of perspective, now felt helpless and guilty about his negative influence on his sons. The insights he achieved in his therapy motivated him to try to change their behavior.

In the psychodrama session, the "sons "were role-played by several prisoners in the group, who understood from their personal experience how his real sons would react to their father's new perspective on life. Fernando opened the psychodrama session by tearfully telling his "sons" how terrible he felt about the negative influence he had had on their lives and how he was now changing his life.

To his delinquent sons, Fernando had been a hero who had established a strong reputation as a *veterano* drug-dealing and murderous gangster in their barrio. In the psychodrama session the "sons" were appalled at the new message Fernando was giving them—"Crime doesn't pay!" One role-playing convict "son" said, "Man, we got our reputation on the streets from you. We have a rep because we are known as your sons. And now you're punking out on us. You're talking like a pussy."

After being rebuked by his "sons" several times for his new viewpoint on life, Fernando was ready to give up and quit the session. The other inmates in the group chastised him and told him to "hang in there." One sharp member of the group said, "You know, Fernando, you have been a terrible father and role model for your sons for many years. You're not going to change them overnight. But if you demonstrate a new positive role in here and when you get back to your family and the community—that's the best way to change their behavior."

After he was released from prison, Fernando did change his way of life. When he was paroled he entered the Amity Therapeutic Community halfway house and later became a drug counselor. He reconnected with his sons as a positive role model and had a positive effect on them. I met with Fernando and one of his sons about a year after his release from prison. In our discussion I learned that at least this son was now in a positive relationship with his father, and Fernando was attempting to establish a similar relationship with his other two sons. Fernando's rehabilitation and his impact on his son, unfortunately, is a rare exception.

In another situation of a father-son relationship, it was apparent that this father, unlike Fernando, continued to have a positive attitude toward his son's criminality. The following scenario reflects a compendium of facts I pieced together about the aftermath of a bizarre criminal event (alluded to in the chapter on violence) involving a failed bank robbery and a shoot-out with police that resulted in the death of the two bank robbers. It reveals the hidden role played by an absentee criminal father of one of the dead criminals—who not only didn't deplore the death of his son and his crimes but eulogized him as a heroic "criminal genius."

To recapitulate the event described earlier, on February 28, 1997, two men were involved in a dramatic shoot-out with Los Angeles police officers after a failed bank robbery. Twelve people, including six police officers, were seriously wounded. After a gun battle involving almost one hundred police officers and the police swat squad, the two would-be bank robbers, who sprayed the area with several hundred rounds of bullets with their automatic AK-47 weaponry, were killed by the police.

On March 10, 1997, in an interview, Larry Eugene Phillips, Sr., the father of one of the criminals, spoke proudly of his dead son. "He was a criminal genius and the bravest man in the world, with a taste for the good life and a hatred for police. He wanted the American Dream." This prideful quote speaks volumes regarding this father's criminogenic influence on his son. A closer analysis of the Phillips family, especially the son's relationship to his father, reveals the impact of the family on the son's violent sociopathic criminal personality. Larry Phillips' half-brother stated, "He idolized the wrong people. His first idol was his father." Larry Phillips, Sr., was a Denver resident who had a long record of arrests. He was an escapee from the Colorado State Reformatory when Larry Jr. was born. As a career criminal, he often told his son how he hated cops. Larry Sr. attributed his son's bad feelings about law enforcement to the way cops treated him. "On my son's sixth birthday, FBI agents came to the house, guns drawn, to arrest me. Larry, Jr., hated cops because of what they did to me. He knew that every time I came in contact with police something bad happened." The way this father described his interactions with police indicates that he felt no responsibility for his actions.

Larry Phillips, Sr., was proud of his son. He bragged, "My son is the way he is because of *my* life-style. Larry was like a clone of me. He was a pretty gifted kid; that's all I can say. He used his brains. Everything he did was completely thought out. Nothing was overlooked. He was a criminal genius."

Another negative adult role model is the "ghetto hustler"—a fixture in the black hood. Malcolm X (1965), in his autobiography, described this type of negative role model as follows: "The most dangerous black man in America is the ghetto hustler. The ghetto hustler is internally restrained by nothing. He has no religion, no concept of morality, no civic responsibility, no fear-nothing" (p. 86). This type of individual's hustle may be drugs, and he is often a father who has abandoned his son.

Maternal Impacts

The mother of bank robber Larry Phillips, Jr., did not discourage Phillips from the criminal life-style supported by his father. Larry's parents divorced when he was ten. His mother served ten years for drug possession, and while in prison, she stabbed a guard with a homemade knife.

Most children growing up in the inner city have a maternal figure in their family who provides the necessary nurturing for socialization. However, many youths who become delinquent have mothers who are besieged by problems. The film *Sugar Hill* (1992) opens with a scene of a child who witnesses his mother fixing heroin and then dying from an overdose. This portrait of a child's socialization dramatically reveals a situation that in the real world too often produces a sociopathic delinquent.

African-American social scientist, Elijah Anderson (1994) succinctly delineates how a mother in a fatherless home, besieged by her own problems, can affect the socialization of her child:

> The overwhelming majority of families in the inner-city community try to approximate the decent-family model, but there are

many others who clearly represent the worst fears of the decent family. Not only are their financial resources extremely limited, but what little they have may easily be misused. The lives of the street-oriented are often marked by disorganization. In the most desperate circumstances people frequently have a limited understanding of priorities and consequences, and so frustrations mount over bills, food, and, at times, drink, cigarettes, and drugs. Some tend toward self-destructive behavior; many street-oriented women are crack-addicted ("on the pipe"), alcoholic, or involved in complicated relationships with men who abuse them.

In addition, the seeming intractability of their situation, caused in large part by the lack of well-paying jobs and the persistence of racial discrimination, has engendered deep-seated bitterness and anger in many of the most desperate and poorest blacks, especially young people. The need both to exercise a measure of control and to lash out at somebody is often reflected in the adults' relations with their children. At the least, the frustrations of persistent poverty shortens the fuse in such people, contributing to a lack of patience with anyone, child or adult, who irritates them. (P. 46)

I have observed the fatherless family situation described by Anderson in many family groups I have directed. Out of desperation and rage about their own failed lives, single-parent mothers can be quite violent with their children in an effort to get them to behave. They will scream at them or hit them for the least infraction, partly out of the frustration and anger they have about their own lives. A youth growing up in this type of family learns that interpersonal problems are solved by violent behavior.

Substance-Abusing Parents

Many youths who become delinquent have parents who are alcoholics or drug addicts, and this is often a significant causal factor in effecting their delinquent behavior. If a pregnant woman is addicted to crack-cocaine, heroin, or alcohol, her child may be born addicted and have severe physiological and psychological deficits that lead to delinquent behavior.

Substance-abusing parents often abuse their children. In New York state in 1997, three of every four people charged with child abuse had drug or alcohol problems. A survey of the courts in 1996 noted that the most horrendous child abuse and neglect cases involved parents who abused drugs. In 1997 in response to this issue, New York Chief Judge Judith Kaye announced the establishment of special drug treatment courts in the state's Family Court system (*New York Times*, 1997).

Substance abuse is an egocentric enterprise. Drug addicts or alcoholics are self-centered and consequently sociopathic in their relationship with their children. This form of parenting is not conducive to effectively socializing a child into a caring, compassionate, loving person. Children who are socialized in the chaotic world of a substance-abusing family tend to have a limited trust of others and to become egocentric and uncompassionate. These personality factors facilitate their participation in delinquent activities.

A significant factor in socializing a child is discipline. There are four basic forms of discipline: strict, sporadic, lax, and none. Research reveals that the most damaging form is sporadic discipline. In this form the child seldom knows when he or she is right or wrong. Substance-abusing parents tend to administer this type of discipline. They randomly apply discipline that is often not connected to the child's "bad behavior." Children subjected to this type of discipline do not develop a sense of justice in their own lives or in the larger society.

The children of substance abusers accept drug use as a way of resolving their own emotional pain. Substance abuse becomes for them a way of ameliorating their painful feelings of low self-esteem and of hopelessness.

In my work with delinquents, especially those in psychiatric facilities, I have observed the impact of drug-abusing parents on hundreds of youths who became delinquent. One example was a thirteen-year-old boy whose gang name was "Little Killer," L.K. for short. L.K. was emotionally and physically abused from the age of four, several times a week, by his drug-addict father. The physical beatings and verbal abuse administered by his father often had little relationship to L.K.'s behavior. He would be beaten or verbally abused for a variety of "offenses" chosen at random by his irrational father. His father assaulted his wife and son whenever he had a need to act out his drug-induced personal frustrations about the world around him. According to L.K. "He would beat the shit out of me for no reason, just because he was loaded and mad at the world. I've always felt like a punching bag, or maybe more like a piece of shit. If my own father thinks I'm a punk and a loser, maybe that's what I am."

The irrational behavior of L.K.'s father led to several consequences. The indiscriminate beatings and verbal abuse had the effect of producing low self-esteem in the youth. He tended to feel humiliated and worthless. As a result of these feelings, he thought he was "a loser." The only place where he found he had power, respect, and a reasonable sense of self was with his homies in his gang, who were known as the Venice Insane Baby Crips. The gang gave L.K. some level of the positive approval he so desperately needed and sought from his substance-abusing parents.

In summary, Little Killer's dysfunctional family helped to turn L.K. into a sociopathic gangster. First, the youth had no one in his family he felt he could trust. Second, there were no significant people in his surroundings who acted as positive role models, demonstrating how a person shows love and compassion to another person. Third, because he was abused by his drug-addicted father, he developed a poor self-concept. In reaction to these feelings of inadequacy, he developed a macho syndrome, which he acted out in the gang as "Little Killer." Fourth, the gang gave this emotionally needy youth some sense of self-respect and power in his chaotic world. All of these socialization factors converged to produce a violent sociopathic delinquent.

Research on the Family and Delinquency

Research projects on the family's contribution to delinquent behavior analyze socialization factors; the general parental treatment of children; differential impacts of maternal and parental treatment; the impact of different discipline approaches; the relationship of fathers and sons; the impact of broken homes on juvenile delinquency; and the effect of the ordinal position of a child in a family on delinquency. Following are a number of notable studies, old and new, that present relevant generalizations about a family's impact on delinquency.

Rolf Loeber and Magda Stouthhamer-Loeber (1986) carried out an extensive analysis of longitudinal data that showed that socialization variables, such as lack of parental supervision, parental rejection, and parent-child involvement are among the most powerful predictors of juvenile conduct problems and delinquency. Medium-strength predictors include background variables such as parents' marital relations and parental criminality. Weaker predictors are lack of parental discipline, parental health, and parental absence. According to the Loebers' research, a small number of families produce a disproportionate number of delinquents. The presence of one child with delinquency, aggression, or covert conduct problems increases the probability that other children in the family will exhibit those behaviors. They determined that deficiencies in parenting skills were associated with the seriousness of the child's delinquency.

An important aspect of the socialization process as a deterrent to delinquency is the quality and process of interaction between parent and child. Lawrence Rosen (1985) made the following observation: "One important and continuing debate on the relationship between family and delinquency has been the 'structure' versus 'function' controversy. The structural perspective typically focuses on such factors as parental absence, family size, and birth order, whereas the functional or 'quality of family life' position argues for the significance of parent-child interaction, amount and type of discipline, and degree of marital happiness" (p. 63).

316

British psychiatrist John Bowlby (1951) stressed early on the importance of the maternal relationship, particularly for the younger child. He commented about maternal care: "It is this complex, rich, and rewarding relationship with the mother in the early years, varied in count-less ways by relations with the father and the siblings, that child psychia-trists and many others now believe to underly the development of char-acter and of mental health" (p. 351). Bowlby asserted that considerable damage is done to the child by a mother's absence, the amount of dam-age varying with the age of the child when the absence occurs, the length of the absence, and the quality of the substitute care that is provided. He related this maternal deprivation to delinquency. In a study of a group of delinquents, he found significantly more maternal deprivation among the delinquents than among a control group from a child guidance center. He concluded that "on the basis of this varied evidence it appears that there is a very strong case indeed for believing that prolonged separation of a child from his mother (or mother-substitute) during the first five years of life stands foremost among the causes of delinquent character develop-ment and persistent misbehavior" (p. 11).

F. Ivan Nye (1958) and his associates studied 605 cases involv-ing parent-child relationships that ranged from mutual acceptance to mutual rejection. Between these extremes were gradations ranging from either the father's or mother's accepting or rejecting a child to the child's accepting or rejecting either parent or both parents. The children were rank-ordered in terms of "delinquent" behavior, from "most delinquent" to "least delinquent." Of the 292 cases of mother-child mutual accep-tance, only 14 percent of the children were in the "most delinquent" group, whereas 86 percent were in the "least delinquent" group.

Of the 313 cases of mother-child mutual rejection, 48 percent of the children were in the "most delinquent" group and 52 percent were in the "least delinquent" group. Between these extremes, the percent-ages of delinquency varied in proportion to the degrees of acceptance or rejection. The combinations of father-child acceptance and rejection had similar effects on children's delinquent behavior. The data indicated that rejection of the child by the parents closely related to delinquent behavior; acceptance between parent and child was correlated with less chance of juvenile delinquency.

In an investigation of high-delinquency areas in New York City, M. Craig and S. J. Glick (1963) found three factors to be related to increased likelihood of delinquency in boys: (1) careless or inade-quate supervision by the mother or mother substitute; (2) erratic or overstrict discipline; and (3) lack of cohesiveness of the family unit (pp. 231–232).

317

Albert Bandura and R.H. Walters (1959) came up with somewhat similar findings in a study of twenty-six delinquent boys and an equal number of nondelinquents from the same social class and IQ range. Both the boys and their parents were interviewed and rated for a variety of psychological variables. The parents of the delinquent boys were found to be more rejecting and less affectionate than those of the nondelinquents. It was the researchers' opinion that the boys' relations with their fathers constituted a more important factor in development than their relationship with their mothers. They noted that the fathers of delinquent boys were prone to ridicule them when they made a mistake and that there was an atmosphere of ill will between fathers and sons.

Fathers and Sons[1]

The most important phase of a father-son relationship is the period of the son's adolescent life struggle. A father's relationship to his son during this period can significantly influence the son's delinquent or nondelinquent behavior. A son wants the security of knowing that his father is there for him, yet he has begun to strike out on his own and define himself on his own terms. Usually, a boy distances himself from his parents and relates more closely to his peers. He also begins to develop a rebellious posture. Many fathers, during this critical phase of their sons' individuation and normal rebellion, behave unwisely and exacerbate an uncomfortable situation into a stressful one. The father may ask himself when his son becomes twelve or thirteen, "Where did my little boy go? And who is this arrogant monster with muscles?"

The son is often at this time beginning to rival his father's physical strength. This phase of a father-son relationship is fraught with seemingly insurmountable problems. If the normal problems that emerge in this phase are not handled properly, the father-son relationship can be damaged, and the boy may turn to severe delinquent behavior.

The boy's socialization during this period is characterized by his developing a sense of his own identity in relation not only to his father but also to the world in general. He begins to act in a rebellious manner. He becomes belligerent about his ideas and opinions, even when he knows he's wrong. He wants to do everything his way. He begins to feel his own ego power and to separate from his father and family, seeking to become a person in his own right. If these normal expressions of rebellion, which reflect his search for identity, are squelched by a severely

---

1. This section is derived from *Fathers and Sons* by Lewis Yablonsky (New York: Simon and Schuster, 1982).

repressive father, the sons behavior can become recalcitrantly delinquent.

One of a boy's adversaries in this adolescent phase is his father, because the father is perceived by the boy to be the primary carrier of societal norms. A father and son can become engaged in a psychodramatic conflict. In psychodrama terms, the father becomes the son's experimental auxiliary ego, or his "punching bag."

The auxiliary ego in the form of the father represents all the others in his life onto whom the son projects negative and positive emotions. With a compassionate, loving father, the son can try out a variety of outrageous attitudes and behaviors without being hurt. His auxiliary-ego father absorbs some but not all of his son's punches. During the adolescent years, a father and son may engage in playful physical aggression, such as boxing or wrestling, which has all the ingredients of the larger conflict that centers around social and emotional issues. In a physical encounter, the father is usually bigger, stronger, and a more experienced fighter, and in nonphysical areas he is also more experienced.

A loving, understanding father lets his son throw a lot of practice punches to test his strength and ability, both physically and intellectually, without returning a knockout punch. He interprets and explains societal norms rather than severely squelching his son's natural curiosity. In contrast, psychopathic-macho fathers may hit their sons with knockout punches because they are blind to the realities of the jousting. They are unaware that their sons are testing their social and emotional strength and that they need a safe person—the father—as an auxiliary ego to help socialize them.

A son who feels safe with his father can test new views and perceptions of the world on him and in this way learn viable norms of behavior. In the son's real world of teachers, peers, and school, if he experiments in a rebellious way, there may be harsh reactions of condemnation or ridicule that can have a lasting negative impact on his life. In contrast, with a loving father as an auxiliary ego, the young man can test out and experiment with his behavior and attitudes. An understanding auxiliary-ego father will provide valuable suggestions and nonpunitive feedback to his son.

Immature, macho, or emotionally weak fathers will react as peers and outsiders, often in defense of their own weak egos. With this type of father the adolescent son will receive a harsh punitive response that will inhibit his creative spirit and fail to provide him with the needed opportunity to test new behavior. This can produce rebellious, delinquent acting out.

The disciplinary process becomes one of the paramount areas of father-son interaction during the boy's adolescent phase. An important dimension of this process is that a son often compares his father's disciplinary response to his behavior with the responses of the fathers of his friends. Two fathers may respond in entirely different ways to the same behavior, based on their own social contexts and values. An interesting case in point is related to smoking marijuana and the different types of disciplinary response by three fathers with whom I held in-depth interviews.

One disciplinary extreme was what I will call the macho-father approach. It involved a father who was an alcoholic. On finding out that his son used marijuana, he battered his son unmercifully. In fact, he also kept his son "under house arrest" for several weeks. During this period he beat his son sporadically. The man used the situation and his son as an outlet for the enormous hostility and rage he had toward life in general, perhaps rationalizing his own drinking problem. The father and son had fierce debates about the relative destructive effects of marijuana versus alcohol. The father's extreme discipline had little positive effect on the son in dissuading him from marijuana use. In fact, the boy, partly to assuage his increased pain and violent feelings toward his father, graduated to the use of cocaine.

Another disciplinary approach was at the opposite extreme. This case involved what I term a buddy-type father. This father smoked dope regularly with his fifteen-year-old son. His indulgence of his son, who was totally undisciplined, manifested itself at a party at their home. After dinner, the father, a successful businessman, came out of his study and called his son down from his room. The father shouted "You rotten bastard. Don't I give you enough money for dope? I know you've been in my stash. There's a whole lid of grass missing from my desk!" The son shrugged his shoulders and went back to his room. Everyone at the party within earshot of this exchange was embarrassed and tried to act as if it hadn't happened.

A third type of father, one I call a caring-rational father, used an approach that was caring but firm. This rational father set firm limits, without battering his son or indulging him. This was the most effective disciplinary approach.

There are two basic contexts in which father-son discipline occurs. One is when the son violates a family rule. The second involves a situation where the son violates a law of the larger society. In this situation the father is not the main disciplinarian and in many cases may have little power over his son's fate. A father in this type of situation can sometimes rescue his son from the pain of the full impact of the larger society's laws, often to the detriment of his son. This is most likely to happen in the case of an upper-middle-class youth. A case reported to me by an affluent forty-year-old lawyer presents some of the main conflicts and issues that affect a father's response to society's discipline of his son. The following is a composite of the father's depiction of a significant event in the relationship between father and son.

> Bill was sixteen at the time, doing lots of drugs and getting into trouble. I was constantly rescuing him from being expelled from school for truancy, bad grades—you name it. The final blow came when he was arrested in a department store for shoplifting. He already had a few minor drug arrests on his record, so they brought him to the Beverly Hills police station. On the earlier charges, before his trial in the juvenile court, he had been released into my custody instead of being taken downtown to the juvenile jail. The scene at the police station was the same terrible one I had been through several times. But this time I decided I was not going to rescue him. I'll never forget that painful experience.
>
> After a conversation with my son during which he told me he would never do it again, the juvenile police officer present asked me if I wanted to take him home. I said, "No, do whatever you do with a case like this." My son looked at me in disbelief. "Dad, you mean you're going to let them take me to juvenile jail?" I explained to him as best I could that it would be easier for me to take him home, but for his own sake, this time he had to face the real consequences of his behavior. He didn't make it easy on me. I told him I wasn't doing anything to him; he had done it to himself. He really didn't believe it was happening, nor did I. I vividly remember him looking back at me as they took him away.
>
> It was a nightmare for me. The next thing I remember was sitting on the front lawn of the police station crying like a baby. People, including cops, came by, asking me if I was okay. I waved them away and kept on sobbing uncontrollably. My crying must have gone on for at least half an hour. The sight of a forty-year-old attorney, in a business suit, sitting on the lawn in front of a police station crying, must have been something to see. I've reviewed that experience fifty times since in my mind. What was I crying about? Was it because I was now the father of a juvenile delinquent? Or was it because of my compassion for my son? Was I crying for him or me? I've since decided it was for both of us.

The family dynamics that produced the son's delinquency were quite complex. However, on reviewing this disciplinary event, we both concluded that the following analysis was accurate. This father had logically decided that it was time for his son to confront in full force the realities and consequences of his accelerating delinquent behavior in the larger society. If the father rescued his son once again from society's discipline, he would be doing him a disservice. The act of rescue would be more to assuage the father's feelings than to help his son. It was painful for the father to let his son go to jail. When he cried he did so out of pity for himself as a father who had failed and was experiencing the pain of being the father of a delinquent son; he was also crying out of compassion for the pain his son would experience while in jail.

The story had a happy ending. The son's encounter with the inevitable disciplinary end point of his escalating delinquency brought him up short, opened up communication with his father, and resulted in a positive change of behavior in the son.

Effective parenting for a mother or a father often involves biting the bullet and experiencing the personal emotional pain necessary for both parent and child to correct dysfunctional behavior. If such behavior is continued, it can be self-destructive to the parent's life as well. When a good father states the old platitude before administering discipline, "This is going to hurt me more than it's going to hurt you," he is often stating a fundamental truth. A nice-guy approach involving a rescue act for his son may take the father off the hook, but it may be bad for the son. Fathers who do this are not fathering effectively and have avoided their responsibilities to the detriment of their sons' proper socialization. Protecting a child from the consequences of deviant behavior is to bring him or her up in an unreal world.

In a follow-up interview I had with the father and son about a year later, the son validated his father's decision to let him experience the consequences of his delinquent behavior. He told his father, "Dad, when you let me go off with that cop to jail I truly hated you, and I felt abandoned. But I now understand you did what you had to do. Being locked up in that dump downtown for three days with those really tough kids was an experience I've never forgotten. It made me think about my life and where I was heading. I decided, never again. I'm glad you did what you did, and I thank you."

Too many parents, especially middle-class parents, rescue their children from disciplinary processes and in this way reinforce their children's delinquent behavior. The manner in which a parent disciplines a child can have a significant impact on whether or not the child becomes delinquent.

Discipline and Delinquency

Proper and improper discipline are significant factors that affect delinquency in boys. Sheldon and Eleanor Glueck (1950) defined three discipline practice categories: "(1) *sound*—consistent and firm control of the boy by the parent, but not so strict as to arouse fear and antagonism; (2) *fair*—control that is indefinite—sometimes strict, sometimes lax; and (3) *unsound*—extremely lax, or extremely rigid control by the parents, which on the one hand gives the boy unrestrained freedom of action and on the other restricts him to the point of his rebellion" (p. 421). In their research on the discipline factor, Sheldon and Eleanor Glueck found that in most cases of delinquents, 4.1 percent of the fathers were found to use sound discipline, 26.7 percent fair discipline, and 69.3 percent unsound discipline. Of the delinquent cases in which the disciplinary practices of the mothers were known, 2.5 percent were considered sound, 27.4 percent fair, and 70.1 percent unsound (p. 138).

Discipline practice is, therefore, a crucial factor in the causal context of delinquent behavior patterns. Discipline is needed if controls are to be adequately internalized into a youth's personality. Situations and appropriate methods of dealing with them must occur regularly enough to let the child develop concepts of conduct and be able to distinguish suitable and unsuitable responses.

Discipline is generally characterized by three variables: consistency, intensity, and quality. *Consistency* pertains to the predictability of the discipline and takes into account the circumstances in which the offense occurred. Discipline that is consistent, rational, and coordinated with an explanation of why the discipline is being imposed is more likely to produce adequate internal controls. *Intensity* refers to the severity and rationality of the punishment. Discipline based on explanation and understanding between parent and child rather than strict, punitive punishment is more likely to produce internalized control in a child. *Quality* is characterized by the degree of understanding and compassion parents utilize in their disciplinary practice.

Discipline by means of nagging and love withdrawal produces in the child control based on fear of losing parental affection, not on an internalized set of standards of behavior. According to Peterson and Becker (1965), "If one endorses the common assumption that capacities for internal control are complexly but closely related to previously imposed external restraints, then parental discipline assumes focal significance as a factor in delinquency" (p. 49).

Ivan Nye (1958) concluded that 49 percent of both male and female delinquents who reported that their mothers "very often" failed to carry out threats of punishment were found in the "most delinquent" category. This compared to 30 percent of the boys and 22 percent of the girls who reported that their mothers "never failed" to implement their threats. Nye also reported that of the children in the study who considered their father's discipline "always fair," only 30 percent of the boys and 20 percent of the girls fell into his "most delinquent" group. On the other hand, 55 percent of the boys and 44 percent of the girls who felt their father was "unfair" fell into the "most delinquent" group (p. 48).

It is clear from this varied research that the discipline practices of parents are significant not only in the socialization of a child but also in the child's process of "individuating" and discovering a sense of self. When discipline related to family rules is too severe or inconsistent, delinquency often results.

Family Size and Ordinal Position in the Family

The ordinal position that a child occupies in a family has been shown to have an effect on his or her personality and the possibility of being delinquent. The first child is born to inexperienced parents and is sometimes called the "trial baby." This child lives the first years of his or her life as an only child. The child relates easily to adults and is likely to incorporate adult values more rapidly than later children.

As the size of a family grows, each child is subjected to a number of different relationships: the relationship between the parents, each parent's relationship to the children, the children's relationship to the parents, the relationship among the children, and a particular child's relationship with his or her siblings. As the number of family members increases, the number of interpersonal relations is increased. Thus, each child's world is different from the world of his or her siblings. This helps to explain the unique personalities that develop in a family and why one child may become delinquent while others are law-abiding.

Lees and Newson (1954) study the differences among delinquents that might be caused by sibling position and found that intermediaries—children with younger and older siblings—were significantly overrepresented in the delinquent population studies. Sheldon and Eleanor Glueck (1950) found that 60 percent of the delinquents studied were intermediaries, while 47.8 percent of the nondelinquent control group were intermediaries. Ivan Nye (1958) found that both youngest siblings and intermediaries were overrepresented in the "very delinquent" group.

These research conclusions tend to explain the overrepresentation of middle children in delinquency populations. In general, middle children seem to have the greatest need for attention and affection and are the very ones who are less apt to get it. Parents are apt to devote "realistically" most of their parental time to the youngest child because of his or her physical and emotional immaturity, while the eldest sibling may claim some "right" by virtue of age for special attention and consideration.

Broken Homes

In the past century, there has been an enormous and escalating increase in parental separations and divorce. In general, one in every two marriages

324

ends in divorce or separation, and children are increasingly being entrusted to the care of a single parent.

Child-rearing patterns have thus undergone drastic changes. Interviews with single working mothers reveal that the biggest problems they face are finding good care for their infants, dealing with worry and guilt feelings about the care of their children, lack of emotional support in the child-rearing process from relatives and friends, and physical and mental exhaustion caused by trying to do two full-time jobs at once.

According to the 1995 U.S. Bureau of the Census Reports, over 20 million preschool-age children have working mothers, and only one-sixth of these children can be accommodated in licensed preschools. Many welfare-supported women with too many children in too few rooms have taken in neighbor's children to supplement their income. The result is more overcrowding, less supervision, and less effective socialization of children. All of these factors have resulted in a growing number of "latchkey" children— children who come home from school to empty houses, where they are unsupervised while they await the return of their parents. The result of these negative social forces is increasing runaways, teenage suicides, juvenile teenage parenthood, and delinquency.

Roland J. Chilton and Gerald E. Markle (1972) emphasized the continuing effects of family disruption on delinquency. They described their process and findings as follows:

> Employing seriousness of offense as a measure of delinquency, we re-examine the relationship between delinquency referral and family disruption. Information from Juvenile and County Courts of Florida provided us with uniform delinquency data for 8,944 children. We compare the family situations of 5,376 of these children with the situations of children in the U.S. population. The analysis suggests (1) that children charged with delinquency live in disrupted families substantially more often than children in the general population, (2) that children referred for more serious delinquency are more likely to come from incomplete families than juveniles charged with minor offenses, and (3) that family income is a more important factor for understanding the relationship between delinquency referral and family situation than age, sex, or urban-rural residence. (Pp. 93–99)

In their conclusion, Chilton and Markle stated, "Our study provides added empirical support for the conclusions of earlier investigators who have suggested that proportionately more children who come into contact with police agencies and with juvenile courts on delinquency charges live in disrupted families than do children in the general population" (p. 98). In addition, the study suggested that children charged with more serious misconduct are more likely to come from one-parent families than are children charged with less serious delinquency.

Girls, the Family, and Delinquency

Most data on family influences on delinquency are derived from studies of boys. There is evidence, however, that similar forces influence female delinquency. Ashley Weeks (1956) suggested that the differential impact of the broken home by sex disappeared when one controlled for type of offense. Most girls are arrested for incorrigibility, running away, and sex offenses, while most boys are arrested for vandalism, theft, and violence (pp. 601–609). K.M. Koller (1971), in a study dealing exclusively with girls, explored the effects of parental issues on delinquency. From a group of 160 girls aged sixteen and seventeen at a girl's reformatory, 121 were chosen at random. The girls had been committed to the reformatory for a number of reasons: 44 percent were reported as being "exposed to moral danger," 39 percent were "uncontrollable," and 12 percent were admitted for stealing and for drug abuse. A control group of 101 girls were chosen randomly from the general population. They were of a similar socioeconomic status and age as the delinquent girls.

Of the "delinquent" subjects, 61 percent experienced "parental loss." Most common was the absence of the father or of both parents. Eighty percent of the delinquent subjects who experienced parental deprivation came from broken homes. Most delinquent girls came from large families with younger-than-average parents. It is apparent from Koller's conclusions and my recent research that the absence of a parent figure can have severe effects on juveniles of either sex and result in delinquency (Koller, 1971, pp. 319–327).

It is not the absence of a parent per se that is associated with delinquency, but rather the kind of relationship that exists between children and the remaining parent. A warm, stable single parent has a much better chance of raising a nondelinquent child than do two parents who are in conflict. Nevertheless, there is powerful evidence of a direct causal nexus between dysfunctional broken homes and delinquency.

Family Dynamics That Affect Delinquent Behavior

Research indicates that internal family dynamics are more closely related to social deviance in general and delinquency in particular than are structural elements of the family. It is probably not surprising that physical and emotional abuse and outright rejection are closely related to delinquent conduct. It has, nevertheless, been somewhat difficult to directly assess this area because of the understandable legal and social attitudes regarding the sanctity and privacy of the home (McCord, 1991).

Public behavior is visible and to some extent controllable, but what goes on behind the closed doors of a home is largely beyond control. One family variable of importance is the "quality" of the relationship between the marriage partners. Most delinquents come from homes with a poor marital relationship, often including domestic violence. Specific case histories and the results of comprehensive studies by many researchers show that excessive conflict and tension in a family interfere with the personality development of a child, with accompanying disruption of their social development. These factors often cause such children to seek approval in a peer group like gangs rather than in their family environment.

In the 1990s, the television viewing public learned a great deal about what goes on in severely dysfunctional families. Talk shows, such as Springer, Oprah, Phil Donahue and Geraldo Rivera, often provided insights into the most disturbed family situations. On any given day, the television audience could tune in on real battling parents and parent-child conflicts, and could even learn something about why a criminal killed a member of his or her family. The "cop shows" are also revealing. Through television an audience can follow police officers into the most bizarre cases of family violence.

In the context of these real family conflicts and dynamics, there are situations where the most dreadful act of violence by a child, including murder, contains a level of understandable rationality. The following case from a study by Muriel Gardiner (1976) of a child who murdered members of his family reveals this kind of absurd rationality:

> "Get that cat out of here, you good-for-nothing son of a bitch," exploded Harry, obviously pleased to have someone on whom to vent his anger. "I won't let her bother you; I'll keep her in my room," pleaded Tom. "The hell you will!" cried his uncle, seizing the kitten. And, before Tom's unbelieving eyes he wrung her neck. Tom, in a flood of tears, carried the warm little body into his room. He tried in vain to revive it. At last, still weeping, Tom lay down on his bed, stroking and caressing the only thing he had ever loved. . . . "What's all this mumbo-jumbo?" Harry cried angrily, looking at the patch of earth and the little homemade cross. "Please, Uncle Harry," implored Tom in terror, "please don't do anything. I just made a little grave for my cat, that's all." With one great kick, Harry splintered the cross, then stamped on the soft earth of the grave. Turning, he slapped Tom's face with the back of his hand, and strode into the house. Tom went into the furnace room. He picked up one of his uncle's guns, and, pausing only to make sure it was loaded, went upstairs where Harry, Bertha, and Catherine were sitting at the breakfast table. Tom raised the gun, and carefully shot his uncle, then his aunt, then Catherine." (P. 108)

A family's inability to resolve its own problems can result in frustration, which in turn can produce violent behavior. When violence erupts, the child is emotionally affected by what he or she sees happening and is also typically the most accessible target. In addition, the rigid rules and norms that characterize a closed system are not subject to modification, and when a child violates them, the parent may respond with force to bring the child back into conformity and compliance. The likelihood that violence will be used as a means of control is increased if one or both parents grew up in a family where excessive force was commonly used as a disciplinary method.

Some fathers almost directly encourage and reinforce their sons violence by presenting them with tales of their own violent, macho behavior. In my work in a juvenile detention institution, I recall eavesdropping on a fifteen-year-old delinquent boy, who was in custody, talking to his father on visiting day. The father put his arm around the boy when they met, and both father and son continued to relate to each other in a very affectionate and friendly manner. The father related his latest physical altercations to the boy. He told his son how he had assaulted a neighbor who had requested that he move his car because it was partially blocking the driveway. The boy's eyes glowed as his father related his violent adventures in great detail. The boy was in custody for violent gang activity in which he assaulted another boy, who was in critical condition in the hospital.

Research reveals that abusive parents are often subject to more severe and frequent life stresses and crises than are nonabusive parents. Prior to the onset of violent behaviors, abusive parents often experience a series of critical events that place a strain on the family, both physically and emotionally. When the stress becomes too great, a parent may abuse his or her children. Marital difficulties are a primary source of conflict in abusive families. Marital frustrations are often displaced onto an abused child, who later on enacts violent behavior in the larger society (Paschall, 1996).

In summary, the dysfunctional families that are most likely to produce delinquent children are a cauldron of conflict and violence. Murray A. Straus and Richard Gelles (1995) studied 8,145 families in the United States. In a summary statement, they write: "It would be hard to find a group or institution in American society in which violence is more of an everyday occurrence than it is within the family. Family members physically abuse each other far more often than do nonrelated individuals. Starting with slaps and going on to torture and murder, the family provides a prime setting for every degree of physical violence" (p. 56). The family is the causal context that trains many delinquents for their future violent behavior in society.

The Invulnerables

Many children socialized by criminogenic families and dysfunctional families, where they are sexually, physically or emotionally abused, develop patterns of rage and become delinquent. There are, however, a small number of youths who overcome many family difficulties and rise above delinquent behavior. Norman Garmezy and Vernon Devine (1976) studied these exceptions to the rule. For want of a better term, they labeled these children "the invulnerables." According to Garmezy and Devine, "these are children who have come through. They are the ones who have not just survived but have flourished, despite a variety of genetic, psychological and sociological disadvantages" (p. 87). Garmezy and Devine offer as an example a youth whom they call Todd.

> He is eleven and lives with an alcoholic father, who sometimes works as a handyman but is usually unemployed. Todd's mother died when he was three, and he lives in an environment of poverty and unrelieved grimness. By all the usual laws of child development, Todd should be well on his way to juvenile delinquency. Todd is instead cheerful, bright, does well in school, is a natural leader, and is much loved by his friends—as well as by school officials. And there are other Todds, we are learning, everywhere—not just in the ghettos and inner cities, but in suburbia as well. (P. 87)

Garmezy and Devine spent two years discussing issues, parameters, and theories on "invulnerables" and another year locating a group of invulnerables to study. They did this by going into the Minneapolis schools and telling principals and social workers that they were looking for children who "when you learned about their background gave you much concern; yet now, when you see them in the halls, you look at them with pleasure" (p. 88). It was an unusual request for school officials, but it was successful. The researchers concluded that out of nearly four hundred candidates, about 10 percent turned out to be invulnerables.

What makes these individuals invulnerable has yet to be discovered, but the researchers suspect that the presence of a role model somewhere provided a positive image for the youngsters. They note: "Invulnerables try to find solutions, rather than blame; they test reality, rather than retreat before it; and they learn to make something out of very little. They bounce back. They have a real recovery ability. We don't know why yet, but they do" (p. 93).

In summary, it is apparent from the research and analysis presented in this chapter that a delinquent's family background is a significant causal factor in his or her violent behavior and delinquency. The noted sociologist

Pitirim Sorokin, at one point in his research, created what he called the Institute for the Study of Altruism at Harvard University. He was interested in what he referred to as healthy social institutions. With the invulnerables in mind, I believe it would be useful to the analysis of delinquency to study what constitutes a healthy family environment that socializes children who become happy, creative, and productive adults in American society. This research might reveal the family socialization process that produces non-delinquent children, and would by contrast provide some further insights into the dysfunctional family factors that result in the development of violent delinquent youths.

CHAPTER 12

EARLY THEORIES OF CRIME AND DELINQUENCY CAUSATION AND THEIR CONTEMPORARY DEVELOPMENT

Poverty and social disorganization are significant factors in producing juvenile delinquency. Children growing up under the social conditions of poverty are likely to have a high rate of delinquency.

A number of theories of causation have been devised to explain deviance and crime. These include religious explanations, which often characterize crime as "sinful"; physiological theories alleging the "born criminal"; alienation theories; and economic theories. In this chapter all of these explanations are examined with special reference to their roots, evolution, and current development.

Religion and Demonology

The concepts of "good" and "evil" behavior are at the philosophical core of all religions. The demon theory, or some modification of it, has been presented as an explanation of crime and juvenile delinquency for a long period of time. This viewpoint posits that people who fail to follow the basic norms of the group are possessed by demons. There is little or no distinction between crime and sin, and the offender is regarded as an antagonist to both the group and the gods. The offender's criminal action is caused by evil spirits, who take possession of the person's soul and force him to perform their evil will. Early forms of punishment involved penitence—and this term is the basis for calling prisons "penitentiaries."

During the Middle Ages, when Christianity dominated the life of the Western world, the theory of possession by the devil tended to merge with the Christian concept of original sin. The influence of theories of demonology and "natural depravity" upon the legal codes and the practices of the courts is evidenced by the fact that as late as the nineteenth century, a formal indictment in England accused the criminal of "being promoted and instigated by the devil." Even in contemporary American society, people will remark that a delinquent "is full of the devil" or "I'm going to shake the devil out of you." In an address to six thousand people at his weekly public audience in Rome, Pope Paul VI (1972) said that the devil is dominating "communities and entire societies" through sex, narcotics, and doctrinal errors. His address included the following references to the devil: "We are all under obscure domination. It is by Satan, the prince of this world, the No. 1 enemy." He criticized those who question the existence of the devil, saying, "This obscure and disturbing being does exist." Billy Graham and other religious leaders echoed these pronouncements in the 1990s.

A 1997 Time/CNN poll asked the question, "Do you believe in hell, where people are punished forever after they die?" Sixty-three percent of respondents answered yes. Other responses indicated that most Americans believe in heaven and hell and in the concept of sin. It is therefore reasonable to infer that concepts of God, sin (in this context delinquent behavior), the devil, and punishment remain significant elements in the administration of justice.

Demonology is generally believed to be of no value to most criminologists in explaining the causes of delinquency. However, the pronouncements of many clergymen, some judges, and the popularity of a concept of the devil make it a meaningful aspect of treating delinquents in many communities in contemporary society.

Crime and Punishment—The Classical School of Criminology

A significant effort to explain crime in a philosophical manner was made by Cesare Beccaria (1963), the founder of what is now known as the classical school of criminology. Beccaria's theory postulated that only conduct dangerous to the state or to other people should be prohibited and that punishment should be no more severe than deemed necessary to deter persons from committing such crimes. The importance of knowing in advance the degree of punishment to be administered led to the adoption of the fixed or "determinate" sentence.

Accepting the Christian doctrine of free will, the classical school postulated that man should choose between good and evil alternatives. The explanation of crime included the notion that man was essentially hedonistic, desiring a maximum of pleasure and the avoidance of pain. A person committed a crime because the pleasure anticipated from the criminal act was greater than the subsequent pain that might be expected.

A major proponent of the classical explanation was Jeremy Bentham. In 1892 he published a book called *An Introduction to the Principles of Morals and Legislation,* in which he proposed a "penal pharmacy" where definitely prescribed punishments were to be applied for specific crimes. The assumption was that humans had free will and would decide whether or not it was personally profitable to commit a crime. It was assumed that if the punishment or pain was always more than the pleasure or benefit from a crime, the potential offender would be rational and be deterred from committing the offense. The classical philosophical and judicial view of crime is still held by many contemporary courts.

The counterpoint position to the classical view is determinism. This position asserts that people have no free will. Rather, the socialization process and all the social factors that impinge on an individual determine his or her personality and consequently his or her behavior. In this framework an individual has no individual choice, but is propelled by social forces and other conditions beyond his or her control. The controversy over the contradictory positions of free will and social determinism is still present in contemporary society. Each view projects its own image of people and their motivations. The classical school of criminology (Bentham, Beccaria) sketched people as having free will, implying that a person who chooses to violate the law can be restrained from this impulse by a proper measure of punishment. The positivists who believed in what today is called determinism, viewed the criminal as something like a billiard ball, propelled by conditions outside his or her control.

As early as 1901, Enrico Ferri stated an opposing view:

> Whoever commits murder or theft is alone the absolute arbiter to decide whether he wants to commit the crime or not. This remains the foundation of the classic school of criminology. . . . The positive school of criminology maintains, on the contrary, that it is not the criminal who wills; in order to be a criminal it is rather necessary that the individual should find himself permanently or transitorily in such personal, physical and moral conditions, and live in such an environment, which become for him a chain of cause and effect, externally and internally, that disposes him toward crime. This is our conclusion, which I anticipate, and it constitutes the vastly different and opposite method, which the positive school of criminology employs as compared to the leading principle of the classic school of criminal science. (P. 3)

Sociologist David Matza (1966) presented a middle-of-the-road view of causation. Matza asserted that many theorists in the field of criminology had gone too far in the direction of determinism. Although he did not attempt to revive fully the classical viewpoint, he incorporated parts of it in his theory. Matza first pointed to the danger of being overdeterministic. Using the juvenile court concept as an example of overdeterminism, he commented:

> To philosophically attribute fault to underlying conditions, but to actually hold the immediate agent responsible, is an invitation to distrust. And to refer to penal sanction as protective care is to compound the distrust. Thus, by its insistence on a philosophy of child welfare and its addiction to word magic, the juvenile court systematically interferes with its alleged program. By its own hypocrisy, perceived and real, it prepares the way for the delinquent's withdrawal of legitimacy. Without the grant of legitimacy, the court's lofty aspirations cannot be effectively pursued. Thus, the ideology of child welfare supports the delinquent's viewpoint in two ways. It confirms his conception of irresponsibility, and it feeds his sense of injustice. Both support the processes by which the moral bind of law is neutralized. Both facilitate the drift into delinquency. (P. 236)

334

Matza posited what he called "soft determinism" as a basic concept of delinquency and drift. He contended that humans are neither wholly free nor wholly constrained but somewhere between the two. The delinquent is never totally a lawbreaker. He or she drifts into delinquency. Matza wrote:

> The image of the delinquent I wish to convey is one of drift; an actor neither compelled nor committed to deeds nor freely choosing them; neither different in any simple or fundamental sense from the law-abiding, nor the same; conforming to certain traditions in American life while partially unreceptive to other more conventional traditions; and finally, an actor whose motivational system may be explored along lines explicitly commended by classical criminology— his peculiar relation to legal institutions. . . . The delinquent transiently exists in a limbo between convention and crime, responding in turn to the demands of each, flirting now with one, now the other, but postponing commitment, evading decision. (Pp. 238–239)

Matza asserted that most delinquents are drifters: "The delinquent as drifter more approximates the substantial majority of juvenile delinquents who do not become adult criminals than the minority who do" (p. 138). To Matza, delinquency was seldom a youth's total career. Most delinquents, he believed, participate in juvenile delinquency as a part-time enterprise.

Matza described five ways in which delinquents deny that their behavior is bad and "drift" into delinquent behavior. These tend to neutralize the responsibility for delinquent activity:

1. *The denial of personal responsibility.* Here the delinquent uses a kind of social word play. "Of course I'm delinquent. Who wouldn't be, coming from my background?" He or she then can neutralize personal responsibility by detailing the background of a broken home, lack of love, and a host of other factors.

2. *The denial of harm to anyone.* In this pattern of neutralization, stealing a car is only borrowing it, truancy harms no one, and drug use "doesn't hurt anyone but me."

3. *The denial that the person injured or wronged is really a victim.* The assaulted teacher was "unfair," the victim of a mugging "was only a queer," and the rival gang member assaulted was "out to get me."

4. *Condemning the condemners.* "Society is much more corrupt than I am."

5. *Group or gang loyalties supersede loyalty to the norms of society.* "When I stabbed him I was only defending my turf." The youth places

his gang or delinquent group and its values (even if delinquent) above the law, the school, and the society.

According to Matza, all of these factors tend to neutralize the delinquent's belief that he or she is delinquent or has done anything wrong. These rationalizations enable the youth to deny any real personal responsibility for delinquent behavior. He further posited that most delinquents are really not delinquent but are acting out the "subterranean values" of the society. On this theme Matza wrote:

> Who can deny that the mass public admires and respects a smart operator, even if his actions are illegal? The delinquent may in his own self-concept merely be acting out the norms he sees beneath the surface of the law. In some respects, the delinquent may see himself as a lower-class white collar criminal. He feels there is nothing really wrong with his behavior. In fact, he feels he is being unfairly treated by being punished for what society does not really condemn. (P. 245)

By adapting concepts found in the larger society, the delinquent rationalizes his own defense. Since the law supports self-defense as a justification for violent action, it is easy for the delinquent to justify in his own mind the use of violence to defend his gang turf. The delinquent also uses the concept of insanity ("I went crazy") to negate his offense, and he widens the extenuating circumstance of "accident" to include recklessness. The sense of injustice found in the delinquent subculture is thus reinforced by the vagaries of many societal laws and norms. Society's irrational prescriptions weaken prohibitions of certain actions by the juvenile and facilitate the drift to juvenile delinquency and, in time, into a criminal career.

One argument against Matza's theory of drift is found in the early writings of Enrico Ferri (1907). He reasoned:

> It is evident that the idea of accident, applied to physical nature, is unscientific. Every physical phenomenon is the necessary effect of the causes that determined it beforehand. If those causes are known to us, we have the conviction that the phenomenon is necessary, is fate, and, if we do not know them, we think it is accidental. The same is true of human phenomena. But since we do not know the internal and external causes in the majority of cases, we pretend that they are free phenomena, that is to say, that they are not determined necessarily by their causes. (P. 36)

On the nature of "free will," Ferri summarized his viewpoint:

The general opinion of classic criminalists and of the people at large is that crime involves a moral guilt, because it is due to the free will of the individual who leaves the path of virtue and chooses the path of crime, and therefore it must be suppressed by meeting it with a proportionate quantity of punishment. This is to this day the current conception of crime. And the illusion of a free human will (the only miraculous factor in the eternal ocean of cause and effect) leads to the assumption that one can choose freely between virtue and vice. How can you still believe in the existence of a free will when modern psychology, armed with all the instruments of positive modern research, denies that there is any free will and demonstrates that every act of a human being is the result of an interaction between the personality and the environment of man? (1901, pp. 38–39)

The "Born Criminal" Theory—Physiological Explanations

A concept that continues to appear in contemporary discussions of causation is that of the "born criminal." The basic assumption of this theory is that criminals and delinquents are physiologically different from the general population, and consequently their criminal behavior may be impossible to alter without radical treatment. This theory, in contemporary society, is most prevalent with regard to the criminal behavior of sex offenders, especially child molesters.

An early proponent of this theory was Cesare Lombroso, an Italian medical doctor who wrote extensively on this subject. On the basis of this criminological research with military personnel and inmates of Italian military prisons, he developed his theory of the born criminal that challenged Beccaria and the classical school.

Lombroso's major early conclusions were that criminal tendencies were hereditary and that "born criminals" were characterized by physical stigmata. To Lombroso, the born criminal was an atavist, a throwback to an earlier, more primitive species, Lombroso (1896) asserted that:

1. Criminals are at birth a distinct type.

2. They can be recognized by certain stigmata (for example, "long lower jaw, scanty beard, low sensitivity to pain").

3. These stigmata or physical characteristics do not cause crime but enable identification of criminal types.

4. Only through severe social intervention can born criminals be restrained from criminal behavior.

After his initial studies, Lombroso greatly modified his theories. A central error in his early studies was that he neglected to note that most of the criminals in the Italian army were Sicilians and thus were a distinct physical type as compared to the general population of Italy at that time. They did not, however, commit more crimes than the general population because of their physical typology, as Lombroso alleged, but because they came from a culture that was more crime oriented.

Lombroso and his followers in the Italian school included more social factors in their analyses of criminality. Although Lombroso was obviously wrong about his born-criminal thesis, he did make significant contributions to the field of criminology. His research: (1) was based on firsthand studies of criminals and moved the field from a philosophical posture of analysis to empirical research; (2) broadened the discussion of crime causation; (3) produce a school of criminology that attracted many distinguished students to the field; and (4) produced a reform of the Beccaria-Bentham classical school.

Charles B. Goring (1913), an English prison official, tested Lombroso's physiological theories of criminality by measuring the physical characteristics of three thousand criminals and comparing these measurements with those of one thousand students at Cambridge University. He found no significant differences in physical types between criminals and noncriminals. Later studies by Ernest Hooten (1939) and Ernst Kretschmer (1936) on physical types and crime postulated a degree of support for Lombroso's original thesis. A close appraisal of their research methods, however, tends to make their conclusions suspect.

In the 1940s William Sheldon (1949) also concluded that there was a relationship between certain physical characteristics and temperamental characteristics. Sheldon divided human beings into four physical types, based upon body measurements: endomorphs, who tend to be fat; mesomorphs, who tend to be muscular, with large bones and an athletic build; ectomorphs, who are inclined to be thin and fragile; and balanced types, a "combination category" composed of people who show no marked dominance of any single type. Each body type, according to Sheldon, is characterized by a distinctive emotional temperament. Endomorphs were described as viscerotonic, submissive, and not very interested in physical activity or adventure. Mesomorphs were described as somatotonic, physically active, self-assertive, and daring. Ectomorphs were characterized as cerebrotonic, inhibited, and introverted.

Sheldon attributed the various body types and their characteristics to heredity, maintaining that they were genetically determined. In a study of 200 juvenile delinquents, he found that about 60 percent were mesomorphs. Since most police officers, army officers, football players, and other energetic leaders of our society are also likely to be mesomorphic, this correlation between mesomorphy and delinquency was not considered to be a causal explanation of delinquency.

In a review of Sheldon's work in the *American Sociological Review*, Edwin Sutherland (1951) virtually demolished Sheldon's conclusions. Sutherland asserted that:

1. Sheldon defines delinquency in terms of "disappointingness" and not in terms of violation of the law.

2. His method of scoring delinquents is subjective and unreliable. For example, he defines "first-order psychotherapy" in terms of subjectively determined interference with adjustment, apparently the same as "disappointingness."

3. The varieties of delinquent youths he presents are overlapping and inconsistent. They do not differ significantly from each other in their somatotypes or psychiatric indices.

4. The relationship of the psychiatric indices to social fitness is not made clear (1951, pp. 10–11).

Harvard social scientists Sheldon and Eleanor Glueck revived interest in William Sheldon's somatotypes in the 1950s. They found that 60.1 percent of the delinquents they studied were mesomorphs, as against 30.7 percent of the nondelinquents. They were cautious in their interpretation of these findings, concluding that "there is no 'delinquent personality' in the sense of a constant and stable combination of physique, character, and temperament which determines that a certain individual would become delinquent" (1950, p. 221).

Although no causal relationship has been established between any physical characteristic and criminal behavior, there is some evidence that the active mesomorphic child is more likely to become delinquent than are children with other body types, all other things being equal. The mesomorph, who is by definition muscular, active, and relatively uninhibited, may be more likely than others to take actions defined as delinquent by society when confronted with a favorable social environment. Research exploring the possibility of using body types as a predictive device has been going on for many years. The data so far have been inconclusive.

James Q. Wilson and Richard J. Hernstein (1984) revived the assessment of biological and genetic factors in crime and delinquency. In their book *Crime and Human Nature*, they assert that to understand street crime we must redirect attention away from an excessive concern with social and economic factors and focus instead on the differences between individual people, which often reflect biological and genetic differences.

Different types of family upbringing also play a role. They state, "One way or another bad families produce bad children. The interplay of genes and environment creates, in some people but not in others, the kind of personality likely to commit crime" (p. 156).

In another assessment of the biological connection to crime, Sarnoff A. Mednick and William F. Gabriella (1984) reported: "We conclude that some factor transmitted by criminal parents increases the likelihood that their [biological] children will engage in criminal behavior. This claim holds especially for chronic criminality. The findings imply that biological predispositions are involved in the etiology of at least some criminal behavior" (p. 894).

Studies of chromosomal deviation have attempted to show a correlation between criminal behavior and the males possessing an extra male (Y) chromosome, that is, they are XYY rather than the normal XY. In spite of the conflicting results of the various studies, there are some suggestive consistencies of behavior and traits. In general, for criminals, the chance of possessing an extra Y chromosome is up to sixty times greater than it is for the general population; also, a higher frequency of aggressive and disturbed behavior and higher rates of violent crime were found among those having an extra Y chromosome (Amir and Berman, 1970, pp. 55–62).

One theory holds that the criminal act itself is biologically and hereditarily determined; that is, there is a direct relationship between the biological structure and the behavior that is supposedly determined by it. A second theory is that what is genetically transmitted is a general tendency to maladjustment and that, given certain environmental pressures, this disposition leads to criminal behavior. Inherent in this theory is the supposition that crime is just one of many possible outcomes of a defective physiological structure. If criminality is inherited, then noncriminality or conforming behavior must also be inherited.

If we accept the premise that the factors determining criminal behavior already exist at birth, then it follows that the influence of environment is not very important. If, however, criminal behavior is frequently found among persons lacking genetic defects, or if biological defects are found among a great many noncriminals, then the genetic theory of crime becomes questionable. Before we can reach any conclusions on the relationship between chromosomes and criminality, we would need to know how many criminals do not have genetic or biological defects. If the number is large, the theory is defective. Herman Witkin (1976), a research psychologist with the Educational Testing Service, commented on earlier studies:[1]

---

1. See also Robert W. Stock, "The XYY and the Criminal," *New York Times Magazine*, October 20, 1968, p. 30.

First, the search for XYY men has often been conducted in selected groups presumed to be likely to contain them, such as institutionalized men and tall men. Second, a number of reports now in the literature are based on observations of a single case or just a few cases. Third, many studies of XYYs have not included control XYs; in those that did, comparisons were often made without knowledge of the genotype of the individuals being evaluated. The control groups used have varied in nature, and comparison of results from different studies has therefore been difficult. There has been a dearth of psychological, somatic, and social data obtained for the same individual XYY men. Finally, there do not yet exist adequate prevalence data for the XYY genotype in the general adult population with which the XYY yield of any particular study may be compared.

To avoid these problems, Witkin chose to gather data in Denmark by using social records that were available for a sample of the general population. He then compared normal males with males having different patterns of chromosomal abnormalities and attempted to identify the possible intervening factors that might account for any predominance of abnormalities among inmates or among men with criminal records. Out of a sample of 4,139 men, he found twelve XYY cases, sixteen XXY cases, and thirteen XY cases that had other chromosomal anomalies. Of the twelve XYY cases, five (42 percent) were found to have been convicted of one or more offenses, as compared to three of the sixteen XXY cases (19 percent) and nine of the thirteen abnormal XY cases.

There did appear to be an inordinately high probability that XYY men would have criminal records. However, there were 389 men with records, and only five of them were XYY cases. The abnormality is so rare that it cannot account for very much criminal activity. Further analysis by Witkin yielded no evidence that XYY males were more prone to violent crimes than XY males. The elevated crime rate reflected property crimes, not aggressive acts against persons. The XYY males were found to have lower scores on intelligence tests and to be taller than XY males. However, even with these differences in intelligence and height taken into account, there was still a difference between XYY and XY cases. The researchers suggested that chromosomal anomalies may have pervasive developmental consequences, but there is no evidence that aggression against others is one of them.

The Psychoanalytic View

The psychological viewpoint on criminal behavior was launched at the beginning of the twentieth century with the psychoanalytic theories of Sigmund Freud. Psychoanalytic theory, as originally formulated by

Sigmund Freud, has persisted as an explanation of delinquent and criminal behavior. Although Freud's theories of human behavior and their explanation of deviant and criminal behavior originated in the early part of the twentieth century, they have been adopted and adapted by so-called neo-Freudian psychologists. Freud's theories have had a continuing impact on explaining delinquency. Consequently, it is of value to examine his early psychological theories on criminal behavior.[2]

According to psychoanalytic theory, the individual begins life with two basic instincts or urges: Eros, the life or love instinct, and Thanatos, the death or hate instinct. The personality of the normal adult is composed of the id, the ego, and the superego. At birth there is only the id, the reservoir of both the life and the death instincts. The id seeks immediate gratification and is concerned with striving after pleasure. It is governed by the pleasure principle, seeking the maximization of pleasure and the avoidance of pain. It has no idea of time or reality. In the first few years of life, the individual develops an ego and a superego. The ego is the part of the self in closest contact with social reality. It directs behavior toward the satisfaction of urges consistent with a knowledge of social and physical reality. In living out the reality principle through the ego, the individual may postpone immediate gratification; he or she does not abandon it. Morality, remorse, and feelings of guilt arise with the development of the superego, the chief force in the socialization of the individual.

The superego is sociologically or culturally conditioned. It includes the development of a conscience and an ego ideal. The ego ideal represents what we should do, and the conscience gives us guilt feelings when we do "wrong." The following oversimplified model serves to illustrate the operation of the Freudian id, ego, and superego: A child sees cookies on the table. His id demands immediate gratification, and is governed by the pleasure principle. He grabs a cookie. His mother slaps his hand and takes the cookie away from him. When he has developed an ego, he waits for his mother to leave before taking a cookie, or he asks for one and coaxes if it is denied him. In either case he has applied the reality principle and postponed gratification. When he has developed a superego, he will not take the cookie if it is defined as wrong for him to do so. If he does take the cookie without being observed, he feels guilty.

Psychoanalytic theory tends to attribute delinquency or criminality to some of the following causes:

---

2. For a detailed presentation of the psychoanalytic explanation of criminality and delinquency, see Kate Friedlander, *The Psychoanalytic Approach to Juvenile Delinquency* (New York: International Universities Press, 1947), and Walter Bromberg, *Crime and the Mind* (Philadelphia, PA: Lippincott, 1948).

1. Inability to control criminal drives (id) because of a deficiency in ego or superego development. Because of faulty development, the delinquent or criminal is believed to possess little capacity for repressing instinctual (criminal) impulses. The individual who is dominated by his or her id is consequently criminal.

2. Antisocial character formation resulting from a disturbed ego development. This occurs during the first three years of life.

3. An overdeveloped superego which makes no provision for the satisfaction of the demands of the id. Offenders of this type are considered neurotic.

Freudians, neo Freudians, and psychoanalytic schools of thought, in general, attribute criminality to inner conflicts, emotional problems, and unconscious feelings of insecurity, inadequacy, and inferiority. They regard criminal behavior and delinquencies as symptoms of underlying emotional problems. Psychoanalytic theory does not explain the criminal acts of the "normal" criminal, who simply learns to be criminal from differential association with criminal teachers. Psychoanalysis offers an explanation for the impulsive behavior of the psychotic, the neurotic, and the psychopath. This behavior, in psychoanalytic terms, would generally be id-dominated behavior evidencing ego deficiency, the inability to control criminal impulses.

For criminologists, the most important assertion of psychoanalytic theory is that to understand criminality we must understand unconscious motivation. In this context everyone, in his or her id, is a criminal. Freud further asserts that if this is true, we must condemn in others the criminal urges that lurk in all of us. This accounts for the psychoanalytic assumption that the public demands severe punishment for certain crimes because the offender has acted as the rest of us would like to act ourselves. A contemporary platitude is: "We stand out in others the evil we dimly perceive in ourselves."

The classical Freudian view of the interplay of crime and punishment was cogently presented by Franz Alexander and Hugo Staub (1956). Several of their ideas are worth pondering for the light they cast on past and present attitudes toward offenders:

1. Psychodynamically, all people are born criminals. The human being enters the world as a criminal, that is, socially not adjusted. During the first years of his or her life a person preserves his or her criminality to the fullest degree, concerned only with achieving pleasure and avoiding pain. Between the ages of four and six, the criminal begins to develop differently

from a normal person. During this period (the latency period), which ends at puberty, the future normal individuals partially succeed in repressing their genuine criminal instinctive drives and stop their actual expression. They convert or transform these criminal libidinal drives into socially acceptable forms. The future criminal fails to accomplish this adjustment. The criminal carries out in his or her actions natural unbridled instinctual drives. He or she acts as the child would act if it could. The repressed and therefore unconscious criminality of the normal man finds a few socially harmless outlets, such as dream and fantasy life, neurotic symptoms, and also some transitional forms of behavior that are less harmless, like dueling, boxing, bullfights, and occasionally the free expression of criminality in war. According to Alexander and Staub, "The universal criminality of the man of today demands violent, purely physical outlets" (p. 156).

2. The Oedipus complex produces criminality unless it is successfully resolved. The Freudian doctrine of the Oedipus complex asserts that all boys have a natural hostility toward their fathers and a love for their mothers that encompasses sexual desire. The guilt and anxiety aroused by these feelings must be resolved, according to Freud, if boys are to grow up to become psychologically healthy men. Alexander and Staub are extreme and dogmatic about the "fact "of the Oedipal condition:

> It took two decades of psychoanalytical research to prove conclusively that the Oedipus complex presented the chief unconscious psychological content of neurotic symptoms. It was found that all those psychological undercurrents which the adult person usually represses are effectively connected with the Oedipus situation of early childhood; these psychic currents, after they are repressed, continue in the unconscious, tied as with a navel cord to the infantile Oedipus complex. (P. 158)

A major concomitant of the Oedipus complex is the assumption that a youth who represses his hostility toward his father will displace his aggression elsewhere. For the Freudian psychoanalyst, this accounts for much of the violent behavior (including homicide) of delinquent youths.

3. Uncovering unconscious motives is the fundamental task of criminology. Alexander and Staub said:

> Theoretically speaking, every human being's responsibility is limited, because no human act is performed under the full control of the conscious ego. We must, therefore, always evaluate the quantitative distribution of conscious and unconscious motivations of every given act. Only such evaluation will provide us with definite criteria for purposes of diagnosis, or of sentencing, or of any other measure which we might consider necessary to take in regard to a

given act. The task of the judge of the future will be the establishment of such a psychological diagnosis; the measures resulting from
such a diagnosis will, therefore, be founded on the psychological
understanding of the criminal. (P. 163)

Among those who take the extreme psychoanalytic view as gospel,
certain criminal patterns are symbolic reflections of unconscious motivation. For example, the use of a gun by an armed robber is considered a
reaction formation to a sense of male impotence. The gun is a symbol of
male potency, and some extremists of the psychoanalytic school contend
that when the armed robber says, "Stick 'em up," he is symbolically trying
to adjust his unconscious sense of impotence. Similarly, the crimes of
breaking-and-entering and theft are considered to be displaced unconscious rape. According to Alexander and Staub (1956), these are issues the
courts must understand before taking any "measures" against offenders.

Alexander and Staub asserted that the first rebellious act or crime
is committed in early childhood and is an important determinant of one's
sense of justice: "The first crime which all humans, without exception,
sooner or later commit is the violation of the prescription for cleanliness.
Under the rule of this penal code of the nursery, man for the first time
becomes acquainted with the punishment which the world metes out to
the individual transgressors" (p. 174). Based on this debatable assumption, according to Alexander and Staub, Ferenczi is right when he speaks
of "sphincter morality" as the beginning and the foundation of adult
human morality. They extend this reasoning to analyze toilet training as
having some impact on delinquency. They write: "A refractory criminal
who persists in his spiteful rejection of social demands is like a baby sitting on its little chamber pot persistently rejecting any demands coming
from the outside; it sits in this sovereign position and feels superior to the
grown-ups" (p. 192).

Alexander and Staub alleged that the moment when the child
begins to impose inhibitions on the demands of his own sphincter, he
makes the first decisive step toward adjustment to the outside world,
because at that moment he creates an inhibitory agency within his own
personality. In brief, the child begins to develop internal reference points
for conduct and a sense of justice or injustice from his toilet training. The
justice (or lack of it) of this training becomes a prototype of future restrictions on one's instinctual life, and a disturbance during this phase of
development may naturally serve as a cause of future disturbance in one's
social adjustment.

Freud's psychoanalytic theory remains a prevalent construct
among social workers and psychiatrists treating offenders, but criminologists today tend to a greater inclusion of social factors and the societal

framework in their search for an understanding of the causes of crime and delinquency. The so-called neo-Freudian school of thought encompasses a more social-psychological viewpoint in explaining behavior.

Reinforcement Theory

Gordon Trasler, a neo-Freudian, focused on behaviorism and reinforcement theory in explaining criminal behavior. Trasler and others applied reinforcement theory to explain the impact of the socialization process on delinquents. Fundamental to this theoretical approach is the idea that learning does not take place unless there is some sort of reinforcement, some equivalent of reward or punishment. This theory has the characteristics of behavioral psychology.

Trasler (1962) used this theory to determine how a person learns *not* to be a criminal. The basic assumption of his theory is that the individual learns not to become a criminal by a training procedure. He or she learns to inhibit certain kinds of behavior, some of which are defined as criminal. Trasler tested his assumption in an experiment with rats, using passive avoidance conditioning. The rats first learned how to obtain food by depressing a lever. An electric shock was then substituted for the food. The rats learned to avoid depressing the lever even though the original drive—hunger—remained. Even when the unpleasant stimulus was removed, the rats would not touch the lever. The researchers concluded that it was in this way that the rats acquired "anxiety."

An individual's aversion to criminality, said Trasler, develops in the same way. The individual is conditioned to feel anxiety in anticipation of punishment, even though the punishment originally used to condition him or her is no longer present. According to this theory, the degree of one's anxiety is in direct proportion to the amount of punishment meted out during one's early conditioning or socialization process. The intensity of the anxiety is a function of the severity of fear stimulated at the time of conditioning. The theory alleges that persons predisposed to criminal behavior were not adequately punished for criminal acts during childhood. No anxiety is aroused by contemplating a criminal act, because there was little or no fear-producing punishment.

Trasler lists the following as points of importance in adequate social conditioning:

1. The effectiveness of social conditioning will depend upon the strength of the unconditioned reaction (anxiety) with which it is associated.

2. Where there is a strong dependent relationship between a child and his or her parents, the sanction of withdrawal of approval will evoke intense anxiety.

3. The relationship between a child and his or her parents is likely to be one of dependence if it is (a) exclusive, (b) affectionate, and (c) reliable.

Differences in conditioning methods, in sensitivity and family attitudes toward crime, and in class attitudes toward crime determine whether or not an individual will be predisposed to criminal behavior.

Economic Determinism

In the celebrated story about poverty and the masses, *Les Miserables*, the hero Jean Valjean is asked why he stole a loaf of bread. His answer is, "Because I was hungry." In many respects, this says almost everything that needs to be said about the causal connection between economics and delinquency. Most criminals commit crimes for financial and emotional profit.

William A. Bonger, a Dutch criminologist, was heavily influenced by Karl Marx and was an early proponent of a theory of economic causation of crime. Bonger (1916) attributed criminal acts, particularly crimes against property, directly to the poverty of the proletariat in a competitive capitalistic system. According to this theory, poverty results from unsuccessful economic competition and is an inherent part of a capitalist society. One solution to poverty is crime. Bonger alleged that the only way to solve the crime problem is through the reorganization of the means of production and the development of a classless society.

> The egoistic tendency does not by itself make a man criminal. For this something else is necessary. . . . For example, a man who is enriched by the exploitation of children may nevertheless remain all his life an honest man from the legal point of view. He does not think of stealing, because he has a surer and more lucrative means of getting wealth, although he lacks the moral sense which would prevent him from committing a crime if the thought of it occurred to him. . . . As a consequence of the present environment, man has become very egoistic and hence more capable of crime than if the environment had developed the germs of altruism. The present economic system is based upon exchange. . . . Such a mode of production cannot fail to have an egoistic character. A society based upon exchange isolates the individuals by weakening the bond that unites them. When it is a question of exchange the two parties interested think only of their own advantage even to the detriment of the other party. . . . "No commerce without a trickery" is a proverbial expression (among consumers), and with the ancients, Mercury, the god of commerce, was also the god of thieves. The merchant and the thief are alike in taking account exclusively of their own interest to the detriment of those with whom they have to do business. (P. 89)

There has been sufficient evidence since Bonger first presented his viewpoint to indicate that poverty alone does not cause crime and that most poor people are not criminals. Most Western societies, however, have assumed greater responsibility for care of the unemployed and the poor than they did in Bonger's time.

A commentary of Bonger's that still appears to hold true is his observation that conspicuous consumption tends indirectly to set goals that are impossible for people in the lower strata of society to achieve. Bonger's postulate of the discrepancy between culturally approved goals and institutionalized means of achieving them as a cause of crime has been incorporated into the theoretical positions of many sociologists.

Economic determinism as part of a contemporary criminology has been supported by the work of David M. Gordon and others. According to this view, capitalist societies depend on competitive forms of social and economic interaction and upon substantial inequalities in the allocation of social resources. Without competition and a competitive ideology, workers might not be expected to struggle to improve their relative income and status in society by working harder. Although property rights are protected, capitalist societies do not guarantee economic security to most individual members. Gordon (1987) asserts that "driven by fear of economic insecurity and by a competitive desire to gain some of the goods unequally distributed throughout the society, many individuals will eventually become criminals" (p. 189).

According to Gordon (1987), the following three different kinds of crime in the United States provide examples of a functionally similar rationality:

1. *Ghetto crime.* The legitimate jobs open to many young ghetto residents typically pay low wages, offer relatively demeaning assignments, and carry constant risk of layoff. Many types of "crimes" available in the ghetto offer higher monetary return, higher status, and often low risk of arrest and punishment.

2. *Organized crime.* Activities like gambling, prostitution, and drug distribution are illegal for various reasons, but there is a demand for these activities and products. Opportunities for monetary rewards are great, and the risks of arrest and punishment low.

3. *Corporate crime.* Corporations exist to protect and augment the capital of their owners. If it becomes difficult to do this lawfully, corporate officials will try to do it another way.

Gordon (1987, pp. 236–238) also points out that current patterns of crime and punishment in the United States support the capitalist system in three ways:

1. The pervasive patterns of selective law enforcement reinforce a prevalent ideology in the society that individuals rather than institutions are to blame for social problems.

2. The patterns of crime and punishment manage "legitimately" to neutralize the potential opposition to the system of many oppressed citizens. The cycle of crime, imprisonment, parole, and recidivism denies to the poor, particularly the black poor, meaningful participation in a society, denies them decent employment opportunities, and keeps them returning to crime.

3. By treating criminals harshly as misfits and enemies of the state, we continue to avoid some basic questions about the dehumanizing effects of our social institutions.

Radical Marxist Theories

A critical and, from my viewpoint, an extremist theory of delinquency causation that builds on Bonger's Marxist theories and generally supports Gordon's position was stated by Richard Quinney (1974). I am including Quinney's viewpoint, not because I am in agreement with his theory, but because it is in vogue with many criminologists.

Richard Quinney developed a comprehensive group-conflict theory that rests on Marxist theory; he calls his theory the social reality of crime. As Quinney sees it, the legal order gives reality to the crime problem in the United States. The theory of the social reality of crime, as formulated by Quinney, contains six propositions and a number of statements within each. These are summarized as follows:

1. Crime as a legal definition of human conduct is created by agents of the dominant class in a politically organized society. Crime, as officially determined, is behavior that is defined by those in power. Legislators, police, prosecutors, judges, and other agents of the law are responsible for formulating and administering criminal law. Upon formulation and application of these definitions of crime, persons and behaviors become criminal. The greater the number of definitions of crime that are formulated and applied, the greater the amount of crime.

2. Definitions of crime are composed of behaviors that conflict with the interests of the dominant class. Definitions of crime are formulated and ultimately incorporated into the criminal law according to the interests of those who have the power to translate their interests into public policy. The definitions of crime change as the interests of the dominant class

change. From the initial definitions of crime to the subsequent procedures, correctional and penal programs, and police for controlling and preventing crime, those who have power regulate the behavior of those without power.

3. Definitions of a crime are applied by the class that has the power to shape the enforcement and administration of criminal law. The dominant interests intervene in all the stages at which definitions of crime are created and operate where the definitions of crime reach the application stage. Those whose interests conflict with the ones represented in the law must either change their behavior or possibly find it defined as criminal. Law-enforcement efforts and judicial activity are likely to increase when the interests of the dominant class are threatened. The criminal law is not applied directly by those in power; its enforcement and administration are delegated to authorized legal agents. As legal agents evaluate more behaviors as worthy of being defined as crime, the probability that definitions of crime will be applied grows.

4. Criminal behavior patterns develop in relation to definitions of crime. Behavior patterns are structured in relation to definitions of crime, and within this context people engage in actions that have relative probabilities of being defined as criminal. The probability that persons will develop action patterns with a high potential for being defined as criminal depends on structured opportunities, learning experiences, interpersonal associations and identifications, and self-conceptions. Personal action patterns develop among those defined as criminal because they are so defined. Those who have been defined as criminal begin to conceive of themselves as criminal, adjust to the definitions imposed upon them, and learn to play the criminal role.

5. An ideology of crime is constructed and diffused by the dominant class to secure its hegemony. An ideology that includes ideas about the nature of crime, the relevance of crime, offenders' characteristics, appropriate reactions to crime, and the relation of crime to the social order is diffused throughout the society in personal and mass communication. Legislation is passed as a reaction to the growing fears of class conflict in American society. The political power structure creates an image of a severe crime problem and, in so doing, threatens to negate some of our basic constitutional guarantees in the name of controlling crime. The conceptions that are most critical in actually formulating and applying the definitions of crime are those held by the dominant class. These conceptions are certain to be incorporated into the social reality of crime.

6. The social reality of crime is constructed by the formulation and application of definitions of crime, the development of behavior patterns in relation to these definitions, and the construction of an ideology of crime.

Quinney's Marxist viewpoint on the capitalist economy and delinquency may be summarized in the following principles (1974, p. 24):

1. American society is based on an advanced capitalist economy.

2. The state is organized to serve the interests of the dominant economic class, the capitalist ruling class.

3. Criminal law is an instrument of the state and ruling class to maintain and perpetuate the existing social and economic order.

4. Crime control in capitalist society is accomplished through a variety of institutions and agencies established and administered by a governmental elite, representing ruling class interests, for the purpose of establishing domestic order.

5. The contradictions of advanced capitalism—the disjunction between existence and essence—require that the subordinate classes remain oppressed by whatever means necessary, especially through the coercion and violence of the legal system.

6. Only with the collapse of capitalist society and the creation of a new society, based on socialist principles, will there be a solution to the crime problem. As capitalist society is further threatened by its own contradictions, criminal law is increasingly used in the attempt to maintain domestic order. The underclass, the class that must remain oppressed for the triumph of the dominant economic class, will continue to be the object of criminal law as long as the dominant class seeks to perpetuate itself.

Radical theorists like Quinney draw heavily on economic and Marxist theory. They argue that delinquency is the product of the perpetual class struggle in capitalist societies. The ruling class creates the conditions out of which delinquency arises, and nothing short of revolution will alter the situation. Such theorists tend to see delinquency as a result of the marginalization of youth. Capitalism is viewed as a "criminogenic" system that perpetuates inequities based on age, sex, race, and occupation. From their viewpoint, merely "tinkering" with the system by investing time and resources into rehabilitation, diversion, or prevention will not rectify the delinquency problem. They assert that when children are freed from the evils of class struggles and are reintegrated into the mainstream of life, the cooperative instincts of the young will become dominant, and a society free of crime and delinquency will emerge.

Culture Conflict Theories

Criminologists like Quinney who seek to explain why certain behavior is defined as criminal tend toward a culture-class conflict explanation. What becomes defined as a crime is related to the power of some groups in the society to include in the criminal law their values and interests. The same power structure, or one closely related to it, by its enforcement of the law imposes a variation of the same values and interests. This point of view leads to the conclusion that the passage of virtually all criminal laws, the policies of nearly all law-enforcement agencies, and the operation of the criminal justice system are in some way influenced by political pressures of competing interest groups. Economic interest groups exercise a predominant influence on the governmental system, including the legislative, enforcement, and criminal justice systems.

The criminal law is a body of rules or norms of conduct that prohibit specific forms of conduct and provide for punishment for them. The type of conduct prohibited often depends upon the character and interests of the groups that influence legislation. Everyone is required to obey the rules set forth by the state, as described in the penal code. Some people, however, belong to groups that have sets of rules or norms of conduct different from those required by the overall society's criminal law. According to Thorsten Sellin (1938), culture conflict arises when an individual is committed to normative rules and laws that are contrary to those of the overall society. Whether behavior is criminal or noncriminal depends upon which conduct norms are applied (p. 21).

Culture conflict is among immigrants to the United States. They come with many customs and traditions that are not acceptable in this country. Prior to World War II, when U.S. influence was less pervasive than it is now, the problem was even more acute. Consider an old Oriental tradition of "family honor." Under this system, if a woman committed adultery, it was the duty of either her elder brother or her father to kill her. This was not something that he might do; he was obligated to do it. If a man were to kill his daughter for that or for any other reason in the United States, he would be prosecuted for murder.

There are still many conduct norms of other countries that clash with those of the United States and lead immigrants into trouble with the law. When culture conflict arises in this way, it is referred to as "primary culture conflict." Another type of culture conflict arises when people are committed to the norms of a subculture within a society that differs in some respects from the norms of the overall society. This sort of conflict is expressed by a person who migrates from a rural area to an urban center, the Puerto Rican who migrates from the island to New York City, or an African-American family that moves from the rural South to the urban North. When conflict arises as a result of conflicting conduct norms within the society, it is referred to as "secondary culture conflict." The overall society has defined the "right ways" of doing things. As Albert Cohen asserts, "The hallmark of the delinquent subculture is the explicit and wholesale repudiation of middle-class standards and the adoption of their very antithesis." Whether we regard the delinquent subculture as a repudiation of middle-class standards or simply as a way of conforming to lower-class standards, it contains rules of behavior at variance from those of the overall culture of our society and often leads to behavior that is legally viewed as delinquent.

George Vold on Group Conflict Theory

Building on culture and group conflict theories that have a foundation in Marxism, George Vold (1973) stated:

> First, that man is always involved in groups and, second, that action within groups and between groups is influenced by opposing individual and group interests. Society is a collection of such groups in equilibrium; that is, opposing group interests are in some way balanced or reconciled. There is a continuous struggle within and between groups to improve relative status. Groups come into conflict when the interests and purposes they serve tend to overlap and become competitive. As conflict between groups intensifies, loyalties to groups intensify. The outcome of group conflict is either victory for one side and defeat for the other or some form of compromise. Politics is primarily a way of finding practical compromises between antagonistic groups. (P. 46)

In a democracy, a struggle between conflicting groups often culminates in legislation translating compromise into law. Those who produce legislative majorities dominate policies that decide who is likely to be involved in violation of the law. Crime, according to Vold (1973), may be seen as minority group behavior. Some of those whose actions have become illegal as a result of legislation violate the law as individuals. Many of those who belong to groups that oppose the law react as a conflict group. The juvenile gang, in this sense, would be an example of a "minority group" in opposition to the rules of the dominant "majority." In a group-centered conflict, "criminal" behavior occurs when action is based on the principle that "the end justifies the means" and the end object is the maintenance of the group position.

This principle is the rationalization offered to justify the actions of a juvenile gang, organized crime running gambling operations, the white-collar criminals who fix prices or deal on inside information, and the junk bond criminal scandals of the 1990s. Whenever there is genuine conflict between groups and interpretations, correctness is decided by the exercise of power and/or persuasion. Criminal behavior is determined by interpretation of the laws by the people in power in the society.

Capitalism, Feminism, and Delinquency

Most of the Marxist-oriented group-conflict theories by Gordon, Quinney, and Vold focus on male delinquency. A body of Marxist theory and research developed by feminists Nicole Rafter and Elena Natalizia (1981) asserted that "the special oppression of women by . . . [the criminal justice] system is not isolated or arbitrary, but rather is rooted in systematic sexist practices and ideologies which can only be fully understood by analyzing the position of women in capitalist society" (p. 54).

On the relationship between capitalism, sexism, and crime, Rafter and Natalizia write:

> Capitalism and sexism are intimately related, and it is this relationship that accounts for the inferior status traditionally given to women by the American criminal justice system. Sexism is not merely the prejudice of individuals; it is embedded in the very economic, legal, and social framework of life in the United States. The criminal justice system, as one part of that institutional framework, reflects the same sexist underpinning that is evidenced throughout capitalist society. Capitalism relies upon the traditional structure of monogamy and the nuclear family to fulfill its economic potential. The division of labor essential to the capitalist system is one that cuts off those who produce from control over the means of production. And it dictates that men shall be the chief producers of goods, while women shall function primarily as nurturers of the next generation of producers. (1981, p. 89)

Rafter and Natalizia further assert that in a capitalist system, law reflects a bourgeois moral code that restricts women to specific roles within the economic scheme. Women are properly chattel of the dominant men in their lives (husbands, fathers, lovers, pimps), and women's work is defined as unworthy of significant remuneration. Violations of the moral code defining women's proper role are labeled deviant and punished by stringent sanctions. Law becomes an instrument of social control over women and a means of preserving the economic status quo.

Historically, the entire justice system in America has been dominated by men. Our legal framework has been codified by male legislators, enforced by male police officers, and interpreted by male
judges. Rehabilitation programs have been administered by males.
The prison system has been managed by men, primarily for men.
Chivalrous motives are the ostensible grounds for a particularly discriminatory instrument for the oppression of female juveniles—
status offense statutes. These statutes specify that juveniles can be
prosecuted for behaviors or conditions that would not be illegal if
committed or manifested by an adult, such as running away, incorrigibility, and being in danger of falling into vice. Although theoreti-
cally applying to juveniles of both sexes and all economic levels,
these laws reflect efforts to uphold bourgeois standards of femininity—standards glorifying submissiveness, docility, and sexual purity.
That these statutes function with sexual bias is borne out by studies
revealing that the prosecution rate for status offenses is much higher
among girls than among boys, and that female status offenders are
punished more severely than are boys who commit more serious
property or violent offenses. And, as in the case of their adult counterparts, low-income and minority girls bear most of the burden of
such sanctions. At an early age therefore, these girls learn that
deviance from economically based sex role patterns will result in legal
sanctions, despite the chivalrous intent of our justice system. (P. 98)

Rafter and Natalizia believed that the legal system oppresses
women through its almost total failure to respond to issues of concern to
women. Wife abuse, sexual harassment, incest, rape, production of unsafe
methods of birth control, forced sterilization for eugenic purposes—these
are critically important problems to women, whose needs the legal system
has either failed to consider or has glossed over with token, ad hoc efforts.
Such problems, moreover, have the greatest significance for poor and working-class women, indicating that class is at least as critical as sex in the
struggle to obtain legal equality for women.

Another analysis of the feminist position and delinquency is presented in *Gender, Crime, and Punishment* by Kathleen Daly (1994). In her
analysis, Daly describes the processes through which women become
labeled as delinquents and criminals, and the disparity of punishment
based on gender. There is considerable political and social awareness of the
conditions related to female delinquency and efforts have been made to
remedy these problems. The twentieth century produced many positive and
notable changes in the status of women, and the twenty-first century portends a greater awareness and amelioration of past gender problems, especially related to female delinquency.[3]

---

3. Also on gender issues and delinquency, see the analysis of Meda Chesney-Lind and Randall G.
   Sheldon in *Girls, Delinquency, and Juvenile Justice* (Pacific Grove, CA: Brooks/Cole, 1992).

CHAPTER 13
SOCIOLOGICAL CAUSATION THEORIES

Many youths, including girls, become alienated from their families and the larger society. Their rebellion includes forming deviant sub-groups and drifting into drug addiction and delinquent behavior.

Many eminent sociologists have presented sociocultural theories of crime and delinquency. Prominent among these social scientists are Emile Durkheim and Robert Merton, who have posited theories about conflicts and dislocations in the social system and how these have impacted on the delinquency problem. Also notable in this context is Edwin Sutherland and Donald Cressey's effort to explain crime and delinquency with the widely accepted theory of "differential association." These theories, including my own theory on "self-concept and delinquency," in many respects dovetail with each other. These varied theories are presented in this chapter in an effort to eliminate the causal context of delinquency within the framework of sociological theory.

Emile Durkheim on Crime and Delinquency

The eminent French sociologist Emile Durkheim considered crime an integral part of all societies. Having defined crime as an act that is punished, he expressed the view that a society exempt from crime was utterly impossible. The dominant group in the society invariably defines certain behavior as undesirable and punishable. It is this societal definition that confers criminal character upon the act, and not the intrinsic quality of the act. According to Durkheim (1950):

> Crime is present in all societies of all types. Its form changes; the acts thus characterized are not the same everywhere; but, everywhere and always, there have been men who have behaved in such a way as to draw upon themselves penal repression. If, in proportion as societies pass from the lower to the higher types, the rate of criminality . . . tended to decline, it might be believed that crime, while still normal, is tending to lose this character of normality. [Actually] it has everywhere increased. . . . There is, then, no phenomenon that presents more indisputably all the symptoms of normality, since it appears closely connected with the conditions of all collective life. (Pp. 65–66)

Durkheim recognized that some criminal behavior (for example, murder) was pathological and was made punishable with the complete consensus of the society. With respect to other behavior classified as criminal there is less general agreement. In a society that permits individuals to differ more or less from the collective type, it is inevitable that some acts are criminal. However, since nothing is "good" indefinitely and to an unlimited extent, people must be free to deviate; otherwise, social change would be impossible.

357

From Durkheim's perspective on crime, if social progress is to be made, individual originality must be able to express itself—even criminal behavior. He stated, "For the originality of the idealist to find expression it is necessary that the originality of the criminal also be expressible. It would never have been possible to establish the freedom of thought we now enjoy if the regulations prohibiting it had not been violated by people who were at one time classified as criminals" (1951, p. 43). It should be remembered that the founding fathers of the United States were at first considered to be criminals in the context of the British Empire. Crime and delinquency is thus, according to Durkheim, sometimes a valuable force for positive social change.

One of Durkheim's most significant contributions to the understanding of crime causation was the theory of "anomie," or normlessness. Anomie, as first presented by Emile Durkheim and later elaborated upon by Robert K. Merton and others, is characterized as a condition in which an individual feels a loss of orientation, without outside controls to trust or believe in. For such an individual, little is real or meaningful; the person cannot relate to society wholly, and its norms and values are without meaning. The person is free of the restrictions imposed by the norms of society, and consequently is prone to commit acts of deviance, including crime (Durkheim, 1951, p. 257).

In his treatise on anomic suicide, Durkheim (1951, p. 246) points out the dangers of such freedom from acceptable restraint: "Those who have only empty space above them are almost inevitably lost in it, if no force restrains them." Durkheim points out that "no living being can be happy or even exist unless his needs are sufficiently proportioned to his means." Society limits the means available to people. Society also sets goals appropriate to each category of people in it. There may be some flexibility, but there are also limits. "To pursue a goal which is by definition unattainable is to condemn oneself to a state of perpetual unhappiness" (p. 246).

In American society, as in the France of Durkheim's time, all classes contend among themselves because no established classification exists. Society, according to Durkheim, is the only agency that is acceptable to people as a regulator of the desires of men. It is the only agency recognized as superior to the individual, with the acknowledged right to make demands and impose restrictions. Yet "discipline can be useful only if considered just by the peoples subject to it. When it is maintained only by custom and force, peace and harmony are illusory; the spirit of unrest and discontent are latent; appetites superficially restrained are ready for revolt" (1951, p. 248).

Robert Merton on Anomie and Delinquency

Robert Merton, in a series of brilliant theoretical sociological treatises, elaborated on Durkheim's theory of anomie and added some new and significant dimensions. Merton (1957, pp. 131–160) related crime to anomie through the four following concepts:

1. Society in the United States places an emphasis on success as represented by possessions and their consumption, and at the same time, for some people, blocks legitimate paths to the achievement of that goal. Success is assumed to be achievable by all.

2. The access to legitimate means of achievement are effectively denied to many members of the lower classes and to members of minority groups.

3. The conflict thus established is often resolved through illegal means of achievement of acceptable goals.

4. On the other hand, an individual may deny the value of the goal and act out that denial in the destruction of property.

Resorting to illegitimate means or destruction of the goal is anomie. It is an inability to correlate the ends of action and the action to the values of society. Since legitimate means and shared goals become contradictory, the individual must relieve his or her anxiety and frustration by denying the one or the other as meaningful. As distance grows between institutional means and cultural goals, anomie grows more prevalent.

Some people, for whatever reason, come to reject the goals defined by the society as appropriate and the means defined as legitimate. If they seek to substitute other means and other goals for those dictated by the society, they may move toward rebellion. A solution does not come easily. It may require a reorganization of society. This seems to be the solution some are striving for on a national level by peaceful means. Effective civil rights legislation and the chance of equal opportunity for all can effectively reduce the disparity between goal and means for many people. The attempt to reduce the wide differences in income may be helpful to others. Unless these objectives are attained, we can, by applying this theoretical position, predict increased criminality and/or increased rebellion.

In his focus on anomie, Robert K. Merton (1957) examined the way in which the social structure exerts definite pressure upon some persons to engage in nonconformist behavior. He asserted that deviant behavior results from discrepancies between culturally defined goals and the socially structured means of achieving them. According to Merton, American society define success as a goal for everyone. Some of the socially approved means of achieving success are hard work, education, and thrift. The emphasis in our society, he pointed out, is on the goals—winning the game—not on the means—how you do it. Since some people do not have equal access to approved means, they have a more limited chance to achieve the goals of the society unless they deviate.

Merton described five basic modes of adaption to the goals and means of the society (1957, p. 188):

Adaptation 1: Conformity to both cultural goals and means. This is the most commonly used adaptation in every society.

Adaptation 2: Innovation, the acceptance of the cultural emphasis on success goals without equally internalizing the morally prescribed norms governing the means for their attainment. The individual accepts the goals of wealth and power but does not accept work as means. The innovator may choose illegal means and become a criminal. This choice is particularly attractive to the person who concludes that he or she does not have access to approved means of achieving his or her goals.

Adaptation 3: Ritualism, the rejection of culturally defined goals with conformity to the mores defining the means. The ritualistic individual does not try to get ahead; he or she is overly involved with the ritualistic means of success.

Adaptation 4: Retreatism, the rejection of both the culturally defined goals and the institutionalized means. The individual escapes by becoming a drug addict, an alcoholic, a psychotic, or by some other method.

Adaptation 5: Rebellion, the rejection of both the goals and the means of attaining them. The rebel attempts to introduce a "new social order."

In general, Merton's fundamental explanation of the tendency to criminality is that the emphasis on goals rather than on the means of attaining them causes many people who cannot achieve material success goals through legitimate means to resort to any means, including crime. Merton's point of reference for accounting for criminality is found in the analysis of dislocations in the social system. This is the fundamental direction taken by many later sociological theorists of crime causation.

Richard Cloward and Lloyd Ohlin on Anomie and Delinquency

Richard Cloward and Lloyd Ohlin build on Durkheim and Merton's theories in their analysis of delinquency causation. Cloward and Ohlin (1960) explored two questions: (1) Why do delinquent norms, or rules of conduct, develop? and (2) What are the conditions that account for the distinctive content of various systems of delinquent norms such as those prescribing violence or theft or drug-use?

Cloward and Ohlin relied heavily on the concept of the delinquent subculture. In their view, "a delinquent subculture is one in which certain forms of delinquent activity are essential requirements for the performance of the dominant roles supported by the subculture. It is the central position accorded to specifically delinquent activity that distinguishes the delinquent subculture from other deviant subcultures" (p. 7). They defined three dominant kinds of delinquent subcultures: the "criminal," the "conflict," and the "retreatist." Cloward and Ohlin recognized that the extent to which the norms of the delinquent subculture control behavior will vary from one member to another. Their description of each subculture is therefore stated in terms of the fully indoctrinated member rather than the average member. The "criminal" subculture is devoted to theft, extortion, and other illegal means of securing an income; some of its members may graduate into the ranks of organized or professional crime. The "conflict" group commits acts of violence as an important means of securing status. The "retreatist" group stresses drug use, and addiction is prevalent.

Cloward and Ohlin's central explanation for the emergence of delinquent subcultures is derived from the theories of Durkheim and Merton. Their basic viewpoint is that "pressures toward the formation of delinquent subcultures originate in marked discrepancies between culturally induced aspirations among lower class youth and the possibilities of achieving them by legitimate means."

Cultural goals are an important aspect of Cloward and Ohlin's thesis. In describing two categories of need, physical and social, they noted that Durkheim made the point that physical needs are satiable, whereas social gratification is "an insatiable and bottomless abyss." Given this condition, when people's goals become unlimited, their actions can no longer be controlled by norms, and a state of normlessness or anomie exists.

Cloward and Ohlin turned to Merton's elaboration of Durkheim's basic postulate to account for the various patterns of deviant behavior. In Merton's view, anomie (normlessness) and the breakdown of social control emerge not because of insatiable goals alone but because of a lack of fit between the goals and the legitimate means for attaining them. As Merton specified, "Aberrant behavior may be regarded sociologically as a symptom of disassociation between culturally prescribed aspirations and socially structured avenues of realizing these aspirations" (p. 36).

Merton's formulation, according to Cloward and Ohlin, helps to explain the existence of a large proportion of law violators among lower-class youths. Delinquents, because they are denied equal access to normative social opportunity, experience a greater pull toward deviance.

> The ideology of common success-goals and equal opportunity may become an empty myth for those who find themselves cut off from legitimate pathways upward. We may predict, then, that the pressure to engage in deviant behavior will be greatest in the lower levels of the society. Our hypothesis can be summarized as follows: The disparity between what lower class youth are led to want and what is actually available to them is the source of a major problem of adjustment. Adolescents who form delinquent subcultures, we suggest, have internalized an emphasis upon conventional goals. Face with limitations on legitimate avenues of access to these goals, and unable to revise their aspirations downward, they experience intense frustrations; the exploration of nonconformist alternatives may be the result. (1960, p. 42)

Cloward and Ohlin viewed the gang as one of the "nonconformist alternatives" these boys may explore. Alienated youths band together in the collectivity of the gang in an effort to resolve their mutual problems. The same theme is used to explain the normative patterning of gangs: the conflict, criminal, and retreatist. A youth's selection of one type of subcultural adjustment over another is related to the degree of availability of these illegitimate "opportunity structures" in various sociocultural settings. They wrote:

> We believe that the way in which these problems are resolved may depend upon the kind of support for one or another type of illegitimate activity that is given at different points in the social structure. If, in a given social location, illegal or criminal means are not readily available, then we should not expect a criminal subculture to develop among adolescents. By the same logic, we should expect the manipulation of violence to become a primary avenue to higher status only in areas where the means of violence are not denied to the young. To give a third example, drug addiction and participation in subcultures organized around the consumption of drugs presuppose that persons can secure access to drugs and knowledge about how to use them. In some parts of the social structure, this would be very difficult; in others, very easy. In short, there are marked differences from one part of the social structure to another in the types of illegitimate adaptation that are available to persons in search of solutions to problems of adjustment arising

> from the restricted availability of legitimate means. In this sense, then, we can think of individuals as being located in two opportunity structures—one legitimate, the other illegitimate. Given limited access to success-goals by legitimate means, the nature of the delinquent response that may result will vary according to the availability of various illegitimate means. (1960, pp. 151–152)

Cloward and Ohlin tended to minimize the importance of individual personality factors and characteristics and emphasized sociological factors: "The social milieu affects the nature of the deviant response whatever the motivation and social position (i.e., age, sex, socioeconomic level) of the participants in the delinquent subculture" (p. 53). Criminal subcultures, according to Cloward and Ohlin, are most likely to occur in the somewhat stable slum neighborhoods that provide a hierarchy of criminal opportunity.

Cloward and Ohlin argued that, for many youths in this type of neighborhood, the desire to move up in the neighborhood criminal hierarchy may cause them to overconform to delinquent values and behavior to show off their criminal ability. Such criminal overconformity accounts for rash, nonutilitarian delinquent acts. The criminal subculture is likely to arise in a neighborhood milieu characterized by close bonds between different age levels of offender, and between criminal and conventional elements. As a consequence of these integrative relationships, a new opportunity structure emerges, which provides alternative avenues to success goals. Hence, the pressures generated by restrictions on legitimate access to success goals are drained off. Social controls over the conduct of the young are effectively exercised, limiting expressive behavior and constraining the discontented to adopt instrumental, if criminalistic, styles of life.

Conflict subcultures, according to Cloward and Ohlin, tend to arise in disorganized slums that provide no organized hierarchy for criminal development. These slums, with their high degree of disorganization and their orientation toward the present, offer limited legitimate and illegitimate opportunity structures. The social disorganization of such slums contributes to the breakdown of social control. Youths in such areas are exposed to acute frustrations, arising from conditions in which access to success-goals is blocked by the absence of any institutionalized channels, legitimate or illegitimate. They are deprived not only of conventional opportunity but also of criminal routes to the "big money." In other words, precisely when frustrations are maximized, social controls are weakened. Social controls and channels to success goals are generally related: where opportunities exist, patterns of control will be found; where opportunities are absent, patterns of social control are likely to be absent too.

The lack of opportunity in these areas causes such youths to seek it in other ways. "Adolescents turn to violence in search of status. Violence comes to be ascendant, in short, under conditions of relative detachment from all institutionalized systems of opportunity and social control" (1970, p. 63). The retreatist subculture emerges, according to Cloward and Ohlin, as an adjustment pattern for those lower-class youths who have failed to find a position in the criminal or conflict subculture and have also failed to use either legitimate or illegitimate opportunity structures. "Persons who experience this 'double failure' are likely to move into a retreatist pattern of behavior" (p. 65). Some youths who either drop out of other types of sub-cultures or find the conflict or criminal subculture no longer functional may also resort to the retreatist pattern.

Cloward and Ohlin concluded that limitations on both legitimate and illegitimate opportunity structures produce intense pressures toward retreatist behavior. All three types of delinquent behavior were viewed by Cloward and Ohlin as adjustment patterns that utilize the most available opportunity structure provided by the anomic social system.

Strain Theory: Ronald Akers and Robert Agnew

The theories of Merton and Cloward and Ohlin are often referred to as "strain theories," because they refer to strains in the social system that produce deviance. Ronald L. Akers (1997) presents a cogent summary of these theories as they relate to strain. Akers asserts that

> anomie, strain and social disorganization theories hypothesize that social order, stability, and integration is conducive to conformity, while disorder and malintegration is conducive to crime and deviance. Anomie is the form that societal malintegration takes when there is a dissociation between valued cultural ends and legitimate societal means to those ends. The more disorganized or anomic the group, community, or society, the higher the rate of crime and deviance. (P. 52)

Merton proposed that anomie characterizes American society in general and is especially high in the lower classes, because they are more blocked off from legitimate opportunities. High levels of anomie and social disorganization in lower-class and disadvantaged ethnic groups, therefore, are hypothesized to be the cause of high rates of crime and delinquency in these groups. At the individual level, the strain produced by discrepancies between the educational and occupational goals toward which one aspires and the achievements actually expected are hypothesized to increase the chances that one will engage in criminal or delinquent behavior (Agnew, 1993).

Recent research provides some support for these hypotheses on class and race, but the relationships are usually not strong. Consequently, the self-perceived aspirations/expectations discrepancy seems to be only weakly related to delinquency. Cohen and Cloward and Ohlin modified Merton's theory to apply anomic to lower-class delinquent gangs. Research shows clearly that gang delinquency continues to be concentrated in the lower-class and minority neighborhoods of large cities. But research has not verified that urban gangs fit very well into the theoretical specifications of Cohen, Cloward and Ohlin, and others in the anomic tradition.

Robert Agnew (1993) has proposed a modification of anomie/strain theory, primarily by broadening the concept of strain to encompass several sources of strain, failure to achieve goals, removal of positive or desired stimuli from the individual, and exposure to negative stimuli. Early research offers some support for this modified strain theory, but further research is required to assess its empirical validity

Albert Cohen: Delinquent Subcultures and Delinquency

Albert Cohen (1955) viewed delinquent youths as comprising a subculture with a value system different from the dominant one found in the inclusive American culture. Lower-class children, according to Cohen, use the delinquent subculture as a mode of reaction and adjustment to a dominant middle-class society that indirectly discriminates against them because of their lower-class position. Lower-class youths, trained in a different value system, are not adequately socialized to fulfill the status requirements of middle-class society. Despite this differential socialization, they are unfairly exposed to the middle-class aspirations and judgments they cannot fulfill.

This conflict produces in the lower-class youths what Cohen termed "status frustration." In reaction, they manifest a delinquent adjustment, acting out their status frustrations in "nonutilitarian, malicious, negativistic" forms of delinquency. In such settings as the school and community center, the lower-class youths find themselves exposed to generally middle-class agents of the society (teachers and social workers). Their efforts to impose on these youths the middle-class values of orderliness, cleanliness, responsibility, and ambition are met with sharp negativism.

Cohen listed nine middle-class values that are specifically rejected by the lower-class child: (1) ambition; (2) responsibility; (3) the cultivation of skills and tangible achievement; (4) postponement of immediate satisfactions and self-indulgence in the interest of long-term goals; (5) rationality, in the sense of forethought, planning, and budgeting of time; (6) the rational cultivation of manners, courtesy, and personality; (7) the need to control physical aggression and violence; (8) the need for wholesome recreation; and (9) respect for property and its proper care. The lower-class child, in reaction against these unfair impositions, substitutes norms that reverse those of the larger society: "The delinquent subculture takes its norms from the larger subculture, but turns them upside down. The delinquent's conduct is right by the standards of his subculture precisely because it is wrong by the norms of the larger culture" (1955, p. 67).

The dominant theme of the delinquent subculture theory is the explicit and wholesale repudiation of middle-class standards and the adoption of their antitheses. In this negative polarity of "just for the hell of it" vandalism and violence, lower-class youths attempt to adjust their status frustration and hostility toward the larger society's unfair imposition of middle-class values upon them; the gang is the vehicle for their delinquencies. The individual delinquent is the exception rather than the rule.

Cohen's position on the gang's relation to the community and the family parallels the conceptions of the early Chicago school. He asserted that relations with gang members tend to be cohesive and positive. Relations with other groups tend to be indifferent, hostile, or rebellious. Gang members are unusually resistant to the efforts of home, school, and other agencies to regulate not only their delinquent activities but any activities carried on within the group and to efforts to compete with the gang for the time and other resources of its members.

Cohen argued that the resistance of gang members to the authority of the home may not be a result of their membership in gangs, but that membership in gangs, on the contrary, is a result of ineffective family supervision, the breakdown of parental authority, and the hostility of the child toward the parents. In short, the delinquent gang recruits members who have already achieved autonomy. Certainly a previous breakdown in family controls facilitates recruitment into delinquent gangs. But we are not speaking of the autonomy or the emancipation of individuals. It is not the individual delinquent but the gang that is autonomous. For many of our subcultural delinquents, the claims of the home are very real and compelling. The point is that the gang is a separate, distinct and often irresistible focus of attraction, loyalty, and solidarity.

In summary, the delinquent subculture described by Cohen represents a collective effort on the part of youths to resolve adjustment problems produced by dislocations in the larger society. In the gang the norms of the larger society are reversed so that nonutilitarian deviant behavior (especially violence) becomes a legitimized activity. The gang thus serves lower-class boys as a legitimate opportunity structure for striking back at a larger society that produces their status-frustration problems.

William Kvaraceus and Walter Miller on the Subculture of Delinquency

Using cultural concepts in a somewhat different fashion than Cloward and Ohlin, William Kvaraceus and Walter Miller projected a lower-class adolescent theory of gangs. They maintained (in a fashion somewhat similar to Cohen's position) that the values of lower-class culture produce deviance because they are "naturally" in discord with middle-class values. The youth who heavily conforms to lower-class values is thus automatically delinquent.

Kvaraceus and Miller (1959, p. 43) listed a set of characteristics of lower-class culture that tend to foster delinquent behavior. These include such focal concerns as trouble, toughness, "smartness" (ability to con), and excitement (kicks). According to Kvaraceus and Miller, gang activity is, in part, a striving to prove masculinity. Females are exploited by tough gang hoods in the "normal" process of relating. Girls are "conquest objects" utilized to prove and boost the masculinity of the street-corner male. The gap between levels of aspiration of lower-class youths and their general ability to achieve produces distinct types of lower-class categories, which reveal the degree of delinquency proneness of a youth:

1. "Stable" lower class. This group consists of youngsters who, for all practical purposes, do not aspire to higher status or who have no realistic possibility of achieving such aspiration.

2. Aspiring but conflicted lower class. This group represents those for whom family or other community influences have produced a desire to elevate their status, but who lack the necessary personal attributes or cultural "equipment" to make the grade, or for whom cultural pressures effectively inhibit aspirations.

3. Successfully aspiring lower class. This group, popularly assumed to be the most prevalent, includes those who have both the will and the capability to elevate their status.

Kvaraceus and Miller (1959) emphasized the fact that lower-class youths who are confronted with the largest gap between aspirations and possibilities for achievement are most delinquency prone. Such youths are apt to utilize heavily the normal range of lower-class delinquent patterns in an effort to achieve prestige and status: toughness, physical prowess, skill, fearlessness, bravery, ability to con people, gaining money by wits, shrewdness, adroitness, smart repartee, seeking and finding thrills, risk, danger, freedom from external constraint, and freedom from

superordinate authority. These are the explicit values of the most important and essential reference group of many delinquent youngsters. These
are the things they respect and strive to attain. The lower-class youngsters
who engage in a long and recurrent series of delinquent behaviors that
are sanctioned by their peer group are acting so as to achieve prestige
within their reference system.

Herbert Bloch and Arthur Niederhoffer: The Adolescent Striving for Adulthood

Herbert Bloch and Arthur Niederhoffer (1958), in a somewhat different
interpretation of the sociocultural forces that propel youths into delinquency, viewed delinquent behavior as a universal and normal adolescent
striving for adult status. Their hypothesis was based on considerable cross-
cultural material that attempted to reveal the differences and similarities of
the adolescent condition in a variety of societies. Their basic position, as
stated in chapter 7, bears repeating:

> The adolescent period in all cultures, visualized as a phase of
> striving for the attainment of adult status, produces experiences
> which are much the same for all youths, and certain common
> dynamisms for expressing reaction to such subjectively held
> experience. The intensity of the adolescent experience and the
> vehemence of external expression depend on a variety of factors,
> including the general societal attitudes toward adolescence, the
> duration of the adolescent period itself, and the degree to which
> the society tends to facilitate entrance into adulthood by virtue of
> institutionalized patterns, ceremonials, rites and rituals, and
> socially supported emotional and intellectual preparation. When
> a society does not make adequate preparation, formal or other-
> wise, for the induction of its adolescents to the adult status,
> equivalent forms of behavior arise spontaneously among adoles-
> cents themselves, reinforced by their own group structure, which
> seemingly provide the same psychological content and function
> as the more formalized rituals found in other societies. This the
> gang structure appears to do in American society, apparently sat-
> isfying deep-seated needs experienced by adolescents in all cul-
> tures. Such, very briefly, is our hypothesis. (1958, p. 17)

In their analysis Bloch and Niederhoffer assess the effects of such cultural
patterns as puberty rites, self-decoration, and circumcision on adolescent
behavior. Gang behavior, with its symbolic evidence of the "urge for manhood" is seen as an American equivalent of the puberty rites of other cultures. The gang is thus viewed as a vehicle for accomplishing the assumed

highly desired status of manhood. According to Bloch and Niederhoffer, gang structure has a high degree of stability. In their criticism of those investigators who attributed characteristics of flux and "movement" to gang organization, they argued:

> Observations of gang behavior in various neighborhoods of New York City, for example, seem to reveal just the opposite to be true. In fact, one of the outstanding characteristics of numerous gangs which have been observed appears to be their highly non-mobile and stationary nature, a fact to which many exasperated shopkeepers and building custodians, as well as the police, can amply testify. Gangs, thus, might just as well be characterized by an absence of movement since, for the most part, they frequent the same corner or candy store for hours on end, every day of the week. (1958, p. 17)

Bloch and Niederhoffer strongly emphasized the highly controversial point that delinquency is a "characteristic of all adolescent groups" and that the organizational structures of all adolescent groups (delinquent or not) are similar. They stated:

> In respect to the type of organizational structure, there is little to distinguish, in one sense, between middle- and lower-class adolescent groups. Although middle-class groups of teenagers are not as apt to have the formal, almost military, structure characteristic of certain lower-class "war gangs." . . . They do have similar and well-defined informal patterns of leadership and control. Even here, however, the distinctions become blurred and, upon occasion, almost indistinguishable when one recalls the ceremonial designations and ritualistic roles performed by college functionaries. (1958, p. 38)

Using data about adolescents from such diverse groups as the Mundugumor of New Guinea, the Manus of the Admiralty Islands, the Kaffirs of South Africa, the Comanche and Plains Indians, and a tightly knit delinquent New York City gang, Bloch and Niederhoffer attempted to draw the inference that the ganging process provides symbolic evidence of the urge to manhood. They concluded (1958, p. 53):

1. Adolescent gangs may be profitably studied by using as a frame of reference the theory of power.

2. The gang's attempt to gain status and power through the domination and manipulation of persons and events is a collective representation of the individual gang member's guiding fiction, which is "to prove he is a man." In passing it is worthy of note that Alfred Adler's system of psychology is "tailor made" for the analysis of the gang

369

since it is principally concerned with the struggle for power and the "masculine protest."

3. The presence of the gang, real, constructive or symbolic, gives the individual member ego support and courage. He gains a psychological sense of power and manhood which he does not possess at all when he is on his own.

4. If single gangs can pose a threat to the peace and safety of the community—and they certainly do so—then the well-meaning efforts to organize several gangs into a confederation may be a very grave error. Without significant changes in behavior and values on the part of such gangs, this maneuver may only multiply to extremely dangerous proportions the looming menace which even now we find difficult to control.

Donald R. Taft and Ralph England on the Sociocultural Forces That Cause Delinquency

Donald R. Taft and Ralph W. England formulated a sociological theory that attempts to explain the high rate of crime in the United States and other Western societies. They saw criminality resulting from a combination of the following aspects of American culture (1964, pp. 27–31):

1. American culture is dynamic. Our standards are constantly changing. "The wrong of yesterday is the right of today."

2. American culture is complex. Crime is the product of culture conflict, and culture conflict is widespread as a result of immigration and internal migration.

3. American culture is materialistic. "Speaking generally, the underprivileged and unsuccessful accept the same values as the successful and aspire to imitate their success" (p. 28). It is apparent that the underprivileged have a more difficult time achieving success goals than the privileged.

4. American social relations are increasingly impersonal. Primary relationships in the family and neighborhood have declined. Anonymity breeds alienation and a greater impetus to crime and delinquency.

5. American culture fosters restricted group loyalties. "Preference for men, not wholly because of their personal qualities, but because they are natives, neighbors, Masons, or of our race, class, or creed, is widespread and not essentially different in quality from gang loyalty" (p. 30). This leaves people out, and produces conflict, hostility, and crime.

6. Survival of frontier values. Among frontier values that have survived to the present are the traditions of extreme individualism and the tendency of some groups within our society to take the law into their own hands. All these factors in American culture "normally" produce a high incidence of crime.

Milton Barron on American Culture and the Criminogenic Society

Milton Barron presented an analysis of the criminogenic aspects of the American society and culture that impact on delinquent behavior. He discussed several official and unofficial American values that are likely to encourage norm-violating and illegal behavior. According to Barron (1974, pp. 68–71), these basic issues are:

1. *Success.* There is an emphasis in our culture on the importance of succeeding and asserting oneself. The well-known quotation of football coach Lombardi is cited: "Winning isn't everything, it is the only thing." Americans hate to admit failure. They feel frustrated if they do not achieve success. There is also a high value placed on moving up, going higher on the scale toward ultimate success. When people realize that they are not going to succeed and are not moving up through hard work, thrift, study, and so on, many turn to crime and delinquency as ways of achieving success.

2. *Status and power ascendance.* The answer to the question "How far can I get?" is found in terms of social status. Evidence of higher status is provided by high grades, expensive cars, expensive clothes, jewelry, and so on. Dollars provide the power. Money and material goods have become values in themselves. People who cannot obtain them lawfully may violate laws to get them.

3. *Resistance to authority.* Independence, individuality, and nonconformity are encouraged. These involve resistance to authority. Americans tend to ridicule literal observance and strict conformity. This tendency applies to observance of laws.

4. *Toughness.* There are class differences in the emphasis on toughness. However, in every subculture people are encouraged to fight back. Violence is celebrated in crime and gangster programs on TV, in films, and elsewhere.

5. *Dupery.* People are rewarded for getting the better of others. The observation of P.T. Barnum that "there's a sucker born every minute" meets

with general agreement if not approval. Official norms and laws are violated with the tacit acceptance of the society or group as long as violations are concealed. People are proud of getting the better of others.

6. *American culture is dynamic.* Changes in norms are so rapid that differences between right and wrong are weakened.

7. *Alternative and conflicting values and norms.* Behavior that is defined as illegal in the American society may not necessarily be "wrong" in the subcultures of some groups.

8. *Impersonal social relations.* In American society relationships have become increasingly impersonal. Urban living, in which one hardly knows one's neighbor, does not provide the informal controls of rural society.

9. *A duality of loyalty and ethics.* Many people apply one code of ethics in their relations with members of their ingroup and a different code with outgroup members.

Barron tempers the impact of his criminogenic society and culture theory by acknowledging that widespread crime and corruption existed at other times in history and occur in places other than the United States. Nevertheless, although these factors are not unique to American society, they are part of the problem.

Walter Reckless on Containment Theory

Walter Reckless (1956, 1961) presented a social-psychological theory on delinquency that is based on the inner-psychological and outer-sociological forces that affect delinquent behavior. Reckless used outer containment and inner containment as intervening variables in causing and preventing delinquency. According to his theory, youths may be pressured into delinquency by unfavorable economic conditions or pulled into it by association with a delinquent subculture if their outer containment is deficient. The lack of outer containment is evidenced by the lack of well-defined limits to behavior, the breakdown of rules, the absence of definite roles for adolescents to play, and the failure of family life to present adequate limits and roles to the youths.

Reckless contended that youths in a high-delinquency area where outer containment is weak may remain nondelinquent if their inner containment is good. Inner containment consists of good ego strength, self-control, good self-conceptualization, and strong resistance against diversions.

Containment theory has the advantage of merging the psychological and the sociological viewpoints of crime causation. It facilitates an analysis of the inner personal forces that propel a person to commit a crime and at the same time permits an examination of the sociocultural forces that shape motivation and personality. Reckless's theory is presented in the following propositions (1956, pp. 744–746; 1961, pp. 355–356):

1. At the top of a vertical arrangement impinging on an individual is a layer of social pressures. Pressure factors include adverse living conditions and economic conditions, minority groups status, lack of opportunities, and family conflicts.

2. The pressures include what Reckless refers to as "pull factors." These draw the individual away from the accepted norms. They include bad companions, a delinquent or criminal subculture, and deviant groups.

3. In the situation immediately surrounding the individual is the structure of effective or ineffective external containment. This structure consists of effective family living and supportive groups.

4. The next layer is the inner containment of the individual. It is a product of good or poor internalization. When external containment is weak, inner containment must be additionally strong to withstand the pushes from within and the pulls and pressures from without.

5. The bottom layer consists of the pushes. These include inner tensions, hostility, aggressiveness, strong feelings of inadequacy and inferiority, and organic impairments.

② Labeling Theory and Its Impact on Delinquency

A number of theorists have believed that labeling youths as delinquent tends to reinforce their delinquent behavior. They assert that labeling develops in the following way. A person convicted of a crime is considered a "criminal," and a juvenile adjudicated by the juvenile court is viewed as a "delinquent" by society. These are stigmatizing labels. Once given the stigmatizing label, the individual may be subjected to isolation, segregation, degradation, incarceration, and chemical or psychological treatment. These impacts facilitate continuing a life of delinquency and then crime.

Labeling theorists assert that the status of criminal or delinquent is a creation of the laws of the society based on what the society considers to be deviant behavior. In a sense, there is no behavior that is intrinsically deviant. It is the society that confers the status on a person who it deems is deviant or, in this case, delinquent. Howard Becker

(1963), a leading exponent of labeling theory, described the process of labeling as follows:

> Social groups create deviance by making the rules whose infraction constitutes deviance, and by applying those rules to particular people and labeling them as outsiders. From this point of view, deviance is not a quality of the act the person commits, but rather a consequence of the application by others of rules and sanctions to an "offender." The deviant is one to whom that label has successfully been applied; deviant behavior is behavior that people so label. (P. 9)

It is clear that the labeling theorist did not consider criminality a property inherent in certain types of behavior but rather a status conferred upon a person who is found to have engaged in the behavior. Another implication of this theory is that the process of labeling is itself a critical determinant of the subsequent deviant or conforming career of the individual. Frank Tannenbaum (1951) perceived labeling delinquents as exacerbating the problem: "The young delinquent becomes bad because he is defined as bad and because he is not believed if he is good. The person becomes the thing he is described as being. Nor does it seem to matter whether the valuation is made by those who would punish or those who would reform. . . . Their [police, courts, parents] very enthusiasm defeats their aim. The harder they work to reform the evil, the greater the evil grows under their hands" (p. 18).

One of the institutions that too often labels juveniles as delinquents is the school. The school, through its administrators, is in a position to have a great impact and influence upon the lives of juveniles—particularly toward career orientation. If the student is labeled negatively in the school, he or she will likely come to regard him- or herself as inferior and is unlikely to succeed at school or elsewhere. The student who is given failing grades seldom makes a comeback. He or she tends to view him- or herself as a failure and often drops out of school.

An implication of labeling theory is that one of the factors determining whether delinquency will be reduced, repeated, or even broadened to include a wider range of acts is the nature of the reactions of the group to a youth's initial act of deviancy. The reactions may have several possible effects. On the one hand, if the reprimanding institution wisely and discreetly imposes firm sanctions on the individual and attempts to involve the individual in acceptable activities, the chances are good that the individual will conform to the acceptable ways of the society and will develop a good self-image. On the other hand, if the sanctions are harsh and degrading, the punishment can have long-term negative impacts on a youth. If a youth is expelled from school, for example, his or her delinquent behavior may escalate, for the simple reason that he or she is excluded from the possibility of being rehabilitated in the school's social system.

When students are excluded, they become further alienated from contact with more responsible persons and standards rather than pulled back in and helped. In other words, there seems to be a tendency to shut out rather than open up opportunities for a juvenile to become involved in a legitimate, acceptable, conforming-to-the-norm situation.

Labeling theory raises serious questions about the advisability of recklessly stigmatizing people with labels like "criminal" and "delinquent," when the objective is principally to deter the behavior. When we attach the stigmatizing label, we may actually contribute to an increase in the undesirable behavior by seriously handicapping the individual's efforts to secure a responsible position in society. Labeling theory does little to explain delinquent or criminal behavior. It does a great deal, however, to emphasize the damage that can be done by attaching stigmatizing labels.

The creation of the juvenile court and the introduction of specialized judicial detention and treatment services for children was intended to avoid giving them the stigmatizing label of juvenile delinquent. Now that the term "juvenile delinquent" has become a stigmatizing label, it may be time to reexamine the entire juvenile justice system. All sorts of data acquired in the course of the delinquency and criminality labeling process are now in computers.

The process of arrest, whether or not the youth is guilty of an offense, places the stigma of delinquent on an individual and is the culmination of a systematic labeling process. The labeling process begins with suspicion, with the suspect being known only to the police or some other investigatory agency. Eventually the courts certify the label of the defendant's criminality. The data are then computerized.

The tremendous increase in the use of computers means that the label attached to persons as a result of arrest and, later on, conviction because a matter of permanent record available to law enforcement agencies and others throughout the country. This is especially true of files on gangs. Nearly all modern effective law-enforcement agencies have computer services. Stigmatizing data also go to data banks of the Federal Bureau of Investigation and the National Crime Information Center. The availability of these data to persons who might misuse them constitutes a threat to freedom and privacy. Regarding this possible impact of computer technology on delinquency and crime, Arthur Niederhoffer (1974) said:

> The other side of computer technology is that it constitutes a threat to democracy—to privacy and freedom to dissent.

Inevitably computerized information systems will place everyone in America from the age of fourteen to seventy into the category of possible suspect. And there is no statute of limitation on tapes, disks, and memory banks; they can be held thirty, forty, and fifty years, or in perpetuity. Moreover, not only state and federal law enforcement agencies, but also the Pentagon, the Army, the Navy, and the Air Force have gathered data on millions of citizens. They, too, are interested in "troublemakers." The C.I.A. and the State Department have their computerized card files. The Civil Service Commission has millions of names listed in its security files. (Pp. 47–48)

Labeling offenders through computers, a process that will no doubt become more systematic in the twenty-first century, of course, has a positive side. It enables law enforcement to easily maintain records and criminal profiles. Because of this process, it is easier to identify suspects, and many crimes are solved more easily. This is especially true of convicted and "labeled" sex offenders with a special emphasis on pedophiles.

In the labeling of sex offenders, American society, in a more sophisticated way, is returning to the practices rampant in colonial days when offenders were placed in stockades or had their offense emblazoned on their foreheads. As previously indicated, in 1996, in New Jersey, twelve-year-old Megan Kanka was sexually assaulted and murdered. This horrendous event spurred a variety of legislation that has become known as "Megan's Law." In the late 1990s, in forty-three states, various forms of Megan's Law were enacted that made it mandatory to identify a child molester and report his presence in a community. This is often done with a flyer that is distributed within the radius of his home. This is labeling at its most extreme and is probably unconstitutional. Despite this, the law is being debated, appealed, and utilized in almost all of the states.

Labeling a sex offender poses a dilemma to society. On the one hand, labeling practice with regard to recidivising pedophiles is totally understandable. Parents and their children want to know if a pedophile is living in their neighborhood, especially since this type of offender has the highest recidivism rate of any criminal. However, on the other hand, if we assume that the offender is somewhat rehabilitated and is striving to control his compulsions, the stigmata of labeling him will only contribute to his remaining a pariah in the community. In effect, he is being punished after he has served his time in prison. In this context, his constitutional rights may be violated. There is no easy solution to this paradoxical situation—although many people will take one side or the other with great enthusiasm and conviction.

It is clear to me, based on my experience, that officially labeling a youth as a delinquent in the juvenile court can affect his self-definition.

I have seen this process occur on many occasions. I recall a specific case example of a youth I had met several times when he was incarcerated in the juvenile jail where I worked. He had been before the judge in the court four times for various offenses. When he was in custody I had many lengthy conversations with him about his behavior. Most of the time he indicated a motivation to change his ways and end his delinquent behavior.

The next time I saw him I was the custodial officer who brought him into court, where he was charged with a burglary. The judge lost patience. The label of delinquent was no doubt appropriate in his case; however, it had an impact on his later behavior. I followed his career from delinquent to his becoming an adult criminal, and I met him later at the Trenton State Prison.

In terms of labeling theory, many offenders, by their deviant behavior, certainly deserve their label. However, labeling, especially with regard to juveniles, should be handled with considerable thoughtfulness and discretion. Arbitrary labeling can affect a youth's self-concept and intensify his delinquent behavior. This is especially true with regard to further stigmatizing youths by referring them to the adult criminal justice system.

③ Edwin Sutherland and Donald Cressey: Differential Association Theory

Edwin Sutherland's social psychological theory of delinquency is one of the most widely accepted explanations of the way criminal behavior patterns are acquired by delinquents. Sutherland's original theory was later elaborated upon by Donald Cressey, his student and collaborator. The central thesis of the theory, known as differential association, is that "criminal behavior is learned through interaction with others in intimate personal groups. The learning includes techniques of committing criminal acts, plus the motives, drives, rationalizations, and attitudes favorable to the commission of crime" (1970, p. 39). The following factors derived from their writings explain Sutherland and Cressey's basic principles of differential association:

1. Criminal behavior is learned. This means that criminal behavior is not inherited as such. Also, the person who is not already trained in crime does not invent criminal behavior, just as a person does not make mechanical inventions unless he or she has had training in mechanics.

2. Criminal behavior is learned in interactions with other persons in a process of communication. This communication is verbal in many respects but includes the "communication of gestures."

3. The principal part of the learning of criminal behavior occurs within intimate personal groups. The impersonal agencies of communication, such as movies and newspapers, play a relatively unimportant part in the genesis of criminal behavior.

4. When criminal behavior is learned, the learning includes (a) techniques of committing the crime, which are sometimes very complicated, sometimes very simple, and (b) the specific direction of motives, drives, rationalizations, and attitudes.

5. The specific direction of motives and drives is learned from definitions of the legal codes as favorable or unfavorable. In some societies an individual is surrounded by persons who invariably define the legal codes as rules to be observed, while in others he or she is surrounded by persons whose definitions are favorable to the violation of the legal codes. In our American society these definitions are almost always mixed, with the consequence that we have culture conflict in relation to the legal codes.

6. A person becomes delinquent because of an excess of definitions favorable to violation of law over definitions unfavorable to violation of law. This is the basic principle of differential association. It refers to both criminal and anticriminal associations and has to do with counteracting forces. When persons become criminal, they do so because of contacts with criminal patterns and also because of isolation from anticriminal patterns. Any person inevitably assimilates the surrounding culture unless other patterns are in conflict; a Southerner does not pronounce "r" because other Southerners do not pronounce "r." This proposition of differential association means that associations that are neutral insofar as crime is concerned have little or no effect on the genesis of criminal behavior. Much of one's experience is neutral in this sense, for example, learning to brush one's teeth. This behavior has no negative or positive effect on criminal behavior except as it may be related to associations that are concerned with the legal codes. This neutral behavior is important especially as an occupier of a child's so that the child is not in contact with criminal behavior during the time he or she is so engaged in the neutral behavior.

7. Differential associations may vary in frequency, duration, priority, and intensity. This means that associations with criminal behavior and also associations with anticriminal behavior vary in those respects. "Frequency" and "duration" as modalities of associations are obvious and need no explanation. "Priority" is assumed to be important in the sense that lawful behavior developed in early childhood may persist throughout life, and also that delinquent behavior developed in early childhood may persist throughout life. This tendency, however, has not been adequately

demonstrated, and priority seems to be important principally through its selective influence. "Intensity" is not precisely defined, but it has to do with such things as the prestige of the source of the criminal or anticriminal pattern and with emotional reactions related to the associations. In a precise description of the criminal behavior of a person, these modalities would be stated in quantitative form, and a mathematical ratio would be reached. A formula in this sense has not been developed, and the development of such a formula would be extremely difficult.

8. The process of learning criminal behavior by association with criminal and anticriminal parents involves all of the mechanisms that are involved in any other learning. This means that the learning of criminal behavior is not restricted to the process of imitation. A person who is seduced, for instance, learns criminal behavior by association, but this process would not ordinarily be described as imitation.

9. While criminal behavior is an expression of general needs and values, it is not explained by those general needs and values since noncriminal behavior is an expression of the same needs and values. Thieves generally steal in order to secure money, but honest laborers work in order to secure money. The attempts by many scholars to explain criminal behavior by general drives and values, such as the happiness principle, striving for social status, the money motive, or frustration, have been and must continue to be futile, since they explain lawful behavior as completely as they explain criminal behavior. They are similar to respiration, which is necessary for any behavior but which does not differentiate criminal from noncriminal behavior.

The impact of Sutherland's theory on criminology was detailed by Cressey (1960) in an article in *Social Problems*. Sutherland's theory had such a profound impact on the field of criminology in the United States that it is pertinent to present Cressey's comprehensive remarks on the origin and development of the theory of differential association:

> The first formal statement of Edwin H. Sutherland's theory of differential association appeared in the third edition of his *Principles of Criminology*, in 1939. Sutherland later pointed out that the idea of differential association was stated in an earlier edition of the text, and he confessed that he was unaware that this statement was a general theory of criminal behavior. At the insistence of his colleagues, he drew up a formal set of propositions based on this earlier notion and appended it to the 1939 edition of the textbook. In one sense, this first formal statement of the theory of differential association was short lived. For reasons which never have been clear, the statement of the theory was qualified so that

it pertained only to "systematic criminal behavior," rather than to the more general category, "criminal behavior."

Further, the statement was redundant, for it proposed generally that individual criminality is learned in a process of differential association with criminal and anticriminal behavior patterns, but then went on to use "consistency" of association with the two kinds of patterns as one of the conditions affecting the impact of differential association on individuals. Thus, "consistency" of behavior patterns presented was used as a general explanation of criminality, but "consistency" also was used to describe the process by which differential association takes place. . . . He also deleted the word "systematic," principally because it led to errors of interpretation. He believed that "systematic criminal behavior" included almost all criminal behavior, while his readers, colleagues, and students considered only a very small portion of criminal behavior to be "systematic."

The theory now refers to all criminal behavior. The current statement of the theory of differential association holds, in essence, that "criminal behavior is learned in interaction with persons in a pattern of communication," and that the specific direction of motives, drives, rationalizations, and attitudes— whether in the direction of anticriminality or criminality—is learned from persons who define the codes as rules to be observed and from persons whose attitudes are favorable to violation of legal codes. "A person becomes delinquent because of an excess of definitions favorable to violation of law over definitions unfavorable to violations of law."

In any society, the two kinds of definitions of what is desirable in reference to legal codes exist side by side, and a person might present contradictory definitions to another person at different times and in different situations. Sutherland called the process of receiving these definitions "differential association," because the content of what is learned in association with criminal behavior patterns differs from the content of what is learned in association with anticriminal behavior patterns. "When persons become criminals, they do so because of contacts with criminal behavior patterns and also because of isolation from anticriminal patterns." These contacts, however, "may vary in frequency, duration, priority, and intensity."

When this idea is applied to a nation, a city, or a group, it becomes a sociological theory, rather than a social psychological theory, for it deals with differential rates of crime and delinquency. For example, a high crime rate in urban areas, as compared to rural areas, can be considered an end product of a situation in which a relatively large proportion of persons are presented with an excess of criminal behavior patterns. Similarly, the fact that the rate for all crimes is not higher in some urban areas than it is in some rural areas can be attributed to differences in probabilities of exposure to criminal behavior patterns.

> The important general point is that in a multi-group type of social organization, alternative and inconsistent standards of conduct are possessed by various groups, so that individuals who are members of one group have a higher probability of learning to use legal means for achieving success, or of learning to deny the importance of success, while individuals in other groups learn to accept the importance of success and to achieve it by illegal means. Stated in another way, there are alternative educational processes in operation, varying with groups, so that a person may be educated in either conventional or criminal means of achieving success. Sutherland called this situation "differential social organization" or "differential group organization," and he proposed that "differential group organization should explain the crime rate, while differential association should explain the criminal behavior of a person. The two explanations must be consistent with each other."
>
> Sutherland's theory has had an important effect on sociological thought about criminality and crime, if only because it has become the center of controversy. Strangely, it seems to have received more discussion, comment, and research attention in the last five years than in the first fifteen years of its existence. Also, there rapidly is developing a situation in which probation, parole, and prison workers have at least heard of the theory, even if they are barely beginning to try using it for prevention of crime and rehabilitation of criminals. A social worker has recently written, "The hallmark of this new departure (in delinquency prevention) is the recognition that delinquency is not primarily a psychological problem of neuroses but a social problem of differential values. Essentially most delinquent behavior arises from the fact that core concepts of what is right and wrong, what is worth striving for and what is attainable, are not transmitted with equal force and clarity throughout the community. (Pp. 93–95)

The theory of differential association helps to illuminate some basic causes of delinquency, yet it does not explain why some people associate with those who approve of violation of the law while others do not. It also doesn't explain why some individuals become intensely committed to definitions favorable to the law while others with similar associations do not. It remains significant, however, because most current theorists have adopted the emphasis that differential association places on social learning through interaction in intimate groups as the principal method of the transmission of criminal and delinquent values.

(4) Ronald Akers' Social Learning Theory

Ronald Akers, building on Sutherland and Cressey's theory of differential association, with the aid of several other criminological theorists, developed his theory of social learning to explain criminality. Akers retained the concepts of differential association and definitions from Sutherland's theory but conceptualized them in more behavioral terms and added concepts from behavioral learning theory. In this regard he states: "These concepts include differential reinforcement, whereby 'operant' behavior (the voluntary actions of the individual) is conditioned or shaped by rewards and punishments. They also contain classical or 'respondent' conditioning (the conditioning of involuntary reflex behavior); discriminative stimuli (the environmental and internal stimuli that provides cues for behavior), schedules of reinforcement (the rate and ratio in which rewards and punishments follow behavioral responses), and other principles of behavior modification" (1997, p. 63).

Akers retains Sutherland and Cressey's concern with social structure and relates the social learning process to variations in the group rates of crime and deviance. Social learning theory retains a strong element of the symbolic interactionism found in the concepts of differential association and definitions from Sutherland and Cressey's theory. Symbolic interactionism is the theory that social interaction is mainly the exchange of meaning and symbols; individuals have the cognitive capacity to imagine themselves in the role of others and incorporate this into their conceptions of themselves. This, and the explicit inclusion of such concepts as imitation, anticipated reinforcement, and self-reinforcement, makes Akers' social learning theory a kind of "soft behaviorism."

The central theme of Akers' learning theory, which offers an explanation of crime and deviance, refers to variables that operate to motivate and control criminal behavior and to promote and undermine conformity. Akers asserts that the probability of criminal or conforming behavior occurring is a function of the balance of these influences on behavior. He writes: "Deviant behavior can be expected to the extent that it has been differentially reinforced over alternative conforming behavior" (1997, p. 65).

Akers' theory focuses on four major concepts: (1) differential association; (2) definitions; (3) differential reinforcement; and (4) imitation. Differential association refers to the process whereby one is exposed to normative definitions favorable or unfavorable to illegal or law-abiding behavior. Differential association has both behavioral interactional and normative dimensions. The interactional dimension is the direct association and interaction with others who engage in certain kinds of behavior, as well as the indirect association and identification with more distant reference groups. On this theme, Akers states:

> The groups with which one is in differential association provide the major social contexts in which all the mechanisms of social learning operate. They not only expose one to definitions, they also present them with models to imitate and with differential

reinforcement for criminal or conforming behavior. The most important of these groups are the primary ones of family and friends, though they may also be secondary and reference groups. Neighbors, churches, school teachers, physicians, the law and authority figures, and other individuals and groups in the community (as well as mass media and other more remote sources of attitudes and models) have varying degrees of effect on the individual's propensity to commit criminal and delinquent behavior. Those associations which occur first (priority), last longer (duration), occur more frequently (frequency), and involve others with whom one has the more important or closer relationships (intensity) will have the greater effect. (1997, p. 68)

According to Akers, (2) definitions are one's own attitudes or meanings that one attaches to given behavior. This includes rationalizations, definitions of the situation, and other evaluative and moral attitudes that define the commission of an act as right or wrong, good or bad, desirable or undesirable, justified or unjustified. In social learning theory, these definitions are both general and specific. General beliefs include religious, moral, and other conventional values and norms that are favorable to conforming behavior and unfavorable to committing any deviant or criminal acts. Positive definitions are beliefs or attitudes that make the behavior morally desirable or wholly permissible. Neutralizing definitions favor the commission of crime by justifying or excusing it. According to Akers, criminals view the act as something that is probably not desirable but, given the situation, is nonetheless justified, excusable, necessary, or not really bad to do.

The concept of neutralizing definitions in social learning theory incorporates the concepts of Sykes and Matza and others. Akers states in this regard: "These definitions, favorable and unfavorable to criminal and delinquent behavior, are developed through imitation and differential reinforcement. Cognitively, they provide a mind-set that makes one more willing to commit the act when the opportunity occurs. Behaviorally, they affect the commission of deviant or criminal behavior by acting as internal discriminative stimuli. Discriminative stimuli operate as cues or signals to the individual as to what responses are appropriate or expected in a given situation" (1997, p. 72).

(3) Differential reinforcement refers to the balance of anticipated or actual rewards and punishments that follow or are consequences of behavior. Whether individuals will refrain from or commit a crime at any given time (and whether they will continue or desist from doing so in the future) depends on the past, present, and anticipated future rewards and punishment for their actions. On differential reinforcement Akers asserts: "The probability that an act will be committed or repeated is increased by rewarding outcomes or reactions to it, e.g., obtaining approval, money, food, or pleasant feelings—

positive reinforcement. The likelihood that an action will be taken is also enhanced when it allows a person to avoid or escape aversive or unpleasant events—negative reinforcement" (1997, p. 56). ④

In the context of Akers' theory of social learning, imitation refers to the engagement in behavior after the observation of similar behavior in others. Whether or not the behavior modeled by others will be imitated is affected by the characteristics of the models, the behavior observed, and the observed consequences of the behavior. The observation of salient models in primary groups and in the media affects both prosocial and deviant behavior. It is more important in the initial acquisition and performance of novel behavior than in the maintenance or cessation of behavioral patterns once established, but, according to Akers, it continues to have some effect in maintaining law-abiding behavior.

Akers stresses that social learning is a complex process with reciprocal and feedback effects. The reciprocal effects are not seen as equal, however. Akers hypothesizes a typical temporal sequence or process by which individuals come to the point of violating the law or engaging in other deviant acts. This process is one in which the balance of learned definitions, imitation of criminal or deviant models, and the anticipated balance of reinforcement produces the initial delinquent or deviant act. He states on this issue:

> The facilitative effects of these variables continue in the repetition of acts, although imitation becomes less important than it was in the first commission of the act. After initiation, the actual social and non-social reinforcers and punishers affect whether or not the acts will be repeated and at what level of frequency. Not only the behavior itself, but also the definitions are affected by the consequences of the initial act. Whether a deviant act will be committed in a situation that presents the opportunity depends on the learning history of the individual and the set of reinforcement contingencies in that situation. (1997, p. 42)

Akers and his associates have developed and carried out considerable research to test his social learning hypotheses. Based on this research there is considerable empirical data to support his theoretical assertions. Although Akers' theory has many parallels to Sutherland and Cressey's differential association theory, it develops the phenomenon of social learning to another level in the causal explanation of delinquency.

⑤ Travis Hirschi: Social Bonding

A theory of causation that is widely accepted by criminologists is Travis Hirschi's theory of social bonding. Hirschi (1969) based his theory on his own empirical studies of self-reported delinquency. He is one of the few theorists who carried out research with a representative sample of delinquents to validate his theoretical viewpoint.

Hirschi's basic theory states that "delinquent acts result when an individual's bond to society is weak or broken" (1969, p. 85). Four principal factors make up this bond: (1) attachment, (2) commitment, (3) involvement, and (4) beliefs. In this context, youths who have strong bonds with their parents, other adults, school teachers, and peers will be controlled in the direction of conformity. The weaker these bonds are, the more likely it is that the individuals will violate the law. These four elements are viewed by Hirschi as highly intercorrelated. In the following analysis, each of Hirschi's four factors is presented with commentary based on my research into delinquency.

1. *Attachment.* Attachment, according to Hirschi, involves close emotional ties to others and identification with them so that we care about their expectations. The more insensitive we are to others' opinions, the less we are constrained by the norms we share with them; therefore, the more likely we are to violate these norms. All of these factors lead to greater self-control over deviant behavior. In this regard Hirschi refers to the internalization of norms as a factor in controlling delinquency. He states: "The essence of internalization of norms, conscience, or superego thus lies in the attachment of the individual to others" (1969, p. 87). He emphasizes that attachment to parents and parental supervision are important in controlling delinquency and maintaining conformity. On the other hand, based on Hirschi's thesis, it could be argued that the emotional attachment to a gang's values and norms would propel an individual into delinquent behavior.

2. *Commitment.* Commitment, according to Hirschi, refers to the individual's degree of investment in conventionality or his or her connection to the norms of society. A youth's investment in conventional educational and occupational endeavors builds up the commitment factor. The greater the commitment, the more he or she risks losing by nonconformity. This is an important variable in predicting delinquency. Youths who have a sense of hopelessness about their prospects in American society, in terms of Merton's anomie theory, would be uncommitted and more prone to commit delinquent acts. This is a factor that I have observed in the extreme in violent gangsters. Not only are they uncommitted to the general society, their alienation results in attacking the system whenever an opportunity arises.

3. *Involvement.* Involvement refers to the degree to which a youth is involved in conventional activities, such as school, studying, spending time with family, and participation in legitimate extracurricular activities.

Youths who are involved in law-abiding activities like school are less likely to become delinquent. This is, of course, a most obvious point, since a youth has only so much time in his daily life, and if he spends it at school and with his family there is limited opportunity for participation in delinquent activities.

4. *Belief.* The concept of belief in Hirschi's social bonding theory is defined as "the endorsement of general conventional values and norms, especially the belief that laws and society's rules for behavior are morally correct and should be obeyed" (1969, p. 94). According to Hirschi, this factor does not necessarily refer to beliefs about specific laws or acts, nor does it mean that people hold deviant beliefs that "require" them to commit crimes. In fact, Hirschi argues that the less a person believes he or she should obey the rules, the more likely he or she is to violate them. My own research indicates that delinquents have beliefs that are antithetical to the society, and these beliefs are as pertinent to their delinquent behavior as positive beliefs are to law-abiding juveniles.

→ DID RESEARCH TO PROVE THEORIES, DEVELOPED MEASUREMENTS

Hirschi provided clear measures for the four principle elements of the social bond. Most research on his theory has used his measurements. Hirschi's research indicated support for his bonding theory. He found that, except for involvement, the weaker the bonds, the higher the probability of delinquency. However, he found delinquency to be most strongly related to association with delinquent friends, a finding not anticipated by his theory and heavily supportive of Sutherland and Cressey's differential association theory. My own viewpoint is that Hirschi's bonding theory rests on Sutherland and Cressey's theory of differential association; however, it expands their explanation of delinquency that facilitates testing the theory with empirical research.

Clarence R. Jeffery:
Social Alienation and Criminality

Clarence R. Jeffery (1959) presented a theory of social alienation focusing on the individual delinquent to explain his or her propensity for delinquent behavior. Jeffery pointed out that the concept of crime must exist before the concept of the criminal is possible. He asserted that antisocial behavior is not criminal behavior until a system of criminal law emerges. All of the theories of crime up to the 1950s put forth in criminology were theories that attempted to explain the behavior of the criminal. They did not explain why the behavior was regarded as criminal. This is why Jeffery believed that criminologists needed a theory of crime that explained the origin and development of criminal law in terms of the institutional structure of society.

Jeffery's causal theory rests on the development of law:

> Law came into existence at a time when the tribal system was disintegrating and social cohesion was no longer available as a means of social control. Primitive law is custom enforced by the kinship group and based on the cohesiveness of the group. It is private and personal in nature and in operation. Law is a product of impersonalization and the decline in social cohesion. It is a product of urbanization. Law emerges in a society whenever intimate, personal relationships are no longer efficient as agents of social control. (1959, p. 138)

Jeffery divided his explanations of criminal behavior into two schools of thought: the psychological and the sociological. The psychological school is based on the proposition that criminals differ from noncriminals in terms of personality traits that are expressed in some form of antisocial behavior. Criminal behavior is caused by emotional or mental conflict. The most damaging criticisms raised against the psychological school are the observations that few neurotics are criminals and that most criminals are neither neurotic nor psychotic.

Jeffery chose Sutherland and Cressey's theory of differential association to represent the sociological school. He described it as basically a theory of learning and stated that criminal behavior is learned from contact with those who maintain criminal attitudes and practices. Criminal behavior is learned by association with criminal and antisocial patterns. He made the following criticisms of the theory of differential association:

1. The theory does not explain the origin of criminality.
2. It does not explain crimes of passion or accident.
3. The theory does not explain crimes by those with no prior contact with criminal attitudes.
4. It does not explain the noncriminal living in a criminal environment.
5. The theory does not differentiate between criminal and noncriminal behavior.
6. It does not take into account motivation or "differential response patterns." People respond differently to similar situations.
7. The theory does not account for the differential rate of crime associated with age, sex, urban areas, and minority groups. (1959, p. 143)

Jeffery advanced his theory of social alienation in an attempt to integrate the psychological and sociological concepts of criminality. His theory states that crime rates are highest in groups where social interaction is characterized by isolation, anonymity, impersonalization, and anomie. According to this theory, the criminal is one who lacks interpersonal relationships and suffers from interpersonal failure. The typical criminal has failed to achieve satisfactory interpersonal relations with others; he is lonely and emotionally isolated; he lacks membership in lawful primary groups and is insecure, hostile, and aggressive; he feels unloved and unwanted, and has an inadequate sense of belonging. He is the product of social impersonalization.

The theory of social alienation is in essential agreement with the psychological thinking that places emphasis on such concepts as feelings of rejection, emotional starvation, and psychological isolation from others. Jeffery's theory of alienation is in agreement with Sutherland and Cressey's theory in that both emphasize the importance of social interaction that occurs in the primary group. It differs from differential association in the following respects. It explains (1) sudden crimes of passion, (2) why an individual can live in a delinquent subculture and yet isolate himself from delinquent patterns, (3) why a person with no history of association with criminals can commit criminal acts, and (4) the origin of criminal behavior in the first place by suggesting that high crime rates exist in areas characterized by anonymous, impersonal relationships.

Jeffery divided social alienation into three types. First there is individual alienation. The individual is alienated and isolated from interpersonal relations. He or she does not accept the values of the society. This person is often characterized as a sociopath. The second type is group alienation, as for example in a delinquent gang. The group to which the person belongs is alienated and isolated from the larger community. The individual who identifies with such a group is often characterized as a cultural deviate or a dissocial person. A lack of integration of the various segments of society produces alienation of the segments. The third type is legal alienation. Here Jeffery refers to the inequitable treatment of African-Americans and of lower-class individuals in courts of law to illustrate the fact that different social groups have differential access to justice.

Jeffery's theory of social alienation represents an attempt to integrate the sociological and psychological schools of thought. His theory retains the idea of social interaction while emphasizing the emotional content of human interaction. In support of his theory, Jeffery pointed to the fact that crime rates are high for young adult males who live in urban slum areas, who are from lower socioeconomic groups, and who are members of minority groups. In these areas one also finds social isolation, a preponderance of impersonal relationships, and anonymity. Individuals living under these conditions are alienated and more prone to become delinquent.

7

The Yablonsky Causation Theory: A Social-Psychological View

Based on my research and work in crime and delinquency, I have found the most useful concept for understanding delinquency is related to the delinquent youth's self-concept. The factor of self-concept has sociological routes and is reflected in the psychological personality of the delinquent.

A basic causal factor in a boy's self-concept is determined by the socializing agents in his early years—mostly his parents. If they treat him with respect and value him, he will be more apt to become a humanistic adult. If he is emotionally, physically, or sexually abused or abused by abandonment, he is more likely to become a delinquent, and after going through the usual administration of juvenile justice, an adult offender. One study, among many others, makes this point. Heather Knight (1997) reports on some relevant research on this case.

> A study based in Sacramento County has found a "smoking gun" relationship between child abuse and criminal behavior, reporting that abused children are sixty-seven times more likely than nonabused ones to run afoul of the law.
>
> Based on the results of its study, released Thursday, the Child Welfare League of America challenged President Clinton to veto bills pending in Congress that would earmark federal funds for new juvenile prison facilities. Instead, the league—a private, nonprofit children's advocacy group based in Washington— urged the federal government to funnel more money to such programs as preschool for low-income kids, home visits for teenage mothers, enrichment and mentoring programs in high school, and family counseling for first-time juvenile offenders. The league's study used arrest records of 75,000 children in Sacramento County who were ages nine to twelve in 1996. It found the arrest rate for abused children was 60 children per 1,000, compared with a rate of .89 per 1,000 for nonabused children. . . .
>
> In light of these findings, Michael Petit, deputy director for the league, said Congress' response to juvenile crime is "ineffective and needlessly expensive." The House recently voted to spend $1.5 billion to combat juvenile crime, with constructing prisons for youths a top priority. A Senate bill, which is pending, would allocate more than $2.5 billion over five years for, among other items, new juvenile prison facilities and prevention programs targeting youths. . . .
>
> Supporters of these bills have defended the prison component as fundamental to fighting juvenile crime. Among those questioning such assertions was Buffalo, New York, Police Commissioner Gil Kerlikowske, who joined Child Welfare League officials at a news conference and stated: "If Congress is

serious about fighting crime, it won't pretend that just building more jails is going to solve the problem. Those of us on the front lines know we'll win the war on crime when Congress boosts investment in early childhood programs and Head Start, health care for kids, after-school and mentoring and recreational programs. We'll win the war on crime when we invest tax dollars in America's most vulnerable kids instead of waiting until they become America's most wanted adults."

I support the viewpoint of Police Commissioner Kerlikowske. This research supports my contention that youths who are physically and emotionally abused, mainly by their parents, develop low self-esteem and are more apt to commit delinquent acts essentially because they don't care about themselves. One insightful and quite paranoid delinquent boy told me, "In the first place my parents never wanted me to be born. They always abused me in every way possible. I feel worthless and couldn't care less what happens to me. I would really like to kill my mother and father for making me this way. Because of them I am full of rage. I am always pissed-off and I am ready to beat the shit out of anyone that gets near me. Everyone hates me, so why shouldn't I hate myself?"

The starting point for most delinquents is the physical, sexual, or emotional abuse they receive from their family. Because of this treatment, they denigrate themselves, feel worthless, and are less likely to care about what happens to themselves. These social-psychological forces push these juveniles toward self-destructive behavior involving drugs and violence. Their "suicidal tendencies" make them prone to commit senseless, destructive delinquent acts, which are often as harmful to themselves as they are to their victims. In my work with delinquents, especially in psychiatric facilities, I have observed the impact of self-concept on delinquent behavior in thousands of youths. As a result of the abuse they have low self-esteem. These feelings of low self-esteem are often acted out in self-destructive, delinquent behavior that involves violence. For example, with regard to violent gang youths, observers of the motivation of gangbanging misperceive gang youths as "fighting for their turf" and committing acts of violence in a rational defense of their homie comrades-in-arms. A more accurate perspective on their violent behavior is that, because of their underlying low self-esteem, they are acting out self-destructive behavior, because they don't care whether they live or die.

A low self-concept is one consequence of abuse; another is extreme rage. Rage in a child is created by physical and emotional abuse by his or her parents. I recall a fifteen-year-old gangster I worked with in New York who accounted for his being wild in the streets in this way: "My father always beat me up since I was a little kid. When I hit fourteen we would wrestle and fight one-on-one. Sometimes I would beat him up—but mostly he won. Our fights would totally piss me off, and when I hit the streets I was looking for trouble. I had fights every day, and when our gang would go bopping, I was always up in the front line. I never cared what happened to me or anyone else." A considerable amount of displaced, so-called senseless violence by delinquents in gang fights, muggings, or armed robbery is cooked up in the cauldron of family violence.

Substance abuse is another consequence of the "abuse/low self-concept" syndrome. Substance abuse and alcoholism are ways of quickly ameliorating the painful feelings of low self-esteem. In a sense, using drugs that change a person's emotional state is a self-administered therapy. It is a therapy that works immediately but briefly, and the "treatment" has long-term negative consequences.

Child abuse, low soft-esteem, a delinquent self-concept, and suicidal tendencies are entwined factors in the cases of most juvenile delinquents. In some respects, teenage suicide is the opposite side of homicide. One delinquent youth, sixteen-year-old Pete, was in the hospital for stabbing himself in the chest with a hunting knife. He almost died from this self-inflicted wound. Although on this occasion he was in the hospital for attempted suicide, he had a long delinquent career that include drug addiction and robbery. In a psychodrama session, I had him act out the specific dramatic episode that involved his suicide attempt. A number of dimensions of his feelings about his father, delinquent behavior, and self-concept as a delinquent emerged in the session.

In Pete's psychodrama, a key dramatic episode involved a screaming battle with his father. In the core dialogue in the psychodrama with his father, Pete screamed at him as he brandished a rolled-up magazine, which represented the knife he had actually held in his hand during the real fight:

> PETE (to his father): You drunken_____, you've been beating on me since I was a little kid. I'll never forget that day you threw me up against the wall when I was ten. And I really didn't do anything.
>
> AUXILIARY EGO IN THE ROLE OF PETE'S FATHER: You deserved every beating I gave you.
>
> PETE: Bullshit. No kid deserves the things you did to me. I'm going to end this pain now. I'm going to kill you!

I intervened in the psychodrama at this point and used a psychodramatic technique known as a soliloquy a la Hamlet.

> L.Y.: Pete, I want you to hold off your next move. Here you are in this terrible situation. Like Hamlet, just say your inner thoughts out loud.

PETE: I hate this man. He's never been a father to me. He doesn't deserve to live. With one move of this knife [the rolled-up magazine in his hand] I can wipe him out of my life and get rid of all my pain. It's either him or me. (Begins to cry.) But there were times when he was good to me. We went to ball games and fishing. I guess I love him, and maybe he's right about me. I'm no fucking good. I'm everything he's accused me of. I'm just worthless. It's never going to work out, and I can't stand it anymore. I have to kill one of us. It's either him or me.

L.Y.: So to remove the pain of your terrible relationship with your father, either he has to go or you have to go. Which one are you going to kill?

In response to this question, Pete, still sobbing, stabbed himself in the chest with the symbolic knife. This was the behavioral act he had committed in reality, which resulted in his placement in the psychiatric hospital. In the post-psychodramatic discussion with Pete and the group, Pete developed some insight into his stabbing himself. Later discussions and therapy with his father helped the father to understand their conflict. The psychodrama and later family therapy were helpful to Pete and his father in resolving their family problems.

The session was a classic representation of many delinquent youths who have these conflicting emotional forces at work in their lives. They have low self-esteem because they have been physically and emotionally abused. They are full of rage toward the perpetrator of the abuse, in Pete's case, his father. They displace a lot of their aggression onto people other than the primary object of their hostility, and this accounts for their violent delinquent behavior. Yet, their low self-esteem persists and is reflected in self-destructive behavior. In Pete's case, it resulted in his self-inflicted wound. In brief, it was almost a toss-up between killing his father or himself. Pete believed that either act—killing his father or himself—would end his emotional pain.

Another factor that produces a delinquent self-concept and perpetuates delinquent behavior is having a criminogenic family background that fosters the adoption of deviant values. This deviant socialization process produces the "socialized delinquent." This syndrome is revealed in the case of sixteen-year-old Bill. I worked with Bill in juvenile detention. Bill's father was a devoted member of a "biker" gang. All his life Bill was surrounded by a biker culture, which included drugs, violence, and sexual acting out. These behavioral patterns constituted a normal part of his family's day-to-day life situation.

When Bill went to school, he began to notice that he came from what he later termed a "criminal family." Others in the community, including his teachers and neighbors, perceived and labeled Bill as a delinquent, and in time, Bill's family background tended to reinforce his self-image as a delinquent. His deviant behavior, which involved drug abuse and violence, was reinforced by his self-concept and the deviant values he learned from his family. Society finally placed the stamp of delinquency on Bill in juvenile court when he was adjudicated and sent to the state reformatory.

Being labeled a delinquent by the juvenile court validates a delinquent's self-concept and the delinquent behavior that emanates from this self-description. Following is a case of this dynamic factor in defining delinquency. I escorted a youth, George, who was fourteen at the time, into juvenile court when I worked in a juvenile detention institution in Newark, New Jersey. Prior to this court appearance, George had been involved in various thefts, gang fighting, and drug abuse. Despite several court appearances for these varied offenses, he had managed to avoid being sent to the state reformatory.

In our conversation prior to his court appearance, George revealed a great deal of anxiety about his behavior, his parents' reactions, and what was going to happen to him in court. The judge determined that probation was no longer feasible and sent George to the state reformatory for eighteen months.

When George and I left the court to return to the detention facility to prepare him for his transfer to the state reformatory, his earlier attitude of concern and anxiety was radically changed. He seemed angry, swaggered, and had a determined look on his face. On the way to the detention facility, I vividly recall his looking up at me with a snickering smile and flatly stating, "I guess I am now a juvenile delinquent." George now had the self-concept of "delinquent" officially conferred upon him by the courts. In further probing as to his feelings and attitudes, he revealed that this meant he had more status in his gang and that from here on "nobody cares and I may as well do anything I want."

This youth's attitude was typical of many who, when defined as a delinquent by the courts, define themselves in this way more definitively and take on the attitudes and behavior of a delinquent. The label becomes more of a fact. Based on their research with regard to this factor, Walter Reckless, Simon Dinitz, and Ellwyn Murray (1956) stated: "The concept of self as a delinquent may work negatively. To attribute certain abstract characteristics and predictions of delinquency to certain individuals or groups could possibly influence persons to accept the ascribed roles, a self-fulfilling prophecy. Applying labels and epithets such as 'juvenile delinquent' and 'young criminal' does not help anyone to think well of himself. Active, aggressive, impetuous, sometimes violent and irrational behavior does not automatically mean that a child is a junior public enemy. Equating healthy defiance with delinquency may encourage a child to think of himself as a delinquent." (P. 745)

In summary, delinquency has several related phases and characteristics:

1. The youth is sexually, physically, or emotionally abused, neglected, or abandoned by his or her primary socializing agents—his or her parents.

2. Because he or she is treated in negative ways with limited respect, the child feels humiliated, demeaned, and unworthy. As a consequence of this pattern of negative socialization, the child develops a low self-concept and feels self-hatred. He or she thinks on some deeper emotional level, "If these important, powerful people in my life think that I am stupid, inadequate and unworthy of love and respect, I must be a terrible person."

3. Mixed in with his or her low self-esteem, the child develops a rage against the people—the parents—who have abused or neglected him or her and this rage is often displaced onto people in the general society.

4. The juvenile court reflects society's viewpoint and puts the final stamp of the label "juvenile delinquent" on the youth.

5. Children with delinquent self-concepts tend to care little about what happens to them. They not only do not value themselves, it carries over into their attitude toward other people in their world. Their "I don't give a damn about anything" attitude, mixed with the rage that derives from being abused, creates a youth who is apt to be violent and has a disrespect for the rights of others.

6. The youth who has little regard for him- or herself or for others, is most likely to be delinquency prone. The emotional pain that results from the abuse and consequential low self-concept motivates law-violating behavior. A significant facet of this low self-esteem involves a "suicidal tendency" that is characteristically acted out in the delinquent behavior of violence and substance abuse.

Application of Theory to Treatment Approaches

An examination of the foregoing theories discussed in this and the preceding chapters in Part 5 clearly indicates that some theories contribute more than others to an understanding of particular types of crime and delinquency. In this regard, I refer to the three types of delinquent personalities delineated earlier: (1) socialized, (2) neurotic, and (3) sociopathic delinquents.

The activities of socialized delinquents may best be explained by such theories as differential association, anomie (Durkheim and Merton), social alienation, and conflict theory. The high incidence of juvenile delinquency in the United States is best explained by modern positivism, the cultural dimension, economic determinism, social disorganization, culture conflict, and group-conflict theories. Other theories that help to explain the socialized delinquent include group theory, the subculture of delinquency (Cohen), the adolescent striving for manhood (Bloch and Niederhoffer), delinquency and opportunity (Cloward and Ohlin), and lower-class culture (Kvaraceus and Miller). Psychoanalytic theory aids in explaining the neurotic delinquent, and my concept of abuse and self-concept helps to account for the sociopathic delinquent. As yet, no single causal theory has been developed that explains all types of delinquent personalities and certainly not all juvenile delinquent behavior. The various theories presented are useful in explaining certain types but not all causes of delinquency. In brief, no causal theory, in my view, comprehensively explains all delinquent behavior.

A particular theory can lead to programs and policies for effectively treating delinquent behavior. For example, if we believe that there is a degree of validity to the proposition that poverty causes delinquency, then we should implement programs for creating jobs for the unemployed and work out a more equitable distribution of the society's wealth. If the negative self-concept problem is ameliorated in the family, this can result in reducing delinquency. In the following chapters a variety of institutional programs, therapies, and intervention strategies for preventing and controlling delinquency are presented.

PART 6

The Prevention, Treatment, and Control of Delinquency

CHAPTERS

CHAPTER 14

COMMUNITY TREATMENT PROGRAMS FOR DELINQUENTS

Caring adult male role models in direct communication with at-risk youths can be a vital force in preventing delinquency.

Early on in the career of an incipient juvenile delinquent, an effort is made in the school and a variety of community-based programs to prevent and control his or her deviant behavior. It is not unusual for a youth to have four to eight juvenile court appearances before he or she is referred to some diversionary program like a community program or placed on probation. When these treatment methods fail, often as a last resort the youth is sent to a custodial institution. This chapter reviews the variety of options in the community that are available for preventing and controlling delinquency.

Youths in the justice system may have many of the same health problems as other adolescents; however, they are particularly at risk for sexually transmitted diseases (STDs), unwanted pregnancies, and drug or alcohol dependencies. Youths in the juvenile justice system engage in sexual activity more often and at younger ages then do other adolescents (Office of Juvenile Justice and Delinquency Prevention, 1997). As previously indicated, many juvenile offenders have histories of sexual abuse. With limited exposure to pregnancy and STD prevention programs, these youths often hold unrealistic views about sexuality and childbearing. Both adolescent boys and girls are often are burdened too early in life with unwanted pregnancies and children.

A wide variety of therapeutic methods have evolved for treating juvenile offenders in the community. Dominant among these are probation and parole. Another strategy involves community delinquency prevention programs in high-delinquency areas. These varied approaches rest on the assumption that there are advantages to treating a juvenile offender or at-risk youth in the community.

The advantages of community-based programs are that they are less costly and have a better chance for success than institutional programs. The social environment is more natural than the onerous and artificial milieu of a custodial institution, and it is in the community that the youths will probably live after their custodial situation. The prime disadvantage of treating offenders in the community is that they are apt to be living within the same environmental set of causal factors that originally produced their crime or delinquency. These negative forces must be vitiated or overcome if these individuals are to function as law-abiding citizens, whether or not they spend time in a correctional institution.

In addition to the standard approaches of probation, a variety of other approaches attempt to prevent delinquency. These include attacks on the problem at various levels in the social system. Macrosociological programs, or efforts at large-scale social change, have been organized to provide opportunities for more people to achieve the culturally approved goals of the society without having to resort to illegal means. These

① ② ③
include increased access to education, training, and employment for all
members of the society, with special emphasis on those in the lowest
socioeconomic categories.

On another level, neighborhood and community programs have
been designed to reduce the incidence of criminality and delinquency in
problem areas. These programs are based on the assumption that certain
urban areas with high delinquency rates tend to foster crime and delinquency and that the development of indigenous anticriminal leadership
and services in these areas would reduce the incidence of criminal and
delinquent behavior.

Varied clinical treatment programs, largely psychological in orientation, have been developed. Community programs include psychiatric MICRO
casework, social group work, and combinations of these services to individuals and families. In these program contexts, professional therapists
attempt to modify attitudes and behavior patterns of persons deemed likely
to engage in delinquent behavior. (Various therapeutic techniques utilized
by professional therapists for delinquents in and out of custodial institutions, including individual, group, and psychodrama therapy, are presented in chapter 16, and the "therapeutic community" for delinquents is
discussed in chapter 17.)

Community Child Guidance and Area Programs for Delinquency Prevention

A specific approach geared to a variety of problems juvenile offenders confront in their communities that evolved in the twentieth century is the
"child-guidance" clinic. The first clinic of this type directed at delinquency
prevention was established by Dr. William Healy in Chicago in 1909 as an
adjunct of the Chicago juvenile court. Since then, almost every large city in
the United States has established one or more child-guidance clinics offering treatment for young children and adolescents. These services are not
limited to children considered delinquent or diagnosed as predelinquent;
they have been considered useful in preventing delinquent behavior.
Problem children are referred to these clinics by social work agencies,
schools, police, and the juvenile courts.

One important guidance clinic program that was in place from
1936 through 1945 was the Cambridge-Somerville Youth Clinic in Boston.
Research was built into the program to evaluate the effectiveness of child
guidance clinics on delinquency. The Cambridge-Somerville Youth Study
was instituted in Boston for this purpose. On the basis of interviews with
teachers, psychiatric evaluations, and psychological tests, some 750 boys

attending schools in Cambridge and Somerville, Massachusetts, were classified as to the likelihood of their becoming delinquent. By a random process, 325 were assigned to an experimental group to receive preventive treatment, and a matched group of 325 boys was studied as a control group. The experimental group was provided with family guidance, individual counseling, tutoring, camp and recreational facilities, correction of health defects, medical care, and when deemed necessary, their families received financial assistance from community agencies. Services were provided for an average of five years. The results of the study indicated that the program was effective with some at-risk children but not with others (Powers and Witmer, 1951).

In contrast to the child guidance or clinical approach, which attempts to work on children's emotional problems, so-called area programs have been developed to change the social environment or neighborhood of the child. Such programs coordinate the activities of existing facilities and agencies and establish additional facilities if this seems advisable. Community organization experts attempt to activate or organize councils representing as many social welfare agencies as will cooperate and sometimes seek to organize the people of the problem area into neighborhood committees for action.

In Chicago in 1933, Clifford R. Shaw originated the first important program of this sort. Called the Chicago Area Project, the program was developed after the research of Shaw and his colleagues had clearly indicated that the slum areas of large cities were characterized by a disproportionately large number of delinquent children and criminals. These area programs are as relevant today as they were in the 1930s. Over the years, a number of neighborhood organizations have emerged in high delinquency areas, such as South Central Los Angeles and Chicago, in an attempt to control the delinquency and violent gang problems.

The Chicago Area Project was based on a number of assumptions that have become standard for programs of this type. In an article on the early area project, Solomon Kobrin (1959), who worked with Shaw, delineated a number of principles that are relevant to this type of community project and serve as guidelines:

> (1) In high-delinquency areas, delinquency is symptomatic of deeper social ills. It is a product of the social milieu. The same blighted areas that have high delinquency rates also have high rates of economic dependency, illness, infant mortality, substandard housing, and poverty. (2) Delinquency cannot be attributed to factors inherent in any race or nationality groups. (3) Delinquency in deteriorated areas may frequently be regarded as conformity to the expectations, behavior patterns, and values of the groups of boys in the neighborhood. (4) Most delinquents in

deteriorated areas are not inferior to children in the more privileged communities in any fundamental way. Delinquency is a part of the social tradition of the neighborhood; a large segment of the population tolerates, reinforces, and even encourages delinquent behavior. (5) Current practices in dealing with delinquency have been ineffective. It is not possible to save a boy apart from his family or community. A community with a new morale and new leadership directed in socially constructive channels is essential. (6) The local neighborhood can be organized to deal effectively with its own problems. There exists in the neighborhood sufficient indigenous leadership to bring about changes in attitudes, sentiments, ideals, and loyalties for the construction of a more acceptable community lifestyle. (1959, p. 69)

An innovative part of the Chicago Area Project was the preparation of offenders for return to the community. Offenders soon to be released were visited in their institutions, encouraged to participate in committee activities upon their return, and helped to establish contacts with employers and other local groups. These legitimate activities furnished the framework within which the offender returning from an institution could become accepted and to think of him- or herself as a full member of the community.

The social climate of a community can be expected to improve as the people in it assume greater responsibility for its direction. A community administered by outsiders is less likely to develop an *esprit de corps*. The Chicago Area Project demonstrated that people capable of supplying the leadership necessary to increase constructive action can be found in deteriorated areas of our cities. While the effect of the Chicago Area Project on delinquency was not precisely measured, in all probability delinquency was substantially reduced as a consequence of the effort. The Chicago Area Project was the pioneer model for many comparable programs that emerged in cities around the United States, including a project I directed in New York City, modeled after the Chicago approach.

The Adult-Youth Association

In 1953, when I acquired the position of director of the Morningside Heights Program in New York City, I made it a condition of my contract that I would spend some time in Chicago studying the Chicago Area Project. Over a two-week period in Chicago, I met Clifford Shaw and was shown around the city by this pioneer in the field of delinquency prevention. As a consequence of this experience, I constructed a program in New York City built on the concept and experiences of these earlier community-based organizations—especially Shaw's. The program I developed was called the Adult-Youth Association (AYA). Like the Chicago Area Project, the AYA program encompassed a variety of intervention methods and focused on one of the essential causes of delinquency and gangs, the absence of positive adult role models in the hoods or barrios.

The situation of boys without positive male role models can be effectively attacked by producing natural relationships through recreation, project planning, and other activities that bring adults and youths together in constructive interaction. The use of citizen-volunteers from a community who are willing to give of their time and energy is essential to an AYA operation. The usual approach of getting volunteers to help a social agency was reversed in AYA. Our social agency and its professional staff attempted to help and support concerned adults who lived in the community to run their own programs that involved relating "naturally" with neighborhood youths.

The AYA-type project is especially successful and peeling off the more easily reached marginal gang youths and involving them in meaningful relationships with adults, thus helping to resolve the neighborhood adult-youth schism. The detached gang worker can serve as the bridge and coordinator for making this possible. The activities utilized are not the primary factors in the AYA program; rather, the involvement of adults from the neighborhood working with youths is at the core of the AYA approach.

The AYA approach can be self-perpetuating. Many individuals who successfully participated in the AYA program as youths tend to turn around at a later age and become role models for neighborhood youths. A goal in the AYA approach is to build it into the natural structure of the community, so that whether the professional agency that initiates the program continues or not, something positive is at work in a somewhat changed neighborhood. It operates in terms of the admonition: if you give people fish, they eat that day; however, if you teach them how to fish, they become self-sufficient and can feed themselves.

Recreation as an AYA Approach

In the process of planning a recreational activity, a natural interaction takes place that is difficult to duplicate. Emphasis should be placed on some degree of organized league activity rather than on random play. The organizational procedures required for finding a gym or field for the league, developing rules, age limits, team-size quotas, scheduling, and so on, involves adults and boys in a natural and productive interaction. The main sports that are attractive to boys include baseball, basketball, and football.

In developing an athletic league, care must be taken to not make any of the gangs in the community more cohesive. In using the league idea, efforts should be made to have the teams form around athletic ability rather than around gang affiliation. A good league will reshuffle the neighborhood's gang structure and thus minimize violent gang activity. Marginal gang members become involved in a social athletic club rather than their destructive gangs.

Building recreational activity into the social fabric of the neighborhood is basic. Emphasis should be placed on (1) maximizing the involvement of local adult volunteers; (2) utilizing neighborhood facilities, for example, gymnasiums, meeting rooms, halls, and so on; and (3) gaining monetary and moral support from local citizens. Whether the professional worker continues on the project or not, there should be sufficient community involvement to keep the adult-youth activity in motion. And "graduates" of the program should be encouraged to come back as responsible adults for the continuation of the program. This enables the program to be self-perpetuating.

Overly structured recreation programs prepared in advance by adults or professionals, into which youths are moved in an assembly-line fashion, are of limited help in involving the youths and resocializing them adequately. However, allowing youths to take a major role in defining what the activities will be, combined with the assistance of interested and inspired adult volunteers, produces activities that become part of the youths' natural milieu.

The Community Gang Committee

In the New York AYA project that I instituted and directed, the organization spearheaded a cooperative effort of social agencies and gang workers that became known as the West Side Gang Committee. Members of the committee included a number of ex-gangsters who had become responsible citizens, local police, interested citizens, and people from various social agencies in the community.

The Community Gang Committee met regularly and concentrated on exchanging information and knowledge about gang organization in the area. In addition to compiling data on gang patterns, the more than thirty members of the committee discussed effective programming for gang control and dealing with such special problems as drug dealing and drug addiction. Following is a summary of aims and activities developed and utilized by our gang committee:

1. *Gang information.* Information (both rumored and factual) about the size, organization, and so on of gangs and delinquent groups was shared among the members of the committee. This interaction was carried on through questionnaires, discussion at meetings, and phone calls.

2. *Gang-work techniques and methods.* The committee attempted to discuss and continually develop more effective techniques and methods for detecting, preventing, dealing with, and eliminating gangs and related individual problems. These methods including group discussion with gangsters, working out social agency-police-youth relationships, and dealing with gang-narcotics problems.

3. *Community education groups.* The committee disseminated information and educated the public on gang problems and issues of relevance.

4. The committee, through a local university, utilized college students who carried out limited-range surveys, research, and group therapy projects.

The treatment methodologies of group psychotherapy and psychodrama are a significant part of the described AYA approach and the various detached gang work programs and agencies devised for reaching delinquents. These treatment methods can be incorporated into programs in community centers, schools, and custodial institutions.

The Role of Local Citizen Leaders in Community Projects: Two Examples

At the heart of any effective community-based program are strong men and women leaders who emerge from the community. James Rainey (1997), in an article in the *Los Angeles Times,* described the work of such a "street crusader" named Evelio Franco.[1]

> In the wake of the 1992 LA riots, leaders of churches felt that they had to do something to respond to the poverty and despair that gripped much of Los Angeles. They were seeking to build social programs, job prospects and some threads of community unity. What they got, in the downtrodden San Fernando Valley community of North Hills, was Evelio Franco. Franco's official title was director of the church's Shalom Zone, a neighborhood agency formed by the church to foster community harmony. Franco took on several job descriptions: counselor, coach, translator, teacher, ombudsman, or simply padrino—godfather.
>
> When the poor and dispossessed Latino immigrants of North Hills had a problem with the police, a delinquent teenage son, the Internal Revenue Service, or an uncooperative landlord, they turned to the forty-two-year-old former aerospace worker. One

---

1. For an additional analysis of the value of community programs, see "Beacons of Hope: Community Centers," National Institute of Justice, January 1996.

community worker described Franco as follows, "He reminds me of one of those forts out in the West. He is out there all on his own making a stand." Franco confronted gang members who were caught distributing crack cocaine to schoolchildren. After a tense standoff of several days, the dealers were driven, at least temporarily, from a street corner not far from the church. Another community worker commented, "Evelio is willing to go into one of the most dangerous communities in Los Angeles, a neighborhood where the people are afraid, and put aside that fear and do whatever is necessary to help the kids and the people in that community."

In some community improvement projects, ex-offenders who have changed their lives to become law-abiding citizens help at-risk youngsters in their neighborhood. Michael Janofsky (1997) describes an example of this community approach in Washington, D.C.

The violent incident that provoked action on the part of an alliance of ex-offenders was an unusually dramatic murder in Washington, D.C. Walking home from school one day in January 1997, twelve-year-old Darryl Hall was viciously beaten by three teen-aged gang members, forced into a car, and killed. His body was found three days later in a ravine near his home with a bullet wound in the back of his head.

A few days later, eight men gathered as they had on Sunday nights for the last six years, and all they could talk about was Darryl's death and the insanity of four lives wasted—his and those of the three teenagers who were arrested by district police officers and charged with the killing. "The next morning, Tyrone called me and said he couldn't sleep," said Arthur Rush, one of the eight, referring to his friend and colleague Tyrone Parker. "We all couldn't sleep because of the viciousness of the crime. We had done some outreach before in that neighborhood; we once got a drug dealer off the street. We all knew we had to do something." The eight men called themselves the Alliance of Concerned Men of Washington, D.C., a collection of middle-aged former felons, substance abusers, and inmates who share an extraordinary history.

These men were all friends as youths growing up in low-income neighborhoods of Northeast Washington. They went their separate ways into hellish worlds of crime, drugs, homelessness, and incarceration, only to emerge as young adults who found salvation, jobs, families, and, eventually, each other again. Convinced it was God's work that transformed and reunited them, they vowed to return to the streets as a group to try breaking the cycle of crime and hopelessness that produced them and teenagers like the killers of Darryl Hall.

Within weeks of Darryl's death, the alliance intervened

with the two factions of a gang that had been terrorizing his Southeast neighborhood. They mediated a truce, brought the warring sides together as friends, helped them find jobs, and encouraged them to dream beyond hoping to reach an eighteenth birthday.

At a banquet on March 5, 1997, in Washington, the president of the six-year-old alliance, Pete L. Jackson, fifty-one, and six people from similar groups around the country were honored for their efforts in saving the lives of young people in their communities—as well as their own. This was the fifth such annual award ceremony, organized by the Washington-based National Center for Neighborhood Enterprise, a sixteen-year-old organization founded on the premise that the most effective solutions to urban ills often come from the communities themselves, rather than government. The center coordinates efforts of groups like the alliance in thirty-eight states and further assists them by raising money and helping find jobs for the young people they are turning away from crime.

The center seeks no government support, other than work opportunities through local agencies, like the $6.50-an-hour jobs of painting, landscaping, and trash removal that David I. Gilmore, the court-appointed receiver of the district's public housing authority, has provided for twenty of the Southeast gang members. Since they began working last month, peace has prevailed in their neighborhood, and residents say they feel safe for the first time in decades.

"What all these people have in common," Robert L. Woodson, founder and president of the center, said of the groups around the country, "is that they are not motivated by career advancement or profit. What motivates them is a commitment of heart and a commitment to the neighborhoods." Like other groups in Washington and beyond, he added, the Alliance of Concerned Men came together because "they saw a need, and they responded to the need." In addition to mediating gang disputes, the alliance has organized two other community programs, including one that arranges for children to visit their fathers in prison. Woodson stated that heart and dedication only reach so far. The other key components of the alliance's success, he said, are the members past experience with crime, which allowed them to open communications with the gang members, and the willingness of someone in the community to create jobs as an alternative to criminal behavior. The combination, Woodson said, has convinced center officials that they now have a model intervention program to replicate in other cities.

One of the group's honorees, fifty-one-year-old Pete Jackson's life was typical among the alliance members. Growing up poor and without a father, he was lured into the streets as a teenager and quickly fell into a life of crime. He robbed stores and banks, sold drugs, and abused alcohol. In

1965, at age eighteen, he was convicted of armed robbery. After a couple of years in a youth prison, he returned to school, got a degree in sociology, and began working as a drug counselor for the same prison system that housed him as an inmate. That was twenty-six years ago. He is now deputy warden.

The alliance members discussed their experiences and agreed that they had much in common with gang members today. But not everything is the same as it was in the old days, and that's why the members say their work is so urgent now. Many recalled that no matter how contentious relations grew between rival groups when they were young, conflicts were generally settled with fists, not guns. When the alliance brought the Southeast gang members together in a room, they noticed all the teenagers were wearing bulletproof vests.

The men could not recall any fights in their day that involved children as young as twelve. "If you were in a fight and were beating the other guy bad enough, you would stop and ask him if he's all right," said James Alsobrooks, now a car salesman. By contrast, Parker, who was once shot in the back by police after robbing a bank, described a recent encounter with the younger brother of a gang member who told him how he watched his older brother die after a rival shot him. The little boy told Parker that his brother had remained still after taking several nonlethal shots, but the shooter realized he was faking death and returned to finish the job, "putting four slugs into his head."

Parker, forty-nine, the alliance founding president, served almost eight years on various charges and remains on parole, himself, through 2013. Seven years ago, his nineteen-year-old son, Rodney, was shot to death.

City police officials, who say one hundred or more gangs may be operating in the district, have not entirely blessed efforts of the alliance in Darryl Hall's neighborhood. Last week, the department announced that it was intensifying police presence in seven high-crime areas, one near where Darryl lived. Some of the alliance members wondered how effective those police efforts would be. "Ministers have tried reaching these kids, the police, sociologists, psychologists, teachers, politicians—and they still can't figure it out," said Rush, a former homeless heroin addict who was now a substance abuse therapist and family counselor. "But we know these kids. They're lost, caught up in the wrong thing like we were. Our experience and life styles have taught us certain things. In a way, we have been preparing for this job all our lives."

This approach of utilizing ex-offenders, whom I have termed "experience therapists," for preventing and controlling delinquency is discussed more fully in chapter 17.

④ The Detached Gang Worker Approach

One methodology expressly designed for controlling violent gangs that has been effectively employed is the "detached gang worker" approach. In this approach a professional, often a probation officer or a social worker, is assigned to the gang problem in a hood or barrio. Ex-gangsters have also been employed as detached gang workers. The goal of the worker is to reach out to the youths in an area and redirect them from destructive gang behavior patterns into constructive activities in their community.

A significant detached-worker program, which has served as a model for gang control in large urban areas nationally since its inception in 1946, is the approach designed and utilized by the New York City Youth Board. It is an approach to gangs in the community that is currently utilized in cities throughout the country. The Youth Board established seven goals for work with street gangs: (1) reduction of antisocial behavior, particularly street fighting; (2) friendly relationships with others street gangs; (3) increased democratic participation within the gangs; (4) broadened social horizons; (5) responsibility for self-direction; (6) improved personal and social adjustment of the individual; and (7) improved community relations (Welfare Council of New York City, 1950).

Reaching the gang through detached youth workers is often effective. However, the process entails pitfalls not specified in policy or in the manuals. Foremost among these potential problems is the possibility of inaccurately diagnosing gang structure. Distinctly different methods are required for treating the more social gangs of youths and the more aggressive, violent gangs. Gang workers, in their initial period of intervention, must accurately diagnose the structure of the gang they are working with (Yablonsky, 1997).

Different levels of involvement among core and more marginal gangsters also dictate different treatment prescriptions. The marginal younger gangster can generally be reached through the conventional methods of recreation, providing a job, and counseling, whereas core gangsters require a different approach that often requires working with them in a custodial institution.

The diagnostic assumption that working through the violent gang leader will redirect the gang can pose another problem. Often working through the leader of a violent gang solidifies its structure. Official sanction of sociopathic gang leaders by a worker may give them more status. Merely gaining access to violent gang participants is frequently mistaken for acceptance and rapport. Contrary to popular belief, getting in touch with a gang is not difficult for a detached worker. However, the meaning given to the relationship by gangsters varies and is of major significance. If the gang

410

worker appears as a "mark" to most members, a "do-gooder" who doesn't know the score, the gang will simply use the worker to get cigarettes, or whatever favors they can obtain. Some naive detached gang workers, rather than resocializing gang members, are manipulated by the gang. They may rationalize their personal motives toward "adventuresome" gang behavior as necessary to maintain their relationship. In fact, this behavior is not necessary. Becoming a "gang member" by identifying with the gang neutralizes the worker's impact as a positive adult role model. The negative nature of the gang worker's mistaken assumptions is revealed by the following statement of a detached gang worker who, in my view, was duped by the gang he was sent to change: "One afternoon the boys were hanging around and a 'crap' game started. I decided it would be strategic for me to participate so that I might get closer to them and improve my rapport. During the course of the game one of the fellows turned to me and said, 'Say, man, you're supposed to be out here to change us and it seems like we're making you like us instead.'"

When an overzealous detached gang worker is duped by the gang or misinterprets the meaning of a situation, the worker is reinforcing rather than modifying their behavior. The gang worker is, in effect, a carrier of the values and norms of the larger society. Initially, gangsters resist the intrusion and possible changes in their subculture. The gang will attempt to get what it can without changing and then seduce the worker into becoming part of the gang. The gang worker should be aware of the negative implications of compromising the relevant norms of the larger society in order to gain false acceptance and superficial approval.

Several issues require revision and redefinition if this approach is to modify rather than solidify or reinforce violent-gang structure and behavior.

1. It is necessary for the detached gang worker to be trained to properly diagnose the structure of the gang he or she is working with.

2. The accurate diagnosis of the gang will reveal different degrees of participation and involvement on the part of each gangster. Marginal members may be worked with through more conventional treatment approaches; core violent gang participants and leaders may require a different and more intense form of treatment, including incarceration.

3. A violent gang can be more integrated by working through some leaders and this error reinforces the gang's cohesion.

4. The detached gang worker is an official representative of the more inclusive society and must avoid sanctioning or participating in deviance to gain what will turn out to be a false acceptance and rapport. He or she should serve as an adequate law-abiding adult role model.

Utilizing these principles and methods, the worker should consciously act upon the gang and dismember it. The marginal members, once they become hooked into more constructive enterprises, will find less energy and time for violent gang activity. The constructive activities should be viewed less for their intrinsic value and more for their usefulness as a means for extricating marginal youths from participation in the violent gang and involving them in activity within the larger society. The core gangsters who require closer supervision and treatment need to be incarcerated for a time in a therapeutic community oriented program.

The Los Angeles County Probation Department Detached Gang Worker Program

The Los Angeles County Probation Department has instituted a most effective detached gang worker program that utilizes probation officers working with gangsters both in the community and in custodial camp institutions. The department's gang workers are knowledgeable about gang structure, and they effectively combine their efforts with a blend of aggressive supervision, caring social work, and access to a number of custodial facilities. Marginal gang youths referred to the department from the courts are worked with in the community where they receive appropriate counseling and job training.

Hard-core recalcitrant gangsters, after adjudication, are placed in custody in a probation camp. The camps have a variety of programs that focus on changing gang affiliation, individual and group counseling, and preparation for the youth's reentry into their communities. Some of these camps have a military-type boot camp approach. The department's varied programs have been successful in redirecting many delinquents from continuing their delinquent activities and being sent to California prisons to returning to their communities with some social skills for leaving their gangs and becoming responsible law-abiding citizens.

Leo Cortez: A Detached Gang Worker in Action

The intervention of detached gang workers in a community can make a positive difference. An excellent example of this is revealed in the following report by Bella Stumbo (1976) on the work of one effective probation department detached gang worker, Leo Cortez. His response to a gang shooting in Los Angeles indicates how a detached worker can effectively intervene in a gang situation.

The night before, a youth with a sawed-off shotgun had shot a middle-aged mother who was picnicking with several small children in an East Los Angeles Park. And now, although the woman's sons and their friends were probably plotting a bloody gang revenge at this very minute, Leo Cortez found himself sitting inside a small county office while assorted law officers and social workers drank coffee and wondered what to do about the youth gang problem in East Los Angeles. At times such as these, Leo Cortez, thirty-seven, a county youth worker and one-time gang member, wonders why he isn't out on the streets working with those he understands so well. So well, in fact, that many residents of that small 8.36-square-mile enclave known as unincorporated East Los Angeles, population about 140,000, are convinced that Leo Cortez has probably averted more gang wars and saved more lives than all the sheriff's deputies combined. . . .

Cortez drove directly to County—USC General Hospital, where he made his way through the maze of corridors to her room, a crowded ward on the ninth floor. Momentarily, he stood at the bedside, silently surveying the damage. Her bruised body was riddled with at least 50 shotgun pellets, two of them only a fraction away from her right eye. . . . Because she was an East Los Angeles mother, she understood gangs. Her two sons belonged to one of the roughest gangs in the area. And, she whispered, with weary acceptance, "They only try to kill each other. . . ." The woman's clouded eyes momentarily cleared, filled with sudden, sharp alarm. "Leo, don't let them go for revenge. Make them stay home."

At a later gang meeting, Cortez heard the typical calls for revenge. "Man, tonight we'll go down there and kill a couple of those vatos (bad dudes)," declared one skinny youth of fourteen. The only problem was that, though they all suspected the assailant had come from one particular rival gang, nobody was sure. "I tell you something," shouted another boy of eighteen, whose nickname was "Little Boy" and whose eyes were glazed over by something much stronger than liquor. "When we go, we'll be cool. We won't go around shooting women and kids. We'll kill the vato who did it."

At the meeting, patiently, in Spanish, Cortez urged them all to leave the park (where they met). Getting arrested wouldn't help anything. Better yet, why not visit the hospital? With surprising passivity, like small, uncertain children, most quickly agreed. Even Little Boy, who was reeling so badly he could hardly walk. And so Cortez gave him a lift home, not knowing, when he let the boy out, that in two days Little Boy would be dead himself—shot to death by youths from another barrio. . . .

Leo Cortez seems to know not only the names of almost every youth in East Los Angeles but also the names of their friends and their enemies. He also knows which kids are hard-core

413

murderers, which ones can be influenced to kill, which ones never could, and, finally, which youths are "locos"—crazy enough to be altogether unpredictable.

According to Cortez, "What most people don't understand is that the kids out here, the gang members, don't consider themselves criminals. Here, even when they kill, national standards just don't apply. Because here, a gang member regards himself as a soldier, you understand? Even if he's only patrolling a few square blocks. No matter how small his turf is, he still regards himself as a patriot . . . protecting his homeland. Because that's all he's got, all he's ever had. . . . Too many kids nowadays aren't following any of the old rules. In the old days, gang members made certain that when they went on a retaliatory raid, they hit their enemy. But now, they often are sloppy, or heedless, simply speeding by an enemy house at night and spraying it with bullets, regardless of who's inside. I think that's why there's more violence here now. . . . They've got no future, nothing but their barrio and their 'homeboys.' So, they can only prove their manhood by standing up and getting killed, or killing."

FATALISM

⑤ Halfway Houses and Community Treatment

Another significant approach that has been developed to prevent and control delinquency in the community is the halfway house. It is based on the realistic premise that most inmates of prisons and training schools were, prior to their incarceration, members of delinquent groups with subcultures deviating materially from that of the dominant culture in our society. While in an institution, inmates are subjected to a continuous acculturation and assimilation of the delinquent value system. The roles played by the inmates and the roles they are required to play upon their release are vastly different in most important aspects.

While inside, youths adjust to prison life, and upon release they may be expected to have difficulty reestablishing occupational and family roles in the community. They need time to adjust and to reconnect to society. Institutions organized to facilitate the necessary transition are called halfway houses, to symbolize their status as an establishment between a prison and the residence of a free citizen. Halfway houses, as they are now constituted, provide a temporary residence for released offenders. Typically, a halfway house is a residence for twenty to fifty youths under the supervision of a correctional authority. While there, the former convicts can look for a job, work on a job, meet with family and friends, and begin to assume roles normally acceptable in the community. This process is facilitated by the methodologies of probation and parole.

414

Probation and Parole

The concept of probation and parole originated in the late eighteenth century when a shoemaker named John Augustus thought it would be a good idea to treat juveniles who committed illegal acts in the community rather than place them in custody. Since that time probation and parole have become methodologies utilized in every federal, state, and local effort to treat and control delinquency.

Probation and parole have become highly developed approaches for working with delinquents in the community. Probation represents a sentence imposed by a court in lieu of confinement. Delinquents sentenced to probation by a judge are relatively free as long as they conform to the conditions imposed by the court. The juvenile is placed under the supervision of a probation officer, who is a peace officer charged with seeing that the court's conditions are met.

Once police decide to refer a youth to the juvenile court rather than using the informal alternatives available at the time of arrest, the youth typically is referred to an intake unit of the court, usually staffed by probation officers. The sole function of intake units is to screen the cases referred by police or other individuals and to determine whether a formal delinquency petition should be filed in the court. If a decision is made to file a petition, an investigation of the case is made to determine the validity of the allegations in the petition. The intake officer may decide that the allegations are without basis or that the case may be difficult to substantiate, and he or she may suggest that the juvenile be informally processed without further court intervention.

Probation officers are also involved in the detention decision. Typically, when a juvenile is arrested, he or she is taken into custody, booked, and often transferred to a local detention unit to await further review by the intake officer. The detention facility may be the local county jail, where the youth may be mixed with adult offenders, or a specialized juvenile detention unit staffed with counselors and other specialists. In cases where the juvenile is referred to an intake unit, the probation officer must decide whether to further detain the child or release him or her to the custody of an adult.

Parole is an approach that is implemented like probation in the community. The major difference between probation and parole is that the parolee has served at least part of his or her sentence in a correctional institution. The juvenile is released from the correctional institution prior to the expiration of the sentence and allowed to serve the remainder of the sentence in the community, provided he or she lives up to the conditions imposed by the parole system.

Probation

As indicated, probation is a treatment program in which the final action in an adjudicated offender's case is suspended, so that the juvenile remains at liberty, subject to conditions imposed by the court, under the supervision and guidance of a probation officer. The correctional system provides for the treatment and the supervision of offenders in the community by placing them on probation in lieu of confinement in a custodial institution. In most states, probationers serve the sentence of a court under the supervision of a probation officer assigned by the court. Judges have broad powers in this situation and set the conditions of probation and the length of the supervision period. They maintain the power to order revocation of probation, usually for a violation of one of the conditions set or for the commission of another offense. The effect of revocation is to send a probationer to a custodial institution.

A few states have centralized probation systems, but most of the approximate three thousand counties in the United States exercise autonomy within limits set by state statutes. For example, the probation system in California is a centralized system that authorizes each county to provide facilities, services, and regulations. Probation is the most common disposition ordered by juvenile courts. In 1994, courts with juvenile jurisdiction handled 1.6 million delinquency cases. Probation supervision was the most severe disposition in nearly 539,000 of these cases (about one-third of all delinquency cases). The number of cases placed on probation increased 32 percent between 1985 and 1994. In the same time period, the overall delinquency caseload increased 41 percent. Compared with other juvenile court dispositions, the relative growth in cases placed on probation was low. For example, the number of cases waived to criminal court rose 71 percent, and the number placed out of the home increased 58 percent. However, because probation is the most common disposition ordered by juvenile courts, the absolute growth in the number of cases placed on probation is much greater than the growth for other dispositions (Sickmund, 1997).

The probation caseload essentially mirrors the overall delinquency caseload in terms of its demographic profile and trends. In 1994, the proportion of cases involving white youths placed on probation was 68 percent (down from 73 percent in 1985), the proportion of black youths was 29 percent (up from 25 percent), and the proportion of youths of other races was 3 percent (virtually unchanged). As with the delinquency caseload overall, the majority of cases placed on probation involved males (about 80 percent). The female proportion of the probation caseload did not change much over the ten-year period from 18 percent in 1985 to 21 percent in 1994. Youths aged fourteen to sixteen comprised about 60 percent of juveniles on probation (Sickmund, 1997).

Probation can be either voluntary or court ordered. Some youths are ordered to probation after adjudication of delinquency (analogous to conviction). In contrast to these court-ordered probation placements, some youths who are not adjudicated delinquent voluntarily agree to abide by certain probation conditions, often with the understanding that if they successfully complete their probationary period, their case will be terminated without any formal processing. In 1994, adjudicated delinquents ordered to probation accounted for nearly half of all delinquency cases placed on probation (nearly 265,000 cases). In the remaining half of delinquency cases, the youths agreed to some form of voluntary or informal probation. The number of cases resulting in a formal order of probation rose 41 percent from 1985 through 1994. In comparison, informal probations increased 25 percent, reflecting the general trend over the period toward more formal processing of delinquency cases. The likelihood of probation for cases in which the juvenile was adjudicated delinquent dropped slightly from 1985 to 1994. Drug offenses were the only category showing a substantial reduction in the likelihood of probation (Sickmund, 1997).

Barry Krisberg and James F. Austin (1993) describe the role of the probation officer as follows:

> In theory, probation officers represent a more sophisticated or professionalized approach to juvenile delinquency than police. They tend to be college educated and are required to write numerous reports—essentially mini-legal briefs—arguing for dispositions that serve both the interest of the youth and that of the community. To present intelligent and persuasive arguments before the court, the probation officer must be aware of principles of law relating to jurisdiction, evidentiary restrictions, appeal motions, and dispositional alternatives. The officer also must be a therapist able to diagnose the etiology of the delinquent's problem and administer the appropriate assistance. Although probation officers are expected to possess academic skills and broad knowledge, this professional image invariably is negated by the reality of most probation departments. (P. 53)

Four basic techniques are employed by most probation officers (Dressler, 1969):

1. *Manipulative techniques.* The environment may be manipulated in the interests of the person seeking help. The end product is usually something material and tangible received by the individual under care, for example, financial aid rendered by the agency or an employer persuaded to rehire a discharged worker.

2. *Executive techniques.* The probation officer may refer the individual to other resources in the community for help that the correctional agency

cannot render. For example, the probation officer may refer the individual to a legal aid society or secure public assistance for her or him.

3. *Guidance techniques.* The probation officer may give personal advice and guidance on problems not requiring complex psychological techniques. The advice is likely to be fairly direct and the guidance comparatively superficial. The end product is intangible, although it may facilitate the achievement of tangible goals. For example, the individual is advised how to budget his or her income or helped to explore the possibilities of training for a job.

4. *Counseling techniques.* These are based largely upon psychological orientations and require considerable skill. The services are intangible, concerned with deep-seated problems in the emotional area, for example, aid in adjusting a family situation or help in overcoming specific emotional conflicts.

It is obvious that a probation officer cannot possibly perform all these services for a large caseload. Most probation departments have an insufficient number of probation officers and not all of them are adequately trained. Contacts are infrequent and services inadequate. Nevertheless, the success of probation, as measured by those who complete probation without revocation, has been surprisingly high.

Because probation has always been regarded as a form of leniency through which the judge permits a convicted person to remain in the community instead of being sent to an institution, the power of the judge to impose conditions is seldom challenged. The courts have even upheld conditions of probation that restrict the constitutional rights of a probationer, where the restrictions have a clear-cut relationship to his or her rehabilitation. Probation officers are generally given great discretion in interpreting the conditions imposed by the court. For example, one condition imposed on a probationer is that he or she not associate with known offenders. For many years this provision interfered with the application of group therapy to offenders on probation; however, in recent years there has been a more logical attitude in place that allows for group therapy.

Contact is generally established when, having been placed on probation by a court, a juvenile or adult appears for his or her first appointment. The probation officer to whom the person is assigned has usually received an advance report from the probation officer who investigated the case. During the initial interview, the ward's attitude is of primary concern and often determines the treatment program. The resistant person is generally seen more frequently than the person who relates easily.

Priority for treatment is usually given to (1) those probationers the probation officers feel they can definitely help, and (2) those probationers against whom the most complaints have been made. The probation officer makes an effort to influence the parents as well as probationer. The probation officer has the power to remove the probationer from the home and place him or her in a foster home, or remove the probationer from the community and place him or her in a custodial institution.

Probation officers have two major problems in their work: the amount of their paperwork and the size of their caseloads. The vast amount of paperwork that is required is responsible for much of the ineffectiveness of probation, since it takes valuable time away from the vital human association between the probation officer and client. Probation officers often cut their interviews short to allow themselves enough time to finish their paperwork. Almost all probation officers are dissatisfied with the size of their caseloads. One probation officer I interviewed had 226 individuals under his supervision and met with approximately ninety wards a month. He had little time to attempt rehabilitation or therapy of any kind. Even with smaller caseloads, a client is seldom seen more than twice a month by his or her probation officer.

A juvenile probation officer with a large caseload often places clients in one of three categories: (1) minimum services (seen once a month or less); (2) medium services (seen once a month); and (3) maximum services (seen frequently). Normally, only about ten clients would fall into the third category and be seen once or possibly two to three times a week. Obviously, youths seen once a month or less do not receive the attention they require. The probation officer's definition of his or her task and the style in which the officer functions are significant vectors in the degree of success.

Parole   FRENCH → "WORD"

Parole is a treatment program somewhat different than probation; the offender, after serving part of a term in an institution, is conditionally released under the supervision and treatment of a parole officer. Three types of agencies are empowered to grant parole: a board set up for the correctional institution; a central parole board for a state; and a group of officials, usually called a parole commission.

It is expected that, while in the state institution, a youth will be provided with job training or some vocational skills that will better prepare him or her for life in the community. Recreational, educational, and vocational training facilities are intended to help in rehabilitation. Medical, psychological, and counseling programs, group therapy sessions, and other therapeutic processes are supposed to prepare the individual to reenter society. A counseling program is one important aspect of a prerelease preparation program.

Parole is a continuation of the correctional process. The goal is to help reestablish the parolee in the community as a law-abiding citizen. Parole supervision includes efforts to discover the strengths in the parolee's personality and his or her ways of dealing with emotional problems. The parole officer cannot permit the parolee to become dependent on him or her for all decisions and solutions to the parolee's problems. The individual on parole must learn to handle successfully difficult situations that may arise. However, the parole officer should be available to help a parolee when required.

A parole officer, very much like a probation officer, has three main functions in his or her relationship with the parolee. The first is to use his or her knowledge of community resources to help the parolee adjust to society. The second is to provide or obtain treatment for the parolee when required. This includes dealing with psychological problems. The third function is supervision. The parole officer is supposed to do what he or she can to keep the parolee from violating the conditions of parole. The officer may visit the parolee's home or work location to determine his or her progress. The officer may also interview family members and other important persons who can help in determining the parolee's progress.

Two of the most difficult problems that confront a parole officer working with juveniles in the community after they are released from a custodial institution are the education and job issues of their clients. In a cogent article on the problem of school and jobs for parolees, Pam Belluck (1996) describes the problem: "For a growing number of teen-agers across the country, getting into school after getting out of jail means crossing a precarious threshold, their home and street lives constantly threatening to unravel their progress or lure them back to a criminal world."

Basic problems for both juvenile probationers and parolees are school and jobs. About two-thirds of juvenile offenders are rearrested within eighteen months of their release, and most become adult criminals. A survey of one hundred youths released from New York's Riker's Island Prison in 1996 found that after six months, only twenty-five had enrolled in school, and four of those had dropped out. Twenty-two of the youths had already returned to Riker's Island Prison (Belluck, 1996).

An effective school program can be a solution to juvenile recidivism. In response to this problem, some corrections and school officials have begun experimental programs to encourage delinquents in custody to return to school, although many schools are reluctant to accept them because of their delinquent background and their behavioral and academic problems. On this issue, Barry Krisberg, president of the National Council on Crime and Delinquency, commented, "School is obviously a critical ingredient in the rehabilitation process for juveniles. If you fail in school or you drop out, you're not going to get a job except in the drug trade. But the vast majority of kids who exit the juvenile justice system never enter school and certainly never enter school successfully" (Krisberg and Austen, 1993, p. 54).

The case of a seventeen-year-old delinquent I will call Ramon depicts the school problems of a recently released parolee. Ramon had been selling drugs and stealing cars since he was eleven. When he was released from Riker's Island Prison, he wanted a high school diploma, but instead he had to support his two infant daughters. He lived in a cramped East Harlem apartment with his 21-year-old girlfriend and his daughters, Marilyn, 2, and Angela, 1. His job skills were limited. He had fewer than the number of high school credits needed to complete tenth grade, and his most recent accomplishment, heart stencils and cartoon-character cards he made in Riker's prison, were taped to the walls. He was trying to get a job and avoid neighborhood drug dealers and gang members.

When he was released from Riker's after serving ten months on a drug charge, he wanted a high school diploma. A Riker's psychologist made an appointment for him with a high school administrator and even accompanied him there, going beyond her responsibilities. Seeing he needed two years to graduate and that he had a family to support, the administrator suggested a work program that included preparation for a high school equivalency diploma. The administrator made an appointment at an alternative high school for troubled youths. Ramon did not show up. He wanted to go back to his old school, but that wasn't possible. The principal of the high school would not let him in the building because of his past behavior. Ramon's various difficulties, including his school problems, aided and abetted his recidivism and return to custody.

The case of Lisa, described by Pam Belluck (1996), depicts the plight of a delinquent girl on parole after her release from custody:

> Lisa was sixteen when she helped two other girls attack and stab a man nearly to death in a Queens subway station. She reentered school and stayed there, trying to escape the drugs and violence around her and forget the memories of seeing her brother and boyfriend gunned down. Lisa was not the one actually wielding the eight-inch kitchen knife in the subway station, stabbing the young man in the back. The girl who did the stabbing, however, was her best friend. But Lisa, then sixteen, and another girl were helping, pummeling the young man, as their friend, who said the man had raped her, punctured his lung and nearly killed him. (P. 5)

Lisa's is a success story. After her year in jail for attempted murder, Lisa entered high school and earned enough credits to graduate in June. The school newspaper published her poetry, and she looked for colleges where she could learn a trade. While other ex-offenders at the school had setbacks, Lisa, who saw a parole officer every other week, managed to do well, using the school as a partial escape from life's hardships: her brother's murder, the fatal shooting of her boyfriend, the pressures from "the fellas" on the block to sell drugs. After school, she visited a friend who was hospitalized after being shot in the head. At home in Washington Heights, she was often summoned by her father at midnight to help clean apartment buildings.

"It's been real hard," said Lisa, earnest in red silk pants, a red silk blouse, a red leather jacket, and white satin pumps. "Just the other day someone said to me, 'Let's go make this money.' I could go on the corner, sell my little bit of stuff. It was tempting." But, Lisa said, she resists. "I see a lot of people, they come home from being incarcerated and do the same thing and go back," she said. "Or they come out and kill somebody. I don't want to have to sell drugs. I don't want to have to sell my body. I don't want that to be me." Apparently an effective parole officer and educational situation has helped Lisa capitalize on her apparent intelligence and intervened in her life in a positive way (1996, p. 4).

A Summary of Probation and Parole Officer Problems

Most parole and probation officers have too much paperwork and too many probationers. The average supervising probation officer has a voluminous amount of paperwork, including maintaining a casework file, writing up all client and family contacts, preparing violation reports and "work-determination" plans, and other tasks. Many probation officers complain that they hardly have time to see their probationers because of paperwork demands. Because of other tasks, a probation officer may actually utilize only 10 percent of his or her total time in face-to-face meetings with clients.

It is not unusual for clients to go many months without seeing their parole or probation officer because they may "report" by mail. Probation departments tend to place a high priority on paperwork. It is a "measurable" way of evaluating the job the probation officer is doing. "Good casework management" usually means that all the planning and recording are up to date and that all "reports" have been filed on time. Everything "looks good," and there is an obvious "product" that can be evaluated and converted into charts and graphs and statistics. However, these paper results tell very little if anything about the probation officer's interpersonal skills or professional knowledge; they reveal little about his or her effectiveness in dealing with the problems of clients or in modifying delinquent behavior.

The goal of probation and parole supervision is the protection of the community, and that supervision should not emphasize rehabilitation or punishment. The focus should be on assessment and management of the offender in terms of risks and needs. The return on that investment will be a high level of community protection from those individuals who present the greatest risk of committing further law violations, good supervision and resocialization programs, and the ability to use community resources wisely.

A major problem of parole and probation, as indicated earlier, is that the average juvenile caseload assigned to an officer has escalated enormously since the program was established early in the twentieth century. With rare exceptions, most probation officers struggle with a caseload of well over one hundred clients. This tends to virtually eliminate the therapeutic impact that probation could have on a delinquent if the officer's caseload were ten to fifteen clients. Despite this overload both parole and probation are reasonably effective in controlling delinquency in the community. And in those cases where a delinquent is out of their control, the probation or parole officer has discretionary power to send the juvenile back to a custodial institution.[2]

In summary, despite the various problems presented, community approaches, including child guidance clinics, community indigenous leader projects, the AYA methodology, detached gang workers, probation, and parole, are valuable community methods for preventing and controlling delinquency. In addition to their lower cost, community interventions are a more natural approach to the delinquency problem—and represent a more humanistic way to treat juveniles than locking them up in custodial institutions, a setting that often exacerbates their problems. It is often necessary, however, to incarcerate a juvenile for his or her safety and the protection of the community. The following chapter describes and analyzes various types of custodial institutions, their inherent problems, and their impact on the juvenile delinquency problem.

---

2. For further analyses of probation and parole officers' problems, see Carl H. Imlay and Charles R. Glasheen, "See What Condition Your Conditions Are In," *Federal Probation, 35* (June 1971), 3–11, and Elaine Anderson and Graham Spanier, "Treatment of Delinquent Youth: The Influence of the Probation Officer's Perception of Self and Work," *Criminology, 17* (February 1980), 54–72.

CHAPTER 15

CUSTODIAL INSTITUTIONS FOR DELINQUENTS

Incarcerating youths in a prison-type setting, without any therapeutic program, often intensifies their delinquent behavior when they are released back into the community.

When probation or other community programs fail to control a delinquent's behavior he or she is, as a last resort, placed in a custodial institution. The custodial institution is for recalcitrant delinquents who persistently violate the law. This chapter examines the variety of institutions and facilities currently available for the custodial treatment of delinquents.

Short-Term Detention Institutions

Almost all municipalities have short-term custodial institutions such as "juvenile halls" and probation camps. My early experience in the delinquency field involved working in what amounted to a juvenile jail in Newark, New Jersey. Juvenile jails, then and now, have not changed significantly. They are basically lock-ups for juveniles who have committed a number of offenses, and the judge has remanded them to custody before making a determination of their cases. Most juveniles in these custodial facilities are awaiting court disposition and are considered to be too problematic to remain in the community.

Juvenile detention institutions are often referred to by pseudonyms in an effort to disguise the fact that they are really jails. They are often named "juvenile hall" or "juvenile detention facilities." The one I worked at was called the Essex County Parental School. The "parental school" name was an effort to indicate that the parents had lost control over the juveniles and the county was taking over parental responsibilities. Such facilities have two basic functions in the juvenile justice system. One is to remand the juvenile into custody to remove him or her from the community while awaiting trial, for the purpose of more closely evaluating his or her social, family, and psychological background by a probation officer. The probation officer then submits an evaluation with a recommendation to the juvenile court judge for the disposition. The judge usually utilizes the recommendation of the probation officer in the final determination regarding the youth. Another function of a juvenile detention facility is for short-term punishment. I have often been in a juvenile court when a judge said something along these lines: "You need to cool off for a few weeks and think about where you are heading, so I am remanding you to juvenile hall for two weeks."

The following statistics present some concept of the number of youths detained in juvenile detention. Poe-Yamagata (1997) analyzed the number and racial background of children detained from 1985 to 1994. During this ten-year period there was a substantial increase of 43 percent in the number of cases detained by the juvenile courts. This was driven largely by the increase in the overall referrals to juvenile court. Youths were detained at some point between referral to court and case disposition in 21 percent (or 321,200) of all delinquency cases handled in 1994. Detention was less likely among youths charged with a property offense (17 percent) than with public order (24 percent), a violent offense against a person (24 percent), or drug law violation (28 percent) offenses.

The proportion of cases the courts chose to detain was only slightly higher in 1994 than 1985 (21 percent versus 20 percent). Consequently, the 43 percent increase in the number of delinquency cases involving detention paralleled the 41 percent increase in the number of cases handled by juvenile courts during that period. This pattern of similar growth in the number of cases involving detention and the number of cases referred was seen in all offense categories except drug law violations. The number of drug offense cases involving detention increased almost twice as much as the number of referrals for drug violations between 1985 and 1994.

Between 1985 and 1994, the use of detention increased most among drug offense cases involving black males. In 1994, males accounted for four out of five cases involving detention. Juvenile courts detained a greater proportion of delinquency cases involving males than females in 1994 (22 percent versus 16 percent). Between 1985 and 1994, the number of cases resulting in detention increased more for males than females (44 percent versus 38 percent). In 1994, black male juveniles accounted for more than two out of five cases involving detention. However, these black juveniles represented only one-third of juvenile court referrals during that year. In 1994, 28 percent of cases involving black youths (males) resulted in detention compared with 17 percent of cases involving white youths (males). In fact, among all offense categories, young black males were more likely to be detained than white male youths during every year between 1985 and 1994.

Ⅲ Detention Camps

An intermediate custodial facility between probation in the community, juvenile jails, and a long-term reformatory in some jurisdictions is the probation camp. The usual stay in a probation camp is six months to one year. In a camp, which in recent years may be an army-like boot camp, youths receive some resocialization treatment like psychological help, counseling, and educational and vocational training. When none of these efforts work, and the juvenile continues his or her deviant behavior, the judge will sentence him or her to a reformatory institution for long-term treatment.

Often the social dynamics that occur in any organization during a crisis reveal a great deal about the social system. The following account of a 1993 riot at a juvenile camp reveal something about the problems and structure of a camp.[1]

One evening, around 11:00 P.M., the customary quiet of a maximum security walled probation camp in the San Dimas foothills was shattered by the sounds of boys screaming and glass breaking. Youths rampaged through the camp's 94-bed open dorm, wielding table legs, forks, wooden stakes, ceramic ashtrays, belts, even beds as weapons. Some inmates of the camp ran in fear for their lives. That night there were eighty youths—many of them hard-core gangsters—who joined in what was in effect a riot.

After it was over, and the sheriff's, deputies, ambulances, doctors, paramedics, and injured had gone, it was determined that fifteen young wards of the county and five probation officers had been injured in the melee. Nine inmates had escaped and were later recaptured.

As one probation staff officer analyzed it, the riot was a result of the racial conflicts at the camp. He said that there were always racial overtones in a camp setting. The degree of racial problems varied with how hot the day was, how lax the staff was, and what they allowed in terms of racial comments. Part of the problem was that the black inmates of the camp resented the "privilege" extended Mexican-American inmates to hold La Raza meetings. The La Raza movement for Chicanos at the camp was a positive situation for developing a history of Mexican-Americans and a feeling of solidarity about their roots. In contrast, the blacks were more fragmented in their gangs, and many were in enemy gangs that fought each other. The Crips and the Bloods fought on the streets and also in camp.

According to a probation officer present, after a black inmate hit a Chicano,

> Bedlam broke loose in the dining hall that morning. Immediately all the wards stood up, picked up forks, spoons, started throwing pitchers of hot coffee, cups, trays. The whole population of the dining hall polarized. The blacks came into one area, the Chicanos into another. I saw a young black kid standing up on a table swinging with both arms. The KPs came out of the kitchen. A lot of kids took off outside. All the black kids went out of the dining hall and all the Chicanos stayed in. All the white kids, who are the minority group in the camp, ran down to the administration building for protection. The black kids broke off some of the stakes holding up trees, they found pieces of pipe, pieces of chairs from the dining hall, and they were trying to break windows and get into the dining hall. The racial war simmered all day. This breakfast disturbance was the prelude to the big riot that happened that night.

---

1. This account of the riot was presented to me by a probation officer who worked in the Los Angeles County camp. I have edited the material to reveal some of the issues that manifest themselves in a juvenile probation camp. The incident took place on July 18, 1993.

A veteran of the rioting at the camp, musing on the two-fold nature of his role as a camp officer—part cop, part counselor said, "There's a difference if the staff member is acquainted with juveniles and knows how to work with juveniles to where you're not classed by them as 'the man.' We are the man as well as the friend of these guys. If a kid does something wrong, we're the ones that have to punish him. We also have to try to show him a better way to handle his anger. I've been working here for seven years, and you are pretty much at the mercy of the boys. We've got nothing but their files to control them." By this comment he meant that control involved the power to write a bad report on a youth and increase his time at the institution.

A number of issues were revealed in the camp riot situation about the dynamic of institutions for male juveniles that are in accord with my observations in similar situations. Following are some of these issues related to the camp riot situation, derived from my own direct work in various juvenile custodial institutions:

1. Sociopaths and extremely emotionally disturbed boys are almost impossible to control, short of putting them in a "time-out" solitary confinement room or transferring them to a maximum security institution.

2. A major method for control with most other inmates is through the threat of a "write-up" and the youth's belief that a "write-up" would keep him in the institution for a longer period of time. This control was usually a fallacious threat, because there were many other factors involved in the boy's time in the institution.

3. As indicated in one of the probation officer's comments about the riot, sometimes you have to look the other way when there is misbehavior. The institutional set-up is so onerous and demanding that "if you enforced every rule you would quickly flip out and be in a straitjacket or an institution of your own."

4. In some cases, on a day when an officer has a low energy level or doesn't feel like working, he can give one of the controlling, physically powerful juveniles in the institution the power to enforce the rules in a quid pro quo arrangement. An example of this agreement would be that the officer in charge allows the "assistant" to have an extra smoke or looks the other way when he violates a minor rule.

I am reminded of a time when I worked in a juvenile facility and corrupted the rules for some short-term relief from the difficulties of my job. It began on a day when I was tired and turned over the responsibility of lining up the boys to a juvenile psychopath. The sixteen-year-old youth helped me line the boys up to march to another area of the institution.

They lined up quickly at his command, and in the process I heard the loud thud of a punch that was thrown at a kid who was not cooperating. My "assistant" had punched him so hard in the chest that he fell to the ground, writhing in pain. He had to be rushed to the emergency hospital, and I was later told that the punch had broken the boy's rib, and that if the blow had been a few inches higher, the broken rib might have pierced the boy's heart. From then on, I attempted to keep all of the power I had as an officer in enforcing the rules.

Boredom is the common mood in all institutions for juveniles. It's hard to gain and hold the inmates' attention with anything beyond the constant viewing of television. One day when I was working in a detention facility, I observed a bizarre approach on the part of the youths in handling their boredom. I was in charge of a group of twenty boys, and we were in the recreation room. In those days all we had for recreation were games and a radio. I ran out of ideas for holding their attention. As an experiment, I decided to do nothing and see what would happen if I exerted no control over the boys. Of course, a few fights broke out, and there were a number of arguments. The most interesting and unanticipated event was that most of the boys began to line up in front of the old radio. The radio had a loose wire, and they were lining up for an electric shock! Anything to relieve their boredom. After they received an electric shock, they would go to the end of the line and repeat their experience.

 Boot Camps

In the 1990s the "boot camp" approach became popular and was experimented with as a get-tough method for treating delinquents. In response to a significant increase in juvenile arrests and repeat offenses, several states and many localities, with the advocacy of politicians, established juvenile boot camps. The programs emphasize physical conditioning and military-style discipline.

In 1992, the Office of Juvenile Justice and Delinquency Prevention of the Department of Justice (OJJDP) supported the development of three juvenile boot camp research demonstration projects to analyze the efficacy of this type of program. The projects were conducted in Cleveland, Ohio, Denver, Colorado, and Mobile, Alabama. Eric Peterson (1997) described the demonstration projects, their evaluations, and lessons learned that will benefit future boot camp programs. The OJJDP-sponsored boot camps focused on a target population of adjudicated, nonviolent male offenders under the age of eighteen. Highly structured, three-month, residential programs were followed by six to nine months of community-based aftercare. During the aftercare period, youths were to pursue academic and vocational training or employment while under intensive but progressively diminishing supervision.

OJJDP undertook impact evaluations for all three sites that compared the recidivism rates for juveniles who participated in the pilot programs with those of control groups. The evaluations also compared the cost-effectiveness of juvenile boot camps with other alternatives. The research determined that most juvenile boot camp participants completed the residential program and graduated to aftercare. Program completion rates were 96 percent in Cleveland, 87 percent in Mobile, and 76 percent in Denver.

At the two sites where educational gains were measured, substantial improvements in academic skills were noted. In Mobile, approximately three-quarters of the participants improved their performance in reading, spelling, language, and math by one grade level or more. In Cleveland, the average juvenile boot camp participant improved reading, spelling, and math skills by approximately one grade level. In addition, where employment records were available, a significant number of participants found jobs while in aftercare.

These pilot programs, however, did not demonstrate a reduction in recidivism. In Denver and Mobile, no statistically significant difference could be found between the recidivism rates of juvenile boot camp participants and those of the control groups (youths confined in state or county institutions, or those released on probation). In the Cleveland pilot program participants evidenced a higher recidivism rate than juvenile offenders confined in traditional juvenile correctional facilities. Several lessons were learned from the demonstration projects:

> The appropriate population should be targeted. Boot camps should be designed as an intermediate intervention. At one site, youths who had been previously confined were significantly more likely to recidivate, while youths with the least serious offenses were also more likely to recidivate. Facility location is important. Cost issues and community resistance were major obstacles to securing residential and aftercare facilities. To increase attendance and reduce problems, aftercare facilities should be located in gang-neutral areas accessible by public transportation. Staff selection and training needs are critical. To reduce staff turnover, fill gaps in critical services, and ensure consistent programming, the screening, selection, and training of juvenile boot camp and aftercare staff must be sensitive to the programmatic and operational features of a juvenile boot camp. This is particularly important with regard to youth development issues. (Peterson, 1997)

430

The research report concluded that the participants were unlikely to succeed if they failed to receive the full range of services prescribed for them. Also, aftercare programs must be broad-based and flexible enough to meet the particular educational, employment, counseling, and support needs of each participant. The aftercare component should also form dynamic linkages with other community services, especially youth service agencies, schools, and employers. Coordination among agencies must be maintained. All three sites experienced difficulties in maintaining coordination among the participating agencies (Peterson, 1997).

A *New York Times* article (1996) described the experience of one New York boot camp graduate but who was not in the OJJDP program.

> Tom, seventeen, got out of boot camp last year and went straight into school, an environment where counselors delved so deeply into his life that they moved him into foster care after learning that his father was selling cocaine from the living room. The school helped him care for his crack-addicted mother, who has AIDS. But after spending six months in a Division for Youth boot camp for punching a high school dean and mugging people for gold chains, things were different. When he was released from the boot camp last year, he was immediately placed in City Challenge, an unusual school taught by public school teachers but supervised by the boot camp. Youths go to City Challenge for five months as part of their criminal sentence and are then placed in other city public schools. City Challenge, a program started four years ago in a brownstone in Bedford-Stuyvesant, Brooklyn, tries to give youths the kind of individually tailored attention and supervision that experts have begun to consider crucial. It also saves money, state corrections officials argue, since it cuts boot camp to six months, instead of the usual ten.
>
> With Tom, boot camp staff members decided he should live with his father, even though he spent most of his life in a foster home in Queens. "The place was neat," Cornick said of the father's apartment. "There was a lot of good furniture in the home. The father talked good." But two weeks later, Cornick said, "He called me back and said 'Hey, my father's selling crack out of the living room' " Tom went back to the foster family.
>
> City Challenge also helped Tom deal with other problems, like his mother's health. After finishing his City Challenge classes each day, Tom would go to East Harlem and pound on the door of a decrepit drug-riddled building until his mother opened it. "I would help her wash up and stuff, get her food," Tom said. "A lot of times I'd be there late at night."
>
> Because of the late nights, City Challenge allowed Tom to attend school part-time. And Hilton Cooper, City Challenge's top counselor, went with Tim to coax his mother to get AIDS treatment. City Challenge also got Tom a part-time job, psychological counseling, and engaged him in basketball. He achieved more

than he ever had, finishing the tenth grade. "It was like the best school," said Tom, a towering teenager slouched on a plastic-slipcovered couch in his living room. "They like working with you. And you can't leave once you got in."

But last spring, when Tom's City Challenge sentence ended, he went to a large public high school in Queens. Things began to unravel. He cut classes and "got the attention of the special ed department," said Sylvia Rowlands, a psychologist at the boot camp. "There was a lot of pressure and it just drove him right out of school altogether. Over the summer, Tom was charged with a misdemeanor when police found a gun in a car he was in. He has spent time putting up Sheetrock in the foster family's garage and playing with his pit bull puppy, Danger. He delivered food for a Chinese restaurant, whose regular delivery boys had been getting robbed. "I wanted to get back in City Challenge," Tom said. Counselors there could not allow that, but encouraged him to keep in contact. Although Tom was apparently not fully helped by his boot camp experience, it aided in putting him back on a more positive rehabilitative track. (Pp. 6–7)

Long-Term Custodial Institutions

The social system of short-term institutions, like juvenile jails, boot camps, and probation camps, is different from that of longer term custodial institutions. Youths who are placed in long-term juvenile custodial institutions will very likely spend a good part of their life in prison. A recent analysis reported by the U.S. Bureau of Justice Statistics (March 7, 1997) revealed that babies born in the United States today have a one in twenty chance of eventually going to prison. According to the study, if 1991 crime, incarceration, and death rates remain constant, about 9 percent of men and 1 percent of women will spend some time behind bars before they die. That works out to 5.1 percent of the population. Nearly 1.1 million men and women were imprisoned in a state or federal facility at the close of 1995, and there were a reported 1.6 million in custody in 1996. According to the Bureau of Justice Statistics (1997), an estimated 28.5 percent of black men, 16 percent of Hispanic men, and 4.4 percent of white men can be expected to serve a state or federal prison term. The projections are based on what is likely to happen to a hypothetical population of newborns over their lifespan. This projection assumes that recent rates of crime, imprisonment, and death will not change. The study did not include the likelihood of imprisonment in a local jail, juvenile facility, or other type of detention center. Also according to the bureau's study, the probability of a person committing a crime and being sentenced to prison for the first time declines steadily with the person's age.

In the 1990s, the prison population grew to about 1.7 million prisoners, but that growth was not the result of a growing number of admissions. Rather, prison sentences were longer, and fewer people were being released. In accord with the bureau's estimates it is apparent that youths who enter long-term custodial institutions are likely candidates for later incarceration in an adult prison. And, of course, because of the "get-tough with delinquents and criminals" attitudes and policies, the United States laws and practices will place an enormous number of people of all ages in prison in the twenty-first century unless there are some radical changes in public policy.

Most juvenile delinquents, especially those who commit status offenses or are incorrigible, are diverted into various treatment programs. Some simply keep coming back to court, are held in detention for a brief period, and are then sent back to their community. The recalcitrant youths who continue to commit serious violent acts or other serious offenses are, in due time, placed in longer term juvenile institutions. In these institutions they may spend one to three years, and in some cases they are incarcerated until they are twenty-one. Most of these youths continue their criminal career when released and end up in adult prisons.

When juveniles have been found to be delinquent for a serious offense and are turned over to a longer term institution, society has decided ①that their behavior needs to be closely supervised, ②that they are to be deprived of some or all of their liberty; ③that a significant change in their values, attitudes, and behavior is desirable; and ④that this experience within the system will result in less likelihood of their violating the law in the future. The juvenile reformatory has been assigned the functions of protecting society and incapacitating and hopefully rehabilitating juvenile offenders.

Longer term institutions for juveniles are often referred to as "training schools" or "reformatories." When these institutions were originally established, they were patterned after adult prisons. Juvenile institutions have many of the same problems as prisons for adults have; however, they place greater emphasis on rehabilitation and less on custody, and they give some attention to treatment. They have populations varying from twenty to five hundred children and a diversity of educational, vocational, and therapeutic programs, including individual casework, group therapy, guided group interaction, encounter groups, psychodrama and role training, and milieu therapy.

After leaving a long-term institution, youths are usually assisted in their adjustment to the community by parole personnel of the institution or by social work agencies in the communities in which they reside. The state training school or reformatory is the "total institution" for juveniles and is the "back-up" long-term institution found in most states. Most states have shorter term, more therapeutic facilities; however, the juveniles know that if they do not fit into these less confining institutions, they will ultimately end up in the "total state institution." The security is not as severe as it is in the adult prison, and rehabilitation programs are more prevalent. Nevertheless, the social system of the state training school is very similar to that of an adult prison.

The California Youth Authority:
A Prototypical Reformatory System

The state training school reformatory system is typified by the California Youth Authority.[2] Most states have a system that somewhat parallels California's system. The California Youth Authority is administered by a director appointed by the governor, subject to confirmation by the state senate. The Youth Authority Board, consisting of eight members, is also appointed by the governor and given overall responsibility for the acceptance of cases, assignment of wards to institutions, releases to parole, revocations of parole, and final discharges of wards.

The California Youth Authority operates two reception centers, one at Norwalk, which receives all wards committed to the authority by all courts in southern California, and the other at Perkins, which receives all wards committed to the authority by all courts in the rest of the state. It also operates five correctional schools for boys, two for girls, and four forestry camps.

The Norwalk Reception Center

The Norwalk Reception Center receives all wards (males) committed to the Youth Authority by juvenile, superior, and municipal courts in southern California. Approximately 90 percent of these commitments are made by juvenile courts. The wards range in age from eight to twenty-one years. Most of those received are between fifteen and seventeen years of age, with very few under twelve or over nineteen. The Norwalk Center is a diagnostic center, not a correctional institution. There is no attempt made to provide academic or vocational training. The wards are held there for a standard period of 28 days. Occasionally, however, wards have been held as long as six months to a year. Legally, a ward can be held until he turns twenty-one. During the time he is there, achievement tests are administered

---

2. This description of the California Youth Authority is derived from their 1996 *Report* and various CYA brochures.

to determine his academic level. He is observed, interviewed, and counseled by social workers and youth counselors, and sometimes by psychologists or psychiatrists. On the basis of these tests, interviews, and observations, a diagnostic report is submitted to the board, which decides on the disposition of the juvenile's case.

The wards live in cottages, about fifty occupants to a cottage selected according to age, sophistication, and past histories. Each ward has a room, or cell, of his own. The doors are locked at night, but unlocked at 5:45 in the morning, when the boys get up. During the day the boys are under the supervision of the youth counselor assigned to their cottage. Five of the seven cottages are concerned only with the therapeutic diagnostic programs. The sixth is devoted to a twenty-day program for youths ready for immediate release; the other is devoted to a ninety-day program called the James Marshall Treatment Program, which allows a boy to be released into the community after a short institutional stay.

On the basis of reports from the medical officer, the living unit, the school, or the social workers, a ward may be referred to the psychological section for further evaluation. The final report consists of a confidential diagnostic summary that is presented to the Youth Authority Board as a recommendation for a proposed treatment program.

All the boys in the program meet with all available staff members for one hour daily, five times a week, to discuss their living experiences and interpersonal difficulties. These group meetings are structured to provide a positive and constructive communication channel in which feelings about the impact of the institutional experience can be examined and problems resolved. The establishment of positive relationships between the wards and the staff also serves to reduce the problems of management of the ward population.

Each ward is assigned to a small peer group—six to eight members—led by a group supervisor. Within this primary group the ward is given an intensive and dynamic experience. He is confronted with his own behavior as well as given an opportunity to examine that of his peers. The group supervisor's efforts are focused on motivating anxiety and stimulating stress situations, in which the individual and his peers assume major responsibility for examining behavior. The whole group thus becomes involved in the problem-solving process.

Every effort is made to discourage boys from isolating themselves from their peers. Group games and projects are fostered whenever possible. Control of "outbursts" and verbalization of feelings are also encouraged. Before any boy may be accepted into the program, his parents must be willing and able to give their full support and substantial time to work with the group worker in the adjustment and the rehabilitation of their son. The group worker attempts to help them accept their son's problems and to provide a better environment for the boy after his release. The group worker also attempts to establish a relationship between the boy and his future probation or parole officer.

The Ontario Youth Training School: A Long-term Reformatory

The Youth Training School at Ontario was established as the first specialized school in the California Youth Authority system. Youths sent to the school are wards of the court and have been certified to and accepted by the California Youth Authority for treatment and training. No youth may be committed who at the time of his offense was twenty-one years of age or older or under sixteen. Wards are sent to Ontario by the California Youth Authority Board based on classification and diagnostic studies made at the northern or southern reception center.

The average stay at Ontario is nine months, although the school budget provides for an average stay of eight months per ward. The school is a medium-security correctional institution. The main security measure is a sixteen-foot fence encompassing the campus area. From the observation tower, located at the end of the administration building, it is possible to see and control almost every area of the "campus." Wards may therefore go to and from classes and work assignments without direct supervision. This is known throughout the school as "free movement." The institution provides both lay and professional counseling.

Each of the four hundred staff members, in theory at least, serves as a counselor to the wards. The use of professional counseling is limited because of the general unavailability of professional personnel. Wards who are believed to be mentally ill are transferred out of Ontario to a more appropriate institution. Individual counseling is available to the wards in their own living units. This counseling is given by the classification officer whose caseload is about one hundred wards. He or she works irregular hours, so is available to the wards when they have free time at night. The classification officer also evaluates the wards, handles their personal business, and performs various other duties. Controlled group sessions, with approximately twelve to fourteen wards involved in each session, are held once a week for one hour.

Wards are allowed two visits of two hours each per month on Saturdays, Sundays, and holidays when there are no vocational training classes. The boys see their visitors in the visiting lounge, toward the front of the institution. The only factor that creates an institutional atmosphere is the control room with double-locked doors, through which visitors must pass upon entering the school. The school finds these visits an effective aid in securing cooperation as well as good for morale and institutional adjustment. The school at Ontario is accredited by the state of California, and wards are encouraged to get their high school diplomas.

New York's "Residential Treatment Centers"

New York's "residential treatment centers" are like California's long-term reformatories in many ways but put more emphasis on therapy (New York State Division for Youth, 1995). New York was one of the first states to give financial support to this type of institution for juveniles. Some six institutions established by private charitable organizations and operated under private auspices have been officially classified as "residential treatment centers" by the State of New York.

Because of intake policies and limits of capacity, the number of referrals is four or five times the number actually accepted. All of the children accepted in the institutions are considered to be emotionally disturbed and in need of psychotherapeutic treatment. Before a child is accepted, the intake study must indicate that he or she is amenable to treatment by the facilities available at the institution. Children with IQs below 70 are not considered acceptable.

The ratio of staff (including all types of service, treatment, custodial, and managerial) to inmates varies between one to one and four to five. Psychiatrists are available as consultants to the psychiatric social workers. Psychologists, in the main, administer tests. Social workers, in addition to providing individual casework and group therapy, are often assigned the task of coordinating all the services. Each center has a school geared to the institutional approach. Insofar as practicable, the education of the child is coordinated with the activities of those directly involved in his or her therapy.

Most residential treatment centers of this type are located in countryside areas at a considerable distance from the cities from which virtually all the inmates come. Although distances are not very great by modern standards, transportation costs are prohibitive for most poor people. Contacts between children and their parents and relatives are therefore limited during the period of institutionalization. Contacts between staff members and the children and their families are likewise limited when the children are returned to their urban communities.

Recommendations for Effective Training Schools

The Office of Juvenile Justice and Delinquency Prevention 1997 report, *Recommendation for Training Schools*, provides a number of relevant and useful recommendations for the development of effective institutions. In summary, it states that "training schools for delinquents should provide a broad range of individual and group counseling programs with emphasis upon positive reinforcement." The report recommends that the following individual and group methods should be a part of the treatment in training schools: Group therapy should be conducted in groups no larger than ten persons and should meet at least once per week. The therapy should be conducted by group leaders whose experience and training are commensurate with the type of therapy being provided. Training school education programs should provide for the diverse educational needs of the juveniles placed therein and should include academic, vocational, and special education components. A curriculum substantially equivalent to that required under the law of the jurisdiction for public school students should be available to all juveniles placed in a training school. The report also asserted that the academic program provided should meet all requirements necessary for the transfer of earned credits to public schools within the state and should be certified to award academic diplomas to juveniles who meet the requirements for such diplomas during their placement. The OJJDP also recommended that all juveniles should receive career counseling to provide them with knowledge of a wide range of career options.

Most delinquents have failed in school, and their lack of success in this important part of their lives has contributed greatly to their antisocial behavior. Because they are barely able to read, some have felt since grade school that they have been shut out of opportunities requiring basic skills. Others, bored in school, have found only illegal applications for their intelligence. Educating delinquents requires using high-interest subject matter, creating a nonthreatening environment, using creative and motivational activities in the classroom, and providing time each day for students to practice reading and writing.

I had a brief experience as a teacher of delinquents in custody that revealed the problems of educating difficult youngsters who were confronting the emotional impact of incarceration. The regular teacher had left, a new full-time teacher had not yet arrived, and I was called upon to teach youths incarcerated in a custodial facility where I worked. I found the experience extremely difficult, because most of my time was spent in disciplining the class and breaking up fights that continually erupted between students. Eventually, the faculty hired a teacher who seemed to have the necessary skills to control the classroom. In fact, when I would look through the classroom window I was impressed with the rapt attention paid to the teacher as he read to them.

One evening, I learned how he controlled the class. After the youths under my charge were in bed, most sleeping soundly, I heard one of the boys screaming. I went to his room and found that he was having a nightmare. As I comforted him, I asked him about his nightmare. He told me, "It's those stories [the new schoolteacher] reads to us. Like the one about the guy buried up to his head with honey on his face, and how the ants ate up his face." The boy went on to tell me about the other lurid stories that the teacher read in the classroom. He obviously was holding the youngsters' attention; however, he wasn't properly or effectively educating our boys. As supervisor of the boy's unit, I found it necessary to fire this teacher. It is apparent that it is difficult to teach delinquents in custody through normal educational methods.

Highfields: A Residential Treatment Center

The prototype for a treatment-oriented small residential group center is the Highfields program, originated by Lloyd W. McCorkle in New Jersey in 1952. The Highfields approach limits the population to twenty boys, aged sixteen and seventeen, assigned directly from the juvenile court. They are youths who had not previously been committed to a correctional institution. The program is *not* designed for deeply disturbed or mentally deficient children. Highfields is a popular institutional model that has been replicated in many states. I worked on the research project on Highfields directed by Ashley Weeks for two years at New York University. The following analysis of the Highfields program is in part based on my research experience.

The boys who lived in the first experimental Highfields stayed there for an average of four months. During the day they worked at a nearby institution performing menial labor. There were few security measures and little or no authoritarian leadership. Meetings were held every evening. The boys were divided into two groups of ten for these meetings, which were organized around the technique of guided group interaction. Guided group interaction sessions are at the heart of the Highfields system. The method is described as follows by Lloyd McCorkle (1958):

> Rehabilitation begins with changes in attitudes. But how can these be brought about? The boys entering Highfields have for years identified themselves as delinquents. Their close friends are delinquent. Group pressure has generally pushed and pulled them into delinquency and prevented their rehabilitation. Most delinquents feel rejected and discriminated against by their parents. They generally manifest strong emotional reactions, particularly against their fathers, but often against their mothers, brothers, and sisters. By the time they are confronted with law-enforcing agencies they have developed strong ego

defenses. They do not take the responsibility for their delinquency. Instead, they tend to blame others—their parents, their associates, and society. The whole Highfields experience is directed toward piercing through these strong defenses against rehabilitation, toward undermining delinquent attitudes, and toward developing a self-conception favorable to reformation. The sessions on guided group interaction are especially directed to achieve this objective. Guided group interaction has the merit of combining the psychological and the sociological approaches to the control of human behavior. The psychological approach aims to change the self-conception of the boy from a delinquent to a nondelinquent. But this process involves changing the mood of the boy from impulses to be law breaking to impulses to be law abiding. (P. 72)

At Highfields, emphasis is placed on normal social activities and values. This is accomplished by four devices intended "to help the boys to be like everybody else." (1) Family members and friends of boys are encouraged to visit them at Highfields and see how they are getting along. (2) An effort is made to educate the surrounding community to accept the boys, rather than to show suspicion or reject them entirely. (3) Perhaps most important, the boys do useful work and are paid for it. (4) The stay at Highfields is limited to a maximum of four months. This time factor is considered an important devise that contributes to successful rehabilitation.

The philosophy, operation, effect, and potentialities of the Highfields program are summarized as follows:

1. Its thoroughgoing use of the group as an instrument of rehabilitation is socially and psychologically sound and has been verified by experience.

2. The method of guided interaction directs group influences toward rehabilitation rather than, as in the large reformatory, to the reinforcement of attitudes of delinquency and hostility to authority.

3. In the guided group interaction sessions, the youth achieves an understanding of himself and his motivations, which enables him to make constructive plans for his future.

4. Highfields greatly reduces the time of treatment from the usual one of five years in training schools or reformatories to three or four months.

5. It requires a minimum of staff as compared with other methods of treatment.

6. Highfields has far lower per capita costs than other institutions for the treatment of delinquents.

7. There is every reason to believe that Highfields can be successfully

established elsewhere provided the new projects incorporate its phi-losophy, its design of operation, and a specially trained staff.

The failure rate at Highfields has been found to be lower than that of the state training schools. Scientific comparisons between the two types of institutions are difficult, however, because the populations on entering are not necessarily comparable. The admission committees of the residential treatment centers can refuse to take a boy if they feel their program does not suit his needs; the state training school must take every boy a court sends to it. This power to select gives the residential treatment center an advantage. The fact that residential treatment centers are privately operated and are able to spend more than state-run schools has enabled them to experiment with costly programs and make considerable progress in institutional treatment.

Institutions modeled after the original Highfields have been developed throughout the United States. Much like the original, they house about twenty persons each, and custodial personnel are held to a minimum. The Highfields experiment has been considered generally successful by a number of research evaluations, including the New York University Highfields Research Project that I worked on, directed by Ashley Weeks (1958).

Evaluations of Custodial Institutions

A common problem in long-term juvenile institutions is conflict and mutual hostility between treatment personnel and staff concerned with custody and discipline. The problem of value conflicts between these authority figures often emerges most sharply in an institution changing over from a "juvenile prison" emphasizing custody to a rehabilitation approach. George H. Weber (1961) carried out a study that revealed the conflict that occurs in a training school where two divergent systems of resocialization exist. He analyzed a state training school that was shifting from a generally custodial-punitive approach to a psychiatric-social work approach entailing diagnosis, group therapy, and individual attention.

The institution Weber studied housed one hundred fifty boys between the ages of twelve and sixteen in five cottages. The staff was composed of five social workers, two psychologists, one psychiatrist, and forty-six cottage parents. Weber noted the following areas of organizational changes and the consequences related to behavior of the boys and the reactions of staff. The shift from tight control of behavior to permissiveness allowed acting out. This pattern was more accepted by the treatment than the custodial staff, as they felt it helped them to see the child "as he really was."

Therapeutic and counseling functions were substantially removed from cottage parents and given to the regular therapeutic staff. Cottage parents were explicitly instructed to not attempt any counseling and to "make sure they did not interfere with the child treatment program." According to Weber, several noticeable effects resulted from these organizational changes:

1. A degree of disciplinary power was taken away from the cottage parents. Instead of controlling a boy through fear of punishment, the cottage parent was forced to establish a relationship based on friendship.

2. The cottage parents were given a subordinate and confusing role in the organization. Their frustrations and anger were often displaced onto the boys.

3. Often the boys would play one authority figure (the cottage parent) against another (the therapist).

After a time the institution began to move more smoothly and positively toward its rehabilitative goal. Weber's research revealed, however, the inherent conflicts that exist between a custodial emphasis and a rehabilitative approach in the institutional treatment of juveniles.

Howard Polsky: The Delinquent Subculture in a Residential Treatment Center

Howard Polsky (1962) carried out several years of significant research into the private cottage-type residential treatment center called Hawthorne-Cedar Knolls in New York. The school was essentially devoted to individual psychoanalytic treatment of emotionally disturbed delinquent children as well as withdrawn, prepsychotic, and fragile children who were not able to live in the community.

The scope provided academic and vocational courses and intense remedial programs. A full range of clinical services was provided by psychiatrists, psychologists, and social workers. Treatment included individual psychotherapy, group therapy, and family therapy provided in accordance with the child's individual needs as seen by the staff. Approximately half the students were Jewish, about 25 percent were black or Puerto Rican, and the remainder were from other ethnic groups.

The focus of Polsky's study was on the cottages' subcultural values and the relationships between the socialization process in the cottages and the treatment program. He found a definite hierarchy of status in the cottages he studied by participant observation. The stratification system was based on "toughness" and the ability to manipulate others (precisely the behavioral patterns the institution was attempting to change). With regard to the group processes and structure, Polsky came to the following conclusions:

1. The boys were highly conscious of each other's position in the rigid social hierarchy. It was this preoccupation with each other's relative strength that dominated and framed much of the boys' interactions, even apparently the most simple kinds, such as the passing of food at the dining table. He observed that "there was very little opportunity for the group to work together to dilute these crystallized roles based on toughness."

2. Another great imbalance appeared to exist around the issue of sharing. He observed, for example, that food was used as a tool to exert pressure and control. There was an individualistic and inequitable distribution of power. The top clique controlled choice items such as butter, and all boys at other tables had to go to them for it. Standing in line for food often became a testing ground as boys tried to step in front of each other and show their superiority. The tougher, older boys in the cottages controlled those of lower status. In the cottages there was a formalistic organization around authority. This was not worked out in rules or as a constitution, but as the accretion of experience—implicit recognition by all the boys of exactly where they stood vis-à-vis the others. When a high-status boy was challenged by someone of lower status, a dramatic outbreak occurred, and generally the upstart was "put in his place" through physical violence.

3. Within each cottage there was very little tendency to make status contingent upon service to the cottage. Nor did status within the cottage seem to depend in any way on skills developed outside it. Status seemed to be determined solely by toughness and ability to control others. The constant hazing of a scapegoat by the group could become so oppressive that the scapegoat would have to either "stand up" or leave. The consolidation of the group against one or several of its members was established procedure. The soil in which scapegoating flourished was the pervasive "ranking" (a pattern of insults) and shaming, dominant characteristics of the pecking order.

4. Finally, there seemed to be a tendency within the cottages for some solidarity to form within subgroups on the basis of close association; there was little or no tendency toward overall cottage solidarity. In the course of time, these cliques became increasingly crystallized. Clique loyalties predominated. In time, the top clique became quite effective in exerting control over the others. The top clique's attitude

toward the staff, whether defiance or cooperation, was established as the basic pattern for the entire cottage.

The cottage, according to Polsky, was culturally and organizationally "delinquent-bound." There was little opportunity for the boys to offset the constant, overwhelming delinquent-expressive behavior with positive socioemotional interactions. Polsky found that the cottage was to a large extent a vacuum in which peer-group authoritarianism and toughness reigned supreme. The individuals tested their emotional problems on each other, and did not work together in meeting challenges placed before them as a cottage group. In the elaboration of their personality distortions, interpersonal cyclical movements were set up in which a preponderance of negative individual acting out resulted in a kind of group pathology. The negative delinquent cottage culture was thus a major source of resistance to treatment.

Polsky's research indicated the absolute necessity of extending individual and group therapy programs to encompass the entire pattern of living in juvenile institutions. The separation of treatment from the youths' day-to-day encounters and life-style in the cottage tends to sabotage the treatment program and render it relatively ineffectual.

In summary, the programs of juvenile institutions are superior to adult correctional efforts; however, with some exceptions they suffer from similar problems. These include: (1) the existence of a criminogenic "crime school" atmosphere and value system; (2) an artificial male-only environment; (3) "doing time" atmosphere, with the time-in-custody factor constantly influencing resident and the staff's actions; (4) a schism between the treatment program and the delinquent subculture; and (5) the power-through-toughness aspect of the social system of the institution.

The State Reformatory System: An Inmate's Viewpoint

In some respects the best evaluator of an institution is the inmate who is subject to its methodology. Claude Brown (1965), a former delinquent, wrote *Manchild in the Promised Land*, in which he described his experiences in New York State's Warwick School for Boys. His analysis of the institution provides some interesting insights from an inmate's point-of-view.

The Warwick School for Boys, a facility of the state of New York, is a total institution for juveniles, serving boys thirteen to fifteen years of age committed by juvenile courts in New York City and the southeastern portion of New York state. Boys sent to the institution spend from eleven to thirteen months there. The Warwick School, situated in a suburban area of Warwick, includes 740 acres of landscaped countryside and holds around

ally killed somebody always seemed to be the nicest cats. . . . There were a lot of real hip young criminals at Warwick.

Warwick had real criminals. It seemed like just about everybody at Warwick not only knew how to pick locks but knew how to cross wires in cars and get them started without keys. Just about everybody knew how to pick pockets and smoke dope, and a lot of cats knew how to cut drugs. They knew how much sugar to put with heroin to make a cap or a bag. There was so much to learn. You learned something new from everybody you met. It seemed like just about all the Puerto Rican guys were up there for using and selling drugs.

I had two or three flunkies after I'd been there for a month. It was no sweat for me; I was ready to stay there for a long time and live real good. I knew how to get along there. I'd had a place waiting for me long before I came. If I'd known that Warwick was going to be as good as it turned out to be, I would never have been so afraid. As a matter of fact, I might have gotten there a whole lot sooner.

At Warwick, it all depended on you when you went home for a visit. The first time, you had to stay there twelve weeks before you could go home. After that, you could go home for a three-day visit, from Friday to Monday, every eight weeks. That's if you didn't lose any days for fucking up or fighting. This was pretty good, because some people were always going home, and they would see your fellows and bring messages back, and your fellows were always coming up every Friday. A new batch of guys would come up and drugs would come up.

When you came back from a weekend home visit, you were searched everywhere. They'd even search in the crack of your ass. You had to go to the doctor and let him look for a dose of clap. But cats would always manage to bring back at least a cap of horse or at least one reefer. Everybody could always manage to smuggle in a little bit of something. . . . We all came out of Warwick better criminals. Other guys were better for the things that I could teach them, and I was better for the things that they could teach me. . . . The good thing about Warwick was that when you went home on visits, you could do stuff, go back up to Warwick, and kind of hide out. If the cops were looking for you in the city, you'd be at Warwick. . . . After about eight months at Warwick, they told me that I'd be going home in about a month. . . .

I left Warwick after staying up there for about nine months and three weeks. I came home and went to the High School of Commerce, down around Broadway and Sixty-Fifth Street. I didn't go for school too much. The cats there were really dressing, and I didn't have any money. The only way I could make some money was by not going to school. If I told Dad I needed about four or five pairs of pants and some nice shirts, he would start talking all that nonsense again about, "I didn't have my first pair-a long pants till I was out workin."

That shit didn't make any sense, not to me. He had been living down on a farm, and this was New York City. People looked crazy going round in New York City with one pair of pants, but this is the way he saw it, and this was the way he talked. I think the nigger used to talk this nonsense because he didn't want to get up off any money to buy me some clothes. So I just said, "Fuck it, I'll buy my own." The only way I could buy my own was by selling pot when I went to school, and I'd take some loaded craps down there, some bones, and I would beat the paddy boys out of all their money. They were the only ones who were dumb enough to shoot craps with bones. After a while, I just got tired. I never went to any of the classes, and if I did go to one, I didn't know anything. I felt kind of dumb, so I stopped going there. The only time I went to school was when I wanted to make some money. I'd go there and stay a couple of hours. Maybe I'd take Turk with me. Turk would sell some pot, and I'd shoot some craps, and when we got enough money, we'd go uptown. (Pp. 231–246) (Reprinted with permission of Simon & Schuster, Inc. from *Manchild in the Promised Land* by Claude Brown. © 1965 by Claude Brown.)

Claude Brown's delinquent life-style returned him to Warwick several times. His unusual ability as a writer managed to help him stay out of New York's adult prisons.

Community-Based Mental Hospitals for Juveniles: A New Direction

The 1990s saw a proliferation of referrals of delinquents to psychiatric hospital programs. According to a report by the 240-member National Association of Private Psychiatric Hospitals of America, teenage psychiatric admissions rose over 500 percent between 1980 and 1995. This trend appears to be increasing despite the cutbacks by HMOs.

The following account is largely derived from a fifteen-year period (1980–1995) during which I directed psychodrama and group therapy programs in the adolescent division of three private and two state California psychiatric hospitals. Increasingly, delinquents who would ordinarily go to juvenile detention or state training schools are now treated in mental hospitals. The juveniles placed in these facilities are usually, but not always, more emotionally disturbed than the average state training school or residential treatment center client. They are more likely to be placed in a mental hospital if they exhibit bizarre behavior or are suicidal. However, many standard sociopathic, substance-abusing, violent delinquent youths are placed in mental hospitals by their parents or the juvenile courts.

The prevalence of mental disorders among youths in the juvenile justice system is considerably higher than in the general population. Common diagnoses of juvenile offenders include conduct disorders, attention deficit disorders, and affective disorders. The occurrence of psychotic disorders among juvenile offenders is about 6 percent. Although this is a relatively small number, psychotic youths need immediate and intensive services. Many have substance abuse disorders that occur along with significant mental disorders.

Confined youths do not fit neatly into a single diagnostic category. Their multiple mental health needs often result from, or have been intensified by, a history of physical abuse, sexual abuse, or severe emotional neglect. Depression is probably their most common mental health problem. It is often expressed through angry, hostile feelings and aggressive, belligerent, or suicidal behavior; withdrawal from others; and weight and sleep problems.

The most serious consequences of untreated or inadequately treated mental disorders are suicidal thoughts and attempts. Approximately 15 to 20 percent of confined juveniles experience hallucinations. Many of the hallucinations are anxiety related: the youths feel scared, threatened, or punished. Others have command hallucinations in which they hear voices directing them to engage in antisocial behaviors.

A significant issue in the placement of youths in psychiatric hospitals is related to whether or not their parents have health insurance. For this reason, the youth population in this type of institution is more likely to come from a white, middle- or upper-class background. Unfortunately, the length of stay in a mental hospital is too often not based on the degree to which the treatment program is helping the child but on the amount of time permitted by the family's health insurance.

Most psychiatric hospital programs for adolescents utilize a wide range of treatment approaches. The program is usually coordinated by the psychiatrist, psychologist, or social worker who has placed the child in the hospital. Individual counseling sessions take place with the client and his or her family several times a week.

Following is a list of treatment services that adolescent patients and their families participated in on a weekly basis in a hospital in which I worked for six years.[3] The program was typical of other hospitals for juveniles.

1.   *Community meetings.* Patients and staff gather to discuss issues and resolve problems that occur on the unit. Communication and leadership skills are encouraged in this process, as each patient takes a turn in assisting in the leading of these meetings.

2.   *Drug/alcohol abuse groups.* An important part of the process is group counseling focusing on alcohol and drug abuse for those patients who

---

3. This list of treatment approaches is taken from the *Manual* of the Coldwater Canyon Hospital, "Adolescent and Child Mental Health Program," Los Angeles, California.

can benefit from this additional service. This program provides Alcoholics Anonymous meetings in the hospital on a regular basis. The emphasis is on drug awareness and education, sobriety, and related personal growth. In addition, the staff offers a transition to aftercare programs and support groups in the community.

3. *Art therapy.* Art therapy is based on the principle that most fundamental thoughts and feelings reach expression in images rather than in words. Through the process of drawing, painting, and sculpting, combined with the art therapist's skill in helping the patient discover and release unconscious feelings and thoughts, the client can then work to resolve conflicts and fears.

4. *Educational therapy group.* Educational therapy is an activity group to help adolescents explore their relationships to school.

5. *Group psychotherapy for emotional problems.* Group psychotherapy sessions are held daily. These groups are designed to complement individual psychotherapy with an emphasis on mutual sharing as well as giving support and constructive feedback to one another. Group goals include encouraging self-exploration and self-expression, identifying current behavior patterns and alternative options, and expanding social skills. As a result, the individual goal is to generate new, more effective interpersonal skills.

6. *Movement therapy.* Therapeutic use of movement helps improve the emotional and physical integration of an individual. In addition to helping patients find appropriate ways to release tension, movement therapy provides an opportunity to express and deal with feelings that have defied words.

7. *Multifamily groups.* Weekly group meetings are designed for all parents and patients. The group provides a forum for the modeling and teaching of good communication skills between parents and their child. An important goal is to help strengthen the parents' ability to provide their son or daughter with limits and structure while still offering love and caring. Issues of the child's growing up and separating from the family are also addressed when relevant. In addition, the group provides an important support network for parents whose children are hospitalized.

8. *Occupational therapy.* A registered occupational therapist (OTR) provides patients with the opportunity to learn and practice skills needed for a successful "occupation" of their time. The OTR evaluates the patient's strengths and weaknesses in the areas of self-care, social, emotional, mental, physical, and occupational functioning.

9. *Psychodrama.* Psychodrama groups meet on a weekly basis. Their purpose is to provide an alternative expressive mode in which dramatic techniques are utilized to facilitate the exploring of painful emotional issues. (This is a basic group treatment modality that I have utilized extensively in my work. Psychodrama is discussed in more detail in chapter 16.)

10. *Recreational therapy.* Recreational therapy provides adolescents with opportunities for learning and practicing social and recreational skills, which help individuals learn to use their time in more satisfying ways and to feel better about themselves.

11. *School.* The school program is provided by the school district. Teachers are trained in special education to meet the unique needs of hospitalized youth.

A Case Study: Rose

A prototypical adolescent who was successfully treated in a psychiatric hospital program of the type described was Rose. Since she was in two of my groups over an eight-month period, I was able to analyze her progress and growth in the hospital. A drug encounter group was especially useful to her. In Rose's overall treatment sessions, she explored, and to a large extent resolved, her difficulties with her parents. In the drug encounter group sessions she was confronted by the therapist, the ex-addicts, and others in the group with eliminating her self-destructive drug abuse. Here she was intensely verbally engaged about her drug abuse and her general delinquent behavior. In the adolescent drug group she regularly attended in the hospital, several recovering ex-addicts from a local drug-addict therapeutic community took part in Rose's overall therapy. They were masters at encounter group therapy. (This method will be discussed more fully in chapter 16.)

Of considerable importance was a counselor named Renee, an ex-addict from a therapeutic community (TC). Renee, twenty-one, had a life experience that was similar to Rose's. Renee at that time had been drug-free for three years. She became Rose's friend, role model, and sponsor. In my drug group, Renee made such comments as, "Rose, I remember when I was your age, I had the exact feelings you're talking about and I handled them." She would then describe how she handled her problems after she became drug free.

In the conceptual scheme of the adolescent drug encounter group was the idea that when Addict A helps Addict B, Addict A is helped. The therapeutic contract between Renee and Rose was not one way. Renee's helping Rose in the group and in personal conversations allowed Renee to review the path she had traveled out of her own addiction. (Later on, I hired Rose as a peer counselor, and she served as a role model for other younger people in the hospital program.)

Bill and Jane were two other teenagers who served as role models for Rose. They were both ex-addicts who had been in the hospital's therapeutic community but now were living in the outside community. They had successfully traveled the track Rose was on and were able to help her through some difficult times in her social growth. They were particularly helpful to Rose in a "slip" regression situation in the encounter group. Rose, on pass, went out with a young man on a date, slipped into having a few drinks, and used some cocaine. She tearfully and fearfully told about this in the encounter group: "I have something to tell the group. I went out with this guy Jack, and I like him a lot. I had a few drinks, and when Jack offered me some coke I felt I couldn't say no. I mean I could say no, but I felt if I did he would think I was a jerk, and I'd never see him again. Anyway, I did horn some coke and I feel horrible. I thought I was cured."

Coming from an aggressive, self-righteous position, Bill blasted Rose in the encounter group. "I'm really pissed-off at you. You've been sitting in this group for four months, and you haven't learned yet that this dick who offered you coke was not your friend. 'Friends' don't offer recovering addicts poison." Other verbal blasts came from members of the group, including Rose's sponsor Renee, who also told some stories about her slips. The group became supportive of Rose and her plight and talked about their own slips. It was valuable to hear from her peers about this. The group had become for Rose both a support and a control group.

Rose later commented, "When I did the coke I really didn't enjoy it like I used to. My first thought was, 'Shit, I'm going to have to cop out to the group,' and I felt terrible." In a way the group had disabled her from going too far wrong, because they had, along with my sermonizing, inculcated an antidrug attitude into her thought processes.

Of great importance in Rose's recovery were the program directors and the adolescent ward psychiatric aides. On a nonscheduled basis, the adolescent ward director or a psychiatric aide with whom Rose had built a relationship would have a therapeutic session on-the-spot, at a time when it was most vital for Rose to have special counseling. The aides and several residents in the program functioned as Rose's "caring circle of friends." Their availability and understanding treatment were vital to Rose's recovery process. Along with the drug encounter group, the individual and group counseling Rose received in the hospital program helped her to get along better with her family and to change her incorrigible delinquent behavior to a more acceptable law-abiding life-style.

In summary, the evidence is that most training schools produce the kind of negative experiences described by Claude Brown (1965). They tend to reinforce deviant values rather than resocialize youths. In contrast, institutions like Highfields and psychiatric hospital programs are more effective in resocializing delinquents. These types of institutional programs appear to be more valuable in treating delinquents than the long-term state facilities, because they tend to reach the needs of the delinquent more effectively. The specific group therapy methodologies, like psychodrama and the encounter group that are utilized in Highfields and psychiatric hospitals, are described more fully in chapter 16.

CHAPTER 16

TREATMENT METHODS AND STRATEGIES UTILIZED IN COMMUNITY PREVENTION PROJECTS AND CUSTODIAL INSTITUTIONS

Group therapy for both males and females that involves in-depth discussions of their mutual problems is an effective treatment method for preventing and controlling delinquency.

A variety of basic methods and strategies are utilized in the therapeutic process of different types of institutional and community facilities for preventing, treating, and controlling juvenile delinquency. These methods and treatment strategies are incorporated in the various overall programs of juvenile reformatories, camps, halfway houses, mental hospitals, probation and parole programs, and "therapeutic communities."

Individual Counseling and Therapy

A basic method for treating delinquents is individual counseling. Parents, teachers, and professional therapists at utilize individual counseling approaches in the home, school, office settings, and institutions. In professional therapeutic or therapy counseling, there are two persons present—the therapist or counselor and the patient or counselee. What occurs in the course of the counseling depends largely on the philosophy, training, and ability of the therapist. For example, if the therapist or counselor is a psychologist, probation officer, or other person trained in transactional analysis, the session includes an analysis of the "games" the delinquent is playing. Similarly, the psychodramatist, the reality therapist, and the gestalt therapist utilize their systems in a therapeutic effort to gain an understanding of the juveniles and to increase their understanding of themselves and of their personal and family problems.

Delinquents pose special problems in almost all therapeutic situations. Richard Korn, an eminent criminologist and therapist, worked with difficult offenders in a variety of settings in and out of custodial institutions. In the following individual counseling session, the problems posed by a recalcitrant sociopathic delinquent who was attempting to manipulate the therapist are revealed. The session took place in an office in a reformatory. Korn opened the session by asking the youth why he had come to see him and then began to work on defining the therapeutic relationship.

> INMATE: Well, I've been talking to a few of the guys. . . . They said it might be a good idea.
>
> COUNSELOR: Why?
>
> INMATE (in a fairly convincing attempt to appear reticent): Well, they said it did them good. They said a guy needs somebody he can talk to around here . . . somebody he can trust. A . . . a friend.
>
> COUNSELOR: And the reason you asked to see me was that you felt that I might be a friend? Why did you feel this?
>
> INMATE (a little defensively): Because they told me, I guess. Aren't you supposed to be a friend to the guys?

455

COUNSELOR: Well, let's see now. What is a friend supposed to do? (Inmate looked puzzled.) Lets take your best buddy, for example. Why do you consider him a friend?

INMATE (puzzled and a little more aggressive): I dunno . . . we help each other, I guess. We do things for each other.

COUNSELOR: And friends are people who do things for each other?

INMATE: Yes.

COUNSELOR: Fine. Now, as my friend, was is it you feel you'd like to do for me?

INMATE (visibly upset): I don't get it. Aren't you supposed to help? Isn't that your job?

COUNSELOR: Wait a minute—I'm getting lost. A little while ago you were talking about friends and you said that friends help each other. Now you're talking about my job.

INMATE (increasingly annoyed): Maybe I'm crazy, but I thought you people are supposed to help us.

COUNSELOR: I think I get it now. When you said "friends" you weren't talking about the kind of friendship that works both ways. The kind you meant was where I help you, not where you do anything for me.

INMATE: Well . . . I guess so. If you put it that way.

COUNSELOR: Okay. [Relaxing noticeably from his previous tone of persistence.] Now, how do you feel I can help you?

INMATE: Well, you're supposed to help people get rehabilitated, aren't you?

COUNSELOR: Wait. I'm lost again. You say I'm supposed to do something for people. I thought you wanted me to do something for you. So you want me to help you get rehabilitated?

INMATE: Sure.

COUNSELOR: Fine. Rehabilitated from what?

INMATE: Well, so I won't get in trouble anymore.

COUNSELOR: What trouble?

At this point, the inmate launched into a vehement recital of the abuses to which he been subjected from his first contact with the juvenile authorities to his most recent difficulties with his probation officer immediately prior to the offense (stealing a car) that led to his present sentence. During the entire recital he never referred to any offense he had committed but, instead, emphasized the mistreatment he believed he had experienced at the hands of the authorities. The counselor listened to this account, his facial expression one of growing puzzlement, which was not lost on the inmate, who continued with increasing vehemence as his listener appeared increasingly puzzled. Finally, the counselor, with a gesture of bewilderment, broke in on the youth's lengthy indictments of all the people who had mistreated him:

> COUNSELOR: Wait. . . . I don't understand. When you said you wanted me to help you stop getting into trouble, I thought you meant the kind of trouble that got you in here. Your difficulties with the law, for example. You've talked about your troubles with different people and how they get you angry but you haven't talked about what got you into this institution.

> INMATE (visibly trying to control himself): But I am talking about that! I'm talking about those bastards responsible for me being here.

> COUNSELOR: How do you mean?

The inmate again repeated his tirade, without accepting any responsibility for his fate, interspersing it with frequent remarks addressed to the counselor ("What about this? Do you think that was right? Is that the way to treat a young guy?"). The counselor once more looked puzzled and intervened again.

> COUNSELOR: I still don't see it. We'd better get more specific. Now take your last trouble—the one that get you into the reformatory. This car you stole.

> INMATE (excitedly): It was that P.O. [probation officer]. I asked him to get me a job in New York. He said no.

> COUNSELOR: What job?

> (The inmate admitted that it wasn't a specific job.)

> COUNSELOR: But I still don't follow. The probation officer wouldn't let you work in New York. What has that got to do with your stealing a car?

Here the youth "blew up" and started to denounce "bug doctors who don't help a guy but only cross-examine him."

> COUNSELOR: Wait a minute. You said before that you wanted me to help you. We've been trying to find out how. But so far you haven't been talking about anything the matter with you at all. All you've talked about are these other people and things wrong with them and how they screwed you. Now, are we suppose to rehabilitate you or rehabilitate them?

> INMATE: I don't give a fuck who you rehabilitate. I've had about enough of this. Never mind, let's call whole thing off.

COUNSELOR: But I do mind. Here you've been telling me that my job is to rehabilitate you and we have talked for about five minutes and now you want to call the whole thing off. Don't you want to be rehabilitated? [Inmate is silent.] Let's see if we can review our relationship and put it in the right perspective. You say you wanted to be rehabilitated. I asked you from what, and you said from getting into trouble. Then I asked you to talk about your troubles, and you told me about this probation officer. He didn't give you what you wanted so you stole a car. Now as near as I can understand it, the way to keep you out of trouble is to get people to give you what you want.

INMATE: That's not true, dammit!

COUNSELOR: Well, let's see now. Have I given you what you wanted?

INMATE: Hell, no!

COUNSELOR: You're pretty mad at me right now, aren't you? (Counselor smiles. Inmate is silent, looks away.)

COUNSELOR (in a half-kidding tone): Here, not ten minutes ago, you were talking about what good friends we could be and now you're acting like I'm your worst enemy.

INMATE (very halfheartedly, trying not to look at the counselor's face): It's true, isn't it?

COUNSELOR: C'mon now. Now you're just trying to get mad. You won't even look at me because you're afraid you'll smile.

Inmate cannot repress a smile. Counselor drops his kidding tone and gets businesslike again.

COUNSELOR: Okay, Now that we've agreed to stop kidding, let's get down to cases. Why did you come to see me today?

Inmate halfheartedly starts to talk about rehabilitation again, but the counselor cuts in.

COUNSELOR: Come on, now. I thought we agreed you were going to stop conning me. Why did you come?

INMATE: Well . . . I heard you sometimes see guys . . . and . . .

COUNSELOR: And what?

INMATE: Help them.

COUNSELOR: How?

INMATE: Well, I tell you my story . . . and . . .

COUNSELOR: And then? What happens then? [Inmate is silent.]

INMATE (finally). You tell them about it.

COUNSELOR: Who do I tell?

INMATE: You know—people who read them.

COUNSELOR: Should I write a report on this session to help you get released. Is that what you want?

INMATE: Hell, no!

COUNSELOR: What do you think we should do?

INMATE (looking away): Maybe I could . . . (falls silent.)

COUNSELOR (quietly): Maybe you should come and talk to me when we really have something to talk about?

INMATE: Yeah . . . Aw, hell . . . (laughs). (Korn and McCorkle, 1959, pp. 562–566)

This interview illustrates the problems and possibilities inherent in the crucial first counseling session with a sociopathic offender of average intelligence. The youth attempted to conceal his true feelings and his motives and to manipulate the therapist under the disguise of a request for friendly help.

The special character of the delinquent's motivations concerning treatment requires a special counseling technique. The usual methods of permissiveness, nondirection, and acceptance require modification. To have permitted the delinquent to "define the relationship" would have been useless, since that definition would have left the counselor no alternative to the roles of dupe or oppressor. Similarly, to have encouraged this sociopathic delinquent to "solve his problems in his own way" would have been merely to collaborate with him in the continuation of his antisocial pattern: the manipulation of personal relationships for the purposes of self-aggrandizement and exploitation.

Another element involved in the individual counseling of delinquents is related to their rationalizing their delinquent behavior by projecting the blame onto the larger society. This manipulation was part of the described interaction between Dr. Korn and the "inmate." Often in a treatment session I have noticed that offenders tend to exonerate or neutralize their delinquent behavior by blaming society, which shortchanged them and caused their delinquency. Poverty, abusive parents, broken homes, limited opportunities—all real causal variables—are cited by delinquents as the problem, rather than their own deviance.

Although these rationalizations (which do have a basis in reality) are more likely to be used by adult criminals, they are also part of the self-concept system of youthful offenders. In the face of these overwhelming variables, delinquents assert that they are not responsible for their delinquent behavior. Society is responsible for their plight, and they conclude that nothing can change these causal conditions, so why should they try to change? Although the offenders' defense may have an element of truth, if they are to change, therapists must get them to accept responsibility for their behavior and some awareness of their own power in the therapeutic process.

Neutralization or nonacceptance of a self-concept of delinquent status impedes the possibility of treatment, since the offender denies he or she has done anything wrong. A parallel is found in the Alcoholics Anonymous philosophy, which posits that before an alcoholic can be helped he or she must, as a first step, acknowledge being an alcoholic and assume some responsibility for his or her own behavior. For a delinquent to be resocialized, he or she must acknowledge that drug abuse, violence, theft, or gang behavior is wrong and bear the responsibility for his or her behavior. If the delinquent's self-concept is one of denial of responsibility, he or she will be difficult to reach and rehabilitate. In the individual session presented here, the counselor was effective in not being manipulated and in getting the client to accept responsibility for his behavior and the reality of his life situation. After accomplishing this position and relationship with his client, the therapist could begin to help the delinquent youth.

Reality Therapy

William Glasser, a psychiatrist who worked with delinquent girls at the Ventura School in California, developed a treatment strategy that he called "reality therapy." Glasser (1965) maintained that, from a treatment standpoint, both the theory and practice of reality therapy are incompatible with the prevalent concept of mental illness. He described the task of the therapist as one of becoming involved with the client and then inducing the client to face reality. A major objective is to get the client to decide to cooperate with the treatment process and take responsibility for his or her way of life.

Glasser believed that reality therapy differs from conventional therapy on six points related to the involvement of a delinquent:

1. Because we do not accept the concept of mental illness, the patient cannot become involved with us as a mentally ill person who has no responsibility for his behavior.

2. Working in the present and toward the future, we do not get involved with the patient's history, because we can neither change what happened to him nor accept that he is limited by his past.

3. We relate to patients as ourselves, not as transference figures.

4. We do not look for unconscious conflicts or the reasons for them. A patient cannot become involved with us by excusing his behavior on the basis of unconscious motivations.

5. We emphasize the morality of behavior. We face the issue of right and wrong, which we believe solidifies the involvement, in contrast to conventional psychiatrists who do not make the distinction between right and wrong, feeling it would be detrimental to attaining the transference relationship they seek.

6. We teach patients better ways to fulfill their needs. The proper involvement will not be maintained unless the patient is helped to find more satisfactory patterns of behavior. Conventional therapists do not feel that teaching better behavior is a part of therapy. (1965, pp. 44–45)

The case of Maria illustrates Glasser's application of reality therapy.

Apathetic and despondent, Maria, a seventeen-and-a-half-year-old girl, was a far different problem from Jeri. Jeri was at least capable of taking care of herself fairly well, albeit illegally. She had good intelligence and some sort of warped self-reliance. Maria, on the other hand, had almost nothing. In institutions since she was about twelve, before then in foster homes, with no family, few friends, not too much intelligence (although test results are misleadingly low on these deprived girls), she came to my attention after she was involved in a serious fight in her cottage. I was asked to see her in the discipline cottage because she seemed so hopeless. She had been sitting in her room, eating little, and making no effort to contact any of the cottage staff. There seemed to be little we could do for her because she had given up herself. The fight that brought her into discipline was the result of a building frustration caused by an older, smarter girl, Sonia, who, recognizing Maria's desperate need for affection, pretended to like her in order to get Maria to be a virtual slave. Marie had attacked another girl whom Sonia had openly preferred to her and who joined with Sonia in making fun of Maria.

When I sat with her in the day room of the discipline unit, she refused to speak, just sitting apathetically and staring at the floor. I asked her my routine getting-acquainted questions, such as, How long have you been at the school? What are you here for? What are your plans? Do you want to return to your cottage? Maria just sat and stared. Finally she asked me to leave her alone. She had seen plenty of psyches (as our girls call psychiatrists) before, but she never talked to them. It was a discouraging interview, if it could be called an interview at all. We were worlds apart. After about twenty very long minutes I said, "I will see you next week." Saying nothing, she walked quietly back to her room. I felt I had made no impression whatsoever. None!

Each week for seven weeks the same scene was repeated, except for different questions, and few enough of them because I could not think of what to ask. My most frequent question was, "Don't you want to get out of here?" Her reply, on occasions when she did reply was, "What for?" My attempts to answer were met with silence. I did not have a good answer because she was obviously involved with no one and had no way to fulfill her needs—her isolated room was probably the most comfortable place for her. At least in a room by herself she did not have to see others doing and feeling what was not possible for her.

At the eighth visit I detected the first glimmer of hope. She said "Hi" in answer to my "Hi" and looked at me occasionally during the interview. I decided on a whim to ask her about her tattoos. Tattoos are the rule with our girls, nine girls out of ten have some. On her legs and arms Maria had twenty or thirty self-inflicted tattoos—dots, crosses, words, initials, and various marks, all common with our girls. I asked her if she would like a large, particularly ugly tattoo removed. Unexpectedly, she said she would; she would like them all out. Her request surprised me because girls like Maria are more apt to add tattoos rather than want them out. Lonely, isolated girls, particularly in juvenile halls, derive some sense of existence through the pain of pushing ink or dirt into their skin and by the mark produced by the act. It is a way they have, they tell me, of making sure they are still there. On the next visit we talked further about her tattoos and her feelings of hopelessness. In addition, she brought up her fear that her housemother, toward whom she had some warm feeling, would not take her back into the cottage because of what she had done. Although a housemother can refuse to take a girl back into the cottage when there are serious fights between girls, she rarely does so. I said I did not know whether or not her housemother would take her back, but that I would have her housemother stop by and see her if Maria wished it. She said she would appreciate seeing her housemother very much.

Maria now started to make progress. Her housemother, who liked her and recognized the loneliness in her quiet, uncomplaining ways, visited her and told her she was welcome back in the cottage. Her housemother also said how much she missed Maria's help with the cottage housework. Maria had been a tireless worker in the cottage. I told Maria that I had discussed her problems with the girls in my therapy group and that they wanted her to join the group. My few interviews, together with the powerful effect of the housemother's visit, had already caused some change in Maria when she left discipline. The girls in my group therapy took a special interest in her, something which might have been resented by a more sophisticated girl, but was deeply appreciated by Maria. The technique of getting girls who are more responsible to become particularly interested in someone like Maria is strongly therapeutic for them because it directly leads to fulfilling their needs and helps them to identify with the staff, thereby helping to sever ties with their own delinquent group.

Taking more interest in school, Maria began to learn to read for the first time. In the group we talked at length about what she might do, and it was decided that a work home with small children, whom she could love and who might love her in return, would be best. Older girls who have no families do well in carefully selected homes where they are paid to do housework and child care. Although by then she was no problem, we kept her a few extra months so that some of her worst tattoos could be removed and to allow her to become more accustomed to relating to people.

The case of Maria illustrates that the key to involvement is neither to give up nor to push too hard. No matter how lonely and isolated a girl may be, if the therapist adheres to the present and points to a hopeful future and, in cases like Maria's, expands her initial involvement into a series of involvements as soon as possible, great changes can take place. Here the need for group therapy was critical for there she could gain strength from relating to more responsible girls and could see how she might emulate their more responsible behavior. Through our persistence Maria, perhaps for the first time in her life, was able to fulfill her needs.

From her good relationship with her housemother, Maria was able to go to a work home where her hard work and love for children were deeply appreciated. Later she married and our assistant superintendent has several pictures of Maria's growing and successful family in her "grandchildren" picture gallery. (Glasser, 1965, pp. 44–45, 80–82)

Group Therapy

J.L. Moreno, a pioneer psychiatrist (and my mentor in psychology, psychodrama, and group therapy), was the first to introduce a form of group psychotherapy into the correctional process in 1931. Before this innovation, the only form of therapy employed in the corrections and mental health fields was individual therapy. Moreno described his group therapy methodology in an article published in 1932 by the National Committee on Prisons and Prison Labor. The article described Moreno's working at Sing Sing Prison in New York. Moreno's later research and action methods, used at the Hudson Training School for Girls, provided valuable material for his now classic book, *Who Shall Survive?* (1934). Since the early 1930s, in part due to Moreno's pioneer work, virtually every correctional institution for delinquents now has some form of group therapy included in its program.

Some group therapy approaches are therapist centered. In this approach the therapist attempts to treat each member of the group individually or together but does not intentionally use the members of the group to help one another. Other programs are group centered. In such groups, the therapist considers every member of the group to be a therapeutic agent for every other member. Also of importance is the therapist's perspective on the group's structure in the therapy process. Guided group interaction is a group-centered method; here the group is treated as an interactional unit. Some groups are psychoanalytically oriented; the therapist seeks to give individual members of the group insight into their problems from a psychoanalytic point of view. Other groups are spontaneous and free, and members are encouraged to develop spontaneity.

Psychodrama and role training are group methods designed to develop spontaneity and to modify illegal behavior. In individual therapy sessions, an offender can rationalize, distort, or simply lie about what is taking place. However, in group therapy he or she must necessarily be aware that his or her description of the group process is subject to the wider commentary and audience. Group methods, therefore, usually have broader impact than individual methods on delinquents.

The group process produces an open situation that tends to merge the institutional underworld with its more formal structure. In addition to blending the subculture of the institution with its upper world, group therapy also opens up the group therapist's activity to wider inspection and more critical analysis, not only by peers but also by his or her clients. What he or she does as a group therapist is much more open to discussion than what he or she does in the individual therapy situation. The process of group therapy, therefore, presents the possibility for much greater impact than the process of individual therapy not only upon offenders but also upon staff and the total social system of the institution.

In dyadic therapeutic interactions (one therapist, one patient), two personalities who may be far apart in intellectual abilities attempt to community about one of the individual's problems (usually the offender's). Generally speaking, therapists tend to come from a different sociocultural milieu than delinquents. Therapeutic communication may therefore be significantly impaired. This is not necessarily the case in group therapy. Delinquents in group therapy are (by definition) in interaction with others who have comparable levels of understanding and usually a similar set of difficulties. In group therapy, delinquents become co-therapists, and this seems to increase the potentiality of group understanding.

Often in group psychotherapy offenders who have difficulty interpreting and diagnosing their own problems are experts vis-à-vis their fellows. In fact, many sociopaths, generally considered the most difficult type of delinquents to treat, are excellent diagnosticians and interpreters of the problems of other delinquents. Sociopaths can thus be enlisted as effective co-therapists, and this sometimes has a positive effect on their own behavior.

In comparing group therapy with individual therapy (formal psychoanalysis in particular), one finds that the average offender's educational background and intellectual abilities are geared more to the group process. In psychoanalysis with offenders, for example, the therapist may develop excellent and appropriate formulations about the offender's problem. However, the analyst may have considerable difficulty inducing the offender to understand him- or herself in the same way that the psychoanalyst thinks he or she understands the delinquent.

In group psychotherapy, which tends to operate on a less sophisticated intellectual level, the offender, with other offenders as co-therapists, is more likely to develop insights and understanding of his or her behavior that are beneficial to treatment. The offender can thus relearn behavior patterns on an emotional and action level in the group process rather than be required to understand an intellectual analysis that may be foreign to his or her thought processes.

Guided Group Interaction

Guided group interaction is a form of group treatment developed by Lloyd McCorkle during World War II, while he was on duty with the army at Fort Knox, Kentucky. The treatment gained prominence in the area of delinquency when it was successfully applied by McCorkle while he was director of Highfields, described earlier (McCorkle, 1958). In the application of this method, little emphasis is placed on academic training as a prerequisite for group leadership of guided group interaction sessions, and for that reason it is widely used in halfway houses throughout the country.

Guided group interaction is based on the idea that delinquent adolescents can realistically appraise their life situations and make decisions based on that appraisal. The leader encourages free discussion of the events of the day and of relationships within the group. It is a "here and now" approach to behavior and concentrates on developing concern *for* others and mutual concerns *with* others. Each individual is encouraged to recognize his or her shortcomings and deal with them.

McCorkle described the process and a prototypical session as follows:

> A guided group interaction meeting usually runs for ninety minutes. Typically, ten or twelve boys file into the room promptly at the scheduled hour, dragging in their own chairs. The director may introduce a new boy to the others, explaining that he

was there to help them with their problems, as the experienced members were to help him with his.

Immediately after such an introduction, Harvey, one of the group members who has been at the center for some months now, becomes the focus of attention, describing, in a somewhat belligerent tone, a clash he has had that morning with his work supervisor. The latter had taken offense at a comment he had meant to be humorous, and had yelled at him. Harvey, in turn, had grabbed the employee's arm. The employee had then shouted, "Get your——hands off of me." Although the narrator was giving a version of the incident favorable to his point of view, the other boys were hesitant to credit it, one after another criticizing him for having deliberately aggravated the employee: "What's wrong with you, Harvey? The man was simply doing his job." Harvey replies that he felt he had been humiliated, or "put down" by the employee, to which the others retort: "You put yourself down." Harvey, now aroused, states that he would not have grabbed the employee's arm if he had not "hollered and cussed at me," at which, he said, he himself had become excited and scared.

At this point, the leader intervenes, for the first time in fifteen minutes, quietly asking the group why they thought Harvey had acted as he did. The boys are quick to reply that, although he had been at the center for five months, Harvey could still be expected to make "smart" remarks and wisecracks. Almost half the group now hurl questions at Harvey, many of them simultaneously, all accusing him of being a troublemaker, a faker, and a "bad mouth." [These are euphemisms for more profane language.] Harvey at this point admits that the employee with whom he had argued probably agreed with the group's opinion of himself.

One boy then asks, "What will it take to get you interested in people?" When all he gets back is a muttered reply, another boy comments, "It would be easy to talk Harvey into committing a crime if he was 'on the outside.'" Here again (ten minutes having elapsed since his last question), the leader quietly asks, "Why?" The boy replies: "It doesn't matter much to him. Harvey seems like a weak person." The comments that follow are not all so negative, the boys admitting that, "Harvey does not enjoy hurting people like he used to."

The significance of this remark can better be judged by the fact that Harvey had had a long history of violent assault. In his most recent act, the one resulting in his arrest and conviction, he had forced a grown man, at the point of a gun, to crawl, bare-chested, on a gravel road. After several hundred feet of such humiliation and torture, when the victim, his chest torn and bleeding, attempted to lift himself up from the road, he had been met with threats that his head would be blown off.

Harvey now voices his concern that he might get sent to the state training school. "Why do you enjoy wising off?" The leader asks this question, to which Harvey admits that he didn't think of the feelings of others. Then one of the group comments, "If Harvey doesn't like someone, he just messes over him. He doesn't care."

"Does Harvey intended to hurt people here, at this time?" the leader asks, to which one boy replies, "No, he didn't mean to. His smart remarks were more off the cuff."

The counselor cuts in: "Harvey is not really sorry about the employee. He is simply sorry because he knows the man will be riding him from here on. He's sorry for himself, not for what he did."

The conversation had now gone on for an hour, and Harvey was permitted to step down from the "hot seat." In his place came Stanley, a black boy who had hit another boy with a mop because, "He told me I was lying. I didn't want him lying on me."

"How did this affect you?" the group asked. "Why did it make you mad when the boy said you were lying?"

Stanley began to get angry. "I thought it was like a team here. I got attached to you guys, when I tell you what I've done, you give me hell even though I said I was sorry."

The boys, thoroughly aroused, all reject his statements. "How come no one in the group can talk to you, Stan? What are you going to do about it, Stan?"

Incensed, Stanley remarks that he is "a cool agent," who does not have to justify himself to anybody. The others better not "mess" with him.

Harvey, now a discussant rather than the target of the group's concern, comments, "You're not near as cool as you think you are, Stan."

Another asks, "What does this 'cool' mean, Stan? Suppose you tell us just what this 'being cool' means."

Stanley becomes thoroughly belligerent at this point: "Anything I feel like doing, I'll do it. Besides, Harvey'd better watch himself, 'cause I don't like him messing with me."

The intensity of the attacks now increases: "What is this threatening stuff, Stan? Let's face it, Stan, you do threaten people."

Above the loud and angry attacks Stanley is heard defending himself: "That still stands. Ain't no one going to mess over me."

Another member of the group, stung but undaunted by his threats, asks, "What are you, Stan, a giant superman?"

Stanley fights back, "You just——with me and you'll find out. I won't let little boys like you——over me. I can handle myself pretty well. I ain't been——up like I have been. I been trying."

Suddenly he seems to change his tactics and, although still furious, pretends complete agreement though in a low monotone, "I'll go by what the group says. If you say I don't know what I'm doing, I guess I don't."

The others are not so easily placated. One comments, "Now you're playing games, Stan. You're acting like a baby. Your threats aren't bothering anybody."

Quite subdued, now, Stanley: "I don't mean it as a threat. I've been saying that kind of stuff all my life." As if he suddenly realizes that he himself has let drop his guard, Stanley shouts back angrily, "But nobody better tangle with Stan!"

Suddenly the air is thick with obscenities. A third boy, Frank, as angry as Stanley, now remarks, "You don't scare me none. Go ahead and make your move."

A fight appearing imminent, the leader, who has been silent during all the foregoing, quietly asks, "What's the group doing now? Aren't you trying to force a challenge?"

The tension eases and one of the group says quietly, "We just want him to stop that kind of——."

Stanley rejoins, "I ain't going to like these boys, if they keep messing with me."

For the remaining quarter hour the leader now took over, giving a summary of what had taken place. He referred to Harvey's clash with the employee and his belief that progress had been made, because this was the first time that Harvey had admitted being afraid. He was confident of Harvey's ability to control himself even when other people shout at him. He pointed out that Harvey had acted belligerently because of his fear of being "put down" before the group. The leader than emphasized the boys' concern for one another by relating how, when Harvey had recently got himself into an embarrassing situation, it had been Stanley who had stepped forward and permitted Harvey to "save face."

He then referred to Stanley's attack with a mop on another boy, pointing out that Stanley had told the other boy he was sorry. "Stan says he's trying to change, and he complains that the group won't recognize this. The group, on the other hand, says it does care for Stan, but it's not afraid of him either. The group feels that Stan is trying to 'put them down' by making them afraid of Stan. But," he continued, "Stan is showing us some of his true feelings in contrast to Frank who has been playing it real 'cool' in keeping his feelings hidden."

Here Frank admitted that, "I've had these feelings for a long, long time," that he often felt angry, and that he tried to conceal it by "playing it cool."

The leader then criticized the group for not having stopped Frank at the point when he had challenged Stanley to "make his move."

"The group should have asked what was going on because Frank left the issue of helping Stan and simply got mad."

Frank, his head low, in an undertone: "I might as well let my anger out here, or I'll never get out of this place."

The leader assured him, "Don't worry about letting it out."

The meeting ended with Stanley, still appearing angry, remarking, "I don't know what to say."

With the other boys looking concerned, the director closed the meeting: "You boys recognize you've got problems, and you're doing something about them." (Keller and Alper, 1970, pp. 69–72)

Transactional Analysis

Eric Berne, a psychiatrist, developed a popular treatment strategy called transactional analysis, based on the assumption that every person has available a repertoire of three ego states. These are, according to Berne (1981):

1. Parent: ego state that resembles that of parental figures; tells us how to do things and what we should and should not be doing.

2. Adult: ego state that is autonomously directed toward objective appraisal of reality; examines and evaluates; bases decisions on facts.

3. Child: still active ego state that is fixated in childhood; the "I want to" feelings and emotions.

The treatment in transactional analysis, according to Berne, consists of efforts to get Parent, Adult, and Child to work together and to allow Adult to solve problems. In transactional analysis terms, a *stroke* is a fundamental unit of social action. An exchange of strokes is a transaction. When interacting with others, transactions take the form of (1) rituals, (2) pastimes, (3) games, (4) intimacy, and (5) activity. Each person, in interaction with others, seeks as many satisfactions as possible from his or her transactions. The most gratifying social contacts are games and intimacy. Most games are ways of avoiding intimacy.

In transactional analysis, the focus is on finding out which ego state (Parent, Adult, or Child) implements the stimulus and which state implements the response. To attain autonomy, the individual must become game free. He or she must overcome the programming of the past. The transactional analysis group is considered effective in analyzing transactions. When applied to delinquents, it has been found helpful in improving life positions, vocations, recreations, and interpersonal relationships.

The Encounter Group Process for Treating Drug Abusers

The encounter group, a form of group therapy, was pioneered by Charles Dederich, the founder of the first therapeutic community, Synanon. Dederich, in his early work with substance abusers, including alcoholics, determined that extreme confrontation was often necessary to get to the reality level of criminal/addicts' problems—since most of their life they had practiced self- and other deceptions. This early Synanon group approach has increasingly been used in group therapy programs in the United States and around the world (Yablonsky, 1965; Yablonsky 1989).

The members of an encounter group are very direct with each other, bordering on harshness. This "directness" is a significant element in the encounter approach that is used in therapeutic communities. Following is a description of the encounter approach as it has evolved in treating delinquent substance abusers in a therapeutic community. Although this decision focuses on the encounter method in a therapeutic community setting, it should be noted that this approach has been increasingly used for delinquents in general as a group approach in training schools, reformatories, mental hospitals, and other institutions for delinquents.

Most encounter groups consist of eight to twelve participants. In a typical session, everyone in the group settles down as comfortably as possible in a circle, facing one another. There is usually a brief silence, a kind of sizing up of one another, and then the group launches into an intense emotional discussion of the basic personal and emotional issues that relate to the members' problems.

In most groups, each person is put on the "hot seat" and confronted in a rotation fashion. Sometimes an individual may request the group to discuss his or her particular problem, but most of the time the person on the hot seat is picked by another group member who has observed something in the person's behave that requires attention.

A person's status in the therapeutic community (TC) or institution is left outside of the encounter group. This makes the group process more democratic and enables lower status people in the TC who have less power to speak up about issues that are bothering them. This opportunity is not usually allowed in the group system in the larger society. It is a valuable situation for adjusting grievances, and generally gives the recovering delinquents a feeling of power that they probably never had in their former life situations.

A conscious dimension of the group process is the use of senior members as role models; this is a significant factor in encounter-group sessions. A role model is a person who has been in the situation of the newer person and has made progress to a higher level of life performance in the group's structure. The role model is a dynamic example of what the newcomer can become after he or she learns, grows, and develops in the TC.

A person who is a role model in a TC has gone through three levels of valuable experience. He or she has (1) been a substance abuser, (2) gone through the complex emotional and therapeutic process of eliminating drugs from his or her life, and (3) developed skills for remaining substance free and leading a responsible life. These experiences can be passed on to a recovering delinquent through the group process.

Role models in a TC encounter group are usually not appointed as leaders in the group. Different group leaders emerge in any given session.

Leadership evolves in a spontaneous way as a result of length of time "clean," seniority in group experience, and a person's effective talent and ability to contribute to the group process. The senior members of a TC who become role models for newcomers have logged more encounter-group time and are usually more effective in their encounter-group ability.

For example, when members get together in a senior-members group (as often occurs), they throw up fewer smokescreens to defend self-deceptions and to obscure their problems. They waste less time on irrelevance and quickly get to the subject under discussion. Their verbal fighting style is more like a rapier than a bludgeon. When a point is made, the group does not dwell on it and savor its "great success"; they move into another problem area.

At least one senior group person who has logged many hours is injected into every TC group in order to facilitate the interaction, pace, and productivity of the session. Also necessary in an encounter group is an awareness of each group member's ability to examine his or her self-deception at that time. The newcomer is often handled lightly (given a "pass") until he or she becomes trained in the method. More experienced, senior residents are considered fair game for all-out attack. When they are on the hot seat, there is an assumption that their encounter-group experiences have toughened their emotional hides. They can defend more capably and are better prepared to handle the group's biting appraisal of their personal problems.

When newly arrived individuals dominate a group, the sessions are more apt to be cathartic and involve excessive and wild verbal responses. As individuals grow and develop skills in the TC organization, they usually develop better control and greater insight. Older members tend to be more intellectual and in most respects more capable in group sessions as facilitators of productive group interactions and as role models. They are also usually more adept at summarizing insights that may emerge in the process.

Often the comment made by a senior person (role model) in a group to a newcomer is, "I remember when I was like you when I was here six months ago." The person then shares why he or she no longer feels in imminent danger of returning to a delinquent life-style. This permits the newcomer to identify with someone who has experienced the same internal conflicts that he or she is currently facing and has resolved these issues. The role model is "listened to" and respected as a living example of the success that can be achieved by the newcomer.

A role model also provides preliminary information about the problems that the newcomer can anticipate upon reaching a higher level of social functioning. A role model might comment to a newcomer, "I vividly remember telling a group exactly what you just said when I was here six months. I talked about how helpless I felt at the prospect of never drinking or using drugs again—and in the back of my mind I had this terrible urge to use. I thought that after I'd been clean six months I could smoke and drink 'recreationally.' I've been there. I tried it two or three times, fell right on my ass, and went back to my old habit. Now that I've been clean two years, I know I can't use, even a little. I can't use at all. Maybe you can benefit from my experience with failure. Take my word for it. You are just like I was, and like me you can't use drugs 'recreationally.' It's a dumb idea."

This kind of open self-revelation by a senior patient-therapist in a therapeutic community is rarely found in conventional group therapy. Professional group leaders seldom use their own problems as examples for their patients. In fact, it is contraindicated in most therapeutic methodologies. In a TC, however, it is standard technique for the acting leader to "cop out" and identify with the "patient's" problem. In the encounter group, therefore, the delinquent has an achievable, positive goal exemplified by a person who has successfully worked through similar problems. The role-model concept is often discussed in TC encounter groups as a basic socialization process for developing a personality that will be drug free.

It is important to note that the interaction of the senior patient and the junior patient is of value to both. When delinquent A helps delinquent B, delinquent A is also helped. When the role model explains why the junior addict can't use drugs again, he or she is reinforcing his or her own resolution to stay drug free. Therefore, a delinquent in a TC playing the role of "therapist" is being helped personally by this role. And since all residents of a TC play "therapist" in the group, they are helping resolve their own problems in the process.

The dynamic factor that should be emphasized in this interaction is that the junior patient can perceive future possibilities because of the model, whose progress represents an achievable goal. For the senior patient this constant reminder of the way he or she was as a newcomer is important in reinforcing his or her resolve to remain drug free.

The characteristic of random group construction in a TC sets up a mathematical probability that the same individuals will not meet more than once. This gives everyone in the TC a chance to meet almost everyone else on a personal, emotional basis. This positively affects the *esprit de corps* of the community, since everyone gets acquainted on a personal basis in the encounter-group situation.

This random group factor also helps defeat the problem of the "therapeutic contract" that emerges in many conventional therapy groups, where the same people meet regularly in the same group. The therapeutic contract problem emerges in a conscious and unconscious reciprocal agreement between two or more people to not expose one another's psychological Achilles' heel. The unstated contract might be, for example, "If you don't expose or attack my embarrassing and painful problem, I won't bring up the problem that you don't want to discuss." This type of covert contract impedes personal growth in the group, since the group becomes constricted in its search for truth. In a TC the problem is avoided because of the randomization of the group construction.

In a TC encounter group, general good behavior is demanded on the assumption that it affects internal psychodynamic processes.

Most TCs use an approach that is the reverse of that commonly used in traditional group psychotherapy. In most traditional therapy, the starting point for treatment is the internal dynamics of the patient. The assumption is made that if a person's inner problems are somehow resolved, he or she will stop "acting out" bad behavior, such as using drugs. TC groups start with an attack on the reality of overt bad behavior that takes place in daily life situations. The group demands positive work habits, truth telling, and nondeviant behavior. If an addict lives positively and constructively in this manner and drug free for one or two years, it is conceivable that this will positively change his or her inner emotional dynamics.

This theme of demanding positive behavior is hammered home in the encounter group. Any deviant, irresponsible (often crudely labeled "dope fiend") behavior is subject to verbal attack. The fact that it is a verbal attack is also a learning experience, since many former addicts using verbal violence in an encounter group are obliquely learning physical violence impulse control. People who would formerly have acted out physical violence to express their angry emotions have learned to express these raw feelings verbally in an encounter group.

A key issue in the acceptance of the TC approach to delinquency is related to the reaction to the encounter-group approach. Many therapists and others raise such questions as: "Isn't it harmful to verbally attack a young delinquent who already has a weak ego?" "How do you know when one delinquent is ventilating his or her own hostility and has no concern for the person on the hot seat?" "How does this approach change the delinquent's self-destructive behavior?" My response to these questions is to point out that in the verbal "attack" in an encounter group, what is under attack is not the person or the person's ego but his or her deviant behavior and self-deception. In an effective encounter group, the "attackers," through hyperbole and exaggeration, denounce the self-deception that fosters self-destructive drug-abuse behavior and delinquency.

Another key factor in the success of encounter groups in TCs is their emphasis on uncompromising candor. No statements are barred from the group effort at truth seeking about problem-solving situations, feelings, and emotions of the members of the group. In the encounter process on a verbal level, "anything goes" if it will help the subject and the group to reach a better understanding of a situation or in their search for the truth about themselves.

The "anything goes verbally" concept about the encounter group is the one point that most participants in the verbal mayhem may find difficult to comprehend. Too often they interrupt what is being done as a "personal attack" when it is in fact an act of caring. The best way to explain this point is to clearly state that the rules of regular society and social interaction are modified or suspended in the encounter-group processes for the purpose of exploring truth to reach the goal of insight.

When the encounter-group process ends, the people in the group return to the roles of a more civil society. This concept is often made clear when people who have been viciously attacking or ridiculing each other in the group situation smile and hug each other after the group session ends. The encounter group, therefore, may be perceived as an emotional battlefield where an individual's delusions, distorted self-images, and negative behavior are attacked by the group to help the person under verbal attack better understand the reality of his or life, at least as perceived by other group members who share the same problem.

The method often involves, at first, exaggerated statements, ridicule, and analogy; and after the person whose self-deceptions are being attacked begins to listen to other group members more rationally, the situation is discussed in more rational, intellectual, and philosophical terms. The encounter, paradoxically, is an expression of love. As one delinquent told another at the end of a harsh group encounter, "If I didn't care about you and also feel that you could change, I wouldn't tell you the things I do. It would be foolish to attack someone who is hopeless or helpless."

The encounter group, in addition to exposing valuable truths, has the effect of emotionally "toughening up" the egos of delinquents who are usually, underneath it all, vulnerable, dependent, and overly sensitive. It helps delinquents to see themselves as relevant others do. The encounter often produces information and valid insights into a person's problems. If, at the conclusion of a term on the "hot seat" an individual who has been under attack has been able to hang on to any defenses for his or her behavior, then they are probably "valid defenses."

The delinquent is forced to examine positive and negative aspects about him or herself in the encounter group, as well as some dimensions about his or her behavior he or she would never have considered. This often leaves the person with a clearer knowledge of his or her inner and outer world. It should also be noted that a significant part of the process involves supporting and "picking up" members at the end of or after an encounter-group session. Here the positive aspects of the group's members are reinforced with care and love.

Psychodrama and Role Training

Psychodrama, a group therapy method, was created in 1905 by J.L. Moreno. The method has been used in a variety of institutional and community clinics for delinquents. I have employed the method with considerable success in a variety of settings, including psychiatric hospital programs for delinquents, prisons, and therapeutic community treatment centers (Yablonsky, 1976, 1990).

Psychodrama is a natural process. Everyone at some time has had an inner drama going on in his or her mind. In this confidential setting you are the star of your psychodrama session and play all of the roles. The others you encounter in your monodrama may be your parents, an employer, a God you love or one who has forsaken you, or a wife, a husband, or a lover who has rejected you or demands more than you are willing to give.

Many people are able to act out these internal psychodramas in the reality and activity of their external life. For such people, psychodrama is not a necessary vehicle, except as an interesting adjunct to their life experiences. But for some people, including delinquents, psychodrama can provide a unique opportunity for externalizing their internal world onto a theatrical stage of life. The others in the session—or, as they are called in psychodrama, "auxiliary egos"—may not be an actual human adversary but some ideal someone or something an individual wants but cannot have, such as an unfulfilled dream or perhaps an obsession for fame or wealth. With the help of the people present at a session playing relevant auxiliary-ego roles, emotional conflicts and problems can often be resolved.

Psychodrama produces peak experiences that often result in individual and social change. In psychodrama a person encounters his or her conflicts and psychic pain in a setting that approximates a real-life situation. For example, a young man in conflict with his father talks directly to a person who, as an auxiliary ego, plays the role of his parent. His fantasy (or reality) of hostility or love can be acted out on the spot. He can experience his pain not in an artificial setting but in direct relationship to his father, since his enactment takes place as closely as possible to the pertinent, specific core situations in his life.

In psychodrama, the resolution of pain or conflict does not necessarily require extensive analysis or discussion, because the person experiences the emotions and resolves the problem in action. Often when someone has had a deep psychodramatic experience, there is no need for lengthy group discussion or analysis. The protagonist has unraveled the mystery of his or her problem in the action of the drama.

In most psychodramas sessions, benefits accrue to all members of the group. Group participants other than the main subject of the session are encouraged to witness aspects of their own lives that became manifest in the session, as if watching a dramatic play that projects their own behavior onto the stage in front of them. This kind of personal participation, either as a subject or as a member of a group in a live psychodrama, produces emotional impact and therapeutic benefits.

Psychodrama often emerges spontaneously in a discussion-type group therapy session. A therapeutic community paraprofessional described an incident that took place in a regular therapy group session. A seventeen-year-old female delinquent, in a three-day marathon group session, spontaneously became involved in a psychodrama. When her defenses were low on the third day of the group meetings, she began talking about her unresolved hostility toward her father, who had sexually abused her (a painful traumatic situation that accounts for the delinquent/ drug patterns of many women and men). At a certain point in her monologue on her father, she said, "It's weird but Dominic here [another addict] really reminds me of my father." At this point a senior member of the group, who had some experience with psychodrama said, "OK, Dominic will play the role of your father."

What followed was an intense, verbal outburst of hostility aimed at "the father" that verged on physical violence as the woman got into her feelings. The director of the session placed a pillow in front of Dominic, and the young woman, without too much encouragement, viciously rained blows on the pillow, as she expressed her venom about how her father's sexual abuse had caused her a life of pain and a low self-concept, and how she had used to drugs to kill the pain. Her feelings were later shared by other people in the group. The psychodrama had developed into a valuable analytic discussion on how early parental abuse had affected various individuals' drug and alcohol problems.

The Psychodrama of Ralph and His Father

Father-son conflict is a significant issue in delinquency causation. The following psychodrama involved a young man who had this problem in the extreme. I successfully treated his problem in several psychodrama sessions.

Ralph had been diagnosed by the psychiatric staff at Atascadero State Hospital for the Criminally Insane as a psychopath. At eighteen, he was in custody for going out of control and attempting to kill his father. He almost succeeded. The verbal interactions he had with various therapists in the hospital about his "past behavior" (which I learned through psychodrama) had been of limited help in reaching him. His immediate therapist had participated in several psychodrama sessions and requested that I

476

direct a session with Ralph to help explore some of Ralph's psychodynamics. Ralph's therapist was present at all of the sessions and productively followed the leads produced in our psychodramas, using them in his private therapeutic verbal sessions with Ralph. In this case, psychodrama became a valuable adjunct to Ralph's individual therapy.

In addition to a psychopathic potential for violence, Ralph occasionally manifested a body tic—his body would writhe as if he were experiencing an epileptic seizure. The tic seemed to appear whenever Ralph felt anger or was under pressure. According to a doctor who examined Ralph, there appeared to be no physiological basis for the tic. In the first psychodrama session I directed with Ralph as the protagonist, I noted that the tic occurred whenever there was reference to his father, and sometimes even when the word *father* was used.

In one session, Ralph led us back to a basic and traumatic scene in his life with his father. He acted out a horrendous situation that occurred when he was eight: his father punished him by tying his hands to a ceiling beam in the cellar—like meat on a hook—and beating him with a belt.

We determined from several later sessions with Ralph, and my consultations with his therapist, that the traumatic experience of the whipping and other parental atrocities produced his tic, because the tic appeared after this particular beating, and there did not seem to be any physiological basis for it. The tic seemed to be a way Ralph controlled striking back at his antagonist, his father. Ralph had two extreme postures that emerged from his father's abuse: one was the tic that kept him from the second, the reaction of extreme, uncontrolled violence.

Other sessions I directed with Ralph revealed that his rage toward his father was often displaced onto others, especially other children at school. The father, who had had Ralph hospitalized, was obviously the object of Ralph's hatred. Ralph seldom spoke to his father. He either manifested the incapacitating tic or ran away. Finally, Ralph attempted to kill his father.

After several psychodramas we progressed to a point where Ralph accepted a male nurse as an auxiliary ego in the role of his father. In a typical psychodrama scene, Ralph would alternately produce the tic or attempt to attack his "father." There was hardly any verbalization of rage—he required an action form to express his emotions. The time factor was in the psychodramatic "here and now." This included varied time frames in the same session.

After Ralph had physically acted out much of his rage, I improvised a psychodramatic vehicle that facilitated "a conversation" between Ralph and his auxiliary ego "father." First I put a table between the two. Then, as Ralph talked to his "father," I gave Ralph the option and the freedom to punch a pillow that he accepted symbolically as his father. This combination of psychodrama devices enabled Ralph to structure in thought and put into words his deep hatred for his father. Ralph blurted out much of his long-repressed hatred in a lengthy diatribe. Finally, we removed the props, and after his rage was spent, Ralph fell into his "father's" arms and began to sob, "Why couldn't you love me? I was really a good kid, Dad. Why couldn't you love me?"

In a later session, Ralph played the role of his father, and for the first time he began to empathize with the early experiences in his father's life. Ralph's grandfather—who beat his son—was the original culprit, and Ralph was receiving the fallout of his father's anger toward *his* father (Ralph's grandfather). When Ralph reversed roles and returned to play himself, his hostility toward his father was diminished, and he, at least psychodramatically, that day forgave him.

All of the material acted out in the psychodrama sessions was more closely examined in Ralph's private sessions with his therapist. Also, I had a number of productive discussions with both Ralph and his therapist on an individual basis. This combination of therapeutic activity seemed to be effective in helping Ralph reduce his homicidal, sociopathic behavior. In my follow-up of Ralph's case, I learned that he had made a reasonable adjustment after leaving the hospital. He stayed clear of his father because, although he could handle the relationship in psychodrama, he couldn't fully handle the relationship in real life. The positive results were that he went to work, got married at age twenty, and, according to the reports I later received, for the most part, adjusted to a law-abiding life. The learning-in-action on his part, combined with private sessions, were effective.

Ralph could not just talk about his anger; he required a vehicle like psychodrama, which gave him the opportunity to physically and psychologically reenact the scenarios of the early parental abuse. Ralph was provided with some insights into his sociopathic violent nature and was able to overcome this problem sufficiently to function in a law-abiding way in our society.

Psychodrama in a Probation Camp

A former student of mine, John Hill, used psychodrama to deal with a problem that often manifests itself in a custodial setting. Following is a report of the event that John and I co-authored. We discuss the rationale for using psychodrama and present a prototypical session for controlling gang violence in a custodial setting.

One of the major problems faced by correctional counselors in the care and treatment of gang youths (boys) in a custodial setting is the behavior of the aggressive, assaultive inmate. His violent attitude and behavior tends to disrupt the possibility of the treatment process in the institution. He presents unique difficulties in terms of control and adaptability, especially in the group living situation, and since his behavior directly affects the behavior of his peers, his negative acting out exerts undue pressures upon the group as a whole.

With these thoughts in mind the possibility of utilizing psychodrama as a treatment tool in dealing with an aggressive ward named David became readily apparent based on four major assumptions:

1. Aggressive and assaultive impulses could be channeled in a controlled monitored setting, allowing full expression without the danger of physical injury.

2. Motives behind these impulses could be explored in a manner readily visible to the wards involved.

3. Immediate catharsis could be achieved, reducing the probability of uncontrolled aggression and pressure in the group living situation.

4. Precipitating problems could be alleviated, examined, and explored as they occurred by a restaging of the problem in a psychodrama.

The psychodrama of David presents an example of the process in action. David, a Mexican American youth, was sixteen. He had been committed to the custody of the probation camp by the courts for murder. He was a large, heavyset boy, intensely gang oriented. His case file revealed a record of seventeen arrests ranging from assaults and robberies to the offense that had him committed to camp.

David entered his dormitory at the probation camp reluctantly. His initial reaction to camp was negative in the extreme. Within three hours of entering the program he had managed to alienate virtually everyone in the dormitory, staff and peers alike. His answer to every reasonable request was an obscenity. The consensus of the staff was that David should be removed to a more maximum security or "lock up" facility as soon as possible. This would probably have been initiated in short order had he not become involved in an incident with the kingpin Chicano in the dorm, Leon, a member of a rival gang. Staff intervened before blows were struck, and David and six other wards were taken to the office for counseling.

It was felt that the psychodramatic approach might prove effective in this case, and the transition from encounter group to psychodrama was made by setting the stage for a reenactment of the confrontation between

David and Leon. Initially, an auxiliary-ego staff member played the part of Leon. David sat in a chair facing the staff member, a probation officer, who assumed the role of Leon.

> DAVID: You bastards [indicating the group as a whole] are always messin' with me.

> STAFF MEMBER AS LEON: Man, you come walking in here like a *vato loco* trying to prove how tough you are, what do you expect?

David did a double take and demanded to know who the staff member playing Leon was. Is he to be a staff person or is he supposed to be Leon? The ground rules were repeated, indicating that what we were trying to accomplish was to replay the incident so that we could see what the problem was. David was reluctantly cooperative.

> DAVID: How come that punk [indicating the real Leon] don't do it himself?

Leon became visibly agitated and started to get out of his chair to confront his adversary. He was waved back. Staff explained that because of the charged atmosphere and raw feelings a substitute for Leon was being used. David was instructed to regard the staff person playing Leon as the real Leon for purposes of the psychodrama. The initial confrontation was reviewed with the group: David had challenged Leon and Leon had reacted by questioning David's right to enter the dormitory as a new boy and throw his weight around. The staff member assuming the role of Leon picked it up from there.

> STAFF MEMBER AS LEON: How come you think you're such a bad ass? You can't come walking in here talking all that crap and shoving people around. You better get your act together.

> DAVID: Fuck you man! You don't tell Mad Dog [his gang name] what to do or not do!

> STAFF MEMBER AS LEON: Mad dog? Mad dog? They usually put mad dogs to sleep. What does that mean Mad Dog? (Leon laughed from the sidelines as David clenched his fists and glared at the group.)

> DAVID: I'm going to waste you, *puto!* (This is directed toward the real Leon.)

The psychodrama interchange continued for some minutes and was evidently a source of some satisfaction to David, who began to relax as he realized that he could express himself verbally without fear of physical retaliation from Leon or the staff member playing Leon. Another ward, James, a black gangster who had been delighted with and enjoyed the exchange, moved into position next to David to support him and act as his double. (A double sits behind the subject of the session and gives support in expressing himself.)

> STAFF MEMBER AS LEON: I don't know how a punk like you stayed alive on the outs. If I'd seen you out there I would have brought back your *cojones* [testicles] in a paper bag.

> DAVID (his face reddening at this reflection on his manhood, he struggles with himself for a moment before answering): At least I got *cojones*. You ain't nothing unless you got your home boys around.

At this point James, who had obviously been anxious to participate, interjected as David's double, helping David to present himself more effectively.

> JAMES (as David): Yeah, you think you runnin' this dorm, tellin' everybody what to do all the time. You think you cool, but you ain't shit!

David was somewhat taken aback at the unexpected support from James and warmed to his role. He began to reflect on his statements, picking up cues from James.

> DAVID: Yeah, how come when I come in here you all of a sudden start giving orders? You ain't no better than me even, if you been here longer.

Leon now entered the session as himself. The interchange between the two boys now took place in fairly normal tones as Leon, have vented his personal angry emotions, began dealing with David on the level of a person of authority trying to reason with a recalcitrant underling. David resisted this process by ignoring Leon's arguments and discussing his own feelings of right and justice. While he played the role of the wronged party with obvious relish, it was apparent that he had little or no insight at this point into his role in the problem.

The staff suggested that the wards physically exchange places (a role-reversal) and that Leon play the role of David, while David assumed the part of Leon. Both boys initially balked at the idea of role-reversal, but at the urging of others in the group, they reluctantly exchanged seats. Leon was the first to begin the dialogue. He assumed an exaggerated stance of braggadocio, fists clenched and lips drawn back. He stared defiantly at David.

> LEON (as David): You *puto*, you ain't gonna tell me what to do!

David was obviously struggling at this point, not sure of how he should react. Then, apparently remembering Leon's tirade against him, he launched into a vituperative monologue that continued for some minutes despite Leon's attempts to interrupt. The other members of the group seemed to be enjoying the performance of the two tough gangsters in their power struggle. When David, in the role of Leon, finally ran out of invectives, the staff asked him what he was feeling at that moment. He then returned to being himself.

> DAVID: I don't know, man, I really got pissed off when he called me a *puto* and started staring at me like that. It made me feel like going off on him.
>
> STAFF: Do you want to go off on him now?
>
> DAVID: Yeh, yeh I do!
>
> STAFF (hands David a towel): Okay, hit the desk with this. Hit the desk like it was Leon.

David took the towel and tentatively hit the desk once, twice, three times. Then he knotted the end and brought it crashing down a half dozen times.

> STAFF: Who are you hitting, David?
>
> DAVID: Him, Leon.
>
> STAFF (turns to the group in the room): What's happening here?
>
> GROUP MEMBER: It seems to me that he's getting pissed off at Leon for doing the same thing he always does himself as a gang leader.
>
> MIKE: I think he's pissed off at himself.
>
> STAFF (to David): What do you think about that?
>
> DAVID: I don't know what you're talking about.
>
> LEON: Look man, I was doing the same thing you were doing from the first minute you walked in here. So maybe you can see how you was coming off.

David struggled with the concept for a moment then again crashed the towel violently against the desk.

> DAVID (angrily): You guys don't know shit!

David did not say this too convincingly, however. The rest of the group had a glimpse of the truth and immediately began to belabor the point.

> STEVE: Hey man, maybe you got angry because you know the way it really is. You aren't the big shot here. Maybe you better face it.
>
> JERRY (changing allegiance): Yeah, don't seem like you can take what you was giving out.

> CARLOS: That's the trouble with you, man, you don't know what's coming down even when everyone else can see it!

Suddenly, David lashed out with a towel, actually strikingly Leon across the face, and then he screamed at the group.

> DAVID: Damn it! Why don't you *putos* get off my back?

Leon reacted by pulling the towel out of David's hands and was about to hit him with the knotted end when staff members intervened and pushed both boys back into their chairs. The other boys leaped up, happily anticipating a fight.

> STAFF: Okay, okay, now just sit down and calm down.

Leon rubbed his face, looking daggers at David, who sat slumped in his chair breathing heavily. The other members of the group settled back to as a staff member asked them to explain what had just happened.

> JAMES: I think David knows what's happening and is afraid to face it. He can't admit he's wrong, so he has to take it out on somebody.
>
> MIKE: Yeh, he acts just like my little brother when he doesn't get his way or what he wants. He has a tantrum.
>
> JERRY: Yeah, he's acting like a kid.

The others all echoed Jerry's sentiments as David sat in his chair, fighting back tears. Leon, sensing that David had just passed through an emotional crisis, relaxed and began to talk. He became quite reflective and adult.

> LEON: I don't know, sometimes it's hard to be real. I mean to really see yourself as other people do. [He reflects for a moment.] When I was on the outs [on the street] when I was a kid, I got into fights all the time. I guess I was a real *vato loco*. Everybody thought I was crazy, even my parents. I was in the hospital maybe five or six times. When I was fifteen I got shot, and everybody thought I was going to die. When I got back on the streets I was a big man. I was tough. Then I started thinking how weird it was that it almost took getting killed and having a hole in my side to make me a person of respect. Anyway, now I had my rep and didn't have to go around personally going off on people. Sure, I done some gangbanging, but most of the time since then I kept laid back out of sight. I got things I want to do. I get a *veija* [woman] and a kid. I guess I know what David feels like. I guess he's still got to make his rep. He's just not going about it the right way. Going off on *vatos* in camp ain't gonna make it. That way somebody is going to do him [kill him]. We all got to get along here and do our time the best way we can. We got

> to stick together. When I was sitting here doing his trip [in David's role] I was getting next to how he was feeling. I guess because I been there myself. Always needing to prove myself as a man.

Leon appeared to have lost all his animosity, and during the course of his soliloquy, David listened intently. David seemed surprised that Leon expressed feelings of empathy for him, especially in view of the towel incident. He had difficulty controlling his tears.

> STAFF (to David): Okay, how are you feeling now?
>
> DAVID: I don't know, man. I don't know how I'm feeling. I feel all washed out. I feel like I don't give a damn about anything. I'm tired.
>
> LEON: You got to get with it. You were talking that everyone was down on you without giving you a chance. Well, it seems to me that you were down on everybody without giving us a chance.
>
> DAVID: I don't know. With the *putos* on the street, you got to get them before they get you, you know that, otherwise they walk all over you. I know you got homeboys here, but no one is going to walk over me.
>
> LEON: Okay, no one is going to walk over you here as long as you can take care of business. There's too many dudes out there that want to see us firing on each other. You're just going to make it harder on yourself and the rest of us unless you're cool, and you make some changes. I know how hard is to go through some changes, but it's worth it. I have to, if I'm going to do right by my wife and kid when I get out of here.
>
> DAVID (shaking his head to indicate doubt, reflects for a moment then tentatively holds out his hand. He finds it hard to meet Leon's eyes.): Okay, okay, man, I see where you're coming from. I'm sorry I hit you with the towel? I guess I was pretty pissed off.

Leon took David's hand and shook it firmly, making the comment that he could clearly see why they called him Mad Dog. At this point David had some recognition of his responsibility to the group as a *veterano* in the camp, and took the first step in accepting the camp program for his treatment.

For David the psychodrama was both a catharsis and an initiation into the group-living setting of the camp. A most important facet of the psychodrama was that it enabled David to see himself for the first time as others saw him; it was the beginning of insight and hopefully triggered a positive change from his past violent behavior. While the psychodrama was not a panacea for David's problems, it did provide the initial step to being integrated into the camp program instead of being transferred, because of his violent behavior, to a maximum security prison. The transfer would have placed him in an institution where he would have been swallowed up and indoctrinated even further into the violent, hard-core gangster group in the prison system.

A Spontaneous Psychodrama with a Homicidal Gangster

In my work with gangs, I often used role playing in crisis situations. Gang life moves so fast that it is not possible to wait until gang members are apprehended and placed in an institution. To prevent crime, one must respond to emergencies. In the following account, the underlying theory and elements of a psychodramatic session (warm-up, action, and post-discussion) are applied to (1) an immediate "live" problem (2) of an "emergency" nature, (3) in the "open community," and (4) often emerging unexpectedly.

A disturbed gang leader, accompanied by two friends, accosted me as I was walking down the street. He pulled out a switchblade knife and announced that he was on his way to kill a youth who lived in a nearby neighborhood on the Upper West Side of Manhattan. I moved into action armed with a psychodramatic approach.

First, I was prepared for this emergency possibility, since on a continuing basis I had made sociometric tests that revealed the relationships of various gangs and gang networks in the area. I knew the gangs that were feuding and the leadership patterns of each group. More than that, the youth facing me had had previous exposure to psychodrama; this was helpful as we could move right into action. In short, the groundwork was set for this emergency use of psychodrama. I asked myself, why did the youth stop me before he went to stab the other youth? I suspected the chances were good that he really did not want to commit this violence and wanted me to help him find a way out.

The "Ape," as this boy was called by the gang, was openly defiant and upset. His opening remark was, "Man, I'm packin'. I got my blade right here. I'm going to cut the shit out of those motherfuckin Dragons. I'm going up and get them now—once and for all."

In short, he had a knife and was going to stab any Dragon gang boys he met that day. It was also reasonable to assume that he would stab any youth who, in his hysterical judgment, was a Dragon. The boys followed me to my nearby office and the session began with the use of another gang boy as an auxiliary ego in the role of the potential victim.

A paper ruler replaced the knife (for obvious reasons), and the "killing" was acted out in my office under controlled psychodramatic conditions.

The psychodrama had all of the elements of a real gang killing. The Ape (the subject) cursed, fumed, threatened, and shouted at the victim, who hurled threats and insults in return. Ape worked himself into a frenzy and then stabbed the auxiliary ego (the gang boy playing the part) with the "knife." The psychodramatic victim fell dead on the floor.

The Ape was then confronted with the consequences of his act in all of its dimensions, including the effect on his family. He began to regret what he had done and was particularly remorseful when an auxiliary ego playing the role of a court judge sentenced him "to death in the electric chair."

The psychodrama accomplished at least two things for this potential killer: (1) he no longer was motivated to kill, since he had already accomplished this psychodramatically, and (2) he was confronted with the consequences of this rash act; this was an added dimension of consideration. Many gangboys are unable to think ahead to the outcome of a situation. These factors possibly served as a deterrent to the actual commission of a murder. Of course, this boy required and received further therapy, which sought to deal with his more basic personality problems. Moreover, considerably more work was attempted on the gang networks, so as to minimize their potential for violence. However, the emergency psychodrama did deter the possibility of Ape's committing a homicide, at least on that particular day (Yablonsky, 1960, pp. 167–168).

Group psychotherapy and psychodrama provide the opportunity for direct role training. Here offenders can view themselves and others by presenting their problems for group discussion and analysis. More than that, they are in a position to correct (or edit) their illegal actions in the presented situations. Offenders can try out or practice legally conforming roles in the presence of criminal "experts," who quickly detect whether they are conning the group or playing it straight.

In a role-playing session in which I was training offenders for future employment, for example, one offender (who was soon to be released from prison) went through the motions of getting a job with apparent disinterest. This fact was quickly and forcefully brought out in the open by other members of the group, producing a valuable discussion on the basic need of employment for going straight. In another session I observed how a violent offender learned to control his assaultive impulse by talking about, rather than acting out, his wish to assault a member of the group. He learned to talk about violent impulses rather than assault first and discuss later.

A characteristic of group treatment, therefore, is that it provides an opportunity for violent offenders to talk or act out their illegal motivations in a controlled setting. After acting out their destructive impulses in the session, they may no longer have the need to carry them out in reality. The group also gives offenders and their peer co-therapists an opportunity to assess the meaning of violence through discussion. An empathic group can help violent offenders understand their compulsive emotions. Among other things, they learn that they are not alone in their feelings.

Many offenders have difficulty controlling their immediate compulsions in order to reach future goals. They tend to live in the moment and often lack the ability to relate the past to the present, and the present to the future. The thought of future punishment or past experience doesn't usually enter their conscious deliberations to serve as a deterrent to illegal action. Training in understanding time dimensions is therefore often useful in crime prevention. Psychodrama as a group process provides such time flexibility. Offenders can act out past, immediate, or expected problem situations that are disturbing them. The process is useful in working with criminals who manifest impulsive behavior. Psychodrama, in particular the "future-projection technique," by means of which a person is propelled into a future situation, provides an opportunity for the offender to plan for a future free of crime. This technique has been used with offenders who are about to be released into a the community to project them into future social situations in the community, on the job, with family, with supervising probation officers, and so on. The role-training process tends to build up the offender's resistance to efforts on the part of delinquent friends to seduce him or her back into delinquent activity.

Psychodrama provides an opportunity for the immediate-situation-oriented delinquents to review some of their past and future behavior with its many implications for resisting delinquent activity. To the offender with con man or sociopathic characteristics, words are cheap. Considerable research indicates that it is very difficult for a subject to lie in action during psychodrama. Because group pressures make distortion so difficult, the offender is forced to assess his or her behavior and its rationale closely. This, combined with opportunities to try out legally conforming behavior patterns before such severe judges as peers, helps the offender to reexamine and reject his or her illegal behavior patterns and learn socially conforming behavior.

PART 7

Therapeutic Communities: An Innovative Method for the Prevention and Control of Juvenile Delinquency

CHAPTERS

CHAPTER 17

THE HISTORY, METHODOLOGY, AND DEVELOPMENT OF THE THERAPEUTIC COMMUNITY APPROACH

This 1961 group picture of the early residents of Synanon, the first therapeutic community, depicts the variety of people of all ages who pioneered this innovative methodology for effectively treating criminal/addicts. (The author is indicated by the circle at upper right.)

Two questions that professionals in the field of treatment often ask are: How do we reach recalcitrant delinquents? and How do we incorporate some of their positive energy into the treatment process? One approach for treating criminals and delinquents that addresses these questions is the therapeutic community. I believe it is a comprehensive methodology that effectively integrates various group therapy methods and has an enormous potential for reducing America's gang and delinquency problem in the twenty-first century.

The first therapeutic community, called Synanon, was founded in 1958 by Charles E. Dederich. Dederich, with the aid of others (including me) developed a notable methodology that has had considerable impact on the treatment of juvenile delinquents, adult criminals, and drug addicts. The original Synanon method has been replicated, with modifications, in the United States and throughout the world. Before we look at specific plans for the implementation of the therapeutic community (TC) approach for treating delinquents, it is useful to understand the history, development, and methodology of the relatively new TC approach, which I believe will be further developed and more widely used in the next century.

The theoretical basis for the TC approach to modifying difficult offenders was forecast by Donald R. Cressey in a classic article, "Changing Criminals: The Application of The Theory of Differential Association," published in the *American Journal of Sociology* in October of 1955. Cressey said, "The community should restore the former addict (criminal) to a place in society and help him avoid associations that would influence him to return to the crime" (p. 93).

Sutherland and Cressey's differential association theory presents implications for diagnosis and treatment consistent with a group-relations principal for changing the behavior of criminals. As described in chapter 13, persons become criminals principally because they have been isolated from groups whose behavior patterns (including attitudes, motives, and rationalizations) are anticriminal, or because their residence, employment, social position, native capacities, or something else has brought them into frequent association with the behavior patterns of criminal groups. The theory is certainly consistent with the associations and behavior of delinquents.

In a later study, Cressey, with the aid of a UCLA graduate student Rita Volkman, carried out research from 1958 to 1962 in the original Synanon in Santa Monica, which appeared to fit remarkably the criteria Cressey had posited earlier for an ex-offender anticriminal therapeutic community. Their findings were reported in the *American Journal of Sociology* (September 1963).

Cressey and Volkman (1963) concluded that Synanon was a modality that fit the five criteria that Cressey had described in 1955 for effectively resocializing criminals —before Synanon came into existence. Cressey's criteria, which were satisfied by the Synanon modality, were:

> (1) If criminals are to be changed, they must be assimilated into groups which emphasize values conducive to law-abiding behavior; (2) The more relevant the common purpose of the group is to the reformation of criminals, the greater will be its influence on the criminal members' attitudes and values; (3) The more cohesive the group, the greater the member's readiness to influence others . . . and between them there must be a genuine "we" feeling. The reformers, consequently, should not be identifiable as correction or social workers; (4) Both reformers and those to be reformed must achieve status within the group by exhibition of "pro-reform" or anticriminal values and behavior patterns; and (5) The most effective mechanism for exerting group pressure on members will be found in groups so organized that criminals are induced to join with noncriminals for the purpose of changing other criminals. A group in which Criminal A joins with some noncriminals to change Criminal B is probably most effective in changing Criminal A. In order to change Criminal B, Criminal A must necessarily share the values of the anticriminal members. (Cressey, 1963, pp. 95–96)

During the early 1960s, Volkman, Cressey, and I were in the same geographical area of Los Angeles and became interested in the Synanon therapeutic community. An article appeared in *Time* magazine (1961) that provided some insight into the early elements of this first therapeutic community:

> Early in August 1959, home owners along the stylish Pacific Ocean beaches in Santa Monica, California were dismayed to get a new set of neighbors, a bedraggled platoon of half a hundred men and women, who moved into a run-down, three-story, red brick building that once was a National Guard armory. White and black, young and middle aged, criminals and innocents, artists and loafers, the unlikely assortment shared one trait: they were narcotics addicts determined to kick their habit for good. Scrounging lumber, paint, and old furniture, the troupe converted the top floor of the armory into a barracks-style men's dormitory.
>
> They turned the second floor into offices, kitchen, dining hall, and living room, and the main floor into women's sleeping quarters. Over the doors in the living room they hung their emblem: a life preserver with the words "S.S. Hang Tough," slang for "Don't give up." . . . Such was the formal dedication of Synanon House, a self-run, haphazardly financed experiment in human reclamation whose success has been hailed by Dr. Donald Cressey, University of California at Los Angeles sociologist, as "the most significant attempt to keep addicts off drugs that has ever been made." The technique was patterned roughly after

the group-therapy methods of Alcoholics Anonymous. Dr. Cressey describes the psychology: "A group in which Criminal A joins with some noncriminals to change Criminal B is probably the most effective in changing Criminal A."

In the often brutally frank personal group exchanges, the addicts slowly reveal themselves . . . and through daily contact with similarly beset persons are reinforced in their determination to quit narcotics permanently. Says the founder of Synanon House, 48-year-old Charles E. Dederich, who was once an alcoholic but never a drug addict: "It is something that works." The Synanon curriculum is divided into three stages. During the first phase, the emotionally shaken, physically weak addict gradually adjusts to his new surroundings. . . . During the second stage, the ex-addict works at a regular job on the outside, contributing part of his wages to the group, continues to live at the house. . . . In its final stage, Synanon sends its member out into society. (Pp. 46–50)

The concept of utilizing former offenders or former patients in treatment programs has a long history, one that precedes the creation of Synanon. The best-known example of this kind of paraprofessional therapy is Alcoholics Anonymous. In my early work with violent gangs in New York City in the 1950s, I used a form of TC approach when I hired former gang members to work alongside university-trained people on the gang problem. These "paraprofessionals" knew the turf and understood the problems that violent gang youths were struggling with, since they had "been there" themselves. This enabled them to help many youths extricate themselves from the gang warfare, drug abuse, and crime that were rampant in their neighborhoods. I also utilized the treatment energy of parolees who were leading successful lives to help resocialize neighborhood violent gangs and delinquents in small group therapy sessions.

During this period, as part of my work with gangs and delinquents, I directed a parolee project for delinquents released into the area in an Upper West Side courtroom that was available in the evenings. I often brought "guest lecturers" into our group therapy. These included former parolees who had been delinquents and had become successful law-abiding citizens. At one of our sessions I managed to involve former middle-weight boxing champion Rocky Graziano. In his earlier years, Rocky had been involved in criminal activities and had done time in the New York City Riker's Island Prison. Most of the parolees in my group had recently been released from Riker's Island, and they were anxious to hear Rocky's "lecture" on how he had changed his life from criminal to celebrity. (This metamorphosis was vividly depicted in the book and later the film *Somebody Up There Likes Me*, starring Paul Newman as Rocky Graziano.) Sportswriter Jimmy Cannon heard about Graziano's appearance and sat in on our session. He accurately and eloquently reported the dynamics of this gang-parolee session the following day in his nationally syndicated column in the *New York Post* (1955). His analysis captured the flavor of the 1950s and the delinquents of that period.

> They were ex-cons who came voluntarily last night to a court-room in upper Manhattan magistrate's court. There would be a talk by Rocky Graziano, who had been in prison. And Lewis Yablonsky, who is concerned with their anguish, would preside. He is the director of the crime prevention program of a philan-thropic organization. . . . They liked Graziano. They sat, somber and slightly hostile, before he started his monologue. They were still defendants because that's what they were the last time they were in a courtroom. You felt their anxiety as Yablonsky explained how important sports are. . . . Losers do a lot of look-ing before they find a guy who listens to them because he's inter-ested. "We ran a baseball league," Yablonsky explained in his solemn young man's way. "Six gangs, we didn't have any gang wars. We had a 10-team basketball league. It was tremendous. They got interested. Sports—a gimmick. It gets them into a good relationship with a good adult. A man they respect."
>
> There was one kid I felt had made it all the way. He wore a one-buttoned jazzy coat. I'd bet on him. He had the drug habit and had shaken it. You had to be touched by his fierce pride. He stood up there when Yablonsky solicited questions and told them the ring was out of his nose. He explained how he had dug in for kicks but he was asking, asking, asking. He was telling but also wondering and going back over it and attempting to put it together. Why, why, why? They wanted to know and Yablonsky was trying to give it to them in his educated way. Not talking down to them but using the language of the streets. . . .
>
> "You go in for sports?" I asked the kid in the one-buttoned jacket. "Stick ball in the streets," he replied. "In the summer." "What about basketball?" "The winter's for dances," the kid said. Of course, summer's for stickball and winter's for dances. But the seasons don't change in the can (prison). That's what Yablonsky told them in his way. And so did Graziano. (Cannon, 1955, p. 38)

My aides in this parolee project were former criminals effective in communicating the benefits of a crime-free life-style to younger delin-quents, some of whom were gangsters, in small group situations that I con-structed as part of my overall crime prevention program in New York. Consequently, when I first heard about Synanon, I was enormously inter-ested in researching the organization, since its apparent methodology res-onated with my own viewpoint in utilizing ex-offenders for working with delinquents.

I first learned about Synanon at a United Nations conference on crime and the delinquency in London in the summer of 1960. The highlight of the conference for me was an evening I spent with Donald Cressey, who was also attending the conference. Cressey described in detail this new experiment for treating criminal/addicts in Synanon, the pioneer TC. At this time, I was teaching at the University of Massachusetts. Not long after this, I was invited to join the faculty at UCLA. Partly because of my enthusiasm for Synanon, I accepted.

I arrived in Los Angeles in the fall of 1961 and promptly began to spend four to five days each week researching the Synanon methodology. A summary of my first article on therapeutic communities appeared in the *New York Times*:

> Criminal therapy, the use of ex-criminals to treat criminals, is a major breakthrough in criminology, according to Dr. Lewis Yablonsky, University of California at Los Angeles criminologist. In an article in the September issue of *Federal Probation*, a leading criminology publication of the federal government, Dr. Yablonsky described the important new treatment for criminals.
>
> The technique originated, he pointed out, at Synanon House in Santa Monica, California, a unique self-help community for rehabilitation of drug addicts. Over the past year several "graduates" of Synanon have effectively introduced "criminal therapy" at the Federal Terminal Island Prison near Long Beach, California.
>
> Dr. Yablonsky, who is also Synanon's research director, said, "We have found that former addicts with long criminal backgrounds and prison experience often make the most effective therapists for younger addicts and delinquents who have embarked on similar criminal careers. The ex-criminal therapist has 'made the scene' himself. He cannot be 'conned' or outmaneuvered by his 'patient' and there is rapport. The result is a communication that penologists and others in authority find difficult to establish with others who by their criminal background are defiant of authority." In this new approach, "being clean" (of crime, drugs, and violence) becomes the status symbol. A reverse of the criminal code occurs and any slip back into criminality means great loss of face in the group. (P. 1)

The Synanon organization disbanded for a variety of reasons around 1990; however, the concept and methodology of Synanon has been replicated, with modifications, in thousands of organizations around the world. The generic term for the methodology is "therapeutic community" or TC. There are now several hundred TCs in the United States. Italy has about forty TCs, and Greece has six. Therapeutic Communities of America is an organization of several hundred TCs in the United States and the World Federation of Therapeutic Communities is a worldwide association.

The therapeutic community approach has had a positive rehabilitative result for tens of thousands of former criminal/addicts in the therapeutic communities that are currently in existence. Most of these TC programs are based in the community. However, a number of community-based TCs have implemented programs in prisons. I worked in the first TC prison project implemented by Synanon in the Nevada State Prison in 1964. Since then, there have been a number of effective prison projects, including Staying Out in New York, Amity in California and Texas, and Walden House in California. These projects are administered by ex-offenders who have successfully completed a community-based TC program.

The success rate has been exceptional for criminal/addicts who have participated in these prison programs and then been paroled into a community TC. About 65 percent of the 1 million prisoners in custody in the United States when released will be rearrested for various crimes. A summary analysis of a five-year research project built into the Amity Prison TC program in California's Donavan Prison revealed that the recidivism rate for the prisoners who completed this program was only 35 percent in a five-year period. In comparison, 65 percent of the control-matched group of prisoners in the general prison population were rearrested within five years (Wexler, 1995). Research data from TC programs in other states reveal similar positive results.

The TC approach is a viable alternative to placement in prison for many and is also effective for working with criminals in residential community treatment centers. Many TCs focus on offenders' substance abuse problems. Given the significant linkage between substance abuse and criminality (around 80 percent of offenders abuse some substance), the TC system has a role in helping to solve the criminal/addict problem for both juvenile and adult offenders.

Therapeutic Communities for Socializing Delinquents

The manner in which a therapeutic community can be utilized for socializing delinquents was brought home to me in the early days of Synanon. During the five-year period I researched Synanon for *The Tunnel Back* (1965), I spent almost every day in the community. I interviewed almost all of the residents and participated personally and professionally in the group processes. A number of Synanon residents at that time were young delinquents. These alienated youths, many of whom were gangsters in their hood, were searching for some kind of status, respect, belonging, and community.

An experience that led me to believe that the TC was a viable methodology for delinquents came in a serendipitous way. Chuck Dederich, founder of Synanon, and I became friends and professional colleagues. Dederich audiotaped almost all relevant group sessions that took place in Synanon, and we logged many hours listening to the tapes and discussing their social psychological significance.

One evening we were listening to a tape of a special group session labeled as the "gangster tape." As I listened to the tape I had the eerie feeling that one of the voices with a New York accent on the tape sounded familiar. I asked Chuck, "Who is that guy?" He told me, "That's Frankie Lago, a New York gangster who has been here over a year. Would you like to meet him?" Frankie appeared, and after a brief discussion with him, I realized he was the older brother of Ralph Lago, a gangster who was involved in the 1957 gang killing of Michael Farmer at High Bridge Park— an event that was featured in my first book, *The Violent Gang*. That brief incident triggered my interest in Frankie and the path he had traveled to Synanon and rehabilitation in the TC system.

The transition of Frankie, an eighteen-year-old Puerto Rican former New York street gang member, reveals a great deal about the therapeutic community process. The following summary of Frankie's odyssey from delinquent to artist is based on many interviews I had with Frankie and observations I made of him over the five-year period he resided in Synanon. (After Frankie left Synanon we maintained a friendship that still exists.)

Frankie's first reaction to Synanon when he arrived in 1962 was confusion. He said, "The first thing they hit me with flipped me. This tough-looking cat says to me, 'There are two things you can't do here, shoot drugs or fight.'" Frankie said, scratching his head, "I was all mixed up—these were the only two things I knew how to do."

Despite this confusion, he found the environment interesting and exciting and quite different from places where he had "done time." There were, for him, "lots of hip people." Among this group was Jimmy, who at forty-eight had been an addict, a criminal, and a con man for more than thirty years. He was assigned as Frankie's sponsor, or mentor. Part of Jimmy's education as a mentor for Frankie took place during the in-and-out fifteen years he had spent in a Michigan state prison.

Jimmy ran the kitchen at Synanon. Frankie got his first job in Synanon scouring pots and pans and mopping floors. According to Frankie, Jimmy could not be "conned" or manipulated like the officers and therapists that Frankie had encountered in various New York institutions, including Riker's Island Prison. Jimmy, of course knew the score. To him, Frankie, with all his exploits, was a "young punk" who would give him no trouble. "I've met kids like this all my life—in and out of the joint," Jimmy told me.

According to Frankie, "At first, I hated this bastard. I used to sometimes sit and plan ways to kill him." When Frankie wanted to fight Jimmy over a disagreement about work, Jimmy laughed and told him that if he wanted a fight, he would be thrown out of the place and get sent back to New York and a long prison term. The usual institutional situation was reversed, and this confused Frankie. In other institutions, if Frankie got in trouble, confinement became increasingly severe, with the "hole" (solitary confinement) as an end point. In the Bellevue Hospital psychiatric ward, where Frankie had also spent time, it was a straitjacket.

What made Frankie behave in order to stay in the TC? It wasn't only the threat of prison. In another setting his low impulse control would propel him out the door. The fact that Frankie was exported from New York to Los Angeles was a significant initial force in keeping him in Synanon. He commented, "At times I felt like splitting. Then I thought it would be hard to make it back to New York. I didn't know Los Angeles and was afraid to go downtown where the drugs were, because I didn't know the people. Where I was was better than anything else I could do—at the time." This factor is known in TC circles as "the geographic cure."

What was also of importance for Frankie was that there were others who understood him, had made the same "scenes," and intuitively knew his problems and how to handle them. Although he would not admit it, he respected people he could not "con." He belonged and was now part of a "family" he could accept. Frankie could also make a "rep" in the TC without getting punished or locked up. In other institutions the highest he could achieve in terms of the values of the other inmates was to become "king" in the inmate world, acquire a stash of cigarettes, obtain some unsatisfactory homosexual favors, and land in the "hole."

In Synanon, he began to learn that he could acquire any role he was "big enough or man enough to achieve," and "growing up" carried the highest approval of his fellows. He could actually become a director in this organization. For the first time in his life, Frankie was receiving status, in gang terms, a rep, for being "clean" and nondelinquent.

Of course, when he first arrived, Frankie attempted to gain a rep by conniving and making deals, in accord with his old mode of relating. When he did, he was laughed at, ridiculed, and given severe verbal "haircuts" by other "old-time con men" in group sessions. They were, he learned, ferociously loyal to the organization, which had literally saved their lives and given them a new life status. He began to develop an *esprit de corps* for the TC. As he once put it, "I never would give three cheers for the Warwick reformatory. But I'm part of this place. It's a home to me." Frankie found that rep was acquired in this social system (unlike the ones he had known) by truth, honesty, and industry. The values of his other life required reversal if he was to gain a rep in the TC. These values were not goals per se that someone moralized about in a meaningless vacuum; they were means to the end of acquiring prestige in this tough social system with which he increasingly identified.

In the encounter groups, three nights a week, Frankie participated in a new kind of group psychotherapy, unlike the kind he had "fooled around with" in the reformatory. Here, the truth was viciously demanded. Any rationalizations about past or current experiences were brutally demolished by the group. There was an intensive search for self-identity. He found that, in the process, he learned something of what went on beneath the surface of his thoughts. Frankie admitted that for the first time in his life he had found other people who had some idea of his underlying thoughts. In his past time in institutions he had experienced individual and group therapy. In those situations he admittedly would "con" the therapist, and, most important, "I said what I thought they wanted to hear so I could get out sooner."

Frankie, who at first had followed his usual (sociopathic) pattern of self-centered manipulation of others, now began to care about what happened to others, who were real friends to him. He began to identify with the organization, and he learned on a "gut level" that if any other member failed, in some measure he, too, failed. Frankie began to gain some comprehension of what others thought in a social situation. The concept of empathy, or identifying with the thoughts and feelings of others, became a significant reality.

Frankie's rise in the hierarchy was neither quick nor easy. He first moved from the "dishpan" to serving food at the kitchen counter. After several months, he began to work outside on a pickup truck that acquired food and other donations. Here he had his first "slip"—no doubt, in part, to test the waters. With two other individuals who worked with him on the truck, a group decision was made one day that "smoking a joint might be fun." They acquired some grass from a connection known to one of the group. When they arrived back from work, their slightly "loaded" appearance immediately became apparent to the group. "They spotted us right away," said Frankie.

They were hauled into the main office and viciously (verbally) attacked and ordered to "cop out" (tell the truth) or "get lost." A general meeting was called, and they were forced to reveal all before the entire group in a fireplace scene. That night Frankie was back washing dishes.

Frankie learned the hard way that the norms of the TC were the reverse of the criminal code he knew. In another slip situation, Frankie, with two other members, went for a walk on the boardwalk in Santa Monica. One individual suggested buying some drugs from someone he knew. Frankie and the other member rejected the proposal. However, no one revealed the incident until two days later, when it came up in group. The group jumped hardest on Frankie and the other individual who had vetoed the idea rather than the one who had suggested buying the coke.

Frankie and the other "witnesses" were expected to report such slips immediately, since the group's life depended on keeping one another straight.
The maxim "Thou shalt not squeal," basic to the existence of the usual
underworld delinquent gang culture, was reversed and ferociously upheld.
For the first time in his life, Frankie was censored for *not* being a snitch.

Another challenge for this former violent gang member was the no-
physical-violence role. At first it was difficult for Frankie to grasp and
believe, since his usual response to a difficult situation was to leap, fists
first, past verbal means of communication into assault. As a result of the
groups and other new patterns of interaction, Frankie's increasing ability to
communicate began to minimize his assaultive impulses. Although at first
the fear of ostracism kept him from committing violence, he later had no
need to use violence, since he developed some ability to interact and communicate effectively. He learned to express himself in a new way on a nonviolent, verbal level. On occasion, Frankie would regress and have the
motivation for assault, but the system had taken hold. In one session I heard
him say, "I was so fucking mad yesterday, I wished I was back in the joint.
I really wanted to hit that bastard Jimmy in the mouth."

In his past, Frankie had had a sketchy, almost nonexistent work
record. Most of his time was taken up with gang fighting, pimping, armed
robbery, or dealing drugs. Aside from some forced labor in prison, he was
seldom engaged in anything resembling formal work. His theme had been
"work was uncool." He learned how to work in Synanon as a side effect of
his desire to rise in the status system. He also learned, as a side effect of
working, the startling new fact that "talking to someone in the right way
made them do more things than threatening them." As a consequence of
living in this new social system, Frankie's social learning and ability to
effectively communicate continued to increase. His destructive pattern of
relating to others withered away. It was no longer functional for him in this
new way of life. The TC experience increasingly developed his empathic
ability. It produced an attachment to different, more socially acceptable values and reconnected him to the larger society in which the TC functioned
as a valid and respected organization. This was probably the first time in his
life that he belonged to a law-abiding social organization.

The TC process unearthed a diamond in the rough. Frankie always
had a proclivity for art. As he later described it to me, "When I was a kid I
always liked to draw—but no one paid any attention to my sketches. The
only thing I got from my art was that I was teased by the other guys as a faggot. I did some secret art work in the joint but tore it up. One day in a group
discussion, they asked me what I really wanted to do 'when I grew up.' I
was scared to say it— but I said, 'I want to be an artist.' It was amazing—
for the first time in my life no one laughed. They even encouraged me to

go to art school." The TC truly worked for Frankie. It converted a potential killer into an artist. Frankie to date has been crime and drug free since 1964. He works as a lithographer, has created many interesting works of art, and has given up the delinquent life he was destined to live before his TC experience.

Group Methods Utilized in a Therapeutic Community

When I became involved with Synanon in 1961, I helped in the development of the encounter method and a variety of other group techniques that were utilized in the early days. At that time I introduced psychodrama into the TC group equation. Since then, based on my research and directing workshops in TCs in the United States and Europe, I have delineated the basic group processes that are employed in almost all TCs. Following is a review of these methods—with some commentary on how these group processes are utilized in various TCs.

In all types of TCs, whether in the community or in a prison, a number of basic group treatment methods and focus groups have been developed to effect attitude and behavioral change. These include:

1. A special group early on in the program for indoctrination of newcomers into modifying their delinquent and gangster attitudes and integrating them into the "positive gang" of the TC community.

2. Special encounter groups.

3. General psychotherapy groups that focus on self-disclosure and insights into the participants' socialization process and past behavior.

4. Psychodrama groups geared toward using role playing for dealing with the residents' variety of problems—especially their past violent behavior.

5. A family focus group that involves discussions with and about the delinquents' families, especially their attitude toward their fathers.

6. Educational focus groups that emphasize and stimulate the TC residents' attitudes toward general knowledge about the larger society.

7. Groups focused on occupation selection and training geared toward preparing youths for life on the outside, when they leave and have to find a job.

Several of these group approaches have already been described in the foregoing chapters. Here I show how they may be implemented with delinquents in a TC program. Given this context, each of these group approaches will be briefly discussed in the following analysis with some emphasis on how they can be implemented, the processes involved, and the goals that are sought and can be achieved through their implementation.

(1) Indoctrination and Orientation Focus Groups

These groups focus on introducing the client to various phases and ramifications of the TC program that will be encountered in the recovery process. Group sessions analyze the overall structure of the TC organization and the value and purpose of various methods, such as the encounter group and psychodrama. The goal of these groups is to integrate the newcomer into truly joining the therapeutic community he or she has voluntarily or involuntarily joined.

An attitudinal change is necessary for most delinquents, especially gangsters. They learn that the macho syndrome may be a necessity for survival in the gang and in correctional institutions, but that it is a hindrance for them in a TC, and especially later on in the real world of employment and relating to a loving family.

(2) The Encounter Group

In the early days of Synanon, Chuck Dederich developed the simplistic but profound concept that tough guys had to be talked to in a tough way to get them to listen. Kindly cajoling a tough youngster to see a point of view usually is not effective. The encounter group approach was created for utilization in TC groups. This treatment method is especially valuable for reaching the delinquent (see chapter 15).

The encounter group is a complex technique that is at the core of most group methods in a TC. The basic process involves a group attack on the self-deception that characterizes a resident. For example, a boy may believe that the violence he committed with his homies was a positive activity, necessary for the defense of his turf; this belief might come under the group's scrutiny and verbal attack. Another issue that might be the subject of an encounter group is black-on-black or Chicano-on-Chicano violence. A benefit of verbally attacking this behavior is that in defending it, the person on the "hot seat" will comprehend the ridiculous nature of the violence.

The macho syndrome is another important subject that can be hammered at in an encounter group. One boy, a newcomer in the TC, was overheard giving instructions on how to mug a person. The youth that had overheard him brought the subject up in the encounter group session. The newcomer's behavior was attacked by various members of the group. The encounter was led by Bill, an older resident of the TC, who had been through the criminal wars as a gangster, a heroin addict, and a convict. He was now a staff member in the TC.

In the encounter session Bill belittled the tough guy gangster attitude as being stupid behavior. And because he himself had a reputation of past behavior as a tough gangster, he was listened to by the group. Professional university-trained therapists are not in a position to attack the gangster's macho syndrome in the same way as an ex-gangster like Bill, who had lived the tough guy role for most of his life, understood the necessity of it in prison and in the gang, and most importantly had changed his own behavior.

Encounter groups force the recovering delinquent boy to examine his behavior and life-style retrospectively and introspectively. In my view, encounter groups are necessary in all TC work, because the sociopathic gangster does not usually respond to the other, more supportive approaches until his basic self-deception devices are vehemently countered by the group. It should be noted that a significant part of the process involves support and "picking up" a person at the end of an encounter session. By doing this, the group's members reinforce positive behavior with care and love. The encounter itself is an expression of love. As one delinquent told another at the end of a harsh group encounter, "If I didn't care about you and also feel that you could change, I wouldn't tell you things I do. It would be foolish to attack someone who is hopeless or who is helpless to change his behavior."

Self-Disclosing and Nurturing Groups

The overall goal of all group approaches delineated here is to help the recovering TC residents deal more effectively with their emotional problems. The nurturing group is instrumental in their opening up. In most respects, what I am referring to is conventional group therapy. A basic difference between standard group therapy and the type employed in a TC group is that the "group therapists" include peers and paraprofessional ex-gangsters. In an informal discussion I had with a former Chicano gangster who was involved in a prison TC program, I asked the question, "What is the toughest part of this program for you?" Without missing a beat he said, "Talking in front of other guys in groups about my early personal life in my family and how my father abused me. Mexicans have a kind of rule that you 'don't put your business out in the street.' So for me talking about these personal things is very hard."

In an effective TC for resocializing gangsters, self-disclosing and nurturing groups are required. These groups deal with "putting your business out in the street." Sociopaths are often manipulative, recalcitrant, and self-deceptive. Consequently, the therapist must deal with a tough facade and deceptive tactics in order to get through to the youth and his underlying real feelings. Once the therapist gets past the youth's criminal mask and game playing, he can help by counseling the real person behind the facade. This kind of breakthrough often takes place in group therapy because a youth's peers tend to understand one another's personal backgrounds.

For gangsters, in most cases, rage emanates from being physically, emotionally, or sexually abused as children by their parents, usually their father. Mixed into this abuse syndrome is abandonment. Tough guys find these negative early life experiences difficult to talk about because they reveal an emotional part of themselves that they have kept private in order to maintain their macho stance.

In many respects rage, in the case of the gangster, has not been repressed. In a nurturing group he begins to understand the source of his hostility and how it has been displaced and acted out against the wrong target. This group therapy process can explain the senseless black-on-black and Chicano-on-Chicano violence that is acted out through the vehicle of the gang. The former gangster can see that his early abusive childhood experiences are the real enemy and cause of his violent behavior.

(4) Psychodrama

In most of the therapeutic communities with which I have been involved or have studied, psychodrama and role-playing have been utilized in group psychotherapy. Psychodrama (described in various sessions with gangsters in earlier chapters) is a useful methodology for resolving the emotional problems of gangsters.

In a psychodrama session a person encounters his or her conflicts and psychic pain in a dramatic setting that more closely approximates a real-life situation; other group members stand in for the person(s) with whom he or she has a problem.

For example, many gangsters have hostility toward their father who has abused or abandoned them. In one psychodrama, a sociopathic gangster named Tomas, who had committed many violent offenses in his criminal career and was in prison for murder, opened up about his hostility toward his father. At one point in the session, after he had revealed a litany of abuses rained on him by his father, I handed Tomas a *battoca* (rubber bat) and told him to hit a chair with it for each abusive offense his father had committed against him. He was to state the offense and hit the chair, which represented his father.

At first his response was one I often heard when I invited a protagonist in a psychodrama to act out feelings of revenge. "Oh no, man, I would never hit my father. He would fuckin kill me!" This comment would usually be followed by a denial of hatred and rage, since many youths try to maintain the image of their parents as caring people. This youth was encouraged by the group to enact his rage, since many of them knew what was coming from comments he had verbalized in group therapy. I assured Tomas that what he was going to do would be held in strictest confidence in the group, and his father would never hear about it.

Tomas began to announce his father's abuses and then hit the chair. At first his blows to the chair were light ones; but toward the end of his role playing, in a kind of exorcism, the enactment of his rage became increasingly intense. As he hit the chair, he screamed at his "father" through clenched teeth, "This is for all the beatings you gave for no reason when I was a little kid, when you came home drunk. (Bang) This is for the times you locked me in the closet. (Bang) This for all the times you threw me up against the wall. (Bang) This is for the time you punished me by putting my hand on a hot stove for some nothing bullshit thing I had done. (Bang) This is for the time you tied up my arms and hung me like a piece of meat in the cellar. (Bang)." And there was more.

After the session, with the aid of further group discussion, others opened up and shared the abuse that had been visited on them. They had a better understanding of the dynamics that motivated them to commit their senseless acts of rage on undeserving victims.

During a psychodrama session, gangsters often discover that they have committed acts dictated by a gang's norms that conflict with their underlying emotions. In one memorable psychodrama a gangster acted out a stabbing he had committed on a homie in prison, because this person, his friend, had snitched on someone in the gang. He tearfully cried his regrets throughout the psychodrama about his violent act. He kept repeating, "I didn't want to hurt him, but I had to do it."

Other gangsters in the group sympathized with his plight because they, too, had been involved in violent acts that went against the grain of humanistic feelings that they had buried in order to conform to the expectations of their gang and the rules of prison life. The psychodrama triggered an in-depth discussion about the tyranny of the gang's expectations for violent behavior. One result of the psychodrama was the participants' realization that they had the power to stop the violence. This may be obvious to most people, but to the gangsters in the group, the fact that they could control their destiny was a revelation!

In psychodrama, the resolution of a problem does not necessarily require an extensive analysis or discussion, because the subject of a session experiences the emotions and resolves the problem in action. Often when someone has had a deep psychodramatic experience, there is no need for lengthy group discussion or analysis. Therapeutic benefits accrue to members of the group other than the central protagonist. Group participants are encouraged to attempt to understand and identify with aspects of their own lives that are revealed in the session. It is tantamount to watching a dramatic play that reveals their own problems on the stage in front of them.

(5) Family Groups

Most therapeutic communities attempt to have family groups, mainly comprised of the residents' parents, meet on a regular basis. These groups are the counterpart of Alcoholics Anonymous's Alanon. It is important to involve the gangster's family in some way into the TC treatment program. Of course, many youths who participate in gangs do not have coherent family situations, and it is difficult to get these usually dysfunctional families to cooperate in the therapeutic process.

Some discussions on family issues involve only residents. Other groups include parents, spouses, siblings, and other relatives. The concept that hovers over every type of family issue session is that the recovering resident is the nucleus of a familial social atom, and his or her problem is inextricably bound up with the family system. This concept encompasses J.L. Moreno's admonition that treatment must always take into account the person's social atom, including family relationships.

The Italian therapeutic community system (there are over 40 TCs in Italy) utilizes a different and perhaps more effective approach to involving the family than those used in American TCs. Before applicants are accepted into residence, they, and their families attend indoctrination groups for a few months, where they learn about various aspects of the TC program. The potential residents get a head start in the program, with the cooperation of their family (Yablonsky, 1978). Typically, in these family groups, work is begun on the potential residents' problems. They may work out a contract with their family for improving behavior and for becoming drug and crime free as a prelude to entering the therapeutic community. These orientation and indoctrination groups facilitate a more effective learning experience when the newcomers finally become full-time residents. This might prove to be a useful approach for some youths entering a gang program. Before entering the TC they might be able to make some progress in disassociating themselves from their homies and becoming more positively involved with their families.

⑥Educational Groups

Statistics from a study of Los Angeles high schools (1996) revealed that around 39 percent of black youths dropped out of high school without graduating. This is generally true of Chicano and African-American youths in urban area schools throughout the country. The percentage is even higher for youths who participate in gangs. Consequently, many delinquents are deficient in reading, writing, and math skills and general knowledge.

On their path to social reality in a therapeutic community most residents become motivated to learn to write, read, and acquire the education they missed when they were out on the streets. This hunger for knowledge is fed in educational groups that focus on various subjects, including philosophical discussions.

I have observed TC residents who had a limited educational background enthusiastically participating in discussions on the writings of Emerson, Plato, Kant, and Spinoza; current events related to a range of contemporary social and political issues; social and psychological theories about mental health, including those of Freud, Moreno, Fromm, and Erikson; racism and its roots; biological sciences; great literature, including Shakespeare; and classical art and music. There is evidence that most youths who participate in the gangster life are as intelligent as other youths and if presented with the opportunity can become involved in intellectual pursuits.

TC educational groups can become an important pathway for a boy to move out of his alienated life in a gang into participation in the larger society. An educational group process often motivates TC residents to complete their formal high school or college education and to better determine the kind of life work they will pursue when they "graduate" from the TC.

⑦Occupational Planning Groups

A probation detached gang worker once told me that one of his most difficult tasks in working with gang youths was keeping them in jobs. He said, "Most of these guys, especially core gangsters, have never worked a day in their lives. And when I do get some of them work, they don't last very long on the job. They get belligerent with their boss, they show up late, or not at all." It is apparent that some effort has to be made to help youths learn how to get a job and understand the necessity of developing some occupational skills if they are to succeed.

In order for a therapeutic community to function, a variety of jobs are built into the organization. Many TCs have gas stations, manufacturing plants, and advertising specialty businesses for the purpose of helping to finance the organization's work. There are office jobs, housekeeping and kitchen jobs, and manual labor. These jobs are filled by residents and provide realistic on-the-job training with the necessary backup of groups where they can discuss the problems they confront in the process of their work.

In occupational-group discussions, residents' efficacy and proclivity for meaningful work are analyzed based on their work performance in the organization. The group's goals are to help residents, to learn how to work and to clarify the kind of work they would like to engage in when they graduate and return to their community. These groups foster on-the-job training and clarify occupational goals. The focus in educational groups on how to get a job (perhaps through role playing), how to hold a job, and the necessity of learning some trade helps residents consider their future occupations in society after graduating from the TC program.

Not all of the foregoing group methods are utilized in every therapeutic community. However, some form of group in every TC attempts to deal with the variety of issues needed to help a delinquent become resocialized into a law-abiding citizen. These treatment methods can help change delinquents into law-abiding citizens. These methodologies can be incorporated into the various institutional and community-based programs described. They have a special relevance and effectiveness for resocializing delinquents when they are properly utilized in the correct setting. Most delinquents, in my view, are amenable to becoming law-abiding, productive citizens if they are helped through their difficult adolescent years by caring, empathetic adult role models who use a variety of methodologies and by institutional systems that have been developed over the years in an effective way. In my work, I have seen extremely recalcitrant delinquents respond when they are treated with intelligence, love, and respect in a bona fide therapeutic community.[1]

An Analysis of the Therapeutic Community Methodology by an Ex-Addict: Zev Putterman

The variety of methods used in a therapeutic community become clearer when they are integrated into a case history. Zev Putterman, a college graduate and an unusually eloquent and insightful individual, described his odyssey from addict to responsible citizen through Synanon.

---

1. For a fuller analysis of therapeutic communities, see Lewis Yablonsky, *Synanon: The Tunnel Back* (New York: Macmillan, 1965) and *The Therapeutic Community* (New York: Gardner Press, 1989).

Following is a lecture Zev presented in a graduate social work seminar I taught at UCLA in 1962. At the time of the lecture he had been in Synanon for thirteen months.

Today, in my talk, I will try to give you the benefit of my contact with various institutional approaches to my emotional disorder, which has been labeled by psychoanalysts as "constitutional psychopathy, complicated by drug addiction." I guess, in your frame of reference, "sociopath" would be more applicable. At any rate, this diagnosis was made fourteen years ago by Dr. Abraham Kardiner, a pretty reputable Freudian psychiatrist, after I had spent eight months in therapy with the man.

Over a period of thirteen years, I wound in and out of private, public, state, county, and federal institutions for drug addicts, as well as private hospitals for people with the whole spectrum of emotional and psychological disorders. What I think is relevant to examine here today, in light of my experience, is what happened to me in the thirteen months that I've been in the TC that has made it possible for me not to behave as I did previously. There is no evidence, as yet, as to whether I have been changed on a deep and meaningful level. But there is plenty of surface evidence that my behavior has manifested a change so drastic from what it was thirteen months ago that, to me and the people who knew me before coming to the program, it's almost unbelievable.

What I wanted to point out to you, in brief, is that what happened in the TC program did not happen for me at the Menninger Clinic in Topeka; the Institute of Living in Hartford; three times at Lexington, Kentucky; at New York Metropolitan Hospital; at Manhattan General; or at the Holbrook Sanitorium. It also didn't happen for me with a number of individual shrinks.

When you think of an addiction history of fourteen years, many people have the image of fourteen years of constant drug use. The thing that makes people drug addicts, to me, is the equation that they learn after their first detoxification. Drug addicts become drug addicts not when they just become addicted to drugs, but when they learn this equation. They kick their habit physiologically, they have decided consciously to change their behavior, they are going to manipulate themselves in every way that they know in order not to repeat what they've been doing, and—bingo—they repeat exactly those processes that got them to the point that they didn't want to get to. This, to me, is the person who has taken his first cure and then gone back to dope. The usual institution he goes to is also part of his addiction process.

Certain circumstances force people to enter a TC. The AA always uses the phrase, "You reach your own bottom." So, let's assume that I had reached a "bottom." I had tried everything else in the Western World. I think just about everything else; you know, chemical cures as well, which I didn't bother to mention.

Anyway, I entered the TC. At first something very strange happened to me. I came into Synanon early in the morning. I had just gotten off the plane. I'd flown 3,000 miles. The usual reception at a place where a person has volunteered for a cure is "Welcome aboard!" This was not the case. I was told to sit down and shut up, in just about those words; you know, literally, "Sit down and shut up." [In Synanon most applicants received a more cordial intake interview. The intake staff, however, felt that in Zev's case, with his demeanor, it would be more useful for him to battle his way into the organization.]

I figured I was talking to a disturbed person who didn't understand who he was talking to. In the first moment of contact, instead of being told "Welcome aboard," I was told to shut up and sit down. Whereupon, being loaded on heroin at the time, I explained that I had just arrived in California; that I had flown from New York; and that I had talked to a board member—whereupon the magic words "shut up and sit down" were read-ministered. I began to realize that reason had nothing to do with the behavior of these people. These are not reasonable people. I had no alternative. If I had, I would have said, "I'll come back another time." But I was three thousand miles away from my connection. I didn't have that resource.

I sat down for a number of hours, and then I was called by some people into a room. Oh, first of all, my luggage was taken away from my possession. And one of my pieces of luggage contained a variety of drugs, nonnarcotic in nature, that were prescribed for me by my psychiatrist. When I left New York, I said "I'll be gone for six months," and he wrote five prescriptions for six months worth of five different kinds of medication, you know, to ease withdrawal, nonnarcotic-psychic energizers, tranquilizers, sleeping medication—a whole satchel full of it.

I've been subjected to many intake interviews, by social workers, psychiatrists, psychologists, and charge nurses. And I was usually asked a variety of questions, and I had my pat answers: Am I white or black—"I'm white." In this instance I wasn't asked anything. They didn't even want to know my name. I mean, literally, they didn't say to me, "Who are you?" They proceeded to tell me who I was. Their only contact with me had been a phone call from Westport, which lasted maybe a minute, and then my contact with the guy at the desk, who didn't listen to what I was saying. So they were telling me who I was. They told me things like I would "never make it," I was a "momma's boy," I was "spoiled," I was "probably incurable," and that if I didn't shut up, they would throw me out, that they were not interested in learning anything from me, because I had nothing to teach them—which, of course, to me was absolutely absurd. I had come here to enlighten the West Coast.

This was a shocking experience. I'm making it humorous, but it shook me up; it shook me down to my feet. In the intake interview there were five addicts staring at me. One said,

"There's an accumulative thirty-seven years of sobriety in this room and eighty-two years of dope addiction, and your three seconds of sobriety doesn't count." Now that was reasonable to me. So you see, I was being hit on a reasonable and nonreasonable level as I saw it. So they were talking about me as if I weren't there, after this thing happened. You know, "Lets take him downstairs, let's do this to him." I wasn't being consulted, and the first thing I thought when I heard about the TC concept, was, "There won't be a we-they alienation, because these are folks like me, and they know how sick I am."

I was then taken outside by a large man, a gargantuan character whom I would never have an opportunity to communicate with, even using dope. I found out he was a street hype from Detroit who had done a lot of time in prison, and he looked very tough. Outside of the TC, it would just be a matter of conning him, or him hitting me over the head. He proceeded to take my little satchel with medicine in it and led me downstairs to the basement of the building, which was pretty grim. It looked like the 23rd Precinct in New York City. He took the satchel and opened the drug bottles and proceeded to pour them into the toilet. I said, "Now, wait, you see, you don't understand. These are nonaddicting drugs—none of these drugs are addicting drugs, and they're legitimate. See, my name is on them." And while I'm saying this, he is grunting and pouring my medicine out.

This is another important aspect of a TC that is different from other institutions. The first thing I picked up in this indoctrination, being a manipulative type of guy, was this: When people didn't want me or didn't seem to want me, I, of course, wanted them. The appeal to me was somewhat like a fraternity appeal in a college. The fraternity that is most difficult to get into is naturally the most desirable. Well, what had been communicated to me immediately by "sit down and shut up," as if I were rushing the house, was that this club was rather exclusive. They were not particularly impressed with me, so naturally they must be pretty smart—because my self-esteem was pretty shitty, although it didn't look that way.

Then my personal property—I think a person's property represents who you are—you know, your resume. For people like me in the theatrical business, your eight-by-ten glossies [photographs] and your theater programs—you know, this is who you are. I had a few pieces of clothing, an electric shaver, things you pick up that are pawnable. These things were taken away from me—brusquely. And I was given *schmatas* [Yiddish for "rags"] is the only word I can think of. I was given unseemly clothing.

There was nothing institutional about the clothing. There was a plaid shirt that didn't fit. And I was very specific in asking for cotton because my skin gets sensitive during withdrawal. I was given a wool plaid shirt, because I asked for cotton, and a pair of khaki pants that didn't fit, and rubber go-aheads, flip-flops, or suicide-scuffs, which were very uncomfortable.

And then I was taken upstairs. There I was. My luggage was gone, my resumes, my identity, my drugs—my pride. I also had my hair cut, just because I protested too much. I had my hair cut off rather short, and by a guy who didn't particularly care for the cosmetic value of a haircut. I didn't need a haircut. The day before I had been to Vincent of the Plaza in New York and had had a haircut.

I went into the living room and was introduced to a few people. I recognized a couple of them as drug addicts. I saw scar tissue on their arms. I saw that they really were drug addicts.

Kicking my heroin habit in Synanon had a big effect on me. It was a process which, again, was very different from that of other institutions. The institutions I had been to all had detoxification procedures of one kind or another. All the detoxification procedures that I'd ever been involved in, although they may be medically necessary for people with heart conditions or for people who are over ninety-three, really were not necessary. In all of the settings I had been in, the bit was to exaggerate your symptoms so that you could get more medication. If you get medication, you feel better; if you don't, you feel bad. I don't think there is anything pathological in this kind of behavior. So the thing to do, of course, is to get medication.

I was told, with the flushing down the drain of the medications I had brought, that I was not getting any medication. And I said, you know, "I'm going to get quite sick—I'm not feeling very good!"

"You will not get any medication."

I said, "You don't understand. You see, I'm going to be really sick. You see, I'm from New York, and they've got good heroin and cocaine in New York, and I'm strung out and I'm going to get really sick."

They again repeated, "You will not get medication. If you want medication, you can leave and get medication. But here, you won't get medication."

This immediately stopped a whole process that would have gone on for two or three weeks if medication were given. This is another important thing: I had my biggest manipulative device taken away for me, because there was nothing to manipulate for, except maybe a glass of water. That's about it. And how much of a con game would I have to run down to get a glass of water?

Then the guy assigned to me as a sponsor started his therapy. He was a big black guy who sure knew his job. The second day I was there, I started to get sick. The drugs held me for twenty-four or thirty hours. He came up to me and said, "Little brother"—he referred to me as little brother, which offended me to the quick—"when are you going to get sick?" I was sick, and he knew I was sick. So he came over again and he said, "Little brother, when are you going to get sick?" Because his attitude was ridiculous, as far as I was concerned, I said, "I'm all right."

Now, what he had done by this simple little intuitive thing

of "When are you going to get sick?" is that he let me know that he knew that I knew that he knew. He immediately stopped the possibility of—you know—he didn't give me sympathy. He didn't give me any kind of "understanding"—and yet he gave me understanding on a very deep level. It became a challenge to me to see how unsick I could be in withdrawal during the next four or five days.

And I noticed another thing. There would be some people in the house who would come over and kind of be concerned about me. I'd get a back rub. If I wasn't vomiting, I'd get a milkshake, and sometimes I would drink the milkshake so that I could vomit and show them how sick I was. There were still these things that were going on that weren't getting me anywhere.

And then they did something to me that was very important. They made me think they had a secret. They made me think that they knew something that I didn't know. I snapped to this, and it was quite true; they did know something I didn't know. They still know many things I don't know. It wasn't just a mystique. They really had information I didn't have. And they weren't willing to share with me, particularly, at least at this time. This got my nose open. I became quite curious about what it was.

My sponsor would drop a concept on me like a Zen cat and run off in the other direction. He would say something like, "Just stay." You know, like a Zen master would clap me on the head and I'd have enlightenment. Well, this is what was going on during the period of detoxification, TC style, which is a cold-turkey withdrawal, which is unlike any other cold-turkey withdrawal because it's bad and its wretched, but it's not all that wretched and not that bad.

I was up off the couch in four days. Now, I had been kicking habits. I was a specialist in observing myself kicking habits—you know, reading Cocteau as another frame of reference in how he kicked his habit—and all of my past evidence crumbled. You see, all of my evidence was destroyed by the experience that I was sleeping by the seventh day, and I hadn't slept without medication, in or out of a place, in seven years. I had not been able to sleep. I was now sleeping within seven days!

On the fifth day, I was rewarded for kicking my habit by receiving a mop. I thought the least I deserved—you know, the least—for what I'd been subjected to was a week at a country club. Instead I was not rewarded at all. Because there really was not any reason for a reward. I heard things like, "Not shooting dope is not worthy of a reward. People don't shoot dope! Therefore, not shooting dope doesn't earn any reward." It's like saying, "Congratulations for not beating your wife" or "Thank you for not murdering my sister." You know, one doesn't do this, so naturally you're not going to get a big hand. No one in the TC is going to applaud you because you're not shooting any dope and you're mopping floors.

Somebody's got to mop the floors, and you're constantly

told you don't know how to do anything else at that time. You begin to think that maybe they're right because at this point, you're pretty vulnerable psychically and physically—so maybe mopping a floor isn't a bad thing to be doing. And then the magic thing begins to go to work, this thing about the secret. I think this is what motivates you to mop the floor well. You begin to see that if you mop the floor well, you won't feel as guilty as if you mop the floor badly.

In most institutional settings, and in most psychoanalytical or socially oriented or tradition-directed treatment centers for addicts, your guilt is usually ameliorated: "You're a sick fellow; you can't help yourself; you have an acting-out disorder; together we'll work this thing out, resocialize you, and everything will be great." So, of course, what people like myself do is, they take all this ammunition, they fuel themselves with the fact that they have an acting-out disorder. What can they do? They have all the data, so they go and act out.

Here they lay guilt upon guilt. In other words, every time the energy flags a little bit—like mopping the floors and the corners aren't done—instead of being told, "Well, you know, he's still sick; he hasn't really kicked yet; he's new and he hasn't done much floor mopping in his time," you are made to feel that the dirty corner represents a dirty corner in your psyche, your gut. You think that you really are ridiculously bad at mopping floors, and you get guilty, you see, and your guilt is fueled.

Whenever you are in a regular institutional setting, your guilt and problems are analyzed and explained away—they are lightened. The burden of guilt is lightened. In Synanon, whenever things began to get buoyant and you permit your insanity to return as self-compensation for your low self-esteem, you're told you're not unique in nature and get smashed on the head with a verbal velvet mallet. It doesn't crush the tissue; you still feel the impact of it, but it really doesn't hurt.

I soon learned that there were people in the TC without the social status I had in the outside world, without the resumes and the eight-by-ten glossies, who were not smashed quite as hard as I was. They came in with a birdcage on one foot, a boxing glove on the other, and they were in bad shape. You can see that they don't have any totems of success or any illusions, so there's no reason for them to be ridiculed the way I was ridiculed, and they are treated in a more caring way. But they still will not be able to get rewarded for bad behavior.

For instance, I think this is significant in looking at the total picture. A friend of mine arrived from New York about three months after I got here. My friend, Herb, was addicted to barbiturates and cocaine as well as heroin. He got pretty damn sick and began to act pretty crazy. This is interesting. One of the directors came down and told Herb that if he acted like a nut, they'd have to ask him to leave, because they couldn't handle nuts. In other words, "Herb, you'll have to go to Camirillo or someplace where they handle crazy people. We don't handle crazy people, so you're not allowed to be crazy here." Now, I've been in three psychiatric hospitals with Herb, and I know how crazy he is. Now, literally, this happened to work. "Don't be a nut." And, you know, he wasn't! He just couldn't act crazy if he wanted to stay, so he didn't. Herb was a pretty sick guy physically, but he was able to curb his emotional symptoms because of this direct approach to him by an understanding ex-addict.

Here is another significant thing in terms of an institution, and in terms of understanding the TC thing. About three or four weeks after my arrival, I began to notice that the place was full of me. In other words, in every other institution I had ever been at, I had a very schizoid feeling. There were the doctors, and I was kind of like them, but by some fluke, they became doctors and I was an addict. I'd look at them, and because I knew a lot of psychology, I felt like I kind of had a foot in their camp. And yet I was with the addicts because I am an addict. There was a kind of we-they thing, and I felt that I was in two roles. I knew that my soul was with the addicts because the doctors did not know where it was at. They really didn't. In the TC, in contrast, I saw a million manifestations of me, in everyone, because despite their background and status in the TC, they were addicts like me; and I truly trusted them.

The contract I had set up all my life with other people was a "we-they" situation: my father and me, my psychiatrist and me, the warden and me, the teacher and me. This contrast was smashed by the TC situation. I became aware that the place was run by a hundred Zevs, different aspects of me. So when I hated somebody's behavior, I disapproved of me. My sense of alienation with the "we-they" equation—the hip and the square, the culture and the subculture, the ingroup and the outgroup, the Jews and the gentiles, the whites and the blacks, and all of the other "we-they" equations that I had learned—primarily were destroyed in the TC. I had nothing to rebel against but myself.

I began to see what Lew Yablonsky articulates as "social mobility" in a TC. [I had discussed this issue when I introduced Zev to the students.] We don't have a caste system in Synanon, where my upward mobility is restricted to being a patient or an inmate. We have a kind of class system based on clean seniority, productivity, mental health, talent, and so on. I've begun to climb this status ladder, and I'm beginning to understand now that I'm hooked into the organization and want to move up. The side effect of this status seeking for me has been growing up from being a baby to my chronological age of thirty-three. In the process, of course, I have stayed clean, and I plan to remain drug free for the rest of my life.

Zev remained in the Synanon program for three years as a counselor with newcomers. He left the program to continue his career in TV and film but maintained a constructive connection by participating in a variety of TC and other support groups. I le remained drug free for the rest of his life, and died of natural causes at the age of sixty-eight in 1997.

Zev was a pioneer in the TC movement for the last half of his life. He worked as an administrator in the development of Amity and other programs in the United States. He was a true role model for many individuals who changed their lives as he had, and in this context he was a significant "experience therapist."

CHAPTER 18

THE THERAPEUTIC COMMUNITY, THE EXPERIENCE THERAPIST, AND SOCIAL SYSTEMS FOR TREATING THE DELINQUENCY PROBLEM

This photo of a cellblock at the California Department of Corrections Donovan Prison depicts 200 men who are in the most avant-garde and effective treatment program for criminal/addicts of the 20th century: the Amity Project. The usual recidivist (repeat offense) rate in the United States for released prisoners is around 65%. The Amity Project rate for prisoners who have completed the program, after release, is around 20%! As a conse-quence of the program these men develop therapeutic skills as "experience-therapists," and many are employed after completeing the Amity Program to work with gangs and juvenile delinquents in the community. This positive experiment portends a hopeful future for criminal/addict treatment in the 21st century.

The social system of the therapeutic community (TC) facilitates changing criminal addicts into law-abiding citizens. The success of the TC process is evidenced by the numbers of ex-gangster delinquents and criminals who have gone through the programs. Resocialization offers the TC graduate the possibility of enacting a new and valuable social role of "experience therapist." This new role for the ex-criminal/addict can be enacted in the process of social growth and development during his time in the TC and beyond. When former offenders graduate from a TC, they have an opportunity to acquire jobs as counselors in the TC that has changed them or work in this capacity in another therapeutic community. TC-trained ex-criminal/addicts are increasingly in demand for this new and valuable societal role.

Donald Cressey succinctly delineated the basic concept of the experience therapist in his comment, "When Criminal A helps Criminal B, Criminal A is helped." When an ex-addict gangster helps others travel the therapeutic road he has been on, he helps himself to stay on the straight and narrow. Even if he is not the greatest helper to others—when he is functioning as an experience therapist he is removed from his past self-destruct life pattern. To fracture an old homily, "When he is talking the talk (of law-abiding behavior), he is walking the walk."

The concept of the therapeutic community and its value were apparent in a Texas prison TC program I observed while researching gangs for my book *Gangsters*. This Texas prison housed several thousand convicts and had a special cell block for a TC that was administered by the Amity Foundation. The prison population was comprised of offenders doing time for various crimes, including, homicide, rape, drugs, robbery, burglary, theft, assault, and gang murders.

I made a number of research visits to a special unit in the center of the prison that housed four hundred inmates involved in the Amity TC program. The project was directed by thirty-five ex-criminal/addicts, including several former gangsters, who had been rehabilitated and trained in the Amity Therapeutic Community in Tucson, Arizona. The Beaumont prison project was modeled after a successful and ongoing program that Amity directed for the California Department of Corrections at the Donovan Prison in San Diego.

Two Amity people assisted me with my gang research at the Texas prison: Sheila, a former addict who had been clean for over fifteen years and was the director of the prison program, and Ed, the former Crip member whose case history appears in chapter 7. At this time, Ed had been free of drugs and violence for over five years as a result of his treatment in the Amity Therapeutic Community and was now a paid experience therapist in the Amity prison program.

After I had researched several special gang focus groups, I received permission to visit a special maximum security unit that housed the most difficult, recalcitrant, and violent convicts in the institution. Most of these individuals were responsible for murders in and out of prison, and were doing life sentences. The unit was supervised by several guards, who maintained twenty-four-hour security within the cell block. The cells were built for solitary confinement, with a small slit in the door for continuing surveillance by the guards. The prisoners' food trays were slid through this slit into the cagelike cells. In the center of the area was a large cell with bars from floor to ceiling that was sometimes used for visitors. Accompanied by Sheila and Ed I entered the big cell to sit down and talk with one of the inmates, who had been released from his solitary cell to talk to us. The inmate, Jesus, was about thirty years old. (I later learned that he had murdered several people.) The part of his criminal background that was especially shocking to me was that he had murdered his father as the result of a gang conflict, in part, because his father had moved out of Jesus's gang's territory and joined a rival gang.

Jesus was stripped to the waist, possibly for security purposes so that the guards could see that he was not secreting any weapons. His body was covered with tattoos of snakes. One prominent tattoo stood out from the rest—a large "TS" on his upper arm, signifying that he was a member of the violent and notorious Texas Syndicate, the counterpart of California's infamous Mexican Mafia prison gang.

Sheila and Ed had met Jesus before, and they introduced me as someone who was writing a book on gangs. He was not impressed, nor did he say anything in response to my questions that was noteworthy. I asked him if he had any regrets and what advice he would give to a young kid who wanted to join a gang. This standard question usually elicited a "don't do it" response from even the most recalcitrant sociopath. Jesus responded with a sneer and belligerently said, "Hey man, that's the kid's decision, ain't it! I'm doing okay right where I am." This response clearly told me he was not going to reveal any useful information, and his machismo attitude dominated his view on life.

Despite the fact that Jesus clammed up, the situation was for me a revealing experience. Sitting at my left was Ed, whose background and behavior for many years has been no different than Jesus's. Yet, Ed was now an open, reasonable, positive person, dedicated to treating a significant and difficult crime problem. Sitting across from me was Jesus, an example of the crime problem we were trying to treat. It was necessary to keep Jesus in prison to prevent him from following his violent proclivities. It was also clear, however, that his sociopathic-homicidal attitude toward life was going to become intensified by his life sentence.

Although for several decades I had touted the positive value of the therapeutic immunity for controlling and treating criminals and the violent gang problem, and I knew of many core gang members who had been positively changed by their TC experience, it all came together for me that day when I was in that cell block with Ed and Jesus. The difference between these two individuals was that Ed had been resocialized in a TC program, and Jesus, because of his treatment in a standard punitive prison, would spend his life in his prison cell. It drove home the fact that many hard-core former offenders like Ed, if effectively treated in a TC, can become a vital therapeutic force, ameliorating America's crime and delinquency problem.

Transformation from Gangster to Experience Therapist

Ed's extensive criminal, gangster, and prison experience is detailed in chapter 7. He is a prototypical representative of the several hundred criminal/addicts I have interviewed and known over the years who have benefited from the TC approach and have chosen to become experience therapists in TCs in the community and in prison programs. After working alongside Ed in a number of gang focus groups and being enormously impressed by his technique in eliciting insightful responses from many youths in the group, I asked him to describe the therapeutic process that worked for him in Amity. Following is a report of several lengthy interview sessions I had with him.

> I will try to describe for you how I feel the Amity program turned my life around and gave me another viewpoint on how to live my life in a better way. And how I became what you, Lew, referred to as an ET—a person who can help others who are currently acting out the role of criminal/addict. This certainly was the role I played around seven years ago.
> Let me go back in time a little to explain how I wound up in Amity in the first place. When I got out of Soledad prison in 1989, I found that some of my Crip homeboys were making a lot of money selling drugs. So to help me out they gave me a little money and some crack to sell to get me started. I was no good as a dealer, and I began to use the shit myself. Of course, I got all strung out and was useless to my homies in the drug business. Pretty soon I had burned all my homies, and they didn't want to help me anymore or really have anything to do with me. I needed money for my habit.
> I always was good at armed robbery, and jewelry stores were my specialty. I joined up with this crew from the Crips and we started to hit jewelry stores around the Southwest—like

Albuquerque, Phoenix, and Tucson. I brought one of my young homeboys, Bootsy, who was sixteen, along with us in our work. In this one robbery in Tucson, everything went wrong. Bootsy was killed by one of the crew. The guy who killed Bootsy felt it was necessary because during the robbery Bootsy panicked and ran out on us and this put us in danger.

After this robbery we all headed back to California, and one of the crew got stopped in Arizona in this van we used in the robberies. They got fingerprints off the van and this one guy told on me and everyone else. They found four of us, and we were all busted and wound up in jail in Tucson. We were charged with first-degree murder for Bootsy's killing and armed robbery. I liked Bootsy, and I had nothing to do with his murder, but being with the guys in the robbery, all four of us were charged with murder.

They had no evidence to prove that I was involved with the murder, so they dropped that charge but held me in jail for some robberies. I pleaded guilty to robbery, because my fingerprints were on some of the stolen property. I was sentenced to a two-to-five-year sentence and was waiting in jail to be sent to an Arizona state prison.

At that time I had already been in jail for a year. I was thirty-five years old and for some reason I began to think about my life. Before they dropped the first-degree murder charge, they were talking about me getting the gas chamber. That scared the shit out of me!

I figured if I kept doing what I was doing, I would spend the rest of my life in prison or be dead. I had heard about the Amity program, and I knew the judge on my case liked that program. That year I spent in jail in Arizona I was checking out Amity. So I wrote the judge a long letter telling him that prison had never helped me change, I wanted to do something about my life, and I felt that I could get the help I needed in the Amity TC program. The judge went for it, and I was sent to Amity.

My whole purpose at that time was to get off of drugs, find out why I used drugs, and stay out of prison. I mainly wanted to learn how to stay off drugs so I could go back to sell drugs without using and make some money. I also had a secret that I'll tell you now. I never wanted my little homie Bootsy killed, and I was planning to get the motherfucker who killed him when I got out of Amity. So when I entered Amity, I wasn't being completely honest about my intentions.

The judge in Tucson cut me loose with an agreement that I would enter Amity and stay there for at least eighteen months. When I first arrived at Amity I was scared, so I didn't do much talking in any of the groups. The level of honesty with the way these people talked in groups about their problems and feelings really fucked me up emotionally. When someone talked about dope or things that had happened to them or their loved ones, I would break down and start crying.

I remember this one woman, Alice, who had been a crackhead, talkin' about how her son had been killed in gang activity, and I began crying like a baby. Another guy, Ron, had a son who was killed in a gang. I didn't say much in groups, but a side of me that I really didn't know was there began to open up in these groups. And whenever I saw Alice anywhere on the property, I would break down and cry. I felt really guilty about her kids being killed in gang activity. It was crazy, but I felt guilty and responsible.

Whatever was going on with me, I felt it was something I needed to do. I knew something good was happening to me, but I hated it too, because it was so foreign to me to act like that. I hadn't cried about anything in years. That experience of their honesty opened me up. Then I began to share in the groups about who I am and things that I did that I was ashamed of for the first time in my life. It made me feel better to get some of this shit out in the open.

The first thing I began to share was out of anger. I was talking a lot of bullshit at first and holding back. Finally I opened up about my plan to kill the motherfucker who murdered my little homeboy. So, at first, I was talking mainly about revenge on the guy that killed Bootsy. One of the things I began to see in the group where I was blaming this guy was that I began to see my own responsibility in my homies' death. I began to feel guilty because I brought him along on the robberies and I felt responsible for his being killed. When I became honest enough on this thing with my homie to tell on myself to the people in Amity, I realized, motherfucker, you have changed!

Their opinion on my plans for revenge was, "You are a crazy motherfucker to be thinking like that." Their opinion was the opposite of what I felt was necessary revenge for the death of my homeboy.

I said, "So your conflict was about the rules of the gang versus a more rational opinion by the people in Amity. They saw your necessity for revenge as holding on to the values of the gang in contrast with your really becoming involved with the rules and norms of society."

That's right, they believed that what I wanted to do as a gangster was really crazy behavior, and I had to figure all of this out. It was really the first time anyone told me that my way of thinking wasn't right. Other people, my mother, at school, cops, judges and all had told me what was right, but these people at Amity were like me and I listened to them.

After that experience, where I decided that killing that cat was crazy, I accepted a wider circle of friends in Amity. I still had trouble talking in groups, but I found one guy from New York, Jimmy T., who had been clean over ten years in Amity. I trusted him and felt I could talk to him about anything. And he helped me a lot to get my crazy gangster thinking of the need for revenge straightened out.

I felt bad that I had done a lot of violence in the past and killed some people. I was afraid of getting convicted on some old beefs and things like that. So I learned to not identify times and places. So many things I had done in gangs began to come out to some trusted guys and I also began to become more honest in the groups. When I began to dump this old shit, I felt like a burden was lifted off of my shoulders.

I said, "Give me an example of a turning point in your life in Amity."

In a retreat, that's like a forty-eight-hour series of groups that opens you up, they showed this movie, *Boyz N the Hood*. This retreat happened before I unloaded my insane secret of revenge and my plan to kill this cat who had murdered my homeboy. The movie was shown to kick off some group discussion. After the movie, people were asking questions and giving opinions on gangs. What they were saying about gangs upset the shit out of me. Rod, the group leader, saw I was agitated, and he asked me if I had something to say. I went stark raving crazy. I said, "Yeah motherfucker, I got something to say. You motherfuckers saw this movie and now you're going to be an expert on my hood, my people, and my gang." I cussed and I threatened people for their forming all these wrong opinions on where I come from. It drove me up the wall, because they didn't know what the fuck they were talking about, and I resented all of their bullshit opinions. What made me so mad, at that time, was that they saw this one movie and thought that gangbanging was insane behavior.

When I think back to the showing of *Boyz N the Hood* and my crazy explosion, I would analyze it this way. I felt that was me up there on the screen, and they were talking about me personally. And when they said that gang violence and murder was crazy, they were saying that I was crazy. I felt at that time that I was still affiliated with my homeboys. I now realize that at that time I was defending my gang insanity. In other words, I now see that what they said about gangbanging and all that shit was right. It was kind of a turning point for me to give up some of my old crazy gang ideas, join the Amity community, and learn how to express myself in a more sensible way.

When I talked honestly about my past, people would be touched and would hug me and tell me they loved me. I thought they were crazy. In my past the only love I would get from my homeboys or anyone is if I did something violent for them, or they might like me out of fear. In Amity I found people who liked me for myself. And the more honest I became, the more I felt I deserved to be loved.

"Correct me if I'm wrong" I said. "The more honest and open you became, the more you began to feel that you could relate to more people and help someone else."

> Exactly. I can't take anyone—like some of the younger dudes in Amity—anywhere that I wasn't willing to go myself. I learned in Amity that in order for anyone to be honest with me I had to be honest with them. I began to feel I could help some of the younger gang kids in Amity get their act together for a better way of life.

Ed has been gang, drug, and crime free since 1990 as a result of the positive social and psychological impact of the Amity TC program. He has become an effective paraprofessional in TC prison groups and working with gangs. Former criminals like Ed are uniquely qualified to become effective "therapists" for three reasons:

1. They know many of the rationalizations and self-deceptions that keep a person on the criminal merry-go-round from the streets, to jail, to prison, and back to the streets. They comprehend on a deep emotional level what a criminal life is like. They have been there themselves.

2. They have gone through the complex resocialization process of personal change in a TC program. They know the painful emotional crises and traumas of confronting their own life-styles more directly. They have experienced the various phases of reorganizing their relationships with their families and friends. They have developed valuable coping mechanisms for dealing with the temptations of sliding back into their former states of existence, and for breaking off relationships with former partners in crime. They have learned how to stay away from crime, drugs, and gangs, and are succeeding as responsible citizens.

3. As a result of these two sets of experiences—a past life as a criminal and firsthand knowledge about the recovery process—former offenders have usually developed some special insights and skills. They are not easily outmaneuvered or conned. They quickly acquire the respect of their "clients," because they can see through the rationalizations and ploys that they once used themselves. The result is a communication that has more therapeutic power than that usually achieved by more traditional professional therapy. These paraprofessionals also know from their day-to-day experiences the self-discipline that is required to continue to lead a crime-free life.

In 1997, Ed became a detached gang worker in a paid job in a Beaumont, Texas, project. One of the gangs Ed was assigned to work with in Beaumont called themselves the Hoover Crips, despite the fact that they had no Los Angeles connection.

The Experience Therapist's Role in the Creation and Administration of Therapeutic Communities

The original Synanon, as previously indicated, was invented by Chuck Dederich, an ex-alcoholic, and administered by Dederich with the aid of several ex-addicts including Reid Kimball and Bette Coleman Dederich. For nearly ten of the early years, when many of the basic elements of therapeutic communities were created, I was on the board of directors along with the Dederichs and Reid Kimball. I have found that in many TCs, in the United States and elsewhere, proper balance between university trained professionals and experience therapists in the management of TCs has been an issue. In Italy, for example, where there are over forty TCs partially financed by the government, legislation was passed to insure that staffing had a ratio of 60 percent university trained professionals and 40 percent ex-criminal/addict administrators. This issue will become increasingly significant as TCs become government financed entities, somewhat like probation, in the twenty-first century.

What is not at issue is that ex-criminals/addicts like Ed can become experience therapists who can work effectively with juvenile delinquents, and that some talented experience therapists may even create and administer TC organizations. Following are two notable examples of individuals who as a result of their resocialization, training, and education in a TC (in these two cases, Synanon) founded their own versions of a therapeutic community.

The first example, Alphonso Acampora, an ex-criminal/addict from New York's Bronx, founded, developed, and is the CEO of one of the world's premier therapeutic communities—Walden House in San Francisco. The second is Naya Arbiter, an ex-drug dealer and heroin addict who, along with two dedicated friends who were nonaddict residents of Synanon, Rod Mullen and Bette Fleishman, founded the Amity Therapeutic Community in Arizona and later in California. In addition to creating their community-based TCs, both Al and Naya were instrumental in developing two significant therapeutic community demonstration projects in the United States with the cooperation of and funding from the California Department of Corrections: Walden House's Corcoran Prison Project in Northern California and Amity's Donovan Prison Project in San Diego. (The Amity Donovan program is described later in this chapter.)

Al Acampora and Walden House

I was born in 1941 in the South Bronx to an Italian-American family. My father was an Italian businessman. He had numerous businesses, but mainly what he did was loan money to people for exorbitant interest. Some people might say he was a loan shark and was in some ways connected to the mob. He also had a wholesale meat market business with contracts to sell meat all over New York.

I come from a large Italian family, and we all lived in the same neighborhood. I didn't know anybody that wasn't in some way a cousin of mine. In that neighborhood, I guess it's the same thing like today's Gotti stories—there were quite a few "Wise Guy Italian Social Clubs." As teenagers, we had our own social club. You know, it was our *familia*. That was the thing to do in those days. You didn't leave your neighborhood. You would just go to the club and play cards and hang out. I meant the whole neighborhood was a family. I was also part of the Golden Guineas, which was the gang in our neighborhood around 1956.

I went to Columbus High School in Pelham Bay, but I wasn't a great student. My life was more on the streets of the Bronx. In our gang, I was always a negotiator. On the streets, and later on in the prison system, I always had the ability of not thinking of a person's color, even though I was raised to believe that anything that wasn't Italian was no good. But I always had this negotiating ability in me. So, I was the warlord and negotiator for the Golden Guineas whenever we were in conflict with another gang. If there was a fight or an impending gang war, I would try to smooth things out to avoid the violence.

My career as a junkie, criminal, and drug dealer began when some wise guy authorized me to pick up some heroin here and deliver it there. The heroin back then was cut seven to one. I was around fifteen when I started to become a kind of mule, or drug runner. Younger guys were in demand in the commerce of drugs for the same reason they are today—if a young guy gets busted, he isn't going to get a big sentence because he is a juvenile. I began to take some off the top when I delivered or sold junk, and that's when I began to use and get hooked.

I turned sixteen in Riverside Hospital, a treatment center for adolescent drug addicts. I spent quite a few of my adolescent years in Riverside Hospital. There was a guy in the hospital named Sampson who was Puerto Rican, a huge weight lifter, and another Puerto Rican named Shorty. He was like a dwarf and very, very skinny, and this black guy named Elmo. We didn't get much treatment at Riverside, but we did break into the hospital pharmacy once in awhile and score some drugs.

The hospital priest came to us Italians because he wanted the white guys to go to church. His problem was that the only people who were going to church were the Puerto Ricans. I negotiated a deal with him where, if he would pick up a lasagna from my aunt in town and deliver it to me, then I would get the white guys to go to church. My cousin used to put bags of heroin in the grated cheese.

The Puerto Ricans had a set of works, the blacks had a set of works, and the Italian guys had a set of works on the island. So, anytime any junk came in there there were three sets of works available to fix. We were democratic and used each others works. Today, half the junkies in New York City are HIV positive. If I was using today like I did then, I might very well have AIDS.

As you know, Lew, since you once worked there, Riverside was on an island near the city. Some nights, I used to swim the distance from shore to shore, and my cousin would be there waiting for me on the New York side. I would cop some junk from him in a condom, have an Italian sandwich, and swim back to the hospital. That was my early contact with therapy. Apparently, at that time, I was quite resistant to changing my asinine behavior.

After a number of winders in and out of Riverside, I was old enough to make the big time—and was sentenced by the courts to spend some time in the New York Riker's Island Prison. It was there that I met John Maher with whom I later on helped to found the Delancey Street therapeutic community in San Francisco. Mimi Silbert, as you know, was John's wife, and she later became the head of the TC. Back then I remember that John had a lot of balls. John was very, very witty and very, very sharp and very, very bright. He would read books—something few junkies ever did. John carried his own weight anywhere he went—including in the start-up of Delancey Street many years later.

All told, I did about a year and a half inside Riker's Island. Around that time I turned nineteen years old and was back on the streets dealing drugs. I was in business dealing with my cousins. Basically, what we were doing back then was dealing $3 bags called the Bongo. You got twenty-five $3 bags for $50. At first, I was dealing to support my habit. Then we really started dealing big for financial gain. When I was twenty years old I was dealing really good. I had plenty of money and a big new 1960 Lincoln.

In our pursuit of financial gain, we also began pulling burglaries with my crew in upstate New York. I wound up getting busted in Connecticut and being sentenced to the Valhalla Connecticut State Prison. When I was doing time there I heard about Synanon for the first time. A convict there told me about a place that he had gone to called Synanon, and what he told me about it sounded good. When I got out of prison this time I wanted to clean up. I felt bad and ashamed for my family—especially my mother who took my behavior hard. I wrote a letter to Synanon, and I got a response back that basically told me I needed a thousand dollars to get into Synanon. I didn't have it. Some women who were really do-gooders held bingo games to make money to send New York dope fiends who needed treatment to Synanon. My entrée to Synanon came from the money collected in a bingo game!

I went into Synanon in 1963 and stayed four years. The main thing that made me stay was the group encounters that were called "games." Lew, I loved those groups. I mean, to me they were as exciting as a fight or as exciting as anything else that I ever experienced in my life. The first game [encounter group] I ever was in was after an interview with this guy who said to me, "What do you want to be when you grow up, you punk." Later, in a group, I began screaming at him in retaliation. The games cleaned out my emotional system and always made me feel better. Another thing that kept me staying in Synanon was that my mother and my father were so happy I was getting help.

My father had pronounced me dead—because he was so emotionally upset by my junkie behavior. As a junkie he felt I had brought shame to our family. Later on, he forgave me, and I was able to help him when he was older. In the end, because he saw the good work I was doing here at Walden House, he forgave me. I made peace with him. It was really, really wonderful and important to me to get straightened out with my father. I thank the Lord I was able to do that before my dad passed away.

I moved up the ladder when I was in Synanon, and I wound up opening up all the kitchens in different facilities. I received my basic training and education on TCs in Synanon. When I heard about Maher opening up Delancey Street—I joined in with him. After my stint in helping to develop the Delancey Street TC, I felt I wanted to establish and run my own TC. And that's when I began my work in Walden House in 1968.

I decided that Walden House was going to be Al Acampora's place—with my vision of what a TC should be. I was going to build something different than John Maher's Delancey Street and different than Chuck Dederich's Synanon. I wasn't going to use labor out of the criminal justice system to build an empire. I was going to go after money, get contracts, provide services for these people, and put them back out into the community. In the beginning there were about twenty people in Walden House. And then we started growing to our current situation that involves around two thousand people in the Walden House system.

I think what I have accomplished with Walden House is building it to become a complete comprehensive treatment service. We are one of the first TCs to open up our own nonpublic school system. We have family services for men, women, and children. Today Walden House is providing services to two thousand people a day. I mean anywhere from the direct payee program, which means that if you're on SSI we administrate about three hundred people's checks and vouchers. We pay their hotel bills and their food bills. We integrated Walden House into the overall social and political system.

One of our best projects and the one I am most proud of is for juveniles. We have about seventy of them at this time. Most of them are children of substance abusers. We have kids that have been abandoned and neglected and screwed up through foster care. I purposely chose to deal with these kids in Walden House because nobody else was really helping them. We've got kids that failed in all kinds of placements and we're their last stop. I think the reason why we are able to hold and help these youngsters here is because we offer an extended family. We have an alumni association of our graduates. They aren't there to raise money for Walden House. What we ask our graduates to do is to function as Big Brothers in a mentoring way to people who are in treatment—especially our youths.

The school is where most kids fail. It's where I failed. I look at it this way. When a kid is embarrassed in school because he can't spell or read, it's easier for him to hit a teacher or another kid. I know from my own experience as a kid that it's easier to turn over a chair than to admit that you can't get up to read or spell or do any of your school work. We have our own principal, our own teachers, our own nonpublic school system. Needless to say we provide group sessions for them, and we are able to stop them from the use of any drugs. The kids are with us for one year to eighteen months. When they hit eighteen, if they so desire, they can join our adult program. There is a six-month aftercare program for the juveniles. We are a licensed nonpublic school called the Walden House Academy.

In conclusion, Lew, I would say that I formed Walden House as a place that would have helped me straighten my life out when I was a youngster growing up in the Bronx. At that time, I believe I would have listened to a guy like me, and I wouldn't have had to waste part of my life and go through the horrendous experiences I had as a criminal/addict. Of course, those experiences were my necessary research to become what you call an experience therapist. My early life experiences as a criminal/addict was a necessary training for my becoming the founder and now the CEO of Walden House.

Naya Arbiter: A Founder and Director of the Amity Therapeutic Community

Naya was resocialized and trained in Synanon for a decade during the 1970s. Along with two close friends she founded the Amity Therapeutic Community in Tucson, Arizona, in 1981. She began her career as a heroin addict at the age of fourteen. She is a remarkable woman, who has now been drug free for twenty-seven years.

One afternoon at Amity's northern California facility, I had a long conversation with Naya about her past. She intrigued me with her description of "doing time" in a Mexican prison after she was arrested for transporting drugs across the border as a juvenile delinquent. At my request, she wrote down a portion of her odyssey from drug addict to Amity director, beginning with the lowest point in her life, her time in the Mexican prison. Her experience as a juvenile in a Mexican prison is insightful and dramatically reveals a counterpoint to the current trend of locking up juveniles with adult offenders. It also depicts the "learning experience" that provides

Naya with her enormous compassion for treating delinquents in the TC she helped to create.

> The first time I was in jail in Mexico, I managed to get myself out in just ten days. The second time all the street people that could have helped me get out were arrested too. There were fifteen of us; I was in this hell-hole for five months. At the time of this incarceration I was seventeen.
>
> When I was arrested, I had told the *federales* that I was a twenty-one-year-old University of Arizona student. For the first month I was the only non-Hispanic woman in the prison. Later, a San Diego housewife was arrested with her lover for smoking a joint. Her husband abandoned her there. After a month or so of no one coming for her, she got up early one morning and made a mud-pack over her half-naked self with the maggot-infested garbage always present in the oil drum by the stairs. She sang as she smeared this garbage on her body. It was clear she had lost contact with reality, or at least with the rest of us who served as an audience. She was removed in chains to a Mexican mental institution.
>
> Another non-Hispanic woman who came later had the unfortunate attribute of having the last name of Thompson. This inspired several of the Mexican guards to mimic shooting a machinegun when they passed her [a reference to the Thompson submachinegun]. They were actually flirting. She had that wholesome American, dark-blond, freckled, Kansas look. I would speculate she didn't do too well with the guards who hit on her.
>
> My associates and I had been arrested with three tons of pot in our possession in Mexico—getting ready to take it across the border to the United States side. When the *federales* finally came for us, they weren't clear which of the apartments in the two-story building we were renting were being used in our enterprise. We had three apartments: one for drug storage; one for sleeping; and one for eating, meeting, and conducting business. Since the *federales'* detective skills were not well developed, they just brought in a city bus and arrested all the inhabitants of the apartment building. There were almost a hundred people arrested that I had never seen before, much less met. It was a mess. Mothers were dragged away from their children, the innocent people screamed, the guilty were silent. We all listened to the sound of shotguns being locked and loaded as we stood for hours with hands high above our heads holding on to barbed wire. Some younger soldiers periodically did target practice in the air over our heads. It rained bullets, and I was certain I would be killed.
>
> We were taken in a bus to an old army camp in the mountains where we were interrogated for three days. Separated and left outside, we were told that there were ground mines. I don't know if there really were, but no one felt much like exploring the possibility of being blown up in an escape.

Of the guilty parties, I was the youngest by far. Our criminal gang was comprised of several Mexican nationals, parolees from the United States who hadn't reported in a long while, and my "boyfriend," a Marine deserter who had left Vietnam with military equipment useful for drug smuggling. The United States federal agents paid a special visit to him before we were loaded on the bus.

The head of our drug-dealing *familia* was Ernie, who lived on the Arizona side of the border and considered himself a professional dealer in *El Trabajo*. I believe he was a first generation Mexican American. Ernie had unusual business sense for a man not thirty and would have excelled in a different trade. He was also violent enough to command the kind of respect that kept me from harm on the two days a week that the women were sent to the men's side of the jail for "visits." I didn't ever get to know him that well. I just remember him sitting on his top bunk in the crowded jail cell, counting money, wearing his large cowboy hat. After his arrest, like John Gotti, he continued to make deals from behind the walls. I knew him well enough to know his presence was my only protection in that violent prison. Twenty years later I got his identification number and wrote him in the Southwest prison where he resides. I thanked him for saving my life and I let him know I had tried to do something better for myself.

I had one great woman friend in prison—Berta, from Guadalajara, who was from the Mexican side of the operation. Perhaps five years my senior, she had a face somewhere between Sophia Loren and Rita Hayworth. I didn't know her except by sight. When we were arrested she was in the downstairs apartment, and I was on the second floor clad only in my boyfriend's shirt and my underwear. The *federales* dragged me down the stairs to the fence. I could hear Berta screaming at them that they had no right not to let me get dressed. She then marched up the stairs (the soldiers stood back) and collected boots, jeans, and a shirt for me, brought them to me, helped me dress, and stood beside me with her hands up while I dressed. It was a good thing she helped me, because I wore those clothes for a long time in the prison.

Berta and I made a pact in our first few days—no tears. We made another one when I introduced her to shooting heroin, which at the time was a gesture of generosity—sharing my solution for dealing with pain. It was readily available in the prison. I have a nineteen gauge needle you could almost see the sun rise through. She taught me cold-water washing techniques for clothes at the one water spigot in the central courtyard. I taught her how to make oatmeal with dates on the rather bizarre gas stove I had made. In the Mexican prison we were in, you were fed sparingly—to say the least. When our own food ran out after three weeks, we lived on water and a bottle of honey. I got a boiled potato and I remember thinking long and hard about sharing it. At last I gave her half, and as it turned out she had found a lemon, so we had a potato and lemon feast sitting on the stone stairs above the "hole." A meal to be remembered.

I was proud that I had not asked anyone in my family for help or contacted them in the United States. My mantra was that it was a mess I created, and I would deal with the consequences whatever they were. The prevailing wisdom at the time was that the consequences were going to be a fifteen-year sentence in a Mexican prison! An abysmal thought that depressed the hell out of me.

Later, I discovered that our arrest had been on the front page of the Tucson newspaper, and a local attorney had called my parents immediately to let them know. Like most addicts I had developed an extensive mythology about my family. That they cared, that they were "good people," that I was the problem in my family. That mythology promoted all the denial patterns and lies we were all engaged in while smuggling drugs. So, I found life in jail in Mexico a relief compared to life within my family. My incarceration was a family embarrassment, as I had been for some time to my family.

At sixteen, I had been brutally raped. My mother and step-father left me in juvenile hall where the police had brought me from the scene. I bled all over myself for hours. Finally retrieved and brought home, my mother's response to my swollen, brick battered face had been to repeatedly ask how I could have "done that to her." I was just grateful that I could still see out of my left eye. Years later she would deny the incident. Just as she denied she had left me alone for hours at a time with my sexually abusive biological father in the bathroom. She must have known what was going on with my father. Her response was to slide notes under the door saying dinner was ready.

As a child I was both witness and victim. I was a living and unwelcome reminder to my mother of an ugly, fourteen-year marriage. My face resembled my father's more than my mother's. My presence must have continually reminded her of my hated father. As an adolescent I went from victim to predator. I dared her to admit that she had allowed my biological father to continually rape me. I dared her to try to be my mother after she had failed me. I dared her to try to stop me from my path of self-destruction. The confrontations didn't work. The more she denied, the more I self-destructed. Some twenty years later she would tell me that she felt a special intimacy with me when I was shooting heroin. I am still trying to understand that bizarre comment! [This statement by Naya reminded me of another heroin addict whose mother told her when she was in jail, "I'm glad you use drugs and get arrested. At least I get to see you once in a while when you are locked up and I know where you are."]

About three months into my incarceration in the Mexican jail, my mother showed her caring by sending me a bar of Fels Naptha soap—with a note to the effect that it lasted for a long time in cold water. I corresponded with her and my stepfather some, and my mother apparently shared my letters with a screenwriter while I was still incarcerated and discussed selling them to him. She shared that with me in one of her letters. Her comments seemed wildly out of context to me, if not downright insane, as I struggled daily to survive in the bowels of hell.

There are many emotional snapshots of that prison experience that linger on in my mind. We used to wake up to the sound of the only prison trustee chopping bones. As a trustee, he was allowed to go into town. Each morning Mendolio would walk through the alleyways behind the butcher shops pushing a wheelbarrow and collect the refuse the butchers would throw into the garbage. He would bring these bones to the jail and chop the large ones open with an ax early in the morning before there were signs of light on the only hill visible from my cell on the second tier. The sound of the bones splintering was our alarm clock. These fragments, marrow exposed, were placed in a large galvanized tub on top of beans. Then water was poured on top and the result cooked all day. When there was food, that was the food. The men were always fed first.

I used to look at the tub of "food" and remember my first-grade books. "See Dick. See Jane. See their dog Spot. Spot takes a bath." I thought, "This community is eating out of Spot's tub." One particularly memorable evening, Spot's tub contained the floated head of a burro. Mendolio had chosen not to chop this delicacy, and it was wonderfully intact: hair, mane, and open glassy eyeball staring at us all. I wondered if it was a message that, well, we had it bad, but after all, someone in town that night had paid for a steak and, like us, they were really eating burro.

Our jail was in the middle of the border town of Nogales. As bad as our life in prison was, we all came to dread the weekends when drunks would be collected from Canal Street in town and dumped in our prison home. The Americans arrested were particularly noisy. Typically, they would scream all night about their rights, the United States, and what they were going to do to inflict harm upon their Mexican jailers. This was usually interrupted by the intermittent sound of their vomiting up whatever it was that they had ingested that night. It was a symphony of retching.

I especially recall a particularly noisy woman who was finally tossed out of the drunk tank by her ankles and wrists onto a cement courtyard. She was large, tall, wide, and fat. After she landed on a cement floor, the bones on her spinal column were visible where they punctured her skin. Her howling was unbearable. I got the idea that she needed to be in traction, so with Berta's aid, we dragged her into the bottom cell, which belonged to a convict named Alma, and leveraged her up onto the bed—stretching her out as long and as tightly as we could in an effort to ease her terrible pain.

Alma didn't want anyone in her cell. Alma's habit was to discourage visitors to her cell by hanging some sort of dead meat over her door, which was always buzzing with flies. She was there for murder and would be there forever. That day she was out in the main courtyard when we brought this unfortunate woman into her cell. She wasn't happy when she came back and found us and this terribly wounded woman. She called the assistant warden on me for disturbing her cell. I didn't feel it was feasible to move our suffering patient, and the assistant warden disagreed with me. I called him any nasty name I could think of in English. He replied in Spanish that if I repeated the expletives I was going to the hole under the stairs. A rebel at heart, I repeated it all again.

He enacted his threat. I later found myself in a fetal position in solid darkness in the triangular space under a stone stairway. There was no light at all in what really was "the hole." I could feel a crucifix that someone had carved into the stone on my righthand side. On the other side there was an indentation, a toilet for human waste.

As I crouched in the hole, José Luis, the assistant warden, called all the women together to wash the walls and the steps. As the hours passed I sat on the cement floor as the water got deeper in the darkness. One of the guards gave me a can with the daily ration of beans and bones and then shut the door. The metal edges of the can were sharp and uneven. Another shoved a candy bar underneath. I could hear the fat wounded woman I had tried to rescue continuing to howl in the darkness about her twisted back.

Ultimately, I was released from the hell and degradation of the Mexican prison system. I was not rehabilitated by their treatment approach. My grandmother put up $5,000 in ransom. My stepfather, a geological scientist, as part of my ransom for release, "donated" some research findings for mining processes he had developed to government officials in Mexico City.

Right before my release I paid for a tattoo on my right arm with two papers of heroin. A rose with a snake curled around the stem. A man named Mario and his "wife" Suzie tattooed me. These two homosexual men were "married" in a formal full-dress Mexican wedding on the guy's side of the jail a few months earlier. I thought I should have something to remember my Mexican experience, and a tattoo seemed appropriate at that time. I probably didn't need the tattoo to remember the experience—but it has served both as a conversation piece and a passport of sorts as the years have passed. When the day of my release came, the warden let all of "La Familia" meet me in the courtyard to say goodbye. I was then transported to court. The local judge took a vacation on that day. I went to the courtroom and was told to walk the few miles to the border. I was told to walk over and never return.

Listening to reasonable advice was not my forte at that time. Apparently, I had to learn the hard way. The severe punishment I had received in prison, to put it mildly, did not deter me from committing other crimes. After making some money through some other drug deals, I went back to the same jail three weeks later as a visitor and gave money to my friends who were all still incarcerated.

I then started smuggling heroin across the border because it was easier to transport than marijuana, and soon the FBI arrested me. I was locked up on the Arizona side this time, in the Nogales jail, where I kicked my heroin habit on yet another cement floor. I was six weeks shy of my eighteenth birthday. I was then transported by federal marshals to the Pima County jail in Tucson, Arizona, where I was placed in isolation.

If nothing else, my New York German-Jewish intellectual heritage, apart from my abusive treatment as a child, had made me an avid reader. While in isolation I remembered a *Life Magazine* article about a place called Synanon, where addicts lived together and helped each other achieve sobriety. I was fed up with my dope-fiend existence and decided that was what I needed.

I petitioned my juvenile probation officer on my Synanon plan. Since I was being held on adult charges and being transferred to the adult system, juvenile probation was not an option. I was given the opportunity to work as an informant for the FBI, and if I complied with being a snitch, I would receive a year and a day suspended sentence. Of course, I knew that becoming an informant for the law was the equivalent of a death penalty on the street. The other option to my becoming a snitch for the FBI, a choice that might lead to my death, was a five-year sentence in the federal Terminal Island Penitentiary. This possibility was looking attractive.

I was visited only once during this incarceration by a woman whom I had never met before. She informed me that my most recent boyfriend was really hers, but that she wasn't sleeping with him anymore because he had gonorrhea and suggested I get checked by a doctor. My medical treatment while in custody was, to say the least, horrendous. To get my checkup I was transported in leg irons, belly chains, and handcuffs to the county hospital for penicillin shots. The memory of trying to pull down my jeans for the male doctor to receive a penicillin shot in my rump while still chained remains vivid. There was also a diphtheria epidemic in the jail. I have extreme allergic responses to certain medications, and the inoculation that all inmates were forced to get is one of them. I was held down and inoculated after I loudly protested that I was allergic. A lot of people heard me, but they went ahead with the injection anyway. I became very sick. I remember coming out of a coma to hear a male nurse leaning over me, as my fever spiraled up and my throat closed, saying, "Jesus Christ, don't let her die here, we will really have a case on our hands." I forced myself to get up and walk, walk, walk in my cell.

I obviously survived the indignities and punishment of

536

prison medical treatment, and I believe this helped to create my compassion for the general way that the system treats criminals.

Miraculously, my juvenile probation officer was able to extend my minority status until my twenty-first year. She contacted Synanon in California. They stated they would interview me and consider acceptance after my eighteenth birthday. After six weeks in isolation, my birthday passed, and in September 1970 I was on a plane to California.

Before I took this flight, I remember standing in the parking lot of the Pima County jail and swearing that I would never be locked up or treated as I had been again. I had been labeled, categorized, transported, documented, observed, tested psychologically and fingerprinted by my sixteenth birthday. I was not an adolescent who was targeted "most likely to succeed." I painfully recall one of the jail workers in Tucson, who used to affectionately refer to me as human garbage.

To get slightly ahead of some of the highlights of my story, seventeen years later, as a director in Amity, I returned to the Pima County jail to open a drug treatment program funded by the United States Department of Justice. This program that I developed from my past personal research as a former inmate in the jail became a national model on how effective treatment can help people get out, and stay out, of jails and prisons.

I had read about Synanon but didn't really believe that the fifteen hundred addicts who were there at that time could live together and not be shooting dope. I assume that within hours in Synanon I would find a compatible heroin addict like me, and I would be able to "fix" my pain. I was wrong.

I sat on the "prospect bench" where I was delivered by my probation officer and mother and listened to some great music coming from a large ballroom. Synanon was blessed with some incredible jazz musicians. As a jazz aficionado, I was turned on by the musical backdrop prior to my Synanon interview with the live music of Art Pepper on tenor sax, Frank Rehak on trombone, and Joe Pass on guitar. Frank had been one of the studio musicians who had done the milestone album *Sketches of Spain* with Miles Davis. I stayed. I stop smoking that day. I never shot heroin again. That was the end of my criminal/addict career and the beginning of my entrance into the exciting world of TCs.

The people that had the biggest effect on me in Synanon wouldn't be legally allowed to work with juveniles today. They probably wouldn't be allowed into most social service organizations. For a few weeks, at eighteen, I was the youngest person in Synanon with a history of addiction. I remember walking up to one particularly conservative and distinguished elderly man and asking him what a square like him was doing at Synanon. He explained that he had started smoking opium with the Chinese probably before my mother was born. He was a man named Charlie Hamer, whose life story from [being an opium addict] then heroin addict, was dramatically chronicled in Lew

Yablonsky's great book on Synanon, *The Tunnel Back*— a book I read and treasure to this day.

My sordid tale of jail in Mexico, a story I told several times in group sessions, was met with derision in Synanon. Their response and essence was, "You have a hell of an imagination. Tell us again in five years when you have cleaned up." It didn't matter though. I wasn't really ready to talk about it than as fully as I have described it here for, of all people, my now friend and colleague Lew Yablonsky.

I was fascinated to be in an environment where so many people were learning on every different level. I stayed in Synanon for ten years. I stayed until it became clear to me that the organization was no longer for me. But before left, I learned a lot. I apprenticed myself to a number of brilliant people. I became fascinated with the process of growth and change. How did people get larger than what had wounded them? What were the basics that made what became known as the TC work? What was the essence carried from the Oxford Group, through the inception of AA, into Synanon, and then out to many of the publicly funded drug programs of the sixties and seventies? And what is the future of the TC approach in the next century?

Some of my answers to these questions, which I am still contemplating, have been presented in many lectures I have delivered in Amity and at many conferences in the United States, South America, Europe, and Japan. Notable among the hundreds of lectures I have presented over the twenty-seven years I have been clean and in my role as a director of Amity were the many lectures I delivered at the World Federation of Therapeutic Communities and in 1997 as an invited lecturer at President Clinton's United States Department of Justice White House Conference on Juvenile Violence in Washington, D.C.

In reviewing my personal transformation, and my work over the years creating therapeutic communities in juvenile halls, jails, prisons, with those afflicted by HIV, addicted mothers, their children, and more. I have developed a philosophy regarding the replication and "basics" of the TC model that provided a pathway for me out of my former hell as a criminal/addict. I am pleased to use this opportunity in this book on delinquency to present my viewpoint.

A common pitfall in the replication of any methodology is that those who are engaged in the effort do not fully understand the historical basic assumptions around which TC systems and methods have been developed. Arguably, not everyone who drives a vehicle is a mechanic, but better drivers have some appreciation for the machinery and therefore the care of their automobiles. As populations change, many of the technologies and methods practiced initially have become empty forms. The basic assumptions that were the underlying causal force for the development of those technologies still hold generally true. Form must be adjusted to continually fit the current population they attempt to help.

It is crucial that everything within the therapeutic community serves a functional purpose for the education of the whole person. The more conscious the staff and the community are of what the intended functions of the forms are, the more successful the community will be and the easier adjustment is to different settings and populations. An optimally functioning TC should serve as a microcosmic mirror reflecting the problems of our time as they are manifested in individuals. The TC approach must change and adjust as the decades pass to remain current with contemporary problems.

The successful formation of a TC depends largely on the skill level of community building. Therapeutic community processes have been referred to as "treatment" since this phase is more socially acceptable (and fundable). In this context, an individual enters "treatment" for an addiction (sickness problem). It must be remembered that therapy in and of itself was a dismal failure with alcoholics, addicts, criminals, and juvenile delinquents until the community aspect was included.

The degree to which staff can form a true sense of community, camaraderie, comfort and communication often determines whether specific individuals are able to successfully migrate from degradation to dignity. Although strict sanctions and consequences are employed, an individual must be in an environment where there is enough safety, enough of a sense of home, to begin the process of change. [Naya's theories remind me that gangsters use the expression "homeboys" because they are searching for a caring community. This unfortunately does not exist in the violent gang.]

States of extreme fear, anxiety, and alienation are not conducive to permanent change. Residents in a TC have already been thrown out by their families, by society, by themselves. A sense of safety coupled with boundaries based on concern is critical. This was brought home to me by the commentary of a former resident of Amity—after she had thought about her experience for several months. She stated: "For the first time in my life, I knew I belonged somewhere. I knew no one was going to tell me to leave, or send me away as they had so many other times before. I knew for the first time in my life I was safe, and even if I didn't have my own private room, and I had to share a bedroom with thirteen other people, I knew that in my heart it was going to be all right because I was learning integrity. And I had my family, the family I had always dreamed about through my years of addiction. And most of all, I had some people that believed enough in me to trust me."

In order to foster a sense of home, safety, and ownership, people must work together as well as live together, eat together, participate in groups together, and study together. A TC should feel more like an Israeli kibbutz community than a hospital. Like a kibbutz, people are working together on the basis of shared values and common goals for some things that are larger than any of them individually; they are working together to become larger people, learning how to live a life based on principle rather than crime.

There are some assumptions and values that are intrinsic to the successful functioning of a TC. The degree to which these assumptions are actualized in the environment is the degree to which the stage is set for community, character growth, and maturation. The ability of the staff to understand and translate these into daily interactions with each other and the community provides the foundation for success or failure.

In any family, community, or culture, there are messages projected explicitly and implicitly. These may come from the elders, from the physical environment, from ceremony celebrations or education. These messages are internalized and translated out in behavior. From parents, peers or significant others, we are shaped by some of the input we receive. The way we treat the sick, the retarded, the unfortunate, the poor, the rich, the comfortable, the orphaned is affected by these messages.

At its best the TC is an environment that provides antidote messages. Everything in the environment is geared toward helping people internalize and buy into messages relevant to their particular brand of self-destructive behavior and move them in the direction of personal creativity, prosocial behavior, and responsibility.

In an effective TC "responsibility" may be defined as teaching the ability to respond appropriately and compassionately to other people. A well-functioning TC expands an individual's repertoire for responding appropriately. Following are a few of the basic assumptions and concepts that I believe in and [that] serve as guidelines for both the design and evaluation of effective TC projects.

1. Public rather than private behavior. Drugs, incarceration, and alcoholism serve the purpose of anesthetizing people from themselves and reality. Self-disclosure before a group has the opposite effect. By overcoming prejudgments about each other, people can overcome the prejudices they have about themselves. In the open verbalizing in TC group activities, as much as possible in public living for a period of time, people bond with each other. And they can see the parts of their self that they are ashamed of are OK and become accepted by other people in the community.

2. Becoming a participant rather than a spectator. People must participate in their own evolution in the various TC groups. Assuming the position of spectator, personally alienated from activity, does not foster growth. In order to have community each person must do more than watch. Everyone has a contribution they can make. When the community is functioning well, it helps to facilitate the participation of all of the members of the community.

3. Personal authority rather than vested authority. Every person has to earn respect. Those who are used to posturing and hiding behind a variety of images, streetfighters to degreed professionals, have to "meet" each other as human beings. [From my viewpoint, Naya is also referring to the necessity to remove the machismo or macho criminal mask.] Even fourteen-year-olds arriving at a TC, whether in prison or on the streets, already have been analyzed, supervised, managed, punished, observed, transported, discussed, tested, and documented. Bodily fluids have been tested, arrest records and fingerprints have been computerized, and still no one in particular has "met" them as individuals and knows much about them as persons. As a whole, the criminal/addicted persons who have been objectified have little respect for vested authority that they identify as part of the objectification mechanism. In a true TC, everyone must demonstrate the viability and importance of "real" relationships. This insures that every person entering has an opportunity to earn a place in the community through a personal demonstration of their involvement.

4. A real and responsible job in the community. A job usually illuminates what a person does but not necessarily who the person is. In order to successfully navigate through the life experience, individuals need to engage in role development. Living in community fosters this growth. Typically, the criminal/addict adolescents suffer from role paralysis within their peer group, gang, family, or institution. They are viewed one way, and this determines their self-concept. As they are given real job tasks to perform, their life roles can be developed in the community.

5. Emotional literacy rather than simple obedience and compliance. Criminal/addicts who are incarcerated learn how to adjust their compulsions to any given situation. It is easy for them to appear compliant and obedient to achieve the limited goals presented to those in custody. However, in a TC, residents are encouraged to be honest and develop their true emotional sense of self.

6. The TC as a family and community of choice. Most delinquent youths do not have a successfully functioning family to return to after their custodial treatment. Gaining an understanding of childhood and family dynamics is critical for them if they are to understand their self. This process has to be coupled with a toolbox of social skills that allow them to pick and develop a supportive community in school, on the job, or wherever they may go after the TC experience. The TC is practice for developing these necessary and vital future relationships.

7. The TC as a safe sanctuary. The TC must be a place that represents a sense of safety to each person who enters, and this is especially true for juveniles. TC professionals need to be versed in vocabularies of sanctuary—how to make a room feel

541

safe, how to be nonthreatening, how to teach youths to feel safe with themselves and each other. The truth is most easily told in an atmosphere of sanctuary—and ugly truths can be explored and understood in direct proportion to how safe the youth feels to expose, what he or she, at first, considers, the "dirty secrets" of his or her life.

A youth in a TC is being resocialized and educated. The word *education* comes from the Latin word *educare*, which means "to lead forth." Within the TC environment, everything that is done, certainly including the group processes, should serve the purpose of this literal meaning of education.

I have developed a number of other assumptions and concepts from my life experience—first as a delinquent and now as an experience therapist—that I will probably write into my own book later in my life. One of my basic assumptions about an effective TC is that it needs to be an Ellis Island for the emigration of emotional states. In a TC, certainly in the Amity TC that I have helped to create, individuals travel from [1]degradation to dignity,[2]destructive behaviors to constructive ones,[3]despair to joy,[4]prejudice to inclusion,[5]manipulation to forthrightness,[6]inconsistency to steadfastness,[7]repression to expression,[8]denial to acknowledgment,[9]cruelty to friendship. Lew Yablonsky and I are in agreement that these are the patterns of emotional healing that I have found for others and myself in the type of effective TC that I feel strongly can contribute to the prevention and control of juvenile delinquency in the twenty-first century.

The Social Structure of the Therapeutic Community

One way to illuminate the social system of a therapeutic community is to compare it with the traditional institutions devoted to resocializing deviants—hospitals, reformatories, and prisons. Most traditional treatment structures have a two-tier caste system of organization. There are doctors and the patients, correctional officers and the prisoners, healers and the sick. This castelike division is based on the premise that if the patient follows his or her doctor-therapist's instructions and analyzes his or her problems properly, positive change will occur.

Most reformatories reflect this type of medical model. In a prison or a hospital, the assumption is that if the prisoner or patient follows the rules of the institution and properly interacts with his or her therapist, he or she will change and become a better citizen who can function more effectively in the larger society. These castelike we-they medical model institutions are considerably different from the therapeutic community approach.

Most delinquents have experienced traditional "correctional" systems. The typical offender has learned how to do time in reformatories, prisons, jails, psychiatric hospitals, or addict hospitals. Even at his or her first arrest, the offender is already equipped with a set of attitudes for handling encounters with society's law enforcers and incarceration. He or she learns the proper set of attitudes and responses on the streets, and these are reinforced in the institution.

The "bad guys" are the cops, squares (nonaddicts), judges, jailers, and administrators. On the "right" side are "righteous dope fiends" and "stand-up guys." Offenders learn quickly to trust the "right guys" and to hate and distrust the correctional officials. In the traditional institution, if the offenders are right guys, they live according to inmate rules. They believe "Thou shalt not snitch" and engage in petty larceny, drug use, and homosexuality. They also develop violent skills for surviving in the institution. If they are "solid" members of the inmate ingroup, they con the staff members whenever they can. Staff are the enemy inside the walls, who represent the enemy (square society) outside the walls of the institution.

Almost all hospital and prison officials are stereotyped by the inmate code—at best as inept, at worst as proper targets of extreme rebellious hatred. For most inmates they are objects to be manipulated for quick release, or they are "tricks" (suckers) to beat for small favors to relieve the boredom and monotony of custody. In the game of manipulation, the institution's officials are perceived as pawns by convicts. This inmate code tends to confirm and reinforce criminal/addict ethics and behavior. The code reinforces violence, lying, manipulation, and other patterns of sociopathic behavior.

In contrast, offenders entering a TC are usually baffled by what they encounter in this different social system. Everyone is a "right guy," including the administrators. If they try to play their usual institutional games, they are ridiculed. They have difficulty hating the officials in a TC, because they are people who have experienced the delinquent life-style. If they want to break out (a common subject of conversation in most institutions), they are invited to leave by the TC staff.

At every turn offenders discover new responses to old situations and, most important, other people who know how they feel and who understand them. Instead of receiving a callous reaction, they are told, "I remember how I felt when I first got here," and this is often followed by a detailed description of the precise feeling they are experiencing at the time. This process encourages trust and fosters participation in the therapeutic TC group processes.

This new response by others in the TC is often disconcerting and frightening to newcomers because it is a different and strange situation—

one the criminal/addicts have never experienced in other incarcerated situations. At the same time, the sight of others like themselves, with similar past experiences, who "made it" gives them the confidence that they too can change. They have role models, people they can emulate, who are unlike the therapists they have known in other custodial situations. They find a community with which they can identify, people toward whom they can express the best that is in them rather than the worst. They find friends who will assist them when they deviate from or fall short of their goals: to develop and mature.

Caste and Class Systems

Of significance in comparing traditional institutions with TCs are the sociological concepts of caste and stratification that characterize different social systems. The inmate subculture develops within any custodial institution and produces a "we-they" attitude in the professional administration and in the inmates. Inmates view themselves as "we" and the administration is "they"—as in "they" are the enemy. The inmate society has norms, patterns of behavior, and goals different from and usually in conflict with those of the overall institution. This is partly due to the fact that inmates cannot rise in the status system and become staff. The inmates and the officials are divided into two segregated strata. The inmates may be viewed by administrators as a caste of untouchables. They are restricted to an inferior position in the hierarchy, and in the traditional prison social system, there is no possibility of their moving up in that hierarchy.

It is conceded by most correctional administrators that this inmate-administration conflict situation contradicts and impedes therapeutic progress for inmates. The inmate subsystem helps offenders cope with the new set of problems that they find in most institutions. They feel rejected by the larger society and try to compensate for this rejection. One way they do this is to reject and rebel against the administrators of society's rejection—the custodial staff.

A true therapeutic community does not have a "we-they" caste system. It provides an open-ended stratification situation. Upward mobility is possible in the organization, and in fact, upward movement in the system is encouraged. As one TC leader told a newcomer during an indoctrination session: "In a couple of years, you just might be a big shot around here and have my job." Not only is upward social mobility possible in a TC social system, but healthy status seeking in encouraged. A TC organization assumes that a person's position in its hierarchy is a correlate of social maturity, "mental health," increased work ability, and a clear understanding of the organization.

The following article by Dan Weikel in the *Los Angeles Times* 25, 1997) reveals some aspects of the Amity TC prison success story:

Captain Michael Teichner was thrilled with his promotion at Donovan State Prison except for one thing. His new duties included supervising the facility's privately run drug treatment program. Teichner—known as "Iceman" around the prison yard—didn't much believe in rehabilitating criminals. During his twenty-year career with the California Department of Corrections, he had seen plenty of reform-minded do-gooders come and go. When he met over lunch with Elaine Abraham of the nonprofit Amity Foundation, which runs the rehab center, he lived up to his moniker. "Quite frankly," the Iceman said of prison treatment programs, "I don't think they work."

Four years later, Teichner is a changed man—like many of the convicts who undergo Amity's yearlong regimen and now lead productive lives. Today, he says, the only problem with drug and alcohol treatment is that the exploding prison population can't get enough of it. Compared to the checkered performance of past substance abuse programs for convicts, Amity and similar projects around the country may offer corrections officials a powerful weapon to reduce crime, addiction, and soaring prison costs.

The latest research shows that by weaning convicts off illegal drugs—which are widely available in prison—and overhauling their lifestyles, such programs can significantly lower reincarceration rates, saving taxpayers millions of dollars a year. Consequently, prison officials grappling with unprecedented overcrowding due to the nation's war on drugs have started to rethink how they deal with addicted prisoners. The task before them is daunting: Nationally, only one in six of an estimated 800,000 inmates involved with illegal drugs receives any treatment, most of it sporadic education classes or weekly counseling sessions that don't do much good. Little in the way of treatment has been provided because many law enforcement officials and legislators believe that tough sentences are the best way to deal with the nation's drug problem. Academic research in the mid-1970s also fostered the long-held, some say mistaken, belief that nothing works when it comes to reforming criminals.

In California, an estimated 100,000 state prison inmates have histories of chronic drug and alcohol use. But there are only 400 slots in the corrections system that offer treatment considered intensive enough to break the dangerous cycle of crime and addiction. At Donovan, a medium security prison in an arid valley east of San Diego, hundreds of convicts apply for no more than twenty slots that become available every month. For those who get accepted, the treatment can rewire their lives. The Amity program, which opened at Donovan in 1990, contracts with the Corrections Department for $1.5 million a

Another assumption is that the social skills learned in a TC structure are useful within the larger society. The reverse appears to be true of the "skills" learned in custodial institutions. The we-they problem does not exist in a true therapeutic community since the administration and the inmates are one and the same, and upward mobility is encouraged.

Personality Change in a Therapeutic Community: Eliminating the "Criminal Mask" or Macho Syndrome

Most delinquents who enter a TC for treatment have a tough facade, or "criminal mask," that they developed to survive on the streets or in prison. A postulate in a TC is that this "face," which reflects a recalcitrant macho syndrome, must be changed and a new one developed. This requires a 180-degree turn from past behavior patterns. In a TC, criminal language, jargon, and values are viewed with disdain and extreme disapproval. (I am not referring to so-called profanity—that language is allowed.) Newcomers may hang on to their past destructive habits for a brief time by lengthy discussions of their past criminal life-style. In short order, however, new words and behavior patterns are ruthlessly demanded in encounter groups.

Charles Dederich, founder of the therapeutic community movement, made the following remarks on this issue to describe part of Synanon's resocialization process:

> Eliminating their criminal language is very important for changing their thought process. We get them off drugs by telling them, "Live here without using drugs and you can have all this." We get them off them the negative language by initially giving them another. Since there is some vague connection between their personality problem and the social sciences, we encourage them to use this language.
>
> The language of psychology and sociology is great stuff. Whether or not the recovering addict knows what he's talking about is exquisitely unimportant. Very quickly, in a matter of about ninety days, they turn into junior psychiatrists and sociologists. They become familiar with the use of a dozen or twenty words and misuse them. Who cares! It doesn't make any difference. Now they're talking about "the unconscious," "transferences," "displacement," "primary and secondary groups." This is all coming out, and they're not saying drugs, "fix, fix, fix" all the time. "I used $100 a day," "Joe went to jail behind this broad," "Where did you do time?" and all that. They get off that, and they talk about ids, superegos, and group structure. They make another set of noises, and their criminal facades drop away.[1]

---

1. Personal interview audiotaped in the early days of Synanon, December 1961.

Language is, of course, the vehicle of culture and behavior, and in a TC, it is instrumental in shifting the behavior patterns that the offenders have used in the past. They begin to use a new, still undeveloped set of social-emotional muscles. TC members are not identified as wards, prisoners, or patients, and this also makes a big difference in their self-identity and outlook. They can identify with the constructive goals of the organization as they automatically become employees in the TC organization, at first on a menial level. Later on, they are encouraged to take part in management and development.

In the traditional institution, inmates feel helpless and hopeless about the future. They have limited power in the institution, since it is run by administrators who are indifferent to inmates' opinions about its management. Moreover, as noted earlier, institution officials are seen as representative of society's rejection, and this sets up additional blockades to progress in the custodial institution. Inmates have a clear authority object for their frustrations and hatreds: the custodial staff.

In a therapeutic community, there is no such split, since the administration consists of co-workers and colleagues. There is no "they" to hate within the organization. Involvement in a TC helps to foster empathy in youths whose basic problem is alienation from society. Identification with the TC involves feelings of concern for the other members and for the destiny of the totality of the organization. The development of these empathic qualities reverses the delinquents' past lack of social concern and has a real impact on positive personality change. Vital to this personality change are various group processes directed by former delinquents.

Group Psychotherapy in Prison and in a Therapeutic Community

All therapeutic communities, like traditional institutions, have some form of regular group process built into their social structure. One major difference between TC group therapy and the usual institutional forms of group psychotherapy is that the TC sessions usually are not directed by professional therapists. There is considerable evidence that inmates participate in group psychotherapy in prison in order to get out of the institution. Inmates may verbalize "insights" that seem to indicate therapeutic progress in an effort to convince therapists and custodial officials that they have changed and are ready for release.

At a prototypical group-therapy session I observed in a California prison, several inmates made a great show of wonderful insights, and as one fellow put it, "This program really makes me see life more clearly." But several inmates admitted in private, "Of course I want

to look good to get out of this joint. And a good parole board helps."

TC group sessions are more closely related to t that confront the members. The lack of caste division promotes open lines of communication throughout th and the goldfish bowl atmosphere allow a more exter underlying problems. TC group sessions aim to unco about members, since this is vital to the protection and members and the TC organization. Since all TC membe nization, many real on-the-job problems are funneled chotherapy. All of these factors give TC groups a reali closed-off social systems of most traditional custodial in

Prison Therapeutic Communities

Prison TC programs have a somewhat different social str other therapeutic communities. TC programs in prisons The Amity TC program that began in 1990 with the finan California Department of Corrections illustrates this c directed group therapy and psychodrama sessions in this many of the inmates, and am on the board of directors o

The Amity TC program takes place in a cell blo Donovan Prison in San Diego. The overall prison houses sand convicts who are incarcerated for a variety of c including murder. The maximum security institution is separate facilities, with five cell blocks in each facility. houses about two hundred convicts. The Amity TC has co the assigned prison guards) over two hundred convicts wl gram. I use the term "maximum security" to describe the the guards in the towers are under orders to not shoot ar if someone has made it over the wall. Their orders are to

The Amity TC program is administered by twenty e rience therapists who are graduates of Amity. The convict are volunteers, participate in a group rehabilitation program in regular TC organizations. The program is more complex island of treatment housed within a potentially violent p convicts can change their behavior and rise in status withi project, they remain prisoners. When they are paroled, how the option of continuing in Amity's after-care program. Thi to continue their treatment in a community-based TC. A period of time, many of these TC graduates exercise the opt in a prison TC program as an experience therapist.

year. It is a so-called therapeutic community, a style of intensive residential treatment thought to be most effective for felons with substantial criminal records.

For nine to twelve months, 220 participants share a dormitory, dining facilities, and recreation areas. Upon release from prison, graduating parolees can volunteer to continue taxpayer-funded counseling at Amity's residential off-site program nestled in a wooded hillside in north San Diego County. At both facilities, convicts are required to attend a steady stream of seminars and encounter groups run by recovering addicts, ex-convicts and some of the most experienced substance abuse counselors in the field. The routine is rigorous. No one gets time off their sentences for participating or reprieves from prison work. Unlike rehabilitation efforts at other penitentiaries, Amity enrollees are not isolated from Donovan's main yard, where there are temptations to use smuggled drugs every day. The goal is to teach convicts to deal with personal problems and to live life without drugs and crime.

But the job is difficult because inmates are among the hardest substance abusers to treat. Their complicated pathologies often include poverty, gang membership, mental illness, and child abuse. Relapse is common, and change happens at a glacial pace over many months. Much of the transformation, if it occurs, takes place in encounter groups that attempt to dissect—with brutal honesty—what caused the convict's substance abuse and criminal behavior. The sessions are filled with discussions about trust, personal accountability, relationships with women, family problems, substance abuse, and the inner rage that leads to violence. By drawing inmates out, counselors say, they can help them understand their problems and find solutions.

"There is nothing easy about facing the truth about yourself," former cocaine addict and crack dealer Terry Ward says of Amity's group discussions. "The badder you act, the more they dig. It's hard to keep up the facade. They just pick pieces out of your story and make you humble. The first few months will tear you apart."

Ward, forty, was a violent hustler and convicted armed robber, known to the denizens of South-Central Los Angeles as "Voltron." He always carried two pistols, a knife, and a cane that he used as a weapon. Skilled with a razor blade, Ward could sculpt a $5 piece of crack so it looked like it was worth $15. On the street, he would not hesitate to beat up someone at the smallest provocation. He once broke a man's jaw for calling him by his given name. Ward was paroled in 1991 after serving two years at Donovan. He stayed so long in Amity's off-site volunteer program that he had to be told to leave. Today, he manages a Wendy's restaurant and lives in Spring Valley, a rural community east of San Diego. He has finally gotten to know his nineteen-year-old daughter, whom he abandoned more than ten years ago. "Voltron was a bad person. He died in prison," Ward said. "There are people who go through Amity and use again. I choose not to. I've been insane long enough."

On one recent morning, fifteen convicts, some just like Ward, gather for group therapy in the Robin Gabriel Room of Amity's prison compound. Gabriel graduated from an Amity jail program in Arizona, where the organization got its start in the 1980s. She devoted her life to the foundation until she died of cancer in 1990. Half the people here are doing time for violent offenses, including murder. All have histories of drug and alcohol abuse.

Though prison is a place where revealing inner feelings can be interpreted as a sign of weakness, most are not afraid to talk. "All my relationships have been built on lies," says one barrel-chested convict with corn-rowed hair. "I fall in love with a woman and then she is with my best friend. Women just play a man's heart and throw 'em to the curb. I've never been around a decent woman," another inmate volunteers. "I've been in crack houses a lot of my life, and you don't trust anyone, man or woman. On the streets, I was a predator. I preyed on women," says counselor [experience therapist] Ernie Logan, an ex-convict and recovering addict whose father was an alcoholic. "I had a lot of trust issues too. My mother and father betrayed me as a child." Logan's reference to childhood strikes a chord with a goateed inmate sitting across from him. He is doing eight years for robbery. Rejection has weighed heavily on his mind for years.

"I'm very conscious of the pain I feel. If Ernie won't say hello to me, I feel like, '——— Ernie.' Something that small makes me think back on when I was a kid, all the shame and grief of being abandoned by my parents. That emotion has energy. The power is hard to control." "But," counselor Logan responds, "if you are in touch with what happened to you and the pain it has caused you, you shouldn't be doing the same things to someone else. You shouldn't be taking it out on somebody else."

If drug treatment advocates had their way, programs like Amity's would be available to every convict seeking help. Incarceration alone, they say, does not necessarily stop addiction or protect the public in the long run. State figures show that the average drug offender in California, whether convicted of sales, distribution, or possession, is returned to the street in eighteen to twenty-four months. Proponents say effective drug treatment programs can be provided at a fraction of the billions of dollars being spent on one of the longest building booms in the history of the state penal system.

If present trends continue, the California prison population will rise from 141,000 to more than 200,000 by 2000. . . . Assuming today's prices—which do not include the expense of building more prisons—drug-related felons could cost taxpayers $500 million to $1 billion a year to incarcerate by the end of the century. We've taken the tough-on-crime approach to drugs.

Now we have to figure out what to do with the increasing numbers of people in prison.

"Treatment is a good way to go. It's cheap and it works," said Harry K. Wexler, a researcher for the National Development and Research Institute, a New York-based think tank that specializes in criminal justice issues. For almost two decades, Wexler has studied prison substance abuse programs nationwide. His findings show that the reincarceration rate for Amity, including dropouts, is about 20 percent lower than for untreated convicts two years after release from prison. It is estimated that about 65 percent of untreated convicts are rearrested within the same time period. The most dramatic reductions occurred among program graduates who received several months of treatment at Amity's outside facility. Of that group, 16 percent were rearrested.

The California Department of Corrections estimates that if Amity treats 2,100 inmates over seven years at a cost of $1.5 million a year, taxpayers would recoup the program's expenses and save $4.7 million in prison costs due to reduced recidivism. Assuming that Amity-style programs were established in all thirty-two state prisons, taxpayers' potential savings could be as high as $150 million over seven years if the current level of success were maintained. And that does not reveal the total savings. Convicts who go straight no longer tax the police, court, and social welfare system. The analysis also does not include other benefits to the corrections system, such as less violence and fewer violations of prison rules.

Amity "is doing better than I ever anticipated," said Donovan Warden John Ratelle. "If we had only a 10 percent reduction in recidivism, that would be a success. It is worth the money to do what we are doing." He grew even more convinced that the program was making progress when he ordered surprise urine tests at the treatment unit in 1991. The random testing was conducted on a Monday because prison drug use is often heaviest on weekends. Authorities expected that 25 percent of inmates would test positive, but only one did—for marijuana.

In many ways, prisons are perfect settings for drug treatment. There is a large captive audience. Inmates are often motivated by many factors, from sheer boredom to measures that have increased sentences for repeat offenders, such as California's three-strikes law.

Even the unwilling get drawn into the process despite themselves, such as Rocky R. Reeder, a heroin addict and habitual criminal who applied to Amity just to stop his transfer to a prison in Northern California. Reeder, forty-one, of San Diego, had been a one-man crime wave. By his own estimate, he stole more than seventy vehicles, and each week burglarized two or three houses for much of his career. If someone was sleeping on the sofa or taking a shower when he entered, the bigger the thrill.

He went to juvenile hall and the California Youth Authority more than a dozen times. He has been sent to prison seven times, the last to Donovan in 1992 for possession of stolen property. "At first, I didn't care about treatment," he said. "But I started listening to the leaders in group therapy. They were just like me. It made a difference. The person had been there, and I could relate." Reeder, who has been off drugs since May 1992, works with his son as a technician for a water purification business. He realizes he can never apologize to his victims, so he occasionally visits Amity's parolee program and counsels those in treatment.

"Many convicts are amenable to changing their behavior," said Lewis Yablonsky, an expert on residential treatment programs and professor emeritus of sociology and criminology at Cal State Northridge. Amity is a small program even in Donovan, but it is a significant demonstration of what can be done. He predicts that well-run treatment projects in every state prison could significantly reduce the inmate population. [I would predict, based on current evidence, that the TC approach, if properly utilized throughout the United States, could reduce the 1.6 million people now doing time in prison to half that number by the year 2020.]

Substance abuse treatment has been added to two other prisons since Amity arrived at Donovan. The Correctional Institute for Women in Frontera opened the Forever Free program for 120 inmates several years ago. An 80-bed facility called Walden House has begun at the California Rehabilitation Center in Norco. This fall, the first 1,056 beds of a 1,456-bed facility will open at Corcoran. The Corcoran program will more than triple the statewide capacity of treatment for convicts—a crucial test to see if drug rehabilitation can work on a large scale. "I don't think we have seen a serious effort at prison treatment until the last few years," said John Erickson, director of substance abuse programs for the Department of Corrections. "There is now an all-out effort to refine treatment strategies." He said adding large numbers of treatment beds to the prison system has gone slowly because reliable research has not been available in California until the last few years.

Whether drug treatment will be expanded on a massive scale is hard to predict, even with more positive research. Legislators, government officials, and correctional officers worry that a broad expansion might compromise the quality of smaller, successful programs like Amity. "People need to be convinced that this is more than an aberration," said Rod Mullen, president of the Amity Foundation. "They need to see this as something as normal as a prison industry program, or a religious program, or a high school education program. But that kind of shift in attitude does not happen overnight."

Indeed, it hasn't. The first drug and alcohol programs for convicts were established in the 1930s at two federal prisons in Lexington, Kentucky, and Fort Worth, Texas. Because such efforts were poorly administered and ineffective, criminal justice experts came to believe that little could be done to rehabilitate convicts. That attitude did not begin to change until the early 1980s, when a substance abuse treatment program called Stay 'N' Out reported some substantial success at the Arthur Kill State Prison on Staten Island, New York. As more positive results emerged from a program in Oregon, the federal government began to fund pilot projects across the country. Since then, encouraging findings have been reported in California, Delaware, and Texas. (Reprinted by permission of the Los Angeles Times Syndicate.)

A Summary of the Differences Between the Social Structure of TCs and Traditional Correctional Institutions

The differences in social structure and organization between effective TCs and traditional correctional institutions for delinquents are:

1. The contractual arrangements for therapy and the expectation of success are different. The indoctrination of delinquents by people who have been in their shoes and succeeded appears to be a significant element, providing newcomers with role models of what they can become. Also, the "indoctrinators" see where they have been when they look at the newcomers, and this is valuable for reinforcing their personal growth.

2. TCs provide the possibility of upward mobility, whereas most institutions have a "we-they" caste system. Becoming a TC member is an incentive for changing one's delinquent motivation to antidelinquent motivation. The TC resident can achieve any role in the organization. In the traditional institution, inmates or patients are locked into the inmate position.

3. There is a qualitative difference between the TC and the group therapy carried on in prisons and hospitals. This is partly a function of the described differences in the overall social systems. The TC resident, as a voluntary participant, has little to gain from faking progress. In other institutions, the appearance of being "rehabilitated" may be rewarded by an earlier release from custody. TC residents are encouraged to reveal and deal with their problems honestly by others who have traveled the established TC route to recovery. They can usually detect when there is a lack of truth in a resident's participation.

4. The TC subculture is integrated into the larger societal structure in a way that traditional institutions never are. The flow of members of the community through a TC and the participation of TC members in the larger

society place this subculture closer to the real life situations of the outer world than the artificial communities of the traditional institutions that attempt personality change.

5. Everyone in a TC usually has meaningful work to do. The work assigned is real work, unlike the often contrived jobs in most institutions. This included procuring food, working in the office, and on maintenance, service, and automotive crews, and being a member of the coordinating staff.

6. There have been attempts at self-government in reformatories and hospitals. In these settings, however, the inmates recognize that final decisions on important matters remain with the administration. In a TC, perhaps for the first time, delinquents can assume some responsibility for and control of their future.

7. The residents of a TC, unlike patients in hospitals and inmates in prisons, are involved with the growth and development of their own organization and have an *esprit de corps*. Because there is a generally held belief by most residents that "the TC saved our lives," the enthusiasm in the organization is quite powerful. Few inmates would give three cheers for Warwick or the Riker's Island Prison; however, in a TC, youths seem to enjoy lauding the organization that saved them at every opportunity. And given their *esprit de corps*, they work hard for the TC's growth and development.

Principal Social Forces at Work in an Effective Therapeutic Community

The following elements comprise the essential social-psychological forces at work in an ideal therapeutic community for delinquents.

Involvement. Initially the TC society is able to involve and control the newcomer by providing an interesting social setting composed of understanding associates who will not be outmaneuvered by manipulative behavior. The indoctrinators understand the newcomer because they were once in his or her position.

Achievable Success Goals. Within the context of this system, the delinquent can (perhaps for the first time) see a realistic possibility for legitimate achievement and prestige. A TC provides a rational opportunity structure for the newcomer. He or she is not restricted to inmate or patient status, since there is no inmate-staff division and all residents are immediately staff members.

Social Growth. In the process of acquiring legitimate social status in a TC, former offenders necessarily develop the ability to relate, communicate, and work with others. The values of truth, honesty, and industry become necessary means to this goal of status achievement. With enough practice and time, those socialized in this way react according to these values. This is an effective system for people who, upon entrance into the TC, had an egocentric-sociopathic posture toward life.

Social Control. The control of deviance is a by-product of status seeking. Conformity to norms is necessary for achievement in a TC. Anomie, the dislocation of goals and means, is minimal. The norms are valid and adhered to within the social system, since the means are available for legitimate goal attainment. Another form of control is embodied in the threat of ostracism. This becomes a binding force in keeping the residents in the program, because the participants—perhaps for the first time—have found a "home" that they trust.

The newcomers in a TC usually do not feel adequate for participation in the larger society. After a period of TC social living, the residents no longer fear banishment and are prepared for life outside (if this is their choice). However, they may remain voluntarily because they feel a TC is a valid way of life. In a TC they have learned and acquired a gratifying social role that enables them to help others who can benefit from the approach.

Another form of social control is the group process. Members are required to tell the truth. This helps regulate their behavior. Transgressions are often prevented by the knowledge that deviance will rapidly and necessarily be brought to the attention of pals in a group session. Members live in a community where others know about and, perhaps more important, care about one another's behavior.

Empathy and Self-Identity. The constant self-assessment required in daily life and in the group sessions fosters the consolidation of self-identity and empathy. Members' self-estimation is under constant assessment by relevant others, who become sensitive to and are concerned about one another. The process provides the opportunity for members to see themselves as others see them. They are also compelled, as part of this process, to develop the ability to identify with and understand others, if only to acquire higher status in the system. Side effects are personal growth, greater social awareness, an improved ability to communicate, and greater empathy. When these socialization processes take hold in the TC, participants learn how to function more effectively in the TC social structure and, consequently, are better prepared for life in the larger society. Life in a TC, unlike life in most correctional institutions, parallels life in the larger society. The TC process has the impact of changing a sociopath into an empathic caring person.

A New Social Role. Delinquents in a TC can acquire the new social role of experience therapist, which they can enact later on in the larger society. The growing development of TCs in prisons and elsewhere provide many job opportunities for TC members who qualify as experience therapists.

The Social Vaccine Concept in Treating the Delinquency Problem

Therapeutic communities provide delinquents with a new identity that insulates them from the need to return to their former deviant life-style. In the process, if successful, they develop a new social attitude and personal identity that enable them to lead happier, more productive lives and to pass their new-found positive attitudes on to others. Ex-criminal or delinquent TC graduates can be valuable assets as role-models in society's overall efforts at preventing and controlling delinquency. They may enact this role as experience therapists in a TC, or simply as citizen role-models who are opposed to crime and drug-use.

My "social vaccine" concept is derived from the use of vaccines for diseases first introduced by English physician Edward Jenner. One dictionary definition specifies that "a vaccine is a living attenuated organism that is administered to produce or increase immunity to a particular disease." Dr. Jenner demonstrated that inserting a low level of virus into a person's physiological system stimulated antibodies that usually defend and prevent the person from having a more virulent form of the disease.

Transposing this physiological concept to a social system, I believe that the social vaccine concept would involve the insertion of individuals, in this case ex-criminal delinquents, who had a socially based disease of sociopathic behavior, as "antibodies" would immunize other potential offenders in their social system against the continuance of their delinquency. Former delinquents, who have become informed, law-abiding citizens or experience therapists as a result of their changed behavior, properly employed in a TC, or simply living in a law-abiding manner in their community creates antibodies to the delinquency problem.

Paraprofessional ex-criminal addicts like Frankie, Ed, Zev, Al, and Naya are individuals who, once their problem has been arrested, can in time and in sufficient numbers serve as antibodies to the delinquency problem that exists in their community and in the overall society. To some degree, the force of the anti-alcohol attitude of AA members has produced this kind of antibody on an international level for helping to prevent and control alcoholism. The same approach, if properly applied through the TC methodology, would prove to be effective in helping to prevent and control the delinquency problem.

The social vaccine application to the delinquency problem may be summarized as follows: The individual who has gone through the TC process of recovery and is now functioning effectively as an experience therapist in a TC or in his or her community provides a kind of antibody or social vaccine for the community and the overall social system. They accomplish this positive goal by their attitude and being a vital force in preventing, and helping others, especially youngsters from their community to change their behavior. The projected TC system for treating delinquents can potentially produce thousands of graduates, who in the role of experience therapists or as active concerned citizens in their community can significantly contribute to the prevention and control of delinquency. It is my belief that the TC philosophy and methodology, like probation or parole, will become a part of the crime prevention arsenal of government in the twenty-first century.

APPENDIX

JUVENILE DELINQUENCY ARREST STATISTICS, 1997

The following analysis of 1997 juvenile delinquency statistics provides the most current data on delinquency arrests available at this time. It reveals a coherent summary of the delinquency picture at the end of the twentieth century. It is derived from an excellent report collated and written by Howard N. Snyder, Director of Systems Research at the National Center for Juvenile Justice, with funds provided by the Office of Juvenile Justice Delinquency Prevention agency (OJJDP) to support the Juvenile Justice Statistics and Systems Development Program. The data in the *Juvenile Justice Bulletin* were derived from various sources, especially published and unpublished statistics from the Federal Bureau of Investigation's *Crime in America* Uniform Crime Reports (Washington, DC: U.S. Government Printing Office, 1998) and United States Census statistics. The data in this Appendix are presented with limited sociological analysis. Students and instructors are invited to analyze the data in terms of their specific interests, and in the context of the criminological and sociological theories and research presented in the body of this book.

Introduction to the Data

In this analysis "juvenile" refers to persons below age 18. This definition is at odds with the legal definition of juveniles in 1997 in 13 States—ten states define 17-year-olds as adults and three states define 16- and 17-year-olds as adults. These FBI arrest data are counts of arrests, categorized by the age of the arrestee and the type of offense, from all law enforcement agencies in the United States that reported data to the FBI for final presentation in the FBI's yearly document *Crime in America.* The proportion of the U.S. population covered by these reporting agencies ranged from 68% to 86% between 1980 and 1997. Estimates of the number of persons in each age group in the reporting agencies' resident population assume that their population age profiles are representative of the nation's general population.

To interpret the material in this analysis properly, the reader must have an understanding of what these statistics count. The arrest statistics report the number of arrests made by law enforcement agencies in a particular year—not the number of individuals arrested, nor the number of crimes committed. Many crimes, both juvenile and adult, are not reported, and consequently do not enter into the general analysis of juvenile delinquency in America. The number of arrests is not equivalent to the number of people arrested because an unknown number of individuals are arrested more than once in the year. Nor do arrest statistics represent counts of crimes committed by arrested individuals, because a series of crimes committed by one individual may culminate in a single arrest or a single crime may result in the arrest of more than one person. This latter situation of multiple arrests resulting from one crime is relatively common in juvenile law-violating behavior, because juveniles are more likely than adults to commit crimes in groups. The phenomenon of youth gangs would, in part, account for this disparity between juvenile and adult offenders.

Arrest statistics also have limitations in measuring the volume of arrests for a particular offense. Under their Uniform Crime Report (UCR) Program, the FBI requires law enforcement agencies to classify an arrest by the most serious offense charged in that arrest. For example, the arrest of a youth charged with aggravated assault and possession of a controlled substance would be reported to the FBI as an arrest for aggravated assault. Therefore, when arrest statistics show that law enforcement agencies made an estimated 220,700 arrests of young people for drug abuse violations in 1997, it means that a drug abuse violation was the most serious charge in these 220,700 arrests. An unknown number of additional arrests in 1997 included a drug charge as a lesser offense. And, of course, the statistics do not account for a large number of youths using illegal substances who are never arrested.

Another factor to be considered in interpreting these data is clearance statistics. Clearance statistics measure the proportion of reported crimes that were resolved by an arrest or other, exceptional means (e.g., death of the offender, unwillingness of the victim to cooperate). A single arrest may result in many clearances. For example, one arrest could clear 40 burglaries if one person was charged with committing all 40 of these crimes. Or multiple arrests may result in a single clearance if the crime was committed by a group of offenders. In my work in several juvenile institutions, I recall many instances where one youth would admit to 30–40 burglaries in several months of delinquent activity.

In summary, while the interpretation of reported clearance proportions is not totally complete, the following data are the closest measure generally available of the proportion of crimes known to law enforcement that can be attributed to persons under age 18. These data should provide a barometer of the changing contributions of persons under age 18 to the nationís crime problems. Taking all of these caveats into account, following is an analysis of the 1997 statistics (and other relevant years) reported for juvenile offenders.

The Juvenile Share of the Overall Crime Problem

The relative responsibility of juveniles for the U.S. crime problem is difficult to determine. However, an analysis of the proportion of crimes that are cleared by the arrest of juveniles presents a reasonable estimate of the juvenile responsibility for crime in America. The clearance data in the FBI's *Crime in the United States* series show that the proportion of violent crimes attributed to juveniles has declined in recent years. Juvenile involvement in violent crime grew from 9% or 10% in the early-to-mid-1980s to 14% in 1994. Since 1994, the proportion of violent crimes cleared by juvenile arrest has declined to around 12% in 1997.

The proportion of murders cleared by juvenile arrests in 1997 (8%) was at its lowest level since 1991, but still above the 5% level of the mid-1980s. The juvenile proportion of cleared forcible rapes peaked in 1995 (15%) and then fell, with the 1997 rate (12%) the lowest in the decade. The juvenile proportion of robbery clearances in 1997 (17%) was below its peak in 1995 (20%), but still far above the levels of the early 1980s (12%). Similarly, the juvenile proportion of aggravated assault clearances in 1997 (12%) was below its peak in 1994 (13%), but still above the levels of the early 1980s (9%). The proportion of Property Crime Index offenses cleared by juvenile arrest in 1997 (23%) was equal to the average level between 1980 and 1996.

Juveniles were involved in about 1 in 5 arrests made by law enforcement agencies in 1997, 1 in 6 arrests for a violent crime, and 1 in 3 arrests for a property offense. Over the last 25 years, changes in the number of juvenile arrests for violent crime have been unrelated to changes in the size of the juvenile population. From 1987 to 1994, while the juvenile population increased 7%, juvenile arrests for violent crime increased 79%. Since 1994, juvenile arrests have dropped 18%, while the juvenile population has increased 4%.

Juvenile Arrests and the Juvenile Courts

Most arrested juveniles are referred to juvenile court. However, in several states, as previously indicated, some persons below the age of 18 are, due to their age, or by statutory exclusion of certain offenses from juvenile court jurisdiction, referred to the jurisdiction of the adult criminal justice system. This is most likely to occur for the crime of homicide. For those persons under age 18 and under the original jurisdiction of their state's juvenile justice system, the FBI's UCR Program monitors what happens as a result of the arrest.

In 1997, 25% of arrests involving youth that were eligible in their state for processing in the juvenile justice system were handled within the law enforcement agency, and then the youth was released. The FBI reports that 67% of juvenile arrests were referred to juvenile court, and 7% were referred directly to adult criminal court. The others were referred to a welfare agency or to another police agency. The proportion of arrests sent to juvenile court has gradually increased from 1980 to 1997. In 1997, the proportion of juvenile arrests sent to juvenile courts was similar in cities and suburban areas (66%) and somewhat greater in rural counties (70%). The proportion of juvenile arrests sent directly to criminal court in 1997 (7%) was the highest in the last two decades. And as discussed more fully in the text, this is related to an increasing number of laws involving "get tough" policies in many states. Because of this in the next century we can expect that an increasing number of juveniles will be referred to, and processed through the adult criminal justice system.

An Overview of the 1997 Juvenile Delinquency Statistics

In 1997, law enforcement agencies in the United States made an estimated 2.8 million arrests of persons under the age of 18. (As indicated, throughout this analysis persons under age 18 are referred to as juveniles.) According to the FBI, juveniles accounted for 19% of all arrests and 17% of all violent crime arrests in 1997. The substantial growth in juvenile violent crime arrests that began in the late 1980s peaked in 1994. In 1997, for the third year in a row, the total number of juvenile arrests for Violent Crime Index offenses—murder, forcible rape, robbery, and aggravated assault—declined. Even with these declines (3% in 1995, 6% in 1996, and 4% in 1997), the number of juvenile Violent Crime Index arrests in 1997 was 49% above the 1988 level. In comparison, the number of adult arrests for a Violent Crime Index offense in 1997 was 19% greater than in 1988.

Other notable recent findings from the UCR Program include the fact that of the 2,100 juveniles murdered in 1997, 56% were killed with a firearm and that juveniles were involved in 14% of all murder and aggravated assault arrests, 37% of burglary arrests, 30% of robbery arrests, and 24% of weapons arrests in 1997.

Juvenile murder arrests increased substantially between 1988 and 1993. In the peak year of 1993, there were about 3,800 juvenile arrests for murder. Between 1993 and 1997, juvenile arrests for murder declined 39%, with the number of arrests in 1997 (2,500) 11% above the 1988 level. Between 1993 and 1997, juvenile arrests for burglary declined 9% and juvenile arrests for motor vehicle theft declined 30%. Juveniles were involved in 14% of all drug abuse violation arrests in 1997. Between 1993 and 1997, juvenile arrests for drug abuse violations increased 82%.

Juvenile arrests for curfew and loitering violations increased 87% between 1993 and 1997. In 1997, 28% of curfew arrests involved juveniles under age 15 and 31% involved females.

In 1997, 58% of arrests for running away from home involved females and 41% involved juveniles under age 15. Arrests of juveniles accounted for 12% of all violent crimes cleared by arrest in 1997—more specifically, 8% of murders, 11% of forcible rapes, 17% of robberies, and 12% of aggravated assaults.

The FBI Violent Crime Index

The FBI statistics assess trends in the volume of violent crimes by monitoring four offenses that are consistently reported by law enforcement agencies nationwide and are pervasive in all geographical areas of the country. The four crimes that comprise the Violent Crime Index are (1) murder and nonnegligent manslaughter, (2) forcible rape, (3) robbery (theft from a person), and (4) aggravated assault. Other crimes may be considered violent by their nature or effect (e.g., kidnapping, weapons possession, extortion, drug selling), but the four crimes that together form the Violent Crime Index have traditionally been used as the nation's barometer of violent crime for both juveniles and adults.

After more than a decade of consistency, the juvenile Violent Crime Index arrest rate increased from 1989 to 1994 and then fell, so that by 1997, it had nearly returned to the 1989 level. Between 1994 and 1997, the juvenile Violent Crime Index arrest rate dropped 23%. Even with this decline, the 1997 rate was still about 30% greater than the average rate of the years between 1980 and 1988.

The juvenile violent crime arrest rate declined 23% from 1994 to 1997. The juvenile violent crime arrest rate in 1988 was nearly identical to the rate in 1980; in fact, this rate had changed little since the early 1970s. However, between 1988 and 1994, the rate increased more than 60%. This steady increase after years of stability focused national attention on the juvenile violent crime problem. This attention, as we approach the twenty-first century, is accentuated by the 1998–1999 outbreak of school murders.

After peaking in 1994, the juvenile violent crime arrest rate began to decline. The declines in 1995, 1996, and again in 1997 resulted in a 1997 juvenile violent crime arrest rate 23% below the peak year of 1994, but still 25% above the 1988 level. Therefore, by 1997, the juvenile violent crime arrest rate decreased by half of the increase it experienced between 1988 and 1994.

The juvenile Violent Crime Index arrest rate indicates that in 1997 there were 407 arrests for these violent crimes for every 100,000 youth in the United States between 10 and 17 years of age. If each of these arrests involved a different juvenile (i.e., if each juvenile arrested in 1997 for a Violent Crime Index offense were arrested only once that year—which is unlikely), then 1 in about every 250 persons ages 10 through 17 in the United States was arrested for a Violent Crime Index offense in 1997.

Between 1980 and 1997, Violent Crime Index arrest rates increased substantially for all ages—more for adults than juveniles. Over the last several years, public attention has focused on increases in juvenile violent crime arrests. However, with the recent declines in this rate, the increase in the arrest rate for juveniles between 1980 and 1997 (22%) is now less than the increases found in most other age groups. Following are the percentage increases found in specific age groups: 18- to 24-year-olds: 23%; 25- to 29-year-olds: 32%; 30- to 34-year-olds: 60%; 35- to 39-year-olds: 66%; 40- to 44-year-olds: 50%; and 45- to 49-year-olds: 35%.

A Closer Analysis of Violent Crime Index Offenses

1. **Murder.** The most disturbing offense committed by a juvenile is murder. While only a portion of all youth offenses that occur are reported to law enforcement, this is not the case with the highly visible and clear crime of murder. In this regard, as Thorsten Sellin has pointed out, the murder rate is the most reliable statistic in the context of all criminal offenses.

   The average murder rate in the United States in the past 20 years is around 22,000. In 1997 there was a total of 18,200 murders reported to law enforcement agencies. One would have to go back to 1971 to find a lower annual number of murder victims in the United States, and to 1967 to find a lower murder rate (i.e., murders per 100,000 persons in the population). Eighty-eight percent of murder victims (16,100) were 18 years of age or older. Fewer adults were murdered in the United States in 1997 than in any year within the last 20 years.

   In 1997, about 2,100 murder victims were below the age of 18. This level was 27% below that of the peak year of 1993, when 2,900 juveniles were murdered. However, this decline only returned the level of 1989. The number of juveniles murdered in the United States in 1997 was still over 300 more than in a typical year in the 1980s. In 1997, 900 persons under age 13 were murdered. This figure has held relatively constant for the last 20 years. In 1997, 68% of all murder victims were killed with a firearm. Adults were more likely to be killed with a firearm (70%) than were juveniles (56%). However, the involvement of a firearm depended greatly on the age of the juvenile victim. While 18% of murdered juveniles under age 13 were killed with a firearm in 1997, 84% of murdered juveniles age 13 or older were killed with a firearm. No other age group in 1997 had a higher proportion of firearm homicides. (The recent rash of school murders, especially at Colunbine High School, will no doubt profoundly affect the 1998–1999 statistics, not included in this report.)

In general, the juvenile arrest rate for murder more than doubled between 1987 and 1993. The decline in the juvenile murder arrest rate between 1993 and 1997 has nearly erased all of the increase experienced in the previous 7 years. The drop of more than 40% in the juvenile murder arrest rate between 1993 and 1997 has brought the 1997 rate to a point 20% above the 1987 rate.

2. **Forcible Rape.** More than any other Violent Crime Index offense, the juvenile arrest rate for forcible rape has been confined to a relatively limited range from the early 1980s through 1997. The juvenile arrest rate for forcible rape in 1997 was lower than in any year since 1983 and 23% below the peak year of 1991.

3. **Robbery.** Juvenile arrests for robbery declined 30% between 1980 and 1988. Between 1988 and 1994, the rate at which juveniles were arrested for robbery increased 70%, to a level 19% above the 1980 rate. Between 1995 and 1997, the juvenile robbery arrest rate fell substantially—down 33% in this short period. As a result, the 1997 rate was lower than at any point in the 1990s and just 13% above its lowest level of the last two decades.

4. **Aggravated Assault.** The juvenile arrest rate for aggravated assault increased steadily between 1983 and 1994—up more than 120%. Similar increases (135%) were found in juvenile arrests for other (i.e., simple) assaults over the same period. The arrest rate for aggravated assault declined 16% from 1994 through 1997, returning the rate to the 1991 level. In contrast, the juvenile arrest rate for other assaults continued to increase, up 9% between 1994 and 1997.

The Property Crime Index

As with violent crime, the FBI assesses trends in the volume of property crimes by monitoring four offenses that are consistently reported by law enforcement agencies nationwide and are pervasive in all geographical areas of the country. These four crimes, which form the Property Crime Index, are (1) burglary, (2) larceny-theft, (3) motor vehicle theft, and (4) arson.

For the period from 1988 through 1997, during which juvenile violent crime arrests rose precipitously, juvenile property crime arrest rates (as measured by the Property Crime Index) remained relatively constant. In fact, the 1997 rate of approximately 2,300 arrests for every 100,000 youth in the United States between 10 and 17 years of age is the lowest since 1984.

A Closer Analysis of Property Crime Index Offenses

1. **Burglary.** The juvenile arrest rate for burglary declined consistently between 1980 and 1997, with the 1997 rate 47% below that of 1980. In the period from 1980 to 1997, the greatest decline occurred between 1980 and 1988. The number of burglaries reported to law enforcement in 1997 was lower than in any year since 1972.

2. **Larceny-Theft.** The juvenile arrest rate for larceny-theft remained essentially constant between 1980 and 1997, with the 1997 rate 7% above the 1980 rate. In 1997, larceny-theft arrests accounted for 70% of the FBI's Property Crime Index arrests. Consequently, larceny-theft arrest trends control trends in the Index.

3. **Motor Vehicle Theft.** Juvenile arrests for motor vehicle theft soared between 1983 and 1989, with the rate up more than 130% over this period. After holding constant in 1990 and 1991, the juvenile arrest rate began to decline. The 37% drop between 1991 and 1997 resulted in the 1997 rate returning to the 1986 level. Consistent with the decline in the juvenile arrest rate for motor vehicle theft, the number of motor vehicle thefts reported to law enforcement in 1997 was the lowest in 10 years. Despite this, there is some evidence that the *modus operandi* of "car-jacking," a violent crime involving stealing the car directly from the driver, has increased to replace the nonviolent crime of stealing a parked car with no passengers off the street.

4. **Arson.** Compared with other property crimes, the rate of juvenile arrests for arson is very small. During the 1980s, the rate of juvenile arrests for arson remained constant. The rate increased between 1990 and 1994 and then declined, with the 1997 rate near the 1991 rate.

Female Juvenile Arrests

The juvenile Violent Crime Index arrest rate for females more than doubled between 1987 and 1995, then fell in each of the next 2 years. In 1997, 26% of juvenile arrests were arrests of females. Law enforcement agencies made 748,000 arrests of females below the age of 18 in 1997. Between 1993 and 1997, arrests of juvenile females increased more (or decreased less) than male arrests in most offense categories.

In addition to overall violent crimes, female arrest rates in 1997 were substantially above their 1987 levels in many offense categories: robbery, 52% increase; aggravated assault, 101% increase; other assaults, 142% increase; larceny-theft, 22% increase; motor vehicle theft, 36% increase; vandalism, 42% increase; weapons law violations, 100% increase; and drug abuse violations, 131% increase.

Between 1981 and 1994, the female violent crime arrest rate increased twice as much as the male rate (130% vs. 64%). Even with the recent declines, the female violent crime arrest rate in 1997 was 103% above the 1981 rate, while the male arrest rate was 27% above its 1981 level. Even with the large increase in female rates, the 1997 Violent Crime Index arrest rate for juvenile males was five times the female arrest rate. The growth in juvenile Violent Crime Index arrest rates between 1987 and 1994 was far greater for females than for males, while the decline in rates after 1994 was less for females than males.

Juvenile Arrests and Minorities

A consistent statistic in the past half-century is that juvenile arrests have been disproportionately higher for minorities than the general population of juveniles. According to census figures, the racial composition of the juvenile population in 1997 was approximately 80% white, 15% black, and 5% other races. The fact that juveniles of Hispanic ethnicity are classified as white skews these statistics—since a large proportion of juvenile offenses are committed by Hispanic youths, especially in New York and the Southwest United States.

In 1997, in contrast to the proportions in the general population, 53% of juvenile arrests for violent crimes involved white youth and 44% involved black youth. The following statistics reflect the white Proportion of Juvenile Arrests in 1997: murder, 40%; forcible rape, 56%; robbery, 42%; aggravated assault, 60%; burglary, 73%; larceny-theft, 70%; motor vehicle theft, 59%; weapons, 64%; drug abuse violations, 64%; curfew and loitering, 75%; runaways, 77%.

Drug Arrest Data

After more than a decade of stability, the juvenile arrest rate for drug abuse violations increased more than 70% between 1993 and 1997. Between 1993 and 1997, the increase in juvenile drug abuse arrest rates was greater for females (117%) than for males (78%). Of juveniles arrested for drug abuse violations, 64% were white, 16% were age 14 or younger, and 13% were female. Of course, the use of illegal substances by juveniles is an offense that is well hidden by the youth population, and because of this the statistics on juvenile use and arrests is apt to be skewed, complex, and much lower than the actual behavior patterns of juvenile drug users.

Data Sources

As previously indicated, this analysis is substantially derived from the Office of Juvenile Justice and Delinquency Prevention report collated and written by Howard Snyder. The overall analysis includes: arrest data from unpublished FBI reports for 1972 through 1994, and from Crime in the United States reports for 1995, 1996, and 1997 (Washington, DC: U.S. Government Printing Office, 1996, 1997, and 1998, respectively). Moreover it includes population data from the Bureau of the Census for 1972 through 1979 from Current Population Reports, pp. 25–917 (Washington, DC: U.S. Dept. of Commerce, 1982), for 1980 through 1989 from Current Population Reports, pp. 25–1095 (Washington, DC: U.S. Dept. of Commerce, 1993), and for 1990 through 1997 from Population of the United States by Single Year of Age and Sex (machine-readable data files released August 1998). I am sincerely grateful to Howard Snyder and his associates, the Office of Juvenile Justice and Delinquency Prevention, and the various other government agencies that have provided this relevant and useful data on juvenile delinquent behavior. I am entirely responsible for the manner in which their data is presented in this Appendix.

REFERENCES

Note: UCR is used in the text in place of the full citation for *Uniform Crime Reports, Crime in the United States,* an annual publication of the U.S. Dept. of Justice, Federal Bureau of Investigation.

Abrahamsen, David. 1973. *The murdering mind.* New York: Harper and Row.

Adams, Kenneth. 1985. Addressing inmate mental health problems. *Federal Probation* (December), 46.

Adler, Freda. 1975. In her own words. *People Magazine,* October 13, 20–21.

Adolescent disorders. 1987. *Diagnostic and statistical manual of mental disorders* (4th ed.). New York: American Psychiatric Association.

Agnew, Robert. 1993. Foundation for a general strain theory of crime and delinquency. *Criminology* 30 (April), 47–48.

Akers, Ronald L. 1997. *Criminological theories* (2nd ed.). Los Angeles, CA: Roxbury Press.

Alexander, Franz, and Hugo Staub. 1956. *The criminal, the judge, and the public.* Glencoe, IL: Free Press.

Alexander, C. Norman, Jr. 1967. Alcohol and adolescent rebellion. *Social Forces* 45 (June), 548.

Amir, Menachim, and Yitzcham Berman. 1970. Chromosomal deviation and crime. *Federal Probation* 34 (June), 55–62.

Anderson, Elijah. 1994. The code of the streets. *Atlantic Monthly,* May.

Archives of Internal Medicine. 1997. Report. March.

Bales, Robert F. 1959. Cultural differences in rates of alcoholism. In *Drinking and intoxication,* ed. Raymond G. McCarthy. Glencoe, IL: Free Press.

Ball-Rokeach, J. 1980. Normative and deviant violence from a conflict perspective. *Social Problems* 28 (October), 45–62.

Bandura, Albert. 1963. What TV violence can do to your child. *Look,* October 22, 46–48.

Bandura, Albert, and R. H. Walters. 1959. *Adolescent aggression.* New York: Ronald Press.

Banks, Sandy. 1997. Crime victims' pain lingers even after the shooting stops. *Los Angeles Times,* April 23.

Barnes, Grace M. 1984. Adolescent alcohol abuse and other behaviors. *Journal of Youth and Adolescence* 13 (April), 36.

Barron, Milton L. 1974. The criminogenic society: Social values and deviance. In *Current perspectives on criminal behavior,* ed. Abraham S. Blumberg. New York: Knopf.

Bartollas, Clemens. 1993. *Juvenile delinquency* (3d ed.). New York: Macmillan.

Beccaria, Cesare. 1963. *Crimes and punishments.* Trans. by Henry Paoluci. New York: Bobbs-Merrill. (Originally published in 1764)

Becker, Howard S. 1963. *Outsiders.* Glencoe, IL: Free Press.

Begleiter, Henri, Bernice Porjesz, Bernard Bihiri, and Benjamin Kissin. 1984. Even-related brain potentials in boys at risk for alcoholism. *Science* 225 (September), 280.

Belden, Evalina. 1920. *Courts in the United States hearing children's cases.* U.S. Children's Bureau Pubn. 65, 7–10. Washington, DC: U.S. Government Printing Office.

Bellak, Leopold, and Maxine Antell. 1975. Parental and youth violence: A cross-cultural analysis. *Human Behavior* (March), 43.

Belluck, Pam. 1996. Aftercare for delinquents. *New York Times,* November 17.

Bentham, Jeremy. 1892. *An introduction to the principles of morals and legislation.* Oxford: Clarendon Press.

Berk, Richard A., and Howard E. Aldrich. 1972. Patterns of vandalism during civil disorders as an indicator of selection of targets. *American Sociological Review* 37 (October), 533–547.

Berkowitz, Leonard. 1964. Pictures of violence. *Newsweek,* February 24, 91.

Berkowitz, Leonard. 1981. How guns control us. *Psychology Today,* June, 11–12.

Berman, Claire. 1976. The 90,000 ghosts who haunt the schools. *New York Times,* July 31.

Berne, Eric. 1961. *Transactional analysis in therapy.* New York: Grove Press.

Bierstedt, Robert. 1957. *The social order.* New York: McGraw-Hill.

Bloch, Herbert A., and Arthur Niederhoffer. 1958. *The gang.* New York: Philosophical Library.

Blumstein, Alfred. 1994. Youth, violence, guns, and the drug industry. *Journal of Criminal Law,* 64 (April), 483.

Bonger, William. 1916. *Criminality and economic conditions.* Boston: Little, Brown.

Bowker, Lee. H. *Women, crime, and the criminal justice system.* 1978. Lexington, MA: Lexington Books.

Bowlby, John. 1951. *Maternal care and mental health.* Geneva: World Health Organization.

Brain studies tie marijuana to other drugs. 1997. *New York Times,* June 27.

Brody, Jane E. 1997. Guns increase the risk. *New York Times,* May 21.

Brotman, Richard, and Frederic Suffet. 1976. Research report on women and drug abuse. *Human Behavior* 2 (August), 46.

Brown, Claude. 1965. *Manchild in the promised land.* New York: Macmillan.

Brown, Stephen E. 1984. Social class, child maltreatment, and delinquent behavior. *Criminology* 22 (May).

Bureau of Justice Statistics. 1992. *Recidivism of felons on probation, 1986–1989.* Washington, DC: U.S. Dept. of Justice.

Butts, Jeffrey. 1997. Delinquency cases waived to criminal court, 1985–1994. OJJDP *Fact Sheet,* February. Washington, DC: U.S. Dept. of Justice.

Cameron, Norman. 1943. The paranoid pseudocommunity. *American Journal of Sociology* 49 (July), 32–42.

Cannon, Jimmy. 1955. Column. *New York Post,* February 22, 38.

Cavan, Ruth S., and Theodore N. Ferdinand. *Juvenile delinquency* (4th ed.). New York: Harper and Row.

Chemers, Martin M. 1970. Relationship between birth order and leadership style. *Journal of Social Psychology* 80 (August), 243–244.

Chilton, Roland J., and Gerald E. Markle. 1972. Family disruption, delinquent conduct, and the effect of subclassification. *American Sociological Review* 27 (February), 93–99.

Cloward, Richard A., and Lloyd E. Ohlin. 1960. *Delinquency and opportunity.* Glencoe, IL: Free Press.

Cleckley, Hervey M. 1959. Psychopathic states. In *American handbook of psychiatry,* vol. 1, ed. Silvano Arieti. New York: Basic Books.

Cleckley, Hervey. 1976. *The mask of sanity.* St. Louis, MO: Mosby.

Cohen, Albert K. 1955. *Delinquent boys.* Glencoe, IL: Free Press.

Cohen, Stanley. 1973. The future of vandalism. *The Nation,* August 13.

Cressey, Donald R. 1955. Changing criminals: The application of the theory of differential association. *American Journal of Sociology* 46 (October), 115–116.

Cressey, Donald R. 1960. The theory of differential association: An introduction. *Social Problems* 8 (Summer), 93–95.

Cressey, Donald R. 1963. Differential association and the rehabilitation of drug addicts. *American Journal of Sociology* 74 (September), 130–142.

Cressey, Donald R. 1970. Organized crime and inner city youth. *Crime and Delinquency* 9 (April), 129–138.

Crowe, R. 1975. Research report. *Human Behavior* (May).

Daly, Kathleen. 1994. *Gender, crime, and punishment.* New Haven, CT: Yale University Press.

Decker, Scott. 1995. Field studies of gangs: A synthesis of the past and suggestions for future research. Unpublished.

De Young, Henry. 1976. Homicidal children. *Human Behavior* (February), 89.

Diagnostic and Statistical Manual of Mental Disorders (4th ed.). 1987. New York: American Psychiatric Association.

Drabman, Ronald S., and Margaret H. Thomas. 1975. Television violence. *Journal of Pediatrics* 24 (September), 36–43.

Dressler, David. 1969. *Practice and theory of probation and parole.* New York: Columbia University Press.

Drug abuse in colleges and universities—1995. 1997. *The Chronicle of Higher Education* (February).

DSM-IV. See *Diagnostic and Statistical Manual of Mental Disorders* (4th ed.). 1987.

Durkheim, Emile. 1951. *Suicide.* Trans. by John A. Spaulding and George Simpson. Glencoe, IL: Free Press.

Durkheim, Emile. 1950. *The rules of sociological method* (8th ed.). Trans. by Sarah A. Solvag and John H. Mueller. Glencoe, IL: Free Press.

Erikson, Erik H. 1963. *Childhood and society* (2nd ed.). New York: Norton.

Erickson, Maynard L., and LaMar T. Empey. 1965. Class position, peers, and delinquency. *Sociology and Social Research* 25 (April), 268–282.

Everstine, D., and L. Everstine. 1983. *People in crisis.* New York: Bruner/Mazel.

Ex-criminals help to reform felons. 1962. *New York Times,* September 30, 1.

Fagan, Jeffrey. 1997. Commentary. OJJDP *Fact Sheet,* April. Washington, DC: U.S. Dept. of Justice.

Fagan, Jeffrey, and Chin Ko-Lin. 1991. The social process of initiation into crack. *Journal of Drug Issues* 38 (March), 241–243.

Farr, Bill, and Kristina Lindgren. 1980. Murder suspect described as "weirdo." *Los Angeles Times,* July 31.

Farr, Karen Ann. 1995. *Crime and delinquency* 38 (April).

Ferri, Enrico. 1901. *Criminal sociology.* Boston: Little, Brown.

Finkelstein, Marvin. 1973 *Prosecution in the juvenile courts.* Washington, DC: U.S. Dept. of Justice, Law Enforcement Assistance Administration.

Fleisher, Benton M. 1966. *The economics of delinquency.* Chicago: Quadrangle Books.

Fontana, Vincent. 1973. *Somewhere a child is crying.* New York: Macmillan.

Forer, Lois G. 1980. *Criminals and victims.* New York: Norton.

Frease, J., K. Polk, and F. L. Richmond. 1974. Social class, school experience, and delinquency. *Criminology* 12 (December), 47.

Gardiner, Muriel. 1976. *The deadly innocents.* New York: Basic Books.

Garmezy, Norman, and Vernon Devine. 1976. The invulnerables. *Human Behavior* (April), 87.

Garrett, Marcia, and James F. Short. Social class and delinquency: Predictions and outcomes of police-juvenile encounters. *Social Problems* 22 (February), 368–383.

Gay, Anne, and George R. Gay. 1972. Evolution of a drug culture in a decade of mendacity. In *Heroin in perspective,* eds. David E. Smith and George R. Gay. Englewood Cliffs, NJ: Prentice-Hall.

Gay, George, Richard Rappolt, and R. David Farris. 1979. PCP intoxication. *Clinical Toxology* 14 (April), 509–529.

Geller, Allen, and Maxwell Boas. 1971. *The drug beat.* New York: McGraw-Hill.

Gerstein, D. R., R. A. Johnson, H. J. Harwood, D. Fountain, N. Suter, and K. Malloy. 1994. *Evaluating recovery services: The California drug and alcohol treatment assessment.* Sacramento: California Dept. of Alcohol and Drug Programs.

Glasser, William. 1965. *Reality therapy.* New York: Harper and Row.

Glueck, Sheldon, and Eleanor Glueck. 1950. *Unraveling juvenile delinquency.* New York: Commonwealth Fund.

Goldman, Nathan. 1963. *The differential selection of juvenile offenders for court appearances.* New York: National Council on Crime and Delinquency.

Goldstein, Paul. 1983. The marketing of street heroin in New York City. *Journal of Drug Issues* (Fall), 46.

Gordon, Barbara, 1981. *I'm dancing as fast as I can.* New York: HarperCollins.

Gordon, David M. 1987. Capitalism, class and crime in America. *Crime and Delinquency* 32 (January), 163–186.

Goring, Charles B. 1913. *The English convict.* London: His Majesty's Stationery Office.

Gough, Harrison G. 1948. A sociological theory of psychopathy. *American Journal of Sociology* 53 (March), 365.

Granberry, Mike. 1986. The parent as drug supplier. *Los Angeles Times,* March 17.

Grogan, Hiram, and Ruth Grogan. 1971. The criminogenic family: Does chronic tension trigger delinquency? *Crime and Delinquency* 14 (January), 220–225.

Guides for juvenile court judges. 1957. New York: National Probation and Parole Association.

Guns in Los Angeles schools: A report. 1996. Los Angeles, CA: Los Angeles Unified Schools.

Hagedorn, John M. 1994. Homeboys, dope fiends, legits, and new jacks. *Criminology* 32 (May), 24.

Hamill, Pete. 1981. Why must guns be so available? *New York Times,* April 5.

Hatsukami, Dorothy, and Marian Fishman. 1996. Crack cocaine and cocaine hydrochloride (powdered coke): Are the differences myth or reality? *Journal of the American Medical Association* 46 (November), 221.

Hazlett, Bill. 1981. County takes custody of four children. *Los Angeles Times,* April 29.

Heath, Robert. 1981. The effects of marijuana. *Science Digest,* October.

Hill, John. 1988. Psychodrama with gangs. In *Juvenile delinquency* (4th ed.), eds. L. Yablonsky and M. R. Haskell. New York: HarperCollins.

Hirschi, Travis, and Michael Gottfredson. 1993. Commentary: Testing the general theory of crime. *Journal of research in Crime and Delinquency* (April).

Holden, Gwenn, and Robert Kapler. 1995. Deinstitutionalizing status offenders: A record of progress. *Juvenile Justice* 34 (Fall/Winter), 39.

Hooton, Ernst A. 1939. *Crime and the man.* Cambridge, MA: Harvard University Press.

Horowitz, Joy. 1981. A family tree of criminal life. *Los Angeles Times,* March 25.

Huff, Ronald. 1991. *Gangs in America.* Thousand Oaks, CA: Sage.

Iglitzin, Lynne B. 1972. *Violent conflict in American society.* San Francisco, CA: Chandler Press.

Irwin, John. 1980 *Prisons in turmoil.* Boston: Little, Brown.

Jankowski, Martin Sanchez. 1991. *Islands in the streets.* Berkeley: University of California Press.

Janofsky, Michael. 1997. Old friends, once felons, regroup to fight crime. *New York Times,* March 10.

Japenga, Ann. 1982. Wingspread clinic for women hooked on legal drugs. *Los Angeles Times,* February 18.

Jeffery, Clarence R. 1959. An integrated theory of crime and criminal behavior. *Journal of Criminal Law, Criminology, and Police Science* 50 (March).

Journal of Pediatrics. 1996. Report. March.

Juvenile drug abuse 1997. Partnership for a Drug-Free America. Washington, DC: U.S. Dept. of Justice.

Kaplan, Robert M., and Robert D. Singer. 1972. Television violence. *Los Angeles Times,* January 7.

Kaplun, David, and Robert Reich. 1975. Child battering and murder. *American Journal of Psychiatry* 34 (September), 87–99.

Kaye, Elizabeth. 1982. Growing up stoned. *California,* April.

Keller, Oliver J., Jr., and Benedict S. Alper. 1970. *Halfway houses: Community centered corrections.* Lexington, MA: Lexington Books.

Kids and crack. 1986. *Newsweek,* March 17.

Klein, Malcolm W. 1971. *Street gangs and street workers.* Englewood Cliffs, NJ: Prentice-Hall.

Klein, Malcolm, Cheryl L. Maxson, and Jody Miller, eds. 1995. *The Modern gang reader.* Los Angeles, CA: Roxbury.

Knox, George. 1995, *An introduction to gangs.* Bristol, IN: Wyndham Hall Press.

Knox, George, David Laske, and Edward Tromanhauser. 1992. *Schools under siege.* Dubuque, IA: Kendall/Hunt.

Knox, George, et al. 1995. *The economics of gang life.* Chicago: National Crime Research Center.

Knight, Heather. 1997. The connection between child abuse and crime. *Los Angeles Times,* June 20.

Kobrin, Solomon. 1959. The Chicago area project: A twenty-five year assessment. *Annals of the American Academy of Political and Social Science* 322 (March), 19–29.

Kocourek, Albert, and John H. Wigmore. 1951. *Ancient and primitive law.* Boston: Little, Brown.

Koller, K. M. 1971. Parental deprivation, family background, and female delinquency. *British Journal of Psychiatry* 118 (March), 319–327.

Korn, Richard R., and Lloyd W. McCorkle. 1959. *Criminology and penology.* New York: Holt, Rinehart and Winston.

Kretschmer, Ernest. 1936. *Physique and character.* London: Kegan Paul, Trench, Trubner.

Krisberg, Barry, and James F. Austin. 1993. *Reinventing juvenile justice.* Thousand Oaks, CA: Sage.

Kvaraceus, William C., and Walter B. Miller. 1959. *Delinquent behavior.* Washington, DC: National Education Association.

Laing, R. D. 1967. *The politics of experience.* New York: Pantheon.

Laney, Ronald. 1995. National center for missing and exploited children. OJJDP *Fact Sheet* 32 (October). Washington, DC: U.S. Dept. of Justice.

Lawson, G., J. Peterson, and A. Lawson. 1983. *Alcoholism and the family.* New York: Aspen.

Lees, J. P., and L. J. Newson. 1954. Family or sibship position and some aspects of juvenile delinquency. *British Journal of Delinquency* 5 (May), 46–65.

Lennard, Henry L., Leon J. Epstein, Arnold Bernstein, and Donald C. Ransom. 1970. Hazards implicit in prescribing psychoactive drugs. *Science* 169 (July), 438–441.

Loeber, Rolf, and Magda Strouthhamer-Loeber. 1986. Family factors as correlates of juvenile conduct problems and delinquency. In *Crime and justice: An annual review of research,* vol. 7. Chicago: University of Chicago Press.

Logan, Charles, and Sharla Raush. 1985. Why deinstitutionalizing status offenders is pointless. *Crime and Delinquency* 31, 514–515.

Lombroso, Ceasare. 1896. *The criminal man.* Rome: Turin-Bocca.

Maguire, Kathleen, and Ann L. Pastore, eds. 1996. *Source book of criminal justice statistics,* 1995. Washington, DC: U.S. Government Printing Office.

Malcolm X. 1965. *The autobiography of Malcolm X: As told to Alex Haley.* New York: Grove Press.

Marx, Karl. 1909. *The capital.* Trans. by Ernest Untermann. Chicago: Kerr Publishers.

Matza, David. 1966. *Delinquency and drift.* New York: Wiley.

McCord, Joan. 1991. Family relationships and juvenile delinquency. *Criminology* 29 (April).

McCord, William, and Joan McCord. 1959. *Origins of crime.* New York: Columbia University Press.

McCord, William, and Joan McCord. 1964. *The psychopath.* New York: Van Nostrand.

McCorkle, Lloyd W. 1958. *The Highfields story.* New York: Holt, Rinehart and Winston.

McGee, Zina T. 1992. Social class differences in parental and peer influences on adolescent drug use. *Deviant Behavior* 17 (April), 63.

McKeachern, L., and R. Bauzer. 1967. Factors related to disposition in juvenile police contracts. In *Juvenile gangs in context,* eds. Malcolm V. Klein and Barbara G. Meyerhoss. Englewood Cliffs, NJ: Prentice-Hall.

Mead, George H. 1934. *Mind, self, and society.* Chicago: University of Chicago Press.

Mednick, Sarnoff A., and William F. Gabriella. 1984. Genetic influences in criminal convictions: Evidence from an adoption cohort. *Science* 224 (May), 891–894.

Megaree, Edwin I., and Roy E. Golden. 1973. Parental attitudes of psychopathic and subcultural delinquents. *Criminology* 11 (February), 427–439.

Merrill, J. C., K. Fox, S. R. Lewis, and G. E. Pulver. 1996. *Cigarettes, alcohol, and marijuana: Gateways to illicit drug use.* Washington, DC: U.S. Government Printing Office.

Merton, Robert K. 1957. *Social theory and social structure.* Glencoe, IL: Free Press.

Meyer, Frederick H. 1972. Pharmacologic effects of marijuana. In *The new social drug,* ed. David E. Smith. Englewood Cliffs, NJ: Prentice-Hall.

Middle-class junkies. 1981. *Newsweek,* August 10.

Milgram, Stanley. 1965. Some conditions of obedience and disobedience to authority. *Human Relations* 18 (September), 57–76.

Miller, Arthur. 1962. The bored and the violent. *Harper's Magazine,* November, 51.

Miller, Walter B. 1959. Lower class culture as a generating milieu of gang delinquency. *Journal of Social Issues* 31 (March), 34–36.

Miras, Constandinos J. 1966. Lecture at the University of Southern California, March.

Moore, Joan. 1978. *Homeboys: Gangs, drugs and prisons in the barrios of Los Angeles.* Philadelphia, PA: Temple University Press.

Moreno, J. L. 1934. *Who shall survive?* Beacon, NY: Beacon House.

Myerhoff, Barbara G., and Howard L. Myerhoff. 1964. Field observations of gangs. *Social Forces* 42 (March), 348.

National cable television report. 1997. New York: National Cable Television, Inc.

National Council of Juvenile and Family Court Judges. 1995. *Directory of juvenile and family court judges.* Reno: University of Nevada Press.

National Drug Policy Council. 1997. *Plan for controlling teenage substance abuse, 1996.* Washington, DC: U.S. Government Printing Office.

National Institute of Drug Abuse. 1996. *Statistics on substance abuse—1995.* Washington, DC: NIDA.

The need for delivery of drug abuse services. 1995. Rockville, MD: U.S. Dept. of Health and Human Services.

Neigher, Alan. 1967. The Gault decision: Due process and the juvenile courts. *Federal Probation* 31 (December), 13.

New York Times. 1997. April 17.

Niederhoffer, Arthur. 1974. Criminal justice by dossier: Law enforcement, labeling, and liberty. In *Current perspectives on criminal behavior,* ed. Abraham S. Blumberg. New York: Knopf.

Nye, F. Ivan. 1958. *Family relationships and delinquent behavior.* New York: Wiley.

Nye, Ivan, James F. Short, Jr., and Virgil J. Olson. 1958. Socioeconomic status and delinquent behavior. *American Journal of Sociology* 63 (January), 381–389.

Office of Juvenile Justice and Delinquency Prevention. 1991. *The war on drugs.* Washington, DC: U.S. Government Printing Office.

Office of Juvenile Justice and Delinquency Prevention. 1993. OJJDP *Fact Sheet* 43, December. Washington, DC: U.S. Government Printing Office.

Office of Juvenile Justice and Delinquency Prevention. 1997a. Health needs of youth in the juvenile justice system. OJJDP *Fact Sheet* 43, March. Washington, DC: U.S. Government Printing Office.

Office of Juvenile Justice and Delinquency Prevention. 1997b. *Juveniles in private facilities, 1991–1995.* Washington, DC: U.S. Government Printing Office.

Osborn, Lee Ann, and Peter A. Rhode. 1984. Prosecuting juveniles as adults. *Criminology* 22 (May), 87.

Parsons, Talcott. 1947. Certain primary sources and patterns of aggression in the social structure of the western world. *Psychiatry* 10 (May), 167–181.

Paschall, Mallie. 1996. Family characteristics and violence. *Journal of Youth and Adolescence (April).*

Patterson, Gerald, and Thomas J. Dishion. 1985. Contributions of families and peers to delinquency. *Criminology* 23 (January), 63–64.

The persistent effects of substance abuse treatment—one year later. 1996. National Treatment Improvement Evaluation Study, Preliminary Report. Rockville, MD: U.S. Dept. of Health and Human Services

Peterson, Donald, and Wesley Becker. 1965. Family interaction in delinquency. In *Juvenile delinquency: Research and theory,* ed. Herbert C. Quay. New York: Van Nostrand.

Peterson, Eric. 1997. *Juvenile boot camps.* Washington, DC: U.S. Dept. of Justice, Office of Juvenile Justice and Delinquency Prevention.

Poe-Yamagata, Eileen. 1997. *Detention and delinquency cases, 1985–1994.* Washington, DC: U.S. Dept. of Justice, Office of Juvenile Justice and Delinquency Prevention.

Poll of attitudes toward crime. 1997. *Los Angeles Times,* March 5.

Polsky, Howard W. 1962. *Cottage six.* New York: Russell Sage Foundation.

Pope blames devil for sex and drug evils. 1972. *Los Angeles Times,* December 1.

Porterfield, Austin L. 1946. *Youth in trouble.* Fort Worth, TX: Leo Potishman Foundation.

Powers, Edwin, and Helen Witmer. 1951. *The Cambridge-Sommerville youth study.* New York: Columbia University Press.

Quinney, Richard. 1980. *Class, state, and crime.* New York: Longmans.

Quinney, Richard. 1974. *Criminal justice in America.* Boston: Little, Brown.

Rabin, Albert I. 1961. Psychopathic personalities. In *Legal and criminal psychology.* ed. Hans Toch. New York: Holt, Rinehart and Winston.

Rafter, Nicole, and Elena Natalizia. 1981. Marxist feminism: Implications for criminal justice. *Crime and Delinquency* 36 (January), 81–87.

Rainey, James. 1997. Street crusader. *Los Angeles Times,* April 2.

Reasons, George, and Mike Goodman. 1978. California's new drug pushers. *Los Angeles Times,* March 2.

Reckless, Walter C. 1961. *The crime problem.* New York: Appleton-Century-Croft.

Reckless, Walter C., Simon Dinitz, and Ellwyn Murray. 1956. Self-concept as an insulator against delinquency. *American Sociological Review* 21 (December), 744–746.

Recommendation for training schools. 1997. Washington, DC: U.S. Dept. of Justice, Office of Juvenile Justice and Delinquency Prevention.

Regnery, Alfred. 1986. A federal perspective on juvenile justice reform. *Crime and Delinquency* 29 (April), 43–44.

Reiss, A. J. 1952. Social correlates of psychological types of delinquency. *American Sociological Review* 17 (June), 710–780.

Report on smoking habits. 1997. Sacrament: California Department of Health.

Research Triangle Institute Report. 1995. Washington, DC: National Institute of Drug Abuse.

Richards, Pamela, Richard Berk, and Brenda Foster. 1979. *Crime as play: Delinquency in a middle class suburb.* Cambridge, MA: Bollinger Press.

Roberts, Cara, and Tracy Connow. 1998. Gun arrest fired young killer's anger. *New York Post,* June 3.

Robers, Marilyn, Jennifer Brophy, and Caroline Cooper. 1997. The juvenile drug court movement. OJJDP *Fact Sheet,* March. Washington, DC: U.S. Dept. of Justice.

Roscoe, Mark, and Reggie Morton. 1994. Disproportionate minority confinement. OJJDP *Fact Sheet,* April. Washington, DC: U.S. Dept. of Justice.

Rosen, Lawrence. 1985. Family and delinquency: Structure of function? *Criminology* 23 (March), 46.

Sanders, William B. 1976. *Juvenile delinquency.* New York: Praeger.

Sanders, William B. 1994. *Gangbangs and drive-bys.* New York: Aldine.

Science news report. 1986. *Los Angeles Times,* October 15.

Scott, Kody. 1993. *Monster.* New York: Penguin Books.

Sellin, Thorsten. 1938. *Culture conflict and crime.* New York: Social Science Research Council.

Sheldon, William H. 1949. *The varieties of delinquent youth.* New York: Harper.

Short, James F., Jr., and F. Ivan Nye. 1958. Extent of unrecorded juvenile delinquency: Tentative conclusions. *Journal of Criminal Law, Criminology, and Police Science* 49 (July–August), 258–260.

Short, James F., Jr., and Fred Strodbeck. 1974. Youth gangs and society. *Sociological Quarterly* 26 (Winter), 48.

Sickmund, Melissa. 1997. *Juvenile delinquency probation caseload, 1958–1994.* Washington, DC: U.S. Dept. of Justice, Office of Juvenile Justice and Delinquency Prevention.

Simon, Rita J. 1975. *The contemporary woman and crime.* National Institute of Health. Washington, DC: U.S. Government Printing Office.

Skolnick, Jerome. 1995. Gangs and crime old as time, but drugs change gang culture. In *Modern gang reader,* ed. Malcolm Klein. Los Angeles, CA: Roxbury.

Smith, David E. 1967. Lysergic acid diethylamide: An historical perspective. *Journal of Psychedelic Drugs* 1 (Summer), 1–5.

Snyder, Howard N. 1997. *Juvenile arrests, 1996.* Washington, DC: U.S. Dept. of Justice, Office of Juvenile Justice and Delinquency Prevention.

Sorrels, James, Jr. 1980. What can be done about juvenile delinquency? *Crime and Delinquency* 23, 156–157.

Spergel, Irving R. 1964. *Racketville, slumtown, haulberg.* Chicago: University of Chicago Press.

Spergel, Irving R. 1995. *The youth gang problem.* New York: Oxford University Press.

Spreading fear, changing lives. 1981. *Newsweek,* March 23.

Straus, Murray A., and Richard Gelles. 1995. *Physical violence in American families.* New Brunswick, NJ: Transaction.

Stumbo, Bella. 1976. East L.A. gangs: Youth worker struggles for peace in barrio. *Los Angeles Times,* September 19.

Sugarmann, Josh. 1997. *Violence Policy Research Center publication.* Washington, DC: Violence Policy Research Center.

Sullivan, Harry Stack. 1947. *Conceptions of modern psychiatry.* New York: William Alanson White Psychiatric Foundation.

Sutherland, Edwin H. 1951. Critique of Sheldon's varieties of delinquent youth. *American Sociological Review* 16 (February), 10–13.

Sutherland, Edwin H. 1965. *Criminology.* New York: Lippincott.

Sutherland, Edwin H., and Donald R. Cressey. 1978. Developmental explanation of criminal behavior. In *Criminology* (10th ed.). New York: Harper and Row.

Taft, Donald R., and Ralph W. England, Jr. 1964. *Criminology.* New York: Macmillan.

Tannenbaum, Frank. 1951. *Crime and the community.* New York: McGraw-Hill.

Tappan Paul W. 1949. *Juvenile delinquency.* New York: McGraw-Hill.

Tappan, Paul W. 1960. *Crime, justice, and corrections.* New York: McGraw-Hill.

Tappan, Paul W., and Ivan Nicolle. 1962. Juvenile delinquents and their treatment. *Annals of the American Academy of Political and Social Science* 38 (January), 157–170.

Television and growing up. 1972. Report to the Surgeon General, U.S. Public Health Service. Washington, DC: U.S. Government Printing Office.

Thomas, Piri. 1967. *Down these mean streets.* New York: Knopf.

Thornberry, Terence P. 1994. Violent families and youth violence. OJJDP *Fact Sheet* 21. Washington, DC: U.S. Dept. of Justice.

Time. 1997. March 24.

Time. 1973. News report. August 20.

Time. 1961. News report. September 15.

Tomson, Barbara, and Edna R. Felder. 1975. Gangs: A response to the urban world. In *Gang delinquency,* eds. Desmond S. Cartwright, Barbara Tomson, and Hershey Schwartz. Monterey, CA: Brooks/Cole.

Trasler, Gordon, 1962. *The explanation of criminality.* London: Routledge and Kegan Paul.

Trends in new laws targeting violent or other serious crime by juveniles. 1997. OJJDP *Fact Sheet,* March. Washington, DC: U.S. Dept of Justice.

Trimborn, Harry. 1975. Britain dismayed by U.S. right to own guns. *Los Angeles Times,* September 25.

UCR. See U. S. Dept. of Justice, Federal Bureau of Investigation, *Crime in the United States* (*Unified Crime Reports*).

U.S. Dept. of Justice. 1978. *Exemplary projects.* Washington, DC: U.S. Government Printing Office.

U.S. Dept. of Justice. 1995. *Sourcebook of criminal justice statistics.* Washington, DC: U.S. Government Printing Office.

U.S. Dept. of Justice, Federal Bureau of Investigation. 1996. *Crime in the United States, 1995* (*Uniform Crime Reports*). Washington, DC: U.S. Government Printing Office.

U.S. Dept. of Justice, Office for Victims of Crime. 1995. *Child sexual exploitation: Improving investigations and protecting victims.* Washington, DC: U.S. Government Printing Office.

Vigil, Diego. 1988. *Barrio gangs: Street life and identity in southern California.* Austin: University of Texas Press.

Vold, George B. 1973. Group conflict theory as explanation of crime. In *Deviance, conflict, and criminality,* eds. R. Serge Denisoff and Charles H. McCaghy. Chicago: Rand McNally.

von Hentig, Hans. 1948. *The criminal and his victim.* New Haven, CT: Yale University Press.

Voss, Harwin L. 1966. Socioeconomic status and reported behavior. *Social Problems* 13 (Winter), 314–324.

Wade, Andrew L. 1967. Social processes in the act of vandalism. In *Criminal behavior systems,* eds. Marshall B. Clinard and Richard Quinney. New York: Holt, Rinehart and Winston.

Weber, George. 1961. Emotional and defensive reactions of cottage parents. In *The prison,* ed. Donald R. Cressey. New York: Holt, Rinehart and Winston.

Weeks, Ashley. 1941. Male and female broken home rates. *American Sociological Review* 5 (January), 601–609.

Weeks, Ashley. 1958. *Youthful offenders at Highfields.* Ann Arbor: University of Michigan Press.

Weikel, Dan. 1997. In prison: A drug rehab that pays off. *Los Angeles Times,* April 25.

Weiss, Joseph, Robert Crutchfield, and George Bridges. 1996. *Juvenile delinquency.* Thousand Oaks, CA: Pine Forge Press.

Welte, John W., and Grace M. Barnes. 1985. Alcohol: The gateway to other drug use among secondary-school students. *Journal of Youth and Adolescence* 14 (June), 228.

Wertham, Frederic. 1973. *A sign for Cain.* New York: Macmillan.

Wexler, Harry. 1995. *Research on Amity.* Washington, DC: National Development and Research Institute.

Wilde, James. 1981. In Brooklyn, a wolf in $45 sneakers. *Time,* October 12, 36–41.

Wilensky, H. L., and C. N. Lebeaux. 1958. *Industrial society and social welfare.* New York: Macmillan.

Wilson, James Q., and Richard J. Hernstein. 1984. *Crime and human nature.* New York: Simon and Schuster.

Witkin, Herman. 1976. Criminality in XYY and XXY men. *Science* 193 (August), 547–555.

Wolfgang, Marvin E. 1957. Victim-precipitated criminal homicide. *Journal of Criminal Law, Criminology and Police Science* 48 (June), 187.

Working with teenage gangs. 1950. New York: Welfare Council of New York City.

Wright, Jack, and James Kitchens. 1976. *Social problems in America.* Columbus, OH: Merrill.

Yablonsky, Lewis. 1960. Sociopathology of the violent gang and its treatment. In *Progress in psychotherapy,* vol. 5: *Reviews and integrations,* eds. J. Masserman and J. Moreno. New York: Grune and Stratton.

Yablonsky, Lewis. 1962a. The anticriminal society. *Federal Probation* (March).

Yablonsky, Lewis. 1962b. *The violent gang.* New York: Macmillan.

Yablonsky, Lewis. 1965. *Synanon: The tunnel back.* New York: Macmillan.

Yablonsky, Lewis. 1968. *The hippie trip.* New York: Pegasus (New York: Penguin, 1969).

Yablonsky, Lewis. 1978. *La communita terapeutica.* Rome: Astrolabio.

Yablonsky, Lewis. 1987. *The therapeutic community.* New York: Gardner Press.

Yablonsky, Lewis. 1990. *Psychodrama: Resolving emotional problems through role playing.* New York: Brunner/Mazel.

Yablonsky, Lewis. 1996. Personal interviews.

Yablonsky, Lewis. 1997. *Gangsters: Fifty years of madness, drugs, and death on the streets of America.* New York: New York University Press.

Youth facilities for juveniles. 1995. Albany: New York State Division for Youth.

Zinberg, Norman E. 1976. The war over marijuana. *Psychology Today,* December, 87.

INDEX

De Young, Henry, 116–17
Diagnostic and Statistical Manual of Mental Disorders (American Psychiatric Association), 69
differential association theory, 55–57, 59–60, 377–84, 386, 387, 388, 492
Dinitz, Simon, 393
discipline:
    crime causation theory on, 358; and school violence, 141;
    in socializing children, 315, 319–24
Dishion, Thomas, 305
diversion process:
    "get-tough," 41–45;
    juvenile court, 32, 39–40
divorced parents, 324–26
Donahue, Phil, 327
Donovan Prison Project, San Diego, 194–95, 202, 519, 526, 547–53
Drabman, Ronald S., 118–19
drifters, 335, 336–37
drive-bys, gang, 147, 230–31
driving:
    drugged, 292;
    drunk, 267
Drug Enforcement Administration, U.S., 281
"drug-free zones," 291
"drug gangs," 214
drugs, 238, 265–98;
    arrest statistics, 16, 18;
    commerce, 57, 196–97, 209, 221, 229, 247–54, 284–85, 288;
    designer, 281;
    encounter group process for abusers, 469–74;
    "fun" vs. destructive, 296;
    gangsters and, 182, 196–97, 209, 213, 214, 215, 221, 229;
    life-and-death factor, 297;
    lower class use, 95–96; and middle class delinquency, 95, 101–2;
    painkiller, 297;
    parents' response to use, 10;
    psychedelic hallucinogenic, 244–45, 266, 277–81;
    psychoactive, 248–54, 260–64;
    quasi-legal, 247–54, 284;
    "recreational use," 241, 283, 288;
    smuggling, 273;
    social lubricant, 297. *See also* addicts; alcohol abuse; cocaine; heroin; marijuana; nicotine
drug treatment courts, 314
"due process," 5, 45–50
Durkheim, Emile, 208, 221, 261, 357–59

economics:
    adolescents denied role in, 18;
    capitalist, 85–86, 348–49, 351, 354–55;
    of dependents, 30–31;
    determinist, 347–49;
    diversion program, 40;
    drug commerce, 57, 196–97, 209, 221, 229, 247–54, 284–85, 288;

gun business, 155; and
    interest group influence on justice system, 352. *See also* employment; Marxism; socio-economics
Economics of Gang Life (Knox et al.), 216
"Ecstasy" drug, 281
ectomorphs, 338
education:
    boot camp, 430;
    in criminality, 44, 371–84;
    groups focused on, 502, 508;
    marijuana affecting, 275–76;
    parolee and probationer, 420–22;
    in psychiatric hospitals, 450, 451;
    TC, 542. *See also* schools; socialization
ego, in psychoanalytic theory, 342
egocentrism:
    sociopathic, 69, 71, 74, 78, 314–15;
    of substance abuse, 314–15
ego defense mechanisms, 62–63
emotional disorders, 53–54, 61–68;
    clinical approach to, 402;
    family, 302, 304;
    gangster, 147, 217, 225;
    after LSD, 279;
    psychoanalytic causation theories and, 343. *See also* "mental disorders"; neurotics; personality; psychosis; sociopaths; suicidal tendencies
emotional effects:
    and drug use, 245, 277;
    of social interaction, 388. *See also* emotional disorders; personality; psychology
Empey, LaMar T., 91–92
employment:
    adolescent need for, 19;
    female, 20, 21;
    group meetings focused on, 502, 508–9;
    immigrant, 23, 24;
    parolee and probationer, 420, 421–22
encounter group process, 469–74, 500, 502, 503–4, 528–29
endomorphs, 338
England, Ralph, 370–71
Epstein, Leon J., 247–50
ergot alkaloids, 277–78
Erickson, Manard L., 91–92
Erikson, Erik, 305–8
Eros, in psychoanalytic theory, 342
Everstine, D., 125
Everstine, L., 125
execution, minimum age, 43
"existential validation," 168–69, 225
"experience therapists," 409, 519, 521–42, 547, 556
exploitation:
    of children, 108, 128–34;
    computer, 130–31;
    of females by gangs, 208, 367;
    of missing children, 133–34. *See also* sexual abuse

584

self-concept, 389, 390;
socialization failure, 5;
sociopaths and, 76–78, 314–16; and
substance abuse, 10, 245–47, 249, 254,
260–64, 269–70, 276, 295–96, 314–16;
violence by, 108, 126–28, 390–91.
See also fathers; genetics; mothers
Parents Resource Institute for Drug Education
(PRIDE), 146–47
parole, 414, 415, 419–23, 433–34
parole officers, 420, 422–23
Parsons, Talcott, 94
Partnership for a Drug-Free America, 238–39
Pastore, Ann L., 134, 135
Pataki, George E., 43
Patterson, Gerald, 305
Paul VI, Pope, 332
PCP ("Angel Dust"), 281–82
pedophiles, recidivising, 376
peers:
"group therapists," 504;
lower class, 368; and
substance abuse, 296;
vandalism with, 159.
See also gangs
personality:
delinquent types, 52–82, 394–95;
drug use effects on, 276–77, 280, 281–82;
families' effect on, 303, 327;
gangster, 213, 216, 225, 232;
TC changing, 545–46;
Yablonsky causation theory and, 389–94.
See also alienation; egocentrism; emotional
disorders; psychology; self-concept;
sociopaths
Peterson, Donald, 306, 323
Peterson, Eric, 429–30
Peterson, J., 269
Petit, Michael, 389
petition, juvenile court, 33, 35–36
pharmaceutical industry, 247–54
Phillips, Larry Eugene, Jr. and Sr., 312–13
Physician's Desk Reference, 251
physiology:
criminality caused by, 337–41.
See also genetics
pimps, 129–30
Poe-Yamagata, Eileen, 425–26
police:
agencies with juvenile component, 32, 33;
attitudes, 10, 11, 28, 34–35, 92
politics:
"get-tough" policy, 13–14, 42–43, 44;
interest-group influence on laws, 352
Polsky, Howard, 442–44
population growth, prison, 432–33
Porjesz, Bernice, 269
pornography, child, 131–33
Porterfield, Austin L., 12
positivists, 334
pregnancies:
unwanted, 400.
See also mothers

prisons:
danger for children in, 44;
gangs in, 194–98;
group psychotherapy, 546–47;
parolees from, 420, 421, 433–34;
"penitentiaries" (term), 332; population
growth, 432–33;
TC programs, 202, 497, 519–20, 547–53;
training for future delinquent behavior in,
44
Prisons in Turmoil (Irwin), 194
probation, 4, 31, 400, 414–23;
camps, 426–29, 478–85;
court-ordered, 416–17;
voluntary, 416–17
probation officers, 36, 415, 417–19, 422–23, 428
professional thieves, 59–60
prostitution:
child, 129–30;
substance abuse and, 254–60, 262–63;
teenage, 20, 21, 129–30, 134, 254–60,
262–63
Pryor, Richard, 287
pseudohallucinations, 278
psychedelic substances, 244–45, 266, 277–81
psychiatric treatment facilities, 5–6, 32, 54, 82,
147, 262, 448–53
psychoanalysis:
causation theory, 341–46;
in individual therapy, 465;
treatment facility based on, 442–44.
See also Freud, Sigmund; psychiatric treatment facilities; psychotherapy
psychodrama, 464, 475–87;
in community treatment programs, 406;
in psychiatric hospitals, 451;
in TC, 502, 505–7
psychology:
clinical treatment, 401;
LSD effects on, 278–79;
in TC, 554–56;
theories of criminal behavior, 387–94;
theories of victim-offender relationship, 163.
See also emotional effects; mental health;
neurotics; personality; psychosis; psychotherapy; self-concept
psychopaths. *See* sociopaths
psychosis:
delinquent, 54–55, 63–68, 71–72, 82;
LSD effects, 279, 280–81;
noncriminal, 387; and
senseless violence, 168
psychotherapy:
group, 406, 464, 465, 502, 546–47;
individual, 455–60, 463, 464, 465.
See also psychiatric treatment facilities;
psychoanalysis; psychodrama
pulls and pushes, in containment theory, 373
Putterman, Zev, 509–17

Quinney, Richard, 85–86, 89, 349–52, 354

Rabin, Albert, 68–69

Sing Sing Prison, New York, 463
601 Diversion Project, 39–40
Skolnick, Jerome H., 214
Smith, David, 273–74, 277
Smith, Susan, 73
smoking:
    heroin, 285;
    nicotine tobacco, 239–40, 266, 292.
    See also crack-cocaine; marijuana
social bonding, 384–86
social class, 83–103;
    crime causation theories and, 351, 352, 358;
    families determining, 303;
    organized crime and, 56;
    TC, 542, 544–45, 553;
    theories of, 84–86; and
    unreported delinquency, 12, 89–93.
    See also lower class culture;
        middle class
socialization, 301–30;
    adequate, 75–76, 346–47;
    family as agent of, 5, 303, 308, 330;
    gangs and, 206;
    gender role, 20;
    in judicial process, 7; and
    marijuana use, 275–77;
    mother's dominant role in, 94, 317;
    process of, 304–7; and
    self-concept, 389;
    "socialized delinquents," 54, 55–61, 72,
        77–78, 392, 394–95;
    sociopathic, 69, 75–78, 315–16;
    TC, 497–502, 519, 542, 554–56; and
    violence, 108, 124–28, 141–43.
    See also education
social learning theory, 381–84;
    differential association theory and, 377–84
Social Problems, 379–80
social relationships:
    impersonal, 372, 388;
    marijuana affecting, 275–77;
    social alienation theory and, 387–88;
    social bonding, 384–86; and
    victim-precipitated violence, 162–64.
    See also communities; families; gangs; peers;
        subcultures
"social vaccine" concept, 556–57
social welfare:
    agencies, 11–12;
    community treatment program, 402;
    juvenile justice system function, 30–31,
        38–39, 43, 45
sociocultural factors, 357–95; and
    Chicano gangs, 183–84;
    in individual therapy, 464; and
    juvenile delinquency, 53–54;
    perceptions of delinquency, 6–7, 28–29, 142;
    substance abusing, 246–47;
    TC, 554–56; and
    violence, 108–17, 141–43.
    See also alienation; communities; culture;
        race; socialization; social relationships;
        socioeconomics; subcultures

socioeconomics:
    and delinquency statistics, 24–25, 26;
    families determining, 303;
    gangsters' families and, 183–84; and
    socialized delinquency, 56–57.
    See also economics; education;
        employment; social class;
        social welfare
sociology:
    crime/delinquency theories, 356–95;
    macrosociological programs, 400–401
sociopaths, 55, 68–82, 112–13, 117, 394–95;
    in detention camps, 428;
    gang, 74–75, 81, 232, 233, 410;
    in group therapy, 82, 464–65;
    individual counseling of, 459;
    parents, 76–78, 314–16;
    senseless violence by, 168–69;
    serial killers, 162;
    social alienation theory on, 388;
    in TC, 500
Soledad Prison, 194
somatotypes, 338–39
Somebody Up There Likes Me, 494–95
Somewhere a Child Is Crying (Fontana), 125
Sorokin, Pitirim, 330
Sorrells, James, Jr., 117
Speck, Richard, 160
"speedball," 284
Spergel, Irving A., 56, 211–12
"sphincter morality," 345
Springer, Jerry, 327
statistics:
    arrest, 15–26, 33–34;
    assault, 14, 16;
    criminal court diversions, 41;
    homicide, 14, 16, 42, 148;
    prison population, 432–33;
    substance abuse, 238–39
"status frustration," 206–7, 365–66
status offenders, 9–15, 266
Staub, Hugo, 343–45
Staying Out, New York, 497
Stouthhamer-Loeber, Magda, 316
strain theories, 364–65
The Stranger (Camus), 169
Straus, Murray A., 126, 328
Strodbeck, Fred, 209–10
Stumbo, Bella, 412–14
subcultures:
    delinquent, 352–53, 361–68, 442–44;
    TC, 542–56.
    See also gangs
substance abuse, 237–98;
    adult, 246;
    chronic, 293–94;
    defining the abuser, 241–43; and
    delinquency statistics, 19, 22–23; and
    delinquency status, 28–29;
    despair without, 296;
    encounter group process with, 469–74; and
    female delinquency, 22–23, 28, 254–64; and
    middle class delinquency, 95;

urban lower class, 89;
    community programs in, 401, 402;
    gangs and, 210–11, 365.
    See also lower class culture; urban ghetto
urban school safety, 151–52

vandalism, as violence, 156–60
victims:
    restitution to, 37–38;
    violence precipitated by, 162–67.
    See also abuse
Vigil, Diego, 182–83
violence:
    arrest statistics, 16, 21;
    by child abuse victims, 134–37, 390–91;
        against children, 107–38, 390–91; and
    delinquency status, 28–29;
    family, 126–28, 327–28, 390–91;
    gang, 14, 74–75, 81, 141–43, 147–48, 178,
        179–98, 215, 217, 221–34, 410–14;
    "get-tough" policy and, 13–15, 42, 48–49;
        guns and, 140, 144, 146–56;
    immigrant, 23; "normal," 140–43;
    paradigm of patterns of, 167–74;
    patterns of, 139–74;
    propensity for, 108;
    school, 140–47, 151–53, 215;
    "senseless," 140, 147, 156, 159, 160–74;
        "social"/"asocial," 168;
    sociocultural factors, 108–17, 141–43;
    sociopathic, 73, 74–75, 81, 112–13, 117; and
        substance abuse, 288, 292–93; TC and,
        501; vandalism as, 156–60;
    victim-precipitated, 162–67.
    See also homicides; suicidal tendencies;
        warfare
Violent Crime Index, 16
Violent Gang (Yablonsky), 498
Vold, George, 353–54
Volkman, Rita, 492–93
von Hentig, Hans, 162–63
Voss, Harwin L., 90–91

Wade, Andrew L., 158–59
Walden House, San Francisco, 497, 526–30
Walters, R. H., 318
warfare:
    gang, 178, 230–31;
    local and international, 116–17
Warwick School for Boys, New York, 444–48
Watkins, John G., 66
"weapon's effect," 155
Weber, George H., 441–42
Weeks, Ashley, 326, 439, 441
Weikel, Dan, 548–53
Welte, John W., 270
Wertham, Frederic, 125
West Side Gang Committee, 405–6
white supremacists, 144, 145, 146
Whitman, Charles, 63–64, 168
Who Shall Survive? (Moreno), 463
Whyte, William, 219, 221
Wilde, James, 96–98
"wilding," 160
Wilensky, H. L., 12
Wilson, James Q., 339–40
Wilson, Peter, 42–43
Witkin, Herman, 340–41
Wolfgang, Marvin, 162–63
Woodard, Luke, 143
Woodson, Robert L., 408
working class:
    delinquency generated by, 88;
    gangs, 206–7;
    unreported delinquency, 12.
    See also lower class culture
Wright, Jack, 267
Wurst, Andrew, 144

Yablonsky, Lewis, 135–37, 180, 219–20, 224,
    389–94, 494, 519–26, 537–38
Youth Gang Problem (Spergel), 211–12

Zinberg, Norman, 271–72

PHOTO CREDITS